NOTTINGHAM AND ITS REGION

BRITISH ASSOCIATION
FOR THE ADVANCEMENT OF SCIENCE

Nottingham Meeting, 1966

LOCAL EXECUTIVE COMMITTEE

Chairman
ALDERMAN W. DERBYSHIRE, J.P.
LORD MAYOR OF NOTTINGHAM (1965-66)

Vice-Chairman
F. S. DAINTON, M.A., Sc.D., F.R.S.
VICE-CHANCELLOR OF THE UNIVERSITY OF NOTTINGHAM

Honorary Local Secretaries
P. M. VINE, M.A., LL.B.
TOWN CLERK OF THE CITY OF NOTTINGHAM

A. PLUMB, M.A.
REGISTRAR OF THE UNIVERSITY OF NOTTINGHAM

Honorary Treasurer
A. A. DENNIS, F.I.M.T.A.
TREASURER OF THE CITY OF NOTTINGHAM

Committee Members
ALDERMAN E. S. FOSTER
CHAIRMAN OF THE GENERAL PURPOSES COMMITTEE

ALDERMAN W. G. E. DYER, C.B.E.
VICE-CHAIRMAN OF THE GENERAL PURPOSES COMMITTEE

K. C. EDWARDS, M.A., Ph.D.
PROFESSOR OF GEOGRAPHY, UNIVERSITY OF NOTTINGHAM

A. HENDRY, M.A., C.A.
BURSAR OF THE UNIVERSITY OF NOTTINGHAM

G. GUEST, M.A., LL.B.
DEPUTY TOWN CLERK OF THE CITY OF NOTTINGHAM

L. POLLOCK, M.I.P.R.
PUBLICITY AND INFORMATION OFFICER OF THE CITY OF NOTTINGHAM

H. C. WILTSHIRE, M.A.
PROFESSOR OF ADULT EDUCATION, UNIVERSITY OF NOTTINGHAM
CHAIRMAN OF MEMBERSHIP AND PUBLICITY COMMITTEE

W. G. JACKSON, B.A., M.Ed.
DIRECTOR OF EDUCATION FOR NOTTINGHAM
CHAIRMAN OF YOUNG PEOPLES' COMMITTEE

G. J. ELTRINGHAM, M.A.
DEPUTY REGISTRAR OF THE UNIVERSITY OF NOTTINGHAM

A PERSPECTIVE VIEW OF NOTTINGHAM MARKET PLACE.

Drawn by R.Bonington.

T.Cartwright Sculp.

Adapted Aug.st 1813 by F.Bonington, Nottingham.

Nottingham and Its Region

Edited by

K. C. EDWARDS

Professor of Geography in the University of Nottingham

*Prepared for the meeting of the British Association
for the Advancement of Science*

NOTTINGHAM

1966

Printed in Monotype Bembo 12 point by
Derry and Sons Limited Nottingham
and published for the British Association

FOREWORD

THE BRITISH ASSOCIATION FOR THE ADVANCEMENT OF SCIENCE has met in Nottingham on three occasions, the first one being exactly one hundred years ago. We are delighted that this year's meeting will be held here. The visit of the Association is a great occasion and we are proud that this city has been chosen as this year's venue. In this survey of Nottingham and its region you will read of Nottingham's great industries with world-famous names, which have been the basis of the city's prosperity. Scientists have played a great part in the development of these industries. In 1589 the Reverend William Lee invented the first stocking-frame here. At Nottingham, Richard Arkwright first erected his spinning frames and Hargreaves his spinning jenny.

Educational facilities in the city are on a wide and generous scale, extending from nursery schools to a College of Education and a University. In the sphere of further education, a College of Art and Design, a Regional College of Technology and many evening institutes have been provided.

The growth of the city from a pre-Norman settlement to a great commercial centre shows progress of which any city may be proud. Nottingham is a regional capital, an ancient city with a modern outlook and is justifiably described as The Queen of the Midlands.

W Derbyshire

Lord Mayor of Nottingham

ACKNOWLEDGMENTS

An editor's first thanks must be to his fellow contributors. Colleagues in the University, officers of the City of Nottingham Corporation departments and of neighbouring local authority areas as well as those in the regional offices of Government Departments and national organisations have all given generously of their knowledge and time. This volume is essentially a work of co-operation and the contributors themselves are indebted to many persons engaged in municipal, professional and industrial life who have given freely of their specialised knowledge. Certain more personal acknowledgments are to be found at the end of some of the chapters. Secondly, in the production of the book, particular thanks are due to Professor C. G. C. Chesters, for many years a member of the British Association and Past President of Section K (Botany) and Mr. J. C. Doornkamp who have given valuable assistance throughout, as well as to Mr. N. Barker of Derry & Sons Ltd., the printers, for his guidance, advice and above all for his patience. To Mr. Doornkamp, of the Department of Geography, has fallen the heavy task of organising the flow of contributions, supervising the illustrative material and checking the proofs; his staunch and unremitting effort has in effect been that demanded of an assistant editor.

Authors and editor alike owe much to Mr. M. Cutler, draughtsman in the Department of Geography, for the skill and care he has devoted to the preparation of the maps and diagrams. Thanks are also due to Mrs. M. Gaukroger and to Miss E. Thomas for their clerical help. In addition, grateful thanks are offered to Mr. G. L. Roberts, of the Local History section of the Nottingham City Library, for his willingness on many occasions to supply information and to settle doubtful points of detail. Some of the figures illustrating the text are derived in part from the maps of the Ordnance Survey and are reproduced by permission of the Controller of H.M. Stationery Office.

Special acknowledgment is due to the Nottingham City Library for permission to reproduce, for the first time in colour, the aquatint 'A Perspective View of Nottingham Market Place' (1813) as the frontispiece. It was drawn by Richard Bonington, father of the painter Richard Parkes Bonington who was born at Arnold, Nottingham.

THE BRITISH ASSOCIATION IN NOTTINGHAM

HISTORICAL NOTE

THE British Association has met in Nottingham on three previous occasions, the first being in 1866, exactly 100 years ago. The next visit was made in 1893 and the third in 1937. Prior to its first meeting in Nottingham, the Association, which was founded in 1831, had held 35 annual meetings in more than 20 different centres. Oxford, Cambridge and Birmingham had each been host on three occasions and a number of other centres had received the Association twice. When at length its turn arrived, Nottingham was an industrial town of 80,000 inhabitants, though still without an institution of higher learning. The Mechanics Institute, however, founded in 1837, was a thriving centre of adult education. Yet 2,300 people attended the meetings, some of which were held in the Theatre Royal, which had been opened the previous year.

The Report of the Association's proceedings shows that local officials and eminent scholars in the town and district gave strong support to the occasion, both in organising and contributing to the programme. Among them was Edward J. Lowe, a distinguished naturalist and meteorologist, who served as one of the Local Secretaries. He lived at Highfields House, the grounds of which now form part of University Park and the house itself the Vice-Chancellor's residence, and it is of interest to recall that Lowe's meteorological instruments, from which regular readings were taken over the period 1840–81, were sited within a few yards of the present weather station maintained by the University Department of Geography.

In retrospect other aspects of the first Nottingham meeting are of much wider interest. Thus a report was submitted which dealt exhaustively with progress so far made in mapping the surface features of the moon. To a mid-Victorian public, despite the abstrusely mathematical content of this report, the subject itself was highly topical, for only a year before, Jules Verne's *De la Terre à la Lune*, the forerunner of modern science fiction, had been published in Paris and had already excited imagination on both sides of the Channel. Today, a century later, a journey to the moon, though not yet accomplished, is no longer fiction. Curiously, another contribution described a proposal for a transatlantic telegraph cable *via* Scotland, the Faeroes, Iceland, Greenland and Labrador, when only in the previous month (July 1866) the submarine cable from Valentia to Newfoundland had been successfully laid by the famous steamship *Great Eastern*. Also on this occasion the eminent geologist, Sir Robert

Murchison, pointed to the feasibility of winning coal from beneath the Triassic rocks of central Nottinghamshire 'at some distant day' when mining techniques became capable of deeper working. That day was in fact not far off and at the present time the mining industry in that area is unquestionably the pride of the National Coal Board.

When, in 1893, the second occasion arrived for Nottingham to entertain the British Association, the town was able to offer ampler and more appropriate accommodation. The University College had been opened in 1881 and the Albert Hall (not the present building), the property of the Wesleyan Mission, which was erected in 1876, provided a large auditorium. Both buildings were used for the meetings and evening functions, officially termed *soirées*, were held at the Castle. Nottingham was by now a town of almost a quarter of a million people, although another four years were to elapse before it was raised to the status of a city. The Association's Report again reflects some of the major issues confronting science in the contemporary world. At this time the application of the internal combustion engine to road vehicles had hardly passed the experimental stage, but already consideration was being given to possible means of travel by air other than by balloon. A significant contribution to the subject was offered to the Association in a paper on mechanical science in which, incidentally, the author felt it necessary to state at the outset that applied science, as studied by James Watt, was as free from suspicion of commercial bias as chemical science studied by Faraday! The paper contained a review of locomotive mechanisms in Nature, with particular reference to flight mechanisms in birds and went on to discuss the amount and kind of power required for artificial flight, without exceeding the weight which it would itself sustain. Within 10 years, using the internal combustion engine for the purpose, Orville Wright made the first successful flight in a heavier-than-air machine.

The third visit of the Association to Nottingham occurred well within living memory. Many of the meetings, including section programmes, were held in the University College at University Park on the outskirts of the city, an impressive and spacious site which had been developed since 1928, when the College, except for a few departments, was transferred from the centre of the city. The institution was still small, with about 600 full-time students and at University Park there were but two halls of residence, one for men and one for women. The Association's programme, despite the fact that the world was drifting towards another war, included several contributions in which the social implications of progress in science was an underlying theme. The growing interest in national planning was reflected in a joint discussion involving no less than five of the sections on planning the use of land in Britain, in the course of which Professor Julian Huxley made a strong plea both for nature conservation and for the establishment of National Parks. Another memorable contribution was the address given by the famous author H. G. Wells to Section L on 'The Informative Content of Education' in which he made a plea for breadth and balance in the school curriculum and stressed the importance of what he termed 'personal sociology'—the awareness of the conditions under which the individual must face his own community and the world at large.

The fourth meeting of the Association in Nottingham will be attended by some who did so in 1937. They, with all other members, will be welcomed to a city which has not only grown substantially in the intervening period, but in adapting itself to the modern age, shows striking evidence of the process known as urban renewal. Their deliberations will again take place at University Park, not in a University College but in what is now the oldest of the new Universities. Since the granting of the charter in 1948, the growth of the University reflects more fully than ever the advantages afforded by its superb site. Besides the huge expansion of departments and laboratories, now accommodating nearly 4,000 students, there are eight halls of residence for men and five for women and several of these are providing accommodation for members of the Association. Nottingham itself, moreover, now plays its part in one of the more recent developments of the British Association, for it is one of the regional centres through which the Association aims to keep the general public continually informed of the nature and scope of scientific progress.

At the inaugural meeting in 1866, William R. Grove, Q.C., opened his presidential address to the Association and members of the Nottingham public with the following words: 'If your rude predecessors, who at one time inhabited the caverns which surround this town, could rise from their graves and see it in its present state, it may be doubtful whether they would have sufficient knowledge to be surprised. The machinery, almost resembling organic beings in delicacy of structure, by which are fabricated products of world-wide reputation, the powers of matter applied to give motion to that machinery, are so far removed from what must have been the conceptions of the semi-barbarians to whom I have alluded, that they could not look on them with intelligent wonder. Yet this immense progress has all been effected step by step, now and then a little more rapidly than at other times; but, viewing the whole course of improvement, it has been gradual, though moving in an accelerated ratio.'

While historians have since disposed of the legend that Nottingham's early inhabitants were cave-dwellers—most of the caves date from medieval times or later—it is likely that the citizens of a hundred years ago would gaze in bewilderment if they could behold the products of science and engineering which provide the material equipment of life today. One other difference between their day and ours would be evident; that is the incomparably higher standard of education which now prevails. In the course of this achievement the British Association has made, and still makes, a distinctive contribution and few doubt that, in some manner or other, the process must continue. For scientific education and technological advance must now march together.

CONTENTS

xi

CONTENTS

PART III

The City of Nottingham

xiii

PART IV

Other Urban Centres

CONTENTS

LIST OF MAPS AND DIAGRAMS

B

LIST OF PLATES

For permission to use photographs for half-tone illustrations the editor is grateful to the following:

The Nottingham City Library for the frontispiece and, for Plates I and XVII; The Curator, Nottingham Castle Museum for Plate X; Capt. P. J. B. Drury-Lowe of Spondon, Derby, for Plate II taken from the late Mark Fryar's '*Some Chapters in the History of Denby*', 1934; Dr. J. K. St. Joseph, Cambridge for Plates III, IV, VIII, IX and XXI (Crown Copyright reserved); J. Allan Cash for Plates V and XXIII; H. Tempest Ltd. (Mundella Road, Nottingham) for Plates XVIII, XIX and XXII; The Trent River Authority for Plates VI and VII; The Central Electricity Generating Board for Plate XIV; The National Coal Board for Plates XI and XII; Hoveringham Gravels Ltd. for Plate XIII; Aerofilms Ltd. for Plate XXIV; Lincolnshire Echo for Plate XX.

LIST OF TABLES

INTRODUCTION

THE NOTTINGHAM REGION

On a clear day, looking westwards from Mapperley Plains, the highest part of Nottingham, one can just discern the lighthouse tower which marks the summit of Crich Stand, one of the Derbyshire hills, some 17 miles away. At night, as the light revolves, its momentary flash makes its presence even more distinct. The tower is a memorial to the men of the Sherwood Foresters who fell in the two World Wars and at its base an inscription recalls the famous rearguard action at Le Cateau, 1914 ('Gentlemen, we will stand and fight'). These were men whose forbears had lived for centuries along the borders of Nottinghamshire and Derbyshire, sharing a common history and winning a common livelihood from farming, mineral working and manufacturing. If we then turn to the east, observing the view which is nowadays restricted to glimpses between the houses, we see the unmistakable outline of Belvoir Castle crowning the distant ridge which forms the skyline. Just over the ridge, out of sight, is the old town of Grantham. Between Nottingham and the ridge itself stretches a broad lowland, about 20 miles wide, in which the vale of Trent and the adjoining vale of Belvoir are scarcely distinguishable from one another. Over this tract of country too, the people of Nottinghamshire, Lincolnshire and Leicestershire have for generations shared in the slowly changing rhythm of agricultural life.

The territory embraced by our view from Mapperley includes much of the area over which the influence of Nottingham is directly felt. For most of the population in this area Nottingham is not only the largest town but is the main focus of commercial, cultural and recreational activity. Less directly, however, the city's influence extends westwards beyond Derby to Ashbourne and the southern part of the Peak District, while eastwards it reaches Sleaford and north–eastwards to Lincoln itself. To the north, most of Nottinghamshire has inevitable connections with the city as the historic administrative centre, but beyond Retford and Worksop the remainder of the county, like the adjacent parts of Derbyshire and Lincolnshire, falls within the orbit of Sheffield. Southwards, the Leicestershire towns of Loughborough, Melton Mowbray and Ashby-de-la-Zouch have relatively close economic and social links with Nottingham, although their strongest ties are with Leicester. To the south–west, Burton-on-Trent, situated in Staffordshire yet only 10 miles from Derby, feels the influence of Birmingham as a regional centre rather than that of Nottingham. Similarly in the extreme north–west, Buxton exhibits close connections with Manchester.

With these somewhat intangible considerations in mind, the area chosen for study in this volume is that shown in Fig. 1. Its limits are clearly somewhat arbitrary, but at the same time they indicate, with the exception of the marginal cases referred to above, the area which can reasonably be termed the Nottingham region. In one respect, however, this definition of the region falls short. For many years Nottingham, as an inland city, has exhibited a direct interest in its nearest seaboard, the Lincolnshire coast. The beaches and sandhills of Skegness, Mablethorpe and Chapel St. Leonards, with their invigorating air, have long attracted holidaymakers from Nottingham and other East Midland towns. As a resort, Skegness owes much of its development to Nottingham business interests and to regard it as Nottingham-by-the-Sea is not altogether an exaggeration. More recently, the scientific work in coastal geomorphology, plant ecology, marine biology and nature conservation at Gibraltar Point, undertaken by departments of the University of Nottingham, have strengthened this connection. Accordingly, space has been devoted in this survey for contributions dealing with these and kindred aspects concerning this part of Lincolnshire.

A REGIONAL CAPITAL

Because of its size, importance and accessibility, Nottingham is a regional centre in quite a different sense. As the traditional headquarters of numerous organisations and institutions serving the East Midlands (an area comprising the counties of Nottinghamshire, Derbyshire, Leicestershire, Rutland and the greater part of Lincolnshire and Northamptonshire), it has also become the centre for the regional offices of government departments and most of the various nationalized undertakings. For the most part, Nottingham was the obvious choice as a regional capital. The only likely alternative would have been Leicester, whose claims must have been almost as great. In relation to population distribution, however, Nottingham held the advantage of proximity to the adjoining coalfield and industrial area which, together with the city itself, support more than one-third of the inhabitants of the East Midland region. Again, over much of the northern half of the region, Nottingham's influence is felt through the medium of its press. The 'Nottingham Journal', founded as the 'Courant' in 1710, only a few years after the appearance of the famous 'Stamford Mercury', was among the very earliest of provincial newspapers. Liberal by tradition, it has contributed much to progressive journalism and is still published, although in 1953 it was amalgamated with its competitor, the 'Nottingham Guardian' (1861), and is now known as the 'Guardian-Journal'. Nottingham is one of the few remaining cities outside London with a morning daily as well as an evening newspaper and is the only instance in the East Midlands.

The city's importance as a university centre adds further support to its role as a regional capital. The former University College was established primarily to serve the East Midlands and its advancement to full university status in 1948, attracting students and scholars increasingly from all parts of the country and abroad, confirmed

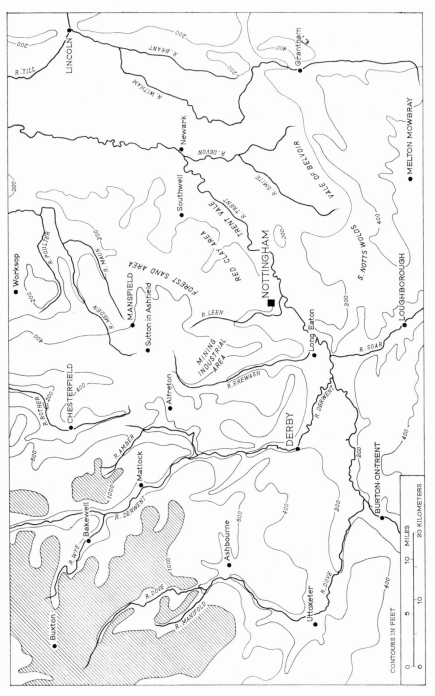

Fig. 1   The Nottingham Region   *(Crown Copyright reserved)*

its significance as a major seat of learning. Here it is of special interest to recall that, as a geographer, the late Professor C. B. Fawcett, who was himself closely associated with the University College and was President of Section E when the British Association met at Nottingham in 1937, suggested that the city should be regarded as a regional capital in a paper entitled '*The Natural Divisions of England*', published almost 50 years ago.

ECONOMIC DIVERSITY AND STABILITY

Later chapters in this volume emphasise the diversity of industrial production which is the outstanding characteristic of Nottingham's economy. This may come as a surprise to some for whom the name of the city has long been synonymous with lace. Nottingham achieved her particular fame as the centre of the machine-made lace trade, for which fabrics of exquisite material and design were produced in huge quantities for all parts of the world. Yet this industry had its technological roots in the much older one of framework-knitting, and when William Felkin, the historian of the lace and hosiery trades, addressed members of the British Association in 1866 it seemed that these two pursuits would eventually absorb the entire energies of the townspeople. Today, a century later, the two industries still flourish, but along with them an astonishing range of manufacturing now exists. The choice of careers for young people is unusually varied and the broadly based economy has resulted in continuous prosperity over a long period. With its persistently low rate of un-employment, its comparative freedom from industrial disputes and its high average incomes enjoyed by both men and women, Nottingham, like Leicester, its near neighbour, ranks in these respects among the most fortunate cities in the country.

DIVERSITY IN LANDSCAPE

If, in regard to material welfare, Nottingham has profited from economic diversity, so too the diversity of environment to be found in its geographical setting, helps to make it an interesting place in which to live. To the ordinarily observant person several contrasted types of landscape can be distinguished within a few miles of the city centre. The fundamental reason for this variety of scene lies in the fact that several geological formations converge upon the site of the city, each giving rise to its own particular surface features, soil and drainage conditions and mineral resources. These, in turn, affect the character of the vegetation and even, to some extent, the types of agriculture and other economic activities (Fig. 2). Man, too, of course, has played, and still plays, a large part in modifying the landscape and often serves to heighten the contrast between one area and another.

The first, and perhaps the most obvious, of these different types of country is the industrial landscape which extends north–westwards across the coalfield to the Erewash valley. This is a densely peopled area. Its rather hilly surface is strewn with straggling towns and mining settlements, with collieries and waste-heaps in or near the hollows and railways threading their way from one small valley to another. In the town of Eastwood is the Sun Inn, where, in 1832, a group of coal-owners met to decide on the building of the Midland Counties Railway, the forerunner of the great Midland railway system. In a nearby street, over 50 years later, D. H. Lawrence was born and nurtured, and, in due course, with deep sensitivity and skilful artistry, portrayed this mining landscape in his earlier tales and novels. The scene is by no means uniformly drab, however, for there remain small stretches of unspoilt country, as at Beauvale and Strelley, beloved of Lawrence, to remind us of how the land appeared before industrial times (Fig. 1 and Plate I).

Northwards from the city, the roads to Mansfield (A.60) and Ollerton (A.614) lead over a sandstone formation known as the Bunter Sandstone which presents a surface of broad undulations which are reflected in the switchback nature of the roads themselves. The Sandstone is particularly porous; consequently there is little surface drainage, streams are infrequent and most of the valleys are dry. The thin, poor soil, so loose in dry weather that strong winds carry it from the fields in dust clouds (hence the term 'blowing sands') does not encourage cultivation without special treatment. Vegetation is also somewhat impoverished by the dry conditions, resulting in a large amount of bracken and gorse, interspersed with oak and birch woods, supplemented in more recent years by coniferous plantations. These conditions provided the ecological basis for the ancient forest of Sherwood, the hunting ground of kings, and the setting for the legends of Robin Hood. Later on, much of the area in central Nottinghamshire was enclosed to form the great estates (the Dukeries) of Welbeck, Rufford, Clumber and Thoresby. Today, despite the difficulties of farming, there is a good deal of arable land and the characteristically large fields are an advantage for modern methods. The Bunter Sandstone country is nevertheless sparsely populated, and even villages are rare. A few large collieries, working coal at depth below the Sandstone, all of them built since 1920, have introduced an incongruous element into the forest environment, but even with their adjacent housing have not greatly affected the area as a whole. An occasional pumping-station is a reminder of the large quantities of water stored naturally in the lower strata of the Sandstone.

Travelling northwards from Nottingham along the Ollerton road, the observer notes a sharp rise of ground a little to the east which continues as a prominent feature for most of the way. This is the same feature which forms the high ground called Mapperley Plains to the north-east of the city and represents the escarpment of the Keuper Series, the formation which succeeds the Bunter Sandstone eastwards. The Keuper Series consists of a considerable thickness of Red Marl underlain by sandstone called Waterstones. The Red Marl forms a broad tract of country on either side of the Trent valley, but it is on the west side that its distinctive scenery is most fully developed. The Marl itself assumes the character of a stiff reddish clay, giving rise to a low plateau dissected by numerous streams. The upper courses of the streams have cut miniature ravines called 'dumbles' (Lambley Dumble, Oxton Dumble, etc.), while the plateau surface in general, like the gentler valley slopes, is well-wooded farm-land. In contrast to conditions on the Bunter Sandstone, villages and farms are abundant and some of the larger valleys like the Greet, in which the little cathedral town of Southwell is situated, and the Dover Beck, with the villages of Oxton and Epperstone, are exceptionally productive. The fields are smaller than on the Sandstone and their hedgerow trees add further to the wooded appearance of the countryside. Orchards, too, are a feature of the area, though many of them are past their prime. The red-brick farms and cottages, with their pantile roofs and white window-frames, ancient sandstone churches, the red soil and abundant green foliage in summer, make this the most colourful of the rural landscapes around Nottingham. Only at Calverton has present-day industry intruded, and it is a strange coincidence that the village where the stocking frame was invented nearly 400 years ago should be chosen as the site of a modern colliery, opened in 1952.

From the physical standpoint alone, the Trent valley is by far the most obvious of the different landscape types. For almost 20 miles, from Beeston (upstream from the city) to Newark, the valley has the form of a shallow trench, with a broad, flat floor, well over a mile wide, bordered by slopes of Keuper Marl, which are often steep enough to form cliffs, as at Radcliffe-on-Trent. These slopes are frequently clad with fine deciduous woods, as at Clifton Grove across the river from Nottingham, at East Bridgford and at Hazelford. With the river curving in wide meanders amid rich meadows, such places are an attraction to anglers and picnic parties as well as to those afloat in small pleasure cruisers. The floor of the vale is put to various uses. In the immediate vicinity of Nottingham it is devoted to industrial development and railway yards. Further away, both above and below the city, are extensive gravel workings which, after extraction, give rise to water-filled pits having potential amenity value. At intervals of a few miles, huge electricity generating stations have made their appearance in recent years, giving the Trent valley a new significance on account of its major contribution to the country's power supply. Elsewhere, the valley floor is mainly devoted to agriculture, with farms and villages located on fragments of gravel terraces away from the river and secure from the floods of former times.

Beyond the Trent valley to the east lies the vale of Belvoir, which is crossed by two main roads leading from Nottingham, the Grantham road (A.52) and the Melton Mowbray road (A.606). It is a broad clay vale, extending in a south–west to north–east direction along the foot of the Belvoir escarpment and is drained by two of the Trent tributaries, the Smite and the Devon. This relatively bold escarpment is formed by the Middle Lias Marlstone, and on the crest, a few miles south–west of Grantham, is Belvoir Castle, the home of the Dukes of Rutland, which is one of the most conspicuous landmarks in the region. The vale itself is chiefly composed of Lias Clay and is almost exclusively devoted to farming, with an emphasis upon milk production. In this connection, villages in the southern portion of the vale have earned a measure of fame as the leading district in the country for the making of Stilton cheese.

Almost due south of Nottingham, not far beyond the limit of the built-up area, the road to Melton Mowbray climbs to a low plateau with an average altitude of a little over 300 feet. The surface in many places is surprisingly flat, but wherever the ground rises slightly extensive views are obtained. This relatively elevated stretch of country is known as the South Nottinghamshire Wolds and its continuation beyond the county boundary as the Leicestershire Wolds. It is roughly triangular in shape, with its apex towards Nottingham and the eastern part of it, which is traversed by the Melton Mowbray road, extends as far as the village of Upper Broughton, from which there is a sharp descent to the vale of Belvoir. That the Wolds possess some kind of individuality is indicated by the village names, such as Stanton-on-the-Wolds, Willoughby-on-the-Wolds and Wymeswold, while in several parishes there is a Wolds Farm. The Wolds plateau is a result of particular geological conditions, for it is formed by a sheet of glacial boulder clay which is the only fairly large occurrence of glacial drift in the Nottingham area. It is really a fragment of the great mantle of similar material which extends far across eastern England. This cover of boulder clay masks the irregularities of the pre-glacial relief, which was mainly developed on the underlying Lias Clay. The Wolds area, like the vale of Belvoir, is almost entirely a farming district, with livestock, especially dairy cattle, as the main interest and is one of the chief sources of Nottingham's milk supply.

The foregoing paragraphs serve to demonstrate the variety of environment to be found within a short distance of Nottingham. Further afield in the region, the diversity of scene is just as great. In many ways the city itself is representative of the combined interests of all these areas and, in turn, the people of the region are interested in the city. Moreover, as Nottingham continues to play its part as a regional capital, this interest will grow rather than diminish. Through a common tradition the people of the region share with its citizens a natural pride in the development of the city. In size, Nottingham is now the eighth city in England and the tenth in Great Britain, and, in an age distinguished by rapid advances in science and technology, its opportunities for enriching the quality of life in the community, in addition to safeguarding its material welfare, are immense. The achievement of the past must inspire the energies of the present. This is a continuous process out of which the unworthy must be rejected and only the best be permitted to survive. The ideal is tersely expressed in the civic motto—VIVIT POST FUNERA VIRTUS—and it is fair to add that high endeavour is as essential now as in the past to ensure the city's future.

PART I

PHYSICAL BACKGROUND

I

GEOLOGY

WITHIN the radius of a few miles from Nottingham, rocks ranging in age from Pre-Cambrian to Pleistocene can be found. Not all the systems are represented, notable exceptions being the Devonian and Tertiary. The city of Nottingham is built largely on sediments of the Permian and Triassic Systems, whilst alluvial deposits of the Rivers Trent and Leen are included within the city boundary. To the east of Nottingham broad outcrops of younger Mesozoic rocks occur as far as the Lincolnshire Wolds. Westwards, Carboniferous rocks produce a varied configuration controlled by the presence of sandstones alternating with softer shales. On the western margin of the region the Carboniferous Limestones of Derbyshire and Staffordshire form the uplands of the southern Peak District.

South and east of Nottingham, the Trent flows over Trias rocks, mainly marls, through which protrude isolated outcrops of Carboniferous Limestone, as at Breedon Hill and the more extensive area of Pre-Cambrian rocks of Charnwood Forest. The nearest outcrops of Lower Palaeozoic rocks are at Nuneaton and Dudley some miles outside the region.

Sub-surface exploration by the National Coal Board and British Petroleum in recent years has given an increasingly comprehensive picture of Carboniferous times. Unfortunately however, few bore-holes penetrate the rocks beneath the Carboniferous Limestone and the pre-Carboniferous geology of the Nottingham region remains one of the principal unsolved problems.

Table I (p. 12) illustrates the generalised geological sequence in the Nottingham region, whilst their surface extent is shown in Fig. 2. The figures in feet indicating thickness are only approximate owing to considerable variations over the region as a whole.

In the account which follows, each of the Systems listed in Table I is described, the detailed geological sequence is given in tabular form, and an attempt is made to indicate the advances in knowledge which have been made since the British Association's last visit to Nottingham in 1937. Brief reference is made to raw materials of economic importance, but these are considered in greater detail in Chapter XVI. The account ends with a brief outline of the structural geology of the region.

Table I   General geological sequence

System	Formation	Approx. Thickness in feet	Rocks
Pleistocene and Recent Deposits			Boulder clay and gravels, R. Trent gravels, Cave and Tufa deposits
.... Unconformity			
Cretaceous (Lincolnshire)	Upper Cretaceous	300	Chalk
	Lower Cretaceous	700	Chalk, sands, clays
.... Unconformity			
Jurassic (mainly Lincolnshire)	Upper Jurassic	700	Clays
	Middle Jurassic	400	Oolitic limestones, sands, clays, ironstones
	Lower Jurassic (Lias)	1000	Clays, limestones, ironstones
Triassic including Rhaetic	Rhaetic Series	40	Calcareous siltstones, black shales
(1000 feet but more in the north, less in the south)	Keuper Series	600	Red marls, skerries, fine sandstones, gypsum
	Bunter Series	600	Pebble beds, sandstones
.... Unconformity in places			
Permian	Upper Permian (Zechstein)	Up to 150	Marls, dolomites, sandstones, siltstones, breccias
.... Unconformity			
Carboniferous (at least 7000 feet)	Upper Carboniferous	5–6000	Dark grey mudstones, black shales, sandstones, coals
	Lower Carboniferous	2–3000	Limestones, igneous rocks
.... Unconformity			
Pre-Cambrian	Rocks comparable with those of Charnwood Forest	—	Altered sediments, volcanic rocks, intrusive rocks

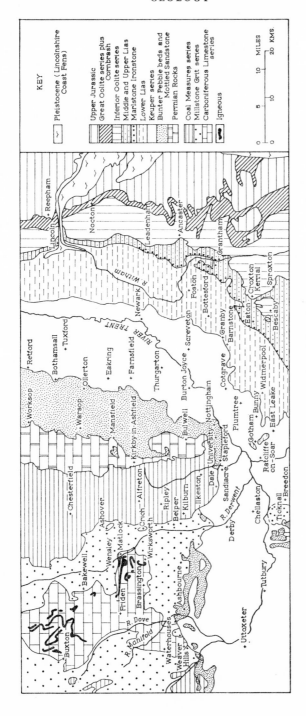

Fig. 2 The solid geology

Based on Crown Copyright Geological Survey map(s) by permission of the Controller of H.M. Stationery Office

STRATIGRAPHY

THE PRE-CAMBRIAN

Rocks of this age are exposed in Charnwood Forest, Leicestershire. As this area lies just outside the Nottingham region no detailed treatment is given here. It is generally believed that rocks of Charnwood Forest type must underlie the Lower Carboniferous throughout much of the region. They have been located at Woo-Dale, at its junction with the Wye Valley near Buxton. An oil boring at Foston, north-west of Grantham, recorded Charnian Rocks possibly similar to those of the Brand Series, and at Sproxton a bore-hole terminated in rocks thought to be similar to the Swithland Slates, again of the Brand Series.

The rocks of Charnwood Forest fall into three main sedimentary and volcanic groups, with associated intruded rocks:

The Brand Series:	Swithland Slates, Conglomerates, grits and quartzites, Hanging Rock Conglomerate.
The Maplewell Series:	Woodhouse and Bradgate olive Hornstone Beds, Slate Agglomerate, Beacon Hill Beds (Hornstones), Felsitic Agglomerate.
The Blackbrook Series:	Blackbrook Beds.
Igneous Rocks:	Porphyroids, Felsites, Syenites and Granodiorites.

It was from the Woodhouse Beds of the Maplewell Series that *Charnia* and *Charniodiscus* were obtained. These 'body-like' fossils, possibly algae, described by T. D. Ford, are comparable with certain Australian fossils found in Pre-Cambrian rocks. In the absence of further information, it is assumed that rocks of the kind mentioned above comprise the Pre-Cambrian basement which underlies the Nottingham area.

LOWER PALAEOZOIC ROCKS AND DEVONIAN STRATA

There is no certain identification of these rocks in the region. In the Nocton oil boring quartzites thought to be comparable with the Cambrian Nuneaton Quartzites were encountered at the base. At the Dukes Wood boring, red sandstones close to the base, below rocks of known Carboniferous age could be from the Old Red Sandstone Formation.

THE CARBONIFEROUS SYSTEM

LOWER CARBONIFEROUS (Carboniferous Limestone Series)

The main outcrops of Avonian strata are to be found in the counties of Derbyshire and Staffordshire. Small inliers are to be found east of the main area at Crich and Ashover (Derbyshire) and to the south, at Breedon Hill, Breedon Cloud, Barlow Hill,

Osgathorpe and Grace Dieu in Leicestershire; and at Ticknall and Calke in south Derbyshire. These rocks also extend eastwards and south-eastwards under the Upper Carboniferous, Permian and Triassic cover.

Recent research has been mainly concerned with the stratigraphical succession of the limestones, which is summarised in Table II. In this table the apparent correlation of the Goniatite, and Coral/Brachiopod zones is shown, and representative formations of these zones. The table does not imply the occurrence of low Viséan and possibly Tournaisian rocks throughout the southern Peak District.

The oldest Avonian rocks occur in the south-west part of the main limestone outcrop. They are found adjacent to the Hanley-Ashbourne road, north of the Weaver Hills, and in the Manifold Valley near Waterhouses. The Tournaisian (C_1) age of these limestones depends, according to J. E. Prentice, upon the presence of *Productus garwoodi*, *Pustula pilosa*, *Schizophoria nuda* and possibly *Pericyclus fasciculatus* whilst A. Ludford includes *Solenopera garwoodi*. It is interesting to note that T. N. George, in a review of the Lower Carboniferous Palaeogeography of Great Britain, considers the presence of Tournaisian beds in the Southern Peak not proved.

Support for the view of T. N. George that there is an absence of Tournaisian rocks in the South Peak has recently been advanced in a paper by Parkinson and Ludford, who would prefer a C_2 age for many of the limestones previously regarded as C_1. The change of opinion is brought about by these authors finding *Solenopera garwoodi* with a fauna considered to be diagnostic of early Visean, C_2/S_1. The new work in the Swinscoe area of Staffordshire suggests that much of the earlier work in the Weaver Hills, Dove Dale and the Manifold Valley will have to be reconsidered and that the correlation shown in Table II, based on that work will also have to be revised.

There follows a full succession of Viséan limestones ranging in age from C_2 (B_1) to D_2 (P_1). The lowest Viséan beds are again found in the west, in the Dove and Manifold Valleys and at Cauldon Low. The lowest limestones of Breedon Cloud and possibly the other inliers in the neighbourhood, are of the same age. During the deposition of the limestones, there were two dominant facies; firstly, well-bedded, light coloured limestones, with a coral-brachiopod (mainly productid) fauna; and secondly, irregular mounds or knolls of unbedded or irregularly bedded limestones which contain a dominantly brachiopod fauna, more varied than the first, with occasional bryozoa, trilobites and goniatites. The first facies is correlated with shelf sea conditions and the second with reefs, although no attempt has yet been made to distinguish back- and fore-reef deposits, as attempted by E. B. Wolfenden in the Castleton area to the north. A third facies is characterised by dark argillaceous limestones, often interbedded with calcareous shales or mudstones, and containing fauna of brachiopods, lamellibranchs, trilobites and solitary corals. Some authors refer these limestones to a basin environment but the presence of trilobites and horny brachiopods suggest that the sea was not markedly deeper than that of the other areas.

TABLE II   Lower Carboniferous
(NOT TO SCALE)

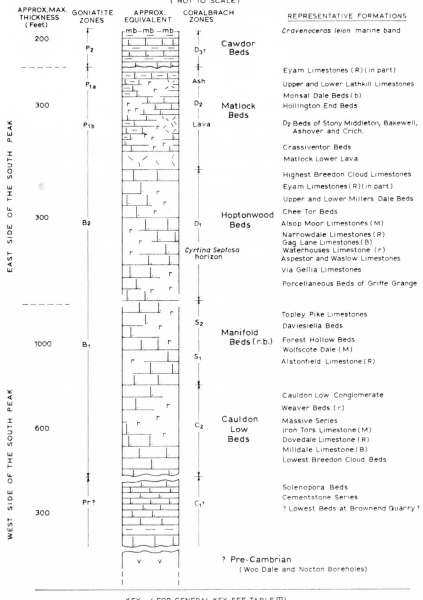

APPROX. MAX. THICKNESS (Feet)	GONIATITE ZONES	APPROX. EQUIVALENT	CORALBRACH ZONES		REPRESENTATIVE FORMATIONS
		mb—mb —mb			*Cravenoceras leion* marine band
200	P_2		D_3?	Cawdor Beds	
					Eyam Limestones (R)(in part)
	P_{1a}		Ash		Upper and Lower Lathkill Limestones
					Monsal Dale Beds (b)
300			D_2	Matlock Beds	Hollington End Beds
	P_{1b}		Lava		D_2 Beds of Stony Middleton, Bakewell, Ashover and Crich.
					Crassiventor Beds
					Matlock Lower Lava
					Highest Breedon Cloud Limestones
					Eyam Limestones(R)(in part)
					Upper and Lower Millers Dale Beds
300	B_2		D_1	Hoptonwood Beds	Chee Tor Beds
					Alsop Moor Limestones (M)
					Narrowdale Limestones (R)
			Cyrtina Septosa horizon		Gag Lane Limestones (B) Waterhouses Limestone (r)
					Aspestor and Waslow Limestones
					Via Gellia Limestones
					Porcellaneous Beds of Griffe Grange
					Topley Pike Limestones
			S_2		Daviesiella Beds
1000	B_1			Manifold Beds (r.b.)	Forest Hollow Beds
					Wolfscote Dale (M)
			S_1		Alstonfield Limestone (R)
					Cauldon Low Conglomerate
					Weaver Beds (r)
					Massive Series
600			C_2	Cauldon Low Beds	Iron Tors Limestone (M)
					Dovedale Limestone (R)
					Milldale Limestone (B)
					Lowest Breedon Cloud Beds
					Solenopora Beds
	Pr?		C_1?		Cementstone Series
300					? Lowest Beds at Brownend Quarry ?
					? Pre-Cambrian (Woo Dale and Nocton Boreholes)

EAST SIDE OF THE SOUTH PEAK

WEST SIDE OF THE SOUTH PEAK

KEY   (FOR GENERAL KEY SEE TABLE III)

Thin Beds		Limestones
Massive Beds		Shales and Calcareous Shales
		Igneous Rocks
		Slates

mb - Marine Band
M - Massive Shelf Limestones
R - Reef Limestones
B - Basin Limestones
m.r.b. developed in part

There is still no general agreement concerning the correlation of the goniatite and coral zonal schemes in Derbyshire, although the degree of disagreement was reduced with the revision of part of the Castleton area. The need for agreement is felt particularly in regard to the Dibunophyllum Zone, where limestones with corals and brachiopods are frequently in close proximity to those with goniatites, but the same feeling of frustration is experienced wherever massive shelf limestones are found close to the reef limestones but cannot be seen to pass one into the other.

At the top of the Viséan in the Matlock-Wirksworth area, Cawdor Beds, P_2, rest on D_2 beds in the north and can be traced southwards eventually resting on the D_1 Hopton Wood beds, at Wirksworth. On the west side of the main limestone area, the D_2 beds are again cut out by the overlying unconformity, or are very thin, such as the upper few feet of the Waterhouses Limestone, referred to by Prentice as the Crassiventor beds. In the Manifold Valley, described by Prentice and W. S. Bisat, goniatites referable to P_{1a} or B_2 would seem to indicate a D_1 age for these beds. The highest Viséan limestones, excluding P_2 beds, are to be found then only on the east side of the limestone area extending northwards from Cromford and Matlock.

A review of the limestones in the southern Peak indicates that a number of areas require further investigation. They are to be found in the country south of a line between Wirksworth and Ashbourne and on to the Staffordshire border, extending as far south as the Trias unconformity and therefore also including Namurian strata. Ford, who is engaged on a revision of the northern part, affirms that shelf, reef and 'basin' facies predominately of D_1 age include algal structures comparable with those described by Wolfenden in the north.

A feature of the limestones in the south is that they are dolomitised to a greater or lesser extent and commonly form prominent upstanding crags. Ford has described among others the dolomite tors of Rainster Rocks, the Harboro' Rocks and Wyn's Tor and has commented on their origin.

The petrology, mineralogy and palaeontology of the Lower Carboniferous has received less attention in recent years. The main reference on the igneous rocks are still the maps of H. H. Bemrose. Only two quarries work these rocks at present, both being outside the region. A series of bore-holes drilled at Ashover showed that considerable thickness of igneous rocks, both extrusive and intrusive, occur at depth. One bore-hole recorded almost 1000 feet of igneous rock with only subsidiary limestones. Although Bemrose's maps indicate the surface extent of the volcanic and intrusive rocks, the stratigraphical position of many of the lava flows and igneous bodies have since been revised, suggesting that a complete review of the igneous rocks might yield new results.

With the final closure of the Mill Close lead mine in 1940, active exploitation primarily for lead and zinc ceased in the limestone area around Matlock. The only mines now operating are further north in the Eyam district. The old lead mines and numerous opencast sections along the mineral rakes are being searched for fluorite, calcite and barytes, with lead and zinc obtained only as by-products. The principal advances made in this field are the descriptions of new minerals, catalogued in a useful mineral index prepared by Ford and W. A. S. Sarjeant. S. Moorbath has published the results of radioactive dating of four samples of lead ore from different localities, the age determinations varying from 150 to 210 million years.

The active exploitation of the southern Peak for limestone has never been more intense than at present. The uses to which the limestone is put are dealt with in Chapter XVI.

UPPER CARBONIFEROUS

In revising the Chesterfield (No. 112) and Derby (No. 125) one-inch to the mile sheets, the Geological Survey has added considerably to our knowledge of the Upper Carboniferous. The need for opencast coal and the extension of the deep mines eastwards has likewise contributed further information through the National Coal Board, while a third organisation, British Petroleum, in their search for oil in the East Midlands has published a large amount of data. The stratigraphical column of the Upper Carboniferous, largely compiled from these sources, is given in Table III.

The Millstone Grit Series (Namurian)

Lithologically sharp changes occur above the *Cravenoceras leion* marine bed. Below this horizon, dark coloured limestones are characteristic, but above they are very rare and calcium carbonate is generally restricted to 'bullion' horizons. Bullions are concretionary blocks of argillaceous limestone, often containing goniatites. Characteristic sediments of the Namurian are black fissile shales, often carbonaceous, containing goniatites; dark grey mudstones and siltstones; and coarse felspathic sandstones, often pebbly. The black fissile shales represent marine conditions, the rest being non-marine sediments. Within the succession very thin coals may be present.

Of particular interest are the marine-beds which may well be the source beds for the oil found in the East Midlands and pumped from overlying porous gritstones, which form the reservoir rocks. These rich organic layers can be detected in bore-holes using various recording devices, in particular the Gamma log. The marine bands remain the most useful marker horizons in stratigraphical correlation.

The sub-surface exploration work and more detailed surface mapping with the discovery of new exposures has convinced geologists that changes were needed in the nomenclature of the Gritstones. Firstly, the occurrence of any one of the three marine beds *Reticuloceras wrighti*, *R. bilingue* and *R. gracile* below the lowest gritstone in the Ashover-Matlock area indicated a higher position in the geological column for this gritstone than the name Kinderscout implied, for in north Derbyshire the above-mentioned marine beds occur on top of the Kinderscout Grit. The lowest prominent gritstone has therefore been renamed the Ashover Grit.

TABLE III   Upper Carboniferous

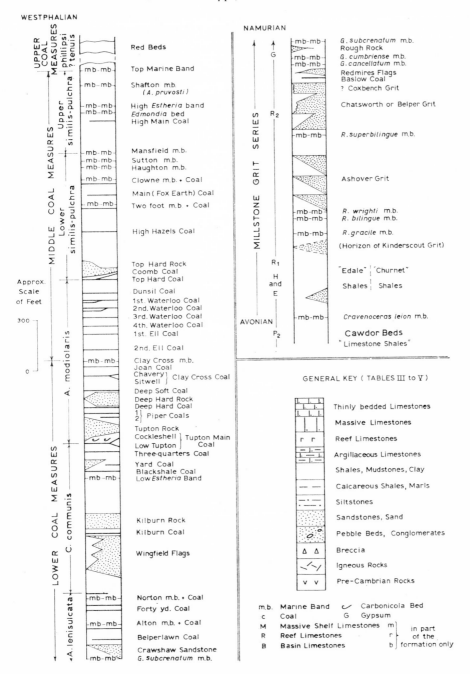

WESTPHALIAN

UPPER COAL MEASURES — phillipsi - ?tenuis	
mb-mb	Red Beds
	Top Marine Band
mb-mb	Shafton m.b. (A. pruvosti)
mb-mb	High Estheria band
mb-mb	Edmondia bed
	High Main Coal
mb-mb	Mansfield m.b.
mb-mb	Sutton m.b.
mb-mb	Haughton m.b.
mb-mb	Clowne m.b. + Coal
	Main (Fox Earth) Coal
mb-mb	Two foot m.b. + Coal
	High Hazels Coal
	Top Hard Rock
	Coomb Coal
	Top Hard Coal
	Dunsil Coal
	1st. Waterloo Coal
	2nd. Waterloo Coal
	3rd. Waterloo Coal
	4th. Waterloo Coal
	1st. Ell Coal
	2nd. Ell Coal
mb-mb	Clay Cross m.b.
	Joan Coal
	Chavery } Sitwell } Clay Cross Coal
	Deep Soft Coal
	Deep Hard Rock
	Deep Hard Coal
	1) 2) Piper Coals
	Tupton Rock
	Cockleshell } Low Tupton } Tupton Main Coal
	Three-quarters Coal
	Yard Coal
	Blackshale Coal
mb-mb	Low Estheria Band
	Kilburn Rock
	Kilburn Coal
	Wingfield Flags
mb-mb	Norton m.b. + Coal
	Forty yd. Coal
mb-mb	Alton m.b. + Coal
	Belperlawn Coal
	Crawshaw Sandstone
mb-mb	G. subcrenatum m.b.

MIDDLE COAL MEASURES
- Upper similis-pulchra
- Lower similis-pulchra
- A. modiolaris

LOWER COAL MEASURES
- C. communis
- A. lenisulcata

Approx. Scale of Feet
300
0

NAMURIAN

MILLSTONE GRIT SERIES

mb-mb	G. subcrenatum m.b.
	Rough Rock
mb-mb	G. cumbriense m.b.
mb-mb	G. cancellatum m.b.
	Redmires Flags
	Baslow Coal
	? Coxbench Grit
	Chatsworth or Belper Grit
mb-mb	R. superbilingue m.b.
	Ashover Grit
mb-mb	R. wrighti m.b.
mb-mb	R. bilingue m.b.
mb-mb	R. gracile m.b.
	(Horizon of Kinderscout Grit)
	"Edale"	"Churnet"
	Shales	Shales
mb-mb	Cravenoceras leion m.b.
	Cawdor Beds
	"Limestone Shales"

G
R₂
R₁
H and E
AVONIAN
P₂

GENERAL KEY (TABLES III to V)

	Thinly bedded Limestones
	Massive Limestones
r r	Reef Limestones
	Argillaceous Limestones
	Shales, Mudstones, Clay
—	Calcareous Shales, Marls
	Siltstones
	Sandstones, Sand
o · o	Pebble Beds, Conglomerates
Δ Δ	Breccia
	Igneous Rocks
v v	Pre-Cambrian Rocks

m.b.	Marine Band	⌣	Carbonicola Bed
c	Coal	G	Gypsum
M	Massive Shelf Limestones	m	in part
R	Reef Limestones	r	of the
B	Basin Limestones	b	formation only

In the Belper area, the Middle Gritstones occur in two distinct layers, the Belper Grit below and the Coxbench Grit above. Evidence is still not available to decide whether the two combined gritstones represent the Chatsworth Grit to the north or if the Coxbench Grit holds a similar stratigraphical position to the Redmires Flags of the north.

The highest prominent gritstone was generally referred to as the Rough Rock. The Geological Survey and British Petroleum geologists have now found the *Gastrioceras subcrenatum* (Pot Clay) marine bed below this coarse sandstone throughout much of the northern part of the region. This marine bed, at the junction of the Namurian and Westphalian, places the highest gritstone in the Coal Measures and it is better referred to as the Crawshaw Sandstone. The Rough Rock is generally made up of a few feet of micaceous siltstones. Whether or not the Crawshaw sandstone completely eclipses the Rough Rock as far south as Dale and Sandiacre remains to be proved, but it seems likely to do so.

The biggest question mark is poised over the area north of the Belper-Ashbourne road (see also p. 17) where discoveries of new fossil localities are likely to be made, providing new information on which the stratigraphy of the area can be based.

In the east of the region information released by British Petroleum shows that the marine beds of the Namurian are remarkably persistent, more so than the gritstones, which thin out east of a line running north and south through Eakring. A comparison of the thicknesses in the Eakring area, both with those of the outcrop area to the west and with those of the Widmerpool area to the south, shows that the successions in the outcrop area and at Eakring might represent block (? shelf) regions whilst the fuller succession at Widmerpool might indicate the presence of a 'gulf' (? basin) region.

The Coal Measure Series (Westphalian)

The Coal Measures begin with a sandstone (Crawshaw Sandstone) lithologically identical with the sandstones of the Millstone Grit Series. However, succeeding sandstones are generally finer grained, more compact and lacking in felspar and pebbles. The more homogeneous texture of the rock is indicated by its lower porosity. In fresh excavations these rocks are grey and exhibit characteristic fine laminations often indicating current-bedding but when exposed to the atmosphere they turn yellowish-brown. Some of the sandstones, such as the Wingfield Flags, can be readily sawn, whilst others are used for walling stones. Table III shows the main stone horizons. They are more frequent in the Lower Coal Measures, although arenaceous beds are again frequent in the Upper Coal Measures (see below, p. 21).

The predominant rock types are dark grey mudstones and laminated siltstones. Marine shales are rare, becoming more common at the top of the Middle Coal Measures. These marine bands are listed in Table III, including the classic trio, the Clay Cross, Mansfield and Shafton Marine bands.

The Clay Cross Marine Band is now used to identify the junction between the Lower and Middle Coal Measures in order that this major stratigraphical division of the Nottinghamshire and Derbyshire coalfield may conform to that of coalfields elsewhere. The boundary between Middle and Upper Coal Measures is placed approximately 75 feet above the Shafton Marine Band at the horizon of the Top Marine Band. These changes account for the different appearance in the Coal Measures outcrop in the first and second editions of the Chesterfield Sheet.

The coal seams are of major economic importance to the Nottingham region. The main seams are listed in Table III. Knowledge concerning the lateral extent of these seams has increased with the development of open-cast coal working in the outcrop area and the continuation eastwards of deep-mining in the concealed field. The Leen Valley collieries, famous for their extraction of the Top Hard Coal, are now concentrating on the deeper seams, at one time the province of the Erewash Valley pits, particularly the Deep Soft, Deep Hard and Tupton Coals. The latter collieries are now working the thinner seams like the Yard and Threequarters Coal. In the south-west part of the coalfield, the Blackshale Coal proved to be of poor quality and in the Kilburn and Stapleford areas the Kilburn Coal, now exhausted, was the principal seam.

Nothing is seen of the Upper Coal Measures in the exposed coalfield in the Nottingham area; they are known only from bore-hole information in the concealed field to the east. North-east and east of Nottingham, 'Barren Red Measures' are recorded below the Permo-Trias south of Eakring in the Farnsfield, Thurgarton and Burton Joyce localities. These red-coloured sandstones and shales always occur above the Top Marine Band and there may be grey Coal Measures, situated between the two series of red, giving thicknesses of up to 700 feet. The argillaceous beds are said to resemble the Etruria Marls and the arenaceous beds the Espley Sandstone of Staffordshire.

Another feature of the concealed Coal Measures is the presence of igneous rocks mainly olivine basalts, south-east of a line from Nottingham through Eakring to Lincoln, with a maximum development in the Screveton-Sproxton area. Both intrusive and extrusive rocks are recorded from Lower Coal Measures. At Screveton, the Lenisulcata Zone of the Lower Coal Measures seems to be largely replaced by volcanic rocks. The igneous rocks, described by W. Edwards, first appear in Namurian strata and are best developed at the base of the Coal Measures, and continue periodically throughout the Lower Coal Measures.

OROGENIC MOVEMENTS AT THE CLOSE OF THE CARBONIFEROUS

Following upon the volcanic and intrusive activity noted above, earth movements began which buckled and dislocated the rocks forming the structures described later on. Both Edwards and Swinnerton and P. E. Kent suggest that the movement began late in Upper Coal Measures times as some of the Upper Carboniferous Red Beds appear to be unconformable on beds ranging in age from the red Upper Coal Measures, at Doddington, down to strata of the Millstone Grit Series at Nocton. In the latter area the greater part of the movement occurred before the deposition of the Upper Red Measures which represent the erosion products of the underlying beds. It has been suggested that some of these beds may be Lower Permian in age. Further erosion continued during the Lower Permian, preparing the surface upon which the deposition of Upper Permian (Zechstein) sediments and evaporites took place. This period of erosion is frequently marked by a variable thickness of red and green coloured Coal Measure rocks, immediately beneath the Permian unconformity.

THE PERMIAN SYSTEM

UPPER PERMIAN (ZECHSTEIN)

The succession of strata considered to be of Zechstein age is shown in Table IV. The Nottingham region is situated at the southern end of a basin of deposition which extends northwards through Yorkshire and on through the county of Durham. It is in these areas that evidence for the age of the rocks can be deduced. Fossils in the Marl Slate, which is correlated with the Dolomitic Siltstones of Nottinghamshire, belong to the Upper Permian. The Permian rocks, resting unconformably on Middle Coal Measures, produce a marked escarpment extending northwards from Strelley (Fig. 5, p. 41).

Basal Breccia

In Nottinghamshire, the Permian sequence begins with a basal breccia. A colliery shaft at Mansfield records the maximum thickness of eight feet. Despite its thinness the breccia is recorded from most bore-holes, shafts and wells in the area. The rock is very hard and is composed largely of angular fragments, rarely exceeding one inch in length, derived from the underlying Carboniferous rocks.

Dolomitic Siltstones

The breccia is succeeded by a series of dolomitic siltstones, referred to by the Geological Survey as the Lower Permian Marls and by others as the Marl Slate. Neither of these terms is satisfactory and the more fully descriptive term is preferred in this account. Within the siltstones, plant fragments are common and mica is abundant along the bedding planes. The siltstones are grey in colour and exhibit fine laminations when recently exposed. After a period of weathering, however, the rocks turn yellow or brown and the laminations are obscured. In the northern part of the area thin seams of red marl may be present.

Lower Magnesian Limestone

The amount of dolomite increases upwards and the dolomitic siltstones pass abruptly into the Lower Magnesian Limestone. The limestone is distinctive, being composed of dolomite $(CaMgCo_3)_2$ with crystals frequently one to two millimetres in length. The rock has the appearance of a medium-to-coarse grained sandstone but there is only a small amount of detrital quartz present. Fossils are very rare, but lamellibranchs (*Schizodus sp.*) are noted from Bulwell. A number of interesting facies variations occur at the southern margin of the outcrop which extends from Strelley, Catstonehill, Broomhill and along the line of the Nottingham–Ilkeston canal to the Leen Valley, where the limestone passes beneath the Triassic sediments. In the extreme south the limestone contains local breccias and sand deposits which probably mark the littoral margin of the Upper Permian sea in Nottinghamshire.

TABLE IV Permo-Trias
(NOT TO SCALE)

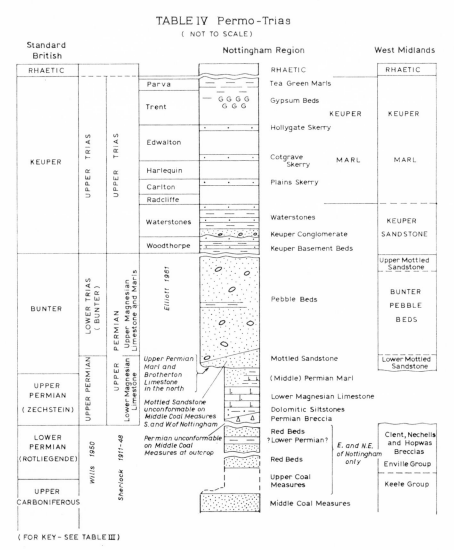

(FOR KEY — SEE TABLE III)

Two local variations are seen at Mansfield, both being characterised by the presence in the dolomite of about 50 per cent silica. In one case the rock dries white in colour, giving the Mansfield White Sandstone which occurs at the top of the Lower Magnesian Limestone and in the other it is brownish-red, the Mansfield Red Sandstone, found a little lower in the succession. L. J. Wills has suggested that an easterly-flowing stream brought the sand into the Mansfield area. It is only from Mansfield Woodhouse northwards, that the typical fine-grained buff or cream dolomite, characteristic of Yorkshire and Durham, completely replaces the littoral facies of the south.

The Permian Marls

The Permian sequence is completed in south Nottinghamshire by up to 50 feet of red marls generally referred to as the Middle Permian Marls. These beds frequently become sandy as in exposures at Annesley and Kirkby-in-Ashfield. At Bulwell the beds become sufficiently coarse to prevent the use of the marl for rough pottery manufacture. Unfortunately for age determination, the sandy development at this horizon seems to be identical to the lowest beds of the Mottled Sandstone (Trias) which in many places can be seen to overly the marls. Interbedded with marls are thin dolomitic limestones.

Permian beds above the Marls

In north Nottinghamshire, north of a line from Worksop to Bothamsall, the Upper Magnesian Limestone (Brotherton Limestone) is recognised as a thin bed, increasing in thickness northwards (Fig. 3A) overlying the Middle Permian Marls. Another series of marls (Upper Permian Marls) likewise occurs above the Upper Magnesian Limestone. The fate of these two divisions to the south is far from clear. The sea in which the evaporites were deposited could terminate along the Worksop-Bothamsall line, but the resulting limestones do not compare with the littoral facies of the Lower Magnesian Limestones further south. In the Mansfield and Bulwell areas the Upper Magnesian Limestone may be represented by the thin beds of dolomite (Fig. 3B). The overlying marls would then be the thin representative of the Upper Permian Marls. All these beds may change laterally into sandy facies, in some localities.

These beds complete the Permian System in Nottinghamshire. Above them, sandstones of the Triassic System rest conformably but, as already noted, similar deposits may locally replace the Permian marls. At this point in the geological column the boundary between the Palaeozoic and the Mesozoic should be drawn. In the north and east of our region it is obscured by lateral facies changes and vertical continuity. The problem is considered further after the description of the Lower Triassic sandstones.

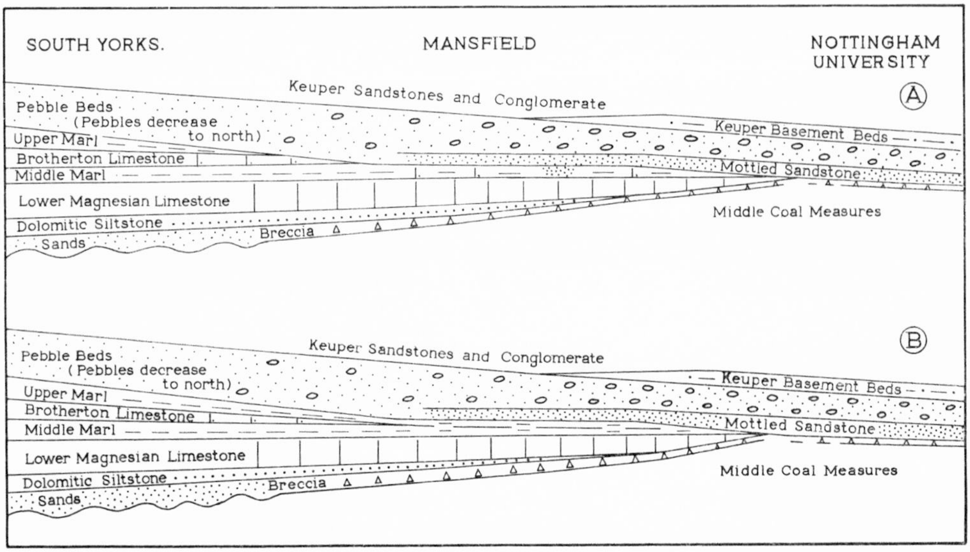

Fig. 3   Possible relationships between the Permian and the Lower Trias Pebble Beds and Mottled Sandstone

THE TRIASSIC SYSTEM

Sediments usually considered to be of this age are shown in Table IV.

The Bunter Series

The Mottled Sandstone

The sediments are darkish red, fine-to-medium-grained sandstones, with occasional yellow-green or yellow seams or patches. Cross-bedding is common with certain large structures, possibly of dune origin. In the lower beds of the sandstone, red clay finely disseminated is common and may form up to 10 per cent of the rock. When the size of the sand grains is about 0·1 of a millimetre and the clay is present the deposit can be used as a moulding sand. Such sand is now obtained from Mansfield but in the past there have been many small quarries extending from Mansfield to Nottingham, the sandstone overlying Permian rocks between these places. Active exploitation of the sand, between Nottingham and Sandiacre, where there are irregular deposits of the same material, this time overlying Coal Measures (Fig. 2), is now confined to Bramcote. The sequence to the west of Nottingham usually commences with a breccia, reminiscent of the Permian breccia, containing very angular fragments. The breccia has also been recorded away from the outcrop, as for example in a bore-hole at Nottingham University and also south of the Trent in a National Coal Board bore-hole at Plumtree. The Plumtree core showed a

D

medium-coarse sandstone at this locality, and similarly between Nottingham and Sandiacre the sandstone can be very coarse. Swinnerton recorded the presence of dolomite crystals in the lower beds.

The Pebble Beds

The first indication of the change from Mottled Sandstone to Pebble Beds is usually an increase in grain size, with the colour becoming a lighter red. Pebbles, mostly quartzite, then appear scattered throughout the deposit, aligned either parallel with the true bedding or with the current bedding. At Nottingham, including the University site, and at Sandiacre, the colour of the Pebble Beds is characteristically yellow or buff, so that a more distinct colour change is noted at the junction. In the Plumtree core, mentioned above, the junction was marked by a breccia. Included in the coarse pebbly sandstone, beds of marl up to four feet in thickness may be found, as in the Barbers Wood Quarry near Mansfield or at Blidworth, while small blocks of marl are usually found in any exposure. Isopachytes for the Pebble Beds show that the deposit increases in thickness north and north-eastwards from 200 feet at Nottingham to 600 feet in the Mansfield district. In the oilfield area, pebbles become less frequent. Most of the pebbles are well rounded but faceted (dreikanter) examples are a common feature of the top three feet of the deposit. An interesting erosion feature is the isolated rock stack about 25 feet high known as the Hemlock Stone situated at Bramcote, a few miles west of Nottingham. The prominent capping offers greater resistance to weathering because the sand is irregularly cemented by barium sulphate, as is much of the higher ground at Stapleford Hill.

There is no Upper Mottled Sandstone in the Nottingham area, the next sediments being Keuper in age and it is for this reason that the term Lower Mottled Sandstone is not used, since it would imply a correlation with the west Midlands which has still to be proved.

Age of the Mottled Sandstone and Pebble Beds

All the available evidence bearing on the age of these two deposits has been noted and a discussion on the age of the rocks and on the boundary of the Permian and the Triassic Systems can, therefore, be made at this point. The various views are summarised in Table IV and illustrated diagrammatically in Fig. 3. The traditional view considers both the Mottled Sandstone and the Pebble Beds to be Bunter (Lower Trias) in age. The correlation with the sequence in Germany was largely the work of the early members of the Geological Survey. R. L. Sherlock contended that there was ample evidence to show that the 'Lower Mottled Sandstone' grades laterally into the 'Middle Permian Marl'. As the first major break in sedimentation occurs above the Pebble Beds, this group was also included in the Permian, being regarded as the lateral equivalent of the Upper Magnesian Limestone and Upper Permian Marls. The presence of dolomite in the lower beds of the Mottled Sandstone would suggest a possible lateral facies change at the southern end of the Permian Limestone outcrop. The dolomite crystals could have been blown with the sand from the drying-out of the Magnesian Limestone sea, either contemporaneously with the deposition of the limestone or at some considerable time afterwards. Wills is rather more familiar with the West than the East Midlands. He regards the dune-bedded Bridgenorth Sandstone (Lower Mottled Sandstone) as Upper Permian in age and the distinct lithological break at the base of the Bunter Pebble Beds as marking the commencement of the Trias and suggests that this correlation could be extended into the Nottingham area.

Palaeontologically, the first evidence for Upper Triassic age occurs in younger beds, close to the base of the Keuper Waterstones where fish (*Semionotus*) and reptile footprints have been found. If Sherlock is right, then there is no Lower Trias in the Nottingham region; if Wills is right, only the Pebble Beds are Lower Trias. Neither of these authors' observations seem to have carried weight with the Geological Survey in revising the Chesterfield Sheet, where the traditional view is retained except for minor sections at the base of the Mottled Sandstone which are deemed to be lateral facies of the Middle Permian Marl. It has been shown above that both marl and dolomite occur in the lower beds of the Mottled Sandstone. These materials could have been produced by the erosion of underlying or locally occurring Permian Marls and limestones. If this could be shown to be the case, using modern sedimentary techniques, then the traditional view that the Trias begins with the Mottled Sandstones may well prove to be the correct one (Fig. 3B). Here is yet another problem for sedimentologists.

The Keuper Series (Upper Trias)

The Keuper beds are characteristically red marls, always containing very fine sand grains, with siltstones or coarser beds (skerries) occurring at various horizons which are indicated in Table IV. Gypsum and other evaporite minerals are nearly always present, but as they are highly soluble they are easily removed from the weathered zone. Fossils are found infrequently and are mainly of fish and footprints. The Keuper Series has been reviewed by R. E. Elliott whose paper contains a full bibliography for this part of the geological column. The red Keuper Marls form an extensive outcrop out of which the greater part of the Trent Valley has been cut. The outcrop extends southwards beyond Nottingham and Derby (Fig. 2), overstepping all the older formations to rest eventually on Pre-Cambrian rocks in the classic unconformity in Charnwood Forest.

The Keuper Basement Beds

The break in sedimentation at the base of the Keuper is most marked in the neighbourhood of Nottingham. The erosion surface at the top on the Bunter Pebble Beds is marked by a concentration of dreikanter pebbles, while the upper few feet may also be cemented with calcite, providing a much harder rock at the junction. In and around Nottingham the Pebble Beds are succeeded by a series of alternating deep red marls and fine-grained yellow sandstones, often containing very small pebbles. Fish and reptile footprints are recorded by Swinnerton. The maximum thickness of these beds is about 42 feet, each unit of marl and sandstone being about six inches thick. They are found on the east and north of the city and as far as Stapleford on the west. These Basement Beds are called by Elliott the Woodthorpe Formation. North-east of Nottingham, the Green Keuper Basement Beds appear to be similar but possess a green tinge which may even be imparted to the soil. They have been found at the surface as far north as Retford and recorded in bore-holes at Gainsborough and Lincoln and as far east as the Vale of Belvoir. The relationship of these beds to the Keuper Basement Beds of Swinnerton is not very clear but they appear to have been included by Elliott in his Woodthorpe Formation.

In many places, particularly west and north of Nottingham, the Keuper Basement Beds are overlain by a hard conglomerate. This has a wider outcrop than the Basement Beds and therefore lies directly on Pebble Beds, as at Dale for example. East of Nottingham the conglomerate thins and appears to pass laterally into sediments of the Waterstones type. The Keuper Basement Beds are thus demarcated above and below by erosion surfaces.

The Waterstones (Waterstone Formation or Keuper Sandstone)

Above the conglomerate, fine-grained yellow or brown sandstones alternate with red marls. The sandstones are well cemented, each bed two or three feet thick, making up a thick arenaceous series about 100 feet thick in all. Tetrapod footprints and fish remains are known from these beds. Specimens of *Lingula* sp. were found by G. M. Rose and Kent from a horizon near the top of the Waterstones.

The upper limit of these beds is marked by the last fine-grained brown sandstone in the sequence. It is a gradational boundary and as such is a little unsatisfactory. Elliott has attempted a definition on sedimentary characteristics which may clarify the situation in those localities where the evaporite minerals have not been leached. In some places a group of green-grey siltstones and sandstones may mark the junction. They contain dolomite, gypsum and calcite. These rocks have been made exceedingly porous by partial leaching of the evaporite minerals and have provided the reservoir beds for the only oil seepage known in the immediate Nottingham district.

The Keuper Marls

(a) *The Red Marls*   Following upon the Waterstones there occurs a thick series of red marls and siltstones, and occasional green-grey dolomitic siltstones (skerries). The sequence, including the 'formations' of Elliott is listed in Table IV. The predominant rocks are red mudstones possessing an irregular fracture and indistinct bedding planes, together with finely laminated mudstones and siltstones. The rocks contain a significant amount of gypsum, although having been leached out of the rock this is rarely seen at surface exposures. Silica is always present as a very fine powder in the marls and in a coarser form in the siltstones and skerries. Some of the latter contain a high percentage of dolomite or gypsum. A valuable contribution made by Elliott was to show that certain skerry beds are remarkably persistent over a wide area. The lowest of these, the Plains Skerry, effectively the junction of the Carlton and Harlequin Formations is the most extensive. The Cotgrave Skerry, with its characteristic gypsum nodules, marks the boundary of the Harlequin and Edwalton Formations. Finally the Hollygate Skerry marks the junction of the Edwalton and Trent Formations.

Only in the top 100 feet of the Red Marls in east Nottinghamshire is gypsum sufficiently concentrated to be exploited commercially. Most of the gypsum seams are nodular, the mineral occurring in a massive granular form as well as the fibrous satin spar, but rarely as anhydrite. The exploitable gypsum is confined to Elliott's Trent Formation. Occurring close to the top of the red marls, the gypsum beds usually outcrop close to the Rhaetic-Lias escarpment and extend from Newark in the north through Cotgrave and possibly to Bunny. Twelve seams are worked by opencast methods between Newark and Cotgrave. From Bunny the outcrop strikes westwards through Gotham and East Leake to Ratcliffe-on-Soar, Chellaston and Tutbury. The occurrence of workable gypsum in these areas is of interest in that it appears to be restricted mainly to one seam, the Tutbury Gypsum, which is mined. It is tempting to correlate the lowest seams at Newark with the Tutbury Gypsum, for the two levels of evaporite formation could then be explained by a thickening of the marl westwards, but the ground between Cotgrave and Bunny is not known in detail.

(b) *The Tea Green Marls*   Above the top gypsum bed, the marls are alternately red and green in colour for a few feet and then become predominantly green. The green beds have for long been called the Tea Green Marls. In total thickness they are under 40 feet and are frequently much less. Variations in thickness appear to be due to erosion prior to the deposition of the succeeding Rhaetic beds. In the Nottingham area, Elliott has been able to locate a fish scale bed, which he uses as a marker to divide the Trent Formation from the overlying Parva Formation.

The Rhaetic

Rhaetic beds in the region are very thin, though for the first time since the Upper Coal Measures, fossils once again become abundant. The lower beds are organic black shales containing principally a lamellibranch fauna including *Rhaetavicula contorta* and *Chlamys valoniensis*. The upper beds are light grey shales with thin limestones or calcareous sandstones. Beds of this type, tinged with red, containing *Protocardium rhaeticum* were exposed in the bridge footings which carry the Sleaford road over the recently (1964) constructed Newark by-pass. The next fossiliferous beds contain *Liostrea* sp. and *Psiloceras planorbis*, the lowest beds of the Lias. In the Upper Rhaetic of the Lincoln area there are thin beds of red marl, noted in the log of the Nocton boring. These may account for the increased thickness of the Rhaetic in the north, whereas the deposits thin southward towards Bottesford, expanding again in south Nottinghamshire and Leicestershire.

THE JURASSIC SYSTEM

The geological sequence of Jurassic strata is shown in Table V. In the Nottingham region, the 2000 to 3000 feet of rocks are very varied and will be described in accordance with the normal sub-divisions of the Jurassic as the Lias, Middle and Upper Jurassic. The fossils and sub-divisions mentioned are to be found in the British Museum Handbook (1964) on Mesozoic Fossils. The description follows the work of Swinnerton and Kent with the exception of the Jurassic-Cretaceous boundary which presents a special problem.

THE LIAS (HETTANGIAN TO TOARCIAN)

The base of the Lias appears to be conformable to the Rhaetic below. The first ammonites found indicate the lowest zone of *Psiloceras planorbis* which rests within a few feet of strata containing Rhaetic fossils. Throughout the area there is little to be seen of the 'White Lias' which does develop further south in Leicestershire, and there are only a few feet of the 'Pre-Planorbis' Beds with their characteristic *Liostrea* sp., *Modiola* sp. and *Pleuromya* sp. fauna. The *P. planorbis* zone is made up of argillaceous limestones with thin interbedded calcareous shales, known as the Hydraulic Limestones. At their outcrop (Fig. 2) these beds form a low escarpment overlooking the Keuper Marls and gravels of the Trent Valley. Fossils obtained from the present working quarry at Barnstone are representative of the upper part of these beds and include *P. planorbis*, *Caloceras* sp., *Lima* sp., *Modiola* sp., *Gryphaea* sp., with reptile remains, mainly *Ichthyosaurus* sp.

Impure limestones are also present in the Arnioceras bucklandi zone at Granby and in the Arietites semicostatum zone, where they are ferruginous. Beyond the Nottingham region to the north the beds of this latter zone develop into the Frodingham Ironstone.

Clays make up the greater part of the succession up to the Marlstone Rock Bed, situated in the upper zone *Pleuroceras spinatum* of the Middle Lias. This ferruginous oolitic rock forms another escarpment (Fig. 5) which extends northwards as far as Belvoir. North of Belvoir a facies change to clay occurs with the consequent loss of the escarpment. North of Lincoln, the limestone again appears but with little iron. An analysis of the rock in the Nottinghamshire area indicates 25 per cent iron, and at Eaton and Leadenham it is extracted as an ironstone. This average analysis is generally considered too low for commercial exploitation but by selective extraction of the top beds and allowing calcium carbonate to be leached out of the rock this figure rises to 33 per cent. In the more calcareous parts of the rock, near the base, the brachiopods *Lobothyris punctata* and *Tetrarhynchia tetrahedra* are common but belemnites can also be found together with the zonal ammonite (*P. spinatum*).

Upper Lias Clays succeed the ironstone, containing ammonites throughout the sequence. Lithological variations are few but the zones increase in thickness northwards. They are extracted near Lincoln for brick-making. The effect of an unconformity at the base of the Inferior Oolite (Northampton Sands) is to cut out the upper zones northwards.

THE MIDDLE JURASSIC

Inferior Oolite Series(Bajocian)

The Northampton Sands Ironstone is the first lithological division of this stage. The ironstone, which is shown by an overall analysis to contain 33 per cent iron, is extensively worked further south outside the region, but is more variable northwards, having a high silica (sand) content in places. It is worked successfully in the Sproxton-Croxton Kerrial district and was exploited in the past at Leadenham and Lincoln. In many places part of the Lincolnshire Limestone and Lower Estuarine Beds are removed before the ironstone is extracted, by opencast methods, but in the Lincoln area it was mined. Further north the iron content decreases and the resulting ferruginous sandstone is called Dogger. Fossils from the Upper Lias may be found in the base of the Northampton Ironstone. They may be derived from the Lias or alternatively the lower beds may in fact be Upper Lias in age. Analyses as well as stratigraphical and petrological descriptions of the ironstone have been made by Hollingworth and Taylor. The ironstone is distinguished by the regular development of boxstone structures.

The Lower Estuarine Beds are commonly very thin (five feet) but may be expanded up to 30 feet. At the southern end of the region they are mainly grey clays with lamellibranchs, while elsewhere white or buff sands are common, with subordinate beds of variegated clays.

The Lincolnshire Limestone forms the next major escarpment (Fig. 5). Table V indicates the four divisions of the limestone. Most of them are oolitic and are grey or blue when fresh, although exposure to the atmosphere quickly changes the beds to a yellow or buff colour. The limestones are very fossiliferous and include species of the coral *Thamnastraea*, *Isastraea* and *Montlivaltia*, and the brachiopod *Parvirhynchia* and *Acanthothyris*, and the lamellibranchs *Ctenostreon* sp., *Lima* sp., *Lopha* sp., *Lucina* sp. and *Trigonia* sp. At the old quarry at Bescaby a very fine worm-bored surface can be examined. The lower beds are used for cement and roadstone, whilst the upper beds comprise the famous Ancaster freestone.

TABLE V   Jurassic and Cretaceous

Feet

			Zones (referred to in text)		

The following represents the stratigraphic column reading from top (3000 feet) to bottom (Rhaetic):

UPPER CRETACEOUS
- Turonian — *H. planus* — Upper Chalk (Flint)
- — *T. lata* — Middle Chalk
- Cenomanian — Upper pink / Lower pink / Totternhoe Stone — Lower Chalk
- Albian — *Neohibolites minimus* — Red Chalk

LOWER CRETACEOUS
- Aptian — Pebbly Carstone / Carstone / Sutterby Marl / Fulletby Beds — Langton Series
- Neocomian — Upper Tealby Clay / Tealby Limestone / Lower Tealby Clay / Claxby Ironstone — Tealby Series
- — Spilsby Sandstone / Nodule Bed — Spilsby Series

UPPER JURASSIC
- Kimeridgian — *P. pectinatus* — Elsham Sandstone, Kimeridge Clay
- Corallian (Oxfordian) — Ampthill Clay, Oxford Clay

MIDDLE JURASSIC
- Callovian — Kellaway Beds
- GREAT OOLITE, Bathonian — Cornbrash / Blisworth Clay / Great Oolite Limestone / Upper Estuarine Beds
- INFERIOR OOLITE, Bajocian — Ancaster Freestone / *A. crossi* Beds / Cementstones / Blue and silver Beds } Lincolnshire Limestone
- — Lower Estuarine Beds / Northampton Sands Ironstone

LIAS
- UPPER LIAS, Toarcian
- MIDDLE LIAS, Pliensbachian — *P. spinatum* — Marlstone Rock Bed (Ironstone); *A. margaritatus*

LOWER JURASSIC
- LOWER LIAS, Sinemurian
  - *A. semicostatum* — Horizon of Frodingham Ironstone
  - *A. bucklandi* — Granby Limestone
  - *S. angulatum* — Hydraulic Limestones
  - Hettangian — *P. planorbis* — Pre-planorbis Beds
- Rhaetic

Lower Lias Clays

Feet scale: 3000, 2700, 2400, 2100, 1800, 1500, 1200, 900, 600, 300

(FOR KEY – SEE TABLE III)

The Great Oolite Series (Bathonian)

The Lincolnshire Limestone is succeeded by the Upper Estuarine Beds. They consist mainly of clays and occasional thin limestones. In the Lincoln area, sandy beds develop. Small lamellibranchs are found in the clays and limestones, i.e. *Modiola* sp., *Liostrea* sp., and *Nucula* sp.

The Great Oolite limestone in Lincolnshire compares very unfavourably with that of the Cotswolds, being composed of thin, rubbly or nodular yellow limestone beds, which are rarely oolitic, and frequent thin marl beds. The fauna is mainly one of lamellibranchs (as above) and the brachiopod *Epithyris* sp. The Great Oolite limestone is succeeded by a third group of clays, the Blisworth Clay (Great Oolite Clay).

The Bathonian stage is completed by the Cornbrash. As seen in Table V. the Bathonian-Callovian boundary occurs within the Oolite Limestone and is easily recognised if the two distinctive faunas are present. In Lincolnshire the Lower Cornbrash averaging one foot in thickness is impersistent, not being reported from Walcot, Aslacky or Sleaford. The important fossils are *Clydoniceras* sp. (rare), *Ornithella obovata* and *Cererithyris intermedia*. The Upper Cornbrash limestone averages six feet and is characterised by *Microthyris* and the ammonite *Macrocephalites* sp.

THE UPPER JURASSIC (CALLOVIAN TO KIMERIDGIAN)

The remaining part of the Jurassic is made up almost entirely of a monotonous thickness, up to 1,000 feet of clays. The three divisions are shown in Table V, along with the sandy limestone which occurs at the base of the Kellaway Beds. These are about 25 feet thick and are frequently decalcified. A temporary exposure in Reepham village east of Lincoln yielded large blocks with characteristic fossils *Gryphaea bilobata* and the belemnite *Cylindroteuthis oweni*. There is little that can be added to the description of the succeeding clays made by Swinnerton and Kent, but interest in recent years has been concerned with the Jurassic-Cretaceous boundary at the summit of the Kimeridge Clay.

The Jurassic-Cretaceous Boundary

The problem concerns the identification of ammonites at the base of the Spilsby Sandstone and at the top of the Kimeridge Clay. Ammonites in the latter indicate the zone of *Pectinatites pectinatus*, the top two zones of *Pavlovia* being absent, presumably eroded by the overlying unconformity, as phosphatised and weathered specimens are found in the base of the Spilsby Sandstone. In this sandstone, the presence of *Subcraspedites* and *Paracraspedites* was used by Swinnerton and Spath to fix the Lower Cretaceous age of the Spilsby Sandstone and to confirm the absence of the Portlandian stage in northern England. Both these genera are considered by R. Casey, whether earlier misidentified or not, to be of Upper Jurassic (Portlandian) age, while specimens of the Upper Jurassic *Kerbites* and *Crendonites* regarded by previous authors to be derived, he considers to be indigenous to the basement bed of the Spilsby Sandstone of Nettleton, north Lincolnshire. The early work of A. Pavlow also claimed that the lower part of the Spilsby Sandstone was Upper Jurassic in age. After a re-examination of all the ammonites from the Spilsby Sandstone, Casey considers that all the zones of the Upper Jurassic are recognisable with the exception of the highest zone, *Riasanites rjasanensis* of the Upper Volgian (the uppermost stage of the Russian Upper Jurassic) which is approximately equivalent to the Portlandian stage in Britain. Thus the unconformity at the base of the Spilsby Sandstone may be regarded as being of a minor character and the junction of the Jurassic and Cretaceous occurring within the Spilsby Sandstone.

This rock is a medium-grained yellow-green rock, for the most part only poorly cemented, with a total thickness of about 70 feet. The basal bed contains phosphatic nodules and fragments of ammonites which contain pear-shaped cavities including *Martsia* sp., a boring bivalve. There are no lithological breaks within the sandstone. The upper part is considered by all authorities to be Neocomian (Lower Cretaceous) in age, although there is some disagreement concerning the names of the ammonites, Casey preferring *Surites* sp. and *Tollia* sp. to Swinnerton's *Subcraspedites*. Yet until further palaeontological (including the analysis of foraminifera, ostracodes and belemnites) and petrological work is carried out, preferably on new exposures and material, the age of the Spilsby Sandstone is perhaps best considered an open question.

THE CRETACEOUS SYSTEM

The Cretaceous rocks outcrop in the Lincolnshire Wolds. The chalk (Upper Cretaceous) forms the main mass of the Wolds with the Lower Cretaceous beds around the foot of the escarpments. The succession is illustrated in Table V.

LOWER CRETACEOUS (NEOCOMIAN TO ALBIAN)

A very varied sequence occurs in Lincolnshire beginning with the Spilsby Sandstone already referred to. The iron content increases towards the top of this sandstone and it grades upwards into the Claxby Ironstone. The ironstone is oolitic, the limonite ooliths being reddish-brown, polished and set in a light brown matrix of (altered) chamosite and siderite. It is now worked only at Nettleton near Caistor.

The Tealby Series above is composed of grey clays with an interbedded limestone. Iron ooliths occur but fossils are rare, being restricted to lamellibranchs in the limestone and occasional belemnites. Iron ooliths are again common at the top of the Fulletby beds, which contain a sandstone, the Roach Rock. The Langton Series begins with 10 feet of iron-free clay, the Sutterby Marl, which contains *Neohibolites ewaldi* and the ammonite *Deshayesites* sp. indicating the Aptian age of the Marl. This rock passes upwards into a ferruginous sandstone which is gritty or pebbly in the upper part. The only fossils found in the Carstone are from the top beds and are of Albian age, the lower part of the Carstone may be Aptian in age, but the

Aptian/Albian boundary still remains obscure. The upper part of the Carstone is very coarse and grades upwards into the Red Chalk. The Albian age of this deposit is given by the belemnite *Neohibolites minimum*, by *Terebratula biplicta* and Inoceramid lamellibranchs. It is only about 14 feet thick in the south, decreasing northwards. Nevertheless its distinctive colour can readily be seen in ploughed fields, the red chalk fragments contrasting with those of the white chalk.

THE UPPER CRETACEOUS

The Chalk (Cenomanian and Turonian)

The last formation of the Mesozoic is the Chalk, which follows on above the Red Chalk without a break. In the south of England there are over 1300 feet of this formation but in Lincolnshire there is a maximum of only 300 feet.

The Lower Chalk (Cenomanian), 70 to 80 feet thick, is the most varied part of the formation with the occurrence of stone beds such as the Totternhoe Stone, two beds of pink chalk and some marl. There are about 125 feet of Middle Chalk and 100 feet of Upper Chalk. The latter belongs to the zone of *Holaster planus* so that it is included with the Turonian. Thus while the combined thickness of the Lower and Middle Chalk compares with that elsewhere in Great Britain, the thinness of the whole sequence is due to the absence of the Senonian. This may well reflect the severity of the erosion which took place subsequent to the deposition of the chalk. A boring at Kilneen in south Yorkshire has recorded 1000 feet of chalk, while casts of fossils, normally found in higher zones, and now obtained only from gravel deposits suggest an earlier occurrence of the higher zones. Chalk is a form of calcium carbonate, made up largely of the remains of organic material such as single crystals derived from the breakdown of invertebrate fossils, complete tests of foraminifera and microplankton, particularly coccoliths of only two microns in diameter. In addition many complete fossils—brachiopods, lamellibranchs echinoids, crinoids, belemnites, comprising over 200 species have been described, many from the Upper Chalk.

PLEISTOCENE AND LATER DEPOSITS

Throughout much of the region 'drift' deposits are very thin, but attain a greater thickness in east Lincolnshire, especially between the Wolds and the present coast. Sand and gravel deposits are extensive, largely associated with the River Trent or found in the Carboniferous Limestone area. The Pleistocene and later deposits are discussed under these headings.

The Sand Pockets of Derbyshire

Between Buxton and Wirksworth sand and gravel workings have revealed extensive deposits of unfossiliferous sands, pebbly sands and red, green and white clays, in which thin seams of manganese oxide and barytes may be present. C. T. Yorke has collected a considerable amount of evidence on this subject, as a director of one of the companies which exploited the sands for making refractory bricks. The deposits are unconsolidated but show well-developed bedding which is inclined in all directions and at all angles from horizontal to vertical. Frequently, the deposits are ill-sorted, large pebbles two inches in diameter and fine sand occurring together. Elsewhere the deposits are more uniform and it is these which are mainly extracted. A small amount of clay is essential to bind the sand grains together. There is some doubt concerning the shape of the deposits. As worked, they appear to be sub-circular pipe or pocket deposits of considerable depth. Few of them give more than an indication of their margins, however, and more information on this point is desirable.

The age and occurrence of these beds has always evoked interest. They are enclosed by dolomites and limestones of D_1 age and are overlain by glacial deposits, containing large blocks of cherty limestones, including replaced corals and brachiopods, and occasional barytes. Recently, blue clays associated with the deposit at Kelslow Knoll, near Friden, have yielded plant remains and the microbotanical content of the clay is now being studied. The main macrofloral content seems to be *Sequoia*. To the writer, the clay seems to underlie the drift but overlie the sands, but the position is not very clear. The petrological character of the sediments, though studied by a number of people, has failed so far to provide the necessary evidence on age. At the time of writing they could be of any age from Carboniferous to Pleistocene.

Boulder Clays and Glacial Gravels

The boulder clays are generally restricted to the higher ground. Those associated with the sand pockets in the Carboniferous Limestone have already been mentioned. Elsewhere in the west of the region, clays containing Lake District erratics and occasional Jurassic oolitic limestones may be found. At Blidworth and Kneesall in mid-Nottinghamshire there are many Carboniferous fragments from the north of England. At Blidworth, gravel deposits, partly originating from the underlying Bunter Pebble Beds have been partially cemented. These extremely hard patches of gravel remain as isolated columns, the softer material having been removed by excavation for building sands and concrete aggregates. Moving eastwards, Jurassic fragments increase in quantity. Boulder clays in the Trent Valley are reddened from the underlying Keuper Marl, while further east they are predominantly grey with chalk and flint fragments, although this type of clay has been found as far west as Risley, between Nottingham and Derby. From the evidence of the gravels, boulder clays, fossil and archaeological finds, and from erosion features, the glacial chronology dealt with in the next chapter has been adduced. The thickest boulder clay deposits, about 80 feet, occur along the Lincolnshire Coast, where they form the flat coastal plain behind Mablethorpe, Sutton and Skegness, extending inland as far as the old Chalk cliff line running from Louth to beyond Alford.

Gravels associated with the River Trent

Within the region, gravels occur along the length of the Trent Valley and are worked in many places, notably at Attenborough and Hoveringham. Mention should also be made of the gravels in the Lincoln area and at Ancaster and Sproxton. Gravels, glacial outwash material and flood-plain gravels are now preserved in isolated patches or as terraces along the Trent Valley. Acheulian implements are known from Beeston and earlier artifacts from the higher terraces at Hilton, while mammoth teeth and tusks are not infrequently found in present gravel workings.

GENERAL STRUCTURE

In describing the rocks of the region, several unconformities have been mentioned. In brief they mark the passage of time during which the rocks were folded, faulted and frequently eroded prior to the next phase of deposition. The most important of these periods of movement began close to the end of the Upper Coal Measures and continued during the Lower Permian period. It is generally considered that at this time the main Pennine axis, arching the Carboniferous rocks, came into being. The southern end of this axis terminates in the Nottingham region, plunging beneath a cover of Triassic sediments. The view that the Pennine axis is an important tectonic element having its origin in the pre-Permian times has recently been questioned by George. Most of his argument is based on evidence derived from areas much further north, but it is pertinent to note that the general alignment of the fold axes in the pre-Permian rocks around Nottingham is 'charnoid' and shows no sign of relationship to, or control by, a major north-south Pennine structure.

The Carboniferous rocks have been crumpled into elongated domes (periclines) and troughs, the long axes of which trend north-north-west to south-south-east, or north-west to south-east. The latest illustration of this structural pattern is described by N. L. Falcon and Kent (Fig. 4). Such anticlinal structures are seen at Ashover and Crich, Hardstoft and the Erewash Valley, and in the concealed coalfield area at Eakring, Dukes Wood and Bothamsall. Further east, oilfield exploration has traced the pattern to Kelham Hills, Gainsborough, Nocton and Stixwold and even to the margins of the North Sea.

The evidence may therefore suggest two distinct periods of folding, the second being at right angles to the earlier one. There are likewise two patterns of faulting which predominate, both sets consisting mostly of normal faults with steep angles of hade. The time of occurrence of this postulated second phase is difficult to fix without detailed analysis. It might have occurred either shortly after the first or following the deposition of the Triassic sediments. For, although the regional dip of the Triassic rocks is to the east, they are also affected by slight folding and faulting along axes trending in an approximately east-west direction. Other periods of uplift are indicated at the base of the Inferior Oolite, and prior to the deposition of the Chalk, but from late Cretaceous times onwards, erosion appears to have been dominant.

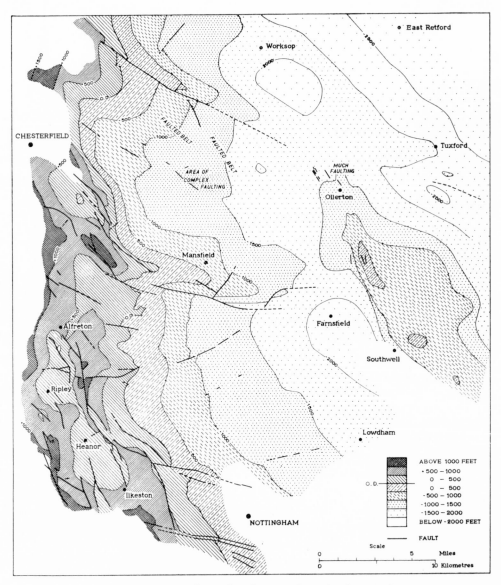

Fig. 4   Structures in the Carboniferous Beds north of Nottingham
Published with the permission of the Geological Society of London

The structures in the Carboniferous rocks have important economic results. In the first place they account for the widespread distribution of coal-bearing deposits, both at the surface and where they are concealed beneath Permian and other later sediments. The gentle folding enables coal seams to be followed into the synclines and then closer to the surface again along the crests of the anticlines. The structures are reasonably simple and of wide amplitude and partly account for the high output figures of most of the collieries. Secondly, the structures have assisted in the accumulation of oil at Eakring, Dukes Wood, Bothamsall and Kelham Hills in Nottinghamshire and at Gainsborough in Lincolnshire, the most recent centre of production. Natural gas (methane) has lately been exploited at Calow, near Chesterfield, but greater interest is now directed towards the continuation of these structures under the North Sea as a possible source of gas or oil, or both.

SELECTED REFERENCES

British Museum—*British Mesozoic Fossils*. British Museum (Natural History) London (1964).

Eden, R. A., Orme, G. R., Mitchell, M. and Shirley, J. A study of part of the margin of the Carboniferous Limestone Massif in the Pin Dale area of Derbyshire. *Bulletin of the Geological Survey of Great Britain* Vol. 21 (1964) pp. 73–118.

Eden, R. A., Rhys, G. H. and Smith, E. G. Summary of Progress. Geological Survey (Chesterfield Sheet) London (1959).

Edwards, W. The Concealed Coalfield of Yorkshire and Nottinghamshire. *Memoir of the Geological Survey of England and Wales*. H.M.S.O. London (1951).

Elliott, R. E. The Keuper Series in Southern Nottinghamshire. *Proceedings of the Yorkshire Geological Society* Vol. 33 (1961) p. 197.

Firman, R. J. Gypsum in Nottinghamshire. *Bulletin of the Peak District Mines Historical Society* Vol. 2 (1964) pp. 189–203.

Ford, T. D. and Sarjeant, W. A. S. The Peak District Mineral Index. *Bulletin of the Peak District Mines Historical Society* Vol. 2 (1964) pp. 122–150.

Ludford, A. Stratigraphy of the Carboniferous Rocks of the Weaver Hills District. *Quarterly Journal of the Geological Society* Vol. 106 (1950) p. 211.

Parkinson, D. and Ludford, A. The Carboniferous Limestone of the Blore-with-Swinscoe District, north–east Staffordshire. *Geological Journal* Vol. 4 (1964) pp. 167–176.

Prentice, J. E. The Carboniferous Limestone of the Manifold Valley Region; North Staffordshire. *Quarterly Journal of the Geological Society* Vol. 106 (1950) p. 171.

Ramsbottom, W. H. C., Rhys, G. H. and Smith, E. G. Bore-holes in the Carboniferous Rocks of the Ashover district, Derbyshire. *Bulletin of the Geological Survey of Great Britain* No. 19 (1962) pp. 75–165.

Rose, G. M. and Kent, P. E. A *Lingula* bed in the Keuper of Nottinghamshire. *Geological Magazine* Vol. 92 (1955) pp. 476–479.

Shirley, J. The Carboniferous Limestone of the Monyash-Wirksworth area, Derbyshire. *Quarterly Journal of the Geological Society* Vol. 114 (1959) pp. 411–431.

Swinnerton, H. H. and Kent, P. E. The geology of Lincolnshire. *Lincolnshire Natural History Brochure No. 1*. Lincolnshire Naturalists' Union (1949).

Taylor, F. M. *The Morphology, Ontogeny and Taxonomy of certain colonial Rugose Corals of Derbyshire.* (Unpublished thesis for the degree of Ph.D., University of Sheffield, 1957.)

Taylor, F. M. An oil seepage near Toton Lane, Stapleford, Nottinghamshire. *Mercian Geologist* Vol. 1 (1964).

Taylor, F. M. The Upper Permian and Lower Trias Formations in southern Nottinghamshire. *Mercian Geologist* Vol. 1 (1965).

References to well-known and in some cases older works of a more general nature have been omitted from the above. These include George, T. N., Lower Carboniferous Palaeogeography of the British Isles, *Proceedings of the Yorkshire Geological Society* Vol. 31 (1958) and Tectonics and Palaeogeography in Northern England, *Science Progress* Vol. 51 (1963); Wills, L. J., *Palaeogeography of the Midlands* (1948–50), and *A Palaeogeographical Atlas of the British Isles* (1951); the contributions of Sherlock, R. L., on the relations between the Permian and Triassic rocks in the *Quarterly Journal of the Geological Society* Vol. 67 (1911) and the *Proceedings of the Geological Association* (1926 and 1928); the work of British Petroleum geologists, Lees, G. M. and Tait, A. H.; Geological results of the search for oil found in Great Britain, *Quarterly Journal of the Geological Society* Vol. 102 (1946); and Falcon, N. L. and Kent, P. E., Geological results of petroleum exploration in Britain 1945–57, *Memoranda of the Geological Society* No. 2 (1960); and the early work on the igneous rocks of Derbyshire by Bemrose, H. H., The Toadstones of Derbyshire: their field relations and petrology, *Quarterly Journal of the Geological Society* Vol. 63 (1907). A useful general account of the region is to be found in the *Guide to the Geology of the East Midlands*, edited by Marshall, C. E., and published by the University of Nottingham (1948). Part of the region was also dealt with by Edwards, W., in his account of the Geology in *Sheffield and its Region: A Scientific and Historical Survey* (edited by Linton, D. L.), British Association for the Advancement of Science (1956).

I   The Nottinghamshire coalfield near Eastwood the home of D. H. Lawrence

II   The Little Eaton—Denby Railway (*c.*1790)

Photo by J. K. St Joseph

IV   The Dovedale gorge cut into the Carboniferous Limestone

Photo by J. K. St Joseph

III   The Dove valley deeply incised into the upland plain of the southern
Peak District

II

GEOMORPHOLOGY

WITHIN the relatively small compass of the Nottingham region, a variety of landscapes is to be found. As long ago as 1929, H. H. Swinnerton (Emeritus Professor of Geology in the University of Nottingham) proposed a physiographic subdivision of the East Midlands, delimiting these landscapes, while more recently K. M. Clayton has drawn attention to the importance of geomorphological history in accounting for the differences of scenery developed on any one of the principal rock types involved. The region lies across the line dividing the highland and lowland zones of Britain, although only a small portion in the west, i.e. in Derbyshire, belongs to the former. Since even this portion does not greatly exceed 1,000 feet in elevation the term 'upland' is more appropriate than 'highland'.

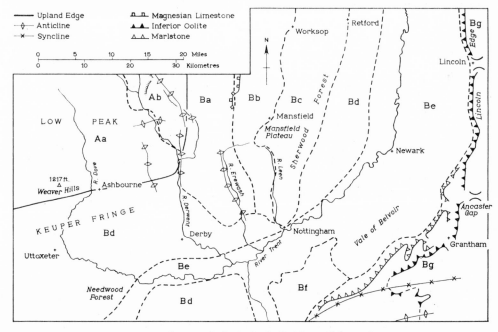

Fig. 5   The morphological sub-divisions of the region

E

In the extreme west the upland assumes the nature of a gently undulating plain (Fig. 5, Aa) cut across the Carboniferous Limestone which forms the centre of the Derbyshire dome. This surface, at approximately 1,000 feet above sea-level, is dissected by deep limestone dales, such as Dovedale (Plates III and IV), which give it a distinctive character. Eastwards, across the Derwent valley, the Millstone Grit outcrops and in places the upland plain can be traced across on to these rocks which have a character very different from that of the limestone. The lens-shaped beds of resistant grits give rise to intermittent scarps called 'edges', with plateau surfaces sloping gently eastwards with the regional dip. In this part of the region (Fig. 5, Ab) structure plays a considerable part in determining the relief because the less resistant strata within the Carboniferous rocks have been lowered by erosion. These include the Edale Shales which overlie the Carboniferous Limestone, the shale beds between the grit bands in the Millstone Grit Series and those between the harder rocks, chiefly sandstones, of the succeeding Coal Measures. The harder strata stand out as scarps between the outcrops of the weaker rocks. The sharp slope which defines the margin of the upland country can be traced clearly on the south side of the Peak District, running from south of the Weaver Hills east-north-east to Ambergate and thence northwards towards Ashover.

Within the lowland part of the region (Fig. 5, B) the slight easterly dip of the rocks gives rise to a succession of north-south belts, especially north of Nottingham, which gradually diminish in elevation as far as the river Trent. This pattern is continued further east across Lincolnshire, though with rather more variable altitude and orientation of outcrop. From west to east (Figs. 2 and 5) these belts include the following:

(a) The Coal Measures country shows some structural control in that the harder sandstones in the series stand out as low scarps with the shales forming intervening shallow valleys. The whole belt is about seven to eight miles wide.

(b) Another scarp, impressive in places, for example at Bolsover, brings in the next significant rock in the succession, which is the Permian Magnesian Limestone. Beyond the scarp the limestone forms a narrow plateau up to five miles wide and from 500 to 600 feet high.

(c) To the east again lies the five to eight miles wide strip of Bunter Sandstone, forming the Sherwood Forest area, with its gently undulating surface and dry shallow valleys with markedly convex sides. With the Bunter may be included the Keuper Sandstone (Waterstones) which flanks it on the east. This latter rock forms a conspicuous feature running north from Nottingham to beyond Ollerton.

(d) The Keuper Marl, with its harder 'skerry' bands should be differentiated on account of its generally better-watered nature, its gentler slopes and lower mean elevation. In places the skerries give rise to higher ground such as Mapperley Plains, the highest part of Nottingham. The Keuper Marl extends south of Nottingham and forms a broad fringe on the southern flank of the upland area including the interfluve tracts between the Dove, Derwent and Erewash. The Marl outcrops again in the higher ground between the Dove and Trent, known as Needwood Forest, lying in the centre of a structural depression.

(e) Within the area occupied by the Keuper Marl is the Vale of Trent. This valley is composed of two distinct reaches, the upper one characterised by terraces, while the lower one has a trench-like form. The Vale of Belvoir, lying further to the east may be included with the Vale of Trent, as the formation of the two is intimately connected with the events of the glacial period.

(f) A small, but distinct, subdivision, lying to the south-east of Nottingham across the Trent valley, is the relatively high ground of the Nottinghamshire Wolds, where the deposition of glacial till has created a landscape of recent date, now being actively dissected to give a somewhat broken relief on its edges, although the central part is still only slightly affected.

(g) Forming a strong contrast with the low ground on the west, the Lincolnshire Limestone (Inferior Oolite) cuesta rises abruptly to form the strong north-south scarp of the Lincoln Cliff or Edge, just over 200 feet high north of Lincoln and over 300 feet to the south. South of Grantham the scarp becomes a double feature as, owing to a change of facies, the Marlstone Ironstone itself forms a prominent scarp on which Belvoir Castle is situated. The latter runs south-westwards while the Limestone scarp, becoming less and less marked, continues southwards. Other minor scarps to the west are formed by the outcrops of the Rhaetic and the Lower Lias Limestone.

Beyond the Lincolnshire Limestone, the only remaining high ground, though beyond the limits of the region, is that formed by the Chalk, outcropping in the Lincolnshire Wolds. These hills are flanked by clays on either side; to the west the valleys of the Ancholme and Witham merge into the Fenlands, while to the east the chalk is buried beneath the glacial and post-glacial deposits of the Lincolnshire marshland. This latter belt of low country, about 10 miles wide, separates the inter-glacial chalk cliffs from the modern coast, with its dunes and protective sea-walls.

THE ORIGIN OF THE PRESENT LANDSCAPE

The depositional history of the region leaves a great gap embracing the whole of the Tertiary period and in order to understand the present landscape this gap must be bridged as far as possible by the techniques of geomorphology. Two lines of evidence can be followed, that provided by the remnants of stages of denudation and that adduced from a study of the drainage pattern. The latter is more helpful in attempting to fill the gap before even the highest relics of the present scene were formed. It is generally assumed, following Linton, that the drainage of the Midlands was initiated on a covering of Cretaceous strata, which in early Tertiary times probably extended further west than it now does. The river Trent was probably one of the rivers flowing east on the upwarped chalk. To the west of Nottingham its original course probably lay a little north of its present position, while east of the city it passed above what is now the Ancaster Gap, to reach The Wash, well south of its present lower course.

Attention has often been drawn to the striking parallel arrangement of the north bank tributaries of the Trent. This direction is shown by Meere Brook, part of the Trent itself downstream from Stoke, Blithe Brook, the river Churnet, the upper part of Dovedale, the Derwent, the Erewash and the Leen; all of these streams flow to the south-south-east. It has been claimed that they represent the original left bank tributaries of the Proto-Trent, flowing down towards the structural depression in which the major stream lay. There is much in favour of this hypothesis, but it also leads to difficulties. One of these has been pointed out by E. M. Yates in discussing the area around Keele, namely that there has probably been faulting during the early Tertiary which must have affected the drainage if it had been initiated on the emerging chalk cover. There is also the problem of the Derwent valley in the reach south of Matlock, and the river Amber, which cuts almost through the centre of the Ashover anticline. Both these streams clearly show some element of epigenesis but they also show curious coincidences. It seems rather improbable that if the course of the Derwent were determined only by a down-warp in the original chalk cover, that it should have become superimposed in the belt of country which separates the limestone uplands on the west from the gritstone edges on the east, broadly coincident with the intervening outcrop of shales. In the Amber valley, also, it seems unlikely that the river would have been superimposed so near the centre of the anticline.

One possible solution to these problems is to consider the sequence of events likely to ensue as streams originating on a chalk cover gradually removed the latter and came into contact with the older rocks beneath. It is possible to envisage a situation when the Derwent, originally flowing south-south-east to the Trent, came into contact with the Carboniferous Limestone rather to the west of and considerably above its present course. The river would tend to work its way down the easterly dip of the limestone until it reached the shale outcrop. It could then have become incised in the shale, for at this time its outcrop would have stood higher than and west of its present position, owing to its general easterly dip. Rapid rejuvenation might then have caused vertical incision of the river and local superimposition into the underlying limestone, as for example in the Matlock area. A similar argument could account for the Ashover pattern. If the Amber had formerly worked its way on to a shale outcrop overlying the present limestone core of the anticline, rejuvenation could then have let it down by vertical epigenesis into the limestone. If this sequence of events were correct, both the Derwent and Amber could be described as originally epigenetic streams subsequently adjusted to the structure and later superimposed as a result of more recent uplift and incision.

To summarise, it seems reasonable to conclude that at the beginning of the Tertiary period drainage was initiated on an emerging cover of chalk, giving rise to an east-west Proto-Trent, fed by south-south-east flowing tributaries and that these later became broadly adjusted to the underlying rocks. The Trent also developed a long south bank tributary, flowing north-north-east, of which the present-day Soar is a remnant.

TERTIARY MODIFICATION OF THE LANDSCAPE

The Tertiary period covers about 70 million years and, as Linton has shown, this is quite long enough for two cycles of erosion to have run their course in a small region of fairly subdued relief. Thus all the landscape of today is either of Tertiary age or younger. The processes that have operated on the landscape to effect the changes it has undergone fall into two broad classes, firstly the processes depending on subaerial forces and secondly the effects of marine transgressions. There is evidence that both have operated in different parts of the area during Tertiary times. The Tertiary period was one of generally falling base level and a study of the landscape facets is a helpful way of attempting to reconstruct the associated denudation chronology. Before considering the evidence for the changes in base-level, however, it is interesting to speculate on their cause and character.

In considering the changes of base level one of the fundamental problems is to distinguish between changes of the land itself, as for example through faulting, and changes of sea-level. Relatively little is known of eustatic movements during the Tertiary, although it has been suggested that sea-level stood at 880 feet above the present towards the end of the Oligocene period, with fluctuations between 164 and 500 feet during the Miocene and Pliocene (Fairbridge). These rapid fluctuations do not accord with the series of events that are usually envisaged; it is often suggested that base level has fallen intermittently, with periodic still-stands, during which erosion could produce recognisable features on the landscape. If this view of landscape development is correct, it seems likely that much of the movement that caused it is the result of uplift of the land. It is, therefore, of interest to consider such evidence as exists concerning the movement of the land. In two separate parts of the region the facts are strongly suggestive. In the west Yates has shown that the Butterton Dyke, together with movement along fault lines in association with such igneous activity, originated during the Tertiary period, while the uplift of the coalfield horsts may well be of mid-Tertiary date. Thus it is probable that the land was being actively warped at least as recently as the mid-Tertiary. Even so there would have been sufficient time following the mid-Tertiary to allow for the formation of the present landscape without the influence of earth-movements. In Lincolnshire the work of

A. Straw shows that movement along faults in the northern part of the Wolds appears to have taken place as late as the end of the Pliocene period and this opinion is strongly supported by the morphological evidence. If movements took place in Lincolnshire at this time, it is possible that they occurred elsewhere as recently.

Evidence of the highest relics of former stages of erosion must naturally be sought in the upland area. It is in the Low Peak that the upland surface, formed with base level nearly 1,000 feet higher than the present, is best developed (Fig. 6). This is, in fact, a very good example of an uplifted gently undulating subaerial surface, the preservation of which owes much to the limestone, strongly contorted west of Ashbourne, across which much of it is formed. It does nevertheless extend eastwards across the Derwent valley on to the Millstone Grit, showing that it is a true erosion surface and not structurally controlled. The relative relief must have been about 200 feet at the time of uplift, with occasional monadnocks rising above it such as the Weaver Hills (Fig. 5). It is usually agreed that this surface was formed during the Tertiary period, probably after the main mid-Tertiary earth movements.

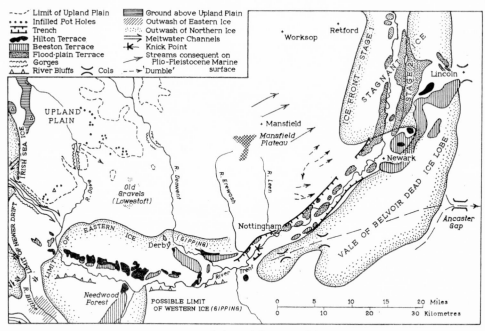

Fig. 6 Geomorphological features of the region

As an alternative view W. G. Fearnsides favoured a Triassic age for the surface. There is certainly evidence that a considerable amount of erosion took place during the Permian and Triassic periods, when much of the Carboniferous strata above the limestone was removed. It is necessary at this point to examine the form of the sub-Triassic surface. To the north of a line from Nottingham to Ashbourne the Triassic rocks appear to overlie and transgress upon a landscape of low relief, presumably the result of Triassic erosion before its burial by sediments of that age. To the south of this line, however, the sub-Triassic floor is very uneven and the Trias rocks bury a landscape of considerable relief. This is particularly noticeable in the Weaver Hills area, where the Trias strata are steeply banked up against the Carboniferous rocks of the Pennines and also in Charnwood Forest where the old landscape of Pre-Cambrian rocks is in process of emerging from beneath its Triassic blanket.

Interesting evidence of the possible former extension of Triassic rocks over the Low Peak area has been discussed by P. E. Kent in drawing attention to silica sand pockets on the 1,000 feet surface in which material possibly of Triassic origin has been found. He argues that material was first deposited on the gently undulating surface of Carboniferous Limestone where sink holes were developing at the edge of remaining outliers of the overlying shales. Down-warping was taking place to the south at this time, preserving the irregular landscape of this area beneath growing deposits. The material in the sink-holes must have been let down deeper as these developed, preserving the fill from later removal, although chalk may eventually have spread over the whole area. With renewed uplift, erosion was continued, removing first the chalk and then producing the 1,000 feet surface during the Tertiary, probably in Mio-Pliocene times. Some doubt has been expressed more recently concerning the age of these deposits, to the effect that they are more likely to be Tertiary in origin. Nevertheless the occurrence of highly siliceous material amongst the surrounding calcareous rocks is of great interest. Doubt has also been cast on the origin and character of the sink holes so that too much weight should not be given to this evidence.

The 1,000 foot surface is a true 'Upland Plain' using the term suggested by S. W. Wooldridge, and can be differentiated from erosion surfaces at lower levels on account of its widespread character as a summit surface. There is an abrupt break of slope at the lower limit of the 1,000 foot surface, which occurs at about 950 feet according to the work of K. M. Clayton in the Middle Trent area, while G. T. Warwick, working in the Manifold valley located a break of slope at the base of his composite higher surface at 930 feet. His upper two levels are clearly part of the 1,000 foot surface; they follow up the valleys of the Dove and Manifold. The subaerial nature of the surface is further confirmed by a similar variation of height range found where it occurs elsewhere.

K. M. Clayton has recognised a Middle Surface lying a little above 700 feet, correlating with the Castern level at 720 feet found in the Manifold valley by Warwick. There is a broad gently sloping surface between 700 and 800 feet between the Churnet and Blithe; this is probably of similar age and origin to the Middle Surface a little further east where it is most extensively developed between the Dove and the Derwent just north of Ashbourne and Belper respectively. A relatively steep slope separates the 1,000 foot surface from the Middle Surface, which occurs more in the form of a dissected bench. It occurs most frequently on the Edale Shales and Triassic rocks. Both these rock groups are less resistant to erosion than the limestone, suggesting that the Middle Surface was formed more rapidly than the much more widespread 1,000 foot surface above it. The evidence also tends to suggest that it is composite and that it slopes gently eastward with the general drainage pattern.

Below the Middle Surface, Clayton has recognised a complex pattern of lower surfaces, all of which occur below 700 feet, and which appear to be subaerial in the area to the west of the Derwent. There are, however, indications of marine incursion at this time, with sea-level reaching about 600 feet in the Nottingham area. The evidence for this is particularly clear in the region around Mansfield where Greenhalgh has recognised features pointing to marine planation (see Fig. 6). The drainage pattern of the wide, gently sloping surface at about 600 to 620 feet, supports this view, showing the initiation of a series of consequent streams flowing north-north-east on the emerging marine surface as the sea again withdrew. Further south, in the area south of Melton Mowbray, R. J. Rice has also recognised a surface, sloping very gently eastwards from 620 to 600 feet, which he has interpreted as being of marine origin or at least trimmed by the sea as it transgressed over the land. The support for this view includes the nature of the drainage, for the west-east streams appear to be superimposed. The character of the surface also supports this interpretation, as the slope is very slight and uniform, with occasional hills, such as Whatborough Hill, rising as old islands above the surface. This view differs, however, from that put forward by G. A. Kellaway and J. H. Taylor who describe an erosion surface which they call the East Midland Erosion surface in the Jurassic area south-east of Nottingham. This surface appears to slope gently eastwards at a gradient of 20 to 50 feet per mile, and the authors suggest that this represents the gradual down-warping of a surface eastwards towards the geosynclinally subsiding North Sea basin. This surface, on account of the adjustment of drainage, is regarded as being of subaerial origin. On the evidence available it is difficult to decide which of the two views is more likely to be correct, but elsewhere in the region there appears to be a number of separate surfaces at relatively low levels as well as evidence for marine incursion to about the 600 foot level.

In the west of the region Clayton has recognised a series of lower erosion surfaces which are most clearly displayed on the wide Dove-Derwent interfluve where they have been left by the slow southward migration of the Trent valley, working its way towards the centre of the Needwood Forest depression. The relics of these surfaces are found as spur flats and occur largely on the Keuper Marl outcrop. The highest of them is at 580 feet and is called the Darley Moor surface and can be well seen in a broad flat south of Ashbourne, from which it derives its name. The surface falls gently eastwards with the main valley and hence is thought to be of subaerial origin and when traced westwards it becomes a valley stage. The next is the Yeavely surface, which is the best developed of the lower surfaces. North of the Trent, like the one above it, it forms broad benches and spur flats on the interfluves, except to the south of the Dove, where it forms the summit surface of Needwood Forest. Here its present height is slightly raised by the addition of fluvio-glacial outwash. The Yeavely surface also slopes gently from west to east, lying at about 470 to 495 feet in the west, with a lower subdivision at 460 feet in places and falling to 430 feet in the area around Derby. The lowest surface, the Mickleover, is most typically developed in the Derby neighbourhood, where it is shown in three stages, at 360, 320 and 280 feet respectively. These are important as spur flats on the Dove-Derwent interfluve and they form a significant element of the landscape around the southern and western flanks of Needwood Forest where, in the Blithe valley, the upper stage is preserved beneath fluvio-glacial outwash. It is likely that at least the lower stages of this erosion surface date from one of the early interglacial periods rather than the pre-glacial.

In the Manifold valley Warwick has also identified two stages below the level which probably accords with the marine incursion of the early Pleistocene. These may well be related to Clayton's lower surfaces further down the river system. In the Manifold valley where the present river level is 440 to 700 feet, the surfaces are at 580 to 860 feet and 460 to 720 feet. In the east also there is evidence of a surface at about 450 feet in the Vale of Catmose in the Melton Mowbray district, while surfaces at 500 to 530 feet, 425 to 460 feet and 280 to 360 feet occur near Mansfield and just north of Nottingham, where relics of them are found in the Leen and Erewash valleys. In Lincolnshire too A. Straw has identified a series of surfaces at various levels between the summit surface of the Wolds at 450 to 550 feet and a low surface at 80 to 150 feet; these he assigns to the late Pliocene and Pleistocene period, following the suggestion of Zeuner that sea-level stood at 420 feet in the early Pleistocene.

It is reasonable to conclude from this brief review of the work done in the area on the development of erosion surfaces that sea-level stood at about 1,000 feet relative to the land in Mio-Pliocene times for a considerable period during which the Upland Plain of the Low Peak was produced. This surface was then probably upwarped to a greater degree than elsewhere in the region and rejuvenation has since caused it to become dissected. On the lower surrounding ground the rivers have left evidence of the intermittent fall of base level in the flight of erosion surfaces, so well preserved on the broad Dove-Derwent interfluve, but also apparent elsewhere in the region. The cutting of the lower surfaces followed an incursion of the sea during the earliest Pleistocene, when the coastline must have lain near Nottingham so that marine erosion fashioned the Mansfield Plateau and possibly the surface south of Melton Mowbray. Since the retreat of the sea the gradual and intermittent lowering of sea-level continued with the formation of the lowest surfaces, some of which belong to the glacial period.

A number of drainage modifications of some significance took place during these events. The gradual shift south of the major rivers down the dip has already been mentioned. This accounts for the north-south pattern of drainage on the Dove-Derwent interfluve south of Ashbourne, these streams becoming lengthened as the main river moved south. In the headwaters of the Trent there is some evidence of a pre-glacial drainage change, by which the Trent, cutting back from Trentham, captured some of the streams formerly flowing south-south-east of Leek. Thus the Blithe and pre-glacial Churnet were beheaded by the Trent, leaving a col in the latter valley at about 700 feet. This col played an important part in the glacial period (Fig. 6). The Trent then followed its present course approximately as far as Long Eaton in immediate pre-glacial times. Its course from this point to the sea has recently been discussed by Straw in assembling the evidence pointing to its former continuation to the east, as suggested by Linton. Evidence for this route is to be found in two cols situated a few miles south of Nottingham (Fig. 6). The more westerly is located just east of Barton-in-Fabis at about 120 feet, having been lowered by subsequent erosion. The more easterly lies near Cropwell Butler at 150 feet, a level which would have allowed the Trent to cross the rock floor of the Ancaster Gap 18 miles further east at about 140 feet, at approximately its present gradient. Between Cropwell Butler and Ancaster this former route of the Trent lies across what is now the low ground of the Vale of Belvoir in which all traces of the old valley have been lost by erosion. This stage of the river's history belongs to the glacial period and it is probable that at the beginning of this period the Trent in the neighbourhood of Nottingham flowed at about 160 to 180 feet higher than the present sea-level.

Further north important drainage modifications have been pointed out by Swinnerton in his discussion of the Lincoln Gap, which is now much lower than the Ancaster Gap. He suggested that in pre-glacial times a river flowing east, the Lincoln river, cut a gap through the scarp at the present site of Lincoln. This river was then captured by streams working south from the Humber along the weak strata in the lower part of the present Trent valley, leaving a dry gap, which played an important part in later events. Subsequent streams thus dominated the northern part of the present Vale of Trent in pre-glacial times, and similar streams also developed along some of the weaker strata within the Coal Measures, giving the north-south direction of the Leen, Erewash and lower Amber. Thus when ice first spread down over the Nottingham area the drainage system differed considerably from its present pattern (Fig. 7), hence the effects of glaciation have greatly influenced the geomorphology of the whole area.

THE EFFECTS OF GLACIATION

Chronology

There appear to have been three glacial advances within the region, the second having the most marked effects on the landscape. The earliest glacial evidence so far recognised is in the form of outwash gravels at about 700 feet near Blackwall, north-west of Derby (Fig. 6). These gravels lie on a ridge 260 to 350 feet above the neighbouring valley floors, indicating that much erosion has taken place since their deposition. They belong to the Pennine Drift, probably correlating with the Lowestoft, Ante-Penultimate (Zeuner), First Welsh (Wills) and Elster (Northern Europe) according to the terminology used. Further south the deposits occur as till beneath more recent accumulations of drift. This early ice probably moved across from the north or north-north-west, eventually extending over the whole of the Midlands but relatively little is known of its effect on the landscape.

More important from the standpoint of landscape was the second ice advance, i.e. the last advance of the Older Drift period. This ice also spread over the district around Nottingham and drift of this period has been correlated with the Gipping Advance of East Anglia, the Penultimate, the Second Welsh and the Saale. Nearly all the till found within the region was brought by this ice sheet (Fig. 6) which approached the area from both north-north-east in the east and north-west in the west, bringing very different materials according to the direction of advance. In the west ice from the Irish Sea and Scotland brought western erratics and left these as far east as a mile or two east of Burton-on-Trent. Ice also spread over the Pennines from the north, bringing northern erratics to the area north of Derby. Further east, however, ice moved southwards down the Vale of York and along the low ground east of the south Pennines; it also moved southwards over Lincolnshire following the pattern of the outcrops. Thus the eastern ice brought a variety of drift types into the area: clayey till with a large Keuper constituent, to the south and east of Nottingham, chalky-Jurassic till in the area east of Lincoln, and intensely chalky till on the eastern Wolds in Lincolnshire and in the area to the south-west around Horncastle. To the south and west of Nottingham the eastern ice at one stage pushed west to reach as far as Abbots Bromley, where its presence is clearly indicated by erratics of flint. Outwash from this ice-sheet also produced the flinty gravels already mentioned as covering the summit surface in Needwood Forest where they reach 25 to 30 feet in thickness (Fig. 6).

The final ice advance to have a direct effect on the region was the major advance of the Newer Drift in the last glaciation. This ice sheet has been called the Irish Sea Ice in the west and in the east is referred to as the Hessle Drift or Hunstanton Drift. The margin of the ice at its maximum impinged on the Pennine flank in the west, pushing an ice lobe up to the Churnet col and reaching the Blithe valley before swinging south-west to cross the Iron-Bridge watershed. On the east, ice appears to have blocked the Humber Gap and pushed up into the valleys on the eastern side of the Lincolnshire Wolds and extended as far as Stickney, north of Boston, where there is a subdued partially buried morainic feature. From here the ice swung off to the south-east to close the Wash Gap by impinging on the North Norfolk coast. Although the ice itself did not cover much of the region at this time it had important effects on the landscape and the Nottingham area provides a useful area for linking together the effects of ice on the east and west sides of the country.

Glacial erosion and deposition

Although glacial erosion is normally associated with highland areas there is nevertheless evidence of such erosion in the Nottingham region. Clearly there must have been erosion to provide the large amount of glacial till, much of which consists of the soft Lias clay outcropping in the area. In the soft clay vales on either side of the Lincoln cuesta the subdrift surface in particular shows evidence of glacial erosion. In the Ancholme valley the subdrift contours show a symmetrical valley, sloping gently south to a level of —50 feet south-west of Horncastle and nearly level at 40 feet O.D. north of Lincoln. The symmetry of this valley suggests glacial scouring because if the formative agent had been fluvial erosion an asymmetrical valley would more likely have been produced. Glacial erosion to the west of the Lincoln Edge may also account for the abnormally low level of the till in the area around Gainsborough.

Another area where glacial erosion has been severe is in the Vale of Belvoir. This low-lying area, floored by weak clays, has only a scattered till cover at present. Ice moving south would have easy access to the Vale, which at the time of the advance must have contained the northern flank of the former Trent valley, directed to the Ancaster Gap. The disappearance of all trace of this part of the pre-glacial Trent valley could be readily explained by its removal due to scouring by ice when the latter was moving vigorously southwards. As the ice became stagnant a decaying lobe was left in this low ground (Fig. 6).

Elsewhere in the region the ice appears to have been mainly depositional in its effects, leaving behind the material it had scoured in its path. The major areas of Older Drift occur to the south of the Vale of Belvoir, where thick till has built up the south Nottinghamshire Wolds, much of the material probably being derived from the area of erosion in the Vale of Belvoir itself. Drift up to 195 feet thick at a point 15 miles south of Ancaster has been shown to have completely obliterated a channel over one and a half miles wide probably cut by river action. Drift is also very thick in the old Soar valley. F. W. Shotton has shown that the direction of flow of this valley has been reversed and it now forms part of the southerly draining Avon valley.

The most important area of Newer Drift lies to the east of the Lincolnshire Wolds in Lincolnshire, where the till banked against the interglacial chalk cliffs, is up to 100 feet thick. Although glacial deposits are widely spread throughout the region, perhaps the most significant changes wrought by the ice sheets are those associated with alterations in the drainage pattern and the development of the terraces of the Trent and other major rivers.

Glacial drainage changes and terrace formation

The course of the river Trent in immediate pre-glacial times has already been mentioned.

As the main eastern ice advanced southwards along the low ground east of the Pennines it scoured the weak clays and deposited this material as it rose on to higher ground still further south. It impounded Lake Harrison in the old valley of the proto-Soar which was considerably longer than the present river. The first important drainage change in the Trent area took place as the eastern ice started to retreat from its maximum position, when the Warwickshire Avon was initiated and extended headward at the expense of the old Soar valley.

A more important change from the point of view of the Trent itself, however, took place at a later stage in the retreat of the eastern ice. The ice, being far from its source, seems to have decayed into stagnant lobes, one of which occupied the low ground of the Vale of Belvoir. This ice provided an effective block across the former route of the Trent towards the Ancaster Gap. Melt-water from the decaying ice, supplemented by ordinary drainage water was forced to flow along the edge of this lobe thus initiating the anomalous trench of the Trent from Nottingham to Newark. This broad, straight trench, about two miles wide, cuts obliquely across the Keuper Marl dip slope and could only have been formed in the presence of some blocking agent on its south-eastern flank. The bounding bluffs on the south-east of the trench reach about 200 feet in height and from this elevation the ground slopes gently down to the Vale of Belvoir at about 100 feet. The cutting of the trench must have started on the dip slope at a height of about 250 feet.

Gravels were laid down by the waters that excavated this trench, and these form the older part of the Hilton Terrace gravels. According to the work of M. Posnansky these appear to have the characteristics of fluvio-glacial outwash. The Hilton Terrace extends from Uttoxeter on the Dove and Rugeley on the Trent as far as Long Eaton. Beyond this point the gravels of this terrace are not present in the trench, but their downstream continuations are found on the hills near Eagle just west of the Lincoln Gap and in other gravels, found east of the gap. The western part of the Hilton Terrace above Nottingham is in two distinct parts, the upper at about 90 feet above the modern alluvium and the lower 40 to 60 feet above the alluvium. At Hilton itself, where the gravels are well exposed, they are composed of 70 per cent Bunter pebbles, with flint as the next most frequent constituent. This is significant for it indicates that the terrace must be younger than the Gipping glaciation which brought the flints into the area from the east. The character of the gravels indicate that the upper Hilton Terrace was aggraded by heavily laden melt-water streams, issuing from the retreating Pennine ice to the north; torrent bedding is shown and lumps of chalky till are included.

It is suggested that the down-cutting between the two parts of the Hilton Terrace was caused by the rapid incision of the river into its trench between Nottingham and Newark, causing rejuvenation to work back up the river. Towards the upper part of the lower terrace gravels the bedding becomes more even and the character of the deposit suggests an amelioration of conditions with the approach of the interglacial climate.

The downstream end of the Hilton Terrace, occurring on either side of the Lincoln Gap, was recognised by Swinnerton in 1937 as marking the former route of the Trent; he linked the gravels at about 100 feet O.D. near Eagle, west of Lincoln, with those at 50 feet near Heighington, on the east side of the gap, showing that the Trent had deserted the Ancaster Gap at this stage (Fig. 7). The likely reason why the Trent used the Lincoln Gap is because the route available to the Humber was blocked by another lobe of stagnant ice, which may in fact have been linked to that in the Vale of Belvoir. The waters from the Trent trench must have flowed over, under, or between the stagnant ice lobes to use the lowest available route of escape *via* Lincoln. Once through the gap, the river turned south-east leaving evidence of its course in a gravel terrace. The pattern of drainage in the Till valley north-west of Lincoln and in the Vale of Belvoir to the south-west has led Straw to argue that these streams were initiated subglacially under the decaying ice lobes, the water draining to the Lincoln Gap which was lowered to about 25 feet O.D. by the time the ice finally melted. Ice to the north of Lincoln gradually shrank from the higher ground to the west, and when the ice-front had retreated to a position running north-south a little east of Gainsborough, the Trent was able to take advantage of the low ground to the north and for the first time adopted its present course to the Humber. This route may have enabled down-cutting to be renewed and it is possible that the formation of the lower Hilton Terrace dates from this time as the Trent gradually cut down through the Keuper Marl.

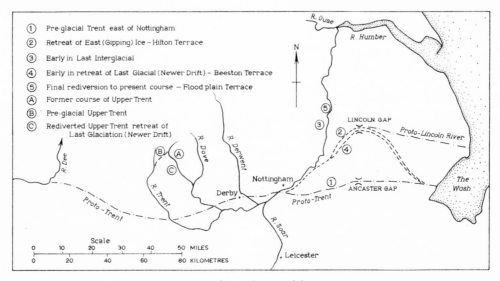

① Pre-glacial Trent east of Nottingham
② Retreat of East (Gipping) Ice – Hilton Terrace
③ Early in Last Interglacial
④ Early in retreat of Last Glacial (Newer Drift) – Beeston Terrace
⑤ Final rediversion to present course – Flood plain Terrace
Ⓐ Former course of Upper Trent
Ⓑ Pre-glacial Upper Trent
Ⓒ Rediverted Upper Trent retreat of Last Glaciation (Newer Drift)

Scale
0   10   20   30   40   50 MILES
0   20   40   60   80 KILOMETRES

Fig. 7   Stages in the evolution of the river Trent

While the ice lobe was still present in the Vale of Belvoir melt-water flowing through the Ancaster Gap from the west deposited coarse gravels to the east of it. As the ice shrank back, a lake developed and sand was deposited both in the gap and to the west of it to a thickness of about 20 feet.

During the last interglacial relatively little erosion was accomplished in the Vale of Belvoir and the lower Trent valley, as these areas were already lowered by glacial erosion, elsewhere there was a certain amount of lowering and incision of the streams.

The Trent area is of special significance in attempting to link the events of the last glaciation on the east with those on the west side of the country, because its upper reaches have been influenced by the western ice and its lower by the eastern. The presence of a pre-glacial col in the Churnet valley has already been mentioned. This col was one of the lowest points along the watershed between the Trent drainage on the west and the Dove drainage on the east. At this time all the drainage north of Leek passed to the Trent *via* Stoke. The Irish Sea Ice, however, advanced as far as the col in the Churnet valley and as it retreated westwards water was impounded between it and the col and flowed over the col. A large volume of melt-water was involved for not only the Churnet headstreams flowed this way. A. Jowett and J. K. Charlesworth have shown how the upper Dane drainage was impounded between the high ground on the east and the retreating ice on the west, forming a lake that overflowed southwards through the Rudyard gorge into the upper Churnet valley. This large volume of water was responsible for cutting the wide valley bends of the Churnet near Leek, which now form a passage much too large for the stream now flowing through it. The water flowing across the Churnet col lowered the level by over 300 feet to form a deep melt-water gorge through which the upper Churnet has been diverted away from the Trent to flow direct to the Dove. This glacial diversion has left the headwaters of the Trent as a misfit stream flowing in a broad valley to Stoke-on-Trent, separated from the Churnet drainage by a now deserted col at Stockton Brook between Leek and Stoke.

The Irish Sea Ice also impinged on the Blithe valley and outwash was carried down this valley to the Trent drainage. This material lies only a few feet above the level of the gravels of the Beeston Terrace and this has given rise to the suggestion that the Beeston Terrace itself grades into the outwash and therefore dates from the retreat phase of the Newer Drift ice advance. The Beeston Terrace gravels, however, have been ascribed to various dates by different authors. Posnansky, partly on the evidence afforded by fossil fauna and artifacts including a whole *Hippopotamus*, parts of *Elephas* and *Rhinoceros* and fresh Levallois flakes, suggests they may belong to the last (Eemian) interglacial. Hippopotamus has certainly been found in deposits at several places in Northern England belonging to the last interglacial. If this view is correct the Beeston Terrace gravels must have been aggraded during the same interglacial as the lower parts of the Hilton Terrace gravels, but there is evidence of down-cutting to the extent of 20 feet between the deposition of the two terraces at

Willington. Against this is the morphological evidence pointing to a date after the Irish Sea Ice for the Beeston Terrace, either as outwash of this ice as suggested by G. H. Mitchell and I. P. Stevenson (1955) or as an interstadial deposit according to Clayton. On the whole the evidence would seem to fit in best with the view of Mitchell and Stevenson.

The Beeston Terrace is an important morphological feature, forming a wide ledge between Rugeley and Burton, in the Dove valley, and along the Trent valley south-east of Derby. At Beeston it is about 30 feet above the present alluvium. Relics of it appear east of Nottingham at Bassingfield but much more extensive remnants occur to the south-west of Lincoln and again through the Lincoln Gap, where the gravels merge into those of one of the Witham terraces called by Straw the Martin Terrace. These gravels show that once again the Trent used the passage through the Lincoln Gap to reach the sea. This was brought about by the blocking of the Humber and Fenland Gaps by the eastern ice of the Newer Drift period. This ice impounded a lake which spread as far as Nottingham and flooded the Lincoln Gap, with a water level about 100 feet O.D. The evidence for a lake at this level is clearly seen east of Lincoln where a sandy delta was formed at this height at the mouth of the Bain valley. This merges into the Martin Terrace and is associated, by means of the terrace, with the Stickney moraine. Thus the lake was impounded at the maximum extent of the Last Ice sheet. The Beeston Terrace was aggraded towards the Lincoln Gap as the level of the lake slowly fell, allowing the terrace to extend up to and then through the gap.

When the northern outlet was again made available by the unblocking of the Humber outlet, the Trent reverted to its former course (Fig. 7). The floodplain terrace gravels were possibly laid down during a second phase of impeded drainage when the northern outlet was partially blocked by a slight re-advance. Thus the Beeston Terrace, if it can be shown definitely to be related to the Irish Sea Ice in the west, would provide a link with the eastern ice on the Nottingham side of the Pennines. Since its aggradation is not related to base level close correlation with neighbouring valleys cannot be expected especially where these were not influenced by glacial damming.

PERIGLACIAL FEATURES

When glaciers approached, but did not actually cover, the region the climate was very severe, and these phases have left their mark in various types of periglacial features. The cemented screes in the Manifold valley are an interesting example as they indicate the effect of climatic fluctuations. These are to be found near Ecton in an area where no screes are being formed at the present time. The material is rudely stratified, consisting of alternate layers of coarser and finer material, the former being more firmly cemented than the latter. The coarser bands consist of very angular limestone fragments, cemented with calcite. The strong cementing and lack of

V   Sherwood Forest showing birch and bracken

VI The river Trent, below Nottingham, showing the new channel with Holme Sluices and the former meander

VII The river Trent at Fiskerton showing newly piled river wall and masonry floodwall

modern screes suggest an origin resulting from a periglacial climate. Frost shattering would have been active and it is known that calcite is more readily precipitated at freezing temperatures; water would also be plentiful in the surface layers if the lower ones were frozen. The softer, finer bands were probably formed in the warmer periods when chemical weathering allowed some size-reduction in the particles. No erratics occur in the material, so it is likely that it was formed during the Newer Drift period, when ice did not cover the area.

The scarcity of limestone pavements in this area may also be accounted for by the lack of glacial scouring during the Newer Drift period, such as was active in the central and northern Pennines.

Other evidence of periglacial activity is widespread. Contortions due to frost activity are found in soil profiles near Derby (E. M. Bridges) and the importance of frost shattering and solifluction is clearly seen in the large-scale formation of head deposits, consisting of shattered chalk, in the Lincolnshire Wolds. More impressive than these, however, are the large-scale superficial structures which have been described in the area to the south-east of Nottingham by G. A. Kellaway and J. H. Taylor. These, too, show evidence of formation under conditions of severe cold. They include features known locally as 'gulls'. These were originally ice wedges, formed either by the growth of ground ice wedges or more likely by fractures resulting from extremely low temperature. Such cracks often become filled with melt-water in summer to form ice wedges, and later sediment slumped into them to form the 'gulls' as they now exist. The pattern of the fossil ice wedge features in the East Midlands is predominantly linear and they can affect the ground to a depth of 150 feet as, for example, north of Stamford.

Other large-scale features include cambering, which affects the dip of strata on scarp slopes, creating a local departure from the regional dip; and the formation of valley bulges and synclinal structures known as sags. Valleys cut in the relatively resistant Lincolnshire Limestone and Northamptonshire Sands, with the weak Lias Clays outcropping along the floors, favoured the development of bulges. The latter are usually bounded either by normal faults or by synclinal structures to form the sags. These sags probably mark the areas which became waterlogged and where ground-ice could accumulate in the largest amounts, so that when it finally melted the ground collapsed. Such vertical subsidence may well have provided the movement required to account for some of the cambering features, a few of which descend below the level of the valley floor.

Areas most liable to permafrost were those where water could not circulate so freely, thus the floors of the valleys would be most affected, particularly the smaller ones. In the larger valleys the slopes and interfluves may well have frozen first and this would influence the form of the resulting permafrost features. An asymmetry noted in some of the East Midland valleys, where the north-facing slopes tend to be steeper than the south-facing ones, may also be due to frost activity; on the south-facing slopes more active melting would allow more effective solifluction action and thaw collapse will be more effective, leading to the formation of a gently sloping valley side. Solifluction probably first became effective on the interfluves and upper slopes. Then ground-ice began to form in the valley bottoms and on the lower slopes, resulting in ice-heaving and the bulging of rocks. Collapse and cambering occurred when melting eventually took place. Some of the material moved in these ways would then be excavated by the river. It seems likely that several phases of permafrost activity have taken place in the area.

POST-GLACIAL MODIFICATION OF THE LANDSCAPE

The last gravels to be laid down by the Trent were the flood-plain terrace gravels, following the present course of the river to the Humber. Since their deposition in late glacial times, sea-level has been low and rejuvenation has worked up the Trent valley as far as Beeston Lock. Clayton has pointed out that the flood-plain terrace gravels are found as a definite terrace downstream from Beeston, but upstream from this point they are covered by recent alluvium. Posnansky has suggested that after the aggradation of the flood-plain gravels a deep channel was cut below Newark. At Cromwell the floor of the flood-plain terrace is at one foot O.D. falling to −35 feet O.D. in the next 14 miles. This channel was then filled with deposits and the flood-plain gravels were incised to form the low terrace which lies at 7 to 10 feet above the level of the alluvium between Nottingham and Newark. Lithologically these gravels differ from the older Hilton and Beeston Terrace gravels in that they lack constituents derived from erosion of the eastern drift and instead appear to be derived from deposits of the western or Irish Sea Ice drift.

As the Trent has aggraded during the post-glacial period it has spread a layer of alluvium below the terrace relics. This spread becomes wider upstream of Beeston Lock, where the knick point is now held up. Upstream from the Lock the flood-plain terrace is missing. The river has developed a meandering course within its trench, building natural levees. Artificial flood-banks have been added to protect the adjacent lands.

Another recent landscape feature, although not entirely post-glacial, is the formation of deep, narrow valleys known locally as 'dumbles' in the Keuper Marl slope leading down to the Trent trench. These small valleys have been eroded as a result of the lowering of the local base-level, due to the incision of the trench, to which they were then adjusted.

CONCLUSION

A traverse across the area from west to east a little north of Nottingham takes one in general from the old to the newer in relation to both the rocks and the scenery. On the west is the subdued relief of the ancient Mio-Pliocene peneplane cut across the Carboniferous Limestone. In the Derwent valley there is evidence of both old and more recent events, its general course probably antedates the upland plain, while its newer terraces belong to the Pleistocene. Eastwards again are the more recent erosion surfaces and subsequent streams of the Erewash and Leen, while again the great trench of the Trent breaks the continuity, by being a relatively young feature, and the gravels on its east side are still more recent. However, the Ancaster Gap takes the development back again to an old stage, before the youngest area of all is reached beyond the Lincolnshire Wolds in the Outmarsh and coast of Lincolnshire.

The scenery of the Nottingham district bears the imprint of subaerial activity, prolonged though variable in intensity, and marine incursions have also left their mark in the landscape. The relatively recent episode of glaciation has also played a major part in shaping the landscape and particularly in modifying the drainage pattern of the major river, the Trent, which has suffered changes of course both at its headwaters and in its lower reaches.

SELECTED REFERENCES

Clayton, K. M. The denudation chronology of part of the middle Trent basin. *Transactions and Papers of the Institute of British Geographers* No. 19 (1953) pp. 25–36.

Jowett, A. and Charlesworth, J. K. The glacial geology of the Derbyshire Dome and the western slopes of the southern Pennines. *Quarterly Journal of the Geological Society* Vol. 85 (1929) pp. 307–334.

Kellaway, G. A. and Taylor, J. H. Early stages in the physiographic evolution of a portion of the East Midlands. *Quarterly Journal of the Geological Society* Vol. 108 (1953) pp. 343–376.

Linton, D. L. Midland drainage. *Advancement of Science* Vol. 7 (1951) pp. 449–456.

Posnansky, M. The Pleistocene succession in the middle Trent Basin. *Proceedings of the Geologists' Association* Vol. 71 (1960) pp. 285–311.

Straw, A. The erosion surfaces of East Lincolnshire. *Proceedings of the Yorkshire Geological Society* Vol. 33 (1961) pp. 149–172.

Straw, A. The Quaternary evolution of the Lower and Middle Trent. *East Midland Geographer* Vol. 3 No. 20 (1963) pp. 171–189.

III

WEATHER AND CLIMATE

INTRODUCTION

WITHIN the area covered by this survey, the Derbyshire uplands in the west are climatically distinct from the rest of the territory because altitude and relief promote higher rainfall and strong local climatic contrasts. To the east and south, over the wide tract of lowland, low relative relief is reflected in a corresponding uniformity of climate. The essential insularity of the British climate, while apparent in west Derbyshire, is elsewhere modified to some degree by the shelter afforded by the southern Pennines, and by the inland position of the area, for Nottingham is over 100 miles from the west coast and 70 miles from the east.

The higher ground of the west intensifies frontal and cyclonic rainfall by uplift and retardation, and promotes cloud and showers in unstable air streams of maritime polar type. These effects account for the greater rainfall. The deeply cut valleys develop strong and persistent temperature inversions on a scale not found in the lowland area. The latter, however, has larger diurnal and annual mean temperature ranges, only marginally exceeded anywhere in Britain. The growing season of seven to eight months on the lowland is over a month longer than that on the upland. The low but rather variable annual rainfall indicates a climate drier than the average for England and Wales. Rain also tends to be concentrated in the second half of the year and to decrease eastwards in amount. So far as the lowland is concerned these are all 'continental' characteristics.

While mean climatic figures are strikingly similar throughout the lowland, there are nevertheless significant variations in detail. Local configuration largely determines the patterns of such phenomena as rainfall, length of snow-lie, and incidence of fog and mist; but regional location in the broader sense is also important. For example, winter showers generated over the Irish Sea fail to penetrate beyond east Derbyshire at night, while heavy snow showers brought by air with a long track across the North Sea from north or north–east strongly affect Lincolnshire but rarely reach west of the Trent. In these respects the vicinity of Nottingham enjoys effective shelter; but it is fully exposed to continental air on a shorter track from east–north–east or east. Anticyclonic development over northern Europe often presages unpleasantly cold, raw, dull weather in late winter and spring, or it may bring sheets of very low stratus cloud (haar) shrouding even the low hills during night and morning in summer.

In any region, especially one of relative climatic uniformity such as the East Midland lowland, climatic changes assume particular importance in arriving at generalisations, for variations from one period to another at a given place are of the same order of magnitude as the differences which occur from place to place. Old records are therefore of special value and have been used considerably in the present account. A brief account of the work of early meteorologists and of their records in the Nottingham region is given in Appendix I on page 522. An examination of readings taken as far back as the late 18th century, many of them yielding only fragmentary series, shows however that mean values for the past 20 to 25 years are as typical of the last 100 to 150 years as those of any other comparable period.

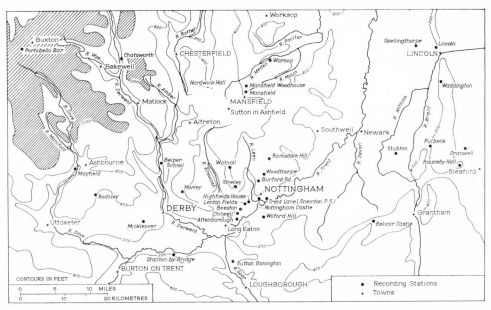

Fig. 8   Location of climatological stations   *(Crown Copyright reserved)*

ATMOSPHERIC PRESSURE

At Nottingham mean monthly atmospheric pressure is above average in the sunny months of May and June and in the relatively dry month of September; it is markedly lower in the duller and more rainy months of July and August and lowest in December. Over the past century both the highest and the lowest pressure of the year have usually been measured between November and March. Neither maximum nor minimum has ever occurred in June or July. Since 1868 the morning M.S.L. pressure has varied between extremes of 1050 mb. (31·01 inches) on 26th January 1932 and 948 mb. (28·00 inches) on 8th December 1886. Hodsock Priory in north Nottinghamshire has a similar seasonal variation and a slightly greater extreme range (1881–1925), from 1051 mb. (31·04 inches) on 23rd January 1907 (then 1048·7 mb. at Nottingham) to 944 mb. (27·883 inches) on 8th December 1886. Shorter records at Watnall and Cranwell show no significant difference in regime. Mean annual isobars for 1921–50 however run almost west–east across the region, pressure falling from about 1014·7 mb. in the south to 1014·2 mb. in the north. This indicates a gradient wind averaging westerly in direction and a mean surface wind from west–south–west to south–west.

WIND

Long records indicate south–west as the most prominent surface wind direction at Nottingham, but the balance of directions has varied periodically. From 1891 to 1925 nearly half the winds in the year were between north–west and south–west, but a 4-point scale for 1868–1901 indicates a marked increase in westerlies through the 1880s and early 1890s, a halving of the frequency of southerlies in the late 1880s, and a minimum of northerlies and a maximum of easterlies in the mid–1880s. Again, at Hodsock (Fig. 9), from 1876 to 1925 south–west was the prevalent wind direction but the decade 1916–25 saw a marked proportional increase in west winds in March, July, October and November, and of north–westerlies in March. Such variations are associated with fluctuations of temperature and rainfall. In the warm period 1896–1938 south–west to south winds were prevalent, especially in winter, as shown in the wind rose for Belvoir Castle (Fig. 9). The greater frequency of west winds from 1935 to 1958 at Woodthorpe, Nottingham, accords with the characteristics of the recent climatic fluctuation.

A prominent feature of the wind roses for Hodsock, Belvoir and Woodthorpe is the secondary maximum of north–east winds and their concentration in spring and early summer, with the maximum in May. This marked frequency of cold, often dry winds has special importance in relation to the hazards of late killing frosts and retarded early growth on light sandy soils. The early record (1786–1805) from Mansfield Woodhouse (Fig. 9) exhibits a similar vernal maximum of north–easterlies.

The mean annual wind speed inland does not reach 10 m.p.h. even at well-exposed stations. In the Nottingham district it is generally no more than six or seven m.p.h. The low summer mean values (minimum in July) continue well into autumn and the higher winter values well into spring.

With regard to hourly records of wind speed, the mean annual hourly maximum at Cranwell (28 years) is 38 m.p.h. and at Leicester (10 years) 33 m.p.h., and the highest hourly means 49 and 42 m.p.h. respectively. Probability analysis shows that at Cranwell and Leicester an hourly average wind-speed of 45 m.p.h. is likely to be exceeded only once in 10 years, but this speed is exceeded almost every year at Spurn Head on the east coast. Gusts of wind, of course, reach higher figures. Mean annual maximum gusts at Cranwell and Leicester are 65 to 70 m.p.h. compared with 70 to 75 m.p.h. at Spurn Head. The maximum gust recorded at Cranwell in 29 years (1928–59) closely matches the recorded maxima of 110 m.p.h. at Tiree and Stornaway. Gusts accompanying severe gales can cause great destruction. A notable example was the gale of 21st January 1802, when fierce gusts during four hours uprooted about 10,000 trees in the Rufford plantations and over 1,000 in Thoresby Park in central Nottinghamshire.

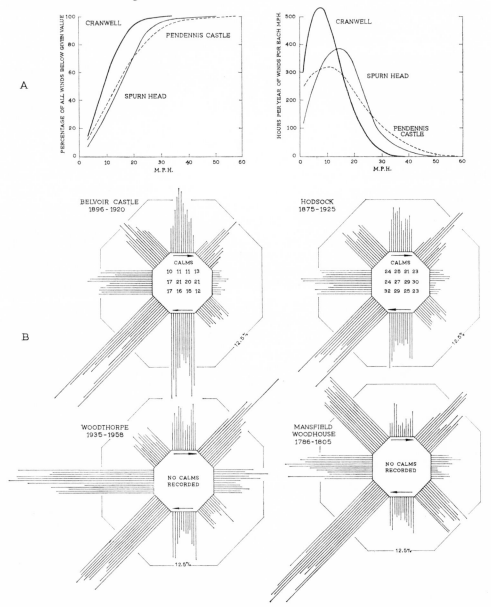

Fig. 9 Wind.   A Wind speeds (10-year period)   B Wind roses, surface winds

Winds of different directions tend to be associated with characteristic temperature and moisture conditions. Observations made by the late Arnold B. Tinn demonstrate the variations of moistness with wind direction at Nottingham through the year. They reveal, for example, that in February the average dew point of a north–east wind is some 12°F (6·7°C) lower than that of a south–west wind, the moistest; but in July and August the north–east wind is the moister. Of particular note are mean dew points between 32°F (0°C) and 35°F (1·7°C) with north to east winds in early spring, for these with dry bulb temperatures of 40°F (4·4°C) or less, and overcast skies, are representative of the raw weather which is an unpleasant though intermittent characteristic of that season in the East Midlands.

PRECIPITATION

Rainfall distribution

For 1881–1915 mean annual precipitation (Fig. 10) ranged from over 60 inches in the High Peak to below 25 inches locally in the Trent valley and other places. At given heights in the Peak District rainfall tends to decrease eastwards, and in the lowland amounts diminish from some 25 to 26 inches in south Derbyshire to 22 to 23 inches in the lower Trent valley and in the Witham valley below Lincoln. But this decrease should not be overstressed, for the general altitude also declines eastward. The tendency for an increasing proportion of convective to frontal–cyclonic rain in summer, and an increasing contribution of shower precipitation from north–easterly airstreams in winter in that direction, as well as local variations with altitude and relief, as for instance along the Lincoln Cliff, virtually obscure any general eastward decrease.

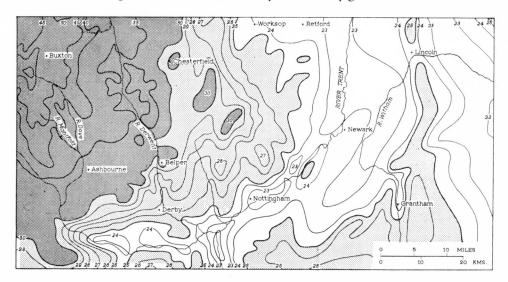

Fig. 10   Distribution of mean annual rainfall, 1881–1915

Most of the higher ground of Derbyshire receives over 30 inches of rain annually. To the east rainfall diminishes though there are isolated areas with over 30 inches near Hardwick Hall, and on ground rising towards 600 feet south–west of Mansfield. Rainfall decreases below 25 inches in the valleys of the Soar and Wreak, and north-wards in the Trent vale. North and eastwards from the Trent–Soar district the amount of rainfall decreases still further from 25 to 23 inches a year, which is characteristic of much of the Trent lowlands. In the flat carrlands around the lower Trent, it is less than 22 inches.

The immediate vicinity of Nottingham thus has a mean annual rainfall of about 25 inches, but distinct local variations occur, some of which are distinguished on Professor K. C. Edwards' map of Nottinghamshire rainfall. For example, with the rise in elevation northward across the city, values as low as 21·5 inches on the Trent valley floor at about 80 feet O.D. are succeeded by 24·2 inches at Nottingham Castle, 25 at Burford Road, 26 at Woodthorpe and 28 inches at Ramsdale Hill (500 feet) in a distance of six or seven miles.

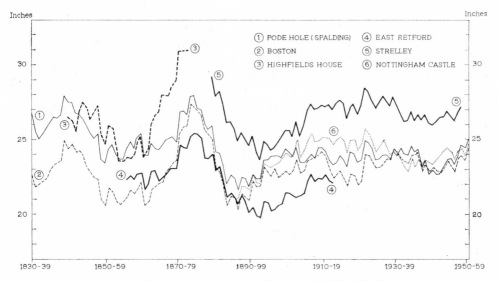

Fig. 11 10-year running means of annual rainfall, 1830–1960

Rainfall trends

Although the general pattern of distribution has not changed significantly since the 1881–1915 period, short-term variations have brought changes in the actual amount of rain recorded over the region. Annual means for 1916–50 at most stations where full records exist, show increases over those for the previous 35 years by amounts ranging up to 2·5 inches; generally 0·5 to 1·5 inches near Nottingham, rather less over the lowlands to the north and east, and somewhat more over higher ground in Derbyshire. This change has probably resulted in no part of the Nottingham district receiving less than 22·5 inches; for example, the mean for Sutton Bonington (1881–1915) of 21·7 inches has risen to 22·9 inches for the period 1916–50.

An altered frequency of dry and wet years is responsible for period changes in annual rainfall. Fig. 11 shows 10–year running means which indicate well-marked fluctuations over the last 130 years, with rainfall peaks around the years 1845 and 1880, and with lower maxima around 1915 and 1926–27. The rise from the later 1860s to the peak in the mid–1880s was especially prominent, and H. Mellish calculated the mean annual rainfall of 12 stations in the Nottinghamshire area for 1875–1883 to be 19 per cent above the average for 1861–90, a fluctuation unmatched at least since 1726. In contrast the period 1881–1915 was drier and the graphs suggest that the general level of annual rainfall during the immediate past 25 or 30 years is a near approximation to the mean of the last 100 to 150 years. For a closer analysis of rainfall it would seem satisfactory, therefore, to rely on figures for a recent period, such as those for 1936–60.

G. H. Dury has recently elaborated the use of a graphical method devised by E. J. Gumbel for analysing and standardising rainfall records for given periods and stations. This form of probability analysis discounts the occurrence of extreme high or low amounts which are to be regarded as the extreme values appropriate to longer periods, but falling by chance within the period under analysis. It is particularly useful in clarifying rainfall regimes in areas like the Nottingham district where seasonal variation is not very great. The Gumbel graph for Nottingham Castle for the 98 years 1867–1964, and the 25 years 1936–60 are closely similar, whereas the graph for 1886–1910, like that for Highfields House for 1840–81, is very different, thus confirming the representative nature of the most recent period (Fig. 12).

Annual rainfall regimes

Gumbel graphs of monthly rainfall standardised to 1936–60 are shown in Fig. 13. Duty presented others for 1932–56 which have also been used to derive the strictly comparable standardised mean rainfalls, reduced to 30–day month equivalents, as set out in Table VI. The figures show that November is the wettest month at all stations, and December markedly drier except in the upland, where rainfall decreases through the winter to the late spring minimum. At lowland stations renewed wetness in January, the second wettest month for some places, is followed by declining amounts, reaching the minimum in March or April, and thereafter rising to a secondary maximum in July or August, one or other of which is generally the second wettest month. At all lowland stations in the Nottingham district September is less rainy than August and October.

The dispersion graphs in Fig. 14 which, through standardisation, are simpler than crude dispersion diagrams, demonstrate the character of the seasonal variation. They include 'most probable falls' for each month. In general form the graphs are very similar from station to station in the lowland, but corresponding graphs for earlier periods present a different picture. For example, at Nottingham Castle for 1886–1910 (within the 1881–1915 standard period) August was the wettest month, October the second wettest; and, compared with recent years, December was wetter and January and February markedly drier. Comparable changes have occurred at other stations.

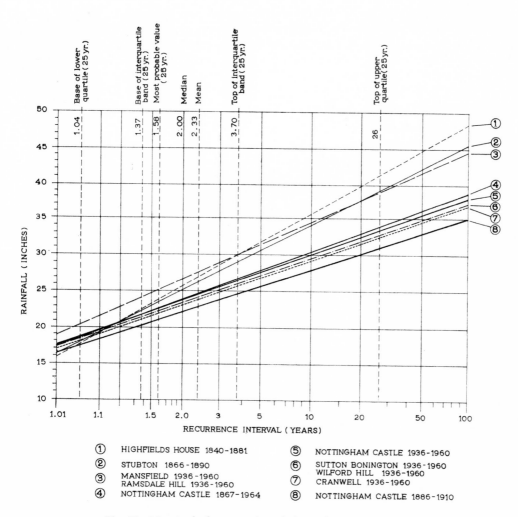

(1) HIGHFIELDS HOUSE 1840-1881   (5) NOTTINGHAM CASTLE 1936-1960

(2) STUBTON 1866-1890   (6) SUTTON BONINGTON 1936-1960

(3) MANSFIELD 1936-1960   WILFORD HILL 1936-1960

    RAMSDALE HILL 1936-1960   (7) CRANWELL 1936-1960

(4) NOTTINGHAM CASTLE 1867-1964   (8) NOTTINGHAM CASTLE 1886-1910

Fig. 12   Magnitude-frequency (Gumbel) graphs of annual rainfall

Standardised for periods shown with extrapolation to 100 years

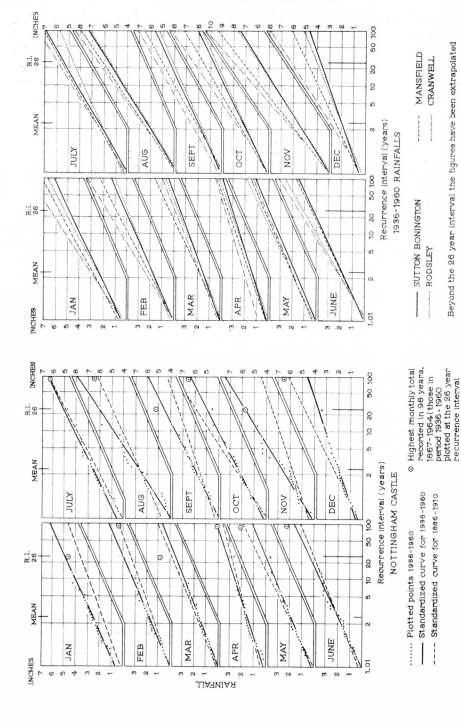

Fig. 13 Magnitude-frequency distribution (Gumbel) graphs of monthly rainfall

Table VI

Rainfall, mean monthly and annual, in inches, standardised to the periods shown, and reduced to 30-day months. Percentage of the annual fall, April–September

	Jan.	Feb.	Mar.	April	May	June	July	Aug.	Sept.	Oct.	Nov.	Dec.	Year	Summer per cent
Buxton (P.B.) 1932–56	4·84	3·91	3·22	3·21	2·91	3·84	5·18	4·41	4·78	5·14	5·52	5·01	51·97	46·82
Stanton-by-bridge 1932–56	2·42	2·30	1·72	1·70	2·08	1·95	2·13	2·27	2·14	2·37	2·75	2·08	26·91	45·59
Matlock .. 1932–56	2·80	2·45	1·89	1·87	2·20	2·38	2·56	2·73	2·55	2·71	3·53	2·84	30·51	46·84
Rodsley .. 1932–56	3·01	2·32	1·86	2·12	1·97	2·33	2·67	2·71	2·62	2·87	3·45	2·89	30·82	46·79
Nottingham Castle 1936–60	2·42	1·98	1·55	1·55	1·87	2·02	2·32	2·51	1·95	2·24	2·70	1·93	25·04	48·80
Sneinton P.S. 1932–56	2·13	1·79	1·57	1·75	1·95	1·89	2·34	2·35	1·80	2·16	2·50	1·73	23·96	50·42
Sutton Bonington 1936–60	2·27	1·96	1·55	1·40	1·74	1·92	2·37	2·27	2·00	2·13	2·60	1·86	24·07	48·61
Mansfield .. 1936–60	2·76	2·33	1·74	1·60	1·98	1·97	2·51	2·48	2·17	2·51	3·09	2·37	27·51	46·20
Cranwell .. 1936–60	2·27	1·97	1·45	1·40	2·03	2·20	2·19	2·32	1·80	2·10	2·55	1·89	24·17	49·40
Nottingham Castle 1886–1910	1·76	1·61	1·74	1·50	1·96	1·92	2·27	2·61	1·65	2·58	1·90	2·32	23·80	49·96
Stubton .. 1866–90	1·84	1·97	1·52	2·05	2·13	2·15	2·45	2·51	2·62	2·80	2·30	2·27	26·61	52·27
Spalding .. 1866–90	1·74	1·82	1·43	1·88	2·11	2·22	2·66	2·42	2·63	2·51	2·30	2·22	24·04	50·00

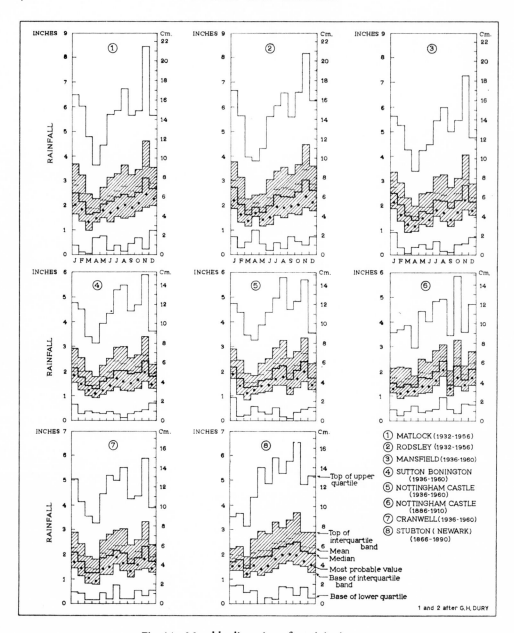

Fig. 14   Monthly dispersion of precipitation

Monthly figures adjusted to 30-day months and standardised to the 25-year periods indicated

Table VII Maximum monthly and annual rainfall, in inches, over given periods

		Jan.	Feb.	Mar.	April	May	June	July	Aug.	Sept.	Oct.	Nov.	Dec.	Year
Highfields House	.. 1840–83	3·6	3·6	3·9	4·3	5·0	5·8	7·4	**8·8**	5·6	5·5	6·6	6·6	40·4
Nottingham Castle	1867–1964	4·64	4·40	4·86	4·03	6·15	6·29	6·15	6·45	5·11	6·45	5·69	**6·56**	35·9
Belvoir Castle	1855–1939	4·06	4·29	4·09	5·04	6·28	4·37	**6·59**	5·84	5·05	6·05	4·46	6·07	35·73
Hodsock	.. 1876–1936	3·54	4·10	4·17	3·74	6·54	4·52	5·92	6·50	5·09	**6·60**	4·31	5·84	34·94
Buxton	.. 1866–1963	12·15	9·54	8·68	10·56	6·04	8·42	8·72	8·77	10·45	12·27	11·36	**15·55**	76·11
Cranwell	.. 1917–63	4·42	3·49	3·99	4·35	4·62	4·33	**9·89**	4·20	4·95	4·57	4·88	4·13	30·84
Sutton Bonington	.. 1924–64	4·20	4·00	4·52	3·12	**6·24**	4·37	4·92	5·22	5·57	4·82	5·62	4·31	32·60
Lincoln	.. 1860–1922	3·95	3·57	3·40	4·66	4·59	6·40	5·65	**7·95**	4·83	5·57	4·41	5·83	32·96
Chesterfield	1856–1922	4·99	4·41	4·69	5·48	7·46	5·04	5·26	**7·65**	4·80	7·23	4·99	7·47	41·30

The still earlier period 1861–90 included the very wet 1870s and early 1880s. September was then the second wettest month of the year at Newark (Stubton), and there was no significant break between the summer and autumn rainfall peaks. March was the driest month, but January and February were also dry; and every month in the second half of the year was wetter than any in the first half. E. J. Lowe's monthly rainfall averages for 1840–89 (combining Highfields House with Beeston Fields) indicate a remarkably constant rainfall from December to April and a broad late summer or early autumn peak. Such changes in rainfall seasonality are of some importance from the agricultural standpoint.

Seasonal balance

The well-known increase in the proportion of summer to winter rainfall across England from west to east can be demonstrated in the Nottingham region.

Table VIII   Percentage of annual rainfall in the summer half-year, 1932–60

Derbyshire		Nottinghamshire and west Leicestershire		East Leicestershire and Lincolnshire	
Hope	41·03	Nottingham Castle	48·80	Melton Mowbray	49·10
Matlock ..	46·84	Sneinton ..	50·42	Cranwell ..	49·40
Rodsley ..	46·79	Sutton Bonington	48·61		
Stanton-by-bridge	45·59	Mansfield ..	46·20		

As shown in Table VIII typical stations in Derbyshire have less than 47 per cent of their rainfall in summer; around Nottingham itself the proportion exceeds 48 per cent (though the figure for Sneinton, a part of the city, exceeds 50 per cent) and at Cranwell and Melton Mowbray it is over 49 per cent. But, apart from the single instance of Sneinton, no station shows a summer half-year rainfall greater than that of the winter half-year. On the other hand, records for the period 1881–1915 indicate that for a number of stations such as Mickleover near Derby, Belvoir Castle, and Skellingthorpe, the summer proportion of annual rainfall exceeded 50 per cent.

Rainfall variability

One index of 'continentality' is the coefficient of variability of rainfall (mean departure from the mean expressed as a percentage of the mean) which is moderately high in the Nottingham region, varying from 12 to 16 generally, though below 12 in the Peak District and exceeding 16 locally in mid-Nottinghamshire and the south–east of the region. Individual years may vary from the mean by much greater margins; for example, the excess of 1872 approached 50 per cent of the normal at many stations. Year-to-year deficits may reach 40 per cent.

Extreme rainfalls relating to periods longer than the one analysed are readily identified on Gumbel graphs. Annual graphs standardised to 1936–60 indicate that the wettest year, 1960, was not abnormal for the period generally. At Mansfield it represented only a '15-year fall' (the maximum appropriate to a 15-year period, or recurrence interval, according to the standardised curve of a range of annual values), though near Nottingham it was slightly more exceptional, a '40-year fall' at Nottingham Castle, and a '50-year fall' at Wilford Hill. The highest rainfalls of the 97-year record at Nottingham represent only '50-year falls' in relation to the whole period, so that no year can be called exceptionally wet in relation to expectation (Fig. 12).

The wettest years at Nottingham since 1867 were 1872 and 1880 with 35·90 and 35·45 inches respectively. In 1882 there were 34·38 inches and the total for 1960 was 32·51 inches. The year 1872 was also the wettest between 1840 and 1880 at Highfield House, and still earlier rainfall data, though incomplete, suggest that it was the wettest year at Nottingham for at least 170 years. The 98-year Gumbel graph for Nottingham Castle, however, indicates a '100-year fall' of about 38·3 inches, and the totals of 1872 and 1880 as only '50-year falls', which suggests that an annual total several inches greater than any so far recorded may now be overdue.

The driest year of the past century was 1887 over most of the Nottingham region, but 1921 was the driest at Belvoir Castle. In general the driest year has less than half the rainfall of the wettest; for example, Nottingham received 15·64 inches in 1887 and 35·90 in 1872. At Nottingham 1964 was drier than 1921 and the third driest in the past century.

Monthly Gumbel curves (Fig. 13) permit assessment of the abnormality of the rainfall in particular months. For example, in the period 1936–60 the rainfall of March 1947 was a '100-year fall' at Nottingham and Sutton Bonington, and a '50-year fall' at Mansfield and Cranwell. The rainfall of September 1957 was an extreme amount relative to 100 years at Sutton Bonington, and 50 years at Nottingham and Mansfield. May 1932 received '200-year falls' at many stations in the Middle Trent area. No remarkable falls were noted at Nottingham during 1886–1910, which denotes the stable character of rainfall incidence in that period. The shortcomings of extrapolation are seen, however, when the secular changes in monthly rainfall described earlier are considered. Thus the 6·56 inches at Nottingham Castle for December 1868 represents about a '100-year fall' in relation to the period 1866–90, but a 250– or 300–year fall relative to 1867–1964, and a maximum appropriate to thousands of years relative to the December rainfalls of 1936–60.

Daily rainfall

High monthly rainfall totals often depend upon exceptionally heavy falls on particular days. At any station in the Nottingham region occasional days with over one inch occur almost every year, and in almost any month, but days with over two inches are much rarer and occur only once in 10 or more years. Table IX shows the frequency distribution of daily rain of given amounts at Nottingham and Belper,

G

and Table X the highest daily falls recorded monthly at certain stations. A. B. Tinn has shown that at Woodthorpe (1936–56), daily totals of 0·5 inch or more occur about 10 times a year, while days with less than 0·1 inch account for over half the total number of rain days. However, on average the 10 wettest days account for 28·2 per cent of the annual total. One quarter of the year's rainfall comes on nine days, a half on 26 days and three-quarters on 55 days. Days with one inch or more contribute six per cent of the annual rainfall.

D. J. Holland recently calculated that Nottingham received 32 falls of at least one inch in 35 years, which approaches the lowest frequency in the country, while Cranwell had 46 and Worksop 47. This low frequency for Nottingham (see Table IX) may be set against the 23 falls of over one inch in 13 years (1952–64) at Lenton. The highest daily falls in the Nottingham area are usually in July or August.

The wettest day recorded at Nottingham (3·05 inches) and Hodsock (3·23 inches) was the 24 hours ending at 09·00 hours on 7th August 1922. At Hodsock on this occasion 5·06 inches fell in 28 hours. Still heavier rains are possible on very rare occasions; for example, the 5·14 inches recorded at Cranwell (11th July 1932), 7·24 inches at Horncastle, south–east of Lincoln (7th October 1960) and 5·97 inches at Rodsley (6th August 1957). All such rainfall is primarily convective and generally associated with thunderstorms, most commonly in relation to a shallow 'low' moving from the Biscay area across southern Britain.

Frequency and duration of rain

The average daily maximum fall in a single year increases from about 1·25 inches in the lowland to 1·5 inches in the Derbyshire uplands. The disparity in average fall per rain day is much greater. For example, while Buxton receives about twice as much rain in a year as Nottingham, it falls on less than 25 per cent more days. Nottingham's average of 160 to 170 rain days compares with fewer than 160 at Sutton Bonington, though the number rises to 180 or more in the higher country north of the city.

Where autographic records exist, actual duration of rain can be computed. In the wetter uplands of the Peak the duration approaches 700 hours a year, but diminishes to 400 to 500 hours in Nottinghamshire. Rainfall duration when reduced to 30–day months is greatest between October and December, with a peak in November, but in this region during the last two decades January has been almost as rainy (Table XII).

Drought

Official droughts, absolute or partial, usually occur in association with persistent anticyclones or spells of 'easterly' weather. During the period 1935–59 no absolute droughts occurred in Nottingham between early October and mid-February. The peak incidence was between mid-July and mid-September and the average frequency about two absolute droughts in three years.

Table IX Frequency of occurrence of rainfalls of more than a stated amount in a day

		Jan.	Feb.	Mar.	April	May	June	July	Aug.	Sept.	Oct.	Nov.	Dec.	Total
TOTAL NUMBER OF OCCURRENCES														
Nottingham Castle														
91 years (1867–1957)														
2 inches or more	..	0	0	0	0	1	0	1	3	1	0	0	0	6
1·5 inches or more	..	0	0	1	0	3	2	3	5	2	1	0	2	19
1 inch or more	..	2	2	4	0	10	13	24	15	13	15	3	4	105
Belper														
37 years (1900–36)														
2 inches or more	..	0	0	0	0	1	1	1	1	0	0	0	0	4
1·5 inches or more	..	0	1	1	0	1	1	5	3	1	1	1	2	17
1 inch or more	..	4	3	4	0	3	5	12	9	7	8	5	6	66
0·5 inch or more	..	40	23	20	18	32	31	51	61	36	52	42	52	458

		Jan.	Feb.	Mar.	April	May	June	July	Aug.	Sept.	Oct.	Nov.	Dec.	Year
AVERAGE NUMBER OF DAYS														
1 inch or more														
Nottingham Castle	1867–1957	·02	·02	·04	0	·11	·14	·26	·16	·14	·16	·03	·04	1·15
Belper	.. 1900–36	·11	·08	·11	0	·08	·14	·32	·24	·19	·22	·14	·16	1·77
0·25 inch or more														
Nottingham	.. 1906–20	2·6	2·1	2·3	1·1	2·5	2·3	3·1	3·2	2·0	2·9	2·2	3·9	30·3
Woodthorpe	.. 1936–56	3·7	2·6	2·3	1·1	3·0	2·4	2·8	3·9	2·0	2·7	3·8	2·4	33·7

Table X Highest daily falls of rain, monthly

		Jan.	Feb.	Mar.	April	May	June	July	Aug.	Sept.	Oct.	Nov.	Dec.
Belvoir Castle	.. 1896–1940	0·91	0·98	1·26	0·71	1·65	1·81	**4·56**	3·62	1·30	1·53	1·06	2·20
Hodsock Priory	.. 1881–1925	1·28	1·69	1·62	1·22	2·02	2·07	2·04	**3·23**	1·49	2·05	1·32	1·64
Nottingham Castle	.. 1867–1957	1·12	1·07	1·52	0·91	2·08	1·57	2·58	**3·05**	2·14	1·82	1·12	1·68
Cranwell	.. 1921–45	1·00	1·01	1·06	0·92	1·78	1·22	**5·14**	2·05	1·31	1·76	1·16	1·12

Table XI Days with rain

	Jan.	Feb.	Mar.	April	May	June	July	Aug.	Sept.	Oct.	Nov.	Dec.	Year
RAIN DAYS (0·01 INCHES OR MORE)													
1871–1905													
Buxton	19	18	18	16	15	14	16	18	16	20	20	19	209
Belvoir	17	16	17	16	15	14	15	15	15	20	21	20	201
Nottingham	19	17	18	16	15	14	16	17	16	20	20	20	208
Lincoln	13	12	12	12	12	11	12	13	11	15	14	13	150
Fulbeck	15	13	16	14	15	13	14	14	13	17	17	17	178
1881–1915													
Buxton	19	18	19	16	16	14	16	19	15	19	19	21	211
Belvoir	19	16	18	16	15	12	15	17	15	20	22	20	205
Nottingham	16	14	15	13	13	11	12	14	11	16	14	18	167
Fulbeck	16	14	18	14	14	12	14	16	12	17	18	18	183
Rauceby	15	14	16	13	11	10	13	14	12	17	17	16	168
Belper	17	15	15	14	13	12	14	15	13	17	17	18	180
Strelley	17	15	15	14	13	12	13	15	12	17	17	19	179
Sutton Bonington 1931–60	14	12	13	13	13	13	12	14	13	12	15	15	159
Woodthorpe 1936–56	19	16	13	13	13	13	14	14	13	15	18	18	179
Watnall 1946–60	17	14	13	12	13	13	14	15	13	13	16	18	171
Cranwell 1931–60	17	15	12	12	12	12	14	13	12	14	17	16	165
Nottingham 1931–60	16	14	12	12	12	12	13	13	12	14	16	16	161
WET DAYS (0·04 INCHES OR MORE)													
Hodsock 1881–1925	10	9	10	10	10	8	10	10	8	11	10	12	118
Cranwell 1931–60	11	9	7	8	8	9	9	9	9	9	11	10	110
Watnall 1946–60	12	10	10	8	8	9	10	10	10	9	12	12	120

Table XII Duration of rainfall, monthly means in hours, adjusted to 30–day months

	Jan.	Feb.	Mar.	April	May	June	July	Aug.	Sept.	Oct.	Nov.	Dec.	Year
Burbage (925 feet) .. 1931–42	80·7	73·0	52·2	59·8	44·5	34·4	43·1	36·3	39·8	69·2	**87·8**	63·7	691·0
Mayfield (374 feet) .. 1911–40	**79·5**	71·8	55·0	55·3	42·3	45·4	47·6	48·6	45·8	63·3	77·4	74·1	723·5
Nottingham T.L. (85 feet) 1913–40 : 1943–52	46·0	41·6	33·8	36·6	31·2	27·1	29·7	29·0	29·2	35·5	**46·8**	40·8	431·0
Sutton Bonington (159 feet) 1928–40	47·4	33·5	28·4	39·2	33·2	25·1	31·5	23·1	30·1	40·2	**54·7**	39·8	433·0
Watnall (368 feet) .. 1948–60	**64·0**	56·8	48·5	36·1	41·1	44·0	33·4	43·0	38·7	45·5	60·2	62·4	581·0
Sutton-in-Ashfield (455 feet) 1943–50	73·6	68·2	38·9	47·9	42·7	41·9	41·7	44·2	45·8	45·4	**82·9**	64·9	645·0
Cranwell (237 feet) .. 1919–60	**67·9**	58·8	43·9	43·4	39·5	33·9	36·0	34·7	36·2	40·7	57·9	51·7	551·3

Evaporation and precipitation

Agricultural drought, i.e. when precipitation fails to meet fully the water needs of crops and grass and when soil moisture has been depleted by evapo-transpiration, is confined to the growing season, when water loss to the atmosphere is high. Measurements of evaporation from a free water surface give only a partial indication of general water losses; and the only long record is that of Revesby reservoir, situated in the southern Lincolnshire Wolds, far outside the Nottingham region. Also there is no reasonably long lysimeter record of potential evapo-transpiration. These deficiencies will be corrected progressively as evaporation and percolation gauges and lysimeters are installed by the Trent River Authority in their development of experimental catchments.

When calculated by Thornthwaite's methods potential evapo-transpiration (water need) amounts to 25 to 26 inches for places in the lowland and about 23 inches at Buxton. Assuming three inches as soil water storage capacity (Thornthwaite's four inches is probably too high) there are water deficits in summer of over four inches in most of the lowland, decreasing to two to three inches in eastern Derbyshire, and reaching nil in upland Derbyshire (Fig. 15).

Computations by Penman's method yield lower values of annual potential evapo-transpiration even if the excessive Thornthwaite winter estimates are discounted, and indicate summer deficits of, for example, four inches at Cranwell, and three inches at Sutton Bonington, and a summer surplus of seven inches at Buxton. G. Dury calculates from hydrological data a 'water loss' of about 16 inches a year on the upper Derwent, which accords closely with Penman results. Periodic summer water deficits occur even where rainfall exceeds 30 inches a year, and over the lowland area east of Nottingham there is risk of agricultural drought in more than five years out of 10, though at places with more than 14 inches of rain in summer the risk is slight. In practice thirsty soils like those of the Forest Sand north of Nottingham, with a very small surface storage capacity, require irrigation in most years for good crop growth.

Snow

The frequency of snowfall and the length of the snow-lie (Table XIII) respond sensitively to variations of altitude and exposure, while the amount of snow responds less sensitively. Days with snow increase by about a day per year for every 50 feet rise beyond 200 feet above sea-level. Thus the distribution pattern tends to show sharp concentrations. Furthermore, the year-to-year variations are large, and snowy years tend to occur in clusters like the late 1870s, 1885–95, and 1915–20. The frequency of snowy years has noticeably increased since 1940, though clustering is not so marked.

During the period 1881–1915 Buxton had snow on an average 38 days a year, while much of the Nottingham lowland recorded about 20 days. For Cranwell (1921–45) the average is 24 days while still further east in Lincolnshire the frequency is even greater, reflecting the influence of exposure to North Sea showers.

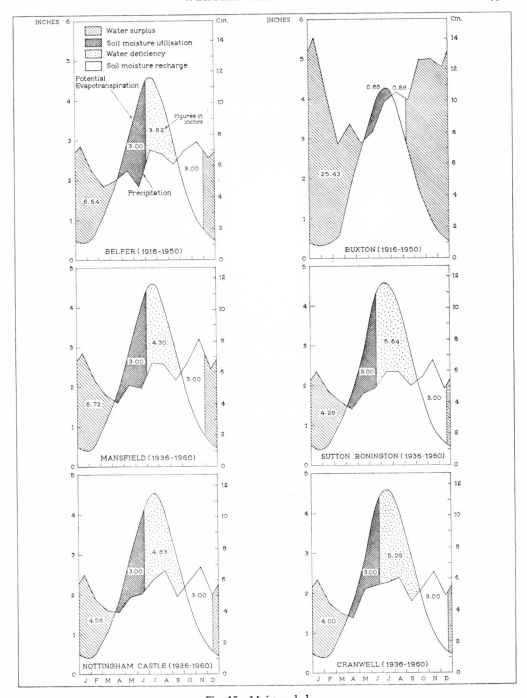

Fig. 15   Moisture balance

Constructed by Thornthwaite's (1948) method, but assuming a soil storage capacity equivalent to three inches of precipitation

Table XIII Snow falling and lying

		Jan.	Feb.	Mar.	April	May	June	July	Aug.	Sept.	Oct.	Nov.	Dec.	Year
DAYS WITH SNOW FALLING														
Belvoir ..	1896–1930	4·1	3·9	5·1	1·7	0·3	—	—	—	—	0·1	0·4	3·1	19·8
Buxton ..	1881–1915	8·1	7·5	8·0	3·3	1·0	—	—	—	—	0·9	3·0	6·0	37·8
Mansfield Woodhouse	1922–33	5·2	7·1	5·4	2·7	0·8	—	—	—	0·2	0·5	2·3	4·9	29·2
Mansfield ..	1785–1805	3·6	3·3	3·7	1·9	0·3	—	—	—	—	0·1	0·8	3·5	17·3
Burford Road and	1927–36	3·5	5·3	2·8	2·6	0·4	—	—	—	—	0·5	0·8	2·6	18·5
Woodthorpe ..	1923–59	5·7	6·4	3·8	1·5	0·3	—	—	—	—	—	0·2	0·8	21·7
Cranwell ..	1921–45	6·0	6·6	4·2	1·7	0·2	—	—	—	—	0·4	1·2	3·8	24·1
Watnall ..	1941–64	8·2	8·5	4·6	1·3	0·2	—	—	—	—	0·1	1·2	3·9	28·1
Mayfield ..	1922–33	4·7	5·7	3·2	2·0	—	—	—	—	—	0·2	1·3	3·7	22·3
Sutton Bonington ..	1922–36	3·2	4·1	3·1	1·4	0·1	—	—	—	—	0·2	0·7	2·6	15·3
Belper ..	1922–29	2·9	3·1	2·0	1·5	—	—	—	—	—	—	0·8	2·4	18·5
MOST SNOW DAYS														
Buxton ..	1876–1933	24	20	18	11	6	1	1	—	1	5	15	17	63
Nottingham ..	1900–59	20	22	14	9	3	—	—	—	—	2	9	16	53 (1917)
SNOW FALL (INCHES)														
Woodthorpe ..	1935–59	6·3	5·2	2·0	0·2	—	—	—	—	—	—	—	1·4	15·3
maximum	1923–59	17·5	21·0	17·0	1·7	1·0	—	—	—	—	—	2·5	9·5	58·7 (1947)
DAYS WITH SNOW LYING AT 09·00 HOURS														
Watnall ..	1941–64	7·4	7·5	2·4	0·1	0·1	—	—	—	—	—	0·1	2·0	19·5
Woodthorpe ..	1935–59	8·6	8·2	3·4	0·3	0·1	—	—	—	—	—	0·2	3·8	24·6
Belvoir Castle ..	1913–30	2·5	1·6	1·4	0·4	—	—	—	—	—	—	0·3	0·9	7·1
Cranwell ..	1931–60	6·8	6·8	2·5	0·1	—	—	—	—	—	—	—	1·6	17·8

In the lowland, snow is most frequent in February at most stations, though in January at some, while the proportions in December and March are considerable. Snow in May is infrequent, although it occurs occasionally anywhere. In November snow is frequent only in the Derbyshire upland where it is also not unknown in June, July and September. The amount of snowfall tends to be more concentrated into the later winter months than over the whole period of days with snow. For example, at Nottingham (Woodthorpe 1921–58) 13·6 of the mean annual total of 15·4 inches fell between January and March. Days with snow lying over more than half the surrounding country at 09·00 hours do not exceed an average of 40 a year in the upland but over most of the region the average is only 15 to 20 days, again depending largely on altitude.

HUMIDITY

Expressed as vapour pressure, atmospheric humidity does not vary greatly over the country, the annual mean value of about 9·7 inches in the Nottingham region comparing with 10·8 inches at Falmouth and 8·5 inches at Eskdalemuir. The annual variation closely resembles that of temperature, autumn being relatively moist as well as relatively warm compared with spring. Indeed the autumn days at Cranwell are unsurpassed for moistness throughout Britain, and the early morning humidity in early spring is notably high. The mean relative humidity of summer afternoons, however, does not fall so low as in south–east England. The mean annual range is normally high, twice as great as that of south–west Ireland. The lowest values of relative humidity are recorded in spring and summer.

TEMPERATURE

Air temperature

From the monthly and annual mean temperatures shown in Table XV it is apparent that conditions differ comparatively little over the lowland. The annual range (1931–60) is 23·8 or 23·9F° (13·3C°) at such widely scattered places as Nottingham, Mansfield, Sutton Bonington and Cranwell. Westward into Derbyshire it decreases slightly, and is about 0·2C° lower, becoming 0·9C° lower at Buxton, where the elevation moderates summer maxima. The annual range in the lowland approaches that of the most 'continental' part of Britain.

The mean annual temperature of 48·9°F (9·4°C) is typical of the lowland, although the Nottingham Castle mean of 49·6°F (9·8°C) is rather higher, for a ridge site, such as this station, tends to prevent very low night minima, while urban influences favour high maxima. The mean for Buxton at an altitude of 1000 feet is 3F° (1·7C°) lower than lowland sites: otherwise no significant difference between the north and south of the region can be discerned. It is rare for any year to exceed or fall short of the annual mean by more than 2·5F° (1·4C°).

Table XIV Humidity

		Jan.	Feb.	Mar.	April	May	June	July	Aug.	Sept.	Oct.	Nov.	Dec.	Year
VAPOUR PRESSURE (INCHES)														
Belvoir Castle 1896–1920	09·00 GMT	6·9	6·7	7·3	8·2	10·4	12·5	14·1	14·0	12·5	10·2	8·1	7·4	9·9
	21·00 GMT	7·1	6·8	7·2	8·0	10·1	12·3	13·9	13·6	11·6	10·1	8·2	7·5	9·6
RELATIVE HUMIDITY (PER CENT)														
Nottingham 1867–1901	09·00 GMT	89	89	84	76	74	77	74	76	75	84	89	89	81·3
Hodsock 1881–1915	09·00 GMT	90	87	82	76	73	72	73	76	81	87	90	91	81
Belvoir Castle 1896–1920	09·00 GMT	93	87	88	80	77	77	78	80	83	89	91	92	85
	21·00 GMT	91	87	88	84	84	84	85	86	88	91	91	92	88
	mean	92	87	88	82	80	80	81	83	85	90	91	92	86
LOWEST RELATIVE HUMIDITY OBSERVED (PER CENT)														
Woodthorpe 1935–59	Average lowest	59	50	38	35	33	34	39	40	45	49	58	61	27
	Absolute lowest	47	33	23	21	9	23	20	25	27	38	42	49	9

Table XV Mean monthly and annual temperatures °C and annual range, 1931–60

	Jan.	Feb.	Mar.	April	May	June	July	Aug.	Sept.	Oct.	Nov.	Dec.	Year	Range
Buxton (1007 feet) ..	1·9	2·0	4·0	6·5	9·4	12·6	14·3	14·0	11·8	8·4	5·3	3·3	7·8	12·4
Belper School (203 feet)	3·1	3·5	5·6	8·2	11·3	14·4	16·2	15·8	13·6	9·8	6·3	4·4	9·4	13·1
Mansfield (357 feet)	3·0	3·3	5·6	8·2	11·2	14·3	16·2	15·8	13·6	9·8	6·3	4·3	9·3	13·2
Nottingham Castle (192 feet) ..	3·5	3·9	6·0	8·7	11·7	14·9	16·7	16·4	14·2	10·3	6·9	4·7	9·8	13·2
Sutton Bonington (157 feet) ..	3·1	3·6	5·6	8·3	11·1	14·4	16·4	15·9	13·6	9·8	6·4	4·4	9·4	13·3
Cranwell (240 feet) ..	3·0	3·5	5·5	8·2	11·1	14·3	16·3	16·0	13·8	10·0	6·4	4·2	9·4	13·3

The annual temperature regimes, too, vary little, except in upland Derbyshire. A January mean temperature of about 37·5°F (3·1°C) rises to 61·3 to 61·5°F (16·3 to 16·4°C) in July, the warmest month.

The annual mean range of daily maximum and minimum temperature varies from about 13 to 15F° (7·2 to 8·3C°) generally, with maxima of about 16 to 19F° (8·9 to 10·5C°) in the summer months, falling to 9 to 11F° (5 to 6·1C°) in winter; but the values are lower in the upland.

The mean temperature of an individual month rarely varies from the period average by 5F° (2·8C°), though deficits of 10F° (5·5C°) have occurred at Nottingham in winter, for example, January 1940 and February 1947. It is rare for any month to exceed the mean by more than 3F° (1·7C°). The year-to-year variations in mean temperatures are much larger in winter, when cyclonic and anticyclonic spells give widely different temperatures, than in summer when insolation is decisive.

The temperatures of individual days are more variable. While the highest mean temperature recorded at Nottingham for any year is 56·2°F (13·4°C) this particular maximum may be reached on any day in a year. For example, at Woodthorpe the maximum temperature of 9th July 1948 was 55·3°F (13°C) and that of 27th January 1944 57·3°F (14·1°C). Excluding a reading of —11·1°F (—24°C) at Buxton on 11th February 1895, the lowest screen temperature recorded in the region over the last 100 years appears to have been —5·8°F (—21°C) at Hodsock on 7th December 1879, closely followed by —5·6°F (—20·9°C) at Southwell on 8th February 1895. But north-wall readings suggest that the coldest night experienced in the region during the past 200 years was that of 24th to 25th December 1860, when the following temperatures were recorded: Nottingham (Carlton) —12°F (—24·4°C); Nottingham (Highfields House) —6°F (—21°C); Beeston —8·3°F (—22·3°C); Chatsworth, Derbyshire, —12°F (—24·4°C); Willersley, Derbyshire, —6°F (—21°C); and Belvoir Castle —1°F (—18·3°C). Other notable extremes of cold were those of 13th January 1814 with 2·5°F (—16·7°C) at Nottingham, when the Trent, like the Thames, was frozen over, and the severe spell in the winter of 1762–63 when the Trent was 'passable for carriages of any burthen, and a sheep was roasted whole upon the ice near Wilford Church'. In more recent years 21st January 1940 was the coldest night in the Nottingham district with 4·9°F (—15°C) at Woodthorpe, 6·0°F (—14·4°C) at the University and 7·0°F (—13·9°C) at the Castle. All low temperatures of this order occur when the ground is snow-covered.

The hottest day of the past century was 9th August 1911, the only occasion on which a temperature of 100°F (37·8°C) was reached at Greenwich Observatory. At Nottingham the maximum was 94·6°F (34·8°C), at Hodsock 94·4°F (34·7°C), at Belvoir Castle 95°F (35°C), and at Lincoln 95·8°F (35·5°C). The only other occasion on which 100°F was recorded in Britain (100·5°F at Tonbridge), was 22nd July 1868, when the maximum in Nottingham reached 94·3°F (34·6°C), though 97·3°F (36·3°C) was measured at four feet at Highfields House in June of that year.

Table XVI   Mean maximum and minimum temperatures in °C, 1926–50

	Jan.	Feb.	Mar.	April	May	June	July	Aug.	Sept.	Oct.	Nov.	Dec.	Year
MEAN MAXIMUM													
Buxton	4·5	4·7	7·3	9·8	13·5	16·5	18·0	17·5	15·1	11·1	7·3	5·1	10·9
Belper School	6·5	6·9	9·8	12·7	16·4	19·6	21·3	20·7	18·1	13·7	9·4	6·9	13·5
Mansfield	5·9	6·4	9·3	12·2	15·9	19·1	21·0	20·3	17·5	13·1	8·6	6·3	13·5
Nottingham Castle	6·5	6·9	9·9	12·7	15·9	19·5	21·2	21·0	18·3	13·7	9·5	6·7	13·5
Sutton Bonington	6·5	7·1	9·9	12·7	16·2	19·5	21·5	20·8	18·1	13·8	9·3	6·8	13·5
Burford Road	6·3	6·9	10·1	13·2	16·8	19·9	21·6	20·6	17·9	13·6	9·0	6·8	13·6
Woodthorpe	6·0	6·7	9·8	12·7	16·3	19·5	21·5	20·9	18·2	13·6	8·8	6·3	13·3
Watnall	6·1	6·6	9·5	12·4	15·7	19·0	20·8	20·3	17·5	13·3	8·8	6·3	13·0
Strelley	6·2	6·9	9·8	12·6	16·0	19·4	21·4	20·7	18·1	13·6	9·0	6·7	13·3
Chilwell	6·3	7·1	10·4	13·6	16·9	20·1	21·9	21·3	18·5	14·2	9·0	6·5	13·8
Attenborough	6·3	7·2	10·4	13·1	16·7	19·9	22·0	21·4	18·6	14·1	9·2	6·7	13·8
MEAN MINIMUM													
Buxton	0	−0·1	0·7	2·7	5·1	8·2	10·6	10·2	8·3	5·3	2·6	0·8	4·5
Belper School	0·4	0·5	1·4	3·3	6·0	8·9	11·3	10·8	8·8	5·4	2·5	1·2	5·1
Mansfield	0·7	0·7	1·7	3·7	6·2	9·3	11·6	11·2	9·4	6·2	3·1	1·0	5·2
Nottingham Castle	1·3	1·3	2·3	4·7	7·0	10·3	12·5	12·0	10·2	6·6	3·9	1·9	6·1
Sutton Bonington	0·5	0·6	1·5	3·5	6·0	8·9	11·5	10·8	9·0	5·8	2·9	1·3	5·2
Burford Road	1·0	0·9	2·0	4·2	6·8	10·3	12·5	11·8	9·9	6·5	3·3	1·5	5·8
Woodthorpe	0·3	0·4	1·3	3·3	5·9	9·1	11·6	11·0	9·1	5·7	2·7	1·0	5·2
Watnall	0·5	0·8	1·6	3·5	5·9	8·9	11·6	10·9	9·1	5·9	3·1	1·3	5·2
Strelley	0·8	0·8	2·0	3·9	6·4	9·5	11·8	11·3	9·5	6·3	3·1	1·6	5·6
Chilwell	0·8	0·6	1·7	3·4	6·3	9·4	11·9	11·3	9·4	6·0	2·9	1·4	5·4
Attenborough	0·7	0·5	1·0	3·1	5·7	8·8	11·2	10·5	8·3	5·2	2·6	1·3	4·9

Table XVII Absolute extremes of temperature, °C

		Jan.	Feb.	Mar.	April	May	June	July	Aug.	Sept.	Oct.	Nov.	Dec.	Year
ABSOLUTE MAXIMUM														
Buxton ..	1869–1954	13·4	15·0	20·0	22·8	27·3	28·9	31·7	31·1	30·0	25·1	17·3	15·6	31·7
Nottingham, Trent Lane and Castle ..	1867–1964	15·0	20·0	21·4	25·6	30·0	32·2	34·6	34·7	34·2	24·1	20·0	15·6	34·7
Highfield House ..	1840–83	15·4	16·2	22·0	33·7	31·9	36·3	34·5	35·4	31·1	25·3	18·3	15·7	36·3
Hodsock (Worksop)	1878–1933	15·3	17·6	22·8	24·9	27·7	31·0	33·7	34·6	33·9	25·3	18·7	14·9	34·6
Sutton Bonington ..	1924–50	14·5	14·5	21·7	22·8	25·6	30·0	31·7	31·1	29·4	21·7	17·8	15·0	31·7
Belvoir Castle	1896–1933	13·9	16·7	20·6	24·0	28·9	30·0	32·2	35·0	33·3	26·1	17·3	15·0	35·0
Lincoln ..	1888–1928	15·0	16·7	20·0	25·0	28·3	30·6	33·3	35·4	33·9	25·6	17·2	15·6	35·4
Fulbeck	1901–25	14·5	16·2	20·6	23·4	28·9	30·6	32·8	35·5	34·4	26·1	15·6	14·5	35·5
Cranwell	1920–46	13·9	15·6	20·6	23·9	27·8	32·8	32·2	30·6	30·0	24·5	17·8	13·9	32·8
ABSOLUTE MINIMUM														
Buxton ..	1869–1954	-18·3	-24·0	-17·2	-13·3	-7·1	-1·3	-0·6	0·6	-2·2	-7·8	-11·1	-20·0	-24·0
Nottingham	1867–1964	-16·8	-16·7	-10·0	-5·1	-3·9	1·0	2·5	1·9	-1·2	-6·4	-11·2	-18·5	-18·5
Highfield House	1840–83	-20·0	-14·4	-10·6	-6·4	-6·4	-0·8	2·4	0·6	0	-7·0	-8·3	-22·2	-22·2
Hodsock ..	1878–1933	-20·2	-20·0	-14·8	-13·8	-4·6	-0·6	2·8	1·8	-2·3	-5·6	-9·6	-21·0	-21·0
Belvoir Castle	1896–1932	-13·9	-12·8	-10·6	-12·2	-3·4	-0·6	1·6	1·1	-1·7	-5·0	-9·4	-12·2	-13·9
Lincoln ..	1888–1928	-12·6	-14·6	-7·8	-6·1	-1·9	1·6	3·8	4·4	-0·6	-4·7	-9·4	-11·7	-14·6
Fulbeck	1901–25	-10·6	-15·0	-8·3	-11·1	-2·3	-0·6	2·2	2·2	-0·6	-3·4	-8·3	-10·6	-15·0
Cranwell	1920–46	-13·3	-12·8	-10·6	-5·5	-2·2	1·1	4·4	3·3	1·6	-3·9	-6·7	-15·5	-15·5

Frosts

Because the occurrence of frost depends strongly on favourable synoptic circumstances, the average number of days with frost, 60 to 70 per year, does not vary greatly from station to station. Site differences influence the number and severity of frosts which occur in marginal periods, notably in April and May when growing vegetation is liable to be damaged. Site conditions also largely determine the relative frequency of ground frosts, which approach 100 a year over much of the region and even reach 150 in some localities.

While Fig. 16 illustrates the variations in frost frequency, and in the frost-free period at Nottingham, it should be pointed out that the data are specific, and further, that occasional exceptional frosts may occur well outside the average frost-free period. Ground frosts may occur in any month of the year at some stations, but at most they are normally absent from early June to mid-September, while few air frosts occur between early May and early October. In Nottingham, at Burford Road and Woodthorpe (1921–59) the first and last frosts occur, on average on 19th October and 19th April respectively, giving a frost-free period of 182 days, but the extreme dates are 19th September and 1st June, with only 109 days absolutely frost-free.

The incidence of serious frosts in late spring is of particular importance, for in the Nottingham region, if crop growth has progressed normally or is actually advanced, screen temperatures of 26°F (—3·3°C) or below in April, 28°F (—2·2°C) or below in May, and 31°F (—0·5°C) in June are likely to cause damage. Table LI, Appendix I, enumerates the most notable examples of such late frosts over many years, with screen minimum temperatures for selected stations, thus illustrating the great importance of site in their incidence. The dependence of such extremes on free night radiation through dry, still air means that grass minima are as much as 10°F (5·5°C) lower on these occasions. Frosts reaching 28°F (—2·2°C) in the screen in May are particularly damaging to fruit blossom.

Around Nottingham itself low sites on inversion nights record temperatures of the order of 10°F (5·5°C) lower than ridges or slopes 100 feet higher. Measurements by A. B. Tinn showed that this difference could develop in two hours on a calm, clear autumn evening between Woodthorpe and Mapperley, 195 feet higher, where the temperature hardly altered. Woodthorpe closely resembles Nottingham Castle in day temperature, but the nights are cooler at all seasons. Strelley (377 feet), on the Leen–Erewash interfluve, is much less prone to low night temperatures. Lenton Fields, on the west side of the University estate, is markedly more subject to frosts than the central University area on the hill, and Messrs. Boots Plant Experimental Station, close to the latter, has not recorded a serious late frost since readings were begun in 1953.

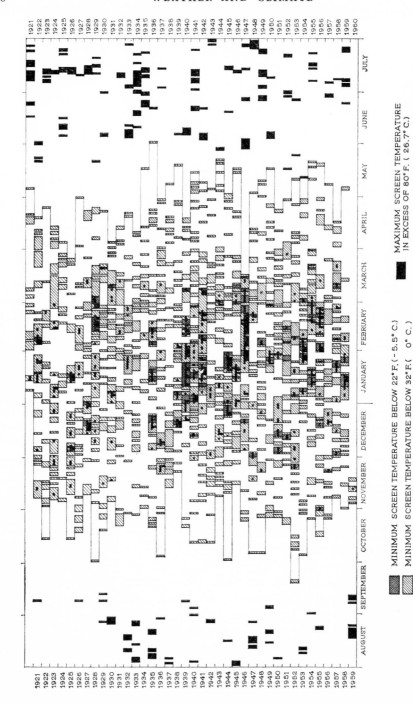

Fig. 16   Cold and hot days at Woodthorpe, 1921–59

Table XVIII Frost

	Jan.	Feb.	Mar.	April	May	June	July	Aug.	Sept.	Oct.	Nov.	Dec.	Year
DAYS WITH SCREEN FROST													
Woodthorpe (Nottingham) 1937–59	15·7	14·0	11·7	4·1	1·4	—	—	—	0·1	2·3	5·8	12·5	67·6
Sutton Bonington .. 1946–64	15·2	14·5	11·4	3·9	1·9	—	—	—	0·1	3·3	6·5	12·2	73·0
Lenton ES .. 1952–64	15·0	13·5	8·5	2·6	0·6	—	—	—	—	2·0	6·1	11·2	59·4
Cranwell .. 1931–60	16	13	8·7	0·4	0·4	—	—	—	—	0·6	5·7	14·0	58·8
Hodsock Priory 1881–1925	13	12	12	7	2	—	—	—	—	3	8	12	69
Mansfield Woodhouse (North Wall) 1785–1805	12·5	10·6	10·4	3·1	2·5	1·7	0·5	0·5	3·3	5·1	7·7	12·7	70·9
DAYS WITH GROUND FROST (<−1°c)													
Buxton .. 1908–20	18·1	16·8	18·4	12·8	5·2	1·0	—	—	1·5	6·4	13·9	16·5	110·6
Belvoir 1896–1930	16·3	15·7	14·5	11·5	4·1	0·9	—	—	1·2	7·0	13·9	14·4	99·5
Watnall .. 1941–64	16·6	15·5	14·3	10·0	4·6	0·7	0·04	0·04	1·0	5·0	9·6	15·2	92·6
Sutton Bonington .. 1924–36	14·1	14·2	15·7	8·2	2·9	2·0	—	—	0·4	4·2	8·9	11·8	79·2
1946–64	21·6	19·9	19·0	13·8	7·0	3·5	0·6	0·6	3·1	9·4	14·1	20·5	133
Lenton ES (<0°c) .. 1952–64	21·8	18·4	13·9	10·0	3·2	0·2	0·6	—	0·9	5·8	12·2	17·6	104
Hodsock .. 1927–36	21·3	19·3	18·4	11·1	5·4	1·0	0·1	0·1	2·7	8·2	14·2	18·8	120·9
Mayfield .. 1922–33	15·1	14·4	16·3	10·1	3·3	0·2	—	—	1·3	6·4	11·3	13·3	93·4
Cranwell .. 1922–33	14·6	14·8	16·1	9·7	4·4	0·4	—	0·1	0·6	4·7	10·7	13·7	89·8
Attenborough 1928–36	16·3	15·7	16·9	11·7	4·9	0·7	0·1	—	1·7	7·3	10·8	13·3	98·3
Lincoln .. 1922–28	12·9	11·3	10·6	7·1	1·1	—	—	—	—	2·7	9·9	13·6	70·3
DAYS WITH HOAR FROST													
Woodthorpe/Burford Road 1927–59	7·3	6·0	6·9	2·9	1·1	—	—	—	0·2	2·4	6·1	7·0	40·0

H

Table XIX Comparison of temperatures of nine stations in and near Nottingham, 1921–50
Temperatures in °C, adjusted from the periods indicated

		Jan.	Feb.	Mar.	April	May	June	July	Aug.	Sept.	Oct.	Nov.	Dec.
MEAN TEMPERATURE													
Nottingham Castle	1921–50	3·9	4·1	6·0	8·5	11·5	14·7	16·8	16·3	14·0	10·2	6·4	4·4
Woodthorpe	1935–50	3·1	3·5	5·6	8·0	10·5	14·3	16·5	16·0	13·6	9·6	5·8	3·7
Burford Road, Nottingham	1919–34	3·7	3·9	6·0	8·7	11·8	15·1	17·0	16·2	13·8	10·1	6·1	4·2
Watnall	1948–57	3·3	3·6	5·6	8·0	10·8	13·9	16·1	15·6	13·3	9·6	5·9	3·8
Strelley	1924–31	3·4	3·8	5·8	8·3	11·2	14·5	16·6	16·0	13·7	9·9	6·1	4·1
Chilwell	1947–58	3·6	3·8	6·0	8·6	11·6	14·7	16·9	16·3	13·9	10·1	6·0	3·9
Attenborough	1928–38	3·5	3·8	5·7	8·0	11·2	14·4	16·6	16·0	13·5	6·8	5·9	4·0
Sutton Bonington	1924–50	3·5	3·8	5·7	8·1	11·1	14·2	16·5	15·9	13·5	9·8	6·1	4·1
Lenton Fields	1922–27	3·2	3·5	5·6	7·9	10·8	14·0	16·2	15·4	13·2	9·3	5·5	3·7
Highfields House	1840–83 unadjusted	2·5	3·6	5·6	8·5	11·7	14·9	16·3	15·8	13·7	9·7	5·7	4·0
AVERAGE OF HIGHEST MAXIMUM, MONTHLY													
Nottingham Castle		12·2	12·3	16·4	19·5	23·5	26·6	27·5	26·6	24·4	19·0	14·7	12·5
Woodthorpe		11·7	12·1	16·8	20·0	23·9	27·0	27·7	26·9	24·5	19·2	14·5	12·2
Burford Road		12·1	12·2	16·6	20·4	24·4	26·9	28·3	26·4	23·7	18·6	14·5	12·3
Watnall		11·7	12·1	16·4	19·5	23·2	26·1	26·9	26·2	23·5	18·6	14·4	12·1
Strelley		11·8	12·3	16·2	19·5	22·7	26·5	27·6	26·2	24·0	19·6	14·5	12·1
Chilwell		12·2	12·7	17·4	20·8	24·6	27·3	28·3	27·5	24·6	19·7	15·0	12·8
Attenborough		12·2	12·6	17·3	20·5	24·4	27·5	29·0	27·7	25·5	20·0	14·9	12·6
Sutton Bonington		11·9	12·1	16·3	19·5	23·0	26·6	27·4	27·0	24·2	19·1	14·9	12·8
Lenton Fields		12·3	12·7	16·9	19·9	23·4	26·3	27·7	27·0	24·5	19·1	15·0	12·6
AVERAGE OF LOWEST MINIMUM, MONTHLY													
Nottingham Castle		–5·3	–4·3	–3·1	–0·6	1·1	5·4	7·6	6·8	3·8	–0·6	–2·1	–3·8
Woodthorpe		–7·3	–6·7	–5·4	–2·3	–0·9	3·2	6·2	4·8	1·7	–2·0	–3·7	–5·1
Burford Road		–5·2	–4·4	–2·3	–0·4	1·7	5·7	8·4	8·0	4·6	–0·2	–2·0	–3·7
Watnall		–5·9	–5·1	–4·3	–1·2	0·4	3·8	6·6	6·1	2·5	–0·6	–1·8	–4·7
Strelley		–5·5	–4·5	–3·8	–0·6	1·3	5·3	7·3	6·8	4·1	–0·7	–2·4	–4·1
Chilwell		–7·3	–6·8	–4·9	–2·1	–0·1	3·9	6·8	5·3	2·8	–1·6	–3·9	–5·7
Attenborough		–6·9	–6·2	–5·4	–3·1	–1·1	2·8	5·1	5·0	0·9	–2·7	–3·9	–5·7
Sutton Bonington		–7·0	–6·5	–4·9	–2·4	–0·6	3·0	6·1	4·7	1·6	–2·2	–3·6	–5·4
Lenton Fields		–7·3	–5·5	–4·5	–2·2	0	3·4	5·8	4·7	2·2	–2·6	–3·9	–6·1

Low temperature of itself is serious only when prolonged, so that it penetrates deeply into the ground. Of special significance for human comfort, however, are days when the temperature fails to rise above freezing point. At Woodthorpe a record of 24 years (1936–59) included 19 with at least one such day; half these days occurred in January, most of the remainder in February and the balance in December and March. Fig. 16 shows the incidence of days of sub-zero minimum, mean and maximum temperature over 39 years at Nottingham (Burford Road 1921–34 and Woodthorpe 1935–59). Also shown are the days with a maximum temperature of 80°F (26·7°C) or above, totalling 138 in 21 years out of the 24 at Woodthorpe, and occurring about every other year in June, July and August, with a few in May and September, but over one-third of them in July. On average at Woodthorpe (standardised to 1921–50) the temperature exceeds 80°F (26·7°C) for 23 hours a year (nine in June, eight in July) and exceeds 70°F (21·1°C) for 248 hours, with a maximum of 81°F (27·2°C) in July.

Soil temperatures

Soil temperatures differ more narrowly and less erratically than air temperatures and vary more with aspect and insolation. Fig. 17 shows the range of monthly mean, maximum and minimum temperatures at one foot depth at 09·00 hours at a number of stations for different periods. At shallow depth the range is wider and more nearly approaches that of air temperature; at greater depth it is less. At one foot the soil is warmest in late July in the lowland area, normally reaching a maximum of 60 to 61°F (15·5 to 16·1°C) and falling to a minimum of about 38°F (3·3°C) in January–February. Freezing point is reached at one foot depth only rarely in long cold spells and in some years the soil may be as warm as 45°F (7·2°C) in January or February. In any month the average temperature at one foot deep varies from year to year within an extreme range of 6 to 10°F (3·3 to 5·5°C) but the range is less in late spring and autumn when neither insolation nor radiation cooling dominates the normal course of the weather.

Growing season

It will be noted that the 'growing threshold' temperature of 42·8°F (6·0°C) is crossed by the soil temperature at one foot depth on average in early April and late November, thus defining a growing season for the soil of about 235 days, which is reduced to 200 days or less in the uplands. Using the same threshold for air temperature, graphs of monthly means suggest an average growing season of about 200 days in the Peak District (Buxton 202), rising to about 230 to 245 days in the lowland (Belper 238, Mansfield 232, Sutton Bonington 241), the latter being at least a fortnight shorter than that for Oxford (259). For individual years this period varies considerably, more particularly because of the variable nature of the weather in late winter and early spring.

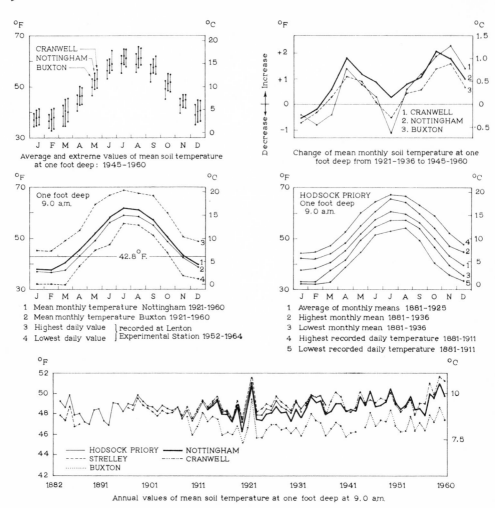

Fig. 17 Soil temperatures

SUNSHINE AND CLOUD

In 1881 T. L. K. Edge at Strelley, and H. Mellish at Hodsock Priory each began to measure bright sunshine with the newly introduced Campbell-Stokes recorder. Except for April 1887 to July 1895, when the instrument was in use at Southwell, the Strelley record was maintained until 1931, and that of Hodsock until 1937. At Buxton, E. J. Sykes used a Jordan photographic sunlight recorder from July 1881, and the Buxton record became strictly comparable only with its replacement by a Campbell-Stokes instrument in February 1908. Around the turn of the century a number of new records began: Nottingham Castle 1898; Nottingham Trent Lane 1903–24; and Belvoir Castle 1907–37. Sunshine records at Cranwell date from 1920 while shorter records, still continuing, exist for Sutton Bonington, the University and the other stations listed in Table XXI.

This coverage amply defines the chief characteristics of sunshine distribution over the region. By 1900 it was established that Strelley and Hodsock received only 29 and 28 per cent respectively of possible sunshine, and Buxton (less reliably) 26 per cent, though over the Midlands generally the average is about 30 per cent (Table XX). The newer stations established that any northward decrease is overshadowed by the reduction westwards from the Lincolnshire coast. Averages for 1881–1915 (Table XX), some standardised from shorter records, clearly define this progression, as well as the reduction caused by increasing altitude and smoke pollution.

Recent figures have indicated a decrease in sunshine as compared with 1881–1915 by one or two per cent. The most recent data indicate that mean annual sunshine decreases from about 4·3 hours a day (35 per cent) at the Lincolnshire coast to about 3·2 hours (26 per cent) in upland Derbyshire. Nottingham, with 3·4 hours (28 per cent), has a somewhat higher figure than might be expected for an industrial city.

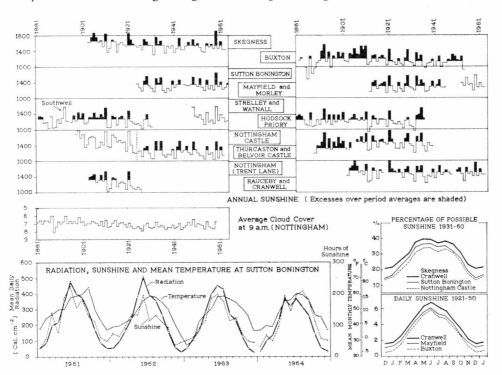

Fig. 18   Sunshine and radiation

Table XX Annual mean duration of bright sunshine in hours per day and as a percentage of possible duration

	1881–1915 hours	1881–1915 per cent	1906–35 hours	1906–35 per cent	1921–50 hours	1921–50 per cent	1931–60 hours	1931–60 per cent
Buxton	—	27	3·30	27	3·14	26	—	—
Matlock	—	27	—	—	—	—	—	—
Ashbourne (Mayfield)	—	—	3·61	29	—	—	—	—
Hodsock Priory	3·43	28	3·34	—	3·56	29	—	—
Strelley	3·49	29	3·40	28	—	—	—	—
Watnall	—	—	—	—	—	—	—	30
Nottingham	3·63	30	—	—	3·53	29	3·38	28
Sutton Bonington	—	—	—	—	3·73	30	3·63	30
Belvoir Castle	4·21	34	4·08	33	—	—	—	—
Rauceby/Fulbeck	4·24	35	—	—	—	—	—	—
Cranwell	—	—	—	—	4·14	34	4·10	34

Table XXI Average daily duration of sunshine, 1957–63

Derbyshire–Staffordshire

	hours	per cent
Stone	3·53	29
Morley	3·64	30
Derby	3·55	29

Nottinghamshire

	hours	per cent
Warsop	3·68	30
Watnall	3·54	29
Lenton (University)	3·73	30
Nottingham Castle	3·29	27
Sutton Bonington	3·65	30

West Lincolnshire

	hours	per cent
Waddington	4·07	33
Lincoln	3·81	31
Cranwell	4·12	34

East Lincolnshire

	hours	per cent
Manby	4·28	35
Skegness	4·26	35

Table XXII Mean hours of sunshine, monthly, 1931–60

	Jan.	Feb.	Mar.	April	May	June	July	Aug.	Sept.	Oct.	Nov.	Dec.	Year
Nottingham	1·24	1·92	2·97	4·30	5·30	5·69	5·10	4·86	3·93	2·70	1·53	1·04	3·38
Cranwell	1·77	2·55	3·63	5·23	6·22	6·61	6·00	5·59	4·58	3·31	2·01	1·57	4·10
Sutton Bonington	1·36	2·21	3·30	4·72	5·69	6·08	5·49	5·14	4·03	2·88	1·66	1·11	3·63
Skegness	1·73	2·48	3·77	5·42	6·43	6·80	6·13	5·70	4·84	3·46	2·05	1·48	4·31

Table XXIII Days with fog

	Jan.	Feb.	Mar.	April	May	June	July	Aug.	Sept.	Oct.	Nov.	Dec.	Year
FOG (–1100 YARDS)													
Sutton Bonington .. 1926–64	5·4	4·1	3·9	0·8	0·4	0·2	0·2	0·4	2·1	4·5	**6·2**	5·7	33·9
Burford Road .. 1923–34	13·2	10·3	9·7	4·9	2·5	1·3	1·2	2·8	8·0	8·8	13·4	**13·8**	90·0
Woodthorpe .. 1935–59	8·7	6·5	7·0	3·0	2·0	1·1	0·8	3·0	3·9	7·6	8·6	**10·3**	62·3
Watnall .. 1941–64	7·7	6·4	6·9	1·7	0·6	0·3	0·5	1·2	2·6	7·1	7·0	**7·8**	49·9
Cranwell .. 1921–60	5·1	4·2	4·6	1·4	1·2	0·7	0·7	1·8	2·7	4·5	**5·5**	5·1	37·8
Buxton .. 1925–60	**7·4**	6·9	5·7	1·8	1·3	1·2	0·9	1·1	2·2	4·0	6·2	7·3	46·1
Mansfield .. 1927–60	7·9	6·1	5·1	1·3	1·1	0·7	0·4	1·3	2·4	6·0	9·1	**9·5**	51·1
Nottingham .. 1919–60	11·1	9·0	7·0	1·3	0·6	0·1	0·2	0·4	2·9	7·0	10·5	**11·4**	61·4
Skegness .. 1919–60	2·4	2·3	1·7	0·3	0·2	0·1	0·2	0·1	0·5	1·3	2·7	**3·5**	15·1
THICK FOG (–220 YARDS)													
Cranwell .. 1920–60	1·5	0·9	1·6	—	0·1	—	—	—	0·4	**2·0**	1·6	**2·0**	10·1
Nottingham .. 1876–90	3·8	2·3	2·3	0·6	0·6	0·3	0·1	0·2	3·5	**4·6**	3·1	4·1	26·7
BURFORD ROAD AND WOODTHORPE													
Maximum fog days ..	18	15	17	11	9	5	3	12	14	16	21	**22**	131 (1925)
Minimum fog days ..	4	2	3	—	—	—	—	—	—	2	4	1	45 (1954)

For 1881–1915 May was the sunniest month on average at most stations. At Strelley, Belvoir and elsewhere, sunshine decreased steadily from May until August, and thereafter more rapidly. The minimum everywhere was in December. However, in the period 1921–50, June was the sunniest month, in both duration and percentage of possible sunshine, and in the Nottingham area, though not in Lincolnshire and Derbyshire, July was sunnier than May. This accords with the changes in raininess mentioned earlier. The reduction of sunshine totals by wet spells in high summer is most marked in the west and north–west, where in the Peak District May is still sunnier than July. Watnall's figures since 1948 show that May is now favoured again, and practically as sunny as June. The total for August is considerably lower than 50 years ago.

The correlation between sunshine and cloud amounts at fixed hours is only moderately close from year to year, as becomes apparent from Fig. 18, although from place to place differences in annual sunshine must, subject to variations caused by air pollution, reflect differences in mean cloud amounts, and, particularly, differences in summer cloudiness. At Nottingham at 09·00 hours there is an average seven-tenths of cloud, with lower amounts probable to the east and higher amounts over the higher country north and west.

Measurements of net radiation have been taken at Sutton Bonington since 1959, and Fig. 18 (1961–64) shows how they compare with sunshine and temperature. The correlation with temperature is not striking, especially in winter, when advection is the dominant influence on temperature.

Fog and pollution

Nottingham is noted for its fogs, and few places exceed its yearly average (1923–50) of 76·6 days with fog (visibility less than 1100 yards). Experience suggests that even this total may be exceeded in the Trent vale east of the city. An annual fog frequency of over 50 days occurs in a belt extending northwards into industrial south Yorkshire. Mansfield (1923–50) has 53·2 days. But the frequency decreases eastwards to about 40 days in west Lincolnshire where Cranwell (1923–50) has only 38·9 days. Buxton's average of 45·6 days (1923–50) appears to differ little from that of the lowland. The annual number of days with fog, however, varies considerably from year to year; for example, at Nottingham, 1925, with 131 days, had almost three times as many as 1954 with 45 days.

Thick fog (visibility less than 220 yards) is also comparatively frequent, averaging 21·1 days at Nottingham (1923–50), and possibly more in the industrialised sections of the Trent and Leen valleys. It often develops in Nottingham some hours after sunrise, when chilled air collecting in the valleys in and around the city on quiet radiation nights is mixed by an incipient breeze. Thick fog declines in annual frequency eastwards to 12·6 days at Cranwell. While thick fog is often general in and around Nottingham, dense fog, with visibility so low as to have a serious effect on traffic movement, is sometimes sharply localised in the valleys, especially during morning and late evening, while the higher parts of the city and its central area have better visibility. The central area is less susceptible to thick fog than the suburbs.

Fog days are fairly evenly distributed through the winter months, but dense fogs at Nottingham occur mainly in the period between mid–October and the end of the year, when absolute atmospheric humidity is appreciably higher than in late winter. They are rare and impersistent in the summer half-year.

Low-level smoke is in part responsible for the high fog frequency of Nottingham. Fig. 19 shows that the degree of pollution by solid smoke particles and by sulphur dioxide varies considerably on average over the city. It is related to the location of heavy sources of pollution rather than to prevailing wind. The consistently high levels in the older, more densely built-up areas and in the city centre, as compared with the peripheral residential districts, is pronounced. Monthly figures show that, while pollution is normally several times more severe between October and April than in the summer half-year, as a result of the combined effect of domestic fires and the development of surface temperature inversions, it can in fact rise to serious levels at any time of year. It is to be hoped that the 'clean air' policy of the city and neighbouring local authorities will bring some improvement.

THUNDER AND HAIL

The Nottingham region lies across the northern portion of a belt extending from the Thames to the Trent in which thunderstorms average more than 15 a year. In the past Belvoir Castle has recorded the highest frequency of thunder in the country, and frequency decreases east and west from the Belvoir area. More than 10 thunderstorms occur throughout the lowland in an average year. They are essentially summer storms, and generally occur later in the day than those of the west Midlands. A recent map of average frequency for the five years 1955–59 by Miller and Starrett indicates an annual frequency of 6 to 12 thunderstorms across the south of the Nottingham region reaching to The Wash, with isochrones of maximum thunder activity progressing from 15·00 G.M.T. at Birmingham to 17·00 G.M.T. at Nottingham and to 18·00 G.M.T. across Lincolnshire. A particular storm showing this tendency has been examined in detail by F. A. Barnes.

Hail is a concomitant of thunderstorms, especially in summer, although thunderstorms do not always produce hail. The distribution of hail is localised even in a single storm and depends almost entirely on conditions in the upper air. Further, hail is not easily classified, especially in winter, when soft hail is very different from large summer hail. It is almost impossible, therefore, to describe the regional distribution of hail except in terms of thunderstorms, although fortunately its occurrence in summer, when hail can be damaging, is infrequent. Indeed at most places, unlike thunderstorms, hail is most common in early spring, when falls are small and brief.

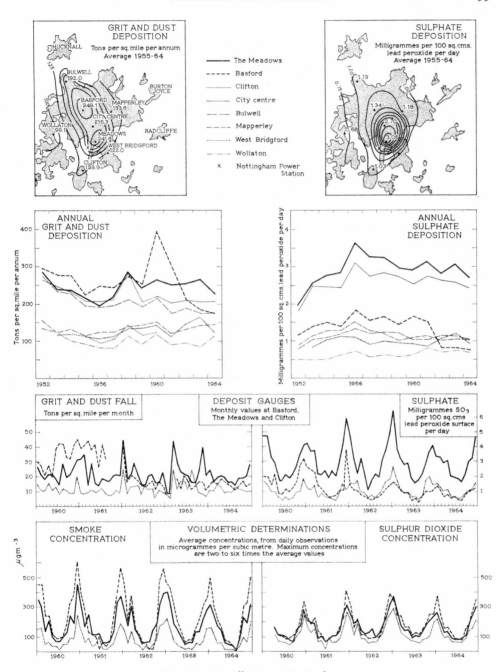

Fig. 19   Air pollution at Nottingham

Table XXIV Thunder and hail

	Jan.	Feb.	Mar.	April	May	June	July	Aug.	Sept.	Oct.	Nov.	Dec.	Year
AVERAGE NUMBER OF DAYS WITH THUNDER													
Buxton .. 1916–35	0·2	0·3	0·2	0·9	2	2	2	2	0·8	0·3	0·2	0·2	10·0
Woodthorpe .. 1935–59	0·1	0·2	0·3	0·9	1·6	2·5	3·2	2·5	1·1	0·4	0·1	0·1	13·0
Belvoir Castle 1896–1930	0·1	0·3	0·7	1·4	3·2	3·9	4·0	3·9	1·3	0·8	0·2	1·0	19·9
Cranwell .. 1921–45	0·1	0·1	0·6	1·3	2·1	2·5	3·6	3·2	1·6	0·4	0	0	15·5
Mansfield Woodhouse 1785–1805	0·1	0·1	0·2	0·5	1·0	1·4	2·3	1·7	0·7	0·2	0	0·1	8·2
MAXIMUM NUMBER OF DAYS WITH THUNDER													
Woodthorpe and Nottingham 1910–59	1	2	2	5	6	8	9	8	7	2	1	2	24 (1936)
AVERAGE NUMBER OF DAYS WITH HAIL													
Buxton .. 1922–30	0·6	0·4	0·6	1·1	1·1	0·1	0	0·3	0·8	0·1	0·6	0·3	6·0
Woodthorpe .. 1935–59	0·4	0·5	0·2	0·8	0·2	0·6	0·2	0·4	0·2	0·2	0·2	0·1	4·0
Cranwell .. 1921–45	0·4	1·2	2·0	2·2	1·1	0·5	0·2	0·2	0·4	0·7	0·3	0·3	9·5
Sutton Bonington .. 1922–36	0·3	0·4	0·5	0·7	0·5	0·3	0·1	0·1	0·3	0·1	0·1	0·1	3·4
Belvoir Castle .. 1922–30	0·1	0·2	0·7	0·4	0·3	0	0	0·1	0	0·1	0	0·1	2·1
MAXIMUM NUMBER OF DAYS WITH HAIL													
Woodthorpe and Nottingham 1910–59	2	5	3	3	3	1	1	2	1	1	2	2	10 (1925)

CONCLUSION

While there are obvious differences in climatic conditions between the Derbyshire uplands and the lowland which extends to the east, it must be emphasised that the latter forms part of the very extensive Midland plain which exhibits considerable uniformity of climate. The foregoing account is an attempt to define the climate, in its various aspects, of only one portion of this plain, arbitrarily defined in extent. Over this area the climate is relatively dry with a rather variable annual rainfall. It is characterised by a comparatively large seasonal and diurnal temperature range and a moderate amount of sunshine. Apart from occasional late killing frosts, the growing season is adequate for the satisfactory cultivation of almost any crop grown in Britain. Indeed, one of its chief advantages is that it favours agricultural diversity, providing adequate sunshine, warmth and rainfall to sustain a good growth of grass throughout normal summers, and to bring cereal and root crops to a rewarding harvest, subject always of course to the suitability of soils. In human terms, by British standards it is a moderately rigorous, but distinctly invigorating climate.

SELECTED REFERENCES

Barnes, F. A. and Potter, H. A. A flash flood in western Derbyshire. *East Midland Geographer* No. 10 (1958) pp. 3–15.

Barnes, F. A. The intense thunder rains of 1st July 1952 in the northern Midlands. *East Midland Geographer* No. 14 (1960) pp. 11–26.

Dury, G. H. *The East Midlands and the Peak*. Edinburgh (1963).

Dury, G. H. Some results of a magnitude-frequency analysis of precipitation. *Australian Geographical Studies* Vol. 2 (1964) pp. 21–34.

Edwards, K. C. Climate. Chapter in *A Scientific Survey of Nottingham*, British Association (1937); and in *Nottinghamshire*, Land Utilisation Survey Memoir, Part 60 (1944) pp. 439–449.

Garnett, A. Relief, latitude and climate: some local consequences. *Indian Geographical Society*, Silver Jubilee Volume (1952) pp. 128–131.

Glaisher, J. The meteorology of successive Quarters. Printed in the Registrar General's Quarterly Returns and in the *Quarterly Journal of the Royal Statistical Society* (1847) *et seq.*

Gumbel, E. J. Statistical theory of floods and droughts. *Proceedings of the Institute of Water Engineers* Vol. 12 (1958) pp. 157–184.

Lowe, J. H. and Lowe, E. J. *The climate of Nottingham during the year 1852*. London (1853).

Mellish, H. The rainfall of Nottinghamshire. *Quarterly Journal of the Royal Meteorological Society* (1893).

Miller, R. C. and Starrett, L. G. Thunderstorms in Great Britain. *Meteorological Magazine* Vol. 91 (1962) pp. 247–255.

Rooke, H. *A meteorological register kept at Mansfield Woodhouse in Nottinghamshire* (1795). Extended to 1805 by annual pamphlets.

Shellard, H. C. Extreme wind speeds over the U.K. for periods ending 1959. *Meteorological Magazine* Vol. 91 (1962) pp. 39–47.

Tinn, A. B. Local temperature variations in the Nottingham District. *Quarterly Journal of the Royal Meteorological Society* (Vol. 64 (1938) pp. 391–405.

Tinn, A. B. The distribution of thunder rains around Nottingham. *Quarterly Journal of the Royal Meteorological Society* (1940).

Tinn, A. B. Rainfall analysis at Woodthorpe, Nottinghamshire. *Meteorological Magazine* Vol. 88 (1959) pp. 65–66.

NOTE

Absolute temperatures have been distinguished from temperature differences in the following way. An absolute temperature of 25°F, for example, has the degree symbol before the F, while a difference of 25F° has been written with the degree symbol after the F.

IV

SOILS

IN a report to the Board of Agriculture, Thomas Brown (1794) described the soils of Derbyshire, the western part of the Nottingham region, under the headings of 'The Fertile', 'The Low Peak' and 'The High Peak'. Within this broad generalisation he writes that "the soil of the County of Derby is various as nature in her most capricious mood could form". The soils in parts of the 'Fertile' and 'Low Peak' areas have recently been examined in detail by the Soil Survey of England and Wales, and the whole area has been surveyed in preparation for a British contribution to a soil map of Europe for the Food and Agricultural Organisation of the United Nations. A version of this map has been included at a scale of 1:2,000,000 in the Atlas of Britain and Northern Ireland, published by the Clarendon Press in 1963.

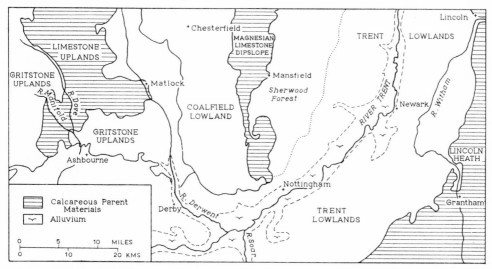

Fig. 20 Sub-divisions of the Nottingham region based on soil parent materials

One of the most convenient methods of describing the soils of the region is to follow the lead of Thomas Brown by using a regional approach. The sub-divisions adopted here correspond to the main groups of soil parent materials (Fig. 20) and are as follows—UPLANDS: Limestone, Gritstone; LOWLANDS: Coalfield, Magnesian Limestone, Trent lowlands, Lincoln 'Heath'. Within each of these the action of soil-forming factors on the parent materials determines the range of the soils that is found. In most cases the soils can be grouped together in associations (Table XXV) corresponding to those described by Mackney and Burnham for the West Midlands.

The two upland areas provide a strong contrast, particularly north of Matlock, where land utilisation has emphasised the differences. The Limestone Upland is mainly enclosed grazing land which has been improved, whereas large areas of the Gritstone have remained as unimproved common grazing. The climate can be considered similar for both areas, but variations of micro-climate occur as a result of the relief pattern. Rainfall is between 40 and 50 inches, rising to 60 inches per annum on the more elevated land near Buxton. The climatic climax vegetation of the Limestone is considered to have been an ashwood dominated by *Fraxinus excelsior*, and of the Gritstone Uplands as oakwood dominated by *Quercus petrea*. Except for small areas on steep slopes little now remains of the former vegetation. A fuller description of the vegetation is given in Chapter V.

Limestone Uplands

The associated soils are rendzinas, brown calcareous soils, brown earth soils and weakly developed, peaty gleyed podzols. Although the sub-heading may imply soil formation from the Carboniferous Limestone, this rock does not act as a soil parent material for much of the region. Recent investigations have demonstrated that the limestone is mantled with a silty drift, probably aeolian in origin, in which the soils have formed. The underlying limestone has only acted as parent material on valley slopes where the accumulation of the silty drift was limited. All of these soils are freely drained and have silt loam textures.

On the steeply-incised valley sides and escarpment faces of the limestone outcrops, shallow rendziniform soils have formed with only a few inches of organic-rich mineral soil. These soils are slightly calcareous and have a granular structure. Where the silty drift is shallow, brown calcareous soils (approximating to Duchaufour's *sol brun forestier calcimorphe*) occur. These soils exhibit only a weak B horizon beneath the organo-mineral A horizon. Where the silty drift is deeper, on level surfaces, leaching has proceeded to a greater extent and brown earth soils are formed. The profile is characterised by an A horizon below which a pale-coloured eluvial horizon occurs. Some movement of clay is indicated by the development of a finer-textured B horizon. The upper horizons become mixed in agricultural soils, but even under semi-natural conditions podzolisation does not seem to be taking place. The brown earth soils are common over much of the plateau formed by the Carboniferous Limestone. However, in the more elevated areas heather can be seen invading pastureland, and the change to the extremely acid litter of the heather produces a weakly-developed peaty gleyed podzol in the upper layers of the profile.

Table XXV Relationship between parent materials, associated soils, soil series and soil properties

Parent Material Region	Geology	Associated Soils (major soil groups and sub-groups)	Typical Soil Series or Complexes	Soil Properties	
				Texture	Natural Drainage
Limestone Uplands	Carboniferous Limestone with silty drifts	BROWN EARTH SOILS	Nordrach	Silt loam	Free
		RENDZINAS with brown earth soils	Sprink Complex	Silt loam	Excessive
Gritstone Uplands	Millstone Grit sandstones, shales and associated drifts	PODZOLS	Anglezarke	Loamy sand	Free
		BROWN EARTH SOILS	Kirkby Overblow	Sandy loam	Free
		SURFACE-WATER GLEY SOILS	Windley	Clay loam	Poor
		PEATY GLEY SOILS	None named	Clay loam	Very poor
		PEATY SOILS	None named	Peat	Very poor
Coalfield Lowland	Coal Measures sandstones, shales and associated drifts	BROWN EARTH SOILS	Seacroft	Loam or Silt loam	Free
		SURFACE-WATER GLEY SOILS	Dale	Clay loam	Poor
Magnesian Limestone Dipslope	Magnesian Limestone and Permian Marl	BROWN CALCAREOUS SOILS	Aberford	Sandy loam	Free
		BROWN EARTH SOILS	Micklefield	Clay loam	Free
		SURFACE-WATER GLEY SOILS	Watnall	Clay loam	Poor
Trent Lowlands	Triassic sandstones and marls, Lias clays, with associated drifts and alluvium	PODZOLS	Crannymoor	Loamy sand	Free
		BROWN EARTH SOILS	Mercaston	Sandy loam	Free
			Bromsgrove	Sandy loam	Free
		BROWN EARTH SOILS with gleying	Worcester	Clay loam	Imperfect
		SURFACE-WATER GLEY SOILS	Salop	Loam or clay loam	Poor
		GLEY SOILS ON ALLUVIUM	None named	Clay loam or silt loam	Poor
Lincoln Heath	Jurassic limestone, sandstones and associated drifts	BROWN CALCAREOUS SOILS	None named	Clay loam	Free
		FERRITIC BROWN EARTHS	None named	Clay loam	Free
		SURFACE-WATER GLEY SOILS	None named	Sandy clay loam	Poor

Recent work has sought to correlate soils found on the Derbyshire Limestone with comparable soils on the Mendip Hills. The names Nordrach series for brown earth soils, and Lulsgate series for the shallower soils, have been adopted in the Wirksworth district. Various soils, including rendzinas, formed on the steep limestone escarpments and valley sides have here been given the name Sprink complex.

Gritstone Uplands

The associated soils are brown earth soils, podzols, peaty gleyed podzols, surface-water gley soils, peaty gley soils and peat soils. Within this sub-division parent materials of extremely differing character occur. Generally, the arenaceous rocks weather to sandy parent materials which result in acid, freely-drained soils, whereas shales and glacial drifts provide fine-textured parent materials which are usually imperfectly or poorly drained. Thus, within the Gritstone area it is possible to see excellent examples of a wide range of soils. The complete succession of horizons associated with the mature profile frequently can be seen on level moorland or woodland sites, but most of the other soils have been modified by agricultural clearance and improvement.

All the parent materials derived from the strata of the Millstone Grit are non-calcareous, and it is convenient to consider those formed on sandstones and sandy deposits in one group and those on argillaceous deposits in another. The sandy parent materials are leached, and podzolisation occurs in all soils on level sites where undisturbed. Development of impervious and indurated horizons in podzols has frequently led to the production of the features of gleying above the illuvial horizons, and the accumulation of a peaty superficial layer. Such peaty gleyed podzols are fairly common on the higher moorlands. Brown earths are restricted to less stable, steep slopes where run-off is more rapid and mixing by slow downslope movement of the surface soil takes place. On argillaceous deposits, the most common soil of the uplands is the peaty gleyed soil with six to eight inches of peat overlying a mineral soil in which strong features of gleying are present. Mottling of the subsoils is characteristic and in some soils a weakly-developed textural B horizon can be distinguished. Areas with high rainfall or which are sited in wet hollows may have developed thick peat, but almost everywhere this is now being eroded. The higher moorlands have been subjected to controlled burning for many years, but recently uncontrolled burning has caused the destruction of the peaty superficial horizons and subsequently to extensive erosion by wind and water.

The less elevated parts of the Gritstone Uplands have soils which, in most cases, have been improved by the addition of manures, by cultivation, and by the installation of drainage systems. In the area mapped in detail it has been possible to correlate with similar soils in the West Riding of Yorkshire. Some of the most extensive soils are the Kirkby Overblow series, a brown earth overlying medium-grained sandstones; the Dunkeswick series, a surface-water gley soil developed in boulder clay; and on the Limestone Shales in south Derbyshire the Windley series, a surface-water gley soil is common. On the higher moorland, the humus-iron podzols are mapped under the name of the Anglezarke series. No series have been named yet for the peat soils or the peaty gley soils of the uplands in the East Midlands.

THE LOWLANDS

East of the Derwent, the general elevation of the land is lower, and the underlying strata are of the Carboniferous (Coal Measures), Permian, Triassic and Jurassic formations. These rocks are partly covered by glacial drifts which have contributed to the parent materials of most of the soils. The lowlands are characterised by a rainfall of 30 inches or less and they support a greater proportion of arable farming than the uplands. Although the climate is fairly uniform differences in parent material are reflected in the varied soil cover which in turn affects the present land use.

The Coalfield

Here the associated soils are surface-water gley soils, brown earths with gleying, and brown earth soils. The Nottinghamshire-Derbyshire coalfield has a low relief with extensive outcrops of shales. Sandstones within the sequence form small escarpments, which in the Chesterfield area and further north become greater in height. Areas of shales and similarly fine-textured boulder clays give an extensive development of surface-water gley soils such as the Dale series. The extent of these soils would be even greater but for the widespread workings of coal by the opencast method. Replaced soils now occupy approximately 27,000 acres in the Nottingham region. The only freely-drained soils are those of the Seacroft series, developed from the sandstones which weather to give a loam or silt loam textured soil.

Magnesian Limestone Dipslope

The associated soils are brown calcareous soils, brown earths and surface-water gley soils. Soil contrasts in this important arable area formed by the Permian rocks are provided by minor variations in the parent material which is only partially derived from the underlying strata. Since boulder clay overlies the bedrock over much of the area the soils tend to have an overall similarity with a dark reddish-brown surface horizon. In the subsurface horizons, however, differences become apparent. The soils found over the limestone are freely drained, partially leached calcareous soils described under the name of Aberford series. The texture of these soils is sandy clay loam and yellow weathering Magnesian Limestone can be found in pockets on the surface of the solid rock. Soils derived from the Permian Red Marl are silty clays and frequently display features of gleying above a well-developed prismatic B horizon. These surface-water gley soils are frequently found under woodland, and have been given the name Watnall series. Small areas of freely drained soils of the Micklefield series are derived from the same parent material.

The Trent Lowlands

The associated soils are brown earth soils, surface-water gley soils, peaty gley soils on alluvium. The lowlands of the Vale of Trent comprise Triassic and Liassic strata with a discontinuous cover of boulder clay. This has given rise to a complex association of brown earths, brown earths with gleying and gley soils. Many of these soils exhibit the effects of leaching and the movement of clay into the B horizon and are regarded therefore as brown earths (*sols lessivés*). The soils formed from the Lower Lias and associated drifts have been tentatively correlated with similar soils in the Vale of Evesham but until the current work on the Melton Mowbray Sheet is published further comment would be premature. On the Keuper Marl, imperfect or freely drained soils with a clay loam texture, have been mapped under the name Worcester series, and poorly drained soils developed from drifts of predominantly Triassic material are called Salop series. Freely drained sandy loams or silt loams derived from fine-grained Keuper sandstones have been mapped as the Bromsgrove series. On the freely drained sandy soils of Sherwood Forest, a complete sequence of soil profiles from brown earth soils to humus-iron podzols occurs. The distribution of these very different soils on the same parent material, the Bunter Sandstone, invites further investigation.

A wide variation in drainage occurs in the soils of the lower terraces and flood plains of the Trent and other major rivers. The soils on the terraces generally are sandy clay loam with sub-angular blocky structures, whereas those on the flood plains have clay loam or silty clay loam textures and a well-developed prismatic structure in the B horizon. Most of these soils are in agricultural use in spite of their drainage defects; however, freely drained soils on sands and gravels north-east of Newark have well-developed podzol profiles. Organic soils, as yet unnamed, occur in alluvial embayments of the Trent valley at Sinfin in Derbyshire, at Ruddington and north of Bingham in Nottinghamshire. Mostly these are represented by dark-coloured humose mineral soils, as cultivation and cropping have reduced the amount of organic matter, so that only very small areas of peat remain.

The Lincoln 'Heath'

The soils found on the Lincoln 'Heath' are of the following kind: brown calcareous soils; ferritic brown earths, brown earths and surface-water gley soils. The Lincolnshire Limestone is an area of freely drained soils of sandy clay loam or clay loam texture derived from an oolitic rock, the carbonate in the soil consisting mainly of the weathering ooliths. The chief disadvantage of these soils is their shallowness and liability to drought during summer, otherwise they are good all-purpose agricultural soils. A typical profile has dark yellowish brown or strong brown colours and sub-angular blocky structure. No detailed mapping has been done on this parent material in the East Midlands, although the Sherbourne series has been mapped in the Evesham district on the same parent material. Freely drained ferritic brown earths are formed over ferruginous strata of the Jurassic sequence, and clay outcrops, as well as patches of boulder clay, give rise to areas of surface-water gley soils. The differences between soils of the 'Heath' and those of the Trent lowlands have been recognised from very early times, and in order to provide a diversity of soils of different potential uses the parish boundaries south of Lincoln have been drawn to include part of the freely drained calcareous soils on the 'Heath', the steeply sloping land of the escarpment face, as well as the imperfectly and poorly drained soils of the lowland to the west.

SELECTED REFERENCES

Bickmore, D. P. and Shaw, M. A. *The Atlas of Britain and Northern Ireland* (Oxford, 1963) p. 40.

Bridges, E. M. Types of soil formation in the Nottingham District. *East Midland Geographer* No. 17 (1962) pp. 15–19.

Bridges, E. M. *Soils and Land Use of the area north of Derby* (Harpenden, 1965).

Mackney, D. and Burnham, C. P. *The soils of the West Midlands* (Harpenden, 1964) pp. 53–91.

Pigott, C. D. Soil formation and development on the Carboniferous Limestone of Derbyshire. I— Parent Material. *Journal of Ecology* No. 50 (1962) pp. 145–156.

Soil Survey of Great Britain, Reports 10, 11, 12 and 13 (1957–1960) Agricultural Research Council, London.

V

VEGETATION

WITHIN the limits of the Nottingham region the surface is formed by a wide range of rock types. The areas covered by superficial deposits, i.e. material transported by water, ice or wind, are relatively small and localised, so that the vegetation and solid geology are closely related. It is appropriate therefore to approach a study of the vegetation by reference to the principal geological formations. Unfortunately for the botanist much of the region has been subject to human interference by urban and industrial development and by widespread agricultural activity, as a result of which in many parts little of the natural ecosystem now remains. Accordingly, detailed accounts of vegetation are given chiefly for those areas with well-developed and extensive examples of natural and semi-natural vegetation, though in addition mention will be made of some very restricted localities of botanical interest.

VEGETATION OF THE CARBONIFEROUS LIMESTONE

The main outcrop of the Carboniferous Limestone in the southern Pennines forms a well-developed plateau with steep slopes around much of its margin. In striking contrast to the widespread occurrence of bare fissured limestone surfaces of the northern Pennines, much of the limestone in the southern Pennines is covered by superficial deposits of loam, chert-gravel or clay. C. D. Pigott has recently shown that these superficial deposits are probably derived from loess, though often mixed with deep accumulations of insoluble limestone residue.

The vegetation of the relatively level plateau with its gentle slopes has been both extensively and intensively modified by man's activities. There can be little doubt that the area was previously well wooded but that as a result of forest clearance, enclosure of the land and continuous grazing by sheep and cattle, the predominant vegetation is now limestone grassland. Most of the trees now present, chiefly sycamore (*Acer pseudo-platanus*) beech (*Fagus sylvatica*) and elm (*Ulmus* spp., but most commonly wych elm *U. glabra*), have been planted to function as shelter belts. The plateau is dissected by numerous valleys (dales) with steep, often precipitous, sides on which the distinctive limestone vegetation is found.

Woodland

Woodland is dominated by ash (*Fraxinus excelsior*) with *Ulmus glabra* and *Acer pseudo-platanus* as the commonest associates of the canopy. *Fraxinus* regenerates successfully and saplings of all ages may occur in abundance. *Acer pseudo-platanus* also regenerates and is a major competitor to *Fraxinus*. In the well-developed shrub layer, hazel (*Corylus avellana*) is the most abundant species. Of the many species which may be found as shrubs or under-shrubs, the following may be considered the most typical associates:

HAWTHORN	*Crataegus monogyna*
ROWAN	*Sorbus aucuparia*
MAPLE	*Acer campestre*
COMMON BUCKTHORN	*Rhamnus catharticus*
DOGWOOD	*Cornus sanguinea*
BLACKTHORN	*Prunus spinosa*
BIRD CHERRY	*P. padus*
PRIVET	*Ligustrum vulgare*

In well-developed scree ashwood the herb layer comprises very few species of common occurrence though there is a large number (up to about 50) of only rare occurrence. The flora of the herb layer ranges between that developed on relatively dry exposed scree slopes, where it is dominated by False-brome (*Brachypodium sylvaticum*), to that developed on moister and more shaded slopes where it is dominated by Tufted Hairgrass (*Deschampsia caespitosa*) and Dog's Mercury (*Mercurialis perennis*). Again the number and variety of associates in this layer is considerable and depends on local habitat factors such as the nature of the scree, slope, aspect and soil moisture. Of these the most prominent are those which frequently form pure stands, e.g. wood anemone (*Anemone nemorosa*), Ramsons (*Allium ursinum*), and lesser celandine (*Ranunculus ficaria*); the first mentioned is abundant in Hurt's Wood on the Staffordshire side of Dovedale. G. Scurfield, in an account of ashwood developed on the Derbyshire limestone, and in particular that at Monksdale, pays particular attention to the successional stages leading to mature ashwood. At sites where the screes are more or less ungrazed *Fraxinus* may be a direct coloniser of the scree together with *Acer pseudoplatanus* (occasionally) and with *Ulmus glabra* (rarely); *Fraxinus* may on occasions be preceded by *Corylus*. On the upper, steeper and drier part of the slope *Corylus* becomes the dominant element in the scrub and plays a considerable part in scree stabilization. Characteristic direct colonisers of the mid-part of the slope are *Prunus spinosa*, *Crataegus monogyna*, honeysuckle (*Lonicera periclymenum*), Stone bramble (*Rubus saxatilis*) and prostrate privet (*Ligustrum vulgare*). Bird cherry (*Prunus padus*), the taller species of *Rosa* (e.g. *R. canina*) and buckthorn (*Rhamnus catharticus*) are characteristic of the bottom of the slopes. There are 'parallel' changes in the herb flora from the top to the bottom of the valley sides. In grassland which is grazed, whether on scree or on more mature and stabilised soils, colonisation by *Crataegus monogyna* is a necessary precursor to colonisation by *Fraxinus*. *Crataegus*, by opening up otherwise closed grassland and by providing the necessary protection from grazing, enables *Fraxinus* to become established, *Crataegus* itself subsequently being suppressed by the ash. Scurfield also gives some information about the environmental tolerances and growth of *Fraxinus* in the district.

Grassland

Degeneration of woodland to scrub and grassland, as a result of grazing by sheep and cattle, is of common occurrence, so that the grassland in particular is extensively developed. A detailed study of the vegetation and soil complex or catena of the slopes of Cressbrook dale by O. E. Balme gives a representative picture of conditions in many of the dales. The typical calcareous grassland of the lower slopes occurs only on the steepest parts (i.e. over 30°), on shallow immature rendzina-type soils with loose limestone fragments, free calcium carbonate, dark (black) alkaline humus with pH7 throughout the profile and overlying a continuously shifting substratum. The soil readily dries out and becomes eroded during periods of drought as it is not protected by a continuous cover of vegetation. The community is dominated by *Festuca ovina* growing in scattered tufts with open spaces between, where non-graminaceous herbs may become established. The community is floristically rich with calcicole species such as the common rockrose (*Helianthemum chamaecistus*), hawkbit (*Leontodon hispidus*) and salad burnet (*Poterium sanguisorba*) covering a relatively large area of ground. The openness of the community is maintained by the instability of the substrate. As the amount of loose scree diminishes and the substrate becomes more stable and the soil deeper, the soil character changes, e.g. the pH of the surface may be as low as 5·8. On these soils there is a closed sward, principally of *Festuca ovina* and *F. rubra*, and a reduction in some of the calcicole species, together with the first appearance of calcifuge plants, notably the mountain pansy (*Viola lutea*). Others invading the grass sward are bedstraw (*Galium hercynicum*) (replacing *G. pumilum*), *Agrostis tenuis* and tormentil (*Potentilla erecta*) which gradually increase in abundance and are joined by woodrush (*Luzula campestris*) to form a *Festuca–Agrostis* association. As the slope lessens and as the depth of soil increases, a brown earth profile with its associated chemical changes is developed. Finally, as the slope flattens out and the deep soils have their surface layers removed from the influence of the basic parent rock and become increasingly acid and base deficient, heath species invade the *Festuca–Agrostis* association and patches of wavy hair-grass (*Deschampsia flexuosa*) and bilberry (*Vaccinium myrtillus*) become prominent components of the vegetation. This community is less rich floristically, all the base-demanding species disappear, the less exacting species, e.g. *Viola lutea* and crested hair-grass (*Koeleria gracilis*) are less common and only *Galium hercynicum* and *Luzula campestris*, of this latter group, remain frequent in the fully developed limestone heath.

There are considerable variations in the 'grassland' vegetation resulting from changes in local habitat conditions, notably those of broken ground and detritus brought about by quarry and mineral workings. These more or less open and disturbed habitats are frequently the sites for unusual species and species now relict in the area. These plants occupy such sites partly because of the lack of competition; examples are Vernal Sandwort (*Minuartia verna*) and Alpine pennycress (*Thlaspi virens*). Cliffs and rocky outcrops often possess interesting groups of plants. One example is that of a well-defined group of annuals which occupy a rather extreme habitat, notably the shallow soils on rock ledges with an open sunny south-facing aspect. The following species studied experimentally by D. Ratcliffe may be found in this community:

COMMON WALL CRESS	*Arabidopsis thaliana*
THYME LEAVED SANDWORT	*Arenaria serpyllifolia*
HAIRY BITTERCRESS	*Cardamine hirsuta*
WALL WHITLOW GRASS	*Draba muralis*
WHITLOW GRASS	*Erophila verna*
ROCK HUTCHINSON	*Horningia petraea*
RUE-LEAVED SAXIFRAGE	*Saxifraga tridactylites*
WALL SPEEDWELL	*Veronica arvensis*

This group of species is not confined to the Derbyshire limestone for it is also found on other limestone and on the fixed and mature stages of sand dunes, particularly calcareous dunes. The physical peculiarities of these habitats, giving open conditions with a well-drained soil, seem to be the most important factors determining its distribution in Britain. Examining their extra-British distribution, D. Ratcliffe concludes that the species comprising this group form a much reduced outlier of a much larger group with a centre of distribution in areas of southern Europe with a climate characterised by predominantly winter rainfall and very dry summers. Accordingly it is not surprising that the British representatives of this group are found in habitats with a seasonal *micro*-climatic variation which might broadly fit into that pattern. These annuals have a characteristic life-cycle; they germinate invariably in autumn, usually mid- or late-September, vegetative growth then proceeds until sometime in December and then with the onset of more favourable conditions in the spring, flowering occurs, seeds are shed in May or June but no germination takes place until the autumn. Ratcliffe showed that the clearly defined life-cycle fitted closely the local climatic conditions and that this relationship is the direct result of two important physiological characteristics: firstly, the necessity for the after-ripening of the seeds, resulting in a synchronised germination in the autumn; and secondly, the necessity for low temperatures before normal flowering can take place so delaying flowering until the following spring though not synchronising it except within a species in each locality.

A second group is found on north-facing ledges and scree slopes which provide both open habitat conditions and constantly moist soils; this group includes such plants as Jacob's ladder (*Polemonium caerulium*). A third group is associated with cliffs which have well-developed vertical fissures, and includes in particular several small ferns, the spleen worts (*Asplenium* spp.), notably the arctic-alpine *Asplenium viride* which favours north-facing sites. Another interesting fern is the rusty-back fern (*Ceterarch officinarum*) found in fissures on south-facing cliffs. Finally, mention must be made of trees which occur in very precarious situations on the cliff faces; these included *Ulmus glabra*, holly (*Ilex aquifolium*), rock whitebeam (*Sorbus rupicola*) and yew (*Taxus baccata*), the latter being especially characteristic of such situations in Dovedale.

VEGETATION OF THE MILLSTONE GRIT

The Millstone Grit formation consists of a series of shales and sandstones, including coarse grits. The Lower Gritstone slopes support grassland. On the drier soils which are not excessively acid, sheeps fescue grass (*Festuca ovina*) and the common bent (*Agrostis tenuis*) are abundant, whilst on more leached soils mat grass (*Nardus stricta*) is the dominant plant. Both the bent-fescue grassland and the *Nardus* grassland may be invaded by heath species, notably *Calluna vulgaris*, whenever grazing is reduced or removed. Locally in the drier sites the two species of gorse (*Ulex europaeus* and *U. gallii*) are found, and bracken (*Pteridium aquilinum*) is found on the deeper soils. Where the drainage is impeded, the ill-drained zones are marked by the occurrence of common rushes (*Juncus effusus* and *J. conglomeratus*). Woodland remnants survive on the steep boulder-strewn sides of the gullies or 'cloughs' where the most abundant species is the sessile oak (*Quercus petraea*), usually in association with the two birches (*Betula pubescens* and *B. pendula*) and with rowan (*Sorbus aucuparia*). Where the ground is well-drained wavy hair-grass (*Deschampsia flexuosa*) is the dominant member of the field layer, though where there is an accumulation of leaf litter and weathered gritstone between the boulders, bracken (*Pteridium aquilinum*) may be abundant. Local patches of bilberry (*Vaccinium myrtillus*) occur if grazing is limited and these extend with a further decrease in grazing pressure. In moister situations creeping soft grass (*Holcus mollis*), the great woodrush (*Luzula sylvatica*) and a variety of ferns may be found.

Degeneration of the woodland is further represented by birch scrub in more gently sloping and open situations, where the floor of the 'wood' is covered with bracken. Ultimately the woodland fragments give way to bracken slopes or to heather (*Calluna vulgaris*), bilberry (*Vaccinium myrtillus*) or cotton sedge (*Eriophorum vaginatum*) 'moors'. Whilst the most extensive 'moorland' vegetation is developed in the northern part of the Peak District representative samples are found on the East Moors between Chesterfield and Matlock. On the gentler well-drained slopes with shallow leached soils *Calluna* is the dominant, often with only *Deschampsia flexuosa* and cowberry (*Vaccinium vitis-idae*) as sparsely represented associates. Where the peat cover may be thicker and wetter *Eriophorum vaginatum* may be co-dominant with *Calluna* or, if burning is both frequent and intensive, it may be the apparent sole dominant. In localised very wet situations another cotton sedge (*E. angustifolium*) is found. Where the ground water represents periodic flooding or flushing the dominant plant may be purple moor grass (*Molinia caerulea*). All these types of 'moorland' vegetation in this locality have very few secondary associates; of those present the most typical are lichens whilst the scarcity of bog moss (*Sphagnum* spp.) is noteworthy. Some of the more intractable parts of these 'moors' have recently been planted by the Forestry Commission, e.g. Middle Moor, whilst others which have shallower peaty soils and better drainage have been reclaimed for cultivation with the plough.

VEGETATION OF THE BUNTER SANDSTONE

Woodland

The Bunter Sandstone Series carries a large proportion of the woodland of the region. The present-day discontinuous patchwork of woodland described by J. W. Hopkinson forms the remnants of Sherwood Forest which in the first recorded perambulation of 1232 is shown to have extended northwards from Nottingham for 25 miles in a broad belt eight to ten miles wide with an area of about 100,000 acres. Only in two localities does it spread beyond the limits of the Bunter Sandstone; the first to the west of Mansfield where it extends on to the Magnesian Limestone, and the second to the north-east of Nottingham where it passes on to the Keuper Waterstones and Marls. The general character of the Forest was of oak and birch-wood, with localised thickets, and patches of open scrub-heath. While it may be assumed that the original forest formed a more or less continuous unit, that part lying immediately to the north of Nottingham was cleared early and gave rise to large areas of scrub-heath. The sterility of the soil derived from the Bunter Sandstone and in more recent times the lowering of its water table are the factors chiefly responsible for the survival of much of this vegetation up to relatively recent times and also for the still more recent partial afforestation with conifers. The subsequent history of the Forest is one of continuous modification and depletion. At first this was mainly due to localised clearing, enclosing and planting with timber or crops. More land was cleared and brought into cultivation as a result of the Enclosure Acts of 1789–96, and many of the parklands were split up into farms. However, many of the owners of the large estates known collectively as the Dukeries, notably the Dukes of Portland at Welbeck, carried out considerable planting programmes, both of cleared land and of heathland, which to a certain extent offset the loss of trees by indiscriminate felling or widespread clearance.

As already stated, the sterility of soil and a falling water-table are the conditions under which the Forest area still supports a 'primitive' form of woodland characterised by an extreme paucity of species. The chief woodlands belong to the dry oakwood association consisting chiefly of oak (*Quercus* spp.) and birch (*Betula pubescens*), with a ground or field layer characteristically of bracken (*Pteridium aquilinum*), wavy hair-grass (*Deschampsia flexuosa*), and creeping soft-grass (*Holcus mollis*) in varying proportions. The only area which may be considered to approximate to the original Forest is the Birklands (= birch lands) which lie to the north of Edwinstowe. In consequence of the extensive and uncontrolled felling, the woodland varies much in character, showing all stages of deforestation ranging from closed oakwood with dense undergrowth of bracken to open 'parkland' and grassheath with scattered trees. A certain amount of replacement by planting over many years suggests that areas with trees up to 200 years old should be considered as semi-natural only. The apparently traditional practice of sparing trees of giant proportions has resulted in several of these remaining to the present day. Some of these, like the Major Oak, are short trees with boles of tremendous girth and extensive crowns, the main branches of which are now supported by props. These trees have a growth form characteristic of those grown in open canopy, whereas others also of great age and size have boles of considerable height with few low large branches suggesting that they have grown in closed canopy.

The woodland varies considerably with regard to the dominant species of oak, for either pedunculate oak (*Quercus robur*) or sessile oak (*Q. petraea*) may be locally dominant, with the other absent, sub-dominant or co-dominant. The hybrid between the two species also occurs and the first published record of this was made by Hopkinson. Birch (*Betula pubescens*) frequently accompanies the oak and much of the woodland may be described as oak-birchwood. The removal of oak, with its resultant opening of the canopy, favours the birch and eventually pure birchwood may develop. Pure birchwood does in fact occur locally, often associated with the drift gravels where this shallow rooting species is capable of thriving on the thin dry soils. The Spanish Chestnut (*Castanea sativa*) is found in many of the semi-natural oakwoods. The most striking features of the oakwoods themselves are the absence of coppice and the general poor development of the shrub layer. Young *Quercus*, *Betula*, and *Castanea*, and hawthorn (*Crataegus monogyna* and *C. oxyacanthoides*), holly (*Ilex aquifolium*) and elder (*Sambucus nigra*) are found occasionally. Honeysuckle (*Lonicera periclymenum*) is abundant, and, because of the paucity of shrubs often assumes a decumbent habit.

The herb layer is equally poorly-developed floristically and is typically represented by bracken (*Pteridium aquilinum*). Under a close canopy, the dense tall growth of *Pteridium* forms a more or less closed community to the exclusion of most other species. In woods where birch is abundant and the canopy is more open, in addition to bracken the following may be locally important: *Deschampsia flexuosa*, *Holcus mollis*, heath bedstraw (*Galium saxatile*) and Tormentil (*Potentilla erecta*). *Pteridium* produces annually a large amount of coarse leaf litter which, together with that of *Quercus* and *Betula*, forms a thick surface layer. Beneath this is a layer of dark, often black, amorphous organic matter; this in turn rests on the weathered parent material which may take the form of dark rusty-brown sand with pebbles. Roots are limited to the top few inches. Hopkinson showed that, whilst the light factor indirectly influences the distribution of the ground flora in the dry oakwood, the major factor is the slow rate of decay of the leaf litter, leading to the accumulation of loose leaf debris up to a thickness of nine inches, overlying a dry humus layer of up to four inches in thickness. Regeneration of oak takes place, if at all, only on the margins of clearings or where the bracken is either weakly developed or absent. Invasion by oak of the grass-heath or *Calluna*-heath, which are the other characteristic semi-natural types of vegetation of the Sandstone, does not seem to take place, perhaps because of rabbits. Birch, on the other hand, colonises felled woodland and grass-heath, though it may be eaten back by rabbits (Plate V).

Scrub, Grass-heath and Calluna-heath

The vegetation of the Bunter Sandstone presents a varied pattern of which the woodland is only one component. Larger or smaller areas may be occupied by true heath in which the dominant species is Ling (*Calluna vulgaris*) often accompanied by Bell heather (*Erica cinerea*). Adjacent to these may be areas dominated by *Pteridium* which is attempting to enter the Calluneta but whose inroads are extremely limited except where *Calluna* has been either burned or severely eaten back by rabbits. Interspread with these areas may be others of grass-heath, which are extremely complex and variable in character but with one important society dominated by *Deschampsia flexuosa*. Another area may be a dense thicket of scrub dominated by gorse (*Ulex europaeus*) or by a mixture of spiny shrubs. Finally, superimposed on this variety of low-standing communities may be a scattering of trees. Of these trees birch occurs in the greatest number with individuals of all ages, scattered thinly or locally more thickly, and with *Quercus* or pine (*Pinus sylvestris*) occurring only occasionally. The scrub association is found on the commons and warrens but is also extensively developed by the wayside. As already mentioned *Ulex europaeus* is by far the most abundant species, though spiny shrubs such as *Rosa* spp., *Rubus* spp., principally the blackberry *R. fruticosus* (agg), blackthorn (*Prunus spinosa*) and *Crataegus* spp., are frequently abundant; broom (*Cytisus scoparius*) and *Lonicera periclymenum* may also be abundant. Associated with these shrubs are many herbs which can flourish in the shelter and relatively slight shade afforded by the shrubs. On the other hand where *Ulex europaeus* forms pure stands it frequently becomes dense enough to preclude entirely all the ground flora. One of the most characteristic grass-heath communities is that dominated by *Deschampsia flexuosa* which often forms a closed community with very few associated species. Hopkinson suggests that the structural character and species composition of this type of vegetation depends on the method of origin and the relative age of the community.

The free drainage of the Bunter Sandstone and the great depth of the water have resulted in the prevalence of dry valleys and the poor development of wet heath. Locally where drainage is impeded, either by the formation of an indurate layer in a podsol or to an accumulation of fine silty sediments along small water courses, limited development of wet heath may occur.

VEGETATION OF THE KEUPER SANDSTONE AND MARLS

The countryside of the Keuper Sandstone and Marls is dominated by agricultural land which, together with occasional gypsum quarries, brickworks and oil wells, greatly limit the extent of semi-natural vegetation. The Sandstone (Waterstones) produce clayey soils somewhat lighter than those of the Marls, supporting a vegetation including Mat grass (*Nardus stricta*) and *Potentilla erecta*. The woods, often on the steeper slopes, are mixed deciduous woods with oak and ash predominating but with some birch and lime (*Tilia cordata*). The ground flora has well-developed fern societies, notably of *Polystichum setiferum*, *P. aculeatum*, and *Dryopteris Borreri* and sometimes *Thelypteris oreopteris*.

The Red Marls are a calcareous silt with occasional bands of sandstone (skerries) which give rise to minor escarpments. The Marls produce a stiff red soil. As R. C. L. and B. M. Howitt have shown these scarp slopes have an attractive calcicole flora in which hairy violet (*Viola hirta*), Dyers greenweed (*Genista tinctoria*), zigzag clover (*Trifolium medium*), small scabious (*Scabiosa columbaria*), stemless thistle (*Cirsium acaule*), wild Basil (*Clinopodium vulgare*), heath false-brome (*Brachypodium pinnatum*), and upright brome (*Bromus erectus*) are typical species, while *Helianthemum chamae-cistus*, slender birdsfoot trefoil (*Lotus tenuis*), yellow-wort (*Blackstonia perfoliata*), felwort (*Gentiana amarella*), pyramidal orchid (*Anacamptis pyramidalis*), and bee orchid (*Ophrys apifera*) can still be found. In addition the Red Marls support a good deal of woodland, mainly mixed, often of oak with hazel coppice (though the Forestry Commission are planting much beech in the woods now being rehabilitated). Of the shrubs, wild service tree (*Sorbus torminalis*) and goat willow (*Salix caprea*) are frequent, with aspen and birch on the lighter soils. The ground flora of the woods varies greatly, often having a characteristic dominant plant such as Wood Anemone (*Anemone nemorosa*), sweet woodruff (*Asperula odorata*), wood sanicle (*Sanicula europea*) or Dog's Mercury (*Mercurialis perennis*).

VEGETATION OF THE JURASSIC ROCKS AND THE LINCOLNSHIRE CHALK

The two main divisions of the Jurassic rocks which form the surface of much of the east and south-east of the region are the Lower Lias and the Inferior Oolite (Lincoln-shire) Limestone. The former succeeds the Keuper Marl east of the Trent and forms the stretch of lowland which reaches as far as the Lincoln Edge, although further south it gives rise to the higher ground of the south Nottinghamshire Wolds. The latter forms the broad dip slope of the Lincoln *cuesta* known as the Lincoln Heath. In both cases much of the area is devoted to agriculture.

Lower Lias

The dark blue shales with bands of flaggy limestone, weather to produce a very sticky blue clay of a calcareous nature. Much of the outcrop is covered by boulder clay which is usually derived from similar calcareous material or from chalk, though in places the surface deposits are more sandy. The area is well wooded, *Ulmus glabra* often forming a large part of the canopy; sanicle (*Sanicula europaea*) is one of the more frequent members of the ground flora, whilst others present include *Daphne laureola* and *Mercurialis perennis*. There are several species notable for their rare occurrence, e.g. *Anemone nemorosa*, *Lonicera periclymenum* and the guelder rose (*Viburnum opulus*) whilst others are surprisingly absent, e.g. sweet woodruff (*Asperula odorata*) and *Adoxa moschatellina*.

Oolite Limestone

The surface of the Heath for many miles north and south of Lincoln is dry and sparsely wooded. In the extreme south beyond Grantham, the plateau broadens and is cut by valleys which are more heavily wooded. In general these are mixed deciduous woods of varying sizes frequently maintained as game coverts. The northern parts of the outcrop are extensively covered by blown-sand. Both here and on the Heath in general, provided there is free drainage, the soils will support open pine and birch woodlands, or dry heath vegetation if tree establishment is prevented by man. Locally in the sand areas, often as a result of an indurated iron pan layer in the soil profile, drainage is impeded and the water table lies at or close to the ground surface; such soils support wet heath vegetation. The dry heath vegetation is characterised by ling (*Calluna vulgaris*), *Deschampsia flexuosa* and bell heather (*Erica cinerea*), though some sites have been invaded by dense growth of *Pteridium aquilinum* and Rosebay willow herb (*Chamaenerion angustifolium*), and where grazing and burning are restricted, by birch. The wet heath has an abundance of purple moor grass (*Molinia caerulea*), cross leaved heath (*Erica tetralix*) and *Sphagnum* spp., and where open-water lies at or above ground level there may be stands of *Phragmites communis*. Three locations where these vegetation types are well developed are Twiggmoor near Brigg, Scotton Common near Gainsborough and Linwood Warren near Market Rasen; the two latter, where a series of management and conservation studies are being carried out, are Nature Reserves of the Lincolnshire Naturalists' Trust.

Chalk

The chalk of the Lincolnshire Wolds forms a broad upland area running approximately north-south. Like the Oolite Limestone, there is a prominent west-facing escarpment, while much of the dip slope is overlain by boulder clay. The heavy boulder clay soils were once densely wooded but the forest has given place over the years to arable and pasture. Periodically, attempts were made by estates to improve the management of their woods. These included the development of a coppice-with-standard system of silviculture. In this system the majority of the trees have the main axis removed to induce the development of coppice shoots from the stump. In the Wolds hazel (*Corylus avellana*) and ash (*Fraxinus excelsior*) were the most widely planted for this purpose. Scattered amongst the coppice are trees which were allowed to reach maturity but because of the openness of the 'canopy' they developed large much-branched crowns. These standard trees are principally oak with some ash and Wych elm. Now, largely due to the different demands for timber, these woods are rapidly disappearing. However, relict stands are still to be found and an example is Hoplands Wood at Claxby-by-Alford which has become the first major woodland reserve of the Lincolnshire Naturalists' Trust.

The typical chalk downlands of the Lincolnshire Wolds have also disappeared with time and many representatives of the original flora are now confined to roadside verges and disused quarries. Many old pits are rich with common plants of the chalk, such as pyramidal orchid (*Anacamptis pyramidalis*), square stemmed St John's wort (*Hypericum tetrapterum*) and Marjoram (*Origanum vulgare*). Some have small patches of open chalk grassland, of thorn scrub and of ashwood. Two good examples of chalk pits are those at Mill Hill near Claxby-by-Alford and Candlesby Hill near Welton-le-Marsh, both of which are Nature Reserves of the Lincolnshire Naturalists' Trust.

THE TRENT VALLEY

The Trent valley, which strikes across the outcrop of the Keuper Marl in a general south-west to north-east direction, is one of the major physical features of the region. The valley, which is about one and a half to two miles wide throughout, has a broad flat floor composed of fine alluvium and gravel, bordered here and there by low gravel terraces. These conditions in relation to the Trent itself and to the water-table beneath the floodplain, afford varying habitats which support interesting assemblies of plants. The lighter sandy soils support whitlow grass (*Erophila verna*), chickweed (*Cerastium arvense*), spotted medick (*Medicago arabica*), and clovers (*Trifolium subterranean* and *T. striatum*) whilst Blinks (*Montia fontana*) and *Trifolium fragiferum* grow in damper hollows. Many of the old Trentside pastures are calcareous and support such species as *Scabiosa columbaria*, meadow-sweet (*Filipendula ulmaria*), prickly rest harrow (*Ononis spinosa*), and *Viola hirta*. The Spring and Autumn Crocus (*Crocus vernus* and *C. nudiflorus*), most famous of the meadow plants, are now nearly extinct though there is still one fine field of Autumn Crocus. The valley contains many areas subject to water-logging, including small pools and ponds of natural origin as well as the man-made ballast and gravel pits. The vegetation of these depends on their age and on local interference so that the many stages of colonisation show a great variety of aquatic species. These include submerged aquatics, milfoils (*Myriophyllum* spp.) floating leaved forms, pondweed (*Potamogeton natans*), reed-swamp, reedmace (*Typha* spp.) and, where the water-table is below ground level, extensive and varied stands of willow (*Salix* spp.). Biologically speaking an excellent example of a gravel pit is that at Attenborough which lies in an area of river wash-land and riparian meadowland adjoining the Trent. The site is of plant ecological interest particularly with reference to the colonisation, establishment and spread of *Typha* spp., reed (*Phragmites communis*) and willow (*Salix* spp.), on the fine sands that have settled out as slurry from the washery effluent. These plants are also found as extensive mature stands. A limited amount of colonisation by these and other plants occurs along the margins of the open water. A number of plants of special interest occur, notably *Salix fragilis* var. *fragilis* (male) and *Salix X Forbyana* (male); the male plant of the latter hybrid was unknown in Britain until discovered by Howitt in 1954 and determined by R. D. Meikle of Kew. Before the pits were developed the existing open water had osier holts at each end, which presumably were the origin of many of the interesting species of *Salix* now to be found in the gravel workings. A rich willow flora comprising species, varieties, and hybrids has been recorded by Howitt. The site has been under observation for some time by various biological organisations, and largely due to their activities a report was prepared for submission to the Nature Conservancy who designated it a Site of Special Scientific Interest (S.S.S.I.), and it will shortly be declared a Local Nature Reserve of the Nottinghamshire Trust for Nature Conservation.

PEAT DEPOSITS

Localised shallow peat deposits are to be found in the Trent valley, though most of them have been drained and used for agricultural land for some time past. For a good example of a relatively undamaged peat area we must go to the Blithe valley at Chartley Moss, near Uttoxeter. The major part of this Moss is a large quaking mire or 'Schwingmoor', in which much of the present surface vegetation grows on a floating raft of peat. The Moss is roughly triangular with each side about half a mile long and occupying a basin at least 45 feet deep in the glacial drift. The basin is partially lined by a detritus mud comprising wood and plant remains in an amorphous matrix. Above this is a large reservoir of water up to ten metres deep and finally an uppermost layer of oliogotrophic *Sphagnum* peat which is actively forming at the present time. The raft supports a mosaic of several plant communities and a series of pools of open water. The pools may be characterised by the vegetation at their margins. The commonest type of pool is that with a marginal, actively growing, *Sphagnum* carpet (principally *S. recurvum*) with *Eriophorum angustifolium* which appears to be encroaching on the open water; this type of pool tends to be associated with the area of *Sphagnum* lawn. A unique type is one that appears to have originated by the sinking of an area supporting *Eriophorum vaginatum* and *Pinus*, possibly as a result of the increasing weight of the raft caused by the pines. Locally at the margins of this pool type, *Sphagnum recurvum* is establishing itself and beginning to extend into the open water. Another unique pool type has sharp, steep sides to the open water bounded by clumps of *Molinia caerulea* and *Juncus communis*; here again localised colonies of *Sphagnum recurvum* are being established. In many ways the most interesting community is itself a mosaic of smaller ones. The general 'background' of the complex is a more or less level lawn of *Sphagnum recurvum* with individual plants of the following species scattered throughout in abundance: *Eriophorum angustifolium*, *Erica tetralix*, cranberry (*Vaccinium oxycoccus*) and sundew (*Drosera rotundifolia*), and only occasionally *Eriophorum vaginatum*, *Calluna vulgaris*, crowberry (*Empetrum nigrum*) and *Andromeda polifolia*. Locally the level nature of the *Sphagnum recurvum* lawn is broken by hummocks of *S. papillosum* frequently accompanied by *S. acutifolium*, *S. magellanicum* and *Aulacomnium palustre*. Like the lawn, these hummocks support *Vaccinium oxycoccus*, *Erica tetralix* and *Andromeda* though these species tend to be more vigorous

K

in this situation. The lawn has a scattering of young pine, the density decreasing with increasing wetness of the lawn. Elsewhere pine is found forming localised stands of adult trees, the most mature stands having a thick carpet of needle-litter covering the ground, which is superficially dry, though the water-table is not far below the surface.

In more open, younger and less well-developed stands the ground flora may include occasional plants of bilberry (*Vaccinium myrtillus*), *Empetrum nigrum* and *Dicranum scoparium*. Where the pine stands are adjacent to *Sphagnum*-dominated areas there is evidence of their active invasion by *S. recurvum* again possibly due to the sinking of the raft brought about by the increasing weight of the trees. These areas may in fact give rise to the pool type with submerged pines, already described. One other very localised community remains to be mentioned. This lies between the sloping margin and the centre of the Moss. It has an open canopy of tall alder (*Alnus glutinosa*) with a few birch and *Sorbus aucuparia* and with a ground flora of plants characterising eutrophic conditions, e.g. *Calamagrostis canescens*, *Carex paniculata*, and *Cladium mariscus*. The substrate has a thin superficial layer of eutrophic peat overlying oligotrophic peat. The eutrophic peat-water has a pH of 6·4 compared with a range of from pH 3·82 to 4·15 for the various *S. recurvum* dominated sites and pH 3·0 and pH 3·58 for the pine needle litter and its underlying *Sphagnum* peat respectively. The origin and the pathway of the base-rich water are difficult to determine since the eutrophic area is more than three feet above the level of the marginal lagg stream and some 200 yards distant. The Moss has been visited by botanists since the middle of last century though the early records relate primarily to the flora. Plants which have been recorded in the past and which are surprisingly no longer present include notably *Drosera intermedia*, bog asphodel (*Narthecium ossifragum*) and the beak sedge (*Rhynchospora alba*). More recent investigations by K. Goodway and M. C. Pearson, however, have been concerned with the history and development of the peat deposit and the ecology of the present surface vegetation. Chartley Moss is now a National Nature Reserve under The Nature Conservancy; and permission is required to visit the site.

FORESTRY COMMISSION WOODLANDS

Whilst this account is primarily concerned with natural vegetation it is felt that some reference should be made to the considerable stands of managed woodlands which occur within the region. What follows is a brief and generalised sketch of the Forestry Commission Woodlands on information kindly supplied by the Commission's District Officers.

In the Nottinghamshire district, which includes the adjoining parts of the West Riding of Yorkshire and north-east Derbyshire, plantations are fairly widely distributed. Beech, Sycamore and Ash are found mainly in the west on the Magnesian Limestone. Oak is found principally in the east and south-east on the Keuper Marl. At Cotgrave, south-east of Nottingham, Sycamore and Ash are found also, and these, together with Oak, form a considerable proportion of the area planted, which includes Scots and Corsican Pine, Norway Spruce and Western Red Cedar. In the central part of the district, on the Bunter Sandstone, the major species is Corsican Pine, with Scots Pine on sites liable to frost where it appears in pure stands and in mixed stands with Corsican Pine. Few other conifers are being planted now. Incidental species such as Larches and Spruces, mostly of pre-war origin, do not tolerate the low humidity coupled with freely drained soils. Such broad-leaved species as there are have been used solely for protection, i.e. fire belts, and include a variety of species, the most successful of which have been Birch with Beech and Sweet Chestnut, and Oak; Red Oak and Sycamore too have been used, but with very limited success.

In south Derbyshire near Repton are Foremark Woods which are mainly young plantations established since 1954 of Scots Pine, of Corsican Pine, of Larch and Beech mixture, of Beech and Scots Pine mixture, of Oak and Scots Pine mixture, and of other conifers including Norway Spruce and Western Hemlock. In addition there is some Birch and Sycamore coppice which is being singled out to form false high forest. The remainder of Foremark Woods comprise areas of unproductive Birch crops naturally regenerated over previously felled areas, with an admixture here and there of Sycamore and Ash coppice.

Further afield in north and east Lincolnshire, plantations are scattered and rather inconspicuous and are usually located on soils of low agricultural value such as poor sands and unyielding clays. In the north the Commission's woodlands are mainly on blown sand as at Laughton where there are dunes up to 30 feet high and at Willingham where the ground is level. The chief species planted are Scots and Corsican Pine, both of which have done well. Other species are Norway Spruce, Larch, Oak, Beech, Birch, Poplar and Alder but the hardwoods represent only a small proportion of the total. Further south, small, irregular and scattered woods between Bardney and Horncastle are mainly on boulder clay. There is a variety of soils and drainage can be troublesome. Late spring frosts in May and June may hold new plantations in check for some years. The planting of hardwoods has been widespread and they have proved successful. Pines and Spruce are the most abundant conifers. Planting of mixtures of both conifers and hardwoods is extensive. The species used are Scots and Corsican Pine, Oak, Ash, Poplar, Douglas Fir, Silver Fir, Lawson's Cypress, Western Red Cedar (*Thuja plicata*), Beech, Norway Spruce, Red Oak, Larch and Lime. Herbaceous flora is strong so that in many places it is difficult to get the trees through the weeding stage.

In the northern part of central Lincolnshire the Commission's woodlands occur mainly on sands, gravels and clays overlying the Lower Lias. On the sands and gravels Pines are the chief trees planted, Corsican Pine on well-drained sites and Scots Pine in wetter places where frost occurs. A number of other species have been tried on a limited scale, including Western Hemlock (*Tsuga heterophylla*), Lawson Cypress (*Chamaecyparis laswoniana*), Douglas Fir (*Pseudotsuga taxifolia*), Western Red Cedar

(*Thuja plicata*) and Grand Fir (*Abies grandis*). With the exception of Western Hemlock and, to a lesser extent, Grand Fir, these have not proved successful and their use has been discontinued. Cover is required for the two exceptions which are largely used to break the uniformity of the Pines. On the clays pure Norway Spruce, and Oak and Norway Spruce mixtures have mainly been grown, but Beech, Western Hemlock and Western Red Cedar, have also been successful on a limited scale. Further south the scattered blocks of woodland are mainly on clays. On cleared fertile sites, pure Norway Spruce, and Oak and Norway Spruce mixtures have been planted, while on poorer sites there are pure stands of Corsican Pine and Scots Pine. Where cover was present, usually as birch scrub, this has enabled underplanting with mixtures of various species of shade bearers, including Beech, Douglas Fir, Western Hemlock, Grand Fir and Western Red Cedar. Again in south Kesteven, there is an appreciable amount of Oak in pure stands, which is growing well. On the other hand a large wood planted before the war with European Larch and Ash both pure and in mixed stands, has proved to be unsatisfactory, and is now being replanted with the species mentioned above. There are several herds of fallow deer in the area and the increasing deer population may lead to difficulties in tree establishment, while the clay soils provide constant and expensive drainage problems. In both the Lindsey and Kesteven parts of Lincolnshire, the County Naturalist Trust and the Naturalist Union are interested in the wild life of several woodland areas which have been set aside for conservation purposes.

SELECTED REFERENCES

Balme, O. E. Edaphic and Vegetational Zoning on the Carboniferous Limestone of the Derbyshire dales. *Journal of Ecology* Vol. 41 (1953) pp. 331–344.

Edwards, K. C. *Nottinghamshire, The Land of Britain*. Part 60 (1944) pp. 420–439, 449–460, 496–503.

Edwards, K. C. *The Peak District* (London, 1963).

Grime, J. P. An Ecological Investigation at the junction between two plant communities in Coombsdale on the Derbyshire Limestone. *Journal of Ecology* Vol. 51 (1963) pp. 391–402.

Hopkinson, J. W. Studies of the Vegetation of Nottinghamshire. I—The Ecology of the Bunter Sandstone. *Journal of Ecology* Vol. 15 (1927) pp. 130–171.

Howitt, R. C. L. and B. M. *A Flora of Nottinghamshire* (published privately, 1963).

Lousley, J. E. *Wild Flowers of Chalk and Limestone* (London, 1950) pp. 155–167.

Pigott, C. D. Soil Formation and Development on the Carboniferous Limestone of Derbyshire. I—Parent Material. *Journal of Ecology* Vol. 50 (1962) pp. 145–156.

Ratcliffe, D. Adaptation to habitat in a group of annual plants. *Journal of Ecology* Vol. 49 (1961) pp. 187–203.

Scurfield, G. The Ashwoods of the Derbyshire Carboniferous Limestone, Monksdale. *Journal of Ecology* Vol. 47 (1959) pp. 357–369.

VI

FAUNA

WHILE the late Professor J. W. Carr worked with such enthusiasm and so thoroughly to obtain a list of the invertebrate animals of the county of Nottinghamshire and information on their biology, the vertebrate animals did not receive the same attention from local naturalists. Perhaps no one felt competent enough at the time to deal with the vertebrates in the way Professor Carr dealt with the invertebrates, as exemplified by his volumes '*The Invertebrate Fauna of Nottinghamshire*', 1916, and the '*Supplement*', 1935. Carr was Professor of Biology in the former University College of Nottingham and for a time Curator of the Nottingham Natural History Museum. More recently, the Trent Valley Bird Watchers and the Nottingham and Nottinghamshire Field Club have done much to provide up-to-date details on the bird life of the county and on the other vertebrates in general.

VERTEBRATES

MAMMALS

There is no outstanding feature about the mammals of Nottinghamshire that is not shared with other parts of the country. Nevertheless, mammals that do occur or are suspected of being present, pose many problems and will repay closer study and investigation. Of the insectivorous mammals the Hedgehog, Common Shrew and Mole are common and the Water Shrew fairly common and widely distributed, though it was not common in 1900. The Pygmy Shrew has been listed as recorded for the county in 1937 and to be fairly common in 1964.

Much work on the bats has still to be done. It is known that the Noctule, Pipistrelle and Long-eared Bat are all common. The Noctule and Pipistrelle occur in Wollaton Park, and the Long-eared is present at Bleasby. A single specimen of the Lesser Horseshoe Bat was picked up at Edwinstowe but not another individual has been seen. The Greater Horseshoe Bat is mentioned because of an unconfirmed claim for inclusion in the county list and there is only a single record for Natterer's Bat. The Whiskered Bat flies during the daytime over the grounds of Nottingham University.

Rabbit and Brown Hare are common. The number of rabbits increases in the spring when they breed in shallow holes, but as soon as they go into deeper burrows the rabbit flea multiplies, myxomatosis spreads rapidly, and the rabbits are greatly reduced in numbers. The Brown Hare seems to be increasing in numbers, perhaps because there are fewer rabbits now than formerly. Occasionally, a hare streaks across Wollaton Park, sits erect momentarily on a roadway and then continues rapidly across the open parkland for safe cover.

House Mouse, Long-tailed Field Mouse, Bank Vole, Water Vole and Short-tailed Field Vole are common rodents and the Brown Rat is very common and a pest, especially in the older parts of towns. Fortunately, the Black Rat is unrecorded. The Dormouse and Harvest Mouse were rare in 1900 and are probably now non-existent in the county, though the discovery in Leicestershire in recent times of the Dormouse revives hopes for its re-appearance. The Grey Squirrel is widely spread and its numbers are not diminished for long by the controlling action taken by land-owners. In 1900 it had not occurred in Nottinghamshire. The Red Squirrel becomes scarce wherever the Grey establishes itself and, though the Red was common as late as 1937, it is regarded by some as extinct in the county; at best it is very rare.

Carnivorous mammals, Fox, Badger, Stoat and Weasel, are common. The Fox and the Badger are increasing in numbers, the former is a denizen of Wollaton Park and the latter often a casualty on the road to remind the surprised casual observer of its existence and nearness. The Otter seems to be uncommon in Nottinghamshire. Sixty years ago it was plentiful. Polecat and Pine Marten are now extinct in the region, they were rare and probably extinct as long ago as 1893.

Red Deer and Fallow Deer are confined to parklands on various estates and herds of both kinds are at Wollaton Park, Nottingham.

The Porpoise enters the tidal waters of the river Trent and occasionally comes up as far as Newark. At the beginning of the century this was stated to be a frequent occurrence.

BIRDS

For an inland county about 50 miles long and up to 24 miles broad Nottinghamshire can present a substantial list of birds and probably now shows a greater diversity of bird life than at any previous period in its history. The differing types of habitat, such as man-made gardens, farms, sewage farms, reservoirs, lakes and gravel pits, not forgetting plantations and buildings, have added variety to the natural scene.

To the north-east of the county lie the flat Carrlands and from there the old Sherwood Forest sweeps down in a great ridge of sand and gravel, covered with an ancient flora, with open forest, grasses, heathers, bracken, oak, fir, birch and alder in the moister valley bottoms. In the northern part of this heathy sandbelt are the Dukeries, the great estates of Clumber, Rufford, Thoresby and Welbeck, all with big lakes. Still in the sandbelt, but to the south of these estates, is Mansfield Reservoir, now a public park. The Trent valley is an area of alluvial flats, within which lie the large Nottingham sewage farm and numerous gravel pits. The remaining part of the county is mostly a mixture of urban areas and villages, arable and pasture land, and public and private gardens, all of which have their quota of birds. A complete systematic list is not given in this abbreviated survey; some of the commonest, as, for instance, the House-Sparrow, as well as some of the rarest, are omitted.

Colymbiformes

The Black-throated, Great Northern and Red-throated Divers are rare visitors to the Trent valley.

Podicipidiformes

Extraction of gravel in the county, which gained momentum during the war, has led to the formation of new areas of water with a consequent effect on animal and vegetable life. The big population increase in the Great Crested Grebe coincided with the creation of these new waters upon which a large proportion of the birds breed. A count of 113 individuals on 10 waters in March 1962 included 58 at Attenborough gravel pits in a pre-nesting gathering. Many birds remain throughout the winter most years. Of the four other grebes on the British list the Little Grebe is a fairly common resident, whilst the Red-necked, Slavonian and Black-necked Grebes are rare winter visitors.

Procellariiformes

Leach's Storm Petrel and the Manx Shearwater have been gale-swept into Nottinghamshire from out at sea on the occasion of their rare appearances.

Pelecaniformes

The Gannet and Shag are rare migrants; three of the former were seen together in April 1962 in the Trent valley moving eastwards, presumably to the North Sea. During the spring and autumn months the Cormorant is a scarce vagrant on the river Trent.

Ardeiformes

At the beginning of the century the Heron was fairly numerous wherever there was water; 40 to 50 pairs nesting at just one heronry at Stoke, near Newark. From being a common resident the numbers have greatly decreased. In the 10-year period between 1950 and 1960 the 95 pairs breeding were reduced to about 55 pairs in 1960; now there are approximately 16 pairs only. The reduction has been attributed to the disturbances of heronries by man and the severe winters of 1946–47 and 1962–63. Another contributory factor was probably the use in recent years of farm pesticides and poisonous dressings that were washed by rain into streams and so to aquatic plants and animals, including fish, and thence to herons, the persistent poisons causing infertility, if not death. Affected fish have been reported fairly often in Nottinghamshire. The Bittern is a rare winter visitor most years.

Anseriformes

Apart from the Trent and its tributaries and the water-filled gravel pits, the lakes on the great estates of Clumber, Rufford, Thoresby and Welbeck in the northern half of the county, Mansfield reservoir, the Nottingham sewage farm and smaller lakes like that at Wollaton in the southern area, are the scenes of ever-fluctuating numbers of wildfowl and of species, often swollen in years of severe weather, like 1962–63, by the early autumnal movement of birds out of western Europe.

Trent Valley Bird Watchers make an annual winter count of wildfowl within their territory and, to give an indication of the picture that emerges, the totals for six species of duck on 25 waters for 1962–63 are given below:

Table XXVI   Selected count of wildfowl in the Trent Valley

Species	September	October	November	December	January	February	March
Mallard ..	2,165	2,218	2,877	3,146	2,488	1,774	1,436
Teal ..	501	388	595	948	131	234	336
Wigeon ..	—	8	92	271	31	254	184
Shoveler ..	4	4	1	26	1	6	2
Pochard ..	56	119	103	166	120	199	269
Tufted ..	354	242	226	355	265	695	406

These figures are above the average maximum in December for Mallard and the highest for five years for Teal.

Gadwall, Scaup, Golden-eye and Smew are scarce winter visitors, though Smew occasionally appear in large numbers, and the Long-tailed Duck and Red-breasted Merganser are rare winter visitors. Upwards of 20 Pintail are usually noted each winter. From November to March the Goosander frequents the Dukeries, as many as 33 being observed during the period. Cold spells cause a few to move to the river Trent.

In the summer months Teal become scarce but a few pairs breed most years in the north of the Dukeries. The Shoveler also breeds, but in falling numbers, the estimate being only 10 pairs in 1960 and they could be either residents or summer visitors. Rare though the Pochard is in summer it breeds most years and is suspected of breeding on two new sites in the south of the county, at Attenborough and Holme Pierrepont. The Garganey, a rare summer visitor, was first proved to breed in the county in 1945. It is of interest that Nottinghamshire was the first English county in which the Tufted Duck bred, but probably earlier than 1849, the date stated. It is still an uncommon resident, whose numbers are augmented in autumn and winter by the influx of birds from the continent.

Since the comparatively recent elucidation of the migration routes of the Sheld-Duck from the Lancashire and Cheshire coasts to the moulting grounds in the

Heligoland Bight, this shore and estuarine bird has taken to nesting regularly in eastern parts of the county. Formerly, it was a scarce passage migrant, but as one of the migration routes from the Mersey valley leads to The Wash, it is not unreasonable to suppose that suitable breeding sites were discovered by the Sheld-Duck, especially as it has bred, in small numbers, inland in Lincolnshire at Scotland Common and Twigmoor since the 1890's. It also breeds in the coastal sand dunes of Lincolnshire and, furthermore, is said to be on the increase.

Grey Geese cross the county in the winter months, providing fine flight-views that far exceed the actual identification ground records on which the status of each species is based. The Grey Lag is a scarce and irregular visitor, the White-fronted rare, Brent Goose a rare vagrant, and the Pink-footed Goose a transient winter visitor, seen in flocks of some hundreds in most years. Locally fairly common as a resident is the introduced Canada Goose, which has spread considerably since the beginning of the century. Now, a herd of 100 to 200 will dwell on one lake in the winter before dispersing in the spring to various waters.

Apart from the common resident Mute Swan, and the scarce winter visitor, the Whooper Swan, Bewick's Swan has attracted attention by the change in its wintering habits. Since 1954 it has become a regular visitor when large numbers began to come to Britain on passage to the west in the late autumn on their way to wintering quarters in Ireland, and again in early spring as passage migrants moving eastwards. A herd of 34 to 38 were reported from the 3rd February to the 18th March 1962 at Besthorpe, and about 65 on the 24th March in the same year at Burton Meadows.

Falconiformes

Harriers make rare appearances and the Peregrine Falcon and Merlin are rare winter and passage migrants. The Osprey is a rare passage migrant, yet at the end of last century it used to be shot by gamekeepers over the lake in Wollaton Park.

A rare vagrant and winter visitor, the Buzzard became a resident for three years from 1955 to 1957. There was no definite proof of it breeding, however. Widespread depletion of the rabbit stock through myxomatosis caused the Buzzard to extend its range in the search for an adequate food supply. Probably the bird spread from Wales, where it had become quite common in parts. Now it has almost returned to its former status, perhaps because rabbits are more plentiful and perhaps because the guns of game preservers took their toll.

The Sparrow Hawk is a scarce resident, just managing to maintain itself as a breeding species. There is one record of it nesting in Wollaton in 1962. On the other hand, the Kestrel is a fairly common resident nesting species, though it suffered a set-back in the years 1959 to 1961 when it became rare as a breeding species. The tremendous decrease in numbers was linked with the extensive use of new toxic seed dressings. In the flat open Lincolnshire countryside the visual change was most striking, particularly in the late summer, for, whereas Kestrels perched on telephone wires was a characteristic sight before 1959, their sudden absence was no less arresting. The species is gradually recovering following the voluntary ban on the use of poisonous seed dressings. Once more the Kestrel is seen hovering over parks in Nottingham and a single falcon has frequented the tower of St. Mary's Church, in the city centre.

Galliformes

Black Grouse vanished from the Forest years ago and the Red Grouse is just a rare vagrant. The attractive Red-legged Partridge is a fairly common resident breeder that seems to be more common in the north than in the south of the county. Its habit of running, especially when crossing roads, brings a crop of deaths these days from the wheels of passing vehicles. Our smallest, and only, migratory game bird, the Quail, is an irregular rare summer visitor. Hot, dry summers favour this bird, and in 1947 five pairs nested.

Ralliformes

The Water-Rail is an uncommon winter visitor, but is possibly more common than imagined for, being extremely shy and retiring, it hides in dense aquatic vegetation, particularly in ditches, from which, when flushed, the bird is often mistaken for a rodent, and therefore pursued, as it runs in a darting manner for fresh cover. The Spotted Crake is no longer seen in the numbers observed 90 years ago when a local taxidermist handled 29 specimens in one year. It has become a rare passage migrant. In 1914 the Corncrake was already dwindling in numbers and this was the pattern in the rest of the country. Ten to 15 pairs would populate the grass fields of a single parish and the bird's rasping call was synonymous with a hot summer day. There has been no breeding recorded for the last 25 years and it has become an irregular rare summer visitor and passage migrant. Moorhen and Coot are common residents, breeding on almost all waters, and in cold weather gathering into large parties on some waters.

Charadriiformes

Of the 40 waders on the Nottinghamshire check-list four are recent additions: the Broad-billed Sandpiper from Europe in 1961, and, from North America, Wilson's Phalarope (1961), the Pectoral Sandpiper and Solitary Sandpiper, both in 1962, though there was a previous record for the Pectoral Sandpiper in 1948. Breeding species are the Redshank in at least nine localities, Woodcock, Curlew in six districts, and the Lapwing. There is considerable movement of Lapwings in the Trent valley. At the summer build-up and at the onset of severe weather numbers in the region of 10,000 are involved.

The spread, from south–east Europe, of the Little Ringed Plover as a breeding species in England reached Nottinghamshire in 1956 and nesting sites near gravel pits are being chosen, though not exclusively.

The successful breeding of the Black-winged Stilt at the Nottingham sewage farm in 1945 was a memorable event. Two pairs reared two and one young respectively and made a splendid sight as the flock of seven flew over the breeding ground. This was the first and only breeding record for the British Isles. Modernisation of the sewage farm and the changes it has brought to the habitat is reacting on the bird life and must have influenced the departure of this lovely wader. Hosts of waders appear twice-yearly as migrants at the sewage farm and along the Trent valley; others arrive as casuals. They include the Oystercatcher, Ringed Plover, Golden Plover, Snipe, Curlew-Sandpiper, Black-tailed and Bar-tailed Godwits, Little Stint, Dunlin, Wood Sandpiper, Knot, Grey Plover, Turnstone and Sanderling. The Avocet and Temminck's Stint are rare passage migrants, whilst the Ruff may produce a flock of 20 to 30 towards the end of December time.

Nine species of gulls have been recorded. No doubt the river Trent has been the main attraction, because, for an inland county, this is a substantial proportion of the 15 species on the British list. The Great Black-backed Gull is present every month of the year, usually under five birds, but mounting to 20 or more in the winter. Lesser Black-backed Gulls are passage migrants in the Trent valley, the spring movement being less spectacular than the autumn movement when the number of birds can increase from 60 in August to 200 in November. Larger numbers are sometimes noted and the spring and autumn passages tend to merge.

Another illustration of the fact that the county status of many species of birds is not fixed, but subject to change, is provided by the Lesser Black-backed Gull. In 1945 it attempted to breed, then again in 1960, but the nests were robbed. However, successful breeding along the Trent finally took place in 1963 and 1964. Both the Herring Gull and Common Gull are winter visitors and passage migrants, the former being rare in the summer. The Black-headed Gull nests at two places in the Trent valley and at two places in north Nottinghamshire. The arrival of passage migrants and winter visitors gives totals in the regions of 1,000 to 6,000. A roost at Netherfield one December was estimated at 2,500.

The Common Tern is the most noteworthy of the eight species of terns recorded for, from being a passage migrant and rare summer visitor, it began to breed in the Trent valley in 1945 and at least 10 pairs have bred regularly since, forming one of the few inland breeding colonies in England. The birds fish the river Trent. Regular spring and autumn migrations of the Black Tern occasionally bring rushes of over 100 birds, but numbers vary from year to year.

Columbiformes

The Wood Pigeon is a common, and Stock Dove a fairly common, resident nesting species. Large numbers of Wood Pigeon were found dead in 1960 and 1961 when toxic seed dressings were in use and the paucity of observations on the Stock Dove for 1962 showed that this Dove, too, suffered from the poisonous dressings. A fairly common summer visitor, the Turtle Dove, arrives in May, becomes widely distributed and breeds wherever it takes up residence for the summer. It is also a passage migrant, parties of up to 30 birds being noted. Another, and recent, colonist from the south–east of Europe is the Collared Dove (the other is the Little Ringed Plover). It has spread rapidly since breeding in Nottinghamshire was first proved in 1959 and is now well-established as a resident throughout the year.

Strigiformes

Throughout the area the Tawny Owl is the commonest owl. The Barn Owl and Little Owl are fairly common. All three occur within the Nottingham city boundary, the Tawny at times roosting during the daytime in trees in gardens, from which it disgorges pellets, and the Barn Owl occasionally finds its way into buildings to the consternation of the human occupants. The Long-eared Owl is a scarce resident, but very local, and still breeds on the southern edge of the Carrlands in the north of the county. The Short-eared Owl is a winter visitor and passage migrant that arrives in October, usually singly, and stays as late as April at stations near the Nottingham sewage farm on the Trent as well as on open land further north.

Caprimulgiformes

The Nightjar used to be more numerous in the Forest than it is now, the planting of conifers on its heathland habitat being one factor causing the decrease. As an uncommon summer visitor, it arrives in May at the localised breeding ground at Newstead and in east Nottinghamshire, and also in the north Dukeries, where it was known to have had second broods in 1962. Mention should be made of the only occurrence of the Egyptian Nightjar in this country. One bird, a straggler, was shot in June 1883 in Thieves Wood, near Mansfield, and the circumstances and particulars are recounted by J. Whitaker in his book '*Notes on the Birds of Nottinghamshire*'.

Apodiformes

The Swift is a common summer visitor. Arriving in Nottingham in late April, the return passage begins in July and is over by September. There is heavy passage of the birds in both spring and autumn. In early May 1962, 300 were at Awsworth on the 6th and 800 at Holme Pierrepont on the 9th; at Misson, 200 were proceeding to the south on the 11th August.

Coraciiformes

A well-distributed resident, the Kingfisher averaged a pair for each mile of the river Trent between Beeston and Newark, urban stretches excepted, in 1944. It occurs on unpolluted streams and is occasionally seen near the lake in Wollaton Park.

Piciformes

The three kinds of Woodpecker are resident nesting species and all occur within the Nottingham city boundary. The Great Spotted Woodpecker is the commonest and the rapid hammering sounds as it drills dead branches at the top of trees in Wollaton Park puzzle many an uninitiated stroller who peers, often in vain, for the cause of the noise. The Lesser Spotted Woodpecker is more local and more retiring than the last. It, too, inhabits Wollaton Park, as well as suitable woods throughout the county. Indications are that the Green Woodpecker is tending to increase in numbers. Superficially, it has a parrakeet-like appearance when standing on the ground, as it does when purposefully picking ants from the lawns in Wollaton Park. The Wryneck is a rare passage migrant suspected of breeding in 1944, 1954 and 1955. A young bird seen at Farndon on the 17th July 1944 lent weight to this surmise.

Passeriformes

Ninety species of these are on the county list. As urban development extends the Skylark retreats, though it is still a common resident species, unlike the Wood Lark that has become scarce as the open forest land in the centre of the county, which supports an isolated colony of the larks, gets smaller by the encroachments of afforestation. Swallows, House Martins and Sand Martins are common summer visitors and find the water-filled gravel pits, that have come into existence during and after the war with the expansion of the gravel industry, a varied habitat useful as a feeding and rest area while moving north–east in the spring and south–west in the autumn.

The Carrion Crow, Jackdaw and Jay are common residents, even within the city boundary, and the same is true of the Magpie, which has increased considerably in numbers, invading suburban gardens and parks during the last 12 years, where previously it was absent. A census of the Rook and rookeries in 1962 has shown that there has been a decrease in Nottinghamshire from 17,028 nests in 1958 to 10,609 nests in 1962. It is possible that the increased use of toxic seed dressings was the cause, the poisons directly and indirectly killing a number of the birds. The smaller of the two rookeries in Wollaton Park disappeared during this period. One of the winter roosts of the Rook is in this Park and approximately 1,000 birds congregate there each evening as dusk descends, not, however, without aerial acrobatics and vocal accompaniment. Since 1940 the Hooded Crow has become a rare winter visitor; formerly it was not uncommon, as can be judged by the fact that nearly 300 were shot on one estate in 1906.

The Great, Blue, Coal, Marsh, Willow and Long-tailed Tits are all residents and, with the exception of the Willow Tit, are common, though Wilford is a new nesting area for the last-named species. Willow Tits show a preference for damp woodlands and old elder trees, whereas the Marsh Tit is equally at home in wet or dry situations. Coal Tits and Tree Creepers have increased in the stands of conifers planted by the Forestry Commission because of the close-setting of the maturing trees and the lack of undergrowth.

An increase in numbers and extension of the range of the Nuthatch seems to be taking place. In Wollaton Park, in spite of the felling of trees in which it nested annually, it maintains its numbers, and its presence is frequently proclaimed by its sweet song.

Blackbird, Mistle Thrush and Song Thrush are common breeding birds, even in the city, and the Redwing and Fieldfare visit gardens and parks as well as the surrounding countryside, in varying numbers during the winter.

The Wheatear ceased to nest after 1948. Its territory was rough ground and rabbit burrows. However, it is a fairly common passage migrant. The Bunter Sandstone terrain suits the Redstart for breeding purposes. Formerly the bird was common in the thick growths on the boles of lime trees in Wollaton Park until trimming and pruning destroyed the nesting sites. Twelve records were made between 1944 and 1960 of the Black Redstart as a migrant in Nottinghamshire. In 1958 it was proved that the Black Redstart had bred. Other instances of it having bred may possibly have been overlooked, for whereas it colonised derelict bomb sites in London, in Nottingham it has occupied the slum clearance areas. Stonechats bred occasionally and the Whinchat fairly commonly, though only in certain localities.

A few nestings of the Nightingale occur each year, but the species is scarce and thinly distributed as a summer visitor in a region that must be on the edge of its northern range. Singing males are heard at widely separated places, sometimes in new localities such as Finningley and Misson in May 1962.

The Grasshopper Warbler is a local breeder and its summer haunts include Eakring, Ossington, Cotgrave Forest, Clumber and Oxton. Sedge and Reed Warblers are finding the mud of beaches and vegetation of the newly-created gravel pits, as well as the islands within them, ideal additional breeding sites. *Phragmites* is particularly welcome to the Reed Warbler. Blackcap, Garden Warbler, Whitethroat and Lesser Whitethroat occur and, with the exception of the latter, can be heard singing in gardens. Willow Warbler and Chiffchaff are also common, but the Wood Warbler is a scarce passage migrant.

The diminutive Goldcrest is a common resident very much at home amongst coniferous trees. Outside the breeding season it is more widely distributed and enters gardens in the city where young spruce grow, and in consequence often falls prey to marauding cats.

The Spotted Flycatcher is fairly common generally as a summer visitor. Some years it is less in evidence than others. Formerly a common species in Wollaton Park it now makes irregular appearances and then in smaller numbers. The Meadow Pipit is a common resident, the Tree Pipit a common summer visitor and the Rock and Water Pipits are rare passage migrants.

A wagtail that has lost many of its breeding places in west Nottingham as a result of house-building is the Yellow Wagtail, which, as a summer visitor, delighted the eye as it strutted about gardens on foraging expeditions for insects. It is common locally elsewhere. The Pied Wagtail is a common resident that also breeds within the city boundary, while the Grey Wagtail is an uncommon winter visitor that turns up at the Nottingham sewage farm, in the south of the county, at Worksop in the north, and at intermediate localities.

Most winters the Waxwing reaches Nottinghamshire. During invasion years this northern European bird appears in many places. In 1965 it was seen in many districts of Nottingham and in Mansfield.

The Great Grey Shrike is a rare winter visitor and the Red-backed Shrike a rare passage migrant. The latter was formerly a summer visitor and scattered pairs nested at Blidworth and Southwell. The species is on the decline in Britain and last bred in Nottinghamshire in 1947.

The Starling is abundant, the Hawfinch scarce as a resident and local on the Colwick Hills and Burton Joyce; the Greenfinch, Goldfinch and Linnet are common. The Goldfinch has increased during the last 25 years and in small groups visits gardens in the city on seed-eating forays in the autumn. Flocks of up to 200 Siskin have been known to arrive in the winter and small flocks have visited the alder trees at Felley. The Twite is a rare irregular winter visitor and the Lesser Redpoll a scarce resident and uncommon winter visitor. It bred at Colwick, Worksop and Inkersall until 1950. No breeding was noted after that until 1962, when it bred again at Inkersall.

Bullfinches have increased enormously since 1950. The increase continues, with reports from Retford, Lowdham, Goverton and Teversall, of rising numbers of birds being seen. The Crossbill is a scarce winter visitor which is reputed to have bred in the Forestry Commission's plantations of conifers, but no positive proof is forth-coming. Chaffinch, Yellow Hammer, Corn Bunting, Reed Bunting and Tree Sparrow are common residents, and the Brambling is an uncommon winter visitor which occasionally is seen in flocks of up to 300 birds.

REPTILES

The Slow-worm was at one time frequently encountered in Sherwood Forest, now it is very rare. In suitable habitats the Common or Viviparous Lizard is widely distributed. The Ringed or Grass Snake regularly turns up in gardens and allotments. The Adder or Viper has been rare and local for many years and its presence is reported on only a few occasions. Attenborough is one of its haunts.

AMPHIBIANS

The three kinds of newt, the Crested, Smooth and Palmate are not uncommon in suitable areas. The Common Toad and Frog are plentiful and widespread throughout the countryside and in townships. The Toad is probably more often found in gardens than is the Frog. The Natterjack Toad does not occur in the region.

INVERTEBRATES

The standard work on the invertebrate fauna of Nottinghamshire is that produced by Professor J. W. Carr in 1916, to which a supplement was added in 1935. This is a comprehensive work covering practically all the major groups, the most notable exception being the Protozoa. There has been no subsequent work as complete as this. However, certain groups have been dealt with since then, usually in the form of a national survey, from which the Nottinghamshire records can be extracted, and isolated new records appear at intervals. If these later records are compared with Carr's list it will be seen that the latter was remarkably complete, the number of additional species recorded since then being relatively few.

Some examples are given below. Fairly complete recent records of the Hemiptera-Heteroptera are available: charts showing the county distribution of this group were published in 1955 in the *Entomologists Monthly Magazine*. These list a total of 207 species for Nottinghamshire, of which only eight are new records and one of these appears to be new to Britain: *Stygnocoris fuligineus* (Geoffroy in Fourcroy), *Lygus rugilipennis* new to Britain, *Plea leachi* MacGregor and Kirkaldy, *Notonecta viridis* Delcourt, *Corixa concinna* (Fieber), *Corixa limitata* (Fieber), *Corixa dentipes* (Thompson), *Micronecta scholtzi* (Fieber). On the other hand nine species recorded in the earlier lists are absent from the 1955 list: *Piesma maculata* (Castelnau), *Velia currens* (Fabricius), *Calocoris norvegicus* (Gmelin in L.), *Lygus pratensis* (L.), *Lygus campestris* (L.), *Orthotylus ochrotrichus* Fieber, *Gastrodes grossipes* (Degeer), *Cymatia bonsdorfi* (Sahlberg). As nearly all of these are common species, their absence would suggest shortage of collectors rather than extinction in the area.

Among the Homoptera, a comprehensive list of Aphids, with their host plants, for certain east Midland counties including Nottinghamshire, appears in the *North–Western Naturalist*, Volume 2 (new series) for 1954. These were prepared as a result of a joint investigation by the School of Agriculture, Sutton Bonington, and the National Agricultural Advisory Service, Shardlow, Derbyshire. Some 60 to 70 species are listed as against just under 50 in Carr's list.

Of about 30 common species of Butterfly recorded by Carr, the following appear to have maintained themselves satisfactorily over the years where suitable sites have remained undisturbed: Wall Brown (*Dira megaera* L.), Small Meadow Brown (*Maniola tithonus* L.), Meadow Brown (*M. jurtina* L.), Small Heath (*Coenonympha pamphila* L.), Ringlet (*Aphantopus hyperanthus* L.), Green Hairstreak (*Callophrys rubi* L.), Large White (*Pieris brassicae* L.), Small White (*P. rapae* L.), Green-veined White (*P. napi* L.), Small Tortoiseshell (*Aglais urticae* L.), Peacock (*Nymphalis io* L.), Common Blue (*Polyommatus icarus* (v. Rott.)), Holly Blue (*Celastrina argiolus* L.), Small Copper (*Lycaena phlaeas* L.), Orange-tip (*Euchloe cardamines* L.), Brimstone (*Goneopteryx rhamni* L.), Large Skipper (*Thymelicus sylvestris* Poda), Small Skipper (*Angiades venata* B. & G.).

The following, if not actually extinct in Nottinghamshire, are on the verge of extinction and will disappear unless protected: Speckled Wood (*Parage aegeria* L.), Small Pearl-bordered Fritillary (*Argynnis selene* Schiff.), Pearl-bordered Fritillary (*Argynnis euphrosyne* L.), High Brown Fritillary (*Argynnis cydippe* L.), Silver-washed Fritillary (*Argynnis paphia* L.), Dark Green Fritillary (*Argynnis aglaia* L.), Comma (*Polygonia c-album* L.), White-letter Hairstreak (*Strymon w-album* Knock), Dingy Skipper (*Nisoniades tages* L.), Grizzled Skipper (*Pyrgus malvae* L.), Chequered Skipper (*Carterocephalus palaemon* (Pallas)).

The Speckled Wood *Pararge aegeria* (L.) appears to have been last recorded in 1957, and the Scarce Vapourer *Orgyia gonostigma* Fabr. at Thornley on 5th July 1949.

Among the rarer Hawk-moths, the immigrant Humming-bird Hawk-moth *Macroglossa stellatarum* L. occurs spasmodically; it is much less common than formerly. Isolated records occur over the years for the Convolvulus Hawk-moth *Sphinx convolvuli* L., another immigrant species, the most recent being at Cotgrave in September 1964 and Long Eaton in September 1965.

The larvae of the Wormwood Shark Moth *Cucullia absinthii* L., mainly a south-coast species and not recorded in Carr, was reported from Wollaton, Nottingham, in October 1958. The following year dozens of larvae in different stages of development were reported feeding on wormwood at Doveridge, Derbyshire.

The Gold-fringed Tabby moth *Pyralis costalis* Fabr., recorded only from Worksop and Epperstone Park by Professor Carr, has been reported from Upton, near Newark, in the summers of 1954 and 1956.

Over 1,400 species of beetles are recorded for Nottinghamshire by Carr, these records resulting mainly from the exertions of the Reverend A. Thornley and his colleagues in the early part of the century. Many rare species were discovered, one of which, the Wharf Beetle *Nacerdes melanura* (L.), a wood borer, recorded in 1912 and 1914 in Nottingham, turned up again after a lapse of many years at Bestwood colliery workshop when one male and seven females were found on 30th May 1958 and three males and three females on 19th February 1959. More work needs to be done on these rare species.

A Ray Society monograph on the Neuroptera was published in 1936 and 1937 (two volumes) just after the appearance of the *Supplement* to Carr's *Invertebrate Fauna*. This seems to show only one additional Nottinghamshire species: *Sympherobius fuscescens* (Wallengren). Two other additional species are quite likely synonyms of species already recorded, the nomenclature and synonymity being in some confusion about this period.

Of the 41 native species of ant occurring in the British Isles, 10 are recorded for Nottinghamshire by Carr. The following additional species have since been recorded: *Formiconexus nitidulus* (Nylander), *Myrmica sabuleti* Meinert, *Myrmica lobicornis* Nylander, *Lasius mixtus* (Nylander), *Formica lemani* Bondroit.

From the bordering county of Derbyshire, *Myrmica sulcinodis* Nylander and *Formica lugubris* Zetterstedt have been recorded and *Myrmica schencki* Emery and *Formica cunicularia* from south Lincolnshire.

About 540 species of spider occur in the British Isles and of these 207 are recorded by Carr for Nottinghamshire. Since then seven more have been added to the list: *Dysdera erythrina* (Walck.), *Zelotes rusticus* (L. Koch.), *Phildromus emarginatus* (Shrank.), *Oedothorax agrestis* (Blackwall.), *Tegenaria atrica* (C. L. Koch), *Meta menardi* (Latreille), *Erigone vagans* (Audouin).

The last two are of fairly recent date, *Erigone vagans* being recorded for Kelham Bridge in August 1962 and *Meta manardi* for Creswell in early 1964. It is rather surprising to note that *Tegenaria atrica* was not recorded for the county by Carr, as this is one of the commonest species.

The macroscopic invertebrate fauna of the rivers and streams in the area has remained remarkably constant over the past few years, despite variation in the degree of pollution, although the larva of one species of Chironomus (*C. riparius*) is not now very abundant. The snail *Hydrobia jenkinsi* has become extremely common. Nymphs of two members of the Ephemeroptera (*Baetis rhodani* and *Ephemerella ignita*) have tended to decrease in numbers; nymphs of species of *Caenis*, on the other hand, appear to be increasing.

Finally, a word may be said about the Leeches. There are 14 native species and only three of these have not been recorded for the area. These are: *Batrachobdella palludosa* (Carena), *Hirudo medicinalis* L., *Dina lineata* (O.F.M.).

THE BOMBIDAE OF THE EAST MIDLANDS

INTRODUCTION

The family *Bombidae*, which includes only two genera, the social bees of the genus *Bombus*, and a closely related genus *Psithyrus*, which is parasitic upon them, are essentially inhabitants of the northern continents of the world. Numerous species occur throughout Europe, northern Asia, North America and the mountains of South America. A few species occur spread out over the South American lowlands. In Britain there are 19 species of *Bombus*, belonging to six sub-genera, and six species of *Psithyrus* belonging to three species groups. All British species occur on the mainland of Europe, some spread into Asia, and one, *Bombus lapponicus* (Fabr.), is widespread on mountain ranges throughout Europe, Asia and North America.

The distribution of the species and sub-species of *Bombus* and *Psithyrus* within the British Isles is not very well documented; most of the information relating to the south and west of the country. This is especially true of the Midlands and the purpose of this account is to record the distribution of species within this region. Some of the species of bumblebees are not very easy to identify, and for this reason the records given here are confined to preserved specimens whose identity can be checked. The collections that have been studied are those made by Carr and Jones in the 1920's and 1930's. These collections are now in the Wollaton Hall Natural History Museum. In addition, there are records founded on specimens in my own collection collected over the years 1955–65.

Most of the specimens studied come from localities within the county of Nottinghamshire, a few from Lincolnshire, mostly concentrated near its county boundary with Nottinghamshire, some from Derbyshire, and a few in my own collection from Gibraltar Point. In spite of the considerable amount of work that has been done on the social organisation of colonies of bumblebees, there is little information about the ecology of the different species. I have annotated the list of species given below to give some information of the kind of habitat they have been found in; and included a Table giving the dates of appearance of the queens in the spring and of the capture of males and females in the autumn.

ANNOTATED LIST OF SPECIES

Bombus (Lapidariobombus) lapidarius L.

This species is fairly common on the 'turf' type of grassland throughout the region, particularly on the hillsides facing the Trent valley and the limestone grasslands of Derbyshire and Lincolnshire. It is parasitized by *Psithyrus rupestris* (Fabr.), and is recorded from several widespread localities by Jones and Carr. I have found it only twice within Nottinghamshire, although it appears very commonly along the Norfolk coast.

Bombus (Terrestribombus) terrestris (L.)

This is one of the commonest bumblebees throughout the region. In about 10 per cent of the queens captured in recent years the yellow band on the prothorax is largely or entirely replaced by black hairs (var. *cryptarum F.*). Although few in number, approximately the same percentage of black-haired forms occurs in the Carr and Jones collections. Its parasite, *Psithyrus vestalis* (Geoffrey in Fourcroy) is widespread, but not very numerous.

Bombus (Terrestribombus) lucorum (L.)

This, too, is a very common bumblebee. It is parasitized by *Psithyrus bohemicus* (Seidl), which was recorded from a number of localities by Carr and Jones, but in recent years I have found only one specimen and this at Hawksmoor, in Staffordshire.

Bombus (Agrobombus) ruderarius (Muller)

This is a relatively uncommon species; Jones and Carr found a few specimens near Nottingham and on the Nottinghamshire–Lincolnshire border. In the vicinity of Nottingham I have found it in rough meadow land and waste land, but never abundantly.

Bombus (Agrobombus) agrorum (Fabr.)

This is a very common species throughout the entire region. In populations from southern England the brown hairs of the thorax and abdomen are intermixed with black, while in northern populations there is no black intermixed on the thorax and very little on the abdomen. Both forms occur, but the southern form appears to be more common in the east of the region; in the west it occurs mainly in Sherwood and Charnwood Forests. In the northern form the thorax is devoid of black hairs, but there is much black mixed in with brown on the abdomen, often forming a black band of the second and third segments. The form *septentrionalis* Vogt, which is completely pale-haired and occurs in the highlands, does not occur this far south, although I have caught it in the Cheviot Hills. *Psithyrus campestris* (*Panz*), which is parasitic on *B. agrorum,* is moderately common throughout the region, and an all-black form is occasionally found.

Bombus (Agrobombus) humilis (Illiger)

This largely southern species appears to be very uncommon in this region. It is represented in the Jones and Carr collections by nine specimens, mostly from the south and east of Nottinghamshire amongst meadow and woodland. The nearest place where I have found this species is Chigwell, in Oxfordshire.

Bombus (Agrobombus) muscorum L.

This species was not found in Nottinghamshire by Carr and Jones. It appears to be an inhabitant of marshy districts and is found at Gibraltar Point and is fairly common around the Wash and along the marshes of the Norfolk coast. The specimens found belong to the sub-species *sladeni* Vogt, the northern sub-species *pallidus* Evans evidently does not occur this far south.

Bombus (Agrobombus) sylvarum (L.)

There are a few specimens of this species in the Jones and Carr collections, mostly from Bunny, Widmerpool, Hammeringham and South Leverton. I have not been able to find this species within the region.

Bombus (Subterraneobombus) subterraneus L.

This is a very rare species and has been recorded from only one locality in the region, Longford Moor, south of Newark, where three queens were obtained by Jones and Carr, two in 1925 and one in 1931. I have no other records for this species.

Bombus (Subterraneobombus) distinguendus Mor.

Jones and Carr obtained this species from a number of localities in Nottinghamshire, including one near Bramcote, on the outskirts of Nottingham, as late as 1931. I have not been able to find this species in Nottinghamshire, although I have searched for it in some of the localities given by Jones and Carr. Recently (1965) I have taken one queen near Matlock, in Derbyshire.

Bombus (Pratobombus) pratorum L.

This is a very common species throughout the whole region. Its parasite, *Psithyrus sylvestris* (Lept) is recorded from a number of localities by Jones and Carr. I have not captured this *Psithyrus* in this region.

Bombus (Pratobombus) jonellus (Kirby)

Jones and Carr did not find this species in Nottinghamshire, nor have I been able to find it on the heathlands around Matlock, or in the Sherwood and Charnwood Forest areas. I captured one worker at Rocester, in Staffordshire, which is on the extreme western border of the region. This locality, in meadow and river land, is an unlikely habitat, but it is not far from Hawksmoor and the worker might well have strayed from the heathlands there. In the east it occurs on the heathlands of Norfolk, but I have not found it at Gibraltar Point.

Bombus (Pratobombus) lapponicus (Fabr.)

This bee is predominantly an inhabitant of mountain districts and, as might be expected, is absent from most of the region. I have found it at Edale in the Peak District, and on the heather and bilberry moors around Matlock.

Bombus (Hortobombus) hortorum L.

This species is very common throughout the entire region. In the west it occurs in the valleys and dales of Derbyshire and the southern Peak District, less commonly or not at all on the highland. *Psithyrus barbutellus* (Kirby), which is parasitic on it, is recorded from many localities in the east of the region but is by no means common. It does not appear to follow its host into the high valleys in the west.

Bombus (Hortobombus) ruderatus F.

This species is much rarer than the previous one, and I have not captured one in this region. Jones and Carr collections contain three females from two localities on the Nottinghamshire–Lincolnshire border and four males from a locality in Lincolnshire. Most of these belong to the var *Harrisellus* Kirby.

DISCUSSION

In general there appears to be no evidence of 'industrial melanisation' in the bumblebees from this region. Although black forms do occur in *Psithyrus campestris* (Panz) and dark forms in *Bombus terrestris* L. these appear to be no more frequent in the population than they were 30 years ago. The black *Bombus ruderatus var harrisellus* Kirby appears to have vanished from the area. The southern forms of *Bombus agrorum* (Fabr.) and *Bombus muscorum subsp. sladeni* Vogt. occur east of the Trent and probably extend a good deal further north along the east coast. *Bombus humilis* Illiger; *sylvarum* L.; *subterraneus* L.; and *ruderatus* F. have not been found in recent years in Nottinghamshire. When they did occur in the 1930's Jones and Carr found them in localities along the Trent or in the southern part of Nottinghamshire and north Leicestershire. The most unexpected absentee from this list is *Bombus jonellus* Kirby which, although it occurs all around the region, does not seem to penetrate within it. A possible reason for this is the relatively small areas of heath, its main habitat within the region. A notable loss appears to be *Bombus distinguendus* Mor., which once appears to have been fairly common throughout the area. The capture of a queen in the vicinity of Matlock, in Derbyshire, in June 1965 shows that it may not be entirely absent, but is certainly less common than formerly.

The dates for the first appearance of queens in the spring, and for males and females in the summer and autumn, although founded on relatively scanty data, indicate times similar to those found for the bees in the south and east of the country.

Finally I should like to stress that the above account is founded on relatively little collecting over a rather limited number of years; obviously much more collecting is necessary before a reliable distribution of bumblebees in the Midlands can be given.

Table XXVII Dates of the appearance of queens in the spring and of the capture of males and females in the autumn

Species	Months											
	Jan.	Feb.	March	April	May	June	July	Aug.	Sept.	Oct.	Nov.	Dec.
B. lapidarius ..	—	—	—	♀	♀	♀♂	♂	♀♂	♂	—	—	—
B. terrestris ..	—	—	♀	♀	♀	♂	♂♀	♀♂	—	—	—	—
B. lucorum ..	—	—	♀	♀	♀	♀♂	♀♂	♀♂	—	—	—	—
B. ruderarius ..	—	—	—	—	—	—	—	—	—	—	—	—
B. agrorum ..	—	—	—	—	♀	—	—	♂	—	—	—	—
B. humilis ..	—	—	—	♀	♀	—	♂	♀♂	♀	—	—	—
B. muscorum ..	—	—	—	—	—	♀	—	—	—	—	—	—
B. sylvarum ..	—	—	—	♀	♀♂	—	—	♂	—	—	—	—
B. subterraneous	—	—	—	—	♀♂	♀	—	—	—	—	—	—
B. distinquendus	—	—	—	—	♀♂	♀♂	♀	—	—	—	—	—
B. pratorum ..	—	—	—	♀	♀♂	♂♀	—	—	—	—	—	—
B. jonellus ..	—	—	—	—	—	♀♂	—	—	—	—	—	—
B. lapponicus ..	—	—	—	—	—	—	—	—	—	—	—	—
B. hortorum ..	—	—	—	—	—	♀	—	—	—	—	—	—
B. ruderatus ..	—	—	—	—	—	—	—	—	—	—	—	—
P. rupestris ..	—	—	—	—	♀	♀	♀	♀	♂	—	—	—
P. barbutellus	—	—	—	—	—	♀	♂♀	♀	—	—	—	—
P. sylvestris ..	—	—	—	—	♀	—	♂♀	♂	—	—	—	—
P. compestris ..	—	—	—	—	—	—	♀	♀♂	—	—	—	—
P. bohemicus ..	—	—	—	—	♀	—	—	♀♂	—	—	—	—
P. vestalis ..	—	—	—	♀	—	♀♂	—	♀♂	—	—	—	—

ACKNOWLEDGMENTS

Dr. Clarke wishes to thank the City of Nottingham Art Galleries and Museums Committee for permission to study the collections in the Wollaton Hall Natural History Museum. He further extends his gratitude to Mr. Halton, Curator of that Museum, for his help.

Mr. H. C. S. Halton is indebted to Mr. A. Dobbs for notes on birds, and to Miss Katherine E. Varney for information on other vertebrates.

SELECTED REFERENCES

Bristowe, W. S. The Comity of Spiders. *Ray Society* Vol. 1 (1939) and Vol. 2 (1941).

Carr, J. W. *The Invertebrate Fauna of Nottinghamshire.* Nottingham, J. & H. Bell Ltd. (1916).

Carr, J. W. *The Invertebrate Fauna of Nottinghamshire.* Supplement. J. & H. Bell Ltd. (1935).

Collingwood, C. A. and Barrett, K. E. J. The Vice-County Distribution of Indigenous Ants in the British Isles. *Transactions of the Society of British Entomologists* Vol. 16 Part 3 (December 1964).

Johnson, J. H. Polymorphism in N.E. Derbyshire. *Entomologist's Record* Vol. 76 (1964).

Killington, F. J. The British Neuroptera. *Ray Society* Vol. 1 (1936) and Vol. 2 (1937).

Kloet and Hincks. *Check List of British Insects.* Stockport, Kloet & Hincks (1945).

Locket, G. H. and Millidge, A. F. *British Spiders* Vol. 1 (1951) and Vol. 2 (1953) (Ray Society).

Mann, K. H. and Watson, E. V. *A Key to the British Freshwater Leeches.* Freshwater Biological Association Scientific Publication, No. 14.

Massee, A. M. The County Distribution of the British Hemiptera-Heteroptera. *Entomologist's Monthly Magazine* Vol. 91 (1955).

Whitaker, J. *Notes on the Birds of Nottinghamshire.* Nottingham, Walter Black & Co. Ltd. (1907).

Annual Reports, Trent Valley Bird Watchers, Nottingham (1954–62).

Check List of the Birds of Great Britain and Ireland. British Ornithologists' Union (1952).

The Victoria History of the County of Nottingham (edited by William Page) Vol. 1. London, James Street (1906).

VII

THE RIVER TRENT

THE river Trent from Burton to Newark flows in an alluvium-filled valley overlying Triassic rocks. It is joined in this reach by three of its major tributaries, the Dove, the Derwent and the Soar. All these rivers join the Trent upstream from Nottingham, which is approximately the mid-point of the reach and 80 miles from the confluence with the Humber estuary. The catchment area above Nottingham is 2,785 square miles, which is 69 per cent of the total catchment area.

CHANNEL GEOMETRY

The Trent flows in a meander pattern which is not particularly well-developed, the river mileage between Burton and Newark being 55·5 miles, compared with a direct distance of 40 miles, giving a tortuosity ratio of 1 : 1·4. Meander lengths vary within the reach from 1,800 feet at Burton to 5,000 feet at Colwick, the corresponding widths being 1,500 feet and 3,300 feet.

The bed falls 114 feet in the 55·5 miles, equivalent to a uniform slope of 1 : 2570. Width, depth and discharge changes in the reach are given in Table XXVIII.

Table XXVIII   Width, depth and discharge relationships along the river Trent

Location	Bankfull Stage		
	Width feet	Depth feet	Discharge cusecs
Burton	162·75	7·95	5,600
Shardlow	168·25	9·86	5,000
Nottingham	181·0	13·1	11,750
Colwick	245·0	17·14	21,500

In what is a comparatively short reach of the river, the geometric parameters cannot be expected to exhibit a high degree of correlation, particularly as the river has many man-made restraints. Relationships must, however, exist and an attempt to ascertain these can be made by axial diagrams of which Fig. 21 is an example. In drawing the diagram the following widely accepted relationships have been used:

$$w \ \alpha \ Q^{\frac{1}{2}}$$
$$d \ \alpha \ Q^{\frac{1}{8}}$$
$$M_L \ \alpha \ Q^{\frac{1}{2}}$$
$$M_L \ \alpha \ w$$

where w is width at bankfull stage, d is depth, M_L is meander length and Q is bankfull discharge.

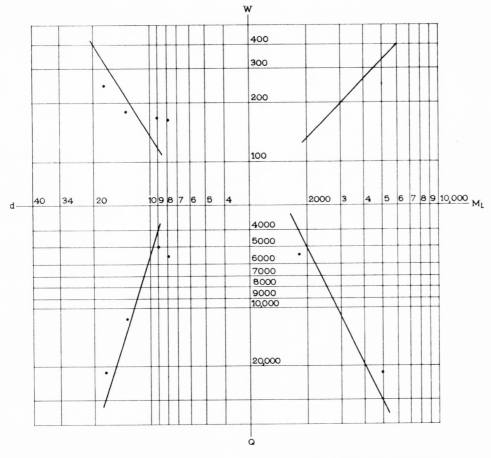

| W | WATER SURFACE WIDTH (FT.) | Q | BANK FULL DISCHARGE (CUSECS) |
| d | MEAN DEPTH (FT.) | M_L | MEANDER LENGTH (FT.) |

Fig. 21 Tentative geometrical relationships for the river Trent between Burton-on-Trent and Newark

Bankfull stage is equalled or exceeded approximately 0·6 per cent of the time (M. Nixon, 1959) and may have a recurrence interval of about one year. The bed material is usually gravel, graded down from two inches in size but there are occasional outcrops of shales and marls. The banks are frequently of a silty-clay material. Clearly further study is necessary before any great reliance can be placed on Fig. 21.

FLOW CHARACTERISTICS

The response to rainfall of the Trent at Nottingham is not very rapid and certainly it cannot be regarded as a 'flashy' river. The flood of 1947 reached a peak after 150 hours and a second and higher peak after 250 hours but this flood was complicated by the influence of snow-melt. The more normal case of a rain-produced flood has a quicker rate of rise and in 1932 the peak was reached in 60 hours. A typical flood hydrograph is shown in Fig. 22.

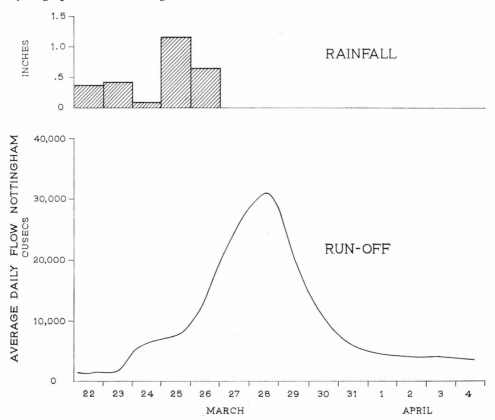

Fig. 22 Rainfall and run-off at Nottingham compared for a part of 1955

The maximum discharge in 1947 was 40,000 cusecs. This magnitude of flood has a recurrence interval of about 75 years and one of 30,000 cusecs can occur once in 25 years. The difference in magnitude of bankfull and flood discharge reveals that the river channel is capable of carrying only a third of a major flood. Discharge in excess of the channel capacity must flow over the natural floodplain of the river or into storage areas which are usually called 'washlands'.

The natural low flow in the Trent at Nottingham is not known because of the effect of discharges from sewage works and industrial discharges and abstractions and because 'foreign' water is brought in from other catchments. The average summer low flow measured at Nottingham is 1,918 cusecs; this includes approximately 420 cusecs of sewage effluent, of which about 160 cusecs originates from sources outside the catchment area. It is thought that during severe droughts the measured flow at Nottingham could fall to about 800 cusecs.

FLOOD PROBLEMS

The valley of the Trent, as in any natural river system, has always been subject to periodic flooding but, presumably because of the comparative infrequency of major floods, ill-advised developments on the natural floodplain near the larger communities have nevertheless taken place, particularly during the 19th century. Most of the contemporary flood problems arise from these indiscriminate developments.

Many examples can be found from Burton to Newark, but probably the best, or the worst, example is at Nottingham. The 18th century city was some distance from the Trent and between it and the river, water meadows formed the natural floodplain. Major floods, such as that of 1795, did comparatively little damage. Early in the 19th century, when the 1795 flood must still have been remembered by many, intensive development took place on the meadows (the term Meadows survives as a district) on both sides of the river. Some attempts were made to protect the development by the construction of riverside embankments but these were inadequate to contain the 1947 flood which was similar in magnitude to that of 1795. Although much the same area was inundated by these two floods, over 7,000 houses and factories and many miles of roads and railways built since 1795 were under water in 1947. The extent of these floods and the growth of building which took place in the period between them is shown in Fig. 23. The flood control measures which now protect the vulnerable areas are described later.

At Burton-on-Trent much the same pattern of events occurred and in 1875 more than half of the town was flooded and as a result protection works were built which fortunately were more successful in limiting the area under water in 1947.

Early flood protection measures were not restricted to the towns. Large estate owners constructed floodbanks adjoining the river to reduce the frequency of flooding on agricultural land and some villages were also protected. These defences were carried out sporadically and were not continuous. As a result, however, a system of protection gradually evolved consisting of minor works to safeguard the countryside and of major defences intended to prevent the flooding of towns.

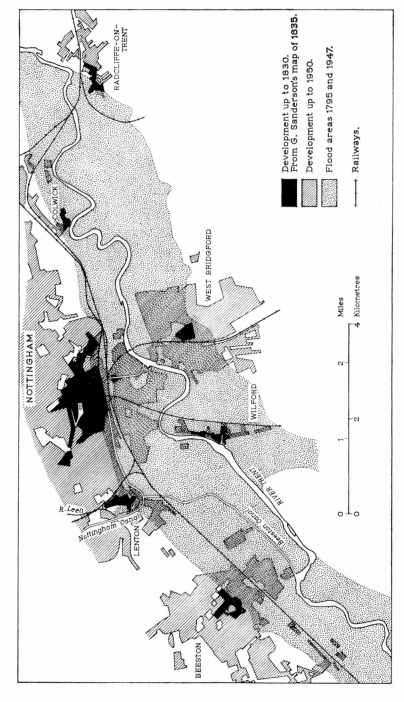

Fig. 23 The urban invasion of floodplain washlands

This system, which exists today (Fig. 24), came under unified control for the first time on the formation of the River Trent Catchment Board under the Land Drainage Act, 1930. The drainage and flood control duties of the Catchment Board were transferred to the Trent River Board in 1950 under the terms of the River Boards Act of 1948, and since the 1st April 1965 have been exercised by the Trent River Authority established under the Water Resources Act, 1963.

FLOOD CONTROL

Flood regulation can be achieved in three ways: by reducing the river flow, by reducing the flood levels and by restricting the area of inundation.

Flood flows are reduced by the provision of flood storage reservoirs or by diverting flows to other areas. These methods cannot be applied to the Trent in its middle reach nor indeed to any extent in the catchment area as a whole because of the physical size of the reservoirs required and the lack of suitable sites. For example, E. C. Hillman has shown that in order to confine within the natural channel a flood as large as that of 1932, which reached a maximum of 30,000 cusecs at Nottingham, a reservoir capacity of 132,484 acre/feet is required. This is equivalent to an area of 69 square miles covered by three feet of water.

Flood levels are reduced by enlarging the channels of rivers or by creating alternative routes for flood flows. To control floods in the Trent valley by channel enlargement, a channel three times the size of the existing river would be required. A channel of this size moreover would be unpracticable as well as being unstable.

It follows from the foregoing that the flood control measures adopted in the Trent valley aim to reduce or limit the area of inundation by the construction of flood embankments or defences. This process does, however, reduce the natural storage capacity of the valley and restricts the area available for flood flows; in consequence levels are raised and flood flows increased. It is for this reason that as much as possible of the natural floodplain or washlands must be preserved as such and used for purposes which can accept periodic inundation. The rise in flood levels and flows can be offset by limited channel enlargement and improvements and this has been done where possible, as part of some of the flood defence schemes now described.

The Burton-on-Trent Flood Protection Scheme

Following the 1875 flood at Burton-on-Trent embankments were built between the river and the town. Part of the town was again flooded in 1947 and it was realised that the margin of safety of the original embankments was too small. The river in 1947 flowed past the town in several channels, some being remnants of a system of natural water meadows, the others consisting of channels used to provide water-power for mills upstream of the town. Water-power is still used immediately downstream where an artificial head of water is maintained by a series of weirs.

Polluting matter originating from part of the Black Country tended to collect above the weirs and in some of the various channels, producing unpleasant conditions during hot dry weather. In 1960 the town was again threatened by flooding and it was estimated that 6,000 houses and factories and a hospital could have been flooded if the embankment had failed. The Trent River Board then prepared a flood protection scheme with the aid of a hydraulic model and investigations carried out by the Hydraulics Research Station at Wallingford. Work began in 1963 (Fig. 24). A continuous line of flood defences protecting the town was built extending from the village of Branston to the high ground on the Derby Road downstream. Where possible the defences are of embankments built of colliery waste but in restricted sites concrete or steel walls were used. The river was reshaped and several redundant channels were filled-in to inhibit the accumulation of silt and the breached Drakelow Weir on the upstream side of the town was removed. By reshaping the river the bankfull capacity was increased from 3,700 cusecs to 5,600 cusecs. The frequency of flooding of the washlands lying between the river and the defences was thereby greatly reduced and the proper development of this area by the town for amenities was made possible. This enlightened use of washlands in urban areas should become more widespread.

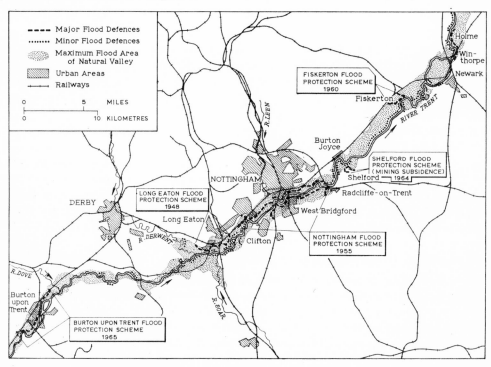

Fig. 24   Flood defences and protection schemes along the river Trent

The Long Eaton Flood Protection Scheme

About 2,000 houses, all situated in the natural floodplains of the Trent and Derwent in parts of Sawley and Long Eaton, were flooded in 1932, 1946 and 1947. The problem was readily solved by the Trent Catchment Board in 1948 by the construction of three and a half miles of flood bank to limit the area of flooding but no work was done on the river channels. Earth banks were built joining three lengths of railway embankment which were capable of retaining flood water, while floodgates were built on the Erewash Canal to prevent water from the Trent reaching the canal behind the defence line. Flood storage areas behind the defences are used for the collection of internal storm water.

The Nottingham Flood Protection Scheme

The incidence of flooding at Nottingham in 1795 and 1947 has already been mentioned. Other major floods occurred in 1852, 1875, 1901, 1910, 1932 and 1946. The peak levels of most of these floods are recorded at Trent Bridge and vary between 79·75 and 80·67 feet above mean sea-level (Liverpool), the normal water level being 68·0 feet. To avoid the flooding it was necessary to pass the whole flow through Trent Bridge, confining the flood to a comparatively narrow width between the built-up areas on both sides of the river.

A hydraulic model investigation of the problem on behalf of the Trent River Board was carried out in the Delft Hydraulic Laboratory in the Netherlands and several alternative protection measures were tested. The scheme finally adopted is primarily an embankment scheme. The model did, however, show that a pure embankment scheme would raise flood levels in the river by as much as six inches and would create exceptionally high velocities in the channel. To reduce the velocities to acceptable limits some widening of the existing channel was unavoidable.

The upstream section of the scheme from Wilford to Beeston consists mainly of earth floodbanks sited as far from the river as possible to provide the maximum area of washlands. In the central section in which the river passes between the built-up areas of Nottingham and West Bridgford, widening was undertaken between Wilford and Trent Bridge since no washlands could be provided, though it was necessary to control velocities. Defence works, however, were incorporated in the widening, consisting either of raised roadways or retaining walls.

In the third section, downstream from Nottingham, washland areas existed and banks were constructed as far as possible from the channel. A new sluice and a straight section of channel were built to replace an existing weir and a large meander. The river was thus shortened by 1,800 yards and at Colwick flood levels were reduced by nearly four feet. The sluices have five 40 feet wide steel lifting gates, 16 feet 6 inches deep, and maintain a difference in head of 11 feet at normal water levels as required for navigational purposes (Fig. 24). The sluices, raised by electric motors, are operated automatically in relation to the upstream level. Each increment of rise in water level causes the gates to open a corresponding amount until, with a two feet rise, they are fully open, while with falling water levels the gates close.

The River Leen Improvement Scheme

The Nottingham Flood Protection Scheme effectively safeguards the urban areas from the Trent. The raising of defences for this purpose created a secondary problem of internal storm water. A comparatively small stream, the river Leen, rises to the north of the City and flows through it to join the Nottingham Canal by which it finally makes an outfall into the Trent just below Trent Bridge. This outfall is closed when the Trent is in full flood so it would be possible for waters from a secondary storm in the Leen catchment to be trapped behind the Trent flood defences and to cause internal flooding. To prevent this possibility the Leen is now being diverted under the canal and made to discharge directly into the Trent at Wilford through a newly constructed channel. The new outfall will enable the remaining portion of the river Leen upstream of the canal to be improved so that the frequent flooding of property along its course can be avoided. The work, which started in 1964, is being financed by the Nottingham Corporation but carried out by the Trent River Authority.

The Fiskerton Flood Protection Scheme

Some communities in the Trent valley can be completely surrounded by water in a major flood. Fiskerton, on the left bank of the river 15 miles from Nottingham, was such a village. In 1959 it was decided to rebuild the old masonry wall which formed the village frontage along the river. The wall was the joint responsibility of the Nottinghamshire County Council, British Waterways and the Trent River Board. The River Board, which carried out the reconstruction, agreed at the same time to protect the village from flooding. This was done by building retaining walls along the river and constructing earth banks around the village (Fig. 24). Almost complete encirclement was necessary, though fortunately it was possible to connect the floodbanks to high ground north of the village. In effect all the washlands to the north of the river have been obstructed, this being permissible only because an area more than adequate for the purpose existed to the south (Plate VII).

MINING SUBSIDENCE PROBLEMS

Subsidence due to mining is a recurrent feature of the Trent valley in the vicinity of the Nottinghamshire coalfield. As the land surface drops without a corresponding reduction in water level, problems of land drainage inevitably arise. The engineering principles governing measures to alleviate these man-made flood problems do not differ from those already described for the prevention of natural flood damage. Where subsidence is considerable, however, it is sometimes impossible to drain local areas by gravity and land drainage pumping stations become necessary. The affected area then becomes similar to the artificially drained fens.

An example of a flood problem created by subsidence is found at Burton Joyce. This village originally lay above the level of a major flood but by 1965 subsidence amounting to 2·83 feet had occurred in parts of the area. In effect the village became part of the Trent floodplain necessitating defence works of the embankment type, local drainage being dealt with by small pumping stations lifting the storm waters over the embankment into the main river system. On the opposite side of the river the village of Shelford had to be protected by an encircling embankment. The minor floodbank protecting the agricultural land between the river and the village was raised by two feet nine inches so that the frequency of overtopping by major floods remained unaltered.

Where major problems caused by subsidence might arise, pillars of support are left during mining operations. For instance, pillars have been, or will be, provided for the Holme Sluices of the Nottingham Flood Protection Scheme, the sewage disposal works of the Nottingham Corporation at Stoke Bardolph and the British Waterways weir and lock at Gunthorpe. On the other hand it must not be thought that mining subsidence is necessarily deleterious to river control. As an example, it may well be possible as a result of future workings under the river Trent to dispense with the need to maintain Stoke Lock and Weir and this would be of great benefit to navigation. Flood protection works on the main rivers made necessary by mining subsidence are carried out by the Trent River Authority at the expense of the National Coal Board.

FUNCTIONAL USES OF RIVER WATER

The Trent has been described as being "often ugly, sometimes beautiful, yet always useful". The final words are indisputable, for Man has put the river to many uses of which the following are the most important.

Waste Disposal

One of the natural functions of a river is to carry detritus to the sea and, in a settled country, rivers are required, in addition, to carry waste products of civilisation. These are conveyed into rivers either direct from industrial plants or from sewage works. There are 534 sewage disposal works in the Trent basin, discharging a total of 254 million gallons per day of effluent, most of which reaches the river upstream of Nottingham. Assuming that an average sewage effluent contains 0·04 per cent of impurities then in effect the Trent at Nottingham is acting as a conveyor carrying 450 tons of waste matter per day to the sea.

Fishing

The quality of the river water at Burton-on-Trent is still affected by pollution originating in the Black Country so the fish population is limited and subsists precariously. However, once the clean waters of the river Dove enter the mainstream the river carries an increasing population of coarse fish, the main species being chub,

M

dace, roach and gudgeon. The river is intensively fished by anglers, some indication of their numbers may be had from the fact that the Trent River Authority issues 160,000 rod licences annually. In an angling match held in 1961 between East Stoke and Newark, 1·85 tons of fish were caught by 1,236 anglers.

Navigation

The navigation of the Trent is dealt with in Chapter XIX and it is sufficient here to state that commercial navigation is one of the more important functions. The river is navigable up to Nottingham and a narrow canal system exists to Burton-on-Trent and beyond. Both systems are controlled by British Waterways. There is also some evidence that at one time the river itself was navigable from Burton to Sawley as derelict locks exist at Kings Mills near Castle Donington and at Greensmith's Mill, Burton.

Water Supplies

(i) *Domestic* The existing quality of the Trent water, recorded in Table XXIX, precludes its suitability for domestic use. This was not always so, for supplies from the gravels fed from the Trent were used by Nottingham until 1845, when deterioration in the quality caused this source to be abandoned.

Table XXIX   Quality of Trent water at Nottingham
(Pollution and Fisheries Department, Trent River Board)

B.O.D.	Nitrogen			Chlorine as Cl	Alkaline as $CaCo_3$	Total Dissolved Solids
	Ammonia	*Nitrite*	*Nitrate*			
11	2·4	0·5	5·4	90	157	569

Triennial Average 1957–1961 parts per million

(ii) *Industrial* A small amount of river water is used by industrial processes but the major use is for cooling in the electricity generating stations. The steam condensate in a thermal power station is cooled by passing it through a condenser which is normally a surface heat exchanger. The coolant may be taken from the river and returned to it directly, causing an increase of river temperature. Alternatively the warmed water can be passed through a cooling-tower and re-used in the station. The river is then required only to make up the loss by evaporation and for purging the system to prevent the build-up of dissolved solids. The large power stations now being built use complete cooling-tower systems as there is insufficient flow in the river to use direct cooling. Some of the less recent stations on the Trent use both direct cooling and cooling-towers and there are still a few old stations using direct cooling only. Between Burton and Newark there are five large power stations and one small one with a total installed capacity of 4,700 megawatts. The amount of water lost by evaporation in the cooling process is considerable. D. Clark and G. England, using estimates supplied by the Central Electricity Generating Board, have shown that the loss from these six stations running at full capacity could be 33 million gallons per day. The actual loss could be even greater due to the increased temperature of the river. The new power station now under construction at Ratcliffe upon Soar will have a capacity of 2,000 megawatts and will be supplied with river water.

Agriculture

Before 1939 the agricultural use of the Trent was limited to watering of stock but since the war spray irrigation of both crops and grass has become commonplace. In the Trent valley there is need for irrigation in six or seven years out of every ten and in periods of a general shortage of rain the demand for water for this purpose may be comparatively high.

Amenity and Recreation

Within easy reach of Nottingham there are several beautiful stretches of the Trent which attract many visitors in addition to those who come to fish. The river is now much used for pleasure boating, dinghy sailing, speed boats and water skiers. Rowing is popular at Nottingham and Burton. The number of pleasure craft of all kinds has increased considerably in recent years and conflicts of interests have arisen.

THE TRENT OF THE FUTURE

It is difficult to consider the future of the river Trent in relation to the one section which traverses the Nottingham region, so much of what follows has wider application. The passing of the Water Resources Act of 1963 and the formation of River Authorities means that river management in its widest sense can now be practised. River management can be defined as the art of directing the sources of water in nature for the use and convenience of man. Engineers will recognise these words as being almost identical with those used in the Charter of the Institution of Civil Engineers to define the object of that body.

Flood protection clearly falls within the definition but in this field most of the major works have already been undertaken. Future works may include a more extensive system of minor floodbanks which will give protection from floods having a frequency of one in 20 years or thereabouts. Considerably greater protection can thus be given to the existing floodplains but these areas must of necessity be reserved to accommodate major floods. The protection of some of the villages within the Trent floodplain may prove too expensive to justify and this may gradually lead to some redistribution of population.

The increase in the demand for water for domestic, industrial and agricultural uses can in the end only be met from the river Trent itself. This means that the quality of the water must be improved mainly by the construction of larger and more efficient sewage disposal works. As the quality improves fishing will benefit and a more diverse fish population will become possible.

The demand for public recreational facilities must inevitably increase. To meet this the river must play its full part. Greater access to the river will be required as well as the facilities for all kinds of water pursuits. Conflicting interests must be resolved by mutual understanding and by sympathetic control. Ultimately much of the floodplain may become a regional park.

There are parts of the river Trent which may be unattractive to some, although probably not in the reach between Burton and Newark. Nevertheless the appearance and beauty of this section could be greatly improved by imaginative landscaping. Carefully sited planting of trees would do much to improve the appearance of the river and there is no reason why the Trent should not become as well-loved as the Thames.

Not all the development of the future can be achieved by the Trent River Authority alone. The co-operation of many agencies will be required. It is hoped that the growth in the public awareness of the importance of rivers in our national life will create a climate which will enable imaginative schemes for the management of our river to reach fruition.

> We thank with brief thanksgiving,
> Whatever God's may be,
> That even the weariest river
> Winds somewhere safe to sea.
>
> *Swinburne*

SELECTED REFERENCES

Clark, D. and England, G. Thermal Power Generation. *Institute of Civil Engineers Symposium on 'Conservation of Water Resources'* (1962).

Hillman, E. C. The effect of flood relief works on flood levels below such works. *Journal of the Institute of Civil Engineers* Vol. 2 (1936) p. 393.

Pollution and Fisheries Department, Trent River Board. *Second Quinquennial Abstract of Statistics relating to River Surveys in the Trent Watershed, 1957–1961.*

Nixon, M. A study of the Bankfull Discharges of Rivers in England and Wales. *Proceedings of the Institute of Civil Engineers* Vol. 12 (1959) pp. 157–174.

Records of the Borough of Nottingham Vol. IX (1836–1900) Nottingham 1956.

VIII

HYDROLOGY

THE tributary rivers and streams related to the non-tidal section of the Trent, together with the present number of permanently established river level recorder stations are shown in line chart form in Fig. 25. In this part of the Trent basin there are five principal tributary rivers, each draining a considerable area. On the left bank of the Trent are the Dove/Churnet and the Derwent/Wye basins which between them drain most of the southern areas of the Pennines. Many of the streams in these basins are highland in character. On the right bank of the Trent are the three lowland basins of the Sow/Penk, the Tame/Anker and the Soar/Wreak. Table XXX gives details of the divisions of the non-tidal part of the Trent basin in area and percentage area form, while Table XXXI gives in similar form details of the various basin areas above 600 feet above sea-level.

Table XXX The non-tidal reaches and drainage areas of the river Trent

Designation	Area (square miles)	Area (x 1,000 acres)	% Area to Colwick	% Area to Cromwell Lock
NON-TIDAL TRENT BASIN AREAS				
Total Non-Tidal Area	3,178·68	2,031·80	—	100
Trent Basin to Colwick Recorder ..	2,890·35	1,849·82	100	90·93
Trent Basin to Shardlow Recorder	1,704·12	1,090·64	58·96	53·61
TRIBUTARY RIVER BASINS				
(a) Left Bank				
Dove/Churnet Basin	393·75	252·00	13·62	12·39
River Churnet Basin (Rocester)	91·76	58·73	3·17	2·89
Derwent/Wye Basin ..	458·95	293·73	15·88	14·44
River Wye Basin	105·00	67·20	3·63	3·30
River Amber Basin ..	53·80	34·43	1·86	1·69
River Erewash Basin ..	80·23	51·35	2·78	2·52
(b) Right Bank				
Sow/Penk Basin	233·87	149·68	8·09	7·36
River Penk Basin	123·69	79·16	4·28	3·89
Tame/Anker Basin	580·98	371·83	20·10	18·28
River Anker Basin ..	157·68	100·92	5·45	4·96
River Sence Basin	66·41	42·50	2·30	2·09
Soar/Wreak Basin	534·82	342·28	18·50	13·68
River Wreak Basin (Syston Mills)	159·78	102·76	5·53	5·03
River Sence Basin	51·13	32·72	1·77	1·61

Table XXXI Areas above 600 feet above Ordnance Datum within the Trent Basin

River Basin	Total Drainage Area		Area above 600 feet A.O.D.		% of Total Area
	Square miles	x 1,000 acres	Square miles	x 1,000 acres	
Derwent/Wye　　　　　　　..	458·95	293·73	293·76	188·01	64·01
Dove/Churnet　　　　　　..	393·75	252·00	213·60	136·70	54·25
Sow/Penk　..	233·87	149·68	5·92	3·79	2·53
Tame/Anker　　　　　　　..	580·98	371·83	20·80	13·31	3·53
Soar/Wreak　　　　　　　..	534·82	342·28	7·68	4·92	1·44
River Trent to Great Haywood	125·36	80·23	28·64	18·33	22·85
River Trent to Shardlow　..	1,704·12	1,090·64	286·40	183·30	16·81
River Trent to Colwick　..	2,890·35	1,849·82	587·84	376·22	23·38

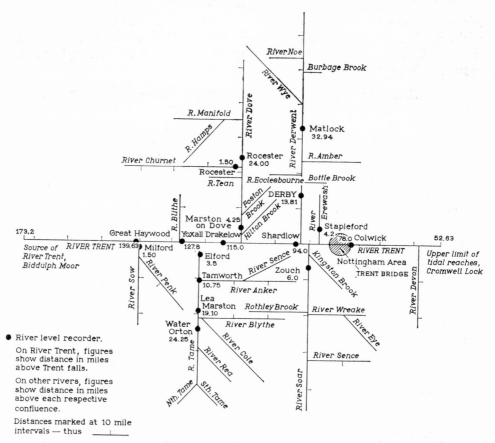

Fig. 25　The non-tidal section of the Trent Basin, in line diagram form, showing the position of river level recorders

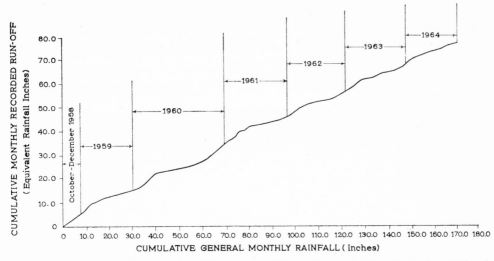

Fig. 26 Cumulative monthly general rainfall and its run-off equivalent for the Trent Basin above Colwick

At the present time, the principal level-recorder on the non-tidal section of the Trent basin is at Colwick, just over two and a quarter miles downstream from Trent Bridge, Nottingham. This station was established in 1958, and Fig. 26 shows the relationship between the cumulative monthly general rainfall values for the area of the Trent basin upstream of Colwick (estimated by means of a Thiessen Grid using 39 rainfall stations) and the cumulative rainfall equivalent of the monthly recorded flows at this station, for the period from October 1958 to December 1964. This period included several weather extremes, the prolonged drought of October 1958 to November 1959; the double flood period of 26th to 27th January and 30th January to 2nd February 1960; the very wet autumn of 1960 which culminated in the great flood of 5th to 7th December; the severe winter of 1962–63 which was generally a period of drought; the winter drought of 1963–64, and finally the very dry autumn of 1964. Fig. 27 shows the Flow-Duration Curve for the six Water Years, October 1958 to September 1964, and Fig. 28 shows similar curves for the summer and winter six months period in this interval. Flows below 873 cusecs have never yet been measured, and the extrapolated values for the lower flows have been shown with dotted lines in the lower parts of the different graphs. The computed mean flow for the winter period is 3,820 cusecs while the daily mean summer flow is 1,800 cusecs. Owing to the improved channel capacity at Colwick, primarily as a result of the Nottingham Flood Protection Scheme (see p. 151) the bankfull flow is 21,500 cusecs. During the period of record the river has only flooded over its left bank on three occasions; for just over 12 hours during 26th to 27th January 1960; for some two and a half days during 30th January to 2nd February 1960; and for nearly two and a quarter days between 5th and 7th December 1960. Although the river was over the bank for less time in December 1960 than during the January–February flood, the peak level was about one foot higher in the December flood, and this ranks as the fifth highest since 1795. A more comprehensive account of flooding in the valley of the river Trent is given in Chapter VII.

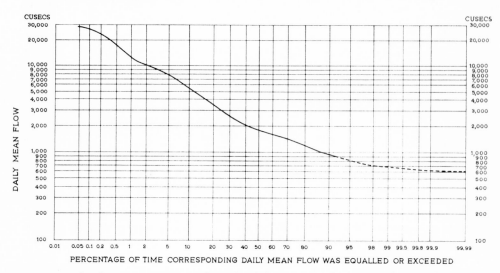

Fig. 27 The Flow-Duration Curve for Colwick between October 1958 and September 1964

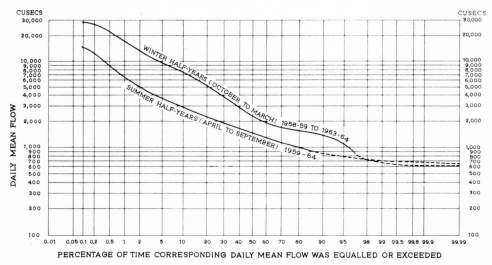

Fig. 28 The Flow-Duration Curves at Colwick for the winter and summer half-year periods, October 1958 to September 1964

STANDARD (EXPERIMENTAL) CATCHMENTS

Among the main objectives of hydrology is the accurate assessment of the water resources of the different types of catchment within a river basin, and the control of the ways in which these resources are developed and used. In making the original assessment of the water resources of a catchment two kinds of data are used.

First to be considered are the catchment characteristics, which include the geological conditions, the surface configuration and the drainage pattern. Such data, which are commonly obtained for other scientific disciplines, may be profitably used by hydrologists.

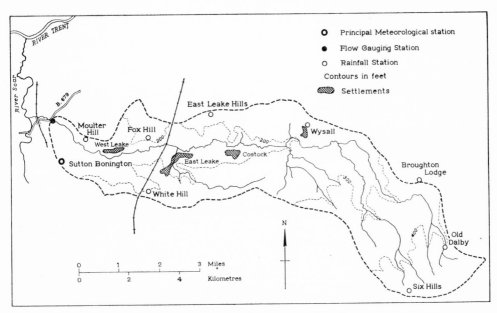

Fig. 29 The Kingston Brook experimental catchment area

Secondly come the hydrological variables of precipitation, run–off, ground water fluctuation, evaporation, soil moisture, sediment transport and water quality, all of which require measurement. Here some of the data, such as rainfall, and water quality, may already have been acquired for other purposes, whereas other data, such as run–off and sediment transport are more strictly of hydrological interest and less likely to be available. Since the total available information for a large catchment area is at present extremely limited and uneven, there arose the concept of using a relatively small catchment area, selected as being typical or 'standard' for a larger one of which it is only a part and in which relatively accurate measurements can be made of the different hydrological elements. From the relationships established between these elements, it is considered that assessments of the less well-instrumented larger areas may be possible. The diversity of geological and relief conditions over the Trent basin as whole has led to the choice of some 16 such catchments, the nearest to Nottingham being that of the Kingston Brook, a right bank tributary of the lower river Soar. This valley is regarded as being typical of the surface drainage of the south Nottinghamshire and Leicestershire Wolds. Fig. 29 shows the outline of this catchment, together with the existing and proposed instrumentation, while Fig. 30 shows the hypsographic curve for the area together with the distribution of rainfall stations. The stream-flow station, yet to be built, is sited at the Kingston bridge (B.679 road), and as there is considerable likelihood of backwater effects from high levels in the river Soar the gauging station had to be designed to allow for this possibility. The type intended for use here is a double-gauged Crump Weir.

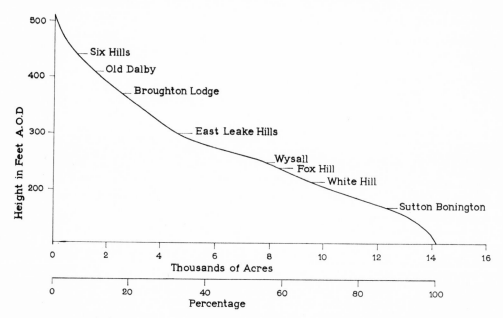

Fig. 30   The hypsographic curve for the Kingston Brook experimental catchment area

Several criteria have been borne in mind in making the choice of a particular catchment:

(a) The area should be relatively small. Kingston Brook has a total catchment area of just over 22 square miles and is probably representative of an area of 90 to 150 square miles in all.

(b) The area should be of fairly uniform physique, i.e. either highland or lowland. The Kingston Brook catchment is entirely lowland in character.

(c) The area should as far as possible be of uniform geological composition. In the Kingston Brook catchment over half of the area (Table XXXII) is formed by Boulder clay deposits, most of which overlie the Lower Lias clay.

Table XXXII

Surface area of the different rock types exposed
in the Kingston Brook Basin

	Area		
Rock Type	*Square miles*	*Acres*	%
Alluvium	1·37	876·8	6·20
Older River Gravel ..	1·14	729·6	5·16
Boulder Clay	12·54	8,025·6	56·75
Sands and Gravels (Glacial) ..	1·76	1,126·4	7·96
Lower Liassic Clays ..	1·97	1,260·8	8·93
Rhaetic	0·74	473·6	3·35
Tea Green Marls ..	0·72	460·8	3·26
Keuper Red and Green Marls	1·85	1,184·0	8·39
	22·09		

(d) The stream pattern should be simple, as is the case with the Kingston Brook.

(e) The land use should be fairly uniform and relatively easy to record. In the case of the Kingston Brook the predominant use is mixed farming with only small areas of parkland (113·92 acres) and woodland (328·32 acres).

(f) There should be no major settlement within the area involving large abstractions of water or possible intrusions of 'foreign' water brought in artificially from outside. The Kingston Brook catchment has only small villages and individual farms.

(g) The instruments should be fairly easy to instal and to maintain. In the Kingston Brook catchment there was already a weather station at the Nottingham University School of Agriculture at Sutton Bonington and this serves as the main station for the catchment, a number of evaporation measuring instruments, such as the American Standard Class A Pan, the English Standard Tank, and a Nature Conservancy type of Lysimeter, having been added.

(h) The known meteorological data should not present violent contrasts from one part of the catchment to another. This condition really collaborates with condition (b) above. Using rainfall as an indicator it would appear that no part of the Kingston Brook catchment has a mean annual variation of more than two inches, from 26 to 28 inches per year.

The Standard Catchment concept is useful both for research and teaching purposes, and several educational institutions are co-operating with the Trent River Authority in this work, notably the Nottingham University School of Agriculture in connection with the Kingston Brook study. For research there is first of all the need for adequate instrumentation for measuring the different hydrological elements; this is of great importance if the results obtained are to be satisfactory. Secondly, there is also the question as to how far the network of instruments for each of the different elements is adequate or requires to be supplemented. Experience should help to provide an answer and in the meantime work on Standard Catchments should proceed as vigorously as possible, for it provides a method of obtaining a much-needed quantitative assessment of hydrological conditions within many different parts of the Trent basin.

SELECTED REFERENCES

Potter, H. R. *Standard (Experimental) Catchments*. Loughborough College of Technology (October 1964)

Potter, H. R. *Introduction to the History of Floods and Drought of the Trent Basin*. Loughborough College of Technology (October 1964)

IX

WATER SUPPLY

PUBLIC water supply in the area covered by this survey is the responsibility of a number of undertakings, the various statutory areas being shown in Fig. 31. The Nottingham Corporation supplies the largest population group in the area, including the city of Nottingham and virtually the whole of the southern part of the county, an area of some 260 square miles with a population of 586,000 (1965).

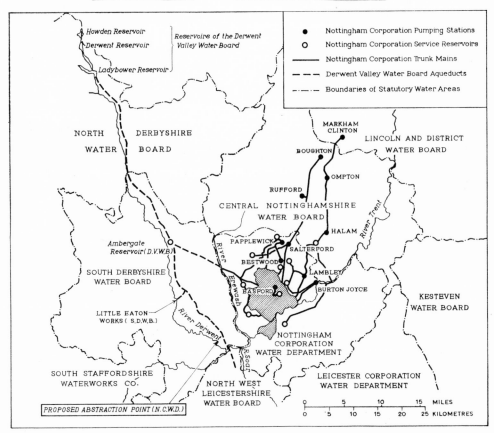

Fig. 31   Water supply and its administrative boundaries around Nottingham

Supplies in the 18th and early 19th centuries

The first recorded public water supplies in Nottingham were given in 1696. Before this date the inhabitants of the town were dependent upon the rivers Trent and Leen, private wells, springs and the storage of rainwater in barrels and other vessels and it is interesting to note that the water from some of the springs was considered to possess curative properties. In 1696 the Company of Proprietors of Nottingham Waterworks was formed and this Company erected an engine house, water-wheel and pumps on the south bank of the river Leen near the site of the present '*Bowling Green*' Hotel in Canal Street.

Water from the pumping station was forced through pipes three and a half inches in diameter into a small open reservoir on the site of the ancient postern near the General Hospital, whence it gravitated to most parts of the town through pipes varying in diameter from three-quarters of an inch to three inches. This supply appears to have sufficed until the early 19th century when complaints of the quality and scarcity of the water caused the Company to construct further works at Scotholme in Basford in order to obtain water from nearby springs and from the river Leen at a point where the river was free of contamination from the town's sewers. Water was collected in an open reservoir covering about one acre and gravitated through 10-inch piping to pumps at the foot of the Castle Rock on the site of the present Water Offices. The pumps were driven by a water-wheel operated by the river and the quantity pumped per day varied from 300,000 to 400,000 gallons.

Towards the end of the 18th century a private water supply undertaking known as the Zion Hill Waterworks was established. Water was raised by a steam engine from a well some 60 yards deep situated near Zion Hill (adjoining what is now Canning Circus) and part was distributed through pipes, the remainder being delivered manually by water carriers known as 'Higglers'.

In 1824 and 1826 two additional water companies were established as rivals to the river Leen Company. One, known as the Nottingham New Waterworks Company, pumped water from a well into a large cistern supplying the north–eastern portion of the town. The other, known as the Nottingham Trent Waterworks Company, was formed to supply the south and south–eastern parts of the town. Water was obtained from the river Trent by filtration through brick tunnels in the natural beds of sand and gravel on the north side of the river and pumped by means of a single-cylinder beam steam engine through a 15-inch main to a reservoir in Park Row. This main is still in use and in good condition.

The three companies and the Zion Hill waterworks existed for a time in considerable rivalry which was enhanced by the fact that they had no statutory limits of supply. This state of affairs was brought to an end by the Nottingham Water Act of 1845 amalgamating the three companies into the Nottingham Waterworks Company and with the passing of this Act the present system of water supply to the city and its immediate environment can be said to have been founded. The

Nottingham Water Act of 1845 was a model of its kind and many of the principal provisions concerned with the general administration of the undertaking and its relationship with consumers and prospective consumers are still in operation.

Supplies from the Bunter Sandstone

By the middle of the 19th century the position had been reached that all the major rivers in proximity to Nottingham were too polluted for use as sources of public water supply yet at the same time the demand for water was rising to unprecedented levels because of the growth of population and industry and the general demand for a public water supply system as an essential feature of civilized life. It was indeed fortunate for Nottingham and Nottinghamshire that an abundant source of good-quality water was available within the Bunter Sandstone. From 1850 onwards the public water supply of virtually the whole region has been derived from this source and from the river Derwent in Derbyshire.

The outcrop of the Bunter Sandstone in Nottinghamshire is shown in Fig. 32. The Sandstone outcrops mainly on the west side of the county and dips below the Keuper Marl to the east (see Chapter I). The width of the outcrop is about eight miles for the majority of its length, narrowing to two miles at its southern extremity. The thickness of the formation varies from 600 feet in the north to 200 feet in the south and its base rests directly on the Permian Marls, varying in thickness from 20 to 30 feet and forming a water-tight barrier between the Sandstone and the Magnesian Limestone and Coal Measures which lie beneath.

The Sandstone has a high porosity and readily absorbs a large proportion of the rain falling upon its surface outcrop. It also acts as an efficient filter where it is not fissured and water pumped direct from the outcrop is of excellent character. On the eastern side of the county where the Bunter is covered by a considerable thickness of impermeable Keuper Marl the Bunter can be said to be sealed off at top and bottom and forms an ideal source of very pure water requiring no treatment of any kind. Water from the wells or boreholes sunk in the exposed outcrop must, however, always be sterilized before being used for public supply purposes, largely because of the fissuring of the Sandstone caused by colliery subsidence. Vertical fissures allow surface pollution to obtain access to the underground water and the presence of horizontal fissures supplying the wells may permit the pollution to reach the well or borehole without any very great dilution taking place.

The Bunter Sandstone is more prolific in its yield of water in the north than in the south. This is because of the greater area of outcrop providing replenishment of the underground reservoir, the greater width of the outcrop in the northern section and the greater thickness of the Sandstone itself. Due to its large area and thickness and high porosity the Bunter Sandstone in Nottinghamshire provides an underground reservoir of enormous volume. Calculations of the quantity of water contained can only be very tentative but some authorities consider that the total amount held in the

Sandstone at the present time may be of the order of several million million gallons. Because of this very high capacity the water levels of the aquifer do not respond very quickly to changes in rainfall. At the time of writing, June 1965, the rainfall on the Bunter outcrop has, for a period of four years, been less than the long-term average, yet there appears to be no immediately recognisable effect on water levels in wells and boreholes. Long-term effects due to overpumping in certain areas are a different problem and are discussed later in this chapter.

Existing pumping stations of the city undertaking

The first of the existing pumping stations abstracting water from the Bunter Sandstone in the immediate vicinity of Nottingham was constructed at Haydn Road, Basford, in 1857 and utilised ram pumps powered by rotative beam steam engines. Two main wells were constructed 112 feet deep and joined by an adit 100 feet long. It was stated at a Local Government Board Inquiry in 1896 that the yield of this station was 2·5 to 2·75 million gallons per day in 1880 but that by 1894 the yield had fallen to 1·96 million gallons per day. The present safe yield of the works is only 1·2 million gallons per day and this gives evidence of the falling yield of this part of the aquifer due to long-term overpumping.

The rising trend of consumption soon necessitated the construction of further stations of a similar character at Bestwood in 1871 and Papplewick in 1883. The combined output of these two stations is now about four million gallons per day. At Bestwood the two wells were sunk 186 feet deep joined by an adit which was further extended for a considerable distance from the well. At Papplewick two wells were sunk 202 feet deep joined by adits 271 feet long. At both Bestwood and Papplewick water was raised by a pair of ram pumps operated by rotative beam steam engines which are in use to this day.

By developing sites at Basford, Bestwood and Papplewick the Nottingham water undertaking was making use of pumping station sites as close as practicable to the city. However, the greater development of wells and boreholes for industrial as well as public water supply purposes in the heavily populated southern end of the county resulted in depletion of the underground reservoir in this area and consequent lowering of the water table. These factors caused the Nottingham authority to seek sources more remote from the city and in 1898 a Bill was promoted to develop a large pumping station at Boughton, some 19 miles from the city centre. Being situated on the Sandstone outcrop, Boughton was developed as a well station with adits. Three wells were sunk to depths of 165 feet, 168 feet and 168 feet, being joined by adits from which boreholes were sunk to a depth of 350 feet below ground. The total length of adits was 824 feet. Water was raised by ram pumps driven by two triple expansion steam engines which are remarkable examples of the massive style of engineering design characteristic of that age, and are in marked contrast to the compact design of modern pumping plant. The maximum output of Boughton Pumping Station is about 4·5 million gallons per day.

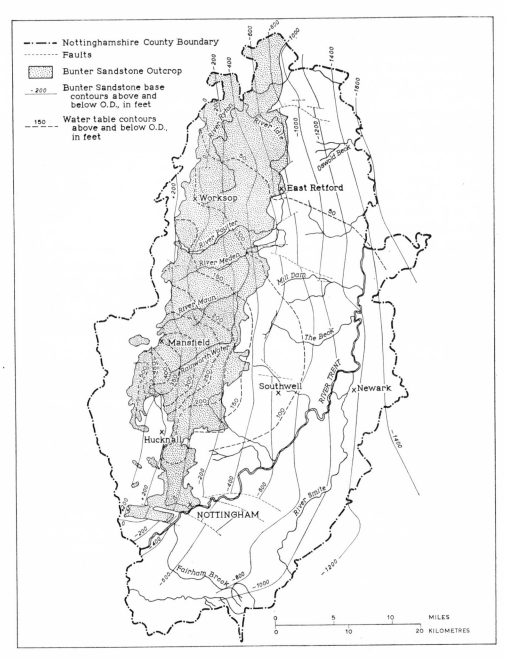

Fig. 32   The Bunter Sandstone and the water table north of Nottingham

N

A new type of station was developed at Burton Joyce in 1898, the water being derived from one borehole of 14 inches diameter and 452 feet deep which was initially artesian. This was the first station to be established on the concealed Bunter Sandstone, the depth of Keuper Marl overlying the Bunter being 154 feet. In 1908 three further 18-inch boreholes 480 feet deep were sunk at this station and in 1928 the original steam plant was replaced by electrically operated pumps. Due to the high rate of pumping in this part of the Bunter Sandstone the station at Burton Joyce is no longer artesian and the maximum yield of the station has diminished from 3·5 million gallons per day to about 3·2 million gallons per day.

In 1945 an all-electric borehole pumping station was completed at Rufford, this being a station on the outcrop. Three 30-inches diameter boreholes were sunk to depths of about 400 feet and the yield of the station was initially about 2·5 million gallons per day. This quantity has diminished in recent years, being evidence of over-development of the aquifer in this area.

In the years following the second world war, borehole stations have been constructed at Lambley, Halam and Markham Clinton, all being on the concealed portion of the Sandstone and located at considerable distances from Nottingham, Markham Clinton being some 23 miles from the city centre. One further Sandstone source is being developed at Ompton.

At Lambley, completed in 1957, there are three boreholes of 30 inches diameter approximately 480 feet deep, the yield of the station being an average of two million gallons per day. At Halam there are three bores, each of 40 inches diameter and approximately 560 feet deep. The average yield of the station is about four million gallons per day.

The modern pumping stations constructed since the second world war have followed a pattern of which Markham Clinton is typical. Three boreholes are dispersed as widely as possible on the available site and it is usual for the nominal output of the station to be provided by pumping from any two of these bores. Nevertheless, a pump is permanently installed in each borehole and the third pump provides standby facilities in the event of failure or overhaul of either of the other two. The boreholes are sunk almost to the base of the Bunter; at Markham Clinton the total depth below ground is about 740 feet, and the top parts of the bores passing through the Keuper Marl are lined with steel tubes grouted in with concrete in order to seal off the borehole from any possible undesirable water or contamination from the Keuper rocks.

Approximate contours of the water table in the southern part of the Bunter are shown in Fig. 32. The borehole pumps at each station are located at sufficient depth to be well drowned when pumping at maximum capacity but are driven through vertical shafting by electric motors mounted at the surface. Each borehole pump discharges into a sedimentation tank of capacity equivalent to about 20 minutes discharge, the intention being the removal of particles of sand or marl from the water. Booster pumps then pump from the sedimentation tank into the delivery main towards a terminal reservoir. If chlorination is necessary it is applied at the inlet to each sedimentation tank.

At all the post-war stations other than Lambley, the centrifugal pumps are operated by electricity taken from the national grid and diesel generating plant is provided for standby purposes. At Lambley the whole of the electric power for the station is generated on the site, by diesel-powered generators.

All the sources constructed since 1850 are still in use and are shown in Fig. 31, together with the principal trunk mains bringing water from the more remote sources into the Nottingham area of supply. The total quantity of water pumped by the Nottingham undertaking from the Bunter Sandstone is at present (1965) 23 million gallons per day.

The water is pumped through delivery mains from the various stations into covered service reservoirs varying in capacity from three to six million gallons and from these terminal reservoirs water gravitates through a complex system of mains and subsidiary service reservoirs to the individual consumers.

Underground works of other water authorities

The Bunter Sandstone has been developed as a major source of supply not only by the Nottingham undertaking but by authorities in the county which now are included in the statutory areas of the Central Nottinghamshire Water Board and the Lincoln and District Water Board. The latter authority also derives water from boreholes in the Lincolnshire Limestone. The Kesteven Water Board also has boreholes in the Bunter Sandstone. The Keuper formation contains some strata which are water-bearing but the yield is small and the quality of the water is chemically not very satisfactory. Hence these strata are only exploited for small supplies to villages and farms.

Supplies from the river Derwent

Reference has been made to the river Derwent as the second major source of supply for the area which is the subject of this survey. Under an Act of 1848 the Derby Waterworks Company constructed works at Little Eaton on the river Derwent immediately north of Derby.

Water was derived from infiltration galleries laid alongside the river and directly connected to it. These galleries have been extended from time to time and now have a total length of five and a quarter miles. Originally water gravitated from the galleries to a nearby pumping station which delivered water to two works known as the High Level and Low Level works respectively. At each of these works the water was treated by slow sand filtration before gravitating into supply.

In 1950 a softening plant was installed at Little Eaton to treat the raw water before delivery to the High and Low Level plants. In 1958 an extensive modernization of the whole of the Little Eaton plant was completed and brought into use by the Borough of Derby Water Department which had replaced the old Water Company. The raw water is now softened, clarified and filtered through rapid gravity filters which completely replace the older filters at the High and Low Level works. The maximum output of the plant is 8·25 million gallons per day.

Concurrently with the development of Little Eaton by the Derby water authorities, a bulk supply authority known as the Ilkeston and Heanor Water Board had been taking water from a tributary of the Derwent known as the Meerbrook Sough, a treatment plant being installed to soften and clarify the water. Both the Little Eaton and Meerbrook Sough works are now owned and operated by the South Derbyshire Water Board.

The Derwent Valley Water Board

In 1899, following much negotiation, the Derwent Valley Water Board was formed to develop impounding reservoirs in the upper reaches of the river Derwent. The Board was formed jointly by Leicester, Sheffield, Derby and Nottingham to act as a bulk supply authority. Certain quantities of water were to be allocated for the use of authorities in the county of Derby, the remaining quantities produced by the Board were to be shared between the four constituent authorities in defined statutory proportions. The Board constructed Howden reservoir in 1912, with a capacity of 1,980 million gallons, Derwent reservoir in 1916, with a capacity of 2,120 million gallons and Ladybower reservoir in 1945 with a capacity of 6,300 million gallons. The yield from the complete works of the Board is now 68·2 million gallons per day, of which 20·416 million gallons per day has to be sent down the river Derwent as compensation water. Of 47·784 million gallons per day available for supply, local authorities in Derbyshire (all of which have now been incorporated in the North and South Derbyshire Water Boards) have a lien on 7·22 million gallons per day. Out of the balance of 40·564 million gallons per day, Nottingham receives 14·28 per cent, Derby 25 per cent, Sheffield 25 per cent and Leicester 33·72 per cent. The water for Leicester, Derby and Nottingham is fully treated by chemical coagulation and rapid gravity or pressure filtration before being delivered by gravity through aqueducts which are shown in Fig. 31 to the three southern constituent authorities.

Future works for the Nottingham undertaking

The quantities of water pumped from the Bunter Sandstone, together with those taken from the Derwent valley reservoirs, have satisfied the needs of the Nottingham district for 120 years but it is now evident that these resources have been utilised to their maximum economic extent so far as Nottingham is concerned. Calculations of the quantity of water replenishing the underground reservoir within the Bunter Sandstone and of the quantities being abstracted by means of pumping show that more is being abstracted than the theoretical replenishment in the southern part of Nottinghamshire, that there is a more or less exact balance in the central area of the county around Mansfield and there is some surplus of replenishment over abstraction in the north near Worksop and Blyth. The quantities available in this northern area are too small to warrant the cost to Nottingham of abstracting the water and pumping it through 40 miles of mains to the city. After a prolonged and detailed survey of all possible sources within reasonable distance of the city, the Corporation has decided that the river Derwent offers, in its lower reaches, the only potential source of the size which is required to meet the needs of the future. A scheme has been prepared and application is being made to the Ministry of Housing and Local Government for powers to abstract up to 15 million gallons per day from the river Derwent, at a point near Church Wilne, some two miles from the confluence of the Derwent with the Trent. The scheme includes the construction of large artificial storage reservoirs to conserve water abstracted from the river at times of high flow and arrangements for an elaborate treatment works which will be necessary to treat the raw water and bring it to the same standard of purity and palatability as the consumers in the Nottingham area now enjoy. It is estimated that the first stage of the scheme which includes work to treat up to 10 million gallons per day will cost over £5,000,000.

Quality of water

The hardness and other chemical characteristics of the water derived from the Bunter Sandstone varies considerably from one source to another.

Table **XXXIII** Water hardness and chloride contents at various sources

Source	Chlorides Parts per million	Temporary Hardness Parts per million	Permanent Hardness Parts per million	Total Hardness Parts per million
Basford	35	162	178	340
Bestwood	28	85	86	171
Boughton	35	112	70	182
Burton Joyce ..	14	183	94	277
Halam	20	117	7	124
Lambley	15	117	11	128
Markham Clinton ..	70	137	10	147
Papplewick ..	21	52	64	116
Rufford	21	70	50	120
Salterford ..	20	57	68	125

The Derwent valley supply is soft, the usual temporary hardness being 19 and the permanent hardness 35. This water has some tendency to plumbo solvency which is corrected by the addition of lime at the treatment works, so that the pH as distributed into supply is always between eight and nine. The average hardness of water distributed in Nottingham is 155 parts per million. The hardness of the raw water in the river Derwent at the proposed point of abstraction at Church Wilne is about 225 parts per million but it is intended to reduce this by treatment to about 140 parts per million.

SELECTED REFERENCES

Edwards, I. G. The Reconstruction of the Derby Corporation Waterworks. *Journal of the Institution of Water Engineers* Vol. 16 (1962) pp. 415–430.

Hawksworth, J. W. M. *Summary of Water Supply Survey of Derbyshire* and *South Nottinghamshire.* Ministry of Health Survey (1950).

Lamplugh, G. W. and Smith, B. *The Water Supply of Nottinghamshire from Underground Resources.* Memoirs of the Geological Survey of England and Wales.

Land, D. H. *Hydrogeology of the Bunter Sandstone in Nottinghamshire.* Water Supply Paper of the Geological Survey (1965).

Lockyer, A. G. A Study of Water Supply in Derbyshire. *East Midland Geographer* (1) No. 8 (December 1957).

NOTE—In 1830 the Trent Waterworks Company appointed as their engineer Thomas Hawksley, a young man of 23, who was born at Arnold. As a civil engineer he combined expert scientific knowledge and ingenuity with resolute public spirit. As a water engineer he gained a national and international reputation and during his years of work in Nottingham the city profited not only from the improvements he effected but also from his far-sighted views. For further details see J. D. Chambers, *Modern Nottingham in the Making* (1945) pp. 9–11. See also Chapter XXVIII of this volume, p. 517.

PART II

HUMAN DEVELOPMENT

X

PREHISTORY

No general study of the prehistory of the East Midlands has ever been made, although unpublished work by M. Posnansky and F. T. Baker cover parts of the area. The present account is heavily indebted to the contributions made by these workers, to which is added material derived from more recent discoveries. Since the Nottingham region cannot be defined in archaeological terms, an arbitrary choice, which nevertheless includes the areas of several distinct archaeological cultures at different times in prehistory, has been made (Fig. 33). It comprises primarily the catchment area of the middle and lower Trent basin together with Lincolnshire.

EARLY HUNTING COMMUNITIES

Lower and Middle Palaeolithic

The distribution of hand-axes in Britain shows that the East Midlands lie on the northern fringes of the Lower and Middle Palaeolithic settlement. No fossil hominids or camp sites have yet been found, and even large groups of associated artifacts are lacking. The most extensive series of implements come from the gravel terraces of the middle Trent basin, between Burton and Nottingham, and small numbers of individual pieces are scattered elsewhere. The predominance of the Trent valley gravels, however, may be due to nothing more than the activities of local collectors at the gravel quarries in the area. All of the implements have been found on relatively low ground (below 400 feet O.D.) with the single exception of a hand-axe from Hopton, Derbyshire, from 695 feet O.D.

The material has been discussed recently by Posnansky and Baker. A series of hand-axes and a few flakes came from fluvio-glacial deposits at two quarries at Hilton, between Burton-on-Trent and Derby. These deposits belong to the retreat stage of the Eastern Glaciation, and the artifacts themselves were probably made during the preceding interglacial period. At Willington, a smaller but comparable series comes from a similar deposit. In the two groups selective collection has saved about 65 hand-axes and a few flakes. Most of the axes belong typologically to Acheulian I-III; the Middle Acheulian pieces are fewer in number, and appear to be less rolled than the bulk of the collection (79 per cent) which belongs to the Early Acheulian phase.

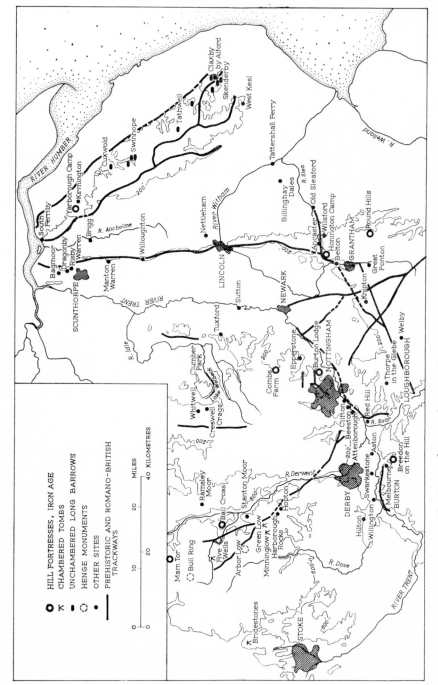

Fig. 33 Prehistory, showing the principal sites mentioned in the text

Further downstream, near Nottingham, a more representative series of hand-axes and flakes has been collected from two quarries working the Beeston Terrace gravels (see Chapter II). These deposits seem to belong to the last interglacial (Eastern Glaciation—Irish Sea Ice Interval). Eight implements from Stoney Street gravel pit at Beeston were recorded by R. A. Smith, and a larger series from the Tottle Brook pit, Beeston, by Posnansky. These implements are less heavily rolled than the Hilton-Willington series, but again are predominantly Early to Middle Acheulian in type.

Early Palaeolithic flake industries are more sparsely represented than core industries. Seven cores of apparently Clactonian facies, all heavily rolled, are known from Hilton, although most of the flakes from the same site would seem to be waste from the manufacture of hand-axes. A single flake from an evolved Clactonian steep core was found with two hand-axe waste flakes at Lodge Farm, Nottinghamshire, in chalky boulder clay of the Eastern Glaciation, a deposit which antedates the Hilton fluvio-glacial gravels, and is so far the earliest implement-bearing deposit in the Trent basin. Of the Beeston flakes, only seven have the flaking angles, prominent bulbs and sizeable striking platforms characteristic of Clactonian flakes. A larger series, however, characterised by simple longitudinal flaking of prepared surfaces, with well-defined bulbs and striking platforms, has been recovered from cannon-shot gravels at Kirmington, Lincolnshire, contemporary with the Pennine Drift—Eastern Glaciation interglacial period.

Middle Palaeolithic flake industries are represented, at best, by a few dubious pieces. Eight flakes from Beeston with thin patination, relative freshness and well-marked faceted platforms, are considered by Posnansky to be Levalloisian flakes struck from longitudinal rather than tortoise cores. A flake from Leicester may belong to a developed Levalloisian or Mousterian facies, and another isolated flake from the lake at Welbeck, Nottinghamshire, is identified by Posnansky as Levalloisian.

Upper Palaeolithic

The Magnesian Limestone region on the Nottinghamshire–Derbyshire border around Worksop, has yielded several important cave sites. Near Creswell, the Millwood brook flows through a gorge in the limestone, and here, since 1872, excavations in the caves on either side of the gorge have established a type sequence for British Upper Palaeolithic cultures. The four principal caves are Pin Hole, Robin Hood Cave and Mother Grundy's Parlour on the Derbyshire side of the gorge, and Church Hole on the Nottinghamshire side.

The material was described in detail by one of the excavators in the Association's Handbook to the Sheffield region, but, since then, further work has been carried out by Dr. C. B. M. McBurney at Mother Grundy's Parlour and at Ash Tree Cave, Whitwell. The sequence begins with a poorly-developed cave Mousterian, dated by its associated fauna to the last interglacial, followed by an Aurignacian phase which develops into a distinctively local culture. This latter, the Creswellian, is dated by radiocarbon from 8,800 ± 300 to 6,750 ± 140 B.P., and must now be regarded as an Upper Palaeolithic survival, if not a true Mesolithic culture.

Small quantities of flint artifacts correlating with the later phases of the Creswell sites are found in a number of localities in north Lincolnshire. These are open sites mainly on the Inferior Oolite Limestone (Sheffield's Hill, Risby Warren, Hardwick Hill, Willoughton) although implements have also been found at Kirmington on the chalk wolds. At Sheffield's Hill and Risby Warren, Creswellian material is apparently mixed with undoubted Mesolithic.

The relatively small quantities of material from the area which contrasts with the major continental sites, together with the poverty of decorative art, suggests infrequent visits by groups of hunters on the fringes of the Upper Palaeolithic world.

Mesolithic

The evidence for Mesolithic occupation of the area has been discussed recently by Posnansky, T. G. Manby and Baker. In Lincolnshire, several major sites fall into three groups: one at the northern end of the oolitic limestone ridge around Scunthorpe, one at the southern end of the limestone around Ancaster, and one at the southern end of the wolds around Spilsby. Geological factors determined the choice of sites in all cases. At Scunthorpe, blown sand accumulated against the scarps of limestone and ironstone, providing elevated and well-drained positions with water supplies usually near. At Ancaster, where a former course of the Trent broke eastwards through the scarp, deposits of river sand flank the slopes of the limestone. At West Keal, a high flat platform of Spilsby Sandstone overlooks the East Fen and low-lying country to the west.

There is no evidence yet from Lincolnshire of sites of Maglemosian affinities such as have been found north of the Humber, notably at Star Carr. The Lincolnshire sites all belong to Tardenoisian cultural groups, characterised in their first phase by micro-burins and simple blunted blades, and later by geometric microliths. No structures have yet been found.

Authentic mesolithic sites further west are more rare. In Nottinghamshire, a few implements, cores and waste flakes come from Tuxford, and from further north around Worksop. In Derbyshire south of the Trent, Castle Pit Hill at Melbourne has yielded a small assemblage of flint material. The cortex of the flint, together with a number of unworked pebbles, pockmarked and sand-blasted, suggests that the source of the raw material was coastal.

Although mesolithic sites are numerous on the gritstone hills of the southern Pennines west of Sheffield, they are less frequent to the south on the Carboniferous Limestone plateau.

Neolithic—the first farmers

During the second half of the fourth millennium B.C., farming was introduced into Britain by immigrants from the continent. By the first half of the third millennium, a culture with its affinities in the Western Neolithic cultures of France, was established in the south. Few settlements are known, and the type site is the causewayed enclosure of uncertain purpose on Windmill Hill, near Avebury, Wiltshire. The dead were buried in collective tombs, either stone-built chambered tombs in use over a long period, or earthen long barrows used once for the burial of an accumulation of bodies.

The evidence for the arrival and development of these farming communities in the East Midlands is sparse. But an occupation site has recently been found beneath a Bell Beaker barrow at Aston-upon-Trent, near Derby. Gullies and pits have yielded sherds of undecorated pottery; one reconstructed vessel is an open carinated bowl, $14\frac{1}{2}$ inches in diameter across the rim. A more rounded bowl, with a similarly everted rim, but without the marked shoulder carination, came from the Giants' Hills I long barrow near Skendleby at the southern end of the Lincolnshire Wolds. The only other possible settlement site in the area is at Great Ponton near Grantham. Gravel quarrying near Cringle brook in 1933 yielded a plain round-bottomed bowl of shell-gritted 'Abingdon' ware, unassociated with, but near, a hut or pit of uncertain date.

These vessels are typologically derived from the Windmill Hill culture of southern Britain, and would seem to represent the spread of later variants of the culture through the Midlands into Yorkshire and beyond, during the second half of the third millennium B.C. But although the material is so scanty, a complex situation is already indicated: the Great Ponton bowl raises the likelihood of connexions with Wessex *via* the Jurassic Limestone belt; the Aston-upon-Trent and Giants' Hills material suggests connexions with East Sussex and East Anglia.

Typologically late, too, are sherds of decorated Peterborough wares from open sites such as Risby Warren (north Lincolnshire), cave sites in Derbyshire, such as Harborough, near Brassington, and Ravencliffe in Cressbrook dale, and from the river Trent at Attenborough and Newark.

Of other Neolithic artifacts, axes of stone and flint are the most common. Until more stone axes have been analysed petrologically, no firm conclusions can be made regarding the trading of axes in the late Neolithic period. But it is probable that markets existed here for the axe factories at Great Langdale, Westmorland, and perhaps Graig Lwyd in Caernarvon. Leaf-shaped arrowheads have been found on a number of sites in Lincolnshire and Derbyshire, but occur less frequently in the Trent valley.

The collective tombs fall into two groups. On the Lincolnshire Wolds, 13 or possibly 15 long barrows were recorded by C. W. Phillips, and one of them, Giants' Hills I near Skendleby, was extensively excavated. All of the barrows are probably similar consisting of long mounds of chalk rubble dug from surrounding ditches, and covering wooden structures, burials and other features. Dimensions, approximately recorded from ground observations by various workers, are given in Table XXXIV. Three of the barrows form pairs: at Swinhope (Hoe Hill, I and II), at Claxby-by-Alford (Deadman's Grave I and II), and at Skendleby (Giants' Hills I and II). At Giants' Hills I, inhumation burials of one adult male, five women and a child, were found 30 feet from the eastern facade of the barrow on a pavement of chalk slabs. Three of the skeletons were disjointed, and many of the bones of these were weathered. The barrow covered a rectangular system of upright posts 200 feet by 40 feet, spaced about five feet apart along the sides, and at the east end taking the form of a facade built by the close-setting of half logs, split side inwards, in a bedding trench of shallow crescentic plan.

In the Peak District, nine sites may be regarded with certainty as true chambered tombs, although a number of others have been claimed in the past. The Bridestones consists of a gallery grave, 18 feet 6 inches long, entered from a semi-circular forecourt at the east end of a long barrow. There were, in the 18th century, two side chambers in addition to, and 55 yards from, the existing terminal chamber. At Five Wells, two gallery graves are entered from opposite sides of a circular mound. Minninglow has five stone structures (two passage graves and three cists) in a circular mound. Recent excavations at Green Low showed that the passage and chamber were entered through a recessed facade over 30 feet long, built of limestone blocks, with a closing slab to the passage in the centre. Burials in the chamber and passage, dug out by Bateman in the 19th century, had all been by inhumation.

Two outliers, both to the north near Doncaster, complete the list. At Sprotborough, a long barrow locally known as 'The King's Grave' has not yet been excavated; nearby, at Dinnington, an oval cairn containing 15 to 25 individuals, was entirely removed in 1862 to obtain stone for walling.

Later Neolithic occupation

Derbyshire in the later Neolithic period was developing into a major settlement area. Two imposing henge monuments indicate religious centres and social organisation in the erection of large-scale earthworks. Arbor Low is the better-known. At a height of 1,230 feet O.D., and commanding a wide view over the surrounding countryside, this Class II henge consists of a circular ditch and external bank 250 feet in overall diameter, enclosing a plateau of an average 160 feet diameter. The two entrances, on the north–west and south–east sides, are each about 27 feet wide. Inside, around the edge of the interior plateau, lie 42 slabs of irregular and undressed limestone, varying in size up to 13 feet in length and six feet in width. Undoubtedly, as at Avebury in Wiltshire, these stones were once upright, although the evidence from excavations is not yet conclusive on this point. Four stones, including two of the largest, lie in the centre of the plateau, and possibly once formed a 'cove', again

Table XXXIV   The long barrows of the Lincolnshire Wolds

Local name	Parish	Grid reference	Length in feet	Maximum width in feet	Orientation	Remarks
Ash Hill	Swinhope	TA 209961	128	53	NNE–SSW	Northern end damaged by erection of air-raid shelter
Ash Holt	Cuxwold	TA 190011	78	38	SSW–NNE	Deep hole in southern end
Beacon Plantation	Walmsgate	TA 369778	257	64	NW–SE	Cut across in two places
Burgh Top (Candlesby)	Burgh-on-Bain	TA 213850	90	45	WSW–ENE	Doubtful
Deadman's Grave I	Candlesby	TF 459675	—	—	E–W	Doubtful
Deadman's Grave II	Claxby-by-Alford	TF 445720	160	54	WNW–ESE	
Giants' Grave	Claxby-by-Alford	TF 447719	173	60	WSW–ENE	
	Ludford	—	—	—	—	Otherwise known as Adams' Head, now destroyed
Giants' Hills I	Skendleby	TF 429711	210	75	NW–SE	Excavated by C. W. Phillips, 1933–34
Giants' Hills II	Skendleby	TF 429707	—	—	NW–SE	Now ploughed out
Hoe Hill I	Swinhope	TA 215954	180	60	E–W	
Hoe Hill II	Swinhope	TA 214955	—	—	—	Destroyed
Normanby Top	Normanby-le-Wold	TA 134964	—	—	—	
Spellow Hills	Landton-by-Spilsby	TF 402723	182	40	NNW–SSE	
(Tathwell)	Tathwell	TF 295823	105	52	E–W	
AVERAGE DIMENSIONS FROM AVAILABLE FIGURES			156	54		

as at Avebury. The date of the monument is difficult to assess. The extensive excavations by H. St. George Gray in 1901–02, which involved clearing out about one-fifth
of the total length of the ditch, yielded only a barbed and tanged arrowhead. One
may suppose the initial earthwork construction to have taken place in the late
Neolithic period, although the stone slabs may have been later additions of the Early
Bronze Age. A monument of this kind would have been in use over a considerable
period.

A second, less well-known, but almost equally impressive henge monument is
situated 10 miles to the north–west at Doveholes. The Bull Ring is closely similar
to Arbor Low in construction and size; although no internal stones survive, an 18th
century account mentions their presence.

The stimulus for the elaboration of henge monuments, if not the origin of sites
like Arbor Low and the Bull Ring, came from a new influx of people during the
late Neolithic period. A relatively rapid movement from Iberia reached many parts
of Europe, and from the Netherlands and the Rhinelands people penetrated the East
Midlands *via* the Lincolnshire coast, perhaps during the 19th century B.C. The new
arrivals buried their dead contracted in single graves. Very few of their settlements
have been found.

The invaders made characteristic pottery beakers, with smooth, S-shaped profiles
and horizontal zoned decoration. The distribution of these Bell Beakers in the East
Midlands is mainly coastal, affecting north Lincolnshire and the Wolds. Sherds have
been found at Manton Warren and other open settlement sites in the Scunthorpe
area, and also at the Giants' Hills I long barrow. Recently, however, a barrow
containing a Bell Beaker, together with an archer's wrist guard, was excavated as
far inland as Aston–upon–Trent, near Derby. But the main cultural impact of this
invasion was not felt for several generations, even in Lincolnshire, while the Beaker
burials of upland Derbyshire are exclusively late. By this time, in the 18th and 17th
centuries B.C., a more elaborately decorated type of beaker, with a globular body
and a long vertical neck had been developed. These Necked Beakers, with other
characteristic grave goods, usually accompany contracted inhumation burials under
round barrows in upland Derbyshire. They are less common in the Trent valley,
although two beakers from Clumber Park, Nottinghamshire, and a beaker found with
a penannular copper or bronze bracelet with incised decoration at Knipton,
Leicestershire, may both have come from graves. At Aston–upon–Trent, the Bell
Beaker barrow was rebuilt for a Necked Beaker burial. In Lincolnshire, the absence
of Necked Beaker burials may reflect only the lack of excavation in the county, since
the distribution is compensated for by a number of casual finds, some of which,
however, may come from settlement sites.

Until the Cornish Beaker site at Gwithian was excavated, the only information
about settlements of this culture in Britain came from the site buried beneath the
Middle Bronze Age barrow at Swarkeston, near Derby. Here, in an area of some

35 feet by 40 feet, was recently excavated a Necked Beaker occupation level featuring stake holes in two long rows approximately four feet apart, and another irregularly shaped complex of holes tentatively interpreted as the remains of a hut.

Less clearly related to the Beaker culture, and perhaps overlapping with the ensuing Early Bronze Age, is a number of barrows in Derbyshire excavated by Bateman, which contained copper or bronze round-heeled daggers or flat axes. In the case of the dagger graves, the general practice of inhumation in rock-cut graves, together with the association of axe heads or axe hammers at Carder Low, Parsley Hay and Standlow, and of V-perforated jet buttons at Net Low, suggests broad contemporaneity with the Necked Beaker graves, despite the mutually exclusive occurrence of beakers and daggers in the two groups. But bone pommels from barrows at Galley Low, and probably Eldon Hill, also suggest a cultural overlap.

Flint daggers occur with the Derbyshire Necked Beakers, and have also been found elsewhere in the region unassociated, as have knives and barbed and tanged arrowheads of flint, and axe hammers.

The Bronze Age

Contemporary with the rich barrow graves of the Wessex Culture of the 17th to 15th centuries B.C. in southern Britain, is the development in the Midlands of cultural elements related to Wessex but evolved from local late Neolithic antecedents. Most of the material comes from graves or is unassociated. In Derbyshire, the barrow material suggests a complexity of cultural trends which passed smoothly, although with some modification, through the Middle Bronze Age and lasted perhaps into the first millennium B.C. About 30 barrows contained the distinctive pottery Food Vessel of Yorkshire type, together with other grave goods. The burials are fairly evenly divided between cremation and inhumation, which compares with the proportions in southern England, where the inhumations in late Neolithic single graves were giving way to the cremation rite, revived perhaps from older Neolithic custom, which dominated the burial practices of the Middle Bronze Age.

In Lincolnshire, about 20 Food Vessels are known, many of them again similar to the Food Vessels of Yorkshire. None, unfortunately, comes from a properly recorded context, although it may be supposed that most are from graves. The distribution, with one exception, is confined to the Jurassic Limestone ridge, where known barrows are few compared with the Chalk Wolds, but where intensive agriculture may well have obliterated many sites. The Trent valley is still poorly represented, although Food Vessels from Newark and Swarkestone indicate occupation of the gravel terraces, and air photography is revealing circular crop-marks along both the main river valley and its tributaries. The sparsity of Bronze Age occupation here may be more apparent than real.

Later in date, and generally related to the early Middle Bronze Age of the 14th and 13th centuries B.C., may be placed a further series of barrows containing

o

cremation burials in cinerary urns with collared or overhanging rims. Again, the change would seem to be cultural rather than ethnic, since the pottery, distinctive as it is, has now been shown to have evolved from indigenous antecedents. The most important groups again come from Derbyshire, where excavations on Stanton Moor, Ramsley Moor and elsewhere have established individual graves or cemeteries of barrows. A few others are known from Lincolnshire and elsewhere in the region. Reliable associations with the more easily dateable bronze implements, however, are lacking, and since Britain as a whole was becoming culturally more isolated from the 14th century B.C. onwards, problems of chronology in the Midlands are especially difficult.

The bucket-shaped cremation urns of the Deverel-Rimbury complex, perhaps typologically derived from collared urns, are now seen to belong primarily to a late phase of the Middle Bronze Age, during the 12th and 11th centuries B.C., rather than much later. Their distribution in Britain is largely confined to the south and east, but similar urns appear in south Lincolnshire, especially in the Ancaster area, and a few others near Scunthorpe in the north. These cremation urns occur in groups secondary to collared urns in or near barrows, or otherwise apparently in flat cemeteries unassociated with earlier burials, as, in our region, at Belton, Frieston and Wilsford, near Ancaster.

The Middle and Late Bronze Age is remarkable, however, for the proliferation of metal tools and weapons, and in the East Midlands considerable numbers are known, both in associated groups and as single finds ploughed up or dredged from rivers. The most important site is at Clifton, near Nottingham, where a fine series of implements of both periods was recovered from the river Trent during the construction of Clifton Bridge in 1958. In addition, three dug-out canoes were found, and piles driven into the river bank suggest the presence here of landing stages or even the foundations for the huts of a river-side settlement. Unfortunately, no pottery or other material was collected. Several important founders' hoards are known. The Nettleham hoard from near Lincoln contains bronzes typical of the earlier Wilburton phase of Late Bronze Age metal-working; while the hoards from Newark and Great Freeman Street, Nottingham, belong to the end of the Late Bronze Age.

The presence in several bronze hoards of foreign types related to the central European Urnfield and Hallstatt cultures, suggests the beginnings of renewed contact with the continent as the prelude to the immigration into the eastern and southern parts of the area of iron-using peoples. Two hoards of metalwork in the area are outstanding because of the presence in them of such types. The Bagmoor hoard, from near Scunthorpe, included the base of a metal bucket typologically representing an intermediate stage between the first Irish imitations of Hallstatt prototypes (such as the Dowris bucket) and later Late Bronze Age native improvements (such as the bucket from Heathery Burn Cave, Northumberland). The Welby hoard, from near

Melton Mowbray, contained in addition to normal Late Bronze Age types, cruciform handle-attachments for a cauldron of central European type, and ornamental discs with circular slides for straps comparable with horse gear from Hungary and Czechoslovakia. These latter, especially, suggest an actual infiltration of people, perhaps warriors, prior to the main series of Iron Age immigrations. To these instances may be added the two fine Hallstatt-type bronze swords from Billinghay Dales, near Sleaford.

The Iron Age

Evidence of early settlement is sparse, but pottery found with a bronze disc-headed pin in the brickyard at Brigg, north Lincolnshire, is of provincial Hallstatt character while retaining Late Bronze Age ceramic features. A few sherds of probably Iron Age A pottery under the rampart of the legionary fortress at Lincoln suggest the proximity of a settlement here. Further west, pottery of Iron Age A type has long been known from the settlement site at Harborough Rocks, Derbyshire, and, in Nottinghamshire, similar pottery has recently been found in gullies otherwise dated to the early Romano-British period underlying a small villa at Epperstone. But good stratigraphical and structural evidence in all these cases is lacking, and the absolute chronology obscure.

The penetration of some parts of Britain by later immigrants from La Tène Europe is reflected in the East Midlands above all by decorated metalwork of an excellence unsurpassed by any other region of Britain. A few objects only may belong to the initial phase: a bronze brooch in the shape of a bird from Red Hill, at the confluence of the Soar with the Trent, and a coral mounted brooch from Harborough Cave, Derbyshire. The majority of the objects, however, belong to a phase of insular development of La Tène metalwork dating from the second century B.C. to the Roman conquest. Most of them are casual discoveries from Lincolnshire, and the river Witham near Lincoln itself has, in particular, yielded splendid pieces of military equipment: the well-known bronze shield with its boar emblem later replaced by bosses, a beautifully ornamented scabbard locket, and an anthropoid-hilted dagger (now lost) among others. From further downstream, at Tattershall Ferry, came the remains of two carnyxes. A group of metal objects, including a finely-decorated bridle bit-ring, could have come from a chariot burial at Ulceby, north Lincolnshire. The Trent basin has produced fewer examples of Iron Age metalwork, but an exquisitely-decorated bronze scabbard comes from Sutton-on-Trent, Nottinghamshire, while from Needwood Forest, Staffordshire, comes one of the finest of gold torques. Some of this metalwork, such as the Witham shield, is likely to have been made outside the area, but many of the pieces are probably local, and suggest craftsmen working in or near the middle Trent valley or the Lincoln Edge.

The settlements of this period are again few, although intensified fieldwork in recent years has added considerably to our knowledge. A mixed Iron Age AB culture was defined in Leicestershire by K. M. Kenyon, with the great univallate fortress at

Breedon-on-the-Hill, overlooking the Trent valley near Melbourne, as a type site. A developed stage of the culture here is characterised by rotary querns, and by coarse hand-made pottery jars, some of which are decorated below the shoulder with twig-brushing or other forms of scoring. The comparative rarity of similar pottery in other areas of southern Britain suggested to Kenyon an independent continental origin. Settlement sites of the same culture have been discovered recently at Ancaster and elsewhere in south Lincolnshire. There is no reason to doubt that the Trent valley–south Lincolnshire culture was flourishing at least as early as the second century B.C., contemporary with the metalwork. A bronze brooch of derived La Tène I type, and part of an iron involuted brooch from the settlement at Ancaster, together with a similar La Tène I brooch in iron from Burrough Hill, Leicestershire, are consistent with this.

There are few hill-fortresses in Lincolnshire and Leicestershire. The three great fortresses in the latter county—Breedon-on-the-Hill, Burrough Hill, and Beacon Hill, in Charnwood—are feebly echoed in south Lincolnshire by the tiny Honington Camp, near Ancaster, Round Hills, at Ingoldsby, and Careby Camp, west of Bourne, and perhaps also in the north by Yarborough Camp, overlooking the Kirmington Gap through the Wolds. In contrast to this is the region north of the Trent. Although very little material has yet been found by excavation or even casual discovery, a group of small fortresses, certainly six, possibly as many as 10, is distributed along the high ground of Keuper marl hills overlooking the left bank of the Trent, and extends north–west to the Mansfield area. The excavation of sections of the defences of Combs Farm and Burton Lodge, both in Nottinghamshire, revealed steep-sided V-shaped ditches with slotted channels in their bottoms; but there is little good evidence of date. Another group of small hill fortresses occupies higher ground in the southern Peak District, but again there is little material, apart from a few sherds of hand-made pottery of Iron Age A character from Ball Cross and Mam Tor, to determine dates or cultural affinities. But, although there is so little material, there does seem to be a real cultural difference between Nottinghamshire and Derbyshire north and west of the Trent, and Nottinghamshire, Lincolnshire and Leicestershire east and south of the river.

At Ancaster, the AB culture must have ended with the appearance of a quite different Iron Age B culture, which founded a new settlement on the lower-lying sandy ground in the gap itself. Excavation has not yet clearly established the sequence and chronology of cultures. But at Dragonby, on the 'Jurassic Way' in the north of the county, this Iron Age B culture, characterised by hand-made footring and carinated jars, omphalos bowls, and other forms, some bearing curvilinear rouletted decoration and stamped designs, may be dated to the very beginning of the first century B.C.

Perhaps around 75 B.C., the Humber area, if not the whole of Lincolnshire, experienced yet another intrusion. At Dragonby appeared an Iron Age C culture clearly related to continental La Tène III, and to the earliest British Iron Age C sites at Aylesford and Swarling in Kent. Its elegant wheel-made pedestal urns and cordoned bowls stratigraphically overlie the earlier Iron Age B culture, although late hybrids indicate the survival of earlier traditions suggestive of an intermingling of people. This Iron Age C culture developed at various sites—at Dragonby, South Ferriby and Kirmington in the north, and at Ancaster, Old Sleaford and Ewerby in south Lincolnshire. During the second quarter of the first century A.D., fresh influences, perhaps due to coastal trade with Essex, caused cultural modifications in pottery and metalwork in Lincolnshire, while Iron Age C penetration by land from the south reached Leicester.

From all these different elements, the culture of the tribe of the Coritani must have evolved. The main Coritanian political centres seem to have been Leicester, which survived into the Roman period as *Ratae Coritanorum*, the administrative capital of the area, and Old Sleaford, where fragments of over 3,000 coin-blank moulds indicate a mint. Here must have been minted many of the coins once thought to be Brigantian, and now attributed by D. F. Allen to the Coritani. Early uninscribed coins of gold and silver were followed in the early first century A.D. by an inscribed series, from which we learn the names, or short-forms of the names, of the Coritanian rulers. The names are usually paired, suggesting the dynastic relationships of kings or the joint rule of magistrates: AUN.AST; ESUP.ASU; VEP.CORF; VOLISIOS. DUMNOCOVEROS; VOLISIOS.DUMNOVELLAU; VOLISIOS.CARTIVEL, although in one series there are three names: DUMNO.TIGIR.SENO. The distribution of these coins covers the area of Rutland, Lincolnshire and Leicestershire, with very few find-spots north of the Trent. Hoards containing Coritanian coins from Honley and Lightcliffe in the Calder valley, Yorkshire, may represent nothing more than the flight of refugees into Brigantian territory after the conquest and annexation of Coritanian land by Rome.

The conquest of the Coritani, carried out within four years of the initial landing of the legions in 43 A.D., resulted in the temporary establishment of a frontier along the Trent and Humber consisting of forts on both banks of the Trent served by the Fosse Way and Ermine Street. This system remained the frontier of the Empire from the late 'forties until the invasion of the north by Petilius Cerealis during the reign of Vespasian, when the remainder of our area passed under Roman rule.

COMMUNICATIONS

Evidence for communications in prehistoric times within the area is particularly interesting. One may presume that the Lincolnshire coast, from the Wash to the Humber, saw incursions of immigrants as well as coastal trading. Inland the area is particularly rich in remains of dug-out canoes, which provided an important form of river transport. Twenty or more are known from the Ancholme valley, and rather fewer from the Trent and Witham. In most cases there is no direct evidence for date, and, although many have been regarded as Iron Age, some, for instance, at Brigg and at Clifton, belong certainly to the Bronze Age.

Prehistoric trackways have received little attention since Phillips' survey of the trackways of Lincolnshire. Here the simple configuration of the county helps to indicate probable lines of land communications especially clearly. Elsewhere, in Leicestershire, Nottinghamshire and Derbyshire, the more broken country makes the identification of trackways difficult. Fig. 33 shows possible prehistoric and native Roman trackways in the region, and is based on the work of C. W. Phillips, M. W. Barley and R. W. P. Cockerton. Detailed explanation must await a future publication, for here only the conclusions are presented.

SELECTED REFERENCES

Allen, D. F. *Sylloge of Coins of the British Isles: The Coins of the Coritani.* Oxford University Press (1963).

Baker, F. T. *The Prehistoric Settlement of Lincolnshire.* (Thesis submitted to the University of Nottingham for the degree of Master of Arts, 1954).

Kenyon, K. M. Excavations at Breedon-on-the-Hill, 1946. *Transactions of the Leicestershire Archaeological Society* Vol. 26 (1950).

Manby, T. G. Chambered Tombs of Derbyshire. *Derbyshire Archaeological Journal* Vol. LXXVIII (1958).

Manby, T. G. Some Mesolithic Sites in the Peak District and Trent Basin. *Derbyshire Archaeological Journal* Vol. LXXXIII (1963).

Phillips, C. W. The Present State of Archaeology in Lincolnshire. *Archaeological Journal* Vol. 90 (1933); *ibid.* Vol. 91 (1934).

Phillips, C. W. The Excavation of the Giants' Hills Long Barrow, Skendleby. *Archaeology* Vol. LXXXV (1936).

Posnansky, M. *Some Considerations on the Pleistocene Chronology and Prehistory of Part of the East Midlands.* (Thesis submitted to the University of Nottingham for the degree of Doctor of Philosophy, 1956.)

Posnansky, M. The Lower and Middle Palaeolithic Industries of the English East Midlands. *Proceedings of the Prehistoric Society* Vol. 29 (1963).

ACKNOWLEDGMENT

The author is grateful to Mr. N. de L'E. E. Thomas for reading the manuscript of this paper and making several helpful suggestions. The following have kindly supplied information in advance of publication: Dr. C. B. M. McBurney, D. Reaney, T. G. Manby, G. D. Lewis, S. Revill and S. E. Thomas.

XI

EVOLUTION OF SETTLEMENT

ROMAN PERIOD

WITH the Roman conquest the region can be described in terms of political geography. It covers a substantial part of the territory of the Coritani and their only known pre-conquest mint centre (Old Sleaford, Lincolnshire), but does not contain what became their tribal capital and the centre of local government, *Ratae* (Leicester). Through it runs an important section of the Fosse Way, the frontier road of the first phase of the conquest. It includes in the Southern Peak a small part of what became a permanently militarized zone. The rest of the region in its broader sense saw both intensification and extension of settlement.

The pattern of Roman military roads, which conditioned the development of urban settlement, followed natural lines of communication with an eye to contemporary political realities. The Fosse Way is an engineer's version of the earlier highway along the Jurassic ridge. The Ermine Street through Lincolnshire, based for a few miles north of Stamford on the prehistoric trackway from the Welland to the Trent, abandoned it to strike north along the Jurassic ridge. Both converged on Lincoln, strategically the most important site in the eastern part of the Coritanian territory, though not occupied as far as we know by any Belgic group, nor by any earlier hill-fort builders. King Street, constructed early in the Roman period along the western margin of the Fens, a line which traffic must already have been accustomed to follow, passed through the Belgic site at Sleaford and then made for Lincoln. A temporary legionary camp has been identified by aerial photography at Holme by Newark, about one mile north-west of the Fosse Way.

The Ninth Legion was established at Lincoln by 49 A.D., in a fort whose earth and timber defences have been observed underlying those of the succeeding colonia. Of the small forts strung along the new road, only Great Casterton (Rutland) has been examined. Lying half a mile east of Ermine Street, along which the Roman town later developed, it represents the most normal size of fort in the area, 630 feet long and 435 feet wide, over its ramparts, with double-ditched defences and timber-framed internal buildings. It was reduced by some 80 feet in length after a time, and its occupation then lasted until the late 70s of the first century. Its history must be typical of many Midland forts before the advance of Agricola into Scotland shifted the northern military zone into the Pennines and beyond. At Thorpe (*Ad Pontem*) the fort has been located, its rampart sealing earlier native huts. On the strength of finds, forts can be presumed on Ermine Street at Ancaster (*Causennae*) and on the Fosse Way at Willoughby on the Wolds (*Vernemetum*), East Bridgford (*Margidunum*) and Brough in South Collingham (*Crocacalana*), but the sites have not been found. The site at Broxtowe destroyed by the spread of Nottingham in 1938 was evidently another fort belonging to the same phase of the advance.

Bridges over the Trent at Cromwell and East Stoke carried roads from near *Crocacalana* and from *Ad Pontem* into central Nottinghamshire; the course of the latter is clear as far as Goldhill in Edingley. A newly discovered fort on the east bank opposite Littleborough (*Segelocum*) must presumably belong to the next stage of the military advance. The fort at Little Chester (*Derventio*) was probably established *c*75 A.D., though after that it was not continuously occupied.

The prehistoric Sewstern Lane must have continued in use. The Fosse Way itself was remodelled early in the second century, being laid between East Bridgford and Syerston on a new line parallel to and about 200 yards east of the old. The importance attached to the Fosse Way in the early period is underlined by the siting on it of the Coritanian capital, Leicester, as well as the capital of the Dobunni, Cirencester.

The shift of the centre of local government to the south-western part of Coritanian territory may be linked with the establishment of a *colonia* on the legionary fortress site at Lincoln in *c*91 A.D., which involved the permanent loss by the tribe of land already taken when the legionary fortress was established. Although Leicester was larger than Lincoln, even after the *colonia* had been extended in the third century down to the bank of the river Witham, Lincoln must always have been a more imposing example of the civilising effect of empire. This follows from its function, as a home for retired veterans of the Ninth Legion; it is proved by the quality of its public buildings, and by the glimpses of social life revealed by a few notable relics. The design of the four original gates is now known, but not of the later extension. The walls are known to have had interval towers. The water supply was carried by aqueduct and pipe-line to a reservoir behind the town wall in East Bight, and thence fed to public baths in the north-east quarter and to fountains in the streets. The gridded street plan is known from remains of buildings and from the remarkably impressive sewer system. Comfortable houses stood both within the old town and on the terraced slopes of the new.

The region contains five other settlements whose history spans the whole Roman period and which were eventually fortified. Ancaster had double ditches and a wall enclosing nine to ten acres, constructed (as at Great Casterton) towards the end of the second century. Both towns had bastions added to the walls in the fourth century. Two of the Fosse Way towns, *Ad Pontem* and *Margidunum*, were walled only in the last century or so of the Roman era. Horncastle, at the southern extremity of the Lincolnshire Wolds, occupied eight to nine acres; its defences are as yet undated. The old Belgic centre of Old Sleaford grew into an extensive settlement in the Roman period but seems to have remained unfortified.

Superior water communications, natural and artificial, contributed to this urban development in the north-eastern part of the Coritanian territory. The Trent was used to distribute manufactured goods. *Margidunum* lay within one and a half miles, *Ad Pontem* no more than a quarter of a mile of the river. It has been established that a Cambridgeshire section of the Car Dyke was cut not later than *c*100 A.D.; hence the Car Dyke and the Fosse Dyke, together over 80 miles long, are seen as a stroke of imperial initiative designed to open up the Fenland for settlement and also to transport provisions to military depots in the north.

The region contributed significantly to the industrial wealth of Roman Britain. In the north-west lay the important lead deposits of the Wirksworth area of Derbyshire, worked certainly from the second century onwards. Coal found at several Fenland sites, and at sites elsewhere such as *Ad Pontem*, may well have come from outcrop workings in the east Midland coalfield and have been distributed by the Trent and the canals. The iron industry was concentrated in the area south of Grantham, though deposits of bog ore may well have been worked elsewhere (e.g. *Margidunum* and *Thurgarton*). In addition to the iron furnace from Woolsthorpe, shaft furnaces of second century date have been found at Pickworth (Rutland), and slag heaps at Clipsham (Rutland) and Castle Bytham.

Gravel was extracted on the Fen margin and in the Trent valley for road-making, the Fosse Way being entirely so constructed in the vicinity of Newark. The high quality limestone of the Jurassic zone was quarried for building purposes, and also, at Lincoln and Ancaster, for sculpture. Suitable slate for roofing was to be found in Charnwood Forest, Leicestershire, whence it was sent to *Margidunum* and to villa sites.

The prehistoric salt industry of the Lincolnshire coast continued there and was extended to the new settlements in the Fenland.

Much of the demand for wheel-made, well-fired pottery was met, in this region as elsewhere in lowland Britain, by local potters. On the outskirts of Lincoln a large industry grew up from the early second century if not before, using the clays found at the foot of the scarp and producing a wide variety of wares. Kilns at Ancaster produced a distinctive grey ware used mainly in the town. Potters working at Lea, Torksey and perhaps Meering and Newark could distribute their wares by the Trent to urban markets as well as to rural settlements. A pottery at Bourne, a small settlement or posting station on King Street in Lincolnshire, must have met part of the local demand for calcite-gritted pottery, a technique of Iron Age ancestry which persisted in parts of eastern England throughout the Roman period. These small industries must have found their outlets restricted by the larger centres in the Nene valley to the south and at Doncaster to the north. Nevertheless, potters working at Hazelwood and Holbrook, Derbyshire, mainly in the second and third centuries, were able, by concentrating on one type of vessel, a storage jar, to sell their output widely within the region and even on Hadrian's Wall.

Tile kilns, which must have been common to judge from urban and rural sites on which clay tiles are found, have proved difficult to locate. One example is known at Sookholme near Warsop; another at or near Lincoln is inferred from fragments of fossil ammonite (*Dactylocerus commune*) in a tile from Epperstone.

Rural settlement in a region of such varying terrain exhibits the greatest possible range. In the north-western part, an enclosed hut group has been found and excavated at Scratta Wood, two and a half miles west of Worksop, and other sites have been identified in the immediate vicinity, showing the southward extent of a settlement type usually restricted to highland areas. Native sites have been identified from aerial photographs in the Trent valley from the Dove to below Newark, and in the lower Soar valley. Similar sites have been observed on the limestone north of Lincoln and a string of sites recorded by surface pottery along the upper Witham may also be noted. Occupation persisted within or near the Iron Age hill forts of central Nottinghamshire but its character is unknown.

The virgin fenland south of the Wash, developed from the second century onwards, eventually carried a dense pattern of villages and hamlets engaged in predominantly pastoral farming and in salt manufacture. Similar sites have recently been discovered near Boston, and more may still be blanketed by silt deposits west and north-west of the Wash. It is thus evident that the story familiar from later Fenland history of peasant communities, large and collectively rich, waging a constant struggle against water, begins in the second century A.D.

Under what social conditions large Romanised farmsteads emerged out of this native society cannot yet be discerned, but the distribution pattern of villas, and hence the soil conditions which favoured that development, have become clear. The best evidence comes from the limestone uplands of Kesteven, where there was a concentration of villas similar in setting to those of the Cotswolds, but much less grand in scale. The only one excavated, at Denton, was a simple aisled house, or 'basilican' villa, with a small bathhouse nearby. Corn production is suggested by the large corn-drying kilns at the Great Casterton villa and Old Sleaford.

Four villa sites are known on light soils: Norton Disney, near *Crocanalana*, where the group of buildings includes an aisled house; Cromwell, Nottinghamshire, and Lockington, Leicestershire, on the valley alluvium, and Mansfield Woodhouse on the magnesian limestone. Nothing is known of their economy, but Mansfield Woodhouse was a fairly large establishment. Villas were probably not much less numerous on the medium to heavy soils of Nottinghamshire than on the soils of similar texture on the limestone heath of Lincolnshire.

An elaborate villa at Southwell flourished in the third and fourth centuries. The villa complex by the Thurgarton Beck now being excavated includes yet another aisled house, and early corn-drying kilns. The poor soil of the Bunter sandstone was as thinly settled as in prehistoric and medieval times.

The site at Ratcliffe-on-Soar, long-known from finds, is now identified as that of a Romano-Celtic temple on the strength of an inscribed lead plaque. Another such site may await discovery on Loveden Hill, in the parish of Hough-on-the-Hill, Lincolnshire. Otherwise, religious sites are evidenced only within or near the towns of Lincoln and Ancaster.

ANGLO–SAXON AND DANISH PERIOD

It is becoming evident that the way for a substantial Anglo-Saxon settlement, beginning in the middle of the fifth century A.D., was paved by the use of Germanic recruits in the Roman army in the later part of the fourth century. This was followed by the employment of Germanic mercenaries as *foederati* to aid the sub-Roman authorities against raiders in the early fifth century.

The corpus of so-called Romano-Saxon pottery, produced by provincial potters in south-eastern England to suit Saxon taste, includes a stamped vessel from the villa at Great Casterton, north of Stamford. At Ancaster (*Causennae*) the small Anglo-Saxon cemetery, which is an extension of the Roman burial ground outside the south gate of the town, has produced nothing but early pottery of the kind now known as Anglo-Frisian. This hand-made pottery with linear ornament is strongly represented in east Kent and Yorkshire cemeteries, but is probably most common in Lincolnshire. In addition to Ancaster, it has been found in the Loveden cemetery at Hough-on-the-Hill, and at nearby Caythorpe. Together, these finds suggest the settlement of *foederati* in the Ancaster gap. The same type of pottery also occurs in north Lincolnshire at Kirton-in-Lindsey and South Elkington.

Excavation of a substantial part of the cemetery at Loveden Hill by Dr. K. R. Fennell, as well as adding to the body of Anglo-Frisian pottery, has made it difficult to evade the conclusion that the cremation burials there begin by *c*425 A.D. The cemetery at Newark-on-Trent includes urns which certainly belong to the fifth century. On the other hand the string of cemeteries stretching from there to Burton-on-Trent seem to belong mainly to the sixth century. How much these cemeteries are due to expansion from settlements nearer the east coast and how much to new immigrants is not yet clear.

The cemeteries in the middle Trent valley, together with mid-Kesteven (Caythorpe, Loveden Hill, Ancaster, Sleaford, Ruskington) suggest penetration by way of the Wash and the river Witham. The west side of the lower Trent is unsuitable for settlement; the principal cemetery in north-west Lincolnshire at Kirton-in-Lindsey probably indicates, as does Sancton in east Yorkshire, the use of Roman roads leading away from the Humber.

The consequent growth and extension of settlements in Nottinghamshire during the sixth century was apparently due in part to movement north from Northamptonshire and Leicestershire, to judge from pottery from the cemetery at Kingston-on-Soar.

The large inhumation cemetery at Willoughby-on-the-Wolds, with burials deposited on the line of the Roman Fosse Way, also contains metal-work with affinities in counties to the south and south-east.

In Derbyshire north of the Trent not a single flat cemetery has been discovered. Barrows with inhumations are there the rule, and finds suggest that the whole group is late, belonging mainly to the seventh century.

The pattern of settlement suggested by archaeological evidence is supported by that derived from place-names. So far as we know, the earliest strata of place-names of English origin are those derived from Old English *-ingas* and *-inga-*, as in *-ingahām*. Most of the common elements, like Old English *tūn*, 'farmstead, village', remained in constant use throughout the Anglo-Saxon period, and place-names containing them could have been given almost at any time during it, even though they do not happen to have been recorded until much later.

The only type of place-name which can be shown to have been confined to the earliest periods of the settlement is that composed of a personal name followed by Old English *-ingas*. To this can be added the group which contain a personal name followed by *-inga-*, the genitive plural of *-ingas*, and ending in a word like *hām*, 'homestead'.

Now, *-ingas* is the plural of *-ing*, which in Old English denotes 'son of, descendant of',—Alfred the Great is sometimes referred to as *Ælfrēd Æðelwulfing* 'Alfred the son Athelwulf'. The plural form *-ingas* was similarly added to a personal name to denote a dynasty, as in *Wuffingas* 'the descendants of Wuffa', the name of the ruling family in East Anglia, one of whose members is probably commemorated by the ship burial at Sutton Hoo.

But, the plural form seems at a very early date to have developed the sense 'the dependents of, people of', as in *Gēdlingas* 'the people of *Gēdel* or *Gēdla*', originally the name of a group of people who settled in Nottinghamshire and who have given their name to Gedling. Folk-names of this type are found in other Germanic areas, and apparently represent a group of people, varying in numbers, associated together under a single leader. Such groups seem to have been typical of the migration period, and included not only blood relatives of the leader but also dependents (along with their wives and children), unrelated by blood but bound to the leader by a personal oath of loyalty.

The place-names which are formed from a personal name followed by *-ingas* were therefore not originally place-names at all, but rather folk-names which became place-names when the folk concerned settled permanently in some particular place. It has long been recognised that such names belong to the earliest periods of English settlement in Britain, for they reflect a social organisation which must have preceded the establishment of the Anglo-Saxon kingdoms. So, their geographical distribution (Fig. 34B) is significant since it will define some of the areas first settled and indicate some of the routes by which the settlers penetrated the country.

Fig. 34 Distribution of place-names

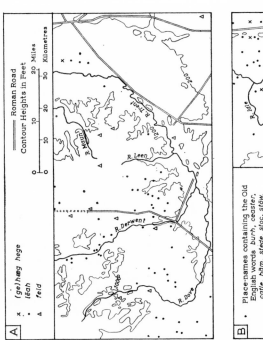

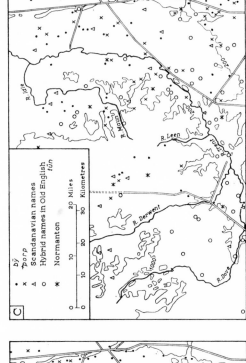

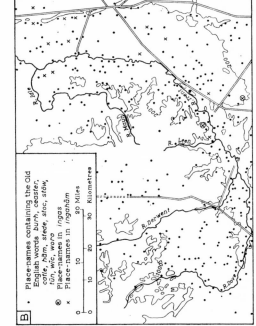

The ending -*ingas* was also used, however, to denote the settlers in a particular district and in place-names derived from such groups the first element of the name denotes a natural feature, as in the Nottinghamshire Meering 'the dwellers near the pool'. This particular usage continued in the later Old English period, and although some such names may well date from an early period, the group as a whole cannot be used as safe evidence of early settlement because of the continued use of the type. As a result, only those place-names which have Old English -*ingas* added to a personal name provide certain evidence of an early date for the settlements so named.

There are also place-names derived from the genitive plural of group-names and these have been compounded with another element, to give a form such as *Snotinghām* 'the homestead of the *Snotingas*', where the group-name *Snotingas* means 'the people of Snot'. Again, there are topographical names of this type like Hoveringham 'the homestead of the *Hoferingas*', in which *Hoferingas* means 'the dwellers on the hump of ground'. A distinction must be made between these types, and the topographical group-names in -*ingahām*, like those in -*ingas*, cannot be used as evidence of primary English settlement, even though many of them are likely to be very old.

The relationship between names like Gedling and Nottingham is so close as to suggest that both were in use at about the same time. The Nottingham type may well have continued to be given for a generation or so after the Gedling type had become obsolete, merely because they are *original* place-names and not the names of groups of people which became the names of places. There can hardly have been much significant difference in their dates, however, and both belong to the period of primary substantial Anglo-Saxon settlement in various parts of the country.

Such names are represented in some parts of our area. In Nottinghamshire are Gedling and Hickling, as well as Beckingham, Collingham, Nottingham and Walkeringham, and perhaps Bingham. In the adjacent parts of Lincolnshire are Bassingham, Beckingham, Cammeringham, Corringham, Fillingham, Grayingham, Waddingham and Willingham-by-Stow. Along, or close to, the lower Trent, and not shown on Fig. 34B are Messingham, Frodingham and Winteringham. No examples of names derived from -*ingas* occur in this part of Lincolnshire, but there are seven such names in the county and a total of twenty-three from -*ingahām*. Not a single example of either type, however, is found in Derbyshire, and the only really ancient name in the south of that county is Repton, 'the hill of the *Hrype*', where *Hrype* is the name of a tribe, which also gave its name to Ripon in the North Riding of Yorkshire.

The evidence of place-names, therefore, supports that of archaeology, but it indicates, further, that settlement took place on both sides of the Trent, and not predominantly to the south of the river. It also suggests that in the first generations of their settlements the Angles, entering the country by way of the Humber estuary and the valley of the Trent, did not penetrate much beyond Nottingham. The settlements upstream in Derbyshire and Staffordshire must have been due to later bands of settlers pushing on into the area which later became the centre of the kingdom of the Mercians.

Further to the east the invaders must also have used the Roman roads both as routes of communication and of settlement and the importance of Ermine Street in this respect is easy to demonstrate. Where it reaches the Humber and where there must have been a ferry across the river to the continuation of the road at Brough, stands Winteringham. Nearer to Lincoln and just off Ermine Street to the east is Waddingham, while to the west below Lincoln Edge are Grayingham, Fillingham and Cammeringham. South of Lincoln, the early settlers seem to have followed the course of the Witham to found Bassingham and Beckingham.

Elsewhere in Lincolnshire, the place-name evidence suggests that the earliest settlements were by way of the coast and along the streams which flow from the Wolds, and by way of the Wash and along the Welland and the Witham. No firm dates can be adduced for these settlements, but on the balance of probabilities, the earliest of those in the east probably belong to the later part of the fifth or to the early part of the sixth century; those further to the west cannot have been much later, and Ekwall's judgment that we should not reckon with a much later time than the middle of the sixth century may, if anything, be a little too conservative.

Little is known of the early history of this region, but Lincolnshire seems to have been an independent Anglo-Saxon kingdom—a genealogy of the kings of Lindsey is still extant—while Nottinghamshire probably formed a part of the kingdom of the Middle Angles, and Derbyshire a part of Mercia. By the mid-seventh century, however, the whole area formed part of the West Midland kingdom of Mercia.

From these, and no doubt other early sites, as well as from new settlers entering the area, for instance from the south, the extension and expansion of English settlement took place. The names of English settlements containing habitative elements, like *burh* 'fortified place', *ceaster* 'Roman station', *cot(e)* 'cottage', *hām* 'homestead', *stede* 'place, site of a building', *stoc* 'place, cattle-farm', *stōw* 'place, holy place', *tūn* 'farmstead, village', *wīc* 'dwelling-place, dairy-farm', and *worð* 'enclosure, homestead', have been plotted on the accompanying map. The distribution of these names shows that settlement has taken place particularly on the slopes above the major rivers and streams, and the geological characteristics of the region explain why this was the case.

The penetrations from the Trent valley, itself the area of greatest settlement, was by way of the valleys of its tributaries, the Idle, Devon, Leen, Soar, Erewash, Derwent and Dove. But, a number of settlements are also found at a short distance from the Roman roads, Ermine Street, Fosse Way and Ryknield Street, so that there can be no doubt that they too played a part in the development of this region in Anglo-Saxon times.

The Old English place-name elements (*ge*) *hæg/hege* 'enclosure' and *lēah* 'wood', but more commonly 'open space in a wood, glade' are descriptive of settlements in wooded districts, while *feld* 'open country, land free from wood' is also common in old forest areas and probably denoted an open space larger than a *lēah*. Only those names recorded in Domesday Book have been included on Fig. 34A, and we must bear in mind that other similar names which do not happen to have been noted in the Assessment of 1086, could well have been in existence by that time, but at least we can see something of the pattern of the expansion of Anglian settlement into the old wooded districts, which had *certainly* taken place before 1086. The most notable features of their distribution are the groups with names derived from *lēah* in the valley of the Derwent, in the area north-east of Derby and north-west of Nottingham, and in the lower-lying district of Derbyshire south of Ashbourne and east of the Dove.

Settlement in the north-east Midlands was, however, profoundly affected during the last quarter of the ninth century by the immigration of Danes into the district. In 876, after some twelve years of campaigning, a part of the Danish army began to make permanent homes here. They established their headquarters at five important sites which came to be known as the Five Boroughs of Derby, Nottingham, Leicester, Lincoln and Stamford, and each became a military and administrative centre. In the following century, perhaps by the end of the first quarter, the administrative division, the shire, already in existence in some other parts of the country, was extended to the territory of the Five Boroughs, and Derbyshire, Leicestershire and Nottinghamshire no doubt represent the areas under the control of the armies with headquarters at Derby, Leicester and Nottingham, while Lincolnshire represents the areas under the control of those of Lincoln and Stamford, which were merged to form a single great shire.

It has long been believed that the size of the invading Danish army was large, to be numbered in thousands, but recently various pieces of evidence have been brought together to suggest that it should rather be counted in hundreds, perhaps no more than two or three hundred and it should be remembered that only a part of this army settled in the north-east Midlands. Now, already by 1086 some 303 places with names in -*by*, over 100 in -*thorpe* and a substantial number of other places with names of Scandinavian origin were in existence, and it is obvious that a small force could not have been responsible for the establishment of so many villages and farmsteads even if many are reckoned as the result of subsequent expansion and extension of settlement. The rate of expansion involved would not agree with the known economic facts of the period.

Further, it has often been assumed that the Danes took over many existing villages, which they re-named. No doubt this happened in a number of cases, but an examination of the place-name evidence in the light of the topographical and geological character-istics of the sites of the Danish-named villages suggests that this has been over-estimated, and that many were in fact new settlements. The implications of this are obvious.

The distribution of Scandinavian place-names recorded in Domesday Book formed from the elements -*by* 'farm, village' and *þorp* 'secondary settlement, outlying dependent farmstead or hamlet' are recorded in Fig. 34C. The names ending in -*by* represent primary Danish settlement, those in *thorpe* secondary. The secondary nature of the *thorpes* can be clearly seen in names like Mattersey Thorpe in Nottinghamshire, for, as the name itself indicates, this place was an outlying or secondary settlement dependent on Mattersey, which is itself an English-named village.

It has been noted above that in some cases a Danish name ending in *by* has replaced an English one, and sometimes documentary evidence of various kinds proves this to be so. Derby replaced an earlier name *Northworthy*, as a statement in the *Chronicle of Ethelweard* dated *c*1000 tells us; Bleasby in Nottinghamshire, which is not itself recorded in Domesday Book, is found as *Blisetune*, a hybrid Danish-English form, in a document dated 958, suggesting that a change of name took place here; and similarly, Normanby-by-Spital, which occurs four times in the Lincolnshire Domesday Survey, is recorded *once* in the form *Normanestou*, again a hybrid form which suggests that a change of name has taken place. Where a change of this kind has occurred it is likely that the Danes had taken over an existing English village, and the comparatively high assessment of Normanby in Domesday Book, as compared with nearby Danish-named places would seem to support this. There is, however, no real evidence that this has happened in the case of names in -*thorpe*.

Though some English villages were taken over by the Danes, the evidence in general suggests that a large number of places with names in -*by* represent new settlements. Except near Leicester, such names do not occur around the military and administrative centres of the district. Indeed, close to Nottingham are a series of English-named places, Bilborough, Basford, Bulwell, Sneinton and so on. Had members of the Danish Army centred on Nottingham wished to take over any of these sites presumably they could have done so. Instead they have made settlements at a distance from the town.

An examination of the 23 *bys* in Nottinghamshire supports this hypothesis. Almost all of them are situated on the slopes of tributary valleys and streams, and the settlers reached these sites by way of the valleys of the major rivers, or in one or two instances in the south apparently by the Roman roads. They also fall into distinct groups—nine in the angle of land between the Idle and the Maun; three in west Nottinghamshire, probably to be associated with Blingsby and Stainsby in Derbyshire; and three south of the Trent. The remainder lie along the Trent or its smaller tributaries and these are more widely scattered than is the case in Lincolnshire or in Leicestershire. One of these is Bleasby, an example of an English name re-modelled by the Danes and probably representing an English village taken over by the new settlers.

When the distribution (Fig. 34C) of the names in -*by* is compared with that of English habitative names, the patterns of the Danish ones appear in a more realistic light. The English occur along the valleys of the major rivers, and most of these sites were probably already occupied when the Danes settled in Nottinghamshire, so they made their settlements in the tributary valleys. This would support the hypothesis that for the most part the Danes came as colonists in the strict sense.

P

Villages with names in *-by* in the south and south-west of the county could well represent settlements made by men from the Danish army itself, and the same could well be true of Linby, Kirkby and Skegby in the west, involving a movement of settlers from Nottingham into a sparsely-inhabited district, much of it at the time heavily wooded. Again these would seem to be new settlement sites.

But, the group in the north are at a considerable distance from the Danish military and administrative centre, and if we interpret them as having been founded by men from the Nottingham army, we must ask why they settled so far away and why they crossed the sparsely-settled Bunter Sandstone of the old Sherwood Forest region to establish their homes on the comparatively infertile soils of this Sandstone near the Ryton and the Maun. After all, sites on the fertile soils of the Trent lowlands must still have been available. Their distribution and their situations suggest an answer.

It is noteworthy that there are very heavy concentrations of names in *-by* on the Lincolnshire Wolds, and to a lesser extent in north-west Lindsey in the wapentake of Manley, all at a distance from the Danish centre of Lincoln. The extent of these settlements suggests that they could not all be due to settlers from the army of Lincoln or to expansion of such settlements. They are in fact better explained as the result of immigration from Scandinavia by way of the traditional routes such as the Humber estuary, the east coast of Lincolnshire and the Wash, an immigration which took place behind the protection of the armies of the Five Boroughs.

The settlements in north Nottinghamshire are similarly better explained as having been founded by immigrants who entered the country by the Humber estuary and the Trent valley, and who then followed the course of the Idle and its tributary, the Ryton, to found a group of five *bys*, while others followed the Idle to the Maun where they established a further four villages. This would explain the pattern here better than assuming that it represents northerly outlying settlements of men who had moved across the county from the army headquarters at Nottingham.

The place-names containing Old Danish *þorp* all represent smaller and secondary settlements, for this is the specific sense of that word. Originally most of them were probably farms or dependent settlements established from a parent village, which often it is possible to identify. It should be noted, however, that the parent village has not invariably a Danish name, for *þorp* was borrowed into the local dialect of this district and remained in living use here certainly till the eighteenth century. But, almost all the Domesday names which contain this word are Danish in the strict sense and therefore are likely to indicate settlement by Danish-speaking people, or their descendants, in this area. They are, of course, of additional importance in the history of the development of settlement, since because of their meaning they form a distinctive and almost unique group.

Also plotted on the map (Fig. 34C) is a further group consisting of the so-called Grimston hybrids, names in which the first element is a Scandinavian personal name, the second being Old English *tūn*. In Domesday Book there are 20 such names in

Nottinghamshire and 10 in Derbyshire, one of which is the name of a place now transferred to Leicestershire and in every case the settlement seems to be old. Exact figures are not available for Lincolnshire for the place-name survey of that county has not been completed, but they are certainly comparatively rare there.

Their distribution in Derbyshire and Nottinghamshire seems to be significant, for they are not usually found in close proximity to Danish names in *-by* and they occur in districts where considerable English settlement had probably already taken place, as in the districts west of Derby, in the Trent valley, and to the south of that river. The history of the settlement of these places is difficult to determine, but with our present state of knowledge, the most likely explanation taking into account their distribution and situations, is that they represent older English villages acquired by Danish owners, and that in each of these names the name of the new Danish owner has replaced the earlier first element of the English place-name. This is not to say that the English population of these villages was driven out, rather that the English continued to live on in the village, but now with a Danish lord instead of an English one. We have no means of telling at what date such settlements were made by the Danes, but the names themselves certainly tell us something of the existing local conditions at the time. Whether a village of this kind should be known as a *tūn* or a *-by* must have depended to some extent on the relative numbers of English and Danes in the neighbour-hood. Where the English were present in large numbers no doubt the word *tūn* would remain in use, so that the Grimston-hybrids very probably help us to indicate areas where Danes settled, but in less numbers than in districts in which names in *-by* occur. This must have been the case in Staffordshire where two or three hybrid names in *tūn* are found, but where there are no names in *-by* and where names completely Scandinavian in origin are very rare.

Other names strictly of Scandinavian origin and recorded in Domesday Book are plotted on the map (Fig. 34C). Though some of them occur in areas where names in *-by* are found, there are a few which show that Scandinavian speaking settlers have moved into other districts. The most obvious are Eakring in Nottinghamshire, which lies between the Trent and the group of *bys* in the north, and Rowland, Holme and Flagg, near Bakewell, in Derbyshire. It is important to note that these three are situated in an area where by 926 some Scandinavian settlement had taken place, as is indicated in the text of an Anglo-Saxon charter of that date which deals with land at Ashford and Hope.

There can be no doubt that Danes formed by far the largest part of the Scandinavian army which began the colonisation of the north-east Midlands in 876, for this is proved by the general history of the Danelaw and by the forms of many of the Scandinavian place-names themselves. But place-names indicate that men of other races also settled here in the period between 876 and 1086. There are in Derbyshire three examples of Normanton 'the village of the Norwegians', together with five similar names in Nottinghamshire and one in Lincolnshire, where there are also four Normanbys.

Clearly Normanton and Normanby could only have come into existence if Norwegians formed a small but distinctive feature of the racial complex of the area in which the names occur.

In Lincolnshire there are also two examples of Firsby 'the village of the Frisians', identical in meaning with the two Frisbys in Leicestershire. It is certain that some Frisians took part in the Viking invasions themselves, for Ubba, one of the leaders of the army, a part of which settled here, is referred to as *Dux Fresonum*. Firsby and Frisby must, therefore, represent settlements by small, but distinctive, groups of Frisians, who like the Norwegians of Normanton and Normanby, formed a part of the Viking settlers in England in the late ninth and tenth centuries.

Similarly, there are two Iretons in Derbyshire and two Irbys in Lincolnshire, though only one of the latter is recorded in Domesday Book. These names mean 'the village of the *Iri*', and *Íri* is the term used of a Viking who had been in Ireland before coming to England or of an Irishman who accompanied the Vikings to England. In Derbyshire, too, is Bretby 'the village of the Britons' and these Britons are most likely to be men of British descent from the north-west of England. It is also possible that the Derbyshire Mammerton means 'the village of Maelmuire', and Maelmuire is Goidelic personal name borrowed by the Norwegians in Ireland. It is, therefore, a reasonable conclusion that Bretby and Ireton and Irby represent settlements by men of British and Irish or Irish-Norwegian descent who came down from the north-west of England to take part in the Scandinavian settlement of the territory of the Five Boroughs.

MEDIEVAL PERIOD

The Scandinavian settlements have left remarkably little trace of the archaeological record. The limited evidence includes Viking swords from the Witham near Lincoln, from Farndon and Nottingham and an axe from Repton. Two of these finds come from churchyards, and suggest that although the diocesan organisation of the church was disrupted and monasteries pillaged, the Christian countryside soon absorbed the new pagans in its midst. The only known Scandinavian cemetery in England lies across the Trent from Derby at Ingleby; it consists of a group of small barrows over cremations and has produced a Viking sword.

The distribution of finds along waterways confirms the evidence of documents for the importance of water communications in the ninth century and onward. The movement of Danish armies cannot be separated from the growth of trade in promoting town development. Three of the Danish Five Boroughs lie within the region: Lincoln, Nottingham and Derby. At Lincoln (as at Leicester) the Roman defences were no doubt still in serviceable condition, though the city had by 1066 outgrown them both to the east and to the south. At Nottingham the hill crowned by St. Mary's formed the pre-Conquest *burh* and was fortified by a bank and ditch possibly as early as 868 A.D. (Fig. 35). Stamford, like Nottingham, had earthen defences before its stone

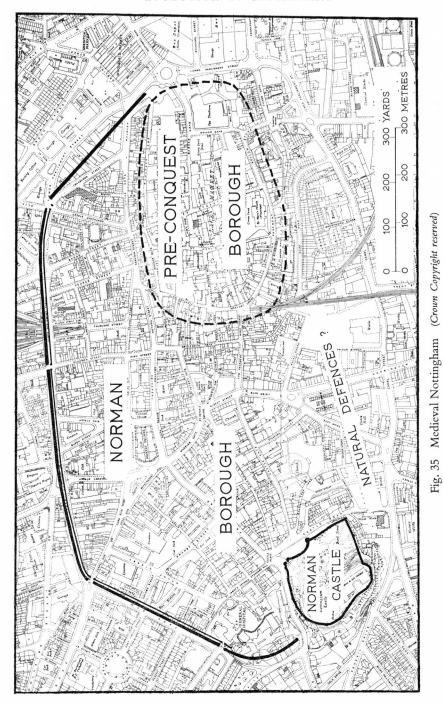

Fig. 35 Medieval Nottingham *(Crown Copyright reserved)*

The pre-Conquest borough was defended by a bank and ditch, the Norman borough at first in the same way, and later by a stone wall (thin line). Nothing is known of the defences across the low ground to the south.

walls, for the church of St. Mary, which stood within St. Peter's Gate was called *Bennewerk* (within the work) in the 12th century. Derby has produced no evidence for defences of this or a later period, although it is described as a *burh* in the Chronicle. Newark came into existence as a fortified place, new in contrast to the ruined Roman 'old works' along the Fosse Way, in the period of Anglo-Danish conflict. Its defences enclosed a rectangle with rounded corners. It is uncertain whether the planned lay-out, which includes a very large rectangular market place, belongs to the years after 1066 when the bishops of Lincoln were lords of the manor, or was an original feature. Torksey, lying at the junction of the Fosse Dyke with the Trent, was evidently more important than Newark in the pre-Conquest period, but was not fortified. The Anglo-Saxon name means 'Turec's island', and the site has low-lying ground on the two sides not protected by the Trent and the Fosse Dyke. Its advantages of water communication are underlined in the Domesday Book, which records the obligation of the burgesses to provide a boat to carry the sheriff of Lincolnshire to York when he required. Excavation has proved that the products of potters working there a century or more before 1066 found their way up to Newark and Nottingham, and also to Yorkshire.

The villages of pre-Conquest Lincolnshire, and to a lesser extent those of the rest of the region, were Anglo-Scandinavian communities, dominated by landowners whose loyalty a Sweyn or a Cnut could easily attract, familiar with the sight of Scandinavian long-boats on the waterways; speaking an English saturated with Scandinavian words. Society was distinguished in structure by the existence of numerous free peasants known as sokemen, and the sokes of the Danelaw are a territorialised version of the responsibility of these men to attend and constitute a court governing the relations of a lord with his men. The status of such places as Newark, Grantham and Southwell in medieval and even later times was enhanced by the courts drawing suitors from the countryside to regular meetings.

The complexity of territorial relations has made it impossible to map the Domesday population in strictly comparable terms for the whole region, but Lincolnshire and Leicestershire were evidently more densely populated than Nottinghamshire, and far more so than Derbyshire and Staffordshire. The population was thinnest in the sandstone area of Nottinghamshire which Norman kings were to make into a royal hunting forest, in west Leicestershire (Charnwood Forest) and in central Derbyshire. Those light soils of the Trent and Soar valleys and of the Fen margin in Kesteven selected by the earliest Anglo-Saxon settlers were by now the most densely populated. The reclamation of the Fenland itself had been resumed and the villages on the silt were already large.

There is no evidence of lead production in Derbyshire before the second half of the eighth century, but the industry grew thenceforward to the quite large scale evidenced in Domesday Book. From the same source it is clear that salt production was well-developed round the Wash and in the Lincolnshire coastal marshland. By the 12th

century, if not before, millstone grit in Derbyshire and granite in Charnwood were
being quarried for millstones and whetstones. The Saxon crosses of Derbyshire also
imply local quarrying and carving from *c*800 A.D. onwards. Quarrying for building
stones is evidenced on a significant scale only in Lincolnshire, where the Lias limestone,
the oolitic limestone of the Jurassic ridge and the ironstone of the Wolds were used
by 1066 A.D. The pottery industry had spread from East Anglia to Lincoln and Torksey
by that time. Stamford was the centre of one of the most important and distinctive
pottery industries in England from the ninth century onwards, and its products were
widely distributed. Iron furnaces also flourished in the town.

The system of through routes inherited from prehistoric and Roman times required
little amplification to suit medieval communities. Prehistoric trackways such as
Sewstern Lane (Fig. 33) linking Stamford with Newark, and various branches of it
making for higher up the Trent, certainly continued in use. The new main road from
Nottingham northwards to Blyth and Doncaster had come into existence by Norman
times; it was adopted as a boundary for adjacent parishes, and is recorded by 1218 as
the eastern boundary of Sherwood Forest. This was the main road to the north prior
to the bridging of the Trent at Newark shortly before 1200 A.D. The name Saltway
for the ridgeway skirting the Vale of Belvoir, and Saltersford for its crossing of the
Witham, south of Grantham, may have arisen at this time.

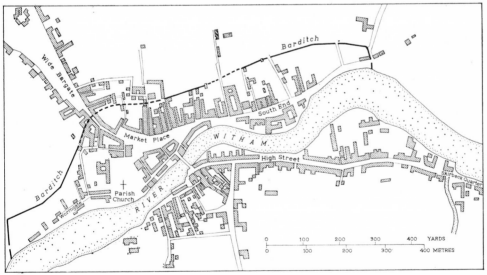

Fig. 36   The medieval Barditch of Boston, as shown on Robert Hall's map of 1741

The Norman Conquest had, either immediately or ultimately, a strong influence
on towns in the region. Nottingham was transformed by having a new Norman
borough planted alongside the old one. William had in 1068 built a castle on the isolated
and virtually impregnable rock to the west of the old borough, and within a century

the old borough and the castle were linked by a new bank and ditch enclosing the new borough. The process of facing the bank with a substantial wall began after c1260, using, in Park Row, a coarse white sandstone from the Bunter. At Lincoln the upper city had a strong castle with two mottes built in the south-west angle of the upper city (incidentally burying the Roman west gate under its great rampart) and the new Minster in the south-east corner. At Boston an entirely new town came into existence, created by the Conqueror's nephew, Count Alan of Brittany, and his Breton followers. By 1204 it ranked next to London in the value of its export trade, and its fair became one of the most important in England. The settlement lay astride the river Witham, but by c1220 the eastern part, which contained the parish church, had been enclosed by a bank and ditch known as the Barditch (Fig. 36).

Elsewhere bishops of Lincoln instituted burgage tenure in their leading manors to encourage merchants and craftsmen to settle. Newark had burgesses by 1086. The town was also surrounded, perhaps in the 13th century, by a relatively slender wall. By 1225 population had long outgrown the fortified area, and ribbon building on roads out was known as the Outer Borough (Fig. 37). At Sleaford settlement shifted half a mile westward to the environs of the castle built by Alexander, bishop of Lincoln (1123–1148), and by 1225 new Sleaford had been given borough status. At Southwell the existence of a minster which enjoyed something like cathedral status in the county had created a community of an unusual kind. The secular canons each had a mansion house there, and, by the 15th century the Archbishops of York a palace; the groups of vicars choral and chantry priests each had institutional accommodation (Fig. 38). The archbishops tried to encourage town development by setting aside land on the north side as burgage tenements round an open space possibly intended to be a market place (Burgage Green), and in 1622 the town was incorporated by charter, but such initiative had come too late. The burgesses of Grantham had their privileges confirmed by the lord of the town in 1312 and the men of Gainsborough secured similar rights from their lord by c1300.

Other places acquired urban privileges, particularly burgage tenure, but failed to distinguish themselves from the many large villages whose lords had secured the right to hold a market and a fair. They included Wainfleet (Lincolnshire) and Kegworth (Leicestershire). The Knights Hospitallers proposed to establish an entirely new town on the Fosse Way midway between Lincoln and Newark, but this design did not get beyond the paper stage. The navigable waterways throughout the middle ages contributed to the growth of Nottingham, Newark and Retford, though Torksey had died by 1540 and Lincoln lost much of its trade to Boston. Apart from the concentration of traders and merchants, or the existence of an important fair, some towns evidently had groups of craftsmen working for more than a local market. Such seems to have been the case with the iron industry at Stamford. Nottingham had, from the end of the 13th century a pottery industry, bell-founding and alabaster-carving. The cloth industry flourished in Stamford, Lincoln, Newark and Nottingham but in the latter two towns served no more than the locality.

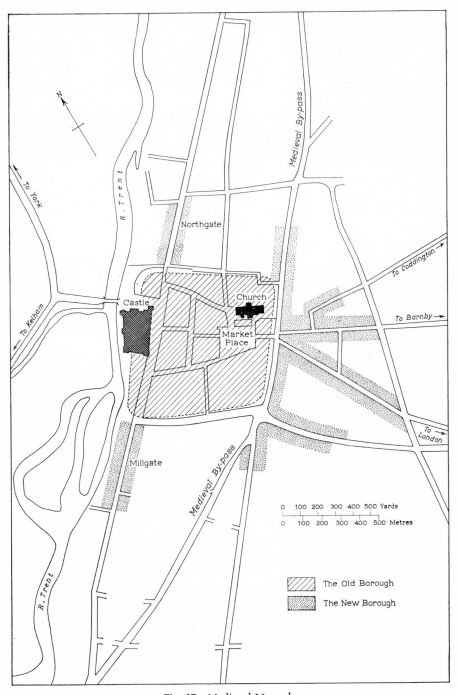

Fig. 37 Medieval Newark

Hatched area is that of the 'new work' while the stipple indicates the ribbon building by 1228

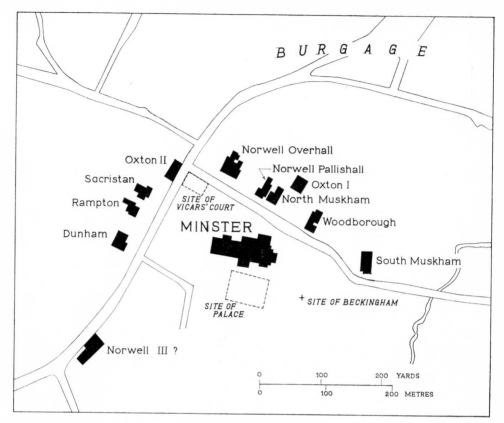

Fig. 38   Medieval Southwell

Showing the mansion houses of the canons, and (to the north) the planned development of the later middle ages

Rural settlement in the post-Conquest period was affected first by the development of monastic life. Lincolnshire is unique for the large number of modest religious houses endowed by the free peasantry. The location of such small establishments has no marked pattern, but the distribution of what became the wealthier monasteries on land hitherto unsuitable or little esteemed for settlement is a striking feature of the region. The majority of them are to be found on the Bunter sandstone, in north-west Leicestershire and in the lower Witham valley.

The Cistercians, in their desire for solitude, sometimes removed villages from their vicinity. At Revesby, on the northern margin of the Fens, the men of Stichesby and Thoresby were induced to leave by the offer of land elsewhere. In the same manner the monks of Rufford were able to dispose of Cratley and Inkersall, and the displaced men founded the new village of Wellow, the houses laid out round a large triangular green surrounded by a bank and ditch (Fig. 39).

Within the parish, the clearance of woodland and extension of cultivation can often be traced by place-name evidence. The parishes on the west side of the Trent, with villages strongly nucleated as everywhere in the region, stretch as much as five miles from the river and the light alluvium to the higher ground of the Keuper Marl. Many of these parishes have a hamlet or an isolated farm named Woodhouse near the western limit.

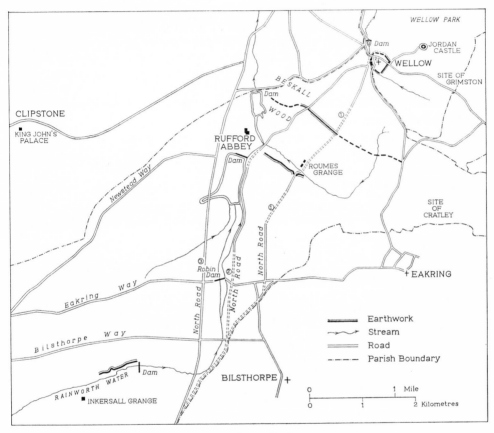

Fig. 39 The Rufford area

Showing deserted villages (Rufford, Cratley, Grimston and Inkersall) and the new village of Wellow. Earthworks survive from defended settlements, mill leets, dams to conserve surface water, and the division of disputed woodland. The north road has shifted westwards from the early medieval line (1) to the modern (3).

The recession of settlement and cultivation in the more difficult economic conditions of the latter middle ages can also be observed. The region has its share of deserted village sites, many of them on the heaviest soils, though more needs to be known of the history of individual villages and their environment before each desertion can be explained. The coal industry had already by the 15th century begun to shift population into areas such as north-west Leicestershire where agriculture alone had sustained only sparse and small villages.

Considerable areas of the region lay under the forest law: in Nottinghamshire, Sherwood; in Lincolnshire, a wide tract laying east of the Kesteven heath and bounded on the south by the Welland; in Derbyshire, Duffield Frith, lying astride the Derwent and the Ecclesbourne, which was originally a private forest appurtenant to the honour of Tutbury and subsequently formed part of the Honour of Lancaster. The history of these forests cannot be traced back beyond the 12th century. At that time Sherwood was simply the centre of a much wider region, afforested by Henry II (1154–1189), which extended on the west and north-west to the Derwent and the Yorkshire boundary, on the north to include Hatfield, and on the east to include the two Clay divisions. This wider area was disafforested between 1219 and 1227, as was the Kesteven forest between 1204 and 1230. In Nottinghamshire the bounds of Sherwood were then defined as the Leen on the west, the Meden on the north, Doverbeck and the road to the north on the east and the Trent on the south. This area was approximately 20 miles long and eight miles wide.

Sherwood lay in a well-defined area characterized by the poor soils of the Bunter sandstone. Its boundaries were partly determined by the location of the king's demesne manors and it remained a favourite royal hunting ground, especially for the Angevin kings, who frequently visited Clipstone. It is not possible to determine the relative extent of heath and woodland in the medieval period. The Domesday Survey suggests that Sherwood was no more heavily wooded than the northern part of the Clay divisions. The forest was an important source of building timber both for local use and for export down the Trent and the Idle.

At the time of Domesday, Sherwood was relatively sparsely settled. However, colonisation of new land continued very rapidly in the 12th century. Its most striking feature was the reduction of land to arable and the enclosure of such assarts. This was the work of all grades of landowners; frequently it seems to have been organised by village communities; the minster church of Southwell and the monastic foundations of the Norman period, especially Newstead, Lenton, Wellbeck and Rufford, played an important part by acquiring licences to cultivate within the forest. By the 13th century, therefore, extensive inroads had been made into the forest woodland and into the rights of the Crown. This was recognised and accepted at the end of the century when Edward I permitted the conversion of large numbers of these assarts into heritable tenures in socage, quit of the forest law and without rights of common within the forest.

This process of infiltration was probably the main reason for the decay of the forest administration in the later middle ages. It was accelerated by the acquisition of forest privileges by great landowners. This culminated in the 16th century when the estates and forest privileges of the Nottinghamshire monasteries passed into secular hands to become the territorial basis of the Dukeries. By then Sherwood was in an advanced state of decay, except for the new parks which the landed families of the county were beginning to establish at Wollaton, Rufford, Clumber and elsewhere. The process was carried further in the 17th century by the enclosure of considerable areas for coppicing to supply the needs of the charcoal industry. By 1609 half Sherwood was enclosed. Further west, Duffield underwent a similar process of decay although here coppicing was unimportant.

The maintenance and ultimate decay of the royal forest of Sherwood involved a long conflict between the Crown and local landowners at all social levels. The forest laws were unpopular; men of every cloth and class were involved in poaching, a crime which carried no moral or social stigma; and all viewed the forest laws as a hindrance to the full economic development of forest land. These were the social conditions which created, by the 14th century, the ballads of Robin Hood. There was no 'real' Robin, but there was a Robin in every poacher and forest outlaw. Stories such as these were popular in several forest districts in northern England. Robin was simply the most successful and widely known of these legendary figures.

SELECTED REFERENCES

Barley, M. W. *Documents relating to Newark-on-Trent*. Thoroton Society Record Series (1955).

Bower, Irene M. *The Place-Names of Lindsey*. (Unpublished Ph.D. thesis The University of Leeds) (1940).

Cameron, K. The Scandinavians in Derbyshire: The Place-Name Evidence. *Nottingham Mediaeval Studies* Vol. 2 (1958).

Cameron, K. *The Place-Names of Derbyshire*. 3 Parts Cambridge (1959).

Cameron, K. *Scandinavian Settlement in the Territory of the Five Boroughs*. Nottingham (1965).

Darby, H. C. *An Historical Geography of England before A.D.1800*. Cambridge (1936).

Darby, H. C. *The Domesday Geography of Eastern England*. Cambridge (1952).

Darby, H. C. and Terrett, I. B. *The Domesday Geography of Midland England* (1954).

Darby, H. C. and Maxwell, I. S. *The Domesday Geography of Northern England*. Cambridge (1962).

Ekwall, E. *The Concise Oxford Dictionary of English Place-Names*. 4th Edition Oxford (1960).

Ekwall, E. *English Place-Names in -ing*. 2nd edition Lund (1962).

Gover, J. E. B., Mawer, A. and Stenton, F. M. *The Place-Names of Nottinghamshire*. Cambridge (1940).

Hallam, H. E. *The New Lands of Elloe* (1954).

Hill, J. W. F. *Medieval Lincoln* (1948).

Payling, L. W. H. Geology and Place-Names in Kesteven. *Leeds Studies in English and Kindred Languages* Vol. 4 (1935).

Sawyer, P. H. The Density of Danish Settlement in England. *University of Birmingham Historical Journal* Vol. 6 (1958).

Sawyer, P. H. *The Age of the Vikings*. London (1962).

Smith, A. H. Place-Names and the Anglo-Saxon Settlement. *Proceedings of the British Academy* (1956).

Stenton, F. M. England in the Sixth Century. *The Transactions of the Royal Historical Society* Fourth Series Vol. 21 (1939).

Victoria County History. *Leicestershire*. Vol. III (1955).

ACKNOWLEDGMENT

The author of the first section is indebted to the following for permission to make use of unpublished material: the late Sir Ian Richmond, Dr. K. R. Fennell and Messrs. C. Green, D. F. Mackreth, S. Revill, B. Simmons, J. Wacher, B. White.

NOTE

The interpretation of place-names in *-ingas* and *-ingaham*, above, follows traditional lines. In recent months, however, considerable detailed work has been done by Mr. J. Mc. N. Dodgson, of University College, London, who has examined the distribution of such names in south–east England in relation to early Anglo-Saxon burial sites. As a result of this research, we may well have to reconsider the historical significance of these names, even though their etymology and meaning remains unaltered.

A preliminary survey in our area, using the techniques tried out in south–east England, has indicated that the topographical relationship of the names in *-ingas* and *-ingaham*, together with others in *-ingalēah*, *-ingafeld*, etc., with early Anglo-Saxon burial-sites is by no means so close as has usually been assumed. From a comparison of the sites of these two types, it may well emerge that names like Gedling and Nottingham, though still very old, are a phenomenon rather of the second phase of English settlement than of the first. Though much detailed research must be completed before any definitive statement can be made, the results of the examination of the materials in south–east England will shortly be published by Mr. Dodgson in *Medieval Archæology*.

XII

ECONOMIC DEVELOPMENT

THE central feature of the area of this survey is the broad shallow alluvium-filled valley of the Trent. It curves in a wide arc from the south-west where the three western tributaries, the Derwent, the Dove and the Chernet cut winding valleys through the Derbyshire hills, to the north-east where a low watershed separates it from the Witham. On the east it is flanked by the clay lowlands which reach to the foot of the Lincoln escarpment and on the west by the successive eastward sloping outcrops of the Keuper red marls, Bunter sandstone, Permian limestone, the stiff clays of Coal Measures and the more rugged country of gritstones and limestone of central Derbyshire.

It was for the most part 'open-field' country; but that is not to say that two-field or three-field agriculture was to be found everywhere at any one time. Indeed, the whole concept of two- or three-field agriculture has to be thought of as a constantly moving rather than a static picture. In the sandland areas of Sherwood Forest it may have existed only in the form of an in-field in continuous strip cultivation, surrounded by brecks or breaks or leys of convertible pasture; in the uplands of Derbyshire open-field cultivation undoubtedly existed; but it was so fluid as to defy classification. The number of fields varied with local circumstances. In the high pastoral areas there might only be one common field, whereas in the areas suitable for grain growing there might be two or three and sometimes more. It is important to remember that the rotation of crops was not determined by the number of 'fields'. A one-field village could use the arable area as it liked, dividing it up according to local needs, the important fact being not the number of fields but the size of the area available at any one time for arable cultivation. Strict cultivation on the basis of a winter-sown area, a spring-sown area, and an area for fallow with protective boundaries consisting of movable hurdles would normally be found wherever co-aration was practised. The furlong rather than the field was probably the unit of cultivation; and the number of furlongs devoted to any one crop could be adjusted to the needs of the community by the decision of the villages themselves. The conventional three-field pattern of the text-book seems to be a relatively late development and to be characteristic of the grain-growing Keuper Marls rather than of the limestone uplands or the sandlands of Sherwood Forest. Where there was an equal need for winter-sown wheat or rye and spring-sown peas, beans and barley, the system of three equal fields would no doubt become standard, but in pastoral regions where corn had to be imported, field arrangements would remain very flexible. This was certainly true of the limestone and gritstone uplands of Derbyshire which had to rely on the export of lead, iron and grindstones to meet its needs for bread corns.

The evidence for strip cultivation can sometimes be found on the landscape itself in the form of ridge and furrow and dry stone walls with the reverse S curve; but the problem of dating such evidence is a tricky one. To equate all ridge and furrow with medieval strip cultivation or even with later open-field cultivation can be disastrously misleading; much of it may be due to Napoleonic War ploughing put down to grass in the post-war depression. Similarly dry stone walling may be evidence of 18th and 19th century enclosure; but where it is accompanied by the reverse S curve, close to an ancient nucleated settlement, it is regarded by those who have made a study of the subject as evidence of the use of the heavy right mould-boarded plough drawn by four pairs of oxen. The dry stone walling would serve the purpose of enclosing individual strips before the era of parliamentary enclosure, and since ploughing in such a confined space would be impossible with an eight-ox team (if they really used it), it is presumed that the purpose was to convert the arable to pasture. Subsequent enclosure took the form of large rectangular areas made out by Enclosure Commissioners and surrounded by stone walls of the prescribed dimensions: six feet in height, 24 inches wide at the base and 16 inches wide at the top with at least 21 through bands in every seven yards of wall (Plate IX).

The region as a whole, therefore, presents examples of most, probably all, known types of British field systems, and provides a variety of soils and surface relief in which farming practice from the most primitive to the most advanced could always be found according to the standard of the times. It is also a region of early industrial development both of textiles and of extractive industries and it has therefore enjoyed the stimulus of a varied economy in which industrial and agricultural centres have been able to supply their respective needs and provide surpluses for extra-regional trade. The river system contributed to this end by providing relatively serviceable communications from early times by the Trent and its tributaries, both for external trade, e.g. in groceries and wine sent from London; cheese, pottery and hardware from the west; and also for the exchange of local products. Thus the coal production of Wollaton was exchanged for the corn of Trent-side villages from the 15th century and perhaps long before. The iron, lead, grindstones and building materials of Derbyshire could reach the Trent *via* the Idle and after 1719 by the Derwent. In the great days of the wool trade the Witham had been the artery of communications between the wool marts of Lincoln and Boston and the foreign importers of wool, but it had long declined. The re-opening of the Fosse Dyke in the 18th century diverted some of the trade of the Trent and gave new life to the corn market in Lincoln.

The processes of agricultural change are slow and the evidence by which they are to be traced are few and scattered. Sometimes the landscape itself can be used to suggest the course of events. An excursion, for instance, along the route through Flawford,

Colston Bassett, Wiverton, and on to Cotes and Bescoby, raises a multitude of questions to those who are willing to look for history on the ground as well as in textbooks. A landlord village such as Kingston-on-Soar can be readily distinguished from the 'open' village like its neighbour at Sutton Bonington; and it comes as no surprise to learn that the former was enclosed in Henry VIII's time and, according to Thoroton, had only one inhabitant who sold ale in the Church; while Sutton Bonington opened its doors to all comers, including poverty-stricken framework knitters, and remained unenclosed until 1777. What lies behind these physical attributes visible today is a matter for speculation buttressed by research; but a visit to the parish of Thorpe-in-the-Glebe, consisting of a single farmhouse, surrounded by 2,000 acres of arable lying in solid slabs of boulder clay left by the modern tractor, stirs ancestral memories of defeat at the hands of a tough stubborn soil, of disease-racked peasants working with clumsy wooden tools and half-starved beasts. It is reported as enclosed for pasture in 1517 and 50 persons expelled. Plague and bad weather could kill a village as surely as an enclosing landlord, but on this occasion a landlord appears to be the main culprit.

A second outcome of the post-manorial freedom which English agriculture enjoyed in the 15th century was the rise of the yeoman farmers as leaders of agricultural enterprise. They may have started as graziers of the lords' demesnes, or they may have emerged as a result of market forces which ruthlessly selected the tougher or more fortunate who could withstand the effects of low prices and contrive to put field to field and build up small properties into large ones at the expense of their weaker neighbours. Whatever their origin they formed a powerful factor in the growth of an enterprising gentry class, steeped in the lore of the soil and ruthless in their response to opportunities for profitable enterprise. These opportunities came in the next century when the dissolution of the monasteries released immense resources for forward-looking gentry, and a rise in the price of corn and meat shifted the emphasis from pasture to arable and animal husbandry. The yeoman and the gentry were now the backbone of English farming. In Nottinghamshire, the families that were borne to the front on the tide of monastic lands can be fairly easily identified from the pages of the local historian Robert Thoroton; and the use to which they put the opportunities for aggrandisement, not unmixed with constructive enterprise, can be seen in the remnants that still remain of the gigantic building boom that they inaugurated in the English countryside. The houses of the great, such as Hardwick Hall, Chatsworth, Wollaton Hall and others, are living examples of the conspicuous consumption at the apex of society; but it can be paralleled through all ranks of the countryside according to their status and resources down to the humble husbandmen whose stock of capital, as indicated in the inventories at death, doubled between 1570 and 1620.

From the point of view of farming history, however, far more important results accrued. The agricultural entrepreneur, whether owner or tenant, was beginning to use his freedom to experiment in different forms of land use. In particular he was

Q

discovering the importance of alternate husbandry, that is, putting down exhausted land to grass for a period and renewing its fertility by grazing, marling and manuring, with increased return on the next arable crop. On some farms in the region the seeds from the stock yard were being sown for this purpose during the 16th century and there is a case recorded in Lincolnshire of a farmer sowing his leys with seed that had been especially selected as early as 1591.

This development of alternate husbandry was not confined to the enclosed farms. In the course of the 16th century, and possibly before, open-field arable in Leicestershire was found capable of admitting grassland suitably fenced off from the sown crops and open to common grazing in the fallow year. By this means the arable under leys was restored to fertility and also, still more important, the supply of fodder was increased so that more beasts could be kept and the manure supply increased. Alongside this practice there was a large-scale taking in of land from the waste in the form of closes, both pasture and arable, so that open-field farmers could have enclosed pasture as an addition to, or in place of, the common grazing of the village. In Laxton, for instance, which remains an open-field village to this day, more than half the cultivated area, namely 1500 acres out of 2800, was already in arable or pasture closes by 1635, and it is reasonable to suppose that other open-field villages had made similar large-scale compromise with enclosure long before the classical period of enclosure in the 18th century. Another innovation that may well have been practised was the construction of water meadows for providing an early feed of grass. It was well known to Robert Bakewell on his farm at Dishley, near Loughborough, in the 18th century and, although no other examples have at present come to light, it is unthinkable that a practice that was so widespread in the south and the west of the country had escaped the notice of the farmers along the Trent and its tributaries (Plate VIII).

There is convincing literary evidence also, that the 17th century was a period in which alternate land use came to be seriously studied. Enclosures in Kesteven, for instance, were defended on the ground that land exhausted by over-cropping could best be restored by temporary enclosure, and the fact that no stout opposition by the peasantry to 17th century enclosure has been recorded, suggests that the actual cultivators of the soil shared this view. The virtues of temporary enclosures were vigorously advanced by the Nottinghamshire writer Gervase Markham who wrote in his *English Husbandman* (1635) on the importance of distinguishing between different kinds of soil and advocated an alternation of grass and arable in the form of temporary brecks or leys, that is, a crude anticipation of the modern practice of 'taking the plough round the farm'. He may have been influenced by the well-known method of light soil husbandry in Sherwood Forest, where, according to the reporter to the Board of Agriculture in 1798, it was an immemorial custom 'to take up brecks or temporary enclosures of more or less extent, perhaps from 40 to 250 acres and keep them in tillage for five or six years'. There was also a great deal of emparking by the aristocratic successors of the mediaeval monastic houses, and, later in the century, of planting so that a new forest came into being around the remnants of the old. Birkland and Bilhagh plantations are today examples of this remarkable development of the 18th century. More important from the point of view of farming practice, it is in this region, as we might expect, that the first use of root crops is recorded. The Rufford Pantry Books of 1624 include a reference to 'turnepps, parsnepps and carrotts' at 4d. per peck and by the end of the century practically every modern vegetable had found its place in the contents of Lord Savile's kitchen. By the beginning of the next century, and probably long before, turnips were being produced as a field crop, as is shown by the complaint of the farmers that in the hard winter of 1708 the starving deer wandered into farmers' barns and fields and ate their turnips and the 'poor people's cabbages and carrots'.

On the eastern fringes of the region, enclosure was taking place under the direction of improving landowners who are by no means to be confused with the sheepmasters of an earlier period. There was John Bluett of Harlaxton, near Grantham, who converted between 200 and 300 acres of arable to pasture as part of a constructive plan, as he put it, 'to mend the common and get heart'. As he pointed out to the Star Chamber Judges, the grassland would still be insufficient to keep the remaining arable as well manured as it should be. Whether the same motives were at work in the enclosures of the Vale of Belvoir is unknown, but village after village in the second half of the 17th century was enclosed, and according to Thoroton (1675), suffered a decline in population as a result of conversion to pasture; but he nowhere mentions enclosure for sheep. In view of the ample supply of meat in the Nottingham market which, according to a historian writing in 1641 was sufficient for five times the population of the town, it may be presumed that this enclosure was mainly for fattening cattle; and the general tendency of corn prices to fall, to the disgust and sometimes the distress of the farmers from the middle of the 17th century, would seem to suggest that the general effect of these changes was to increase agricultural output faster than the population could consume it. If there was de-population on the scale of which Thoroton speaks, it helps to explain the contemporary expansion of the villages on the verges of Sherwood Forest and on the Derbyshire border where waste-land was available for settlement and where the framework knitting industry, a voracious consumer of cheap labour, established itself in such centres as Arnold, Mansfield, Sutton-in-Ashfield, Kirkby-in-Ashfield and Selston.

The disparity between agricultural output and population growth was especially noticeable in the period 1725–45. A succession of severe epidemics of smallpox and of typhus and other forms of fever slowed down the advance that had marked the last years of the 17th and the early years of the 18th century, and in some years, e.g. 1727–29, there was a net decline in many villages. The epidemic years of 1736 and 1740–41 checked the recovery, but for reasons that are still unknown, the subsequent period was relatively free from these crippling visitations, and an accelerating rate of population growth can be traced from this time both in town and country to the end of the century.

The period of low prices between 1730–50 known as the Agricultural Depression put the tradition of good relations between landlords and tenants to a severe test. That such a tradition existed in most parts of the region there seems to be no doubt. Arthur Young complained that rents were too low; landlords were afraid of 'having hats off and God bless your Honour but twice instead of thrice and on rent day they liked to have a bow six inches lower than common, with a long scrape. What crowned all is to have a dozen tenants in an alehouse and nothing disrespectful to the landlord passing. This is popularity and we are not to wonder that landlords find it more captivating than 5/– per acre per annum'. This harmonious relationship appears to have been widespread throughout the whole region and the Duke of Rutland in the Vale of Belvoir, the Duke of Kingston in Nottinghamshire and the Duke of Devonshire in Derbyshire could be cited as examples of landlords who were loath to remove their tenants even when it was in their interest to do so. A somewhat more significant aspect of the landlord-tenant relationship was the practice on the part of local landlords to assist good tenants by allowing arrears of rents or sometimes of writing them off altogether. They also invested in improvements to keep tenants in good heart and sometimes took over the payment of land tax when unremunerative prices bore heavily on tenants whom they wished to keep. The recognition of mutual interests of landlord and tenant, a form of quasi-partnership in the cultivation of the soil by enlightened landlords and progressive tenants, is unquestionably one of the ingredients in the complex factors that made for agricultural progress in England, and was certainly present, though by no means universal, in the region we are considering.

There was considerable migration during the period of low prices in the first half of the 18th century from the agricultural to the industrial areas. Lincolnshire as a whole seems to have suffered a net decline in population. Nottinghamshire and Derbyshire, where textile and extractive industries had long taken root, continued to advance steadily, but from the 1740s onwards the advance was more rapid. Nottingham itself nearly trebled its population between 1740 and 1800. Industrial villages more than doubled and agricultural villages rose by about a half. Population growth on this scale was quickly reflected in the rise of agricultural prices and these in turn exercised an impact on agricultural change that can be roughly indicated by the statistics of enclosure. If Nottinghamshire, where the subject has received special attention, may be taken as a guide to the whole region, possibly one-third of the open fields had already been enclosed before the middle of the 18th century. The villages in which this had occurred were to be found mainly in the heavier clay lands on the east, from Kesteven and the Vale of Belvoir to the Leicestershire Wolds, though a few were to be found in the rich dairying lands of the Trent stretching from Newark to Uttoxeter. Of villages which remained open, and these were in the great majority, about half were enclosed by Act of Parliament in the course of the century that followed, the other half choosing the method of enclosure by private agreement. The choice was largely determined by the distribution of ownership: where the land was concentrated in the hands of a few or possibly of one owner, the expense and trouble of an Act of Parliament was unnecessary; where the consent of many freeholders had to be obtained, a petition by the owners of three-quarters of the area to be enclosed was sufficient to initiate the relatively speedy procedure of enclosure by Act. It is thus possible to show the acceleration of the trend under the influence of price fluctuation as follows:

Table XXXV   Price fluctuations of wheat, and the Enclosure Acts for the period 1721–1800

	1721-50	1751-60	1761-70	1771-80	1781-90	1791-1800
Average price of wheat per quarter	34/–	39/–	43/–	45/–	48/–	63/–
Number of Enclosure Acts	2[1] 5[2]	13 22	27 82	34 95	21 28	31 76
Acreage enclosed by Acts *	970[1] 4,852[2]	18,077 32,061	29,022 124,722	38,268 149,768	25,093 42,093	51,547 139,547

Note: This can only be an approximate figure since in the case of some Acts no acreages are available.   This figure can be accepted as a minimum value.

[1] The upper figure relates to Derbyshire and Nottinghamshire only.

[2] The lower figure includes Lincolnshire as well as Derbyshire and Nottinghamshire.

The movement continued in the next century, with the result that the open-field village became a rarity and its survival, in the case of Laxton, down to our own day is a subject of wonder and also of delight. Why has Laxton survived? Perhaps we should first ask to what extent has it survived? The open fields today amount to only 483 acres out of a total cultivated area of nearly 4,000 acres; but they are in three fields divided into a total of 165 strips and subject to the traditional rotation of two corn crops and a fallow and stinted common after harvest. It is recognizably an open-field village with appropriate institutions of a court leet with a jury for each of the fields. A clue to the reason for its survival may be found in the fact that its immediate neighbours were slow to succumb to enclosure: Egmanton and Walesby remained open till 1821; Ossington until 1845; Moorhouse until 1860; Boughton and Wellow until 1871; and Eakring is still partly open to this day. Evidently, there was something in the soil of this region of friable Keuper marl, which enabled these communities to defy enclosure. It could, and still does, grow good crops of grain without underground drainage; the archaic ridge and furrow into which the land was cast served to keep the surface moisture on the move; and today, when cultivation by tractor has flattened the ridges, the greater depth of the ploughing removes the necessity of ridge and furrow for drainage. Other reasons are probably to be found in the structure of tenure. Small farms predominated, and when small freeholders were being bought out elsewhere, they somehow managed not only to survive but to increase in number in Laxton: from 25 in 1635 to 54 in 1736. There were still 46 in 1838. A large-scale re-organisation in the 1720s which enlarged the enclosed area probably enabled more open-field farmers to have enclosed fields for hay and pasture which would strengthen their animal husbandry and increase manure supply and thus make for higher production and efficiency. Whatever the reason, Laxton remains a bastion around which the waters of commercial agriculture have washed in vain; and its present owner, the Ministry of Agriculture, intends to keep it so (Plate VIII).

The full tide of the Agricultural Revolution which broke on the region in the middle of the 18th century did not affect all parts equally. Whether enclosed or not the undrained clays remained steeped in traditional ways; the dead fallow was considered indispensable to good management and wheat, barley and fallow the best rotation. Only the drainage campaign of the 1830s and 1840s would solve that problem. But where the soil lent itself to the four-course rotation and above all, where these advantages were combined with the oversight of enterprising and far-seeing estate managers, the region was in the forefront of the movement of High Farming. The Duke of Rutland transformed the farming of the Belvoir Ridge by putting down the lower clay lands to grass and turning the lighter soils that had formed the traditional grazing rounds into first-rate mixed farming country, while the enclosed pastures endeared themselves to the hearts of connoisseurs by the production of Stilton cheese. The Duke of Portland, in Sherwood Forest, took the lead in sandland farming and his famous water meadows, 400 acres in extent, stretching for seven miles along the Valley of Maun in Clipstone Park was described by Caird, the Times Commissioner in 1851, as 'the most gigantic improvement of its kind in England and the pride of Nottinghamshire'. It formed part of an arable farm of 2,000 acres cultivated in a seven-year course, lying four years in pasture (a system not unlike that recommended by Gervase Markham in the 17th century) and produced great crops of turnips, '44 tons per acre of swedes being reckoned not uncommon'. In Derbyshire the revolution wrought by the coming of roots and clover was even more striking. The lowlands of the Trent had been recognized as early as the 17th century as among the best dairying and fattening land in the whole country but it was not until the last quarter of the 18th century that the uplands felt the impact of the new agriculture. It was then that the landscape was cut up into regular squares and oblongs by the Enclosure Commissioners and the 'High Peak of Castleton and the Black Lings of Tideswell', to quote the exultant Arthur Young, were brought into the current of agricultural change. Arthur Young, of course, must never be taken too literally and it would be a mistake to imagine that the hill farmers of Derbyshire, small pastoral farmers for the most part, were suddenly converted to advanced mixed farming on a form of regular rotation. They turned their milk into Derbyshire cheese which they brought to market in carriers' carts until the railways made it possible to send milk direct to the towns. In the 1870s, the surplus was taken off by factory-made cheese and the Derbyshire cheese industry was given a new lease of life. In other respects, the upland farmers were slow to change their ways and it was said that the flail could be heard in the barns of small farmers until the last quarter of the 19th century. Undoubtedly the most stimulating influence came from the large owners, perhaps particularly the manufacturing aristocracy, such as the Arkwrights and the Strutts, who put not only their profits into land but also brought their business methods to the problems of agriculture. The gentry and aristocracy of the region were also in the forefront of High Farming in most parts: Colonel Mellish of Blyth introduced the swede turnip by distributing seed to farmers; and the light soil farmers, who in the past had scarcely been able to maintain 50 sheep, could find support for 500 to 700 after the development of four-course rotation. The Duke of Portland was the first to use bone manure and he spent vast sums in floating the sewage of Mansfield to his famous meadows at Clipstone. The last years of the century were clouded by the disastrous fall of prices following upon the terrible seasons of 1878 and 1879 when crops were rained away and flocks were ruined by liver-fluke. Foreign supplies came in and kept prices at ruinously low levels. The continuous expansion of industry came to the rescue of farmers in the region and saved many from the ultimate disaster that had been foreshadowed in the gloomy reports of Rider Haggard. Nevertheless rents were down by 25 to 30 per cent and arable farmers had to make drastic adjustments to compete with the products of harvests in all parts of the world which at all seasons flooded into English ports. The region made its response to the challenge partly through the adaptability of its farmers but also by the establishment towards the end of the century of the Agricultural College at Sutton Bonington which, as the University School of Agriculture, holds a high place as a centre of teaching and research.

The more recent development of agriculture in the region would require an article in itself. It marks a breach with the old tradition of Midland farming that must be counted as a new chapter in the Agricultural Revolution. It is characterised by a great ploughing campaign, especially for barley, the putting of field to field and farm to farm, which is giving a touch of the prairie to the historical Midland landscape. Old pastures that held the secrets of vanished villages in their undulating mounds and hollows are being flattened by the modern plough, and the history that lies in tumbling turf is being obliterated before our eyes. Kingston Park is a good example; it forms the confluence of three streams of history: Tudor enclosure for sheep; 19th century reconstruction of a paternal landlord; contemporary farming for grain under the present farm price support system. In other parts, estates are being broken up and new farms created; the motor car has erased the boundaries between markets that had been left by the railways. Under the impact of the great new motorways that traverse the region, the countryside is visibly shrinking but the agricultural industries are adapting themselves to the new age, and agricultural history is being made faster than we can record it.

LEAD MINING

The Peak District lead mining industry has probably the longest history of any mineral exploitation in Britain and has exhibited a unique blend of traditional and modern methods. In the last decade, ending in 1938, it achieved its climax in output yet ceased through catastrophe.

In the Peak, lead-bearing mineral veins occur frequently within the uppermost strata of the Carboniferous Limestone, and are generally associated with local anticlinal structures found on the northern and eastern margins of the limestone upland. Minerals have irregularly infilled many joints, fissures and cavities within the rock, and have proved especially rich close to impermeable lavas ('Toadstones') which originally acted as local ceilings to the upward movement of mineral fluids. The jointed character of the limestone, so favourable to the penetration of mineral fluids, equally assists the downward percolation of water, leaving the upland surface largely dry and drowning the deeper mineral veins below the water-table. Hence miners in the past faced contrasted problems, one being a lack of water for ore dressing at the surface, and another, more serious, the ever-increasing difficulty and expense of draining the mines once the shallower veins were exhausted.

Peak mineral veins are complex, including both metallic and non-metallic minerals. The main metallic ore is galena, though small quantities of white and brown lead ores occur locally. The silver content is small, but zinc ores have been worked, while in the famous mine at Ecton in Staffordshire lead was subsidiary to copper. The non-metallic minerals, or gangue, are of far greater bulk than the ores. Historically they have varied in significance, acting merely as a burden to early miners who had to lift large quantities of waste to the surface and dump it in hillocks after sorting. Recently the barytes and fluorspar content of the waste has proved of commercial value and has stimulated a revival of activity in some of the old mines.

Figure 40, showing the distribution of mineral veins, indicates that they occur mainly along the eastern side of the limestone upland, from Castleton in the north to Brassington, some 20 miles to the south. The dominant veins, or rakes, run generally east–west, some extending several miles westward across the upland, others dipping eastwards below the shales and grit of the Derwent Valley. Beyond the main limestone outcrop, lead veins of past importance occur in the eastern inliers of Ashover and Crich, and on the western side of the upland, mineral veins in the Manifold Valley were once very productive.

Lead mining in the Peak, probably first developed by prehistoric people, grew to importance under the Romans. The principal evidence, some fifteen pigs of lead found in Derbyshire and another ten elsewhere, suggests that the Peak became one of Britain's chief producing areas, serving both home and overseas markets. Remains of smelting hearths have been traced on Matlock Moor, and it seems probable that *Lutudarum*, the centre of the lead industry, lay somewhere near either Matlock or Chesterfield, the first in the heart of the mining area, the latter on the road between it and the north.

Compared with the Roman era, evidence for lead-mining in Anglo-Saxon times is meagre, but what little there is has value. The lack of evidence covering the invasion period is not surprising, for with the decline of towns and villas, the market must have collapsed. Monastic development, however, brought about revival by A.D. 714 when

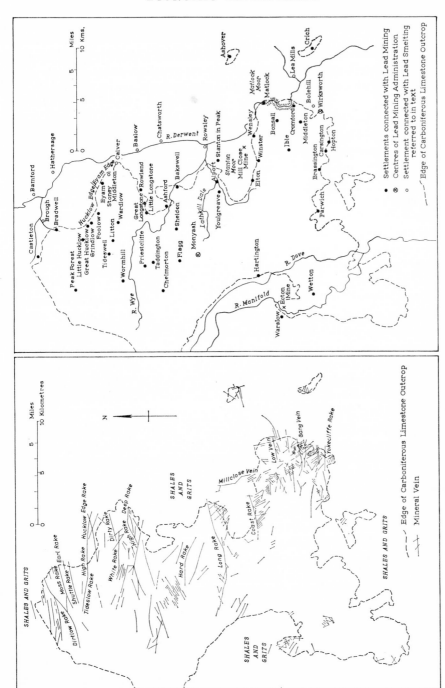

Fig. 40 The distribution of mineral veins and the settlements connected with lead mining in the Peak District

a record of Repton Abbey referred to the mines of Wirksworth. A century later these mines were producing lead to the annual value of 300 shillings for Canterbury Cathedral, and although Repton was subsequently destroyed by the Danes, Wirksworth survived, and its manor later became royal demesne. Thus the Anglo-Saxon period saw the establishment of what was to become the chief lead-mining centre in the Peak.

Domesday testifies to further development. Seven mines were recorded, a small enough number certainly, but in the absence of any mention of lead mining elsewhere, the Derbyshire record appears significant. The distribution of mining also requires a comment. Five mines were situated near the south-eastern margin of the upland, three of them around Wirksworth, and the other two in the Derwent gorge area, near Matlock and Crich. The remaining two, situated further north, are more difficult to locate. They lay in the manors of Ashford and Bakewell, probably in outlying berewicks on the edge of the upland. There were no mines further north in 1086, but Domesday states that in 1066 north manors yielded five cartloads of lead, each containing 50 slabs. These may have been destined for the roofing of the Confessor's Abbey at Westminster, since the manors, like those of Wirksworth, Matlock, Ashford and Bakewell belonged to the king.

The fact of royal ownership had great significance for the subsequent development of lead mining. By the late 13th century much of the limestone upland belonged to the Crown, and during the phase of economic expansion which took place before A.D. 1300 the growing demand for lead used in building castles, cathedrals and abbeys, was assisted in Derbyshire by the growth of practices favouring mining expansion in the royal manors, the lands subsequently known as the King's Field. The Enquiry of Ashbourne in 1288 crystallised these practices into a body of mining rights and customs which controlled lead mining until the passing of the Mining Customs Acts of 1851 and 1852. Crown rights were mainly limited to royalties, while miners were entitled to search for and work lead mines anywhere (with a few exceptions), land owners being required to allow the miner a specified amount of land for mining and ore dressing. Mines thereafter became the property of the miner subject to continuous working. Administration was carried out by the Barmaster and a jury of miners operating in Barmoot Courts, the chief of which were at Wirksworth and Monyash.

Mining, hitherto confined to the eastern margins of the upland, expanded into the interior and to the west as discoveries of surface rakes were made in the wastes and open fields of villages such as Tideswell, Monyash and Hartington. The growth of the mining population must have been considerable, for when the royal mines were expanded in Devon and Cornwall between A.D. 1290 and 1340, Derbyshire miners were sent there at intervals in groups ranging from 40 to 150, the recorded total reaching nearly 600.

Compared with the mining population, the number of smelters was small. After rough dressing, lead ore was carted to boles or wind-hearths for smelting. These hearths, sited on west-facing hills to gain strong draughts, were simple stone structures with vents for flues. The smelting process left a considerable residue of lead in the slag, and this later generations of smelters were able to recover. The distribution of hearths is partly recorded by the survival of a dozen or more 'Bole-hill' place-names, and these appear to show that most of the smelting was done, not on the Carboniferous Limestone upland, but on the steep hillsides of the Millstone Grits. A few sites lay west of the Derwent Valley near the mines, as at Bole Hill, north-east of Wirksworth, but the majority were further away on the slopes of the gritstone moors east of the Derwent, above such villages as Hathersage and Baslow. Here they were situated between the actual mining area and the export route provided by the Trent.

The 16th century saw important developments in the Derbyshire industry. The national market for lead was active and mining expanded, encouraged directly by the discovery of new veins by working miners, and indirectly by nobles and gentry who saw in lead mining the promise of fortunes from royalties or trading profits. In addition, as in other metal industries, technical advance was significant. Powered blast, first by foot-bellows and then by water, was introduced into lead smelting during the second half of the century. Despite an attempt at monopoly, smelting mills using water-driven bellows grew rapidly. Soon the hill-top boles, which used double the amount of fuel required by the new mills, ceased activities and smelting migrated down to the Derwent and its tributaries, to places such as Calver, Chatsworth and Cromford.

During the following century the lead industry experienced both prosperity and difficulties. One aspect of its prosperity is that mining attained its greatest geographical spread. There was much production in the eastern inliers around Ashover and Crich; all the mineral areas of the limestone upland were exploited, and in the west the copper-lead mine at Ecton made a beginning. Not surprisingly, therefore, Derbyshire attracted both capital and labour from outside. About 1630, for example, the Attorney General gained possession of mines on the rich Dovegang Vein on Cromford Moor, and took Cornelius Vermuyden into partnership to drain them. Later, in 1649, a News-letter appeared containing complaints that miners were coming from all parts of England to search for ore in Derbyshire. On the other hand fundamental problems were emerging. With increasing depth many mines were reaching the water table, and further working entailed new methods of drainage. The chief of these was the *sough*, an underground channel cut through the rock, usually at great expense, to carry water to neighbouring streams. Vermuyden himself began the most famous drain, Cromford sough, in the 1630s and this enabled the Wirksworth district to remain the leading producer in Derbyshire.

In the 18th century lead mining in the Peak entered a new phase. This can be seen in its distribution and scale. Mining continued to be widespread over the mineral areas of the Limestone outcrop, but was increasingly extended, as at Hucklow Edge, under the cover of newer rocks bordering the Derwent Valley. Mining enterprises also showed a greater range than before. Hundreds of small-scale mines remained, carried on by partnerships of working miners, but in addition some ten to twenty larger ones were developed, dependent on capital and the introduction of technical improvements. Miners frequently became wage-earners, but many retained their primitive mines for occasional working.

Areal contrasts therefore emerged. On the limestone upland, the north, west and interior saw little advance. Mines here were mainly small-scale workings with primitive equipment and low output. In contrast, on the eastern margins large undertakings were intermingled with small ones, some of the former continuing with a high rate of output for a number of years. Mining continued in the eastern inliers, Ashover experiencing a large expansion through capital investment in the Gregory Mine which flourished between 1762 and 1800. In Staffordshire the Ecton Mine in the Manifold Valley reached its peak of copper production, including some lead, under large-scale operations by the Duke of Devonshire.

Technical advances in mining were largely confined to improvement in drainage. The use of gunpowder for blasting made it possible to build long soughs draining eastern workings to the Derwent, such as the four-mile Hillcar sough, constructed under Stanton Moor between 1751 and 1772. Achievements of this kind, however, were only a part-success, for mining soon penetrated below the soughs and pumping became necessary.

Various primitive types of pump were used in Derbyshire, but a big advance in the efficiency came with the introduction of the Newcomen engine in 1720. This relatively simple engine operated pumps in a dozen or more mines at intervals between 1720 and 1776, but unfortunately its cheapness was offset by high fuel costs and towards the end of the century the more efficient Boulton and Watt engines were introduced. Nevertheless, several mines continued to use improved Newcomen engines built by Francis Thompson, a noted local engineer, while others relied on water-wheels.

The part played by the London Lead Company in initiating further advance during the century must be stressed. This Quaker company operated in Derbyshire between 1720 and 1792, introducing the Newcomen engine and excavating soughs in the Winster area. The company also revolutionised lead smelting by introducing the reverberatory furnace, an efficient smelter, first using coal and later coke fuel. New furnaces were built on the moors east of the Derwent, between the lead mines and the coalfield. Despite this progress the industry began to show signs of decline towards the end of the century. With deeper mining, costs of production rose, profit margins were reduced and indeed losses became more frequent. Compared with developments in drainage, little improvement took place in methods of mining, and the general inefficiency of organisation was severely criticised by a German observer. By 1800 the outlook for lead mining was uncertain.

The 19th century witnessed the decline of Derbyshire's traditional lead industry and, after 1860, the rise of the modern. Mineral statistics published from 1848 onwards, show that the output of lead ore in the Peak reached a maximum of 10,929 tons in

1859 (Fig. 41), subsequently falling to 4,395 tons in 1900. Though this decline followed the national trend, it is to be noted that Derbyshire's share of the total output rose from an average of 9 per cent between 1850 and 1860 to 12 per cent between 1890 and 1900.

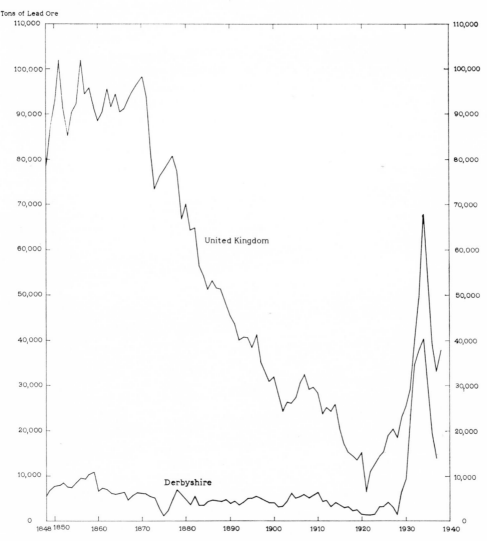

Fig. 41   Lead ore production in the United Kingdom and Derbyshire, 1848–1938

Although production statistics show change, they give small hint of the geographical revolution that overtook the lead industry during the century. For this purpose occupational statistics are more illuminating. These show the number of lead miners remaining roughly constant from an estimated 2,280 around 1830 to 2,333 in 1861, declining later to 285 in 1901. Until 1860 mining was still widespread (Fig. 42) although some contraction was taking place. In the east, the closing of the Gregory Mine in 1803 greatly reduced Ashover's importance, while on the limestone upland, veins in the interior and the west were becoming exhausted. The Ecton mine continued to yield a little lead though copper production had ended. Even on the eastern borders of the upland, always the richest part of the lead field, a number of company mines experienced crises as yield diminished and drainage problems increased. Losses brought about closures such as the Alport Mines in 1852. Nevertheless several of the more fortunate mines struck good veins worth working despite cost of drainage, as, for example, at Eyam where prospects were bright during the 1850s. Records show, however, that a number of company mines changed hands before 1860 and were taken over by poor miners in order to work the shallow veins and the waste of former operations. Such 'hillocking' was the mainstay of many small mines, and another factor which kept them in being was that many of their owners did agricultural work at intervals, while their wives and children brought home wages from textile mills along the Derwent.

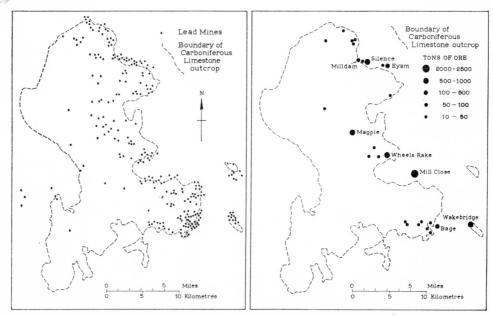

Fig. 42   Peak District lead mines, c.1800 and chief producing mines in 1882

At this stage of economic difficulty the tenacity of the Derbyshire miners came to the fore. They insisted on retaining their customary rights which, accordingly, were codified in the Acts of 1851 and 1852. Thus the small mine was enabled to continue through the later years of the century, an archaic survival in which miners refused to recognise defeat. In general, however, the area of effective operations contracted more rapidly after 1860 (Fig. 41), reaching a climax in the 1890s. By 1900 there was only one undertaking of any significance, the Mill Close Mine, re-opened in 1860, and producing over 4,000 tons annually by 1900. During the 1870s and 1880s, several mines were worked successfully for a few years, producing 100 to 1,000 tons annually, but the development of large-scale production overseas brought a fall in lead prices which forced much of the activity in Derbyshire to cease. Lead furnaces correspondingly declined in number and in 1900 there remained only Brough Mill, near Bradwell, a small concern, and Lea Mill, near Cromford, worked by the Wass Company, which owned Mill Close Mine.

During the present century Derbyshire's lead output climbed to unprecedented heights. Between 1900 and 1912, however, there was little change, production continuing at 4,000 to 6,000 tons annually. This came almost entirely from Mill Close but it should be noted that a number of small firms worked old mines and hillocks for fluorspar and barytes with a little lead as a by-product. New progress in lead mining came after 1922 when Mill Close was acquired by the New Consolidated Goldfields Company, a firm of international experience which introduced new capital and modern equipment. The main expansion of production occurred after 1930 when electric pumping was installed and rich ore-bodies were opened up. Output in Derbyshire soared, reaching a peak of 40,336 tons in 1934. In this year Mill Close produced three-fifths of the country's output of lead ore and much of its zinc. At the same time a modern smelting plant was opened adjoining the mine, replacing the old plant at Lea Mills. Unfortunately production then began to decline, reaching about 14,000 tons in 1938, and in that year vast quantities of water broke into the northern part of the workings. The company decided that costs of further development would be prohibitive and in 1942 the mine was finally closed. War, however, brought an unforeseen renewal of activity at the smelter. Messrs. Enthoven of Rotherhithe acquired the plant for treating lead scrap, and it has since become the chief lead smelter in Britain. Today small quantities of ore are supplied by local firms working fluorspar, but the bulk of the lead comes from scrap brought to the works from many parts of the country.

ALABASTER WORKING

Among early industries the working of alabaster was a specialised activity of the Nottingham region, based on supplies of gypsum which occur on either side of the Trent valley. Onwards from the 13th century, until the Reformation brought it abruptly to an end, the industry provided a large output of ornamental work for churches at home and abroad, consisting of altarpieces, carved panels, memorial tombs, effigies, and the like. Through many generations the alabaster carvers of Nottingham, Derby and Burton-on-Trent maintained a remarkable degree of skill in the production of statuary in different forms. The stone, which is relatively soft, fine-grained of even texture, is an attractive medium for sculpture and is peculiarly responsive to the sensitive touch of the craftsman. It is evident from the care which they devoted to their work that the medieval carvers in the Trent valley came to regard alabaster with a similar affection which their contemporaries in Italy felt for the marble of Carrara.

Whether pure white, or delicately tinged with pink, red or green from other mineral impurities, alabaster provides an elegant material and, like marble, retains its translucent appearance when polished. It is also amenable to gilding and colouring which were frequently applied to statuary in pre-Renaissance times. Owing to its solubility, however, even when exposed to the cleanest rainwater, alabaster is unsuitable for exterior work and its use was therefore restricted to the fashioning of carvings appropriate to the interior of churches and later on to secular ornaments in the homes of the wealthy.

As the raw material, alabaster, which is gypsum or calcium sulphate in its massive form, was worked from three principal localities, all bordering on the Trent valley. These were at Tutbury, actually overlooking the lower Dove valley near Burton; at Chellaston, about four miles south-east of Derby; and Red Hill, eight miles south-west of Nottingham, close to the confluence of the Trent and Soar. The first two were by far the most important sources, the Red Hill alabaster being exploited only during the later stages of the industry, mainly after the Reformation. In all cases the mineral was found in the Upper Red Marls of the Keuper formation. The more precise geological relationships between the various occurrences of alabaster are referred to in the section dealing with the present-day gypsum industry in Chapter XVI. As a stone, alabaster is soft and easily cut, although like many building stones, it hardens somewhat on being exposed to the air. For most purposes only small blocks were required by the industry and these could easily be transported from the quarries to the workshops. In each of the three districts the quarries were on a hillslope giving access to the thicker seams of alabaster which lay at a depth below the reach of percolating water. The quality of the stone varied from one place to another. In general that at Tutbury and Chellaston appears to have yielded larger blocks than that at Red Hill, while compared with the typical white alabaster from those centres, that from Red Hill was usually pink or reddish in colour.

The first quarries to be worked were probably at Tutbury, for the earliest example of carved alabaster in England is to be found as part of the moulding in the west doorway of the Priory Church which dates from the latter half of the 12th century, while only a mile or two away, in the village church at Hanbury, is the oldest known alabaster memorial, that to John de Hanbury (c1280–1300). By the middle of the 14th century stone was being produced from both Tutbury and Chellaston and worked by skilled artisans in Nottingham, Burton and elsewhere. These men, referred to in contemporary documents as *alabasterers, alabastermen, kervers* (carvers) and *imagemakers,*

VIII   Open fields at Laxton, showing the South Field

IX   Chelmorton, Derbyshire, showing dry wall field boundaries marking old cultivation strips

X   Nottingham medieval alabaster: the Flawford Virgin and Child (*c.*1400)

were essentially craftsmen rather than artists. Most of their work depended on skilful execution rather than artistic inspiration, although many of their products were exquisitely fashioned. Their carvings ranged from small figures to elaborate panels for altarpieces. The Nottingham 'school' of carvers, as many entries in the Borough Records show, rose to prominence in the 15th century and the town soon became the most important centre of the industry, not only in the Trent valley, but in the country as a whole. Even as early as 1367 Edward III had commissioned Peter the Mason, a Nottingham craftsman, to carve a reredos for St. George's Chapel at Windsor. Some of the carvers at least were men of respectable status, for in the late 15th century one was twice mayor of the town and another was sheriff.

As the vogue for ecclesiastical alabaster work grew, other centres of carving developed in London, Lincoln and York, making increased demands upon the quarries in the Midlands. Thus, while the trade in raw material expanded, competition in the production of carvings also grew. The pre-eminence of the Nottingham 'school', however, appears to have remained almost unchallenged during the latter part of the 15th century and the first half of the 16th. Some of the products were virtually mass-produced as the result of persistent repetition of standard patterns. For example, the great number of small plaques depicting the head of St. John the Baptist, with only minor variations in design, became a speciality of the Nottingham carvers. Other items such as some of the altarpieces were undoubtedly made to the specifications for a particular church, while memorial tombs would obviously fall into the same category. The Nottingham Borough Records suggest, moreover, that household articles were sometimes made of alabaster, for an entry dated 1491 refers to the 'gilding of three alabaster salt-cellars'.

Although there were lesser 'schools' of carving at both Tutbury and Chellaston, as well as in Derby, the bulk of the raw alabaster found its way to Burton and Nottingham or was sent to more distant centres in England and even abroad. Relatively small blocks were required at the workshops and these were transported from the quarries both by road and river. For a long time Nottingham carvers relied on stone from Chellaston and records show that in 1414 an agreement was made by a Nottingham middleman with representatives of the Abbot of Fécamp in Normandy for the export of alabaster slabs *via* Hull.

More important than the export of unworked stone, however, was the trade in finished products. These found their way to France, Spain and Italy, to the Netherlands and Denmark and even to Iceland. Altarpieces especially, either as single panels or in the form of triptychs, together with images of the Madonna and saints were the principal forms of English alabaster which came to grace the interiors of numerous continental churches during the 15th century. Two examples, cited by F. W. Cheetham in his *Medieval English Alabasters*, serve to demonstrate the wide range of the overseas market. In 1456 an altarpiece was made for the famous shrine at Santiago de Compostella in North Spain, where it still exists, while another at about the same

R

period was sent to Holar Cathedral in Iceland, though it is now in the Reykjavik Museum. Unfortunately it is difficult to identify among the great number of carvings, some 3,000 at least, which survive in Europe, the particular 'schools' from which they originated but it is clear from occasional documentary evidence that many were made by Nottingham workers.

The Reformation brought an end to the alabaster industry so far as its characteristic products were concerned and with it came the sharp decline of one of the lesser arts of medieval England, in the pursuit of which the Trent valley centres have played a leading part. By an Act of Parliament passed early in 1550 the manufacture of images was forbidden, although the export trade in these seems to have continued for another year or two, perhaps through illegal sales of carvings removed from churches at home. One branch of the industry, however, was unaffected both by the laws supporting the Reformation and subsequent puritan fanaticism. This was the making of memorial tombs, but of course only well-to-do families could afford the cost of these. Nevertheless, within the Nottingham region today such tombs are the most frequent survivals of the carvers' craft. They are to be found in many village churches as monuments to noted families, their style and design reflecting different periods in the long history of the industry.

Monuments to members of the ancient Clifton family can be seen at Clifton; to the Willoughbys at Willoughby-on-the-Wolds, the Chaworths at Langar and the Sacheverells at both Barton-in-Fabis and Ratcliffe-on-Soar. In Southwell Minster is the memorial to Archbishop Sands (d. 1588), while at Bottesford, 17 miles from Nottingham on the road to Grantham is the tomb of the second Earl of Rutland (1563) which shows particularly fine carving. Near the western extremity of the region, at Norbury, near Ashbourne, are the beautifully executed 15th century tomb chests of the Fitzherberts. As to representative examples of altarpiece panels and other church ornaments belonging largely to the second half of the 15th century, the collection of alabaster carvings in the Nottingham Castle Museum, some of which are undoubtedly of local origin, is impressive (Plate X).

It seems probable that the Nottingham school of carvers itself did not long survive the Reformation, though the making of memorial tombs continued at Burton and Chellaston. As time passed, especially with the adoption of new Renaissance styles in building, less and less use was made of alabaster and London masons in particular showed an increasing preference for marble and other ornamental stones. In the matter of tombs the Nottingham area adhered to local tradition and Cheetham has found that in Nottinghamshire alone 21 alabaster tombs were placed in churches between 1540 and 1640, more than are known to have been erected in the county during the Middle Ages. In the 18th century an alternative outlet for decorative alabaster was found in the growing number of country mansions. Pillars in dining halls and ballrooms, elaborate mantelpieces and large ornaments served to adorn many of the stately homes. Alabaster columns 20 feet in height, obtained from the quarry at Red

Hill, were erected in the Earl of Yarborough's mausoleum at Brocklesby in north Lincolnshire (1794); the 25-feet Corinthian pillars in Kedleston Hall, the seat of the Curzon family, near Derby (c 1765) also came from Red Hill, while the stone for the columns at Holkham Hall, Norfolk, the home of Thomas Coke, was produced at Tutbury.

As the trade in alabaster dwindled, the use of poorer quality gypsum in the building industry increased. As a plaster material for flooring, gypsum came into general demand because the plaster afforded an even surface, it was fire-resistant and above all it allowed a saving of timber. This led to an expansion in the mining and quarrying of gypsum, not only in the alabaster localities, but at many neighbouring places in the Trent valley area, but the mundane purpose which the mineral now came to serve contrasted strangely with the beautiful work accomplished by the medieval carvers.

EARLY COAL AND IRON INDUSTRY

The geology of the Nottinghamshire and Derbyshire coalfield has been dealt with in Chapter 1, and it is only necessary here to recapitulate the main facts. In Nottinghamshire, the coal measures dip in a general east-west direction, and come to the surface along the southern and central parts of the western boundary of the county. Here, along the line of the river Erewash, which for a large part of its course forms the boundary between Nottinghamshire and Derbyshire, the coal measures come to the surface as outcropping seams. The exposed coalfield, at its southern extremity, projects eastwards in the direction of Nottingham and the river Trent, a fact of considerable importance for the early development of the coal industry in the area. Further east, the general dip of the coal measures takes them underneath younger beds, and no pits were sunk in the concealed coalfield before the 19th century.

Coal from the outcrops must have been burned from the earliest times, and its use as a road-building material for the Roman Rykneld Way shows how readily available it was. I. A. Richmond has claimed that 'Nottinghamshire coal has been noted in the Fenland villages' in the Roman period, and that it probably arrived there as return ballast in barges carrying corn up the Trent *via* the Foss Dyke. If it can be substantiated, this remarkable early example of the trading of coal for agricultural products, utilising the river as a highway, foreshadows a later pattern that was to persist until water transport was superseded by the railways. From the end of Roman times to the 13th century there is a complete lack of evidence on the use of coal, and it can have had little economic significance, unlike lead, which we know was traded over long distances. Nottingham coal makes a dramatic first appearance in 1257, when Queen Eleanor, wife of Henry III, came to the city intending to stay at the royal castle there, but was so offended by the smoke of sea-coal that she changed her plans, and moved on to Tutbury. There must already have been a considerable use of coal, presumably for lime-burning, baking, brewing and iron-forging. The incident is a reminder that for centuries coal was regarded as an offensive fuel, barely tolerated for industrial use, and rejected by the well-to-do as a domestic fuel when alternative supplies of wood were available.

A remarkable early lease, which survives from the beginning of the next century, refers to operations on the area of the exposed coalfield projecting towards Nottingham, on which the great expansion of mining during the 16th and 17th centuries was to take place. It is dated 1316, and is a lease of a mine to seven men of Cossall, who were to pay a rent based on the number of men at work. The rent could be remitted if the men were prevented from working by flooding, or by 'le dampe'. They were to be responsible for repairing the gutter, or sough, and a cancelled clause stipulated that they were also to fill in worked-out pits. This lease to a group of working miners is an early example of the 'charter' or collective contract system, which was to give rise later on in the East Midlands to the hated butty system. The reference to 'le dampe' is its earliest appearance in the language, and no doubt refers to choke-damp, which might have been met in comparatively shallow workings where no provision for ventilation had been made. The other references show that here at least the first primitive stages of getting coal by quarrying or 'drifting' into an exposed seam had now been superseded, and bell-pit mining, with a sough for drainage, had already been introduced. This stage was to have a very long life, and was not to be finally abandoned until the 19th century.

There are several reference to pits at work in many parts of the outcrop during the Middle Ages, but the scale of operations obviously remained small, with the pits merely serving the immediate vicinity. Many bloomsmithies could also be seen in operation, particularly in Duffield Frith, working up the iron-stone found in the coal measures. A nail-making industry early came to be centred on Belper, and Irongate, in Derby, recalls the importance of medieval iron-crafts in the town. With the coming of the 16th century, there was a considerable expansion in the output of both coal and iron. Whilst pits further back on the outcrop continued to be limited to the immediate market, a mine at Wollaton, close to Nottingham and the Trent, which had probably been opened in the 15th century, commanded an extensive and expanding market. There was a steady increase in output, which probably reached 10,000 tons a year in the 1530s. Bell-pit mining was still the rule, aided by an extensive sough, with gangs of colliers raising the coal at fixed piece-rates. Much of the coal must have gone to meet industrial needs, but increased domestic use in Nottingham and the Trent valley no doubt accounted for a part of the demand. Towards the end of the century, the easily mined coal had been exhausted, and the move to the deeper coal brought the undertaking up against intractable drainage problems. New and expensive pumps were brought into use, but as the profit margin declined, sales also fell off. At the beginning of the 17th century, Huntingdon Beaumont, younger son of a Leicestershire coal-owning family, appeared at Wollaton and persuaded the owner to shut down the pits, and to take a lease of the coal in neighbouring Strelley. Output was stepped up to 20,000 tons a year, and a wooden wagonway about two miles long, the first in Britain, was laid down through Wollaton. But the hoped-for sales failed to materialise, despite a bold scheme to ship coal to London *via* the Trent, and Beaumont decided to try his fortune on the north-east coast. Gray, the historian of Newcastle, writing in 1649, tells us that Beaumont introduced pumps, wagonways and boring rods which were all new to the district, and which no doubt had been developed in the Nottingham coalfield. Despite his new devices, Beaumont was unsuccessful, and he ended his days in Nottingham Gaol in 1624. With his passing, the first phase of the expansion of coal-mining around Nottingham appears to have come to an end, and it was not until after the turmoil of the Civil War was over that progress was resumed.

The expansion of iron-making in the 16th century is not so well documented, and must have been effected at first simply by an increase in the number of bloomsmithies. In 1580, Sir John Zouche, whose family had been making iron at Codnor since the beginning of the century, established a water-operated mill at Makeney for making wire. He was, however, infringing the patent of the Mineral and Battery Works Company, and was forced to give up the manufacture. He continued the forge in operation and soon afterwards erected a blast furnace at Codnor Park, the first in the East Midlands. The furnace, with other Zouche property, was passed over as security for debt to Sir Francis Willoughby, who undertook to erect a second furnace, but this was not carried out. The furnace disappears from the manuscript record around 1610, but not before it had recorded another 'first' for the East Midlands, namely the first clear reference to the use of coal in connection with the new method of iron manufacture. The reference is to a proposal to use coal at the chafery stage at the Makeney forge. No real novelty is implied, however, as coal had often been used at forges in the Middle Ages, as an earlier example from Derbyshire shows.

After the Civil War, industrial expansion was resumed, and the demand for coal increased steadily. The Trent valley market now seems to have been served from pits in Strelley and Bilborough, which were soon to come into the hands of a new dynasty of coal-owners, sprung from the yeomanry, who were later to occupy the leading position in the Nottingham coalfield as the Barber Walker Company. Further back on the outcrop, output still served a mainly local demand, but by the end of the 17th century, comparatively large mines were worked at Denby, Smalley and Heanor. These pits served the Derby market, and some of their output found its way into Leicestershire and Northamptonshire, where it was traded against agricultural products. The drainage problems associated with deep mining were now acute, and the newly invented Newcomen 'fire-engines' quickly found their way into the field. Mining was resumed at Wollaton in the 1730s with the aid of a fire-engine, but the engines were expensive, and soughs were still needed. In 1739 a Bill was promoted by local coal-owners alleging that a certain John Fletcher was trying to obtain a monopoly position by stopping-up a sough, and turning the water into his competitor's pits. Fletcher denied the charge, and claimed that he had spent £20,000 on the construction of a sough and other works for his Derbyshire and Nottinghamshire undertakings.

Iron production, too, expanded rapidly in the second half of the 17th century. Before the Civil War the industry had served mainly local needs, though some bar iron was traded over long distances. After the Restoration, George Sitwell, at Renishaw, was making cast-iron fire-backs and pots and pans for a wider market, and sugar rollers from his furnace were even exported to Barbados. Slit iron was sold to the Dudley nail-makers, and iron was also supplied to the Birmingham and London markets. Prospects for further growth seemed good, but in common with other iron-producing districts, a rapid decline in production occurred around the end of the 17th century. The native iron industry was suffering from competition from Sweden, with its higher grade ores and abundant wood supplies. By 1740 there were only four furnaces in blast in Derbyshire, with an estimated annual output of 800 tons of pig iron. But with the gradual spread of the use of coke for smelting, the industry revived rapidly, and by 1788 a total of eight furnaces (of which only one was still using charcoal) was producing an annual output of 4,500 tons.

Although the factory system may be said to have begun in the East Midlands with Lombe's silk-mill in Derby, and Arkwright's spinning-mill in Cromford, the first factories were water-powered, and with the coming of the steam-engine the main centres of the Industrial Revolution moved elsewhere. But the East Midlands, too, was powerfully affected by the rising demand for coal and iron, and a series of important developments in transport transformed the situation for the inland collieries. Turnpikes greatly improved the road system, but more important for the movement of coal, in just over 20 years from 1770 a fine network of canals linked the colliery districts, namely the Chesterfield, Erewash, Cromford and Nottingham canals. The Grand Trunk Canal linked the Trent and the Mersey, and the Nottingham Canal provided easy access for all the important Erewash valley collieries to the markets in Nottingham and the Vale of Trent. Colliery wagonways joined the pits to the canals, and coal could now move more rapidly and cheaply over the whole area. Demand went up by leaps and bounds, though effectively the coalfield remained as much a land-locked area as it had always been.

J. Farey gives a fascinating picture of the state of mining at the beginning of the 19th century, following the establishment of the canal system but preceding the coming of the railways. Several large-scale collieries were now at work, relying increasingly on steam-engines for pumping and winding, but in other areas, away from centres of population, smaller undertakings continued in operation using horse-gins and water-wheels. In a few places, the older method of getting coal by pillar-and-stall working, which had developed naturally from bell-pit mining, was still practised. Elsewhere, the longwall system, said to have been first developed in Shropshire, was the rule. Farey, as a Londoner, was shocked by the waste of the so-called 'soft coal', and poorer grades. Supplies of coal in the region were so plentiful that only best-quality hard coal sold readily. An attempt had recently been made, as it had at the beginning of the 17th century, to open up a trade to London *via* the Trent and Hull, but coal using this route could not compete with the centuries-old trade from the north-east coast.

Farey also gives a valuable account of the expansion which iron-making had undergone. Bell-pit mining for the ironstone was still almost universal, despite the waste involved, but in other respects the industry had been transformed. The smaller charcoal furnaces, blown by water-wheels, had now completely disappeared, and tall furnaces, using coke and blown by cylinder bellows worked by steam-engines, were now universal. The first of the new furnaces had been erected in Morley Park, and in 1806 12 furnaces were in blast, out of a total of 18 in the county, producing 10,300 tons of pig iron, sufficient to give Derbyshire fourth place amongst English iron-producing counties. Of the companies listed by Farey, two, at Alfreton and Butterley, were to combine important coal interests with their iron-making. The Butterley Company had been founded in 1792 to work the ironstone at Codnor, where Derbyshire's first furnace had been founded in the 16th century, with two outstanding engineers, William Jessop and Benjamin Outram among its founders, who had been active in building canals and tramways in the area. The Butterley Company expanded rapidly, and built a new village, Ironville, for its employees, which remains virtually unchanged to this day. In 1848, the Company had six furnaces in blast, producing 21,000 tons of pig-iron out of the county's total production of 78,000 tons. By mid-century, most of the local ore had been worked out, but supplies by rail were now available for a firmly-based industry.

The linking-up of the East Midlands by rail also enabled its coal to break out finally from the confines of its local market. The part played by local coal-owners, meeting at the Sun Inn, Eastwood, in 1832, in the establishment of the Midlands Counties Railway has often been told. The intention at first was the modest one of linking the Erewash Valley collieries with Leicester, but the proposal was subordinated to wider plans to link up Leicester, Nottingham and Derby with London, and it was not until 1847 that a line was finally constructed to serve the Erewash collieries. Before this, two other events had marked the coming of a new era. In 1842, the evidence submitted to the Children's Employment Commission revealed the atrocious conditions under which both men and boys worked in the pits. A working day from 6.0 a.m. to 9.0 p.m. was not uncommon, contrasting with the 12-hour shift from 6.0 a.m. to 6.0 p.m. which had been the rule at the beginning of the 17th century. Ventilation was primitive and quite inadequate, and accidents were commonplace. To make matters worse, the older 'charter' system of employment had now given place at many pits to sub-contracting coal-getting to butties, who would use any means to extract more output from the colliers and boys they employed, and who resorted widely to the truck system in paying wages. When representatives of the Miners' Association of Great Britain arrived in the area in 1844, they found a ready response, and widespread strike action soon followed throughout the coalfield. Wages, hours and conditions, truck and the butty system were all included in the miners' grievances, but the strike soon collapsed and there were to be no further attempts at trade union organisation until the 1860s.

The coming of trade unionism was not the only sign that the industry was now fully entering the modern period. By 1850 consignments of Derbyshire coal began to reach the London market by rail, and although 'Best Wallsend' was to maintain its supremacy for a long time, 'Derbyshire Brights' now began to compete for the Londoner's favour. Now the coalfield had at last burst out from its confines, and had access to an ever-widening market. In 1859, a colliery was opened on the concealed coalfield for the first time, and a new epoch had arrived.

SELECTED REFERENCES

AGRICULTURE

Bennett Jones, R. *The pattern of farming in the East Midlands* (1954). University of Nottingham.

Carr, J. P. Open Field Agriculture in Mid-Derbyshire. *Derbyshire Archaeological Journal* Vol. 83 (1963) p. 72.

Chambers, J. D. The Vale of Trent 1670-1800: A regional study of economic change. *Economic History Review* Supplement No. 3 (1957). (This is a valuable and authoritative account, covering most of the region, dealing with agriculture and the advance to industrialisation, together with the related course of population change.—*Ed.*).

Chambers, J. D. *Nottinghamshire in the 18th Century: a study of life and labour under the Squirearchy.* 2nd Edition London (1966).

Slater, G. *The English peasantry and the enclosure of Common Fields* London (1907).

LEAD MINING

Carruthers, R. G. and Strahan, A. Lead and Zinc Ores of Durham, Yorkshire and Derbyshire. *Special Report of the Mineral Resources of Great Britain.* Memoirs of the Geological Survey London (1923).

Donald, M. B. *Elizabethan Monopolies.* The history of the mineral and battery works from 1565-1604. Oliver and Boyd Edinburgh and London (1961).

Farey, J. *General View of the Agriculture and Minerals of Derbyshire.* Board of Agriculture London (1811).

Fisher, F. N. Sir Cornelius Vermuyden and the Dovegang Lead mines. *Journal of the Derbyshire Archaeological and Natural History Society* Vol. 72 (1952) pp. 74-118.

Lander, J. H. and Vellacott, C. H. Lead Mining. *Victoria County History. Derbyshire* Vol. 2 pp. 323-349.

Nixon, F. The Early Steam-Engine in Derbyshire. *Transactions of the Newcomen Society* Vol. 31 (1957-8 and 1958-9).

O'Neal, R. A. H. Derbyshire Lead and Lead Mining. Bibliography. Derbyshire County Library Matlock 1960.

Raistrick, A. *Two Centuries of Industrial Welfare: The London (Quaker) Lead Company 1692-1965* London (1938).

Raistrick, A. and Jennings, B. *History of lead-mining in the Pennines* (1965).

Stokes, A. H. Lead and Lead Mining in Derbyshire. *Transactions of the Chesterfield and Derbyshire Institute of Mining, Civil and Mechanical Engineers* Vol. 8 (1880-81) pp. 67-166.

Traill, J. G. The geology and development of Mill Close Mine, Derbyshire. *Economic Geology* Vol. 34 (1939) pp. 851-889.

ALABASTER WORKING

Cheetham, F. W. *Medieval English Alabaster Carvings in the Castle Museum Nottingham* (1962).

Cheetham, F. W. English Medieval Alabaster Altarpieces with special reference to Nottingham. *Museums Journal* Vol. 61 No. 4 (1962).

Farmer, R. L. Chellaston alabaster and its use by Nottingham Carvers. *Journal of the Derbyshire Archaeological and Natural History Society* Vol. 38 (1916).

Firman, R. J. Gypsum in Nottinghamshire. *Bulletin of the Peak District Mines Historical Society* Vol. 2 Part 4 (1964).

Gardner, A. *Alabaster Tombs* (1940).

Pitman, C. F. Nottingham Alabasters. *Museums Journal* Vol. 59 No. 9 1959.

Stevenson, W. Art Sculpture in Alabaster, preserved in France, considered in its relationship to the Nottingham School of Alabasterers. *Transactions of the Thoroton Society* Nottingham Vol. 11 (1907).

The study of English alabaster carving owes much to the pioneer work of W. H. St. John Hope who first demonstrated that much of the output previously attributed to continental craftsmen was in fact made from stone originating in the Nottingham and Derby area and the carvings produced by local artisans. Of special interest are his two contributions, 'On the early working of alabaster in England,' *Archaeological Journal* Vol. 61 (1904), and 'On some alabaster sculptures of Nottingham Work', *Archaeological Journal* Vol. 64 (1907). Subsequently many papers on the subject were published by P. Nelson during the period 1913-1927, chiefly in the *Archaeological Journal* and by W. L. Hildburgh between 1915-16 and 1955, largely in the *Proceedings of the Society of Antiquaries of London* and the *Antiquaries Journal*. These are all listed in the bibliography given in F. W. Cheetham's *Medieval English Alabaster Carvings*.

EARLY COAL AND IRON INDUSTRY

Farey, J. *General View of the Agriculture and Minerals of Derbyshire* Vol. 1 London (1811).

Griffin, A. R. *The Development of Industrial Relations in the Nottinghamshire Coalfield*. Ph.D. Thesis University of Nottingham (1963).

Nef, J. U. *The Rise of the British Coal Industry* 2 Vols. London (1932).

Richmond, I. A. *Roman Britain* (1955) pp. 159-160.

Smith, R. S. *The Willoughbys of Wollaton, 1500-1643, with special reference to Early Mining in Nottinghamshire*. Ph.D. Thesis University of Nottingham (1964).

Victoria County History, Derbyshire Vol. 2 London (1907).

Victoria County History Nottinghamshire Vol. 2 London (1910).

Williams, J. E. *The Derbyshire Miners: a Study in Industrial and Social History* London (1962).

XIII

PRESENT-DAY ECONOMIC STRUCTURE

THERE are several ways of defining a region and according to some criteria the expression 'Nottingham region' or even the 'East Midlands region' is of doubtful significance. But in terms of economic characteristics—the concentration of industrial activity and the related distribution of population—a Nottingham region is clearly identifiable. Its nucleus is contained within a triangle with Nottingham and Derby, only 16 miles apart, at its base and with its apex in Chesterfield, some 30 miles to the north. Southwards, across the Trent, the influence of Leicester, 26 miles from Nottingham and almost as large a city, delimits the Nottingham region, while Chesterfield is on the fringe of the Sheffield industrial area. In the more sparsely populated neighbouring country there are several relatively isolated towns which have numerous contacts with Nottingham and to which reference will be made in this account. Such are Newark, Grantham and Lincoln to the east, and Ashbourne, Belper and Matlock to the west.

The development of Nottingham as an industrial and commercial centre and its present economic structure are described in Chapter XXII. Here it is sufficient to mention the main points of interest. Modern Nottingham is remarkable for the variety of its industries and for its well-balanced economic structure. The former preponderance of textiles and clothing is now less marked. The famous lace industry is today quite small; hosiery is still important, but less so than at Leicester; tobacco, chemicals and pharmaceutical products have maintained the strong position they reached between the two world wars; and in the last 20 years there has been a considerable expansion in a variety of engineering trades. Along with its industrial growth Nottingham has become increasingly important as a provider of services, not only for its own inhabitants but for those of its hinterland. More than half the occupied population of Nottingham is employed in the service trades, including building and contracting, a considerably higher proportion than in Derby.

Derby, a town much smaller than Nottingham, has a less varied economic structure. Its early industrial development, like that of Nottingham, owed much to the establishment of textile manufacture. The former silk trade has died out, but there are several hosiery factories, and lace manufacture, which, like that of hosiery, spread out from Nottingham, is still carried on. But a large proportion of the present employment in textiles is contributed by the British Celanese works at Spondon, on the Nottingham side of Derby. This extensive plant is a development of one set up in the first world war for making cellulose. Later it turned to the production of synthetic fibres and more recently it has been adapted for the making of a wide range of chemical products in addition to textile materials. In the 1920s British Celanese built up their labour force to about 10,000; many of the workers were daily travellers, not only from Derby, but from more distant places, including Nottingham. But in recent years, under the ownership of Courtaulds, considerable re–organisation has taken place, making for economy of labour, and employment is now about 6,000.

Although textiles are still of considerable importance in the Derby area, accounting for 15·6 per cent of employment in manufacturing, Derby itself is now primarily an engineering centre. Seventy per cent of manufacturing employment is in the metal and engineering trades. Long before the railway age Derby and its neighbourhood had become notable in several branches of engineering. Some of the earliest steam engines were set up here in connection with the mining of lead, iron and coal. In the latter part of the 18th century Arkwright and Strutt built their famous cotton mills in the Derwent valley, driven by water power. These activities called for new skills in both the making and using of tools and machines and thus gave further stimulus to the growing engineering trades of Derby.

The construction of the North Midland Railway through Derby was undertaken by George Stephenson, and the making of the Clay Cross tunnel north of Derby revealed rich deposits of coal and iron. Stephenson was instrumental in forming the Clay Cross Company, which is referred to later on, and much of the mechanical equipment installed here and at the Crich limestone quarries was built locally to his designs. With the completion of the railway in the early 1840s Derby became still more closely linked with enterprises in the developing coalfield, and as the railway network extended the town acquired an important status in the national communications system. This was emphasised by its selection as the site for the Midland Railway works; Derby became a railway town and the various forms of railway engineering and administrative services are still a major source of employment.

With unified control under British Railways some former railway centres have lost their position. But re–organisation has enhanced the importance of Derby. New railway engineering laboratories have been established and now most of British Railways design and development resources for mechanical and electrical engineering, hitherto scattered throughout the country, will be concentrated at Derby. It is anticipated that the whole scheme, costing about £4m, will make Derby the most important railway technical and scientific centre in the world. Derby is also to become the headquarters of the railways purchasing organisation and part of the finance department is to be located there.

The industrial structure of Derby is, however, by no means dominated by railway engineering and administration. More important, in recent years, has been the growth of Rolls–Royce. This famous concern originated in Manchester and the effect of its transfer to Derby in 1908 is comparable with that produced by the coming of the railway works in the 19th century. Rolls-Royce are now the biggest employers of labour in the district. They have established branches in several other places, including Crewe, where car production has been located since 1946. But Derby is the headquarters for administration and research and the seat of the firm's great aero-engine division. These activities occupy some 20,000 mainly highly skilled personnel and are a dominant element in the local economic structure.

Undue dependence on the aircraft industry could be a source of weakness and there have been fluctuations in employment in recent years. But Rolls-Royce have attained a foremost position as suppliers of aero engines. Moreover, their research activities now extend over a wide field, ranging from nuclear power to the discovery of new materials. They are well established in a number of growth industries.

Several smaller firms have contributed to diversification within the engineering group. Some represent the old trade of iron founding. Ley's Malleable Castings Ltd. is important here. Another, Qualcast Ltd., is the successor of a firm established in 1840 as makers of iron fireplaces and ovens; now they are the biggest makers of lawn mowers in Britain. Boiler making is another old local industry, now represented by International Combustion Ltd., an important supplier of water tube boilers for power stations; and in a related field is Aiton and Co. Ltd., which undertakes special pipework for power stations, ships and industrial plants. A prominent member of the electrical trades is the cable works of Crompton Parkinson Ltd.

The concentration of employment in engineering, and especially heavy engineering, affords little opportunity for women and girls in manufacturing industry. The proportion of females so employed is only 21·8 per cent. In Nottingham the proportion is nearly twice as great, for here, in addition to the traditional women's trades, lighter engineering and a wide range of miscellaneous manufactures have created an increasing demand for female labour. In contrast with Nottingham, however, Derby has far fewer employed in miscellaneous manufactures.

In Nottingham, again, diversification of employment has been assisted by the striking growth of services of all kinds, now accounting for 54·5 per cent of total employment. In Derby the proportion of the working population so occupied is 47·9 per cent. This contrast is due partly to the pull of Nottingham as the larger centre, and the recent marked improvement in the Nottingham–Derby road may well enhance the influence of Nottingham as a provider of services for its smaller neighbour.

Chesterfield, which marks the northern limit of the region as defined for this survey, forms the centre of a heavily industrialised area with a population of nearly 100,000. Its character is inevitably influenced by Sheffield, only 12 miles away. On the other hand, Chesterfield has close affinities with the rest of east Derbyshire and with other parts of the East Midlands. The very proximity of Sheffield seems to have strengthened the sense of community in this corner of Derbyshire, of which Chesterfield is the natural centre.

Coal, iron and heavy engineering are the dominant industries of the Chesterfield area. Before nationalisation coal mining was already largely concentrated in big undertakings with interests spread over a wide area and integrated with other industrial activities, the most notable example being the Staveley Coal and Iron Company. Under the National Coal Board further concentration has taken place, involving the closing of some smaller collieries. Staveley's main product is cast iron pipes and a smaller firm in this industry is the Clay Cross Company, founded by George Stephenson in 1837. A still older firm is the Renishaw Iron Company and there is also the Sheepbridge Coal and Iron Company, which owns foundries, forge and rolling mills and, through its subsidiary, Sheepbridge Stokes Centrifugal Castings Ltd., is an important producer of cylinder linings.

The range of activities springing from these basic industries of coal and iron is extensive. For instance, Staveley has built up an important chemical industry using the by-products of coking and iron smelting. The manufacture of smokeless fuel, started in 1937, has been developed by the National Coal Board. Much of the local engineering, too, is connected with the basic industries, for instance, the making of colliery equipment, blast furnace plants and rolling mills and equipment for the gas industry. Chesterfield has also an old-established concern making seamless steel tubes and gas cylinders, which is now a member of the Tube Investments group. Wagon building and repairing is an important activity and road transport is prominently represented by the important firm of Kennings Ltd., a local enterprise which began as an oil-distributing agency. In the electrical trades there are two firms making components for lamps and one has extended into the manufacture of valves and television tubes.

Until recently hosiery manufacture, so widespread in other parts of the coalfield, had not extended to the Chesterfield area; but with the shortage of labour in the traditional centres several factories have now been opened in the district. In Chesterfield itself, however, Robinson and Sons Ltd. are important employers of female labour. Established over a hundred years ago for the manufacture of pill boxes, this firm has continually widened the range of its products, which now include surgical dressings, sanitary towels, paper and cardboard boxes and printing. Another group of trades which helps to improve the balance of local employment is sugar confectionery and food preserving; Chesterfield is a good centre for the distribution of these products in the Midlands and north of England.

Chesterfield's industrial structure is thus fairly well diversified and the proportion of females in its manufacturing industries, 34·3 per cent, is considerably higher than Derby's. The decision of the Post Office to establish its accountant-general's department in Chesterfield has made a further substantial contribution to female employment; it has a staff of over 1,000, a large proportion of whom are women and girls.

Midway between Nottingham and Chesterfield and therefore more in the centre of the Nottinghamshire–Derbyshire coalfield is the town of Mansfield. The borough itself, with a population of some 55,000, is smaller than Chesterfield, but it forms part of an urban concentration with nearly 150,000 people. Mansfield is an old market town and the first phase of its industrial development was associated with textiles, not only hosiery, but also cotton and wool spinning. These are still the chief manufactures of the town and its neighbourhood, but from the 1890s coal-mining has become the dominant activity. It expanded notably between the wars with the opening of large new pits to the east and north of Mansfield and today it accounts for 37·5 per cent of employment in the Mansfield Employment Exchange area. This has emphasised Mansfield's traditional role as a market town and has stimulated its industrial development in other directions.

The salient feature of this development is the further growth of industries requiring female labour. Although females constitute only 29·2 per cent of the total insured population, as compared with the national figure of 35·5 per cent, in manufacturing industry they considerably outnumber the males. This is also the position at Sutton-in-Ashfield, a smaller mining town to the west of Mansfield. More than half the female employment in manufacture at both these places is in textiles. Another important industry employing mainly women and girls is tin box making. This started in a small way as early as 1870 and there are now two firms, one being a branch of the Metal Box Company. More recent introductions are a firm making radio and radar equipment at Mansfield and another at Sutton-in-Ashfield producing metal fasteners. Each of them employs about 600, a large proportion of whom are women and girls. Mansfield has also the only representative of the shoe industry in this region, the Mansfield Shoe Company, which has a labour force of about 800 persons.

Neither Mansfield nor Sutton is of great importance as an engineering centre; there are more men employed in textiles than in engineering. But the coal industry has assisted engineering development to some extent, and being itself highly mechanised, it has contributed to the supply of trained labour and provides custom for a few firms supplying or maintaining colliery equipment. In addition, Mansfield has one medium-sized firm making machine tools and another making hand tools. Hosiery machine building is represented at Sutton and there is also a member of the Sheepbridge group making aircraft components.

Employment in the smaller towns and villages of the coalfield is naturally less diversified. These settlements are strung out northwards from Nottingham and Derby on either side of the county border. Some of them have a long tradition of activity in manufacture, for in the 18th century the framework knitting industry, forerunner of the modern hosiery manufacture, became widely distributed in this area. Dispersal was facilitated by the domestic system of organisation, which persisted into the second half of the 19th century. But the great stimulus to industrial development came with the opening of main railway routes through the area, from London to the north, and the exploitation of its rich coal measures. This, in turn, led to more railway building, linking the collieries with the main lines, and to an increasing concentration of population. Then, as hosiery manufacture became a factory industry, factories were set up in the old framework knitting centres, securing the advantages of cheap sites, easy communication with Nottingham and Derby, and an abundant supply of female labour. These advantages, and particularly the latter, have become more marked in recent years, with increasing congestion and intensified demand for labour in the main centres.

The presence of textiles and other small-scale manufactures has produced a more varied industrial structure than exists in some coalfields. There is also some heavy engineering at Clay Cross, as already mentioned, and at the important Butterley plant, near Ripley, where structural steelwork is made. Coal mining, however, is the chief industry, although in this part of the field most of the collieries are old and declining. The economic prospect is thus causing some concern. The decay of many of the mining villages seems inevitable and there are three fair-sized towns, Ripley, Alfreton and Heanor, for which the continued decline of the local coal industry could have serious consequences in the next decade. Hitherto it has been the 'surplus' of female labour that has attracted new enterprise; now the need is to find jobs for men. Unfortunately the area is not physically attractive and a particular difficulty is to find sites for new works owing to the prevalence of mining subsidence.

The borough of Ilkeston, further south and therefore nearer to Nottingham and Derby than the places just mentioned, presents less of a problem. Here adjustment to the decline of coal mining has already taken place; 30 years ago coal accounted for half the males employed in extractive and manufacturing industry; now the percentage is 16·5. The local economy is, however, still dominated by heavy industry; the principal firm, the Stanton Ironworks Company, employs more than a third of all occupied males. Stanton is an old-established concern now linked with the Staveley Iron Company and Stewarts and Lloyds of Corby. Its main products are iron and concrete spun pipes, which are widely distributed in the home market and abroad. Considerable additions have been made to the plant in recent years and employment has been well maintained. Undue dependence on this one firm is mitigated to some extent by the presence of hosiery and clothing factories; these employ mainly women, but in hosiery manufacture, especially, men are required for certain occupations and they form more than a third of the labour force. Proximity to Nottingham and Derby further extends the range of employment opportunities, yet it does not appear to have diminished Ilkeston's importance as a commercial and administrative centre. This is shown by the fact that about 40 per cent of the local occupied population is employed in various forms of services.

South of Ilkeston and between Nottingham and Derby lies another industrialised area: Stapleford in Nottinghamshire and Long Eaton in Derbyshire. Here the influence of coal mining is no longer felt; the emphasis is on textiles, and light engineering; railway employment is also of some importance, for the area is a nodal point in the railway system of the East Midlands. Long Eaton's rise as an industrial centre began when sections of the lace trade began to move out of Nottingham in the latter part of the 19th century. Although some of the lace factories have now been adapted to other uses Long Eaton is still relatively important as a centre of lace manufacture, especially dress lace, of which Long Eaton makes more than Nottingham. In the area as a whole the industrial structure is well diversified with several new manufactures introduced in recent years. For instance, there is a growing firm at Stapleford with nearly 2,000 employees making components for the radio and other industries. Long Eaton has two firms manufacturing stainless steel ware. Textile products, in addition to lace, include hosiery and narrow fabrics and elastic webbing. There are also two fair-sized firms making spring seating. Further industrial development in this area may well be encouraged by the extension of the London–Yorkshire motorway, which passes through it.

In the country south of the Trent there is no large centre of population until Loughborough is reached, and this town looks towards Leicester rather than Nottingham. There are, however, two developments that must be mentioned. One is the extension of coal mining with the recent opening of a big colliery at Cotgrave. The other is the building of power stations in the Trent valley. These developments are inter-connected. The newer collieries in the Nottinghamshire–Derbyshire coalfield are among the most productive in the country and more and more of this cheap fuel is being used to generate electricity. With ample water supply and the availability of suitable sites the Trent valley offers technically ideal locations for massive generating plants, though the loss of amenity is all too obvious. The current is, of course, fed into the national grid, so that the growth of power production in this area makes little direct contribution to its industrial development.

To the east of the area so far described the country is largely agricultural, but with several industrial centres having certain characteristics in common. The most important is the ancient city of Lincoln, with a population of some 70,000. Lincoln began as a Roman settlement; in the Middle Ages it grew into a small town around its castle and cathedral; then, with the improvement of agriculture and the growth of population in the county it became increasingly important as a market town. Although this function is by no means submerged in modern Lincoln, the city's growth and prosperity have in more recent years come to depend mainly on its engineering industry. Of the 16,000 males employed in manufactures no less than 13,000 (81 per cent) are in various branches of engineering, which also accounts for 55 per cent of females so employed. More than half the total employment in engineering is provided by Ruston and Hornsby Ltd. They began as Ruston's, makers of farm implements and agricultural machinery, in the early 19th century, eventually merging with the old firm of Richard Hornsby & Sons at Grantham. By the time of their amalgamation both firms had become important producers of gas and oil engines and pumping equipment. Rustons had been a pioneer in the development of diesel engines, and an extensive export trade had been built up. Today Ruston and Hornsby's output includes various types of diesel

XI Cotgrave Colliery, Nottinghamshire, 1964

XII Bevercotes Colliery, Nottinghamshire, showing electronic controls which operate
coal cutter, loader, conveyor and hydraulic roof supports

XIII Gravel extraction below river level at Hoveringham

XIV Staythorpe electricity generating station near Newark, one of the major power stations located along the Trent

locomotives, marine engines, diesel plants and gas turbines and a large proportion is exported. Agricultural engineering, mainly concerned with tractor equipment, and the making of excavators and drills, is undertaken by a subsidiary, Ruston Bucyrus Ltd.

Robey and Co. Ltd. is another old-established firm, smaller than Ruston and Hornsby but with a somewhat similar range. In addition to oil-, steam- and compressed-air engines, the firm makes gas-fired boilers. More specialised is Allen Gwynne Pumps Ltd. which manufactures pumping machinery. Primary metal trades are represented by Leys Malleable Castings Ltd. and Smith Clayton Forge Ltd. Some diversification within the engineering group has been introduced by Clayton Dewandre Ltd., formed in 1928 to acquire the motor engineering section of Clayton Wagons Ltd. and their Lincoln works. They manufacture brakes, heaters and other components for motor vehicles. Another of the newer industries is represented by a branch of A.E.I. which makes electronic valves and transistors.

Lincoln has few manufactures outside the engineering group. There are three firms engaged in food processing, each with between 250 and 500 workers, a leather works and a woodworking firm, while textiles and clothing provide a small amount of employment. The employment structure as a whole is, however, much better balanced than this account of the local manufactures would suggest. Since the war Lincoln has experienced a remarkable growth in its servicing activities. Employment in this field has increased by $2\frac{1}{2}$ times since 1938 and it now accounts for 60 per cent of the total. This illustrates the importance of Lincoln as a commercial and administrative centre for an extensive and prosperous agricultural area.

Grantham, 24 miles east of Nottingham, has an industrial structure very like that of Lincoln, though on a smaller scale. Here 70 per cent of the total employment in manufacture is in engineering, which, as with Lincoln, began with the making of farm implements and agricultural machinery. For many years Richard Hornsby and Sons were the leading firm and eventually, as already described, they were absorbed by Rustons of Lincoln. The works are now occupied by another subsidiary of the Ruston group. Today the biggest engineering firm is Aveling-Barford Ltd., who have achieved a notable expansion since the war as makers of earth-moving and road-making equipment. They also carry on the tradition of agricultural engineering. General engineering includes one fair-sized firm and there is a smaller concern making excavators.

Manufacture, however, accounts for little more than a third of total employment in Grantham, the rest, apart from agriculture and some iron ore working being in the construction trades and services. Grantham is the county town of Kesteven and therefore ranks as an administrative centre. It is also of some importance in the railway system. Like Lincoln it has a considerable status as a market town and its position on the Great North Road suggests the possibility of further industrial and commercial development.

S

Newark, between Grantham and Lincoln and 20 miles from Nottingham, is another of these small engineering centres. Here the industry is dominated by two firms. One, Ransome and Marles Bearing Co. Ltd., as its name indicates, is an important manufacturer of ball and roller bearings. Besides the Newark works it has subsidiaries in Canada, South Africa, Australia and New Zealand. The other firm, Worthington-Simpson Ltd., makes pumps, compressors and heat exchange equipment. Nearly two-thirds of all employment and half the female employment in manufacture is provided by these two firms. Brewing, including a firm of maltsters, is the next most important manufacturing industry and there are two medium-sized clothing firms. Agriculture is, of course, the predominant activity in the surrounding area, but there are important sand and gravel workings, with cement-making, in the Trent valley.

Newark, although somewhat larger than Grantham, has a smaller proportion of its working population in the services group. There are fewer in distribution and transport. But, at 60 per cent, employment in services is considerably higher than for places of its size in the more industrialised parts of Nottinghamshire and, indeed, higher than for Nottingham itself.

One further example of a small engineering centre should be mentioned. This is Gainsborough, situated on the Trent in the extreme north-east of the region as defined for this survey. Here the industry, represented by two firms, accounts for nearly three-quarters of manufacturing employment. In one case, that of Marshall and Sons Ltd., the industry, as in Lincoln and Grantham, had its origin in agricultural engineering. The firm was established in 1862 and became well-known as builders of threshing machines and traction engines. These are still made, though diesels have replaced steam, and the range now includes other diesel-driven equipment such as crawler tractors and earth movers. The other firm, Rose Bros. Ltd., specialises in wrapping and labelling machinery.

Gainsborough is a somewhat isolated place, off the main routes, and in the past its heavy dependence on one industry made it vulnerable to trade depression. In recent years the balance of employment has improved, as elsewhere, by the growth of service trades and occupations. Gainsborough now has 57 per cent of its insured population in this group.

The towns on the western side of the region have a different economic structure from those to the east. Belper, eight miles north of Derby, is on the western fringe of the coalfield, already described. There is one colliery in the area, employing about 700, and there are two firms of iron founders making stoves and firegrates. Ambergate, nearby, has a fair-sized wireworks. But textiles are the chief manufacturing industry. Cotton spinning dates from the latter part of the 18th century when Strutt and Arkwright set up their water mills in the Derwent valley. The present mills, owned by the English Sewing Cotton Company, are engaged in cotton doubling. The local hosiery manufacture, represented by three firms, has a similarly long history, going back to the days of the stocking frame. Strutt himself was already established in this trade as inventor of the rib frame before entering into partnership with Arkwright.

Higher up the Derwent valley, at Matlock and the neighbouring village of Cromford, hosiery is again the main manufacturing industry, one firm employing about 900 people. But extractive industry is of considerable importance, for the area is rich in minerals, apart from coal. There is clay, providing material for the well-known pottery at Denby, near Belper, and abundance of limestone, which is quarried at Matlock and other places. Lead mining has been carried on from ancient times and fluorspar is obtained. An interesting recent development is the establishment of a firm, Magnesium Elektron Ltd., for mining and processing dolomite.

On the services side, Matlock's significance has lately been increased by the Derbyshire County Council's decision to make the town its administrative head-quarters. Matlock also attracts a good deal of tourist traffic. These influences are reflected in the fact that about three-quarters of the population registered in the Matlock Exchange area are employed in services.

The small town of Ashbourne may be said to mark the western edge of the region. It looks eastwards towards Derby, only 13 miles away, although when travel was more dependent on the railway it had better connections with the more distant Pottery towns. Dairy farming is the predominant form of agriculture in the area and Nestle's have a milk processing factory in the town. There is also an old-established firm of corset makers employing nearly 800 and another engaged in yarn processing. A small hosiery factory has lately been established and engineering has been introduced by a firm making compressors and sprayers.

As stated at the beginning, the region as defined for this survey has no definite boundaries. Thus, in the treatment of fringe areas, selection must be somewhat arbitrary. Within the region, however, there are clearly recognisable centres of varying importance whose features determine the character of the whole.

From the economic standpoint the dominant impression is that of a well-diversified industrial and employment structure. There are few industries of importance in the national economy that are not represented in the Nottingham region. This diversification owes little to deliberate planning; it reflects the distribution of natural resources, the working of economic forces and, to a considerable extent, the influence of local enterprise.

The variety of industry in the region helped to sustain prosperity between the wars and in the last 20 years of more rapid national economic growth the region has been well placed for quickly responding to changing trends in the national industrial structure. For many of the industries favoured by these trends were already established. On the other hand, the region had no large stake in declining industries. Coal mining, it is true, has declined nationally, and the older part of the Nottinghamshire–Derbyshire coalfield reflects this trend, but in the field as a whole production is expanding.

A particularly encouraging sign is the prosperity of the small towns in the more sparsely populated parts of the region. With the increasing mobility of people in rural areas the country towns have become more important in their original function. Moreover, the continued shrinkage of the agricultural labour force makes more local labour available for further industrial development in the country towns. Such development will help to relieve congestion in the larger centres.

The problem area of the region is the older part of the coalfield. But this is nowhere very far from the main growing points of the region, and within the area itself new industrial growth has appeared. The process would certainly be assisted by road improvements and here the new motorway will make a major contribution.

XIV

AGRICULTURE

INTRODUCTION

FOR the purposes of this chapter the area under consideration is that of the administrative counties of Derby and Nottingham. Some 90 per cent of the land area of Derbyshire lies above 200 feet in elevation while in Nottinghamshire 70 per cent of the land lies below this level. This is but one of the many physical differences to be found between the two adjacent counties, differences which are reflected in the structure and pattern of farming in the various parts of the area.

The agriculture of a region may be studied from several viewpoints. The soil scientist, the agronomist, the geographer and the economist might each emphasise different aspects of the agricultural environment. The present account has been written from the standpoint of the agricultural economist. After reviewing briefly the main changes over the past half-century, the present distribution of the agricultural resources of land, livestock and manpower is considered in seven regional sub-divisions.

Agricultural economists have, for a number of years, explored ways and means of classifying agricultural holdings on the basis of the enterprises which have constituted their main sources of revenue. Using data from the Agricultural Returns of 1947, R. Bennett Jones found that 60 per cent of the holdings in the area were full-time farms in the sense that they carried sufficient acreages of crops and numbers of livestock to give full-time employment to one man, i.e. the occupier. The full-time farms were then classified as follows.

Table XXXVI Full-time farm classification

Type of farming	Percentage of full-time farms of each type	
	Derbyshire	Nottinghamshire
Dairying ..	80·1	35·0
Arable ..	1·4	13·5
Mixed ..	2·2	29·6
Livestock ..	8·4	13·5
Other ..	7·9	8·4
	100·0	100·0

Clearly at that time dairy farms were predominant in Derbyshire but in Nottinghamshire no one type of farming could be regarded as predominant.

Data for 1962 allowed a revised estimate of the incidence of part-time farming (see Table XXXVIII) but no detailed type of farming classification is available for a recent year on a county basis. In farming, the process of change and adjustment is continuous. Mechanisation has proceeded apace and farms which were full-time in the late 1940's no longer provide enough work to keep the occupier in full employment. The number of milk producers is declining rapidly and further changes in the number and proportion of farms of a given type must be expected. The changes outlined in the following section must be regarded therefore as part of a continuing process.

CHANGES IN THE PAST FIFTY YEARS

Crops and Stock

Derbyshire and Nottinghamshire have shared in the considerable changes affecting British agriculture in the last 50 years, the most notable features of which are: (1) the marked decline in the acreage of permanent grass; (2) the expansion of cereals; (3) the decline of the acreage under 'other crops and fallow'; and (4) the build-up of the livestock population (Appendix III). It should not be assumed that the decline in the crops and grass acreage recorded in agricultural statistics is a direct measure of the land lost to various non-agricultural uses. Over the years some of the land previously returned as permanent grass has been recorded as rough grazings, while there have been gains and losses as the service departments have varied their demands for land and as sites have been acquired and restored after open-cast mining.

The past half-century spans two world wars and an intervening period of intense economic depression both in agriculture and industry. The tillage area rose to a peak during the first world war only to sink, in the late 1930s, to a level far below that recorded in 1914. The ploughing-up campaign of the second world war surpassed the achievements of the first, although in Derbyshire, the tillage acreage shrank after 1945. In Nottinghamshire the war-time level has been maintained. In recent years, particularly since 1954, there has been a revolution in cereal production. In Derbyshire, barley production has increased nearly ninefold and in Nottingham over threefold. This expansion has been largely achieved by substituting barley for wheat and oats. Farmers have found that intensive cropping with barley incurs smaller disease risks than similar practices with wheat or oats, and the demand for barley has increased as pig numbers have expanded and systems of barley-beef production have been evolved.

In 1914, sugar beet was not grown in the area but in Nottinghamshire the crop has since become important. There are now two sugar factories in the county (at Kelham, near Newark, and Colwick, on the eastern outskirts of Nottingham). In 1962 about 17,000 acres of beet or about 40 per cent more than the war-time acreage, were grown, whereas only 10,000 acres of potatoes were grown in 1962, which was about one-third of the peak acreage of 1948.

There has been a marked decline in both counties in the acreage of other crops and bare fallow. The greater part of these other crops consists of turnips, swedes and mangolds, which are the 'fodder crops' used for stock feeding. This change is most marked in Nottinghamshire and is linked to the decline of the Norfolk four-course rotation and the sheep population. Usually, the roots in this rotation were turnips intended to be eaten-off by sheep. Farmers came to realise that sugar beet was more profitable than turnips laboriously folded with sheep, and that considerable numbers of sheep could be maintained on the by-products of the beet crop, namely the tops and the pulp.

Changes in the sheep population mirror trends in other counties. In hill and upland areas such as Derbyshire, the sheep population has recovered from the low levels to which it was driven in the 1940s, particularly in the winter of early 1947, and has now reached record levels. In arable counties such as Nottingham, flock numbers have increased in recent years but still fall far short of their 1914 levels.

Table XXXVII Sheep, pig and poultry population in arable and non-arable counties of England in 1914 and 1964

	1964 population when 1914 population = 100	
	★Arable counties	*Non-arable counties*
Sheep ..	73	127
Pigs ..	245	244
Poultry ..	455	313

★Counties with more than the median percentage of crops and grass under tillage and fallow in 1964.

The proportionate increase in cattle numbers has been similar in both counties but in Derbyshire dairy cattle predominate. For this reason there is a marked difference in the herd structure. In Derbyshire in 1962 cows and heifers represented 51 per cent of the herd, while in Nottinghamshire, where beef cattle are more numerous, cows and heifers accounted for only 35 per cent of the herd. In 1914, Derbyshire had more pigs than Nottinghamshire but in 1924 the position was reversed. The recovery of the pig population from the low point reached as a consequence of policy during the second world war has been most marked in Nottinghamshire where in 1962 numbers increased more than threefold. Again until very recently, Nottinghamshire had a smaller poultry population than Derbyshire but during the past decade the activities of one or two large-scale operators have brought about a spectacular increase, particularly in broiler numbers.

Number and size of holdings

Between 1914 and 1962 agricultural statistics show that the number of holdings with more than one acre of crops and grass fell by roughly one third in both counties. The total crops and grass acreage also declined but despite this the average size of holding increased from 43 to 56 acres in Derbyshire and from 65 to 83 acres in Nottinghamshire. Derbyshire is a county of relatively small holdings. Over 82 per cent of the holdings are below 100 acres in size but in 1962 only about 44 per cent of the crops and grassland was on these holdings (Appendices III and IV). In Nottinghamshire 72 per cent of holdings with only 20 per cent of the crops and grassland were below this size, but at the other end of the scale the six per cent of the holdings which were over 300 acres included nearly 35 per cent of the land. In both counties, between 1914 and 1962, holdings of under 100 acres have declined in importance in terms both of number and size. The average size of holding in the under 20 acres group fell by nearly 20 per cent; those between 20 and 100 acres became about seven per cent larger and those over 300 acres increased in size by about 15 per cent. Holdings between 100 and 300 acres did not change in size. In Derbyshire there were fewer holdings in every size group in 1962 than in 1914; in Nottinghamshire the 'over 300' group was the only one with more farms.

The total number of holdings recorded is not a satisfactory measure of the population dependent on farming as a main source of income, and changes in the recorded total do not necessarily reflect changes in the number of farmers. Many holdings are not farms in the usual sense but recreational or part-time pursuits of people whose main source lies outside agriculture. There are also many instances of more than one holding being occupied by a single person.

Two possible definitions of full-time holdings may be noted: (1) those of more than 20 acres of crops and grass; and (2) those requiring 275 or more days of work per annum. In 1962 the numbers of holdings conforming to these definitions were respectively 4,313 and 3,599 in Derbyshire and 2,510 and 2,361 in Nottinghamshire. It is clear that in both counties, but particularly in Derbyshire, there are holdings of more than 20 acres of crops and grass but without sufficient livestock and crops to keep one man fully employed. The estimated labour requirements of the crops and stock on a holding is frequently used as a measure of size; many would claim that this represents a better measure of economic size than the area of the holding. Any holding with fewer crops and stock than can be cared for in a year by an adult man working for 275 days of eight hours, i.e. 275 'standard man days', is normally classified as a part-time unit. Any holding which provides 275 or more days of work is therefore regarded as a full-time unit which, by implication, is capable of providing a living for one man, the occupier, and his family. The data in the following table refer to the position at June 1962.

Table XXXVIII Percentage of part-time holdings and average size of holdings, June 1962

	Derbyshire	Nottinghamshire	England and Wales
Part-time holding with less than 275 days of work	*per cent* 52	*per cent* 50	*per cent* 49
Total acreage on part-time holdings	13	6	8
	acres	*acres*	*acres*
Average size of part-time holdings	13	10	12
Average size of full-time holdings	99	157	129
Average size of all holdings ..	55	93	72

Part-time farming in this theoretical sense is widespread, but there is a tendency for the proportion of holdings which are part-time to be greater in the urbanised areas lying along the border between the two counties. The location of the larger full-time holdings is more clearly marked. These are found to the south and west of Derby and, in Nottinghamshire, on the Sherwood Forest sand, west of the Trent north of Newark, and east and south of the Trent in an arc extending from Newark through Bingham and south of the city of Nottingham.

Yet another measure of the size of a farm business may be derived from statistics showing the average number of each type of livestock returned by those holdings not making a nil return for a particular item. The table shows that Derbyshire had considerably smaller herds or flocks than Nottinghamshire. The figures also show that a higher proportion of Derbyshire than of Nottinghamshire farms keep cattle, sheep and fowls.

The agricultural labour force

The number of workers on farms, excluding the occupier and his wife was first regularly recorded in the Agricultural Statistics for 1921. In that year there were 25,355 regular and casual workers in the two counties. The number declined steadily and reached a low point, 16,366, in 1939. During the war, numbers increased steadily and, with members of the Women's Land Army supplemented by prisoners of war, reached 23,228 in 1947. A steady decline has since reduced the total number to 15,071 in 1962. The reduction in farm employees has been more marked in Derbyshire than in Nottinghamshire.

Table XXXIX Importance of livestock enterprises, 1962

| | Percentage of holdings returning livestock | | |
	Derbyshire	*Nottinghamshire*	*England and Wales*
Cattle and calves	70	54	62
Pigs	25	33	31
Sheep	22	17	27
Fowls—six months and over	67	59	58
Broilers	1	1	1

| | Average numbers returned per holding | | |
	Derbyshire	*Nottinghamshire*	*England and Wales*
Cattle and calves	39	47	42
Pigs	26	49	48
Sheep	123	159	215
Fowls—six months and over	140	281	196
Broilers	1,796	20,600★	4,107

★This result is due to the presence of a few very large flocks

The employment of regular workers is also a convenient measure of the size of farm businesses. In 1962, only 38 per cent of the holdings in Derbyshire employed regular workers and, on average, these holdings had two such workers, while in Nottinghamshire, 44 per cent of holdings had regular workers with an average of three per holding. The distribution of regular workers shows that in Derbyshire less than 10 are employed per 1,000 acres, except in isolated parishes in the area west and north of Wirksworth. Comparatively few areas employ more than 15 workers per 1,000 acres. These include the market gardening parish of Melbourne, a group of parishes in the extreme south–west of the county and the arable area in the north–east. The urban districts are also areas of high employment. In Nottinghamshire, the rate of employment per 1,000 acres is higher than in Derbyshire. It is also higher in the western than in the eastern half of the county. Here again the rate of agricultural employment is higher in the urban than in the rural areas.

THE STRUCTURE AND PATTERN OF FARMING

The traditional contrast between the agriculture of Derbyshire and Nottinghamshire persists today. In Derbyshire the pattern of farming is based primarily on livestock enterprises, notably dairying and sheep. Nottinghamshire farming, by contrast, is organised in larger farm units and is predominantly arable. Its livestock enterprises, particularly beef, sheep and pigs, tend to be integrated within arable farming systems. Not unexpectedly the productivity of Nottinghamshire farming is higher than that of Derbyshire both in terms of land and labour, while the average net output per holding is over 75 per cent greater than in Derbyshire. These broad distinctions, however, conceal significant variations within the two counties.

Table XL

Farm holdings and output in Derbyshire and Nottinghamshire, 1962

	Derbyshire	Nottinghamshire
	acres	acres
Average size of farm holdings ..	55	85
PER 100 ACRES CROPS AND GRASS:	acres	acres
Cereals	16	39
Other tillage crops	5	12
	number	number
Dairy cattle	24	9
Other cattle	26	22
Sheep	51	33
Pigs	10	17
NET OUTPUT:	£	£
Per acre	37	43
Per standard man day labour requirement	6·2	7·4
Per holding	2,030	3,600

REGIONAL SUBDIVISIONS

The agriculture of any area is influenced not only by the physical environment but also by its human environment. It can be claimed, with considerable justification, that the economic and social characteristics of an area, particularly in the lowlands of England, are of greater importance than the physical environment in determining the varying structure and pattern of farming. Certain elements of the socio-economic structure of Derbyshire and Nottinghamshire may be regarded as crucial in an appreciation of their agricultural diversity. In order to demonstrate this diversity the area covered by the two counties has been divided into seven sub-areas, each being defined on a basis of physical and socio-economic conditions.

The Derbyshire and Nottinghamshire border is notable for its concentration of urban settlements. These form an almost unbroken belt of industrial towns and villages extending southwards from Sheffield to Nottingham and Derby. Socially and economically this belt bears the pronounced characteristics of a mining and manufacturing area. However, it contains a substantial acreage of land devoted to agriculture, although the farm population forms only a negligible proportion of the total. Since certain differences in agricultural conditions occur between the Derby-shire and Nottinghamshire portions of this belt, each is treated as a separate sub-division. The County and Municipal Boroughs, Urban Districts and contiguous parishes in which the estimated population directly dependent on farming is under five per cent of the total, form the basis upon which these 'urban' subdivisions are delimited (see Appendix IV and Fig. 43A). The other subdivisions, two in Derbyshire and three in Nottinghamshire, are also delimited by administrative boundaries.

North-west Derbyshire is an upland area forming part of the Peak District and in administrative terms this subdivision may be defined as the two Rural Districts of Chapel-en-le-Frith and Bakewell together with the northern part of the Ashbourne Rural District. The third subdivision consists of the remaining portion of Derbyshire which includes the undulating lowland in the south and some relatively high ground between the north-west upland and the eastern urbanized zone.

In Nottinghamshire, the western urban belt is succeeded eastwards by the central subdivision which extends from the north of the county to the outskirts of Nottingham. On the west side, between Worksop and Warsop, it reaches to the Derbyshire boundary, thus breaking the continuity of the urban belt. Eastwards again this subdivision is succeeded by the east Nottinghamshire area which comprises the Trent valley and the adjoining lowland. The latter consists essentially of the Newark Rural District and a succession of parishes lying to the west of the river in the Retford and Southwell Rural Districts. The remainder of the county, comprising the Bingham Rural District and the portion of the Basford Rural District lying south of the Trent, forms the south Nottinghamshire subdivision which includes much of the Vale of Belvoir and the boulder-clay Wolds. Thus the regional subdivisions (Fig. 43A) each with its characteristic structure and pattern of farming, are as follows:

    1 The north-west Derbyshire upland
    2 Central and south Derbyshire
    3 The east Derbyshire urban belt
    4 The west Nottinghamshire urban belt
    5 Central Nottinghamshire
    6 East Nottinghamshire (Trent valley)
    7 South Nottinghamshire

The main source of data used to describe quantitatively the farming structure is the parish summaries of the annual (4th June) agricultural census for 1962. These form the basis for the selected, detailed distributions (Fig. 43B–K) and for the summary data for each of the regional subdivisions given in Appendix III. The data may be considered as falling into three groups. First, details of the farm population and holdings provide the structural elements. The estimates of the population dependent on agriculture in each subdivision have been expressed as percentages of the total population shown in the 1961 Population Census. Secondly, the total acreages of the main crop items and the numbers of livestock in each subdivision have been expressed as a proportion of the total for the two counties. Thus, the extent to which the proportion of a particular item differs from the proportion of the total acreage in a subdivision indicates the under- or over-representation of that item, and therefore its relative importance. These particulars are also considered in terms of density (per

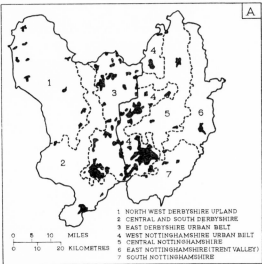

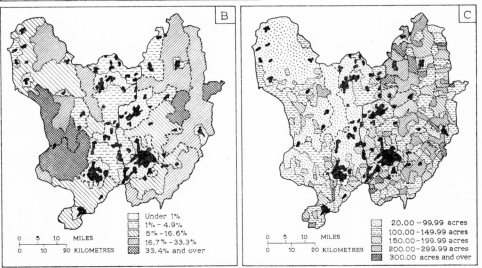

A   Regional sub-divisions
B   Percentage of the total population dependent on agriculture
C   Holdings by average-size groups
D   Dairy cows
E   Beef cattle
F   Sheep
G   Permanent grass
H   Clover, sainfoin and temporary grasses
I   Cereals
J   Sugar beet
K   Potatoes (early and main crop)

1   NORTH WEST DERBYSHIRE UPLAND
2   CENTRAL AND SOUTH DERBYSHIRE
3   EAST DERBYSHIRE URBAN BELT
4   WEST NOTTINGHAMSHIRE URBAN BELT
5   CENTRAL NOTTINGHAMSHIRE
6   EAST NOTTINGHAMSHIRE (TRENT VALLEY)
7   SOUTH NOTTINGHAMSHIRE

Under 1%
1% – 4.9%
5% – 16.6%
16.7% – 33.3%
33.4% and over

20.00 – 99.99 acres
100.00 – 149.99 acres
150.00 – 199.99 acres
200.00 – 299.99 acres
300.00 acres and over

Fig. 43   Agriculture

The items D to K are all defined by reference to 100 acres of crops and grass
The definition used for dairy cows is cows and heifers in milk and calf; and for beef cattle is all cows and heifers in milk or in calf intended for rearing calves for beef and all steers and steer calves

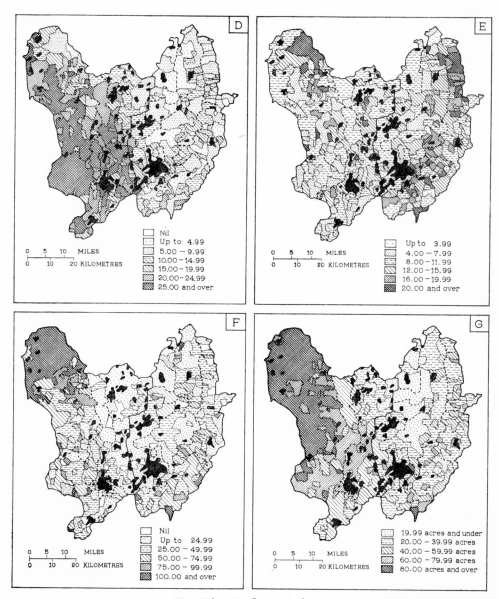

Fig. 43 (*continued*)   Agriculture

100 acres crops and grass). Thirdly, the agricultural census data of crops and livestock have been converted into economic terms of the net output of each main enterprise (for the method, see Appendix IV). The use of standard conversion factors may give rise to a degree of error in the absolute net output figures, but the expression

of these for each subdivision as a proportion of the total in both counties indicates the relative importance of the various enterprises in each. The relative level of net output per acre and per holding in each subdivision has also been assessed.

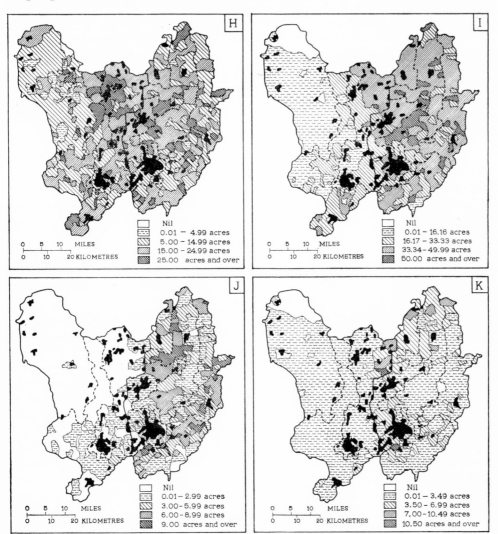

Fig. 43 (*continued*) Agriculture

The north-west Derbyshire upland   Peak 1 (S)

This area of relatively small farms, with an average size of 55 acres, includes 23 per cent of the superficial area of the two counties but only 18 per cent of the crops and grass. It includes most of the land above 800 feet and embraces the fringe of the Manchester conurbation, the moor lands of the High Peak and the Staffordshire–Derbyshire border. Much of it is adjacent to a heavily populated area and there is a growing demand for access to the moorlands for recreational purposes. In this connection the creation of the Peak National Park should be noted. Water supply undertakings modify the landscape and contribute to the economy of the area. Nearly all of the crops and grass acreage is under permanent grass and over 25 per cent of all the cattle and 40 per cent of the sheep of the two counties are to be found here. Only 10 per cent of the net output of the area is derived from pigs and poultry and roughly 94 per cent of the remaining output consists of milk, store cattle and sheep. As might be expected in an area where one third of the agricultural land is rough grazing, net output is low, £31 per acre or £1,720 per holding.

Family farms predominate since relatively few workers are employed, but net output per standard man-day amounts to only £5·6. About 18 per cent of the agricultural population of the two counties reside in the area. However, over 90 per cent of the total population is not directly dependent on agriculture, for a large proportion of the residents are commuters who gain their livelihood in the Manchester conurbation.

Central and south Derbyshire

Apart from some high ground in the narrow strip separating the north–west from the east Derbyshire urban belt, this subdivision is one of undulating lowland. It includes 20 per cent of the total area of the two counties and 21 per cent of the agricultural population. One eighth of the total population is engaged in agriculture, a higher proportion than in any part of the region except south Nottinghamshire. The farm holdings in this area are larger than in the north–west, with 63 acres of crops and grass. The quality of the land is also better, 25 per cent of the area being under tillage crops. Cereals are widely grown and account for about 80 per cent of the tillage area. In terms of its share of the total crops and grassland of the two counties, this subdivision has a higher proportion of fodder roots, grass and dairy cattle than elsewhere. Livestock are the main contributors to the net output, much of the cereal crop being retained on the farms for animal feeding. The estimated net output per acre is nearly £39 or slightly below the average for the region as a whole.

There is an intensive cropping area focused on the parish of Melbourne. In this parish 39 per cent of the crops and grassland is under horticultural crops. The corresponding figure for the whole of the subdivision is only one per cent. Nearly two thirds of the horticultural crops are brassicas such as sprouts, cabbages, savoys, cauliflower and broccoli (see page 271). The average size of holding is only about 40 acres, but the intensity of operation is reflected in the level of employment required. Roughly 64 regular whole-time workers per 1,000 acres are employed and about a third of these are women and girls who work regularly either full-time or part-time. The produce of the Melbourne district is widely distributed. Small quantities are consigned to markets as far afield as Sheffield (43 miles), Birmingham and Stoke-on-Trent, but Derby is the main wholesale market. Retail distribution in Melbourne itself, Derby, Long Eaton, Ashby-de-la-Zouch and surrounding villages is also important to some growers.

The east Derbyshire and west Nottinghamshire urban belt

The urban belt along the Derbyshire–Nottinghamshire border represents approximately a quarter of the total area of the two counties and contains over three quarters of the population. As a result of the high degree of industrialization less than one per cent of the inhabitants are dependent on agriculture. Yet, despite the urban development and industrial concentration this area contains over 20 per cent of the agricultural land and nearly 25 per cent of the agricultural population in the two counties. The nature of the farming activity, however, displays many of the characteristics peculiar to agriculture carried on in an urban environment. In a very real sense, this urban belt forms a transitional zone from the predominantly livestock farming of Derbyshire to the arable systems of Nottinghamshire. Sharp changes occur in the underlying geology, physical features, soils and climate. Moreover, the two subdivisions together constitute a social divide. Within this belt the farm population is in many ways urbanized in its behaviour and outlook, taking part in the economic, social and recreational activities of the local towns. The presence of the urban zone therefore serves to reinforce the differences between the more truly rural populations on either side.

Although agriculture within this belt exhibits a certain degree of uniformity the Derbyshire and Nottinghamshire sections contain significant differences in the structure and pattern of their farming. In east Derbyshire farms tend to be small, of average size $45\frac{1}{2}$ acres, and in terms of the region as a whole it contains an over-representation of small-holdings under 20 acres in size. Similarly, in west Nottinghamshire small-holdings are over-represented, but the average size of farms is greater ($62\frac{1}{2}$ acres), since there is also a relatively high proportion of farms of 300 acres and over. These larger holdings generally form part of the several large estates of the 'Dukeries' in central Nottinghamshire which intrude into the urban belt.

The differences in the pattern of farming between the two subdivisions partly reflects the farm size structure. In east Derbyshire a high proportion of the agricultural land is devoted to grass. This, in turn, is associated with dairying which is the major farm enterprise accounting for over a third of the net output. By contrast, in west Nottinghamshire, where grass covers less than one half of the agricultural area, dairying yields hardly a fifth of the net output. On the other hand, cereal growing is of considerably greater importance in this section, while sugar-beet acreages rise dramatically on crossing into Nottinghamshire. Besides the decrease in dairying from

T

Derbyshire into Nottinghamshire, other grazing livestock also become less important, and wherever cattle are kept the emphasis on beef production increases eastwards. Although the sheep density does not differ markedly between the two subdivisions, their husbandry changes from one dependent on pasture in Derbyshire to one of sheep management within predominantly arable systems in Nottinghamshire.

Pigs and poultry account for about 20 per cent of the net output in both the urbanised subdivisions. The prevalence of these enterprises, however, rests on a different basis in the two areas. In east Derbyshire pigs and poultry form an important element in the relatively intensive livestock production characteristic of the small farms. In west Nottinghamshire pigs are generally integrated into an arable system of farming, a substantial proportion of home-grown barley being used directly to fatten them. Poultry husbandry in west Nottinghamshire also differs from that in east Derbyshire. Both areas enjoy the advantage of a local market for eggs, and many small egg-producers, who rely on doorstep sales, exist in both areas. In west Nottinghamshire, however, recent years have witnessed the development of a few large egg- and broiler-producing units, most of which in fact belong to one particular business which has developed sites in various places, as in the Edwinstowe–Ollerton district.

Despite the differences between the two urban subdivisions, both display a relatively high intensity of agricultural production. The average net output per acre is over £42 in east Derbyshire and approaches £47 in west Nottinghamshire. The larger size of farm holdings in west Nottinghamshire, however, results in a greater difference in the average net output per holding, £1,920 and £2,940 respectively.

Central Nottinghamshire

In this subdivision the main soil types are those derived from the Bunter Sandstone and Keuper Marl. The Bunter Sandstone soil, often referred to as the Forest Sand, covers more than 25 per cent of the total area of the county and its extreme lightness, lack of humus and its low retentiveness of water and plant nutrients constitute considerable handicaps to farming. Only in 22 of the 60 years 1875–1935 was there sufficient rainfall in April and May to dispel the possibility of failure through drought. The sand area has long been susceptible to the economic ups and downs of farming. Under favourable cost/price conditions considerable technical advances have been made and reasonable profits obtained but difficult economic conditions have impoverished farmers more quickly than in more fertile areas such as the clay soils of the Keuper Marl to the east.

The economic depression of the 1930s was severe in its impact on the farming of the area and recovery came only with the improved crop prices and other production incentives offered during the second world war. Many farmers on the Forest Sand feared that hard times would return with peace-time conditions. These forebodings have not yet been realised. In response to relatively favourable crop prices arable production has been maintained at a high level. Net output is high and incomes are comparable with those of other arable areas. Apart from the low proportion of land devoted to permanent grass there does not now appear to be any consistent pattern of cropping or livestock husbandry which distinguishes the farming of the Forest Sand area from that of other parts of the country. Systems of farming on the Sandland have become more versatile with increased use of artificial fertilisers and irrigation. In 1962, it was estimated that nearly 100 plants capable of irrigating 15,000 acres were in operation. The increasing demands for water for this purpose are becoming a matter of some concern to the local water authorities as well as to farmers. Livestock production has also been stepped up; between 1947 and 1962, the population of laying hens in Sandland parishes was quadrupled and pigs increased fivefold.

Central Nottinghamshire is an area of large farms. The average size of holding is over 94 acres and more than seven per cent of the holdings are over 300 acres in size. Only one-sixth of the crops and grass acreage of the two counties falls within this subdivision but it grows one quarter of the cereals and potatoes and one third of the sugar beet. It also produces over one third of the horticultural crops, mainly in the area fringing Nottingham. The total net output per acre (£46·5) almost equals that of the west Nottinghamshire urban belt.

East Nottinghamshire (Trent valley)

This subdivision consists largely of the Trent lowlands to the north and east of Newark. It also includes the town of Newark itself, which is an important agricultural market centre for much of Nottinghamshire, north Leicestershire and west Lincolnshire. The area contains nearly 14 per cent of the crops and grassland of the two counties and contributes the same proportion of the total net output. The main enterprises, in order of their contribution to net output, are cereals, dairying, cash roots, horticultural crops and poultry. The total net output per acre is, however, below the Nottinghamshire average.

The farms are relatively large, although with an average size of 86 acres they are somewhat smaller than in the two adjoining subdivisions. About one third of the land is devoted to permanent grass, while cereals occupy nearly 40 per cent of the acreage. More sugar beet is grown per 100 acres than in any other part of the region. Although beef cattle rank only sixth in output terms, the output per acre in fact exceeds that of every other area except north–west Derbyshire. Most of this beef production is concentrated along the Trent between Newark and Gainsborough. Intensive yard fattening of cattle in winter is a common practice, but the permanent pastures along the river also provide an opportunity for summer grazing.

Despite the predominance of agriculture, a substantial proportion of land along the river Trent is devoted to other uses. In particular, this section of the valley contains one of the main concentrations of electricity generating stations and gravel extraction in the United Kingdom. Waste 'fly-ash' from the power stations is a useful medium for re-filling exhausted gravel pits prior to their reclamation for agricultural use. Currently, the possible reclamation by this means is under 10 acres per annum, which is less than the rate at which gravel pits are being created. The pits, however, are potentially valuable for recreational purposes (such as water sports) or nature reserves. Such facilities are in increasing demand in localities such as these which are easily accessible from large urban centres. These non-agricultural uses thus result in a temporary or permanent withdrawal of land from agriculture. The development of gravel extraction and its associated activities, however, provides an important source of employment in a rural area at a time when the labour needs of agriculture are progressively diminishing.

South Nottinghamshire

This is the smallest of the seven subdivisions into which the region has been divided, but its agricultural population, estimated at just under 4,500, forms a larger proportion of the total than in any of the other six areas. The average farm size is fairly large (95 acres), not because of the number of farms of more than 300 acres, but because of the relatively high proportion of farms between 100 and 300 acres. Net output is relatively low at £36·3 per acre. This is intermediate between north–west and central–south Derbyshire. The main contributing enterprises are, in order, cereals, dairying and cash roots, with beef cattle and poultry sharing fourth position. This is largely due to the relatively extensive system of farming. Over 55 per cent of the crops and grassland acreage is under grass and there are more dairy cattle and sheep than in other parts of Nottinghamshire.

South Nottinghamshire and the neighbouring part of Leicestershire enjoy a degree of agricultural fame as the main area in the country producing blue and white Stilton cheese. Of the 15 dairies which produce these cheeses, 12 are located in the Vale of Belvoir, three being in south Nottinghamshire. Until the 1930s the production of this particular variety of cheese was based entirely on local milk supplies, and it was widely believed to derive its properties from the nature of the local pastures. Today, with the concentration of wholesale milk purchasers in large, modern-equipped dairies, much of the milk used to manufacture Stilton cheese is brought in from outside the area. The quality of the cheese, however, has in no way suffered since this is assured by the skill of the cheese-makers and the build-up of the essential bacteria in the manufacturing dairies.

CONCLUSIONS

The traditional view of agriculture as an industry in which change is limited and very gradual has now lost much of its validity. On the contrary, far-reaching adjustments have been under way in recent years. Profound changes have occurred in the pattern of cropping; livestock populations have multiplied; and the labour force has dwindled as mechanisation has developed, while the size of the farm as a business unit has become larger.

The farming changes in the region, to which reference has been made, have not been unique. Other changes have also been proceeding apace, for example the reduction in the number of registered milk producers. In the seven years 1957 to 1964 this has been at the rate of three per cent per annum in Derbyshire and four per cent in Nottinghamshire. Yet in both counties cow numbers have remained almost constant. Small milk producers have left the industry but their output has been taken over by the expansion of the remaining herds. Similar trends are occurring in other enterprises but detailed figures for individual counties are not available. There is every indication that the trend towards farms carrying fewer, but larger, enterprises will continue and the rate of change may even accelerate.

Table XLI   Number of years when yields per acre in Nottinghamshire exceeded those in Derbyshire

	A *During past 44 years* *(1920–63)*	B *During past 25 years* *(1939–63)*
Wheat	26	19
Barley	16	13
Oats	28	17
Potatoes	31	21
Hay from temporary grass ..	16	14
Hay from permanent grass ..	13	12

Source: Agricultural Statistics

Change is inevitable in an industry where technological advance is rapid and competition from other industries or other agricultural areas is keen. The process of adjustment may be painful for the individuals concerned; farmers and workers leaving the industry must find new occupations and sources of livelihood, while those remaining must find the resources needed for an enlargement of their business. Both groups are affected by Government actions. Examples of what Government action has done to shape the pattern of farming are not hard to find. The introduction of the sugar beet crop has had a far-reaching effect on many Nottinghamshire farms. The upland areas of Derbyshire have benefited by a series of measures such as the hill sheep and hill cattle subsidy and the various schemes of assistance to farmers on marginal land. The relatively favourable prices of arable products in recent years have done much to change the Nottinghamshire Sandlands from an area of farming depression to one of comparative prosperity. Hitherto Government action has been mainly designed to support, directly or indirectly, the income position of existing farmers and there has not yet been a serious attempt to modify the size and structure of the industry. The White Paper published after the 1965 farm price review lists the objectives of agricultural policy and adds that the achievement of these would facilitate the 'transfer of resources for use elsewhere in the national economy'.

Nottinghamshire is better placed than Derbyshire to face future change. The average size of the full-time farms is about 50 per cent larger, and the yields of the main crops are slightly better. The variety of crops that can be grown is also wider. In these two counties the link between town and country may well be closer than in other areas. The existence locally of urban communities and industries offers a wide variety of alternative employment opportunities to farmers and workers wishing to leave agriculture and may even act as a magnet attracting man-power away from this industry. In a predominantly agricultural area these opportunities do not exist, so that the decreasing labour demands of agriculture result in the under-employment of workers and the drift of labour from agriculture leads to serious rural depopulation.

SELECTED REFERENCES

Barnes, F. A. and Jeffreys, D. M. Farming type regions in the Dove Basin. *East Midland Geographer* No. 21 (1964).

Coppock, J. T. *An Agricultural Atlas of England and Wales* (London, 1964).

Daw, M. E. *Benefits from Planning* (University of Nottingham School of Agriculture, 1964).

Edwards, K. C. *The Land of Britain: Nottinghamshire.* Part 60 (1944).

Harris, A. H. and Henderson, H. C. K. *The Land of Britain: Derbyshire.* Part 63 (1941).

Jones, R. Bennett. *The pattern of farming in the East Midlands* (University of Nottingham School of Agriculture, 1954).

Jones, G. E. and Simmons, A. Joyce. Towards an interpretation of change in Farm Structure: a Nottinghamshire case study. *The Farm Economist* Vol. 10 (1964).

Leay, P. The market gardening industry of the Melbourne District, South Derbyshire. *East Midland Geographer* No. 1 (1954).

Makings, S. M. *Farming forest sand* (1936).

Makings, S. M. *Economics of Poor Land Arable Farming* (London, 1944).

Mejer, E. *Sand Land Farming: a study of the impact of war-time conditions on the Nottinghamshire Sand Area* (University of Nottingham School of Agriculture, 1949).

Farming in the East Midlands: Financial Results, published annually in December by the University of Nottingham Department of Agricultural Economics, provides a statement containing harvest year indices for farm products and tables showing changes in output, costs and net income on farms in the different size-groups and by type areas in the region, including the subdivisions treated in the above account.

XV

HORTICULTURE

ON a commercial scale, horticulture in the Nottingham region is largely confined to the production of plants and cut flowers for the larger urban markets; and the nurseries, provided that soil and aspect are favourable, are generally situated within easy reach of the towns, especially the two large centres of Nottingham and Derby. Some specialised forms of production, however, are of more than local importance and serve far larger markets, examples being the large-scale cultivation of roses in the neighbourhood of Nottingham and the raising of garden trees and shrubs near Matlock.

Of considerable interest from the horticultural standpoint is the concentration of highly intensive and specialised market gardens at Melbourne in south Derbyshire, where some 1,600 acres are used for the production of brassicas and salad crops. This development illustrates the close dependence of certain types of crop production on soil and aspect, in which discerning growers have chosen an area of rather light soil, sheltered from cold winds, to produce a succession of seasonal crops with great skill and precision. Altogether, with the raising of peas, beans, potatoes and small fruit, intensive cultivation in the Melbourne district occupies well over 3,000 acres. This activity appears to have begun before the middle of the last century and during the period of railway expansion, especially in the 'sixties, the district gained a reputation for its quick-set hedges (whitethorn) fencing the tracks, Melbourne growers travelling to all parts of the country to plant them. Today the output of brassicas and salad crops is sent mainly to Derby, only 10 miles away, but, with improved road transport, markets further afield are being reached and these include Nottingham, Leicester and Birmingham, while a few growers even send produce to Stoke-on-Trent and Sheffield. One horticulturalist at King's Newton, close to Melbourne, specialises in the growing of Michaelmas daisies.

At Borrowash, between Nottingham and Derby, long-established nurseries, situated on medium-light Keuper soils, reflect the importance of proximity to urban markets, while the more recent and as yet small-scale development of rose cultivation near Bamford, approaching the Hope valley, may well reflect the importance of the travelling public as a market, consisting in this case of the increasing numbers of people visiting the Peak District by car and motor-coach. Large acreages of some vegetables and fruit are grown on a farm-scale to the east and north of Nottingham, as, for example, around Southwell and Newark, mainly on contract for processing peas, beans, carrots, red beet and black currants. On the sandy area north of Newark, especially in the parishes of Collingham, North Clifton, Harby and Thorney, huge quantities of carrots are raised and sent to Nottingham, Sheffield and Manchester. In the same district attempts have been made in recent years to grow bulbs, but so far only as an adjunct to normal farming. Beyond the Trent, the Lindsey division of Lincolnshire, with 19,000 acres of peas for freezing and canning in 1963, was the leading county in the country for this crop. Among other forms of production in the region, one of the most highly specialised crops of all, the mushroom, is raised on a number of holdings, including one started in 1964 in old lead-mine galleries near Buxton, which is said to have the largest output in Europe. Celery is an important crop raised in the Isle of Axholme.

As already mentioned rose cultivation is of particular importance in the Nottingham district where there is one of the largest, perhaps the largest, concentration of nurseries of this kind in the country, producing well over 5,000,000 rose bushes a year, valued at nearly a million pounds from a little less than 500 acres of land. Several factors are likely to have favoured the development of this activity. The virtual absence of black spot disease due to the relatively dry summers is probably an important consideration, coupled with the nature of the soil, which is sufficiently heavy to provide plenty of moisture for growth, yet not too stiff for lifting in wet weather. As shown in Fig. 44, almost all the nurseries belonging to the principal growers are located on the soils of the Keuper Marl to the east, south and south–west of the city. Apart from the physical conditions, the scale of operations and the commercial success which has been attained reflect the initiative and skill of the growers themselves, several of whom have a national and international reputation. The chief areas of production are at Edwalton and Bradmore, near Ruddington, raising 1,500,000 plants a year and Beeston, with over 1,000,000, while other large nurseries are at Southwell, Lowdham and Gotham.

It was in the district called Hunger Hill to the north–east of the city that Nottingham's rose culture originated just over a century ago. At that time rose-growing was a favourite spare-time pursuit of 'stockingers' (hosiery workers) and other artisans. Hunger Hill, then just outside the town, became especially noted for its little rose gardens and in the early 'sixties some cultivators started to grow the trees under glass and soon earned fame in many parts of the country for their early and elegant blooms. In April 1860 what may be claimed as the first rose show in England was held in an inn near Hunger Hill by a group of 'stockingers'. Dean Hole, whose early home was at Caunton Manor, near Newark, was invited to this exhibition and, greatly impressed, insisted on seeing the gardens. In his famous work, *A Book about Roses*, he wrote of Hunger Hill: 'These are tiny allotments on sunny slopes just out of the town, separated by hedges and boards, in size about three to the rod, such an extent as a country squire in Lilliput might be expected to devote to horticulture'. The exhibition, known as 'St. Anne's Rose Show', named from that part of the town, became an annual event and did much to stimulate the development of rose culture in the surrounding area.

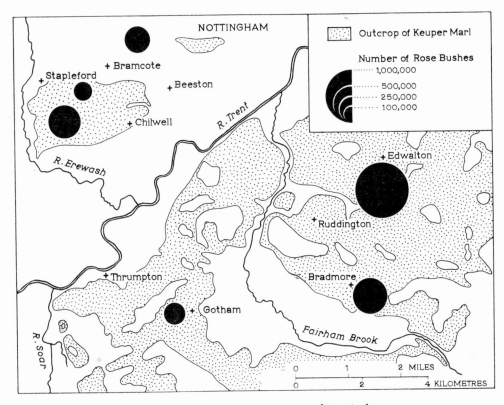

Fig. 44   The rose-growing areas around Nottingham

Trees and flowering shrubs are raised under comparatively rigorous conditions at an altitude of 750 feet on Gritstone soils near Tansley, east of Matlock. These are grown for re-planting in all parts of the country and some of the nurseries, now over 150 years old, are among the best known in Britain.

The Nottingham region also includes a number of magnificent private gardens, such as Chatsworth in its incomparable setting, and Melbourne Hall, with the only remaining unaltered example of the Le Notre type of landscape lay-out.

ACKNOWLEDGMENT

Thanks are due to Mr. Christopher Wheatcroft for information concerning various aspects of rose cultivation.

XVI

EXTRACTIVE INDUSTRY

COAL

THE Yorkshire, Derbyshire and Nottinghamshire coalfield, which is the largest and most productive in the country, has also the greatest proved reserves. Since the nationalisation of the coal industry in 1946, this field has been divided for administrative and operational purposes to form two separate divisions of the National Coal Board, the northern (or Yorkshire) portion forming the Yorkshire Division and the southern (or Nottinghamshire, Derbyshire and Leicestershire) portion the East Midlands Division. The line of demarcation between the two Divisions was fixed in accordance with earlier wage-agreement boundaries. The East Midlands Division also includes the small but highly productive south Derbyshire and Leicestershire field which is not dealt with in this survey. In terms of output the East Midlands leads all other coalfields, raising 45 million tons in 1965, 38 million tons from the main field and seven million tons from the smaller one, comprising 25 per cent of the national total. While there are obvious objections to the separate treatment of what is part of a single geological and geographical entity, there is, as will be shown, some justification for making this distinction quite apart from the fact that National Coal Board statistics are drawn up on a Divisional basis.

Structure and workable seams

The main East Midlands coalfield extending southwards from the Yorkshire county boundary to Nottingham is nearly 40 miles long, with a breadth from east to west varying from 12 to 20 miles. It may be divided into an 'exposed' portion to the west, largely in Derbyshire, in which the productive Lower and Middle Coal Measures appear at the surface and a 'concealed' portion to the east, mostly in Nottinghamshire, in which the Coal Measures continue eastwards beneath the unconformable Permo-Trias cover (Fig. 2). The exposed portion was naturally worked earlier and consequently contains the oldest mines. In general the combined thickness of the Permo-Trias rocks increases eastward and towards the Trent the uppermost seams are as much as 1,800 to 2,000 feet from the surface.

South of Sheffield and the line of the Don Faults the structural features of the coalfield differ somewhat from those in the rest of the Yorkshire field, for in Nottinghamshire and Derbyshire the shallow basin-like depression which comprises the field as a whole is traversed by a number of minor up-folds between which the coal-bearing strata lie in broad troughs. These up-folds seldom form simple anticlines but usually consist of elongated domes strung out along a curving or even sinuous axis. Such structures largely determine the character and location of mining operations for the crests of the domes are often barren of coal, while on their flanks and especially in the intervening troughs seams are abundant. From north to south the principal folds are the Manton (Rotherham–Kiveton) Fold, running south–east from Rotherham; the Norton–Whitwell Fold, running in a similar direction; the Brimington–Mansfield Fold, running south–south–east from near Chesterfield and then turning east to Mansfield; and the Erewash Fold, running southwards from Ironville, closely followed by the course of the Erewash river, thus exposing workable seams on either side of the valley.

Apart from the effect of the minor folds the seams are relatively undisturbed and extend for considerable distances without serious deterioration in quality or marked decline in thickness. Many of the seams it is true exhibit some deterioration eastwards. Faulting in general is much less troublesome than in many other coalfields. Indeed, the favourable geological conditions contribute substantially to the ease of working and in a large measure these compensate for the comparative thinness of the seams.

Over the East Midlands field there are some 30 workable seams, nearly all of which occur within a total thickness of about 2,000 feet of Middle Coal Measures. A few seams are found below these, belonging to the Lower Coal Measures, which outcrop along the western margin of the field. Some of them, like the Alton and Kilburn, have been exploited in the past and again in recent years by modern opencast methods. The Kilburn, varying from two feet six inches to four feet in thickness, provides good quality domestic fuel in the south but further north it becomes thinner and changes to a gas-making coal.

Of the seams in the main sequence six are particularly important and from them a high proportion of the total output is obtained. The most valuable of them all is the Top Hard, the equivalent of the Barnsley Bed in Yorkshire, which is a composite seam containing 40 to 50 per cent industrial hard coal interbedded with bright (domestic) coal. The Top Hard is generally between five and six feet thick and is remarkably consistent, so that many collieries have been designed to work this seam alone and have done so for many years before being obliged to exploit others. Lower down in the sequence is the Deep Hard, also a composite seam but thinner than the Top Hard, more variable in character and containing a lower proportion of 'hards'. Nevertheless it is the most important source of steam coal in the exposed field wherever the Top Hard is absent or exhausted.

The Blackshale or Silkstone Coal, averaging four feet in thickness, is the lowest of the six principal seams and is therefore worked mainly along the western section of the exposed field, particularly between Chesterfield and Ripley where it forms the best coking coal to be found in the field. Above the Blackshale is the Tupton

Coal, one of the most widely exploited seams in the older mining districts. Known alternatively as the Low Main, this provides good domestic coal, with a general thickness of three to four feet, although in the district extending south–east of Chesterfield towards Mansfield it is suitable for making gas and foundry coke. As the reserves of the Tupton Coal become depleted, increasing importance is attached to the working of the Tupton Threequarters which occurs a little lower in the sequence. It, too, yields house coal of low ash content with a varying proportion of 'hards'. High grade domestic supplies are also obtained from the Deep Soft which consists of several seams including two main beds of bright coal separated by dirt bands. Lastly, the High Hazels, another seam now being increasingly mined, is again primarily a domestic coal. It has been worked for many years at Gedling colliery, just east of Nottingham, where its low ash content and free-burning nature have given it a high reputation among British house coals. Its thickness is generally three to four feet. This seam is worked extensively in the concealed field north of Mansfield, where part of it changes in character to become suitable for gas-making.

Apart from the six major seams, which are extensively worked, many others are exploited locally, though they have not yet been 'proved' over wider areas. A good example is the Main Bright, a house coal of exceptionally high quality, which was first mined at Hucknall and so far has only been worked over a limited area between Hucknall and Nottingham. The reserves of this seam are uncertain and further proving is therefore necessary.

From this summary of the principal seams it will be seen that the coals produced from the East Midlands field are predominantly of the domestic, industrial and gas-making types. The field is in fact pre-eminently a producer of first-class house coal, while from the hard coal the best grades of locomotive fuel for main-line express trains were obtained prior to the era of high-speed diesel traction. The resources in coking coal are relatively meagre but there is a tendency for most of the seams in the exposed field to exhibit coking qualities towards the north and it is therefore mainly in the Chesterfield area that true coking coals are found.

From all parts of the field huge quantities of small-size industrial fuel are produced. Being highly suitable for automatic stoking this type of coal is now in enormous demand for supplying the succession of giant electricity generating stations now being established at intervals on the banks of the Trent within a short distance of the collieries. The newest of these stations consume some 8,000 to 9,000 tons a week.

The immense reserves of the East Midlands coalfield ensure that its working life, providing coal continues to be in demand, will continue long into the future. The proved resources of the six major seams alone are of the order of 400 to 500 million tons each, while the reserves of many others are yet to be ascertained. The total proved workable coal, as estimated in the Regional Survey Report of 1945, is 5,500 million tons, together with over 4,000 million tons in the North–Eastern (Yorkshire) Division.

Limits of the coalfield

The question naturally arises, however, as to what is the eastern limit of the concealed field. The answer is still largely conjectural, depending on two basic factors. Firstly, borings show that the easterly dip of the Permo-Trias cover carries the base of these strata down to 4,000 feet below sea-level in the neighbourhood of Lincoln, a depth beyond the limit of present economic working. Secondly, insufficient is known of the extent and behaviour of the Coal Measures underlying the Permo-Trias. From the evidence available it can be inferred that over much of the field accessible seams are not likely to occur much beyond the line of the Trent. In the area lying between Nottingham, Newark and Grantham, exploration for oil in recent years has proved the existence of unidentified coal seams in several places, while in others, as at Foston, north–west of Grantham, borings have encountered igneous rocks, which reveal the Coal Measures to be absent. Closer to Nottingham near the southern margin of the field is an area rich in thick seams, such as the Deep Soft, Deep Hard and Tupton. These were all recognisable in sinking the Clifton colliery at Nottingham in 1870–72 and their recently proved eastward extension determined the location of the new Cotgrave colliery.

Coal production

Mechanisation and improved methods of extraction have greatly increased the productivity of a coalfield already endowed with favourable geological conditions. These developments have affected the older exposed field and the concealed field alike. In the former, machine cutting and opencast working have enabled thin seams and seams hitherto only partially worked to be fully exploited, and in this way the decline of the industry in some districts has been arrested. Since the setting up of the National Coal Board in 1946 some 41 million tons of disposable coal have been won from opencast sites, chiefly in Derbyshire. This is the equivalent of nearly one year's output from deep mined coal in the East Midlands Division. Some of these sites near the margin of the field were encumbered by grass-covered heaps and mounds left from primitive mine workings two centuries or more ago. On each site a regular sequence of operations is followed. First, the topsoil is stripped and stacked, then the overburden is removed by excavators. Next, the surface of the seam is cleaned, after which the coal is extracted by mechanical shovels. The overburden is then replaced and the surface trimmed as nearly as possible to its original contours before the soil itself is brought back and made ready for cultivation. From the first stripping to complete restoration the process may take about five years. The reversion to farmland, however, is not entirely complete, for during the operation hedgerows and even trees were uprooted and afterwards only uninspiring wire fences divide the fields.

Besides the introduction of many improved mechanical devices, including large conveyor belts which operate directly from the coal face to the shaft bottom, in some cases for a distance of over two miles, much re-organisation and even reconstruction of collieries has taken place in recent years, enabling greater outputs to be achieved in the most economical manner. High productivity is reflected in the output per man shift which for the East Midlands is 2·58 tons, by far the highest in the country, compared with the national average of 1·74 tons. These figures are for all workers, but the pre-eminence of this coalfield is emphasised even more by comparing the output from coal-face workers alone, 7·63 tons, with the corresponding national average, 5·19 tons. Broadly speaking the East Midlands field provides one quarter of Britain's coal with barely one-seventh of her miners. High output and low production costs combine to give further distinction to the coalfield in that it leads all others in profitability. In fact under nationalisation it contributes much to keep the uneconomic fields in operation. On the other hand, low cost production is partly offset by relatively high distribution charges resulting from the inland position of the field.

Continued expansion in output has been accompanied by a greater use being made of coal within the East Midlands region itself. More attention is now devoted to coke production in response to the rising demand in the domestic and industrial markets. The large Avenue coking-plant at Wingerworth, between Chesterfield and Clay Cross, opened in 1956, was designed for this purpose. The plant is supplied from neighbouring collieries (Fig. 45) and has an output capacity of 2,200 tons of coke daily. In addition the works contribute large quantities of gas to the public supply grid covering a wide area. Much more impressive is the part now played by the coalfield in the expansion of electricity generation. The progressive development of huge power stations along the Trent, among them the largest in Europe, has already been mentioned. To supply these stations an increasing proportion of the total coal output is directed. In 1955 more than a quarter of the total, some 12 million tons, was consumed in this way; by 1960 the proportion was 36 per cent and today it is nearly 40 per cent. At Cottam, the latest of the generating stations, planned to be in operation by 1968 the consumption will be 9,000 tons a week or over half a million tons a year.

While the East Midlands coalfield has assumed the role of the largest supplier of coal in the country for electricity production, it continues to serve, as it has done for so long, the London market, the east and the south, with domestic and industrial fuel. There is also a considerable movement of industrial coal to south Lancashire and Cheshire where local supplies can no longer meet demands. But it must not be overlooked that the coalfield is the greatest natural resource which the East Midlands region itself possesses. It was through coal that the industrial development of Nottingham and the other leading centres became possible and it is basically through coal that their economic activity is currently sustained.

Experiments in the underground gasification of coal were undertaken over a period of 10 years (1949–59) at Newton Spinney, seven miles north–east of Chesterfield, but these, like similar experiments made in the west Midlands, near Kidderminster, were discontinued. Natural gas was discovered at Calow, near Chesterfield, in 1964 and this has since been used to supplement the supply of processed gas to the regional gas grid.

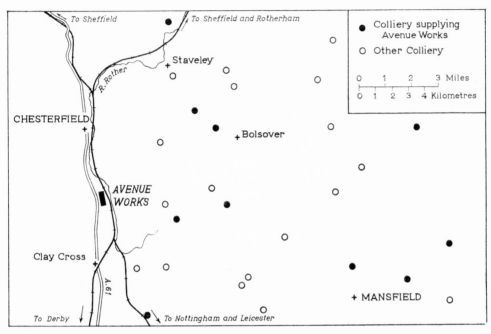

Fig. 45   Position of the Avenue Coke and Carbonisation Works

Outline development of collieries in Nottinghamshire

The era of deep mining in Nottinghamshire began in 1859 with the opening of the Shireoaks colliery, north of Mansfield, which was sunk through the cover of Permian rocks. This colliery, due to the energy and enterprise of the Duke of Newcastle, marked at the same time the initial exploitation of the concealed coalfield. Immediately following Shireoaks, plans for further mining gave a fresh impetus to the industry and in the 'sixties a number of new collieries penetrating the Permo-Trias cover were opened. These were at High Peak, Hucknall (Nos. 1 and 2), Cinderhill, Annesley, Bulwell and Silverhill No. 1, most of them along or bordering on the Leen valley. When the British Association met at Nottingham in 1866, Edward Hedley presented a geological account of the sinking of Annesley Colliery, then in progress. At the same meeting the noted geologist, Sir Roderick Murchison, Director General of the Geological Survey at the time, gave his views on which parts of England and Wales coal was or was not likely to be found. Of Nottinghamshire he said, 'It is possible that at some distant day, and when the more easily attainable coals are exhausted under the Magnesian Limestone, the mineral will be worked under the New Red Sandstone north of Nottingham, though at depths which at present would render operations unremunerative.' In fact the 'distant day' arrived well before the turn of the century. Meanwhile in the period 1870–80 no less than 16 more were brought into production, a larger number than in any other decade either before or since. These collieries, together with some 25 others built between 1880 and 1910, were distributed mainly between Nottingham and Mansfield and northwards along the western fringe of the county. Two, however, were somewhat exceptional in location. Clifton Colliery (1872) was sited on the north bank of the Trent at Nottingham. From this position on the floodplain the shaft penetrated some 25 feet of alluvium and gravel, 160 feet of Bunter Sandstone and, the Permian being absent, 30 feet of Coal Measures before reaching the Top Hard seam. Unfortunately because of the porosity of the overlying Bunter, excessive water prevented the working of this seam and the shaft had to be deepened by another 500 feet to exploit the Deep Soft and Deep Hard. The colliery at Gedling (1902), the first, and for a long time the only, one to the east of Nottingham, was also the first to be sunk through the Keuper Sandstone as well as the Bunter and Permian rocks (Fig 46).

At the time of the first World War and the immediate post-war years, some of the larger mining companies began to exploit the reserves of mid-Nottinghamshire to the east of Mansfield in the area of Sherwood Forest. This led to the building of more modern collieries of much larger size than hitherto, with considerably deeper shafts, in which electricity superseded steam power and mechanical coal-cutting and underground transport were introduced. Some of these employed 1,800 to 2,000 men compared with 1,200 to 1,500 men in the largest of the older mines. In most cases the Top Hard seam was at a depth of at least 1,500 feet but often in the neighbourhood of 2,000 feet.

In view of their large-scale operations, including the working of seams over a greater area than previously from a single shaft, the collieries (of this period) were located at distinctly greater distances from each other. These collieries, together with the year of opening, were the following: Rufford (1915), Clipstone (1922), Harworth (1924), Firbeck (1925), Ollerton (1925), Blidworth (1926), Bilsthorpe (1927), and Thoresby (1928). These developments inevitably resulted in a transformation of the Forest scene. To the farms, woods and stretches of heath were added mines, mineral lines and sidings, the eventual growth of spoil heaps; and of course a considerable influx of population requiring housing estates, schools and other forms of social provision. Correspondingly there were repercussions on the growth and expansion of Mansfield, the nearest town, itself a centre of mining.

Coal production in Nottinghamshire rose from 12·3 million tons in 1913 to 14·5 million tons by 1930, compared with a decline in Derbyshire (including the separate south Derbyshire field) from 18 million tons in 1913 to 14·6 million tons in 1930. It was in this period, therefore, so far as the coalfield as a whole is concerned, that

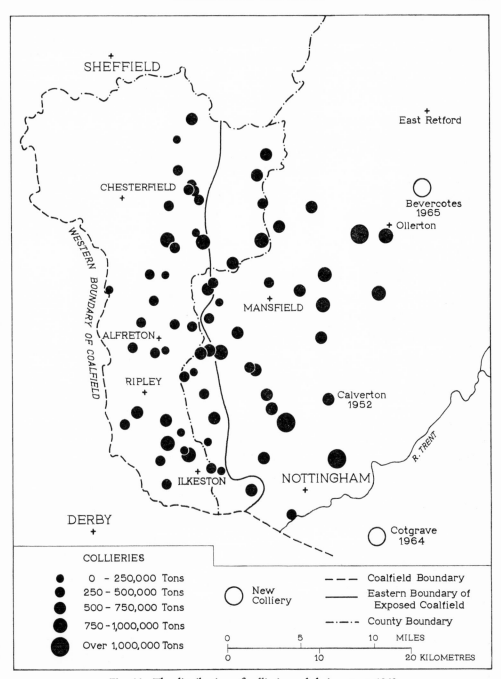

SHEFFIELD

East Retford

CHESTERFIELD

WESTERN BOUNDARY OF COALFIELD

Bevercotes
1965

Ollerton

MANSFIELD

ALFRETON

RIPLEY

Calverton
1952

R. TRENT

ILKESTON

NOTTINGHAM

DERBY

Cotgrave
1964

COLLIERIES

● 0 – 250,000 Tons
● 250 – 500,000 Tons
● 500 – 750,000 Tons
● 750 – 1,000,000 Tons
● Over 1,000,000 Tons

○ New Colliery

– – – Coalfield Boundary

——— Eastern Boundary of Exposed Coalfield

–·–·– County Boundary

0   5   10   MILES

0   10   20 KILOMETRES

Fig. 46   The distribution of collieries and their output, 1960

U

the Nottinghamshire section assumed the lead in output, a situation which has since become more and more accentuated.

During the remainder of the inter-war period no further collieries were built, except for the shaft sunk by the Bestwood Company at Calverton in 1939. Workings from the Bestwood colliery in the Leen valley had by this time proceeded so far to the east that additional means of access from the surface became necessary. Owing to the intervention of the second World War, the shaft was used only to convey personnel, for whom housing was provided in Calverton, while coal continued to move underground to Bestwood in the Leen valley. After the war, under National Coal Board direction, Calverton was completed as an independent colliery with a surface rail link to the Leen valley, coal being first raised in 1952. Two other collieries have since been opened, one in 1960 at Bevercotes, south of Retford, in location the most easterly of all; and the other in 1964 at Cotgrave, south–east of Nottingham, the first to be located across the Trent and, in view of a recent National Coal Board statement, possibly the last (Fig. 46, Plate XI).

An interesting outcome of recent capital investment in the construction of new collieries and the re-organisation of older ones is the growing number with an annual output of one million tons or more. These large collieries include Linby, Newstead and Moorgreen in the older part of the coalfield, Clipstone, Rufford, Thoresby and Calverton in central Nottinghamshire, while the two newest, Bevercotes and Cotgrave, are each designed to produce 1,250,000 tons a year when they become fully operative. Bevercotes is the world's first fully-automated colliery (Plate XII).

Coal exports

While the Nottinghamshire and Derbyshire coalfield continues to provide an increasing proportion of the national requirements, recent years have also seen a significant revival of overseas exports. These amounted to 1,381,000 tons in 1964 or well over a quarter of the total exports from Britain. Shipments abroad are mainly from collieries in central Nottinghamshire and north–east Derbyshire for these are well situated in relation to the ports of Immingham, Hull and Goole. Small quantities are sent through Boston and also *via* the Mersey to Eire. The importance of Immingham as an outlet for coal, the role for which the port was originally designed and equipped, is reflected by the present size of individual cargoes, ranging from 5,000 tons to 15,000 tons, and by the recent proposal to enlarge the port and to introduce permanently coupled trains between dock and colliery, in order to increase efficiency in handling the export trade.

The type of coal sent overseas is mainly small coal for use in electricity generating stations; much smaller quantities of industrial hard coal are sent and nowadays no domestic coal. The consumers are the nearby European countries, especially France, her Common Market partners and Denmark. Exports from the East Midlands to Eire remain fairly constant and amount to about 200,000 tons annually. Among the chief factors encouraging the revival of exports are the inability of continental countries to meet the demand for electricity-producing fuel, and rising freight rates affecting imports from the U.S.A.

Coal in the future

Changes in fuel technology cause the future of the coal-mining industry in Britain to be uncertain. The increasing use of oil in industry and even in some electricity generating stations, the importing of natural gas from the Sahara and the still more recent discovery of gas beneath the North Sea are the chief factors which will inevitably lead to some contraction in mining. The need to ensure a return on heavy capital investments in past years by the National Coal Board may well postpone a large-scale reduction in output for some years, however, but in any case it is reasonably certain that the highly productive East Midlands field, apart from the closure of certain pits which will become exhausted, will continue as a major source of coal for a long time to come.

In its most recent plan for the rationalisation of the coal industry the National Coal Board proposes to close only the exhausted collieries in the East Midlands while expanding production from others. In past years a number of older mines in Derbyshire have been closed, due to exhaustion of the seams. In the next few years others are to follow for the same reason, examples being Alfreton, Swanwick and Coppice collieries. A number of mines in both Derbyshire and western Nottingham-shire will be merged with neighbouring pits and their life thereby prolonged. This means that none in Nottinghamshire will be entirely closed, although doubt exists concerning the Bestwood colliery, where increasing quantities of dirt brought out with the coal present a growing problem in terms of profitability. In all, out of the 77 collieries in the East Midlands Division (including the south Derbyshire and Leicestershire field) 11 will either reach exhaustion or be merged with others in the next five years. In terms of manpower, however, most of the displaced miners can be re-deployed, for the expansion of many of the remaining collieries is already creating a shortage of labour. Movement from the North-East, especially from Durham, is already taking place to the new pits and the need for recruitment will continue for some years to come. The plan for closures, which is much more drastic in some other coalfields, has been received with disquiet by the mining community in those areas, but it appears likely that the East and West Midlands, together with Yorkshire, could absorb most of the redundant men.

SECONDARY MINERALS

Although the mineral wealth of the Nottingham region is dominated by coal, dealt with in the above section, several minerals of secondary importance are exploited. Iron ore, known as clayband ironstone, a carbonate of iron mingled with earthy matter, occurring in seams or as nodules in the Coal Measures, was formerly worked in the Derbyshire portion of the coalfield. It served as the basis of the iron industry which developed along the Erewash and Rother valleys in the 19th century. Often ironstone and coal were produced from the same mines, but after 1880 supplies of the former dwindled, in some cases because the mineral was exhausted and in others because of uneconomic working costs. The industry then became dependent on more distant sources of ore. To the south–west of Grantham, near the eastern limit of the region, the bedded ironstone from the Middle Lias Marlstone is exploited by opencast workings.

Of the other minerals worked, gypsum, limestone, sand and gravel, brick and pottery clays and refractory materials are the chief. Most of these are produced in sufficient quantities to make a major contribution to the national output. In addition to a variety of other minerals the region possesses the only significant oilfields in Britain and these form the subject of the last section in this chapter.

Gypsum

The largest workable deposits of gypsum in the country are found in the Nottingham–Derby area and their exploitation has given rise to a small but important resource-based industry. The mineral occurs mainly in the upper beds of the Keuper Marl and three separate horizons may be distinguished:

The Newark gypsum
The Tutbury gypsum
The Retford gypsum

The Newark gypsum is found immediately below the Tea Green Marls and consists of several seams varying in thickness from a few inches to three feet. The seams dip very gently to the south–east, the quality improving with depth so that the lowest of them attains to 99 per cent pure calcium sulphate. The workings are located east of the Trent at several places between Newark and Bunny in south Nottinghamshire.

The Tutbury gypsum belongs to a horizon a little below that of the Newark gypsum and is a massive variety called alabaster, generally eight to 10 feet thick, reaching 15 feet in places. It extends intermittently from Gotham in Nottinghamshire to Tutbury, near Burton-on-Trent in Staffordshire, and is worked in the neighbourhood of both these places. Outcrops close to each other on either side of the Trent at Red Hill (south) and Bellington Hill (north) suggest that, before the cutting of the Trent valley, this horizon was continuous from south Nottinghamshire into Derbyshire, where Chellaston, like Red Hill and Tutbury, provided much of the alabaster used by the ancient carvers (see page 232).

The Retford gypsum, belonging to the lower Keuper Marl, is found discontinuously in Nottinghamshire west of the Trent. It is of no significance commercially, although throughout most of the 19th century small outcrop workings yielded mineral for floor-plaster and agricultural fertiliser. At East Bridgford, between Nottingham and Newark, veins of fibrous gypsum (satin spar) occur. This also belongs to the Retford horizon and was formerly used for making small ornaments.

The numerous uses for gypsum include the making of plaster-of-paris and other special plasters; for building-plaster, plaster-board and cement; in powdered form as 'mineral white', it provides a filler in paper-making and a stone dust for mines. In the past the output came from small mines and quarries at many places between Newark and Tutbury, the greatest concentration being around Gotham where both horizons are accessible. From the entire area the annual production for many years amounted to well over one-third of the national total.

Following the second World War a new impetus was given to the industry by the needs of the building trade. The rise in demand for both plaster and plaster-board found the older producing units poorly organised to meet the needs and as a result substantial changes have taken place. Mines and quarries are now fewer in number but larger in output; new methods of extraction have been introduced as well as improvements in plaster-making; some firms have amalgamated and have been absorbed into British Plasterboard Holdings which is now the leading producer. The process of amalgamation, however, began before the war, the famous firm of Cafferata Ltd., of Newark, having merged with British Plasterboard Ltd. as early as 1936. The output of gypsum now exceeds one million tons annually, well over half the national total, compared with about 350,000 tons before the war. Of this quantity almost 90 per cent is used in the building trade.

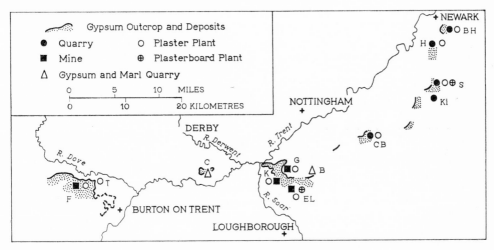

Fig. 47 Distribution of gypsum workings

Of the three producing areas, the Gotham district of south Nottinghamshire accounts for three-fifths of the total output, the remainder being more or less equally divided between the Newark and east Nottinghamshire workings and those of Tutbury and Fauld in Staffordshire. The distribution of the present workings and processing units is shown in Fig. 47. Of the four mines, three are in the Gotham district of south Nottinghamshire; of the seven quarries, five are in east Nottingham-shire, those at Staunton and Kilvington being new. The output from Kilvington is used wholly for cement-making. The Hawton quarry at Newark is the largest gypsum working in the country. A plaster mill, with crushers and calcination plant, is found at most of the mineral workings, while East Leake and Staunton also produce plaster-board. The unit at East Leake, much the larger of the two, was built in 1947, and is the first integrated works of its kind in Britain and claims to be the largest in western Europe. It employs nearly 800 of the 1,800 men engaged in the gypsum industry of the region.

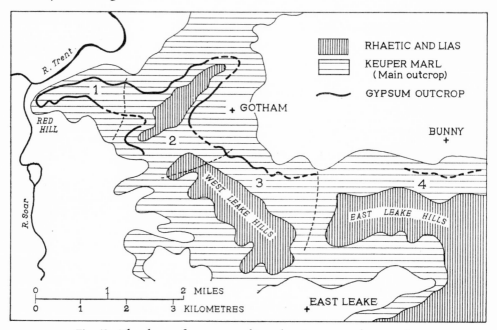

Fig. 48   The phases of gypsum working, showing eastward progression

In the Gotham district over the past 100 years or so, a progressive shift of the workings in an east–south–easterly direction clearly reflects the local geological conditions (see Fig. 48). At Red Hill, overlooking the Trent, gypsum and alabaster were obtained from small quarries and simple adits onwards from the Middle Ages and until the 1850s this remained the largest source of supply. By 1880 a second phase of development began with new workings, chiefly small mines, which were started on the flanks of the Gotham and West Leake Hills. These soon outstripped Red Hill in production, the latter failing altogether before the end of the century. Because of the dip of the beds and the increasing thickness of overburden, comprising Rhaetic and Lower Lias sediments, not present at Red Hill, the mineral had to be won from deeper levels. Towards 1900 production from the East Leake Hills began with the opening of the Hotchley mine, marking a third phase and in 1935 the cutting of the deep quarry at Bunny Hill, still further east, marked a fourth. It was now the turn of the East Leake Hills to supersede the Gotham and West Leake Hills in output, although some of the mines in the latter area were able to delay their closure until the last war or after, Thrumpton in 1940, Barton in 1942 and Weldon in 1957. Today, even though the Gotham mine is still active, over 60 per cent of the production from this district comes from the Hotchley mine.

The effects on the landscape of past and present gypsum working are unmistakable and are most obvious in the Gotham district. In this predominantly rural scene, besides the several active plaster mills can be seen the traces of old mines and adits on the wooded hillslopes, sections of old mineral lines traversing the fields and even part of a long-abandoned wharf on the bank of the Trent, while over trees and pastures rests a film of white dust.

The reserves of gypsum have not been fully estimated but they are sufficient for many years to come at the present rate of extraction. In the Newark district there is further scope for opencast working, whereas in the Gotham area future production must rely increasingly on deeper underground seams.

Limestone

Several different limestone formations within the Nottingham region are of economic importance but by far the most widely exploited is the Carboniferous Limestone of Derbyshire. Over the entire outcrop in the Peak District innumerable small workings to provide burnt lime for farmland date back for centuries. As J. Farey remarks in his *General View of the Agriculture and Minerals of Derbyshire* of 1812, almost every village and farm had its lime-pit and kiln. The use of lime was even more necessary on the acid soils of the surrounding gritstone area and largely for this reason limestone quarrying eventually became concentrated towards the margin of the main outcrop and upon the Ashover and Crich inliers. Under these conditions the scale of operations was related to little more than local needs. Later in the 18th century significant changes took place. Larger kilns demanded more fuel, and coal replaced the already diminishing supplies of timber; the use of gunpowder for blasting led to the working of larger quarries, while improvements in transport by road and canal enabled both stone and lime to be moved in greater quantities. The provision of lime for agricultural purposes became an industry in itself and soon the uses of limestone were greatly extended, as a flux in iron-smelting, as road metal, as ballast for railways and as a raw material for the developing chemical industries.

Large-scale limestone extraction began in 1794 with the opening of the quarry at Dove Holes, north of Buxton; during the following century the area around Buxton became, as it is today, the most important producing district. Although this area lies a little outside the Nottingham region, the development of the quarrying industry there shows close affinities with its growth in other parts of Derbyshire, especially the Matlock district, which fall within the region. Thus the completion of the Midland Railway from Derby to Manchester *via* Millers Dale in 1862, which stimulated a vast expansion in limestone output in the Buxton district, had already exercised a similar effect on Matlock. Again, the trend towards larger undertakings, shown by the amalgamation in 1891 of several producers to form the Buxton Lime Firms Ltd., set a pattern to be followed later in the south–eastern area. The most recent phase of development is characterised by large enterprises using mechanised quarrying techniques which, despite the continued increase in output, require substantially less labour than before; and by road haulage now playing as important a part as railways for the movement of stone and limestone products. Because of the extensive nature of operations around Buxton and Matlock, which will continue so for years to come, both districts were excluded from the Peak National Park when its boundaries were defined in 1950. Nevertheless limestone workings already in existence within the Park were allowed to continue. Most of the output coming from quarries within the Park is used as road metal, for the stone can be produced in chips of uniform size, having a high crushing strength which is exceeded only by granites and quartzites. Some of it is also used as an aggregate in the manufacture of artificial stone for building.

The purest beds of the Carboniferous Limestone occur towards the periphery of the outcrop, especially in the Buxton and Matlock–Wirksworth districts and this largely accounts for the continued concentration of activity upon these centres, for modern chemical industries, agricultural lime producers and blast-furnace flux all demand high-quality limestone. These are also the consumers requiring the greatest quantity of stone. The demand for agricultural lime has shown a striking increase since the granting of the lime subsidy to farmers by the Ministry of Agriculture in 1937.

At the present time, while a number of smaller concerns continue to operate, production is mainly in the hands of two major undertakings: Imperial Chemical Industries Lime Division, formed from the Buxton Lime Firms Co. in 1926; and the Derbyshire Stone Co., originating 10 years later. Output is of the order of seven million tons annually, of which over two million tons come from the huge Imperial Chemical Industries quarry at Tunstead, near Buxton. Within the industry some specialisation occurs according to market demands and the varying quality of the stone. Thus, at Middleton-by-Wirksworth a bed of exceptional purity, worked by a drift mine since 1959, provides material for the Lancashire glass industry, whereas the entire output from the relatively new quarry on Eldon Hill is used as road metal. Another recent development is the output of crushed and finely ground stone at Grange Mill, near Wirksworth. In the Hope valley at Bradwell, the limestone of the Nunlow Beds quarried from the nearby Pin Dale, is used with clays from the adjacent Edale Shales for the manufacture of cement. Beginning in 1929 and now consuming 2,500 to 3,000 tons of limestone a day, this unit is able to serve an important market lying on either side of the Pennines. Another highly specialised activity, dating from 1963, is the working at Hopton, near Wirksworth, of dolomitic limestone for the extraction of magnesium which is used in the manufacture of light metal alloys. The industrial uses to which the Carboniferous Limestone can be directed are thus becoming more and more diversified.

Though the limestone was used in earlier times for building, it seldom serves this purpose nowadays; even the well-known fossiliferous Hopton Wood 'marble' used for interior work on account of its high polish, is no longer obtained, the quarry having been closed in 1962.

The famous 'black marble' from Ashford, near Bakewell, which provided an elegant stone for ornamental work, was exploited intermittently from the 16th century, but ceased to be used after the early years of the present century.

The production of road metal from the Carboniferous Limestone is supplemented by material obtained from the igneous rocks, chiefly in the form of dolerite sills and occasional basaltic masses which occur within the limestone. The chief workings are at Calton Hill, near Taddington. Some of the output is crushed and graded to provide a good quality concrete aggregate.

Two other minor products of the Carboniferous Limestone are chert and ochre. Chert, a siliceous mineral closely resembling flint, is worked from the Holme Bank quarry at Bakewell for use in the Staffordshire potteries. This source was first exploited by Sir Josiah Wedgwood nearly 200 years ago. Ochre, a reddish-yellow hydrated oxide of iron, occurs in pockets in the limestone and where it is found in sufficient quantity, as in the Via Gellia at Cromford and at Matlock, it is extracted as a source of colouring matter.

Among the other limestones of the region, the Permian Magnesian Limestone, as mentioned on page 297, has been extensively worked as a building stone and was also burnt to provide builders' lime. The Lower Lias Limestone ('hydraulic' limestone), with adjacent clays, is exploited for cement manufacture at Barnstone, in the Vale of Belvoir; and just beyond the north–east margin of the region the Inferior Oolite (Lincolnshire Limestone) is used at Kirton-in-Lindsey for the same purpose.

Vein minerals

Lead ore (galena) has been worked in the Peak District of Derbyshire since Roman times but is now of little significance. Its exploitation is more fully discussed in chapter XII. Lead occurs in veins, though sometimes in irregular masses, in the Carboniferous Limestone and is usually accompanied by fluorspar (fluorite), barytes and calcite. The veins generally fill vertical fissures in the Limestone. The richest ore, often associated with small quantities of zinc, has been found to occur in the eastern part of the main outcrop and in the small inliers of Ashover and Crich. Today the gangue minerals, fluorspar and barytes, are more important than lead, although reserves of the latter, too costly to work under present conditions, undoubtedly exist.

Fluorspar, with a calcium fluoride content of 60 per cent or more, is in demand as a flux in steel-making and if this content exceeds 85 per cent it is of value to the non-ferrous metal and ceramic industries. The mineral is now obtained in a number of places, largely from the waste heaps of old lead-workings, as at Bradwell, Youlgreave, Nether Haddon and on Longstone Edge. The chief producing centre, however, is the Glebe mine at Eyam, which yields some 8,000 tons a year, most of which is sent to Sheffield.

The variety of fluorspar called Blue John, with its rich purplish colour, sometimes verging to yellow, is confined to the Castleton area and is used for making small ornaments, though it was once shaped into more massive objects such as the large candelabra commissioned by Robert Adam which can be seen in the Victoria and Albert Museum. The mineral is obtained from the Blue John mine, having also been worked from the Treak Cliff mine and the Old Tor mine nearby.

Barytes, like fluorspar, is also obtained from old lead mines and surface waste heaps. After grinding to a fine white powder it is used in paint manufacture and, being chemically stable, it serves as an effective filling material in the paper and textile industries. Calcite, the commonest of the gangue minerals, is the least important commercially, and is only used in small quantities for decorative work; one of the chief sources is the Long Rake, near Youlgreave.

An important new development was started in 1965. This was the installation of the Cavendish mill at Stoney Middleton for the treatment of fluorspar, barytes and other minerals including lead concentrates. Here the output of the Glebe mine, opened in 1937 at Eyam, will be dealt with, as well as supplies from the Ladywash mine and the recently opened Sallet mine on Longstone Edge. The last-named area is known to hold large mineral reserves and the new plant is located largely with a view to their exploitation. Built on the site of the old Cupola Works, a former lead-smelting centre, the mill is one of the largest and most up-to-date of its kind in Europe. Apart from steel-making flux much of the output will be used for the production of fluorine compounds made by Laporte Industries Ltd. at Rotherham.

GRAVELS

The Middle Trent valley is one of the leading areas of gravel-working in Britain. The huge demand for gravel in recent years, especially for concrete aggregate and road metal, has promoted an important extractive industry in many of our larger river valleys. Along the main valley of the Trent, workings are found at intervals over a distance of 50 miles from Burton-on-Trent to Newark, as well as in the confluence areas of the principal tributaries, the Dove and the Derwent. Gravel-working also occurs in the vicinity of Lincoln. Since most of the material lies below the normal level of the water-table, the workings become partially filled with water. This condition affects the mode of winning the gravel, which is generally by drag-line excavator, and the material worked in this way is known as 'wet' gravel. That exploited from the more elevated deposits is called 'dry' gravel. With recent advances in water pumping, however, it is now possible to effect dry working in some of the quarries. A certain amount of gravel is dredged from the bed of the Trent, thus affording a third source of production.

Wet gravels

These gravels originated in the great accumulations of pebble material which were deposited by the Trent in the early Post-Glacial stage of its history. The extension of the gravel sheet from Newark to Lincoln follows a former course of the river, which carried it eastward through Lincoln Gap. Along the main valley the huge ribbon of gravel, which includes quantities of sand, has since been covered by more recent alluvium, except on the valley margins where the gravel is exposed in the form of terraces. Portions of these terraces occur intermittently along both flanks of the valley while in places smaller patches of gravel form the actual floor of the floodplain, appearing as islands surrounded by alluvium. These often provide sites for villages, which in turn may restrict exploitation.

Two terraces may be distinguished: firstly, is the upper terrace, formed of Older Gravels, with its surface about 25 to 30 feet above present river-level; secondly, is the lower terrace, formed of Newer Gravels, some 10 to 12 feet above river-level.

Actually, in the neighbourhood of Burton and Derby, the upper terrace lies at about 50 feet above the floodplain, while further down at Beeston it is about 25 to 28 feet.

While the gravels consist overwhelmingly of quartzite pebbles derived from the Bunter Pebble Beds, sub-angular pebbles of flint, chert and sandstone, derived from glacial drift, also occur. Towards Lincoln the proportion of flint tends to increase, although it is estimated that the non-quartzite material is everywhere less than five per cent of the total. The average size of the pebbles throughout is from $0 \cdot 25$ to $1 \cdot 50$ inches, the proportion of those too large for commercial use, i.e. above $2 \cdot 0$ inches, being extremely small. In very general terms the Trent gravel deposits increase in thickness from some 20 feet in the Burton and Derby area to over 30 feet towards Lincoln where, in one locality, a face of nearly 40 feet has been worked. Again very broadly speaking, for economic gravel-working the sand content should not exceed 35 to 40 per cent of the total material (Plate XIII).

Besides such considerations as extent, thickness, size and composition, accessibility in relation to depth of overburden is also important to economic working. On the stretches of upper terrace, though they are partly occupied by built-up areas, overburden, consisting chiefly of downwash from the valley slope, is either absent or is little more than one foot in depth. Moreover, on the terraces the water table is appreciably lower than in the floodplain. The most favourable working conditions are therefore found on the upper terrace and it is here that many of the largest extraction sites occur, at Hilton, Attenborough (Beeston) and Hoveringham (Fig. 49).

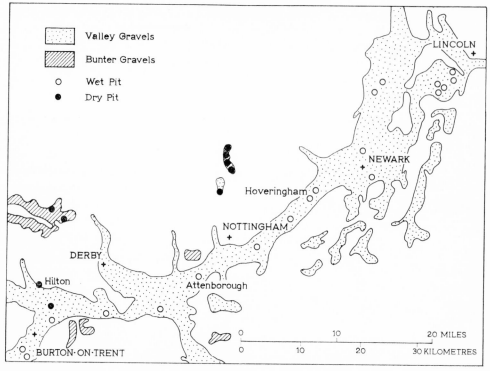

Fig. 49   Distribution of gravel workings

On the floodplain, however, the mantle of alluvium varies considerably in thickness because of the undulating surface of the gravels beneath. Occasionally it is little more than one foot but near Newark it is sometimes as much as 10 feet. In places where stagnant water formerly existed, peat may underlie the alluvium. Whether or not peat is present, a depth of overburden exceeding 15 feet generally precludes economic working.

Over the country as a whole the industry has become highly competitive and in recent years, by the process of absorbing smaller workings, a number of large concerns operating in many different places have emerged. The numerous workings in the Trent valley are thus owned by a relatively small number of firms. One of the largest, Hoveringham Gravels Ltd., in addition to properties in other parts of the country, owns no less than eight of the 20 pits now being worked in the Trent valley area. The Hoveringham undertaking now holds a position of national importance, for its entire output, approaching one million tons a year, amounts to 10 per cent of the country's total production and its output of ready-mixed concrete is about 25 per cent of the total. Its headquarters at Hoveringham, in one of the rich sections of the Trent gravel field, some nine miles north–east of Nottingham, presents some interesting and unusual features. Above all, the operations are fully integrated. With up-to-date extraction and crushing plant; associated works for the making of ready-mixed concrete and mortar, pre-cast concrete, pipes for field drainage and pre-stressed concrete beams; a fleet of trucks (most gravel-working firms rely on haulage contractors); and workshops for repairs of plant and trucks, the firm is particularly well-equipped. While road haulage is almost universal among gravel firms, one of the Hoveringham Company's pits lies adjacent to the railway at Colwick on the eastern outskirts of Nottingham and from this point conveyance by rail allows the firm to extend its market area to the Potteries and Manchester. A small but interesting item of Hoveringham's trade is the export of gravel for water-filtering to distant parts such as Turkey, India, Malaya, Singapore and Hong Kong.

Throughout the Trent valley gravel is extracted from workings which reach below the water-table, consequently the worked-out sites become filled with water and form lagoons of irregular shapes and depth. These, together with untidy heaps of waste material are the scars left by the industry. They generally spoil the appearance of the landscape and the lagoons may be dangerous. Some may be put to amenity uses. One of the lagoons at Hoveringham, for example, is large enough to be used for sailing. Others at Attenborough (Beeston), which have attracted uncommon species of birds and interesting hydrophytic plants, have become small nature reserves.

Dry gravels

Another source of gravel is that associated with the Bunter Sandstone. Such material occurs on higher ground away from the Trent valley and well above the water-table. It is known as dry gravel and is extracted by mechanical shovels. Indeed, there is sometimes insufficient water at hand for washing operations. Another drawback is the likelihood of an excessive admixture of sand for economic working. Nevertheless, such gravel is worked around Blidworth, south of Mansfield, and at Hulland and Mugginton, north–west of Derby.

Dredged gravel

Quantities of gravel, probably not less than 50,000 cubic yards per annum, are dredged from the bed of the Trent. This activity takes place mainly downstream from Newark. There is a wharf at Kelham, opposite Newark, equipped with a grading plant but most of the output is conveyed by barge down-river to the Humber before treatment.

SAND

Valuable moulding sands for use in the iron and steel industry are found in the Nottingham and Mansfield area. These occur in the Bunter Pebble Beds and Lower Mottled Sandstone, but since they are frequently overlain by patches of glacial sand derived from the Bunter they are not readily differentiated from the geological standpoint. The chief workings occur in the neighbourhood of Blidworth, south-south-east of Mansfield, and at Bramcote Hills, west of Nottingham. The output is directed largely to Chesterfield and Sheffield but some of it moves further afield to steel and foundry works near Glasgow. In the Mansfield district there are considerable reserves of good quality moulding sand.

Locally, in the Nottingham and Mansfield area, the Bunter Pebble Beds have long been exploited for building sand and this is also the case in the Derby area, where the Pebble Beds capped with glacial sands and gravel are worked at Hulland and Mugginton. Sand is also worked from the Bunter outlier at Midway, just north of Swadlincote, in south Derbyshire. The output of sand from the Nottingham–Mansfield area, where there are also large reserves, is of substantial importance to the local building trade and today amounts to nearly 100,000 cubic yards annually.

BRICK AND POTTERY CLAYS

Clays from the Middle Coal Measures, the Permian Marl and Keuper Marl have been used extensively in the past for brick-making. Many old brickyards which exploited the Keuper Marl are to be seen around Nottingham at Arnold, Carlton, Edwalton, Bunny and Chilwell. Some of the largest are on the high ground at Mapperley, hence the saying that 'Nottingham once stood on Mapperley Plains', for this was the source of so many of its buildings in the 19th century. Victorian Nottingham was certainly a redbrick town. Nottingham bricks were once exported to other parts of the country and, just as the ironwork for the roof of St. Pancras Station came from the Butterley Works at Ripley (see page 247), so the bricks for the station buildings came from Mapperley. Most of the works exploiting the Keuper Marl failed to compete with the modern large-scale enterprises based on the Oxford Clay in the Bedford and Peterborough districts and one by one they were closed. A few of the Nottingham works have survived, however, such as those at Bunny, Wilford and Carlton.

The Permian Marl yielded good quality bricks at Bulwell, but the firm producing them, dating from 1860, also made coarse pottery and came to specialise in the output of flower pots, which were exported to all parts of the world. Though the export trade has dwindled the home market remains good and the firm is by far the largest producer of garden pottery in the country. The traditional products are noted for their high porosity but in recent years they have been largely superseded by plastic pots. The latter, though not porous, are nevertheless suitable for many plants and offer advantages of being light in weight and not easily broken. The Bulwell industry, long based on local resources, is now largely dependent upon plastic materials brought from a distance.

On the older portion of the coalfield brick-making has long been an ancillary activity at some of the collieries, utilising the clays of the Middle Coal Measures.

Several of these works, now owned by the National Coal Board, are still in production, as at Annesley, Kirkby-in-Ashfield and Watnall. Similar clays form the basis of pottery manufacture at Denby, in Derbyshire, and Langley Mill, in Nottinghamshire. At the latter centre, which produces oven and table ware, local clay has been superseded by the use of ball and china clay; at Denby, where the industry dates back to the early years of the 19th century, and now specialises in table ware, local clay is still included among the materials used. Both centres serve important export markets.

At Hathern, between Nottingham and Loughborough, the making of specialised industrial ceramics is an important development derived from a brickworks, originally making hand-made bricks, dating from 1875. In 1881 the production of terra cotta work was begun and this has continued, although the output is no longer based on local clay from the Keuper Marl. It is now almost the only source of terra cotta, which is still in small demand for the repair and renovation of old buildings. Today a more important activity is the manufacture of stoneware for the chemical industry, which was begun during the first World War but was greatly expanded during and since the second World War. The raw materials, both for terra cotta and ceramics, are brought from other parts of the country. For the highly specialised products required by the modern chemical industry the works at Hathern are the leading centre in the country.

REFRACTORY MINERALS

At Steetley, in the neighbourhood of Worksop, the Magnesian Limestone provides one of the chief sources of dolomite in the country, both for the production of basic Bessemer and open hearth steel and for the making of refractory bricks. The Steetley Company and its associates is in fact the largest undertaking in western Europe for the output of refractory materials. Although the stone was exploited for lime throughout the 19th century, the first refractory products were not made until the early 'eighties and the modern brick-making plant, opened in 1937, is built on the site of one of the older quarries. The output from Steetley, together with that from another of the Company's works at Cadeby, near Conisbrough, is chiefly directed to the Sheffield steel industry. It has almost entirely superseded the use of gannister, which was obtained from the Coal Measures of both Derbyshire and south Yorkshire, and, where this is still required, for coke-oven bricks for example, the raw material is now brought from the coalfields of Durham and South Wales. Other kinds of 'basic' bricks using chrome and magnesite are also made at Steetley. For these, chrome is imported from Turkey and Rhodesia, but magnesite, which at one time came largely from Austria, is now obtained from the sea-water extraction plant at West Hartlepool and from the dolomitized Carboniferous Limestone, near Wirksworth, a new source exploited only since 1963. Bricks made from dolomite clinker are produced at both Steetley and Worksop.

Another source of refractory material is found in the 'pocket' silica deposits of the Carboniferous Limestone of Derbyshire. These occupy large cavities in the limestone (see page 47), some of them being well over 100 feet deep; they are worked, chiefly for making firebricks, at Friden and Parsley Hay, near Hartington, and at Harborough, to the west of Wirksworth. At Friden part of this silicious material contains up to 10 per cent alumina and is suitable for use in gas retorts.

At Bulwell is one of the country's leading producers of sand–lime bricks. The works are on the site of a former stone quarry in the Magnesian Limestone which, until about 10 years ago, was one of the sources of rockery and walling stone for which the district is noted. In 1936, however, the making of calcium silicate bricks was begun, using some of the local materials. This development expanded rapidly and today the main constituents are brought in from outside, the lime from Buxton and the sand from the firm's workings in the Bunter Sandstone, situated between Nottingham and Mansfield. The sand–lime brick, invented in this country in 1866 but first developed on a commercial scale in Germany, is now in great demand. It possesses distinct advantages over the traditional clay brick on account of its strength and durability. It is resistant to weathering, both as regards frost action and the effects of alternate wetting and drying; the surface crystallisation of soluble salts, a defect of some types of clay bricks, which may lead to disintegration, hardly occurs; also, carbon dioxide in the atmosphere acting slowly on the brick converts the bonding material into calcium carbonate and eventually increases its hardness. Such bricks afford maximum light reflection without glare and are easily washed, consequently their use in large buildings is extending. Local examples of their use are to be seen in the new Nottingham Playhouse, the Applied Science buildings of the University and the Castle Donington electricity generating station, as well as some of the other power stations erected on the banks of the Trent. The works at Bulwell are now largely automated and the output is sent to all parts of the country.

BUILDING STONE

The two main sources of building stone within the region are the Millstone Grit and the Permian Magnesian Limestone. Both are still worked but neither is of great importance today, chiefly owing to high costs of production, especially in terms of labour, and to the competition afforded by newer alternative building materials. Throughout the Millstone Grit area of Derbyshire abandoned quarries far outnumber those which are still active and even the well-known stone from Stancliffe and Darley Dale is now produced in very small quantities. It was originally intended that the first building of Nottingham University College on the present site should be constructed of this stone but, quite late in the planning stage, it was found that, largely owing to the curtailment of quarrying during the first World War, aggravated by rising costs in subsequent years, insufficient seasoned stone was available in the 1920s. This explains why the lodges at the Beeston entrance and the walling in front of the lake are of Darley Dale stone, while the Trent Building (1927) is of Portland stone. Within the Millstone Grit series, the Kinderscout, Chatsworth and Coxbench Grits have provided the most valuable stone, the first-named being especially suitable for heavy construction work, such as dock and railway projects, and the others, yielding excellent freestone, being preferable for smaller-scale buildings. The use of gritstone flags for roofing, characteristic of older domestic buildings in the hill country, both rural and urban, has long been superseded by other materials.

The chief gritstone quarries now operating are those in the Matlock district, such as Stanton Moor, Tansley Moor and Darley Dale. There is still a small output of grindstones and pulpstones for which the Kinderscout Grit is mainly employed. These are used in tool and glass grinding and in the pulp, paper and linoleum industries respectively, serving both home and export markets.

Along the narrow outcrop of the Magnesian Limestone, which runs from north to south, thinning out on the north–west side of Nottingham, stone-working has been important in the past. The limestone itself becomes progressively thinner and more sandy in character from north to south and accordingly its suitability as a building material diminishes. The best quality stone is found at Bolsover, but there is little demand for it today. Further south it is still worked at Mansfield, while at Bulwell, on the outskirts of Nottingham, where it is known as Bulwell Stone, its sandy nature makes it suitable chiefly for garden walling and rockery stone. These uses are much in evidence in Nottingham and neighbouring towns. Even at Bolsover, the stone from the historic quarries on Bolsover Moor varies in quality, especially as regards resistance to atmospheric impurities. It was used in building part of the Houses of Parliament at Westminster in the middle of last century, but before very long in the polluted air of London, it showed deterioration; it was also used for Southwell Minster, where it has survived in good condition for over 800 years.

OIL

Oil exploration

Surface evidence of oil is something of a rarity in the East Midlands. Heavy oil residues, elastic or hard bitumen, are known in the Carboniferous Limestone, but later rocks are almost devoid of oil except for two examples in the Trias. The first of these is an impregnated sandstone extending over nearly a square mile at Stapenhill, south of Burton-on-Trent, and a second, much smaller, example, recently described by F. M. Taylor, is located in cuttings for the M.1 extension works near Stapleford. The impetus for the search for oil consequently came mainly from accidental discoveries in coal mines and coal exploration borings.

Perhaps the largest of the mine seepages was that at Riddings colliery, near Alfreton, where oil flowed from the Kilburn coal workings at some 300 gallons a day for several years. This production was exploited commercially by Dr. James Young, who devised a simple distillation technique for breaking it down into more

V

useful products, probably the first development of a commercial mineral oil industry in Britain. When the Riddings supply came to an end Young moved to Scotland, where he founded the Scottish Shale Oil industry, only recently defunct.

Another indication of oil which influenced later activity was in the coal boring at Kelham, near Newark (1908), in which a little oil flowed from the neighbourhood of the Millstone Grit/Carboniferous Limestone contact. This led to an abortive early drilling campaign (1920–23), which failed, partly from lack of resources and partly from the impossibility at that time of determining the deeper structure in advance of drilling. Subsequently this show influenced the choice of Eakring for the first test boring in 1939, and the Kelham Hills oilfield was later discovered two miles to the north of the coal boring.

Strategic pressures in the first World War led to a government-sponsored search for indigenous oil. On the evidence of oil residues in the limestone of the Peak District, this search was concentrated on flanking anticlines where an adequate cover of later shales and other rocks was available as a potential seal for liquid hydrocarbons in the Carboniferous Limestone. Two borings in north Staffordshire encountered unexpectedly thick igneous rock (Apedale and Werrington), others in Derbyshire found traces of oil (Ironville, on the same structure as the Riddings seepage) or gas (Heath, near Alfreton). Only the one at Hardstoft, in the same district, actually found oil. This lay at the top of the Carboniferous Limestone, but production was not established until 1922 when the strategic emergency was over. The well reverted to the landowner, the Duke of Devonshire, and two more wells were drilled without success. The original well continued to produce through the years between the Wars, and was cleaned out and stimulated in 1938 for a final flush of production until effective abandonment in 1945. This final phase yielded 1,236 tons of oil.

The folded Carboniferous rocks with their oil potential are covered eastwards (Fig. 2) by a gently dipping blanket of Permian, Triassic and Mesozoic rocks. Their structure can, however, be worked out from geological data in the mines of the working concealed coalfield and from geophysical surveys in the extensive area further east not yet reached by mining. Exploration has been carried out almost entirely by a single company, a subsidiary of the British Petroleum Company Limited. The location of oilfields in the region is shown in Fig. 50; in addition to these there is another oilfield south–east of Nottingham, just to the south of Plungar.

The Eakring oilfield was essentially defined by geological methods, which indicated a very large fold deduced from levels in the Ollerton and Bilsthorpe collieries, together with coal exploration boreholes. The southward definition was imperfect and the geological data were there supplemented by seismic survey. The first borehole was located a quarter of a mile south of Eakring village and established indigenous oil production in 1939 a few weeks before the outbreak of the second World War at a depth of about 2,000 feet in basal Coal Measures Sandstone.

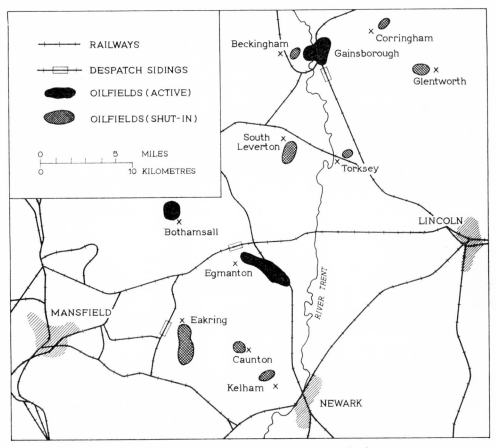

Fig. 50 Location of oilfields in the East Midlands

Geophysical work, which began in Lincolnshire with magnetometer and gravity surveys, proved an anomaly indicative of a major basement uplift at Nocton, south of Lincoln. Seismic survey was used to define this and to carry out a reconnaissance of west Lincolnshire and to explore eastwards and south-eastwards from the Eakring discovery. The latter led to early successes in discovering a southward extension of the Eakring structure (the Dukes Wood oilfield, near Kirklington) and a separate oil-bearing structure at Kelham Hills (both in 1941). Later a fourth field was found at Caunton in the same area (1943). Contrary to expectation oil was found in the basal Coal Measure sandstones and Millstone Grit, with only minor quantities in the Carboniferous Limestone. These four fields made a critical contribution to national petroleum supplies during the emergency, and had together produced 403,345 tons by the end of the war (1945), having reached a maximum production of 111,512 tons in 1943.

Successes in other areas were long delayed despite a protracted drilling effort. One factor was the unexpected development of igneous rocks around the Millstone Grit/ Coal Measures boundary, in some places replacing the expected sand. Sand development was found to become very sporadic towards the south-east, so that at Bottesford, for example, numerous oily sands located were too thin for commercial production, while at Claypole, Eagle Moor and other places they were absent. The large structure south of Lincoln at Nocton proved to have only an attenuated remnant of Millstone Grit and, although the Carboniferous Limestone was oil-bearing, the quantity was very small.

A further advance came with an improvement of seismic methods, which permitted a much more accurate definition of deeper structures beneath the blanket of later rocks. It has been found, in fact, that Eakring and Nocton are of exceptional size among East Midlands folds, and later successes have been in much gentler structures. These have the complication that thickness changes in the component rocks result in relative displacement of the structural culminations at different depths, and whereas older methods had registered on the top of the Carboniferous Limestone, the seismic work now had to be adequate for definition of the structure in the basal Coal Measures.

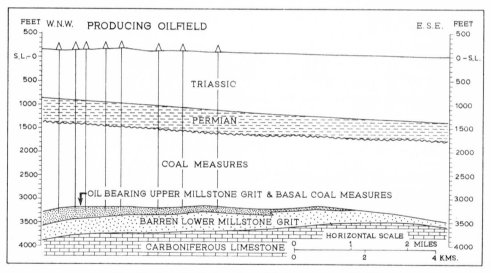

Fig. 51   Longitudinal section of the Egmanton oilfield

The section shows the displacement of the crest between the Millstone Grit and the Carboniferous Limestone, and shows also a limitation of the oil-bearing area due to eastward thinning of the producing sand

The first of the large new discoveries, the Egmanton oilfield (Fig. 51) was made in 1955 specifically because of this better definition, after earlier unsuccessful drilling too far to the east, while the gentler structures further north-east would not have been found by cruder methods. Bothamsall oilfield was found in 1958 on the line of the Eakring anticline, north of Ollerton (a seismic success where drilling on limited geological data had previously produced a near miss), and a smaller field was found a little further east at South Leverton (1960). All these discoveries were of oil in the sands of the basal Coal Measures and, to a lesser extent, in the Millstone Grit.

Meanwhile, detailed seismic work had continued east of the Trent, resulting in the definition of a broad structure centred just east of Gainsborough. Drilling proved an oilfield covering some four square miles, extending westwards from the discovery well (1959) under the town and under the river flats beyond. To reach the part of the field under the town it has been necessary to drill deflected wells from open ground on the eastern side. The oil-bearing horizons extend upwards in the Coal Measures to above the Top Hard coal horizon, and gas sands are also present. Depths are greater than in the fields west of the Trent (3,000 to 4,500 feet) but Gainsborough is now England's largest oilfield, with a production of over 40,000 tons per year.

Smaller fields have been found east of Gainsborough at Corringham (1958) and Glentworth (1961), Torksey (1961) as well as at Plungar, in north Leicestershire (1953).

Oil production

The East Midlands oils are dark brown to green waxy crudes with gravities of 0·82 to 0·91. The gasoline distillates have predominant naphthenic characteristics with high octane values, a valuable feature during the war years. The heavier oils are found at Kelham, Caunton and Plungar, localities with thick igneous developments where some metamorphism of the oil may have occurred. In the shallower fields the oil *in situ* was under-saturated and no separate gas caps existed, but free gas is present in moderate quantity at Gainsborough, partly in separate sandstones in the oil-bearing series.

Wells flowed at the surface for only short periods and production has been mainly by electric-powered plunger pumps. Natural gravity drainage only recovers a modest proportion of oil *in situ* in a field, and as the fields have been worked artificial stimulation methods have been used. This involves shattering the oil-bearing rock in individual wells either by gelignite charges or, as has been the case more recently, by hydraulic fracturing, involving high-pressure fluid injection. In the older fields falling pressures resulting from long production have been restored by peripheral injection of water into the producing sands. These processes have together approximately doubled oil recovery as compared with primary methods.

The greater part of East Midlands oil production has been shipped by rail for refining at Pumpherston, in Scotland, at a plant designed for handling similar waxy crude from the shale oil industry. The most recent development, resulting from the ending of a preferential rebate of duty on home-produced oils at the end of 1964, has been the limitation of production to the larger fields (Egmanton, Bothamsall and Gainsborough), which provide feedstock for a special lubricants plant in Cheshire. The balance of potential production, unable to compete economically with imported

Middle East crude, is now shut in but can be brought back into production when the need arises. Meanwhile, exploration for more fields continues on a limited scale.

In its East Midlands exploration, British Petroleum has drilled 601 wells, 480 of them producers, totalling 1,815,394 feet. During the 25 years to the ending of preference, 1,721,900 tons of oil were produced. In the final unrestricted year (1964) production from the Midlands fields was 127,492 tons. Kimmeridge, in Dorset, was the only other significant British source, but produced a relatively small amount (some 9,000 tons in 1964) (see Appendix V).

SELECTED REFERENCES

National Coal Board. *Annual Reports.* H.M.S.O.

Peak Park Planning Board. *Report of Analysis and Survey* (1954).

Ministry of Fuel and Power. *North Midlands Coalfield; Regional Survey Report.* H.M.S.O. (1945).

Ministry of Fuel and Power. *The Concealed Coalfield of Yorkshire and Nottinghamshire.* H.M.S.O. (1951).

Edwards, K. C. East Midlands Coal Production in Relation to Britain's Fuel and Power Problem. *East Midlands Geographer* No. 6 (December 1956).

Estall, R. C. The Distribution of Coal from the East Midlands Division. *East Midlands Geographer* No. 8 (December 1957).

Groves, A. W. Gypsum and Anhydrite. *Memorandum of the Geological Survey.* H.M.S.O. (1958).

Jackson, L. The Limestone Quarrying Industry of North Derbyshire. *Geographical Journal* Vol. 129 (March 1963).

Ministry of Town and Country Planning. *Report of the Advisory Committee on Sand and Gravel. Part 3, Trent Valley.* H.M.S.O. (1950).

Whiteside, R., Paterson, T. D. and McLean, J. H. Gravel Operations in the Trent Valley, Great Britain. *Institute of Mining and Metallurgy Symposium on Opencast Mining, Quarrying and Alluvial Mining* Paper No. 4 London (1964).

Lees, G. M. and Cox, P. T. The geological basis of the present search for oil in Great Britain by the D'Arcy Exploration Company Limited. *Quarterly Journal of the Geological Society of London* Vol. 93 (1937) pp. 156–194.

Lees, G. M. and Taitt, A. H. The geological results of the search for oilfields in Great Britain. *Quarterly Journal of the Geological Society of London* Vol. 101 (1946) pp. 255–317.

Kent, P. E. Oilfields in Great Britain. *Geography* Vol. 32 (1947).

Dickie, R. K. and Adcock, C. M. Oil production in the Nottinghamshire Oilfields. *Journal of the Institute of Petrology* Vol. 40 (1954) pp. 179–180.

Falcon, N. L. and Kent, P. E. Geological Results of Petroleum exploration in Britain, 1945–57. *Quarterly Journal of the Geological Society of London* Memoir No. 2 (1960).

Taylor, F. M. An Oil Seepage near Toton Lane, Stapleford, Nottinghamshire. *The Mercian Geologist* Vol. 1 (1964) pp. 23–29.

ACKNOWLEDGMENTS

Particular acknowledgment is due to the following: Mr. W. L. Miron, o.b.e., t.d., Chairman of the East Midlands Division of the National Coal Board, for information and advice in connection with the section on coal; to Hoveringham Gravels Ltd. for help in connection with gravel-working in the Trent valley; to Mr. J. Eze, graduate of the Department of Geography, University of Nottingham, for permission to use material from his unpublished dissertation on the gypsum industry of the Midlands (1964); and to the Chairman and Directors of the British Petroleum Company, Ltd., for permission to publish the account of oil exploration.

XVII

MANUFACTURING INDUSTRY

MANY of the manufacturing industries of the Nottingham region are treated in subsequent chapters. In the main these industries are discussed together with the urban centres in which they occur. The industrial structure of Nottingham receives particular attention in chapter XXII, and that of the other urban centres is treated in chapter XXVI. However, in view of their traditional significance within the region the hosiery and lace industries are treated separately in this chapter.

HOSIERY

Hosiery manufacture is the oldest of what may be called the characteristic industries of the Nottingham region. It originated with the invention of the stocking frame by William Lee, of Calverton, a few miles north of Nottingham, in the late 16th century. For a long time the main centre of framework knitting, as the new craft was called, was in London, for the trade was largely in silk hose and luxury goods. Here it came under the close supervision of the chartered Framework Knitters' Company. As the trade expanded, the regulations of this body became increasingly irksome to the more enterprising master-stockingers and in the early 18th century the industry gravitated towards its original home in the East Midlands, where the Company had less influence. Another factor favouring the shift in location was the changing nature of the trade, with an increasing demand for woollen and cotton goods. Leicestershire wool was particularly suitable for knitting yarn, and the coming of Hargreaves and Arkwright to the East Midlands ensured a supply of reliable cotton yarn. Lombe's silk mill at Derby made a further contribution to the local supply of materials for the framework knitting industry.

During the 18th century the hosiery industry consolidated its position in the East Midlands, with Nottingham and Leicester as its chief centres, Leicester becoming eventually the more important. But framework knitting was always, to a considerable extent, a village industry. It was organised on the domestic system characteristic of all the textile trades before the Industrial Revolution, and in this trade the system survived until well into the second half of the 19th century. For many years before the application of steam power and the concentration of production in factories, framework knitting had been one of the most backward industries in the country, chronically overcrowded and offering little incentive to improvement in technique or organisation.

In time, however, the rise of other industries and the introduction of compulsory schooling diminished the supply of cheap labour and the industry gradually adapted itself to the changing environment. The adaptation of the stocking frame to rotary motion and the application of power was, however, a difficult task. It was not until 1864 that a really successful power-driven machine for making fully-fashioned stockings and other garments was introduced. This was the Cotton's Patent frame, which became the typical machine in this branch of the trade, where the parts of the garment are knitted in flat pieces and then sewn together. The other main type of machine, the circular frame making fabric in tubular form, was less complicated because no fashioning was involved, and several versions were in use in the 1850s. Parallel with these developments in knitting machines was the introduction of power-driven sewing machines for seaming the parts of fashioned garments, welting stockings, and making up garments from cut fabric.

At first the coming of the factory had the effect of drawing more of the industry into Leicester and Nottingham, but at the turn of the century more and more hosiery factories were being set up in the smaller towns and villages of Leicestershire, Nottinghamshire and Derbyshire in which framework knitting had been carried on. Labour and factory sites were cheaper in these places. But dispersal had its social advantages, too; many of these smaller hosiery centres had become heavily dependent on coal-mining and hosiery manufacture helped to improve the balance in local employment, especially by providing work for women.

Another effect of the factory system in its earlier phase was to reduce considerably the number of hosiery workers. In the decade before the first World War the total for the whole country was about 45,000; though there was also a large auxiliary force of women outworkers. By 1924 the number of factory workers had almost doubled and far less work was put out. Except for the depression in the early 1930s, the industry continued to expand throughout the inter-war period and its productivity to increase. The Census of Production for 1935 gave the average number of persons employed as 115,273, excluding outworkers; allowing for unemployment, the number of workers attached to the industry was approaching 130,000. Hosiery manufacture now ranked third among British textile industries; its growth was in marked contrast with the experience of the cotton and the woollen and worsted trades. Growth brought little change in the pattern of location, however, for nearly half the firms and about two-thirds of the workers were in the three East Midland counties.

The hosiery industry suffered severe contraction in the second World War and its recovery was handicapped by shortages of raw materials and equipment. By 1950, total employment, at 123,400, had about reached the pre-war level, allowing for the fact that there was now very little unemployment. In 1964 the total was 128,200, of whom 60 per cent were in the East Midlands. The wider distribution of the industry, as compared with the pre-war position, is largely due to labour shortage in the traditional centres, particularly female labour, for 70 per cent of hosiery workers are women and girls. Another influence is the government's policy of encouraging industrial expansion in less prosperous areas.

Although the industry's expansion, measured in terms of employment, has been far less than between the wars, the growth of output in recent years is impressive. Gross output in 1935 was valued at £39·5m; in 1958 sales totalled £195·9m. Over the same period net output per person employed increased from £150 to £728. After allowing for price changes these figures indicate a marked increase in productivity. This is due largely to improved equipment; knitting machines have been made to run faster and they are more automatic in action; handwork has been reduced in many ways. There have also been some changes in the content of production which have increased labour productivity; for instance, the growing output of seamless, as distinct from fully-fashioned, stockings, and the simplification of styles in underwear. Another factor has been the steadier market conditions of post-war years, which have enabled firms to work nearer to full capacity. The great bulk of output is absorbed by the home market; exports in recent years have been about seven per cent of total sales, the same proportion as in the 1930s.

Small-scale enterprise has always been a characteristic feature of the hosiery industry and it is still very prevalent. Of the 604 firms recorded in the 1958 Census of Production, one-third were businesses employing between 25 and 50 workers. Firms employing up to 400 numbered 544 and they produced half the industry's output. One reason for the multiplicity of small firms is the great variety of goods produced and the opportunities for specialisation in particular lines. Technical conditions also favour the small firm; machines are generally compact and highly productive, and it is usually possible to get an efficient balance of processes in quite a small plant. Bigger plants are found in firms specialising in stockings, but many of the larger firms are made up of units, each specialised to a particular branch of the trade. Small firms generally sell through wholesalers; with bigger firms, direct selling to retailers under the manufacturer's own brand is more usual. Many firms, including some of the largest, however, make to the orders of chain stores which provide the specification and the brand name under which the goods are sold.

The favourable experience of the hosiery industry in recent years points to further growth in the future, though the competition of imports has always to be reckoned with. Both technical and commercial efficiency have increased, assisted by the industry's trade association and its research centre in Nottingham. The range of uses for knitted fabrics is still extending and the versatility of the industry has been equal to the demand. In recent years growth has been accompanied by a tendency towards concentration of control. According to the 1958 Census of Production the 15 biggest firms in the industry, with between 1,000 and 4,000 employees, owned 68 establishments. This is partly a reflection of the dispersal policy which many firms have been forced to adopt because of the shortage of labour in their original location. But it also indicates the absorption of firms into larger (commercial) units. Since 1958 further absorption has occurred; a notable case is that of Courtaulds, who have taken over a number of hosiery firms in the last year or two. This is consistent with a movement towards vertical integration that is affecting other textile industries.

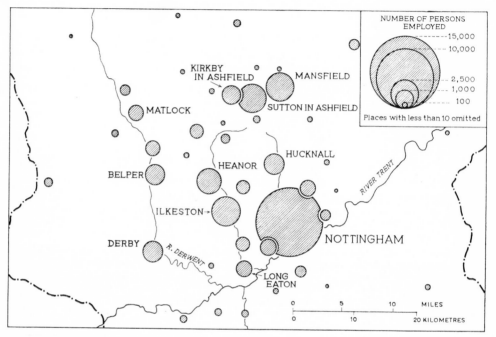

Fig. 52   The distribution of hosiery manufacturing in the Nottingham region

LACE

Although the lace industry now occupies only a minor place in the economy of the Nottingham region, lace is the one product for which Nottingham is known the world over.

The industry is of great interest to the economic historian and to the student of industrial organisation. Indeed, it is not too fanciful to suggest that in the story of the lace industry we have an epitome of British economic history in the 19th century. All the ingredients are here: the skill and perseverance of the inventors, the proliferation of small, specialised businesses, the intense competition, the recurrent booms and slumps, the penetration of overseas markets and then the spread of the industry abroad, aided by the export of British machines. Each of the textile trades was transformed in the Industrial Revolution but none so abruptly as lace-making. For here we have a true handicraft, in which no machinery of any kind had been used, supplanted in a few decades by mechanical factory production. Nowhere was the increase in output and consequent cheapening of manufactured goods more strikingly demonstrated.

Nottingham was never a centre of hand lace-making; the local manufacture grew out of the old-established framework knitting industry. Towards the end of the 18th century some success was obtained in making net on the stocking frame; but it was Heathcoat's bobbin net machine, introduced in 1809, that really established the manufacture. Here again there was a close connection with framework knitting, for Heathcoat was a framesmith and other inventors, too, learned their skill in this craft.

The distinctive feature of Heathcoat's invention was the mechanisation of the characteristic process in hand lace-making: the twisting of threads, as distinct from looping, which is the basis of knitted fabrics. Heathcoat's machine made plain net, on which patterns were often embroidered by hand.

As in a loom, the plain net machine has two sets of threads. The warp threads pass vertically from a bottom beam to a top roller on which the fabric is wound. The other threads are wound on very thin brass bobbins set in two carriages, one in front and one behind the warp threads. As the carriages move in and out the bobbin threads pass between the warp threads. In this process the bobbins are interchanged between the front and rear carriages and at the same time are shogged, one set to the right, one to the left. Thus the bobbins all pass round the machine in turn while the warp moves upwards.

In 1813 John Leavers, another framesmith, built a machine on a somewhat different principle. The change was of great importance for it led eventually to the production of patterned lace. This was effected about 1840 by Hooton Deverill, who redesigned the Leavers machine and applied the Jacquard system of thread control.

Thus while Heathcoat started what is now the plain net section of the industry, Leavers was the progenitor of the branch which still bears his name, although he himself did not fully realise the possibilities of his machine. As time went on, it proved remarkably adaptable to the growing and ever-changing demands of the trade in dress laces and trimmings.

The third main section of the industry, the curtain branch, or lace furnishing section as it is now called, has also its distinctive machine. The curtain machine, though based on the Leavers principle, is simpler in action. It makes net with square meshes and, though less versatile than the Leavers machine, it is capable of a wide range of patterns on the bolder lines suitable for curtains.

By the middle of the 19th century all three branches of the lace industry were flourishing in Nottingham, although one notable migration from the area had occurred when Heathcoat moved to Tiverton after the Luddites had destroyed his factory at Loughborough. About 1875 another location of the industry was established in Ayrshire. But Nottingham maintained its position as the main centre of the trade.

The peak of development was reached in the first decade of this century. The 1911 census of population recorded 46,000 full-time lace workers, including about 17,000 men, in England and Scotland. Nearly half the total were in Nottingham and another quarter in such nearby places as Long Eaton, Beeston, Sandiacre and Derby. A notable feature of employment at this time was the large number of outworkers engaged in clipping, scalloping, mending and other forms of handwork. Besides those directly employed in the industry there were many more in the ancillary trades, such as the bleaching, dyeing and dressing of lace.

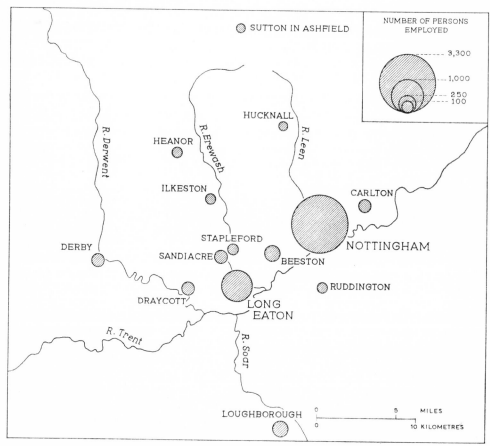

Fig. 53   The distribution of lace manufacturing in the Nottingham region

In this highly localised industry a complex organisation had developed. Lace-making was generally carried on in very small units accommodated in tenement factories. The machines, all built in Nottingham, were large and expensive, but they were often acquired on hire-purchase terms and shift working made for intensive use of the equipment. The trade was dominated by 'finishers', who determined styles and patterns according to their judgment of the market, distributed orders among machine-holders and also got the lace processed ready for sale. Most of the finishers were also small firms; their offices and warehouses were concentrated in one of the oldest parts of Nottingham, which became famous as the Lace Market. The export houses included a number of firms of foreign origin.

Fluctuations in prosperity have always been characteristic of the lace trade. The effects of fashion changes and the uncertainty of overseas markets were enhanced by the comparative ease of entry into both the manufacturing and the commercial side of the industry and by the intensity of competition. But for almost a century lace was a growing industry and Nottingham's position in it was well maintained. In the early 1920s the trend was abruptly reversed and within ten years the industry had shrunk to half its former size. The Leavers section suffered most, but the curtain branch was also severely affected by fashion changes. During the second World War little lace was made, though some machines were kept busy on mosquito nets and hairnets. The industry was forcibly concentrated and this experience helped to produce the more compact structure which exists today.

Small firms are still numerous; but well over half the total output of lace and net is produced by 25 firms, each employing 100 or more workers. These bigger firms usually own several plants and some are both manufacturers and merchants. Diversification has also become common, with lace firms branching out into knitwear, lingeries, and made-up textiles.

Although the decline of the lace trade has been drastic, involving a fall of its labour force in the Nottingham area to a mere 5,000, it would be wrong to think of it as a depressed industry. On its reduced scale it is fairly prosperous and whenever fashion turns towards lace the limits of capacity are soon reached. There is, indeed, some anxiety about the future supply of twisthands, the skilled men who work the lace machines. Technical progress in the industry has been stimulated by the establishment of a research centre in Nottingham and also by the introduction of new types of machine from abroad.

SELECTED REFERENCES

Varley, D. E. *A History of the Midland Counties Lace Manufacturers' Association*, published by the Association (1959).
Wells, F. A. *The British Hosiery Trade*, London (1935).

ACKNOWLEDGMENT

Thanks are due to Dr. D. M. Smith, University of Manchester, formerly of the Department of Geography, University of Nottingham, for permission to reproduce the maps shown in Figs. 52 and 53.

XVIII

ELECTRIC POWER GENERATION

WITH its widespread industrial activity, the Nottingham region makes increasing demands upon power resources, especially electricity. In the generation of electricity, however, the region itself provides a major contribution to the national output. This results from the abundance of coal and the suitability of the banks of the Trent for power station sites. Unlike the Tennessee valley there is no water power to be obtained from the Trent, but like the Tennessee, the river yields large quantities of water for cooling the steam used by the generators of conventional power stations. Large-scale electricity production is a recent development and indeed the great and growing chain of stations shown on Fig. 54 did not exist 20 years ago. Previously most of the East Midlands coal destined for power stations was sent out of the region to London, the West Midlands and even to Lancashire.

In 1945 there were two chief kinds of electricity authority, namely, power companies and municipal corporations. The former supplied the rural areas and smaller urban communities, the latter the larger towns. Nottingham, Derby, Lincoln and Burton-on-Trent each had its own local station, and the Nottinghamshire and Derby Power Company, which produced current at Spondon three miles downstream from Derby on the river Derwent, served areas outside these towns. Only the small station at Burton and the larger one at Nottingham used the Trent. The distribution might well have been different had the course of economic history run smoothly according to a regional plan.

THE INTER-WAR PERIOD

Before 1914 not much electricity was used; few rural areas were supplied, and power stations were small. They were generally sited in town centres. Nottingham had two such stations; one just north of the Old Market Square; the other immediately east of the present Huntingdon Street bus station. A third was attached to the refuse destructor plant in the Eastcroft Depot, some distance south-east of the city centre. It was already foreseen, however, that the rising demand for electricity and the technical needs of power stations, especially for water, would require a new siting policy. With this need in view even before 1914 the predecessors of the Nottinghamshire and Derby Power Company had already taken an option on a Trent-bank site near the railway marshalling yard at Netherfield, four miles east of Nottingham. The Company knew that sanction to supply Nottingham was necessary to justify this project.

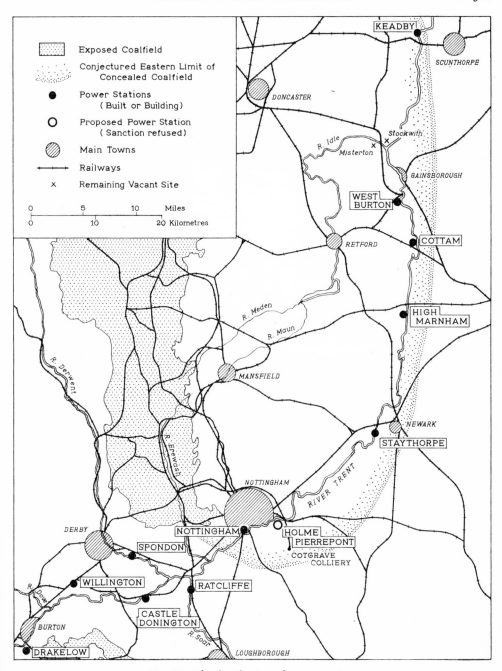

Fig. 54 The distribution of power stations

In 1918 Parliament was considering legislation to help integrate electricity supplies regionally, and in 1919 the Electricity Commissioners were appointed to promote this aim. Accordingly a conference of municipal authorities in the East Midlands sought advice for a regional scheme from J. H. Rider and C. H. Wordingham, consulting engineers, who recommended in 1919 that a 'super' power station of 200 MW should be built on the Trent near Long Eaton to serve the towns of Burton, Derby, Leicester, Loughborough, Nottingham and Mansfield, and in due course the less densely peopled areas between them. The Power Company refused to co-operate; the municipalities thought the expense too great; so the scheme was abandoned. Further help was sought from C. H. Wordingham, who then advised that each town should build its own station. For Nottingham, he recommended the site now used at North Wilford for which the Corporation at once sought the approval of the Electricity Commissioners. At the enquiry (c 1920) objections were made by the Nottinghamshire and Derby Power Company, who urged the superiority of their proposed site at Netherfield as a source of supply for both Nottingham and the area for which the Company already had statutory rights. The city won, and North Wilford came on load in 1925. Netherfield was thus no immediate use to the Power Company, which took swift action in purchasing the generators at Spondon on the river Derwent of the British Cellulose Company's works (later British Celanese). Thus capacity, which rationally ought to have gone to Trent-side during the inter-war period, was instead scattered among the municipalities and Spondon. Political rather than economic factors prevailed.

AFTER NATIONALISATION

New schemes to use the Trent began to emerge just before and during the second world war. To be effective, however, the influence of local political geography had to be reduced, and it was not until after nationalisation on 1st April 1948 that an integrated scheme, now national rather than regional, could be smoothly implemented. Staythorpe 'A' (360 MW), near Newark, was already building; Drakelow 'A' (240 MW), near Burton, and Keadby (360 MW), near Scunthorpe, were included in the plan from 1949; Castle Donington (600 MW), south of Derby, and Willington 'A' (400 MW), west of Derby, were authorised from 1950; Drakelow 'B' (480 MW) and Staythorpe 'B' (360 MW) from 1951; High Marnham (1,000 MW), near Tuxford, from 1953; Willington 'B' (400 MW) from 1955; Drakelow 'C' (1,500 MW) from 1958; West Burton (2,000 MW), near Retford, from 1960; Ratcliffe-on-Soar (2,000 MW), near Long Eaton, from 1962, and Cottam (2,000 MW), near Retford, from 1963. An application to install 2,000 MW at Holme Pierrepont, near Netherfield, and the new Cotgrave Colliery, was rejected in 1961. All these stations, now either operating or being planned under the direction of the Central Electricity Generating Board, are located on the Trent at points convenient for rail transport from the coalfields (Fig. 54). Including extensions to North Wilford, but excluding gas-turbine plant for peak-load generation, the total capacity sanctioned for Trent-side during the period has amounted to 11,868 MW, which is equal to one-third of the capacity installed in England and Wales in March 1964, and almost equal to the total (12,840 MW) for England and Wales in March 1950 (Plate XIV).

All these stations draw water from the river for cooling, though the expense of cooling towers cannot be avoided at any station where capacity exceeds 360 MW, because the Trent is not big enough to meet the demand. A station of 360 MW requires about 14 million gallons an hour and a 2,000 MW plant would need about 78 million gallons on full load.

While water and rail access justify the sites, situations near the coalfield but distant from the markets in the South and in Lancashire are justified by the greater economy of electrical transmission (for base loads or near-base loads) than of rail transport of coal to power stations close to the market. Progress with the techniques of rail freighting are likely soon to reduce the advantage of transmission, so that the proposed station of 2,000 MW at Didcot on the middle Thames has now become economically more feasible. The arrangements for 'merry-go-round' trains which will achieve this improvement are first to be tried at the West Burton power station, and at Cottam, Ratcliffe and Drakelow 'C' among others. The Trent stations will thus benefit, but their advantage will be reduced in comparison with stations farther from the coalfields.

For the next decade, at least, the Trent and the neighbouring Yorkshire rivers will stand out together as a salient feature on a distribution map of power production in Britain. The stations themselves will stand out much longer as major features in the landscape. Though the consultant Wordingham, and Balfour, the Power Company director, might not have foreseen in 1920 a Cottam or a West Burton, both so far from a local market, it is noteworthy that their competitive recommendations foresaw a Ratcliffe, and a Holme Pierrepont. It is also noteworthy that the latter was rejected on both occasions, but for different reasons, largely through opposition from Nottingham. In the best interests of the country and the city, perhaps the removal in due course of North Wilford power station would be fair exchange for consent to build at Holme Pierrepont.

SELECTED REFERENCES

British Electricity Authority (Successors, Central Electricity Board and Central Electricity Generating Board) *Annual reports and accounts* 1947 to 1964.

Rider, J. H. and Wordingham C. H. *Report on electricity supply in the East Midlands district.* Westminster (1919).

—— Transporting energy to the load centres. *Electrical Review* (17th January 1964) pp. 99-100.

—— Power station coal transport agreement. *Engineering and Boiler House Review* (February 1964) 58.

Rawstron, E. M. The distribution and location of steam-driven power stations in Great Britain. *Geography* (1951) Vol. 36 pp. 249-262.

W

Rawstron, E. M. Power production and the River Trent. *East Midland Geographer* No. 2 (1954) pp. 23-30.

Rawstron, E. M. Changes in the geography of electricity production in Great Britain. *Geography* (1955) Vol. 40 pp. 92-97.

Rawstron, E. M. The salient geographical features of electricity production in Great Britain. *Advancement of Science* Vol. 12 No. 45 (1955) pp. 73-82.

Rawstron, E. M. Power stations and the River Trent: a note on further development. *East Midland Geographer* No. 14 (1960) pp. 27-32.

Rawstron, E. M. Electric power in Britain, This changing Britain. *Geography* Vol. 49 (1964) pp. 304-309.

XIX

COMMUNICATIONS

THE network of ground communications in the Nottingham region presents a composite pattern based on portions of national routes which traverse the region, broadly in a north–south direction, and routes which radiate in many directions from the larger centres of population such as Nottingham, Derby and Lincoln. Supplementing this broad pattern is a complex network of local roads and railways which is greatly intensified in the area occupied by the coalfield. As an inland manufacturing region, access to ports is essential and for this purpose organised road and rail services must reach such ports as London, Liverpool, Hull, Grimsby and Bristol. Movements of coal, since much of the output from the Nottinghamshire and Derbyshire field is absorbed by the home market, especially in London, eastern England and the south, make heavy demands upon the railways and more recently the roads.

ROADS

In general the road network of the Nottingham region resembles that of the railways. Along the industrial belt extending northwards from Leicester, through Derby and Nottingham to Sheffield and Doncaster there is an intricate pattern of Class A and Class B roads. To the west, across the hill country of Derbyshire the network of main roads, though more open, is still relatively close because of the need for connections with the trans-Pennine industrial areas of south Lancashire and the Potteries. Eastwards, however, especially beyond the Trent, the pattern of good-class roads is much more open, reflecting the less densely-populated agricultural territory.

Until the construction of the London–Yorkshire Motorway (M.1) the region was traversed by only one major national highway, the Great North Road (A.1) running through Grantham, Newark and Bawtry to Doncaster. Also carrying a large volume of long-distance traffic is the A.6 road (London to Manchester) passing through Leicester and Derby, thence following the Derwent and Wye valleys to Buxton.

Roman roads

As in other parts of the country it is of interest to note how far the modern road system is based on the great highways of the Roman period. In the Nottingham region only to a limited degree is this the case. Nottingham itself was founded long after Roman times and, so far as is known, the nearest Roman road was the Fosse

Way, some eight miles distant on the opposite side of the Trent valley. From the Roman site of Little Chester (*Derventio*) at Derby the Ryknield Street led south-westward to the Watling Street and it still serves as the Derby–Burton road. Northward it led through the vicinity of Chesterfield to Templeborough, between Sheffield and Rotherham. Another road no longer in existence led to Buxton (*Aquae Arnemetiae*) and a third led towards Ashbourne. Yet another was directed to the Trent–Derwent confluence, and as far as Draycott this forms part of one of the present-day routes from Derby to Nottingham. From Leicester (*Ratae*) the Fosse Way, which is still a major highway, led to Lincoln, where it joined the Ermine Street and the King's Street. South of Lincoln, to within a few miles of Ancaster, the Ermine Street is disused, although the King's Street survives as the existing road (A.15) to Sleaford. North of Lincoln the Ermine Street (A.15) continues in use for a distance of 16 miles, but the road branching from it which led west–north–west to cross the Trent at Littleborough (*Segelocum*) has long been abandoned. The road from Lincoln to Wragby (A.158) follows the course of the Roman route to Horncastle on the site of *Banovallum*.

The fact that so much of the road system has been brought into being in later times is shown by the following Table, indicating the proportion of Roman highways followed by the existing routes radiating from the principal centres:

Table XLII

Centre	No. of radial roads (Class A)	No. of radial roads of Roman origin
Leicester ..	9	2
Derby ..	9	3
Nottingham ..	10	0
Lincoln ..	7	5

It will be seen that Nottingham, mainly the product of medieval and modern times, stands in particular contrast to Lincoln, one of the leading urban centres in the Roman period.

Apart from the major centres a number of lesser route foci and nodal points are to be found within the regional network. These include Mansfield, Chesterfield, Retford, Worksop, Grantham and Newark, together with Ashbourne, at the southern extremity of the Peak District uplands. The extension of coal-mining into central Nottinghamshire since 1920 has largely been responsible for the increasing importance of Ollerton as a focal point of modern roads.

The turnpikes

Apart from the survival of some of the Roman highways, the present system of roads originated mainly from ancient tracks, medieval pack-horse routes and innumerable local parish roads which, after the introduction of the Statute of 1555, were maintained by labour supplied from each parish. The parochial basis of highway management operated until the first quarter of the 18th century where its dismal shortcomings, especially as regards through-routes, were steadily reduced by the development of the Turnpike Trusts. The turnpike, however, did not supplant the system of statute labour, but supplemented it, choosing in the vast majority of cases existing roads for improvement. Among the earliest routes to be turnpiked was a stretch of the Great North Road from Grantham through Newark to Markham Moor under an Act of 1725–26. About the same time the road from Leicester to Loughborough was turnpiked and from the latter town, following Acts of 1737 and 1738, the roads to Derby and Nottingham were similarly brought under Turnpike Trusts.

The period 1750–80 saw a considerable increase in turnpikes, especially within the area bounded by Nottingham and Derby in the south and Mansfield and Chesterfield in the north. This was the area of growing industrial activity based on coal-mining and iron-working over which expanding traffic made increasing demands upon communications. The turnpikes emphasised the importance of Nottingham as a regional focus of highways and of Mansfield, the second town of Nottinghamshire in size, as a county market-centre having close contacts with the industrial districts along the Nottinghamshire–Derbyshire border.

Two further points relating to the 'turnpike period' of road development should be noted. Firstly, since many routes led across the Trent it was inevitable that roads converged upon traditional crossing-places, whether by ferry or by bridge. Only at Nottingham, Newark and Burton were bridges to be found, all of these being of medieval origin. The turnpike period therefore saw the bridging of the Trent at several of the more important ferry points. Upstream from Nottingham, Wilden ferry was superseded by the Cavendish bridge in 1758 and Sawley ferry by the Harrington bridge in 1788. Below Newark the Trent was bridged at Gainsborough in 1787 and at Dunham in 1830. Between Nottingham and Newark, a stretch of over 20 miles no bridge existed until that at Gunthorpe was built in 1873. For this structure some of the stone from the medieval bridge at Nottingham was used, the latter having been replaced by the modern Trent Bridge a year or two earlier.

Secondly, as was shown by the late Arthur Cossons, a local historian, the process of turnpiking was often related to the character of the ground. Over damp clay lands, as in east Nottinghamshire and much of Leicestershire, the bad condition of earlier roads provided a strong case for improvement under the Trusts; whereas on drier, firmer ground, such as that afforded by the Bunter Sandstone surface of central Nottinghamshire, roads were more easily maintained and at much lower cost. Many such roads were turnpiked either much later or not at all. A striking instance of this contrast is provided by the Great North Road between Newark and Bawtry. As already mentioned the section from Newark to a point just beyond Markham

Moor, crossing a tract of medium-heavy clay country, was turnpiked at an early date. From Markham Moor as far as the low-lying ground approaching Bawtry, the road traversed the outcrop of Bunter Sandstone. On this section the portion from Barnby Moor to Bawtry was turnpiked much later, while the section between Markham Moor and Barnby Moor across the driest part of the sandstone was never turnpiked, though this was partly because the route itself was later diverted through Retford.

Modern roads and improvements

During the era of motor transport, which may be said to date effectively from the time of the first World War, great improvements have been made, if all too slowly, to the roads within the Nottingham region. Besides improvements and general modernisation, however, several new routes have been developed. One of these, which resulted from the reconstruction in the early 'twenties of an ancient road leading northwards from Nottingham through Ollerton to the Great North Road near Bawtry, provided the city with a much-needed direct route to the north. This road (A.614) runs for almost 40 miles, through parts of Sherwood Forest, unimpeded by built-up areas. Another new route was provided by the restoration of an old track (Bridgford Street) leading from the Fosse Way to the Trent at Gunthorpe. With a new bridge at Gunthorpe (1929) rendered free from tolls, this route which joined the Ollerton road (A.614) enabled northbound traffic from Leicester along the Fosse to avoid passing through Nottingham. By the end of 1964 the Nottingham–Derby road (A.52) had been re-aligned and largely rebuilt to meet the heavy demands of inter-city as well as long-distance traffic. Substantial improvements have also been made to the Great North Road itself in the past few years by the construction of the Grantham and Newark by-passes and by a re-alignment of the route direct from Markham Moor to Blyth at the southern end of the Doncaster by-pass, thus completely avoiding Retford. This modification represents a reversion to the course taken by the road during the turnpike period. The qualitative changes, moreover, involving widening and the introduction of dual carriageways have brought the greater part of the A.1 to the standard of a motorway.

In Nottingham itself, from the standpoint of both local and regional circulation, by far the greatest development, undertaken in stages since the 'twenties, has been the provision of a western ring-road related to a new bridge over the Trent. The ring-road, around what was at the time the periphery of the city, is composed of Valley Road (1925), Western Boulevard (1932), Middleton Boulevard (1928) and Clifton Boulevard (1938). From the approaches to the new bridge on the extreme south to the Mansfield Road at the northern end, this route affords some five miles of dual carriageway, mostly of 120 feet width. The new Clifton bridge, opened in 1958, is in fact incomplete and when funds are available it will be converted to double its present width. Meanwhile, the approach road on the south side has been extended as far as the junction of the Loughborough and Melton Mowbray Roads, thus reducing the pressure of traffic through West Bridgford, apart from the initial purpose of relieving congestion at the old Trent bridge. Nottingham's importance as a regional centre for road passenger traffic is shown in Fig. 55.

Undoubtedly the most important contribution to modern road communications so far as the region is concerned, is the coming of the London–Yorkshire motorway. For not only is this a major national highway but its course along the axis of the coalfield, passing between Derby and Chesterfield to the west and Nottingham and Mansfield to the east, provides the densely-populated industrial belt with a new artery. Also it may well have a significant effect upon future industrial development and the settlement pattern in the area. In detail the route chosen for the motorway has been greatly affected by the need to avoid built-up areas wherever possible and this is especially the case north of the Trent. Even so, the crossing of innumerable roads and railways and the negotiation of relief features have presented a formidable problem of costs. The construction of the motorway is reminiscent of the difficulties which faced the builders of the Great Central railway through the region little more than 60 years ago. Indeed the words of L. T. C. Rolt, in describing the London–Birmingham section of the M.1, are particularly apt in this connection: 'no similar engineering work of comparable magnitude had been seen in England since the days of main line railway construction ended'.

The first section of the motorway, some 50 miles in length, from just south of Luton to a point near the Northamptonshire village of Crick, was opened in 1959. Work on the section through the East Midlands from Crick to the Doncaster by-pass, where the route joins the A.1, was begun in 1962. Progress was delayed partly because of a controversy over the route to be followed through Charnwood Forest in Leicestershire. The ultimate decision to carry the motorway through the Forest involved a climb to 700 feet, the highest altitude reached in its entire length. Northwards from Charnwood the road reaches the Trent floodplain at its widest extent, necessitating considerable embanking. It crosses the Trent at Sawley, just upstream from the old bridge. The new bridge, nearly 500 feet long, has a span of 126 feet over the river, together with smaller spans to accommodate flood water. This section of the M.1 will be completed in 1966.

Whatever may be the advantages to the region consequent upon the London–Yorkshire motorway, many other improvements to the road system are required and some of them, long overdue, are now urgent. Two outstanding deficiencies are the lack of a first-class motor road from Nottingham to Birmingham and a direct route from Nottingham (as well as one from Leicester) to the Lincolnshire coast. The present road to Birmingham through Castle Donington, Ashby-de-la-Zouch and Tamworth is totally inadequate and the considerably longer route *via* Derby and Burton is in some respects preferable. Summer holiday and weekend traffic to Skegness from Nottingham and other East Midland centres increases yearly and if the railway to this resort is eventually closed, as at present contemplated, the need for direct access

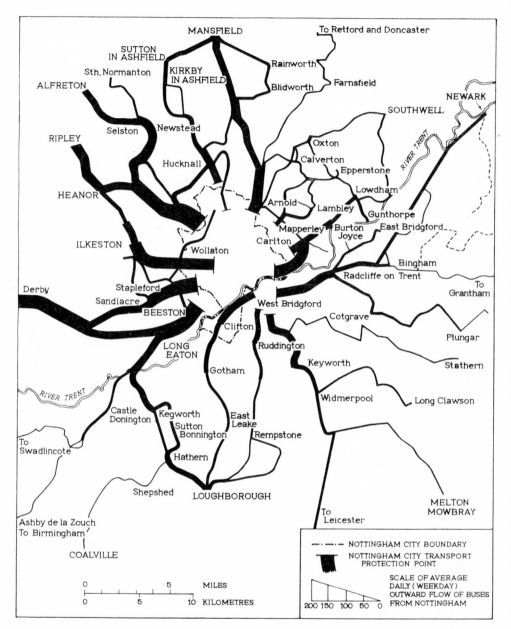

Fig. 55   The daily flow of buses from Nottingham, 1965

The map illustrates the importance of Nottingham as a centre for road passenger services

by a modern motor road will be all the greater. The existing alternative routes lie through Grantham, Sleaford or Lincoln. Once these towns are passed the roads thence onward are narrow and tortuous except for a few local improvements here and there. Any plan for regional development should include, as an item of high priority, a direct road from the industrial area to the coast.

RAILWAYS

Several pioneer railway enterprises originated in the area of the middle Trent and from among those which occurred within the triangle marked by the towns of Nottingham, Derby and Leicester, there ultimately arose the greatest of all British railway concerns, the Midland Railway.

Early railways

In the Derbyshire and Nottinghamshire mining districts, as in other parts of the country, the use of rails on which to run wagons over the short distance from mine, quarry or iron-furnace to the nearest wharf was common enough in the late 18th century. From about 1780 wooden rails gave way to iron rails and flanged wheels and soon the entire coal- and iron-producing area bristled with small railroads varying from half-a-mile to four or five miles long, serving as feeders to the canal system. One of the earliest uses of rails was for horse-drawn wagons on the tramway constructed in 1794 from Little Eaton, north of Derby, to the coal mines at Denby, about five miles away. At Little Eaton coal was transhipped to a branch of the Derby canal by means of which it could either reach Derby itself or be conveyed to the Trent. The engineer of the tramway was Benjamin Outram. The flanged rails were made at the Butterley Ironworks at Ripley, apart from the first delivery which was obtained from Joseph Butler of Chesterfield. The gauge inside the flanges was four feet four inches and the lengths of rail were fastened by iron spikes to blocks of stone placed longitudinally and not transversely as sleepers (see Plate II). The 'mule' or container portion of the wagon, carrying about two tons of coal, was lifted from the undercarriage and transferred to the canal boat, thus avoiding break of bulk. By 1800 there were no less than 12 such lines linking various coal and iron works with the Cromford canal; while many others led to points on the Erewash and Nottingham canals. The first line of this kind to cover a greater distance and then to become a true railway in the modern sense, was projected in 1813 from Mansfield to Pinxton wharf on the Erewash canal. Completed in 1819, the Mansfield–Pinxton Railway was soon extended by a one-and-a-half mile branch to Codnor ironworks. At first horse traction was used, with gravity playing its part on the steep incline between Pinxton and Kirkby. When acquired by the Midland Railway in 1849 the line was converted to the standard gauge and steam locomotives introduced. Though primarily built to convey coal and iron to Mansfield, local stone was moved in the opposite direction, including some used for building the Houses of Parliament at Westminster. Passenger traffic was introduced in 1832.

The year 1832 was indeed a momentous one so far as railway history in the East Midlands is concerned. For also in this year the Leicester–Swannington line, built to provide Leicester with cheap coal from the Leicestershire collieries (Bagworth, Ibstock and Long Lane) only 16 miles distant, was completed. This was the first line in the region to be worked by steam locomotives and, like the Mansfield–Pinxton venture it soon began to carry passengers. So alarmed were the colliery owners of the Erewash valley at this threat to their market in Leicester, which they had hitherto supplied by means of the Soar Navigation, that at a meeting held at the Sun Inn, Eastwood, on 16th August, they resolved to connect their pits with Leicester by railway by extending the Mansfield–Pinxton line southwards across the Trent. This was accomplished in 1840.

The meeting at Eastwood was in reality the birth of the later Midland Railway, for the project to which it gave rise became part of a much larger scheme for linking Derby and Nottingham with Birmingham and with Leicester and London *via* Rugby. Meanwhile another line of unique character had been constructed. This was the Cromford and High Peak Railway which followed a difficult route across the Derbyshire hills from Cromford wharf on the Cromford canal to reach the Peak Forest canal at Whaley Bridge whence navigation was available to the Mersey. Begun in 1825 and completed in 1831, this line was 34 miles in length and was worked by stationary winding engines on the steep inclines (one in eight at Cromford) and by horses on the other sections, but horses were eventually superseded by locomotives. At its highest point, near Parsley Hay, the track reached an altitude of 1,268 feet above sea-level, or 990 feet above its eastern terminal in the Derwent valley. Besides providing an outlet for lead and various quarry products from the Low Peak area, the promoters of this railway hoped it would convey Derbyshire coal into Lancashire and Cheshire and bring imported goods from Liverpool to the Midlands. Though some success was obtained, it was relatively shortlived, for after a few years the canals became outmoded and eventually the lead trade itself declined irreparably. To this situation the owners responded in 1846 by extending the line for two miles below Cromford wharf to join the Midland line which was then advancing along the Derwent valley from Ambergate. Thus, instead of serving as a link between waterways, the High Peak Railway became principally a feeder to a main line, and as such traffic was maintained until well into the 'sixties. For many years only the eastern portion of the line has continued in use. Limestone, crushed or in blocks, and silica bricks from Friden are still conveyed to the main lines, while quarry equipment and other supplies are carried in the opposite direction. Today both the Sheep Pastures incline at Cromford and the winding grass-grown track across the hills beyond are witness of a remarkable piece of early 19th-century engineering.

Routes to London

Much of the railway development in the region can be viewed from the standpoint of Nottingham's expanding needs over the past century. In particular the history of the city's connections with London is unique, for no other large town can claim to have had scheduled rail services to the capital on eight different routes at one time or another.

The two earliest routes to London were opened in 1839 and 1840 respectively. The first followed immediately upon the completion of the Nottingham–Derby line, for later in the same year the Derby and Birmingham Junction Railway reached Hampton-in-Arden (Hampton Junction) on the London–Birmingham main line. The next year saw the Midland Counties line from Derby and Nottingham to Leicester extended to Rugby, also on the London–Birmingham line. Thus in quick succession two routes, both using the London and North Western track to Euston, came into existence. Naturally passengers and goods from Nottingham preferred the shorter one *via* Rugby. As traffic mounted, however, delays and frustration at Rugby increased, for of course the London and North Western gave priority to movement on its own line between London, Birmingham, Lancashire and Scotland. Eventually the Midland Company, inheritor of the Midland Counties and the North Midland, built a line in 1857 from Leicester through Bedford to Hitchin on the Great Northern main line from King's Cross and obtained running powers over the latter. This was the third, and so far the shortest, route to the capital.

Just as the London and North Western held the mastery at Rugby, so did the Great Northern at Hitchin and in time a similar intolerable situation developed so far as Midland traffic was concerned. A solution was not reached until the Midland line was extended from Bedford through Luton and St. Alban's to St. Pancras in 1868. The fourth route to London was followed 12 years later by a fifth, this time a Midland alternative, largely to meet increasing demands at Nottingham. Traffic between Kettering, Leicester and northward through Trent had so outgrown the capacity of one pair of tracks that, to avoid doubling the route, it was decided to build a line from Kettering to Nottingham *via* Melton Mowbray. Thus by 1880 Nottingham secured a direct route to London on the Midland system. Long before this, however, an entirely different approach to the capital had been achieved. This had resulted from the opening of the Nottingham–Grantham line in 1850 by a company called the Ambergate, Nottingham, Boston and Eastern Counties Railway. Despite its grandiloquent title it never reached Ambergate or Boston but at Grantham it met the main Great Northern line from King's Cross to the north (1852) and eventually the Great Northern itself took over the Nottingham–Grantham section. This made the sixth route to London. Following a famous incident when a Great Northern locomotive ran into Nottingham Midland station and was impounded, the Great Northern built its own separate terminal, known as the Low Level station. The station building, quite small but impressive in appearance, can still be seen and is now used as a railway parcels depot.

For many years bookings to London were available from the Nottingham Low Level station on a long and leisurely route, opened in 1879, which left the Grantham line near Bingham and traversed the Vale of Belvoir and the Leicestershire hunting country to Market Harborough and Northampton (Great Northern and London and North Western Joint Railway) and thence to London by the London and North Western. Not surprisingly few people appear to have patronised this route.

Finally, at the turn of the century, long after the main lines of the national system had been laid, came the last flourish of the Victorian railway builders. This was Sir Edward Watkin's plan to extend the Manchester, Sheffield and Lincolnshire Railway to London. In 1897 this company became part of the Great Central Railway. With large new stations at Sheffield, Nottingham and Leicester, the Great Central line *via* Rugby and Aylesbury reached its terminus at Marylebone in 1898 for goods traffic and the following year for passengers. Although this was a bold project, splendidly constructed and operated by superb locomotive power, the line was extremely costly to build and was to prove an unprofitable venture. While it failed as a competitor to the Midland, the Great Central nevertheless rendered valuable public service in the Nottingham area. To cite but one example, it afforded an alternative fast passenger route to London, including the 'Master Cutler' expresses from Sheffield which called at Nottingham and Leicester until they were routed through Grantham a few years ago. At the present time, moreover, during the process of nationalisation and closures under the Beeching proposals, it is particularly relevant to mention the additional far-reaching aims of Watkin's Great Central project. For Watkin sought to carry his line from Sheffield not only to London but on to the coast at Dover and thence by a Channel Tunnel to the continent, a scheme which he actually promoted.

Coal and industrial traffic

In the vicinity of Nottingham the pattern of early railway development was strongly influenced by the growing needs of industry, especially coal, iron and engineering, while the actual routes were closely determined by the easy gradients afforded by the Trent and its tributary valleys. The first line of all, linking Nottingham with Derby (1839), was built along the floodplains of the Trent and lower Derwent, while its extensions a few years later to Birmingham in one direction and to Leicester in the other, also utilised the Trent valley as far as Burton and Newark respectively. The important north–south route between Leicester and Leeds, a little to the west of Nottingham, followed the Soar and Erewash valleys, intersecting the Nottingham–Derby line at Trent Junction. The station built at this junction, like that at Hellifield in Yorkshire, served no centre of population but became a prominent focus of traffic on the Midland system, just as Trent Lock, a few hundred yards away, had been a focus of navigation for the Trent and Grand Union system during the canal period (Fig. 57). The nearby town of Long Eaton, which developed later, is served by a station on the Erewash valley line.

At Nottingham itself the Leen valley, along which early industrial development took place, afforded a natural route northwards through several colliery districts to Mansfield. From the Leen valley, moreover, the line from London to Nottingham *via* Melton Mowbray, by following the old Nottingham canal, reached the Erewash at Trowell to join the main route to Chesterfield, Sheffield and Leeds.

In detail the railway pattern of the Nottingham area cannot be fully understood without reference to the geographical position of the city in relation to the aims and policy of the great companies, chiefly the Midland and the Great Northern, who promoted this form of transport. By the middle of last century Nottingham was connected to the west with Derby, the headquarters and stronghold of the Midland Railway, and to the east with Grantham on the trunk line of Great Northern. From this time onwards, as coal production from the Nottinghamshire and Derbyshire field steadily increased, both companies, along with others of lesser importance, sought to convey the output to various parts of the home market, especially to the south and the east and above all to London. For this purpose the Midland was better placed and its lines along the Leen and Erewash valleys gave it an early lead. Eventually in 1878 the Great Northern opened a line passing round the eastern and northern outskirts of Nottingham, thence westwards from Kimberley to Derby (Friargate Station) and on to Egginton Junction. From this line branches were sent up the Erewash to Pinxton and along the Leen to Mansfield, thus promoting intense competition with the Midland. Later still the Great Central also penetrated the coalfield, with its line from Nottingham to Sheffield serving collieries in the area between Mansfield and Chesterfield. All these railways with their junctions and sidings and their links to innumerable mines resulted in a dense network of metals being laid upon an increasingly industrialised landscape. So far as passenger services were concerned the network afforded several instances of over-capitalisation by the provision of unnecessary alternative or parallel routes. Thus from 1900 until the railway re-grouping in 1923, over the distance of 14 miles between Nottingham and Mansfield, there were three different lines with a total of 26 stations and halts.

Since most of the coal output was to be directed southward, large-scale movement came to be organised through two huge marshalling yards. These large installations, ceaselessly active by day and night, one to the east and the other to the west of Nottingham, epitomise the city's role as the principal outlet for the great coalfield. The Colwick yards (formerly Great Northern) lie adjacent to the Grantham line and occupy almost the entire width of the Trent floodplain. The Toton yards (formerly Midland), which are even larger, extend for well over a mile along the Erewash valley just north of Long Eaton.

In the course of time, as mining operations spread eastwards into central Nottinghamshire, further branch railways became necessary in order to connect the new collieries with the existing main lines. During the years following the first World War a number of lines were constructed in the Sherwood Forest area east of Mansfield. Some of these joined the Mansfield–Newark railway and others the Mansfield–Lincoln railway, which gave access to the Great Northern main line at Dukeries Junction. The latest of these developments took place after the second World War, with lines from Calverton colliery to the Leen valley (1952), from Bevercotes colliery to Ollerton on the Mansfield–Lincoln line (1960) and from Cotgrave colliery, the newest of all the post-war mines, to the Nottingham–Grantham line (1962).

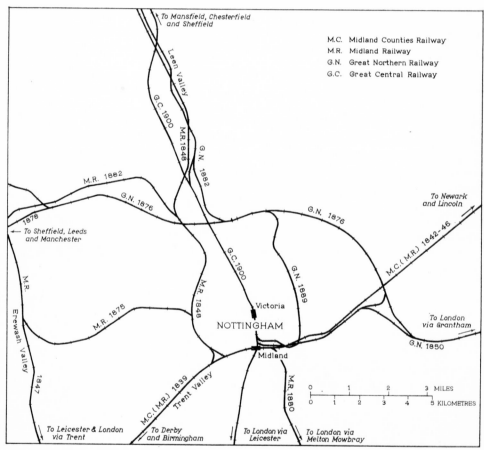

Fig. 56 The growth of railways in the Nottingham district

It was not only the coal trade which demanded the services of railway transport. From the earliest years of main-line construction in the region, railways played an equally important role in the growth of the iron industry. George Stephenson's North Midland line from Leeds to Derby, opened in May 1840, was itself the means by which one of the famous ironworks was started. For when the tunnel piercing the Rother–Amber watershed at Clay Cross was built, revealing a band of ironstone, adjacent to coal seams, the site was chosen for the Clay Cross Company's blast furnaces. Butterley (founded over 50 years previously), Codnor Park, Stanton (1846) and other works exploiting the Derbyshire clayband iron all profited by their proximity to the railways. Not only did the latter widen the market for iron products but railway construction and the demand for railway equipment in all parts of the country stimulated the output of iron.

By the 1870s ore from Leicestershire and Northamptonshire began to supersede the use of Derbyshire ironstone as supplies of the latter approached exhaustion and more distant railway connections assumed a new importance. Again it was the Midland which provided the essential links, not only by carrying the ore to the Derbyshire ironworks but by transporting the coal and coke from that area to the blast-furnace plants which were established on the orefields at Kettering, and Wellingborough, and later on at Corby and Holwell (Melton Mowbray). With the extension of the Erewash line in 1863 to join the Derby–Leeds route at Clay Cross, the two Midland main lines, one *via* Leicester and the other *via* Nottingham, which met at Kettering, formed a major axis for the movement of coal and iron from one extremity of the East Midlands to the other, from the northernmost ironworks at Staveley and Sheepbridge, near Chesterfield, to the most southerly, at Wellingborough.

Like coal and iron, the heavier forms of engineering were equally dependent upon railways. In consequence many firms chose a railside location, especially where suitably flat ground was also available as was the case with towns situated in the principal valleys. While this pattern of industrial development is common enough elsewhere, impressive examples occur in the area around Nottingham. At Nottingham itself the main industrial belt follows the railways along the edge of the Trent floodplain and along the Leen. In Derby a continuous succession of works, mainly of engineering, some four miles long, adjoins the main Midland line in the Derwent valley. The pattern is repeated on a smaller scale at Beeston, Newark and Grantham and not the least spectacular case is that at Lincoln where industrial development became concentrated in the Witham Gap following the arrival of the railways of the Manchester, Sheffield and Lincolnshire (1851) and the Great Northern (1854).

Reshaping the railway pattern

In the Nottingham area, as in some other parts of the country, the re-shaping of the railway system in response to prevailing economic conditions actually began soon after the major grouping of companies which took place in accordance with the Railway Act of 1921. Under the new arrangement the traffic of the region was shared by the London, Midland and Scottish and the London and North Eastern systems. By mutual agreement a number of branch lines and short connecting links, chiefly on the coalfield, were eventually closed to passenger traffic owing to unprofitable working. Quite apart from the rising competition from local bus services, alternative routes often existed so that one line or other was in fact redundant. Examples of closures falling within this category were the former Great Northern line from Nottingham to Derby (Friargate) and Egginton Junction; the Midland Railway line from Little Eaton to Ripley and Butterley and that from the Erewash valley (Langley Mill) to Heanor and Ripley; also a few short links within the dense network serving the Mansfield, Shirebrook and Chesterfield district. In less heavily industrialised areas the Mansfield–Southwell section of the Mansfield to Newark line *via* Rolleston Junction was closed to passenger traffic in 1929 and that from Derby to Ashby-de-la-Zouch was closed the following year.

On the short line which ran from Trent Lane Junction (on the Great Northern to Grantham) northwards to the Great Northern line to Derby and known as the Nottingham Suburban line, passenger traffic at intermediate stations (Thorneywood, St. Ann's Well, Sherwood) ceased as long ago as 1916, though the movement of freight continued. 'Through' services for passengers between Nottingham and the Leen valley were operated until 1931. The southern end of the line at Trent Lane Junction, including a bridge, was destroyed by enemy bombs in May 1941 and thereafter until 1951 only the northern, i.e. Thorneywood–Daybrook, section was worked.

After the war, passenger services were further reduced by the closing of lines in some of the more sparsely populated districts. The branch line to Wirksworth from Duffield on the main Derby–Manchester route was closed in 1947 and the short line from Ambergate to Pye Bridge, which provided one of the links between the Derwent and Erewash main routes, was closed the same year, though in this instance the closure involved an industrialised area. The process continued after nationalisation (1948) and in 1953 the former Great Northern line from Melton Mowbray to Newark *via* Bottesford Junction and the branch from Stathern to Saxondale Junction on the Nottingham–Grantham line were closed. Two years later, services on the Lincoln–Chesterfield line were discontinued, although the section from Shirebrook to Chesterfield (Market Place) had ceased to operate in 1951. In the extreme west the Ashbourne–Buxton line was closed in 1954 except for the portion between Hartington and Buxton which remained open for the movement of limestone and lime. It is an interesting reflection of conditions in the Peak District, however, that British Railways are under obligation to run trains on this line in the event of the alternative road route becoming completely impassable because of ice or snow. Still more recently, the short section remaining open between Rolleston Junction and Southwell on the Mansfield–Newark line was closed in 1959 save for goods trains.

Various lengths of track carrying both passenger and goods traffic, within the intricate pattern of lines serving the Leen valley were also closed during the 'fifties and among these a former section of the Great Northern line, that between Awsworth and Pinxton, was closed entirely. Moreover, the former Great Northern line from Netherfield and Colwick to the Leen valley, which formed part of the Great Northern route from Nottingham to Derby, was closed to both passenger and goods traffic in 1960 when the Mapperley tunnel was declared unsafe. The section from Daybrook to Leen Valley Junction, i.e. to the west of the tunnel, was closed to freight in 1964, but to the east of the tunnel, the line remains open as far as Gedling colliery for the despatch of coal.

In 1953 British Railways embarked upon a general plan of modernisation and among the changes which ensued were the substitution of diesel multiple unit trains for steam locomotives on local services, the concentration of marshalling yards and a reduction in the number of goods depots. By 1960, however, it was apparent that modernisation measures alone were insufficient to reduce the mounting losses incurred by the railways and that more radical changes were necessary. As a result the Government initiated under the direction of Dr. R. Beeching an investigation into the steps required for remodelling of the railway system and the means by which the modernisation programme could be adapted to the new shape. The Beeching Report, entitled *The Reshaping of British Railways*, appeared in 1963 and among its drastic recommendations were proposals for a further curtailment of services in the Nottingham area.

In Nottingham the proposal to close Victoria Station and to concentrate passenger traffic at the Midland Station is now on the way to being implemented. Already a number of services have been withdrawn. By the construction in 1965 of a link between the old Midland and Great Northern lines, where the respective tracks run alongside each other at Netherfield, traffic from Grantham can now be directed to the Midland Station and in the summer of 1965 trains carrying holiday-makers to Skegness, formerly using Victoria as the terminal, did in fact leave from the Midland. The proposal to suspend passenger services to Skegness by eventually closing the branch line from Boston which provides the only rail access to the resort, has, however, given rise to much concern both at Skegness and in Nottingham and neighbouring towns from which so many summer visitors originate. Another issue causing public concern relates to the proposal to discontinue passenger services on the former Great Central line from Nottingham to Rugby through Loughborough and Leicester. This proposal is being strongly challenged by numerous objectors through the Transport Users' Consultative Committee. Should the line ultimately be closed, it may be necessary to keep open the section from East Leake to Nottingham for the movement of gypsum and plaster products. Equally, if Victoria Station is closed, existing tracks passing through it may be retained for freight traffic.

In the meantime the process of modernisation goes on. Improvements to the large marshalling yards at Colwick and Toton, together with the closing of the Beeston yards in 1965, have enabled the two former to handle greater quantities of coal than ever before. The use of diesel locomotives for all main-line trains, whether passenger or freight, has resulted in the construction at Toton of a locomotive depot for maintenance, heavy and light repairs, and fuelling. Designed to service no less than 300 diesel locomotives, it is one of the largest in Europe, and much larger than the other main depot at Cricklewood. This installation reflects the importance of the Nottingham–Derby area as a focus of railway operations in the eastern half of the country, for in accordance with technical strategy, the eastern half will rely more and more upon the use of diesel traction, while the main routes of the western half will rely more upon electrification. Thus along the Euston–Manchester trunk route electric locomotive depots at Willesden, Rugby and Crewe form the counterparts of Cricklewood and Toton.

WATERWAYS

Although there are documentary references to the early use of the Trent for navigation from the time of the Domesday Survey onwards, they are too brief and infrequent to provide a full picture of the river as a routeway. In any case, in the Nottingham area, the main overland routes of the early Middle Ages were directed more or less north and south across the river, so that fords and bridge-points were more significant than the Trent itself. Nevertheless, so far as Nottingham is concerned, two of these early references are of interest. In a charter granted to the town by Henry II in 1155, one of the clauses insisted that the river must be kept clear for the passage of boats for a width of five and a half yards (one perch) on each side of midstream; and much later, in the 16th century, the *Middleton MSS* (page 175) show that Sir Percival Willoughby, the owner of collieries at Wollaton, just west of Nottingham, had a fleet of barges on the Trent which he leased to a contractor who shipped the coal downstream.

The Trent and the early industrial age

From the end of the 17th century onwards, through a series of Acts of Parliament concerned with river improvement and the construction of canals, we gain a clearer idea of the importance of the Trent and of the trade carried upon it along the 117-miles stretch from Burton to the Humber. In 1698 a scheme was devised to make the Trent navigable as far as Burton, but Nottingham, viewing this as a challenge to her long-held monopoly as the head of navigation, reacted strongly and threatened to prevent traffic from passing beyond Trent Bridge by means of chains across the river. An Act of 1699 in fact authorised the provision of a navigable channel between Burton and Wilden ferry (Shardlow) although this project was not undertaken for some years. By an Act of 1772 the construction of a weir and a lock at Newark enabled boats to use the eastern arm of the Trent on which the town stands instead of the western arm which had served hitherto as the recognised channel. In particular the Trent Navigation Act of 1783 marked an important stage in the growth of the river as a commercial highway at a time when the demand for transport was rapidly expanding.

Under its provisions the Company of Proprietors of the Trent Navigation was founded and given responsibility for improving and maintaining the river in return for tolls levied on all vessels trading along its course from Shardlow to Gainsborough, a distance of nearly 70 miles. This company was really the forerunner of the modern Trent Navigation Company which continued in existence until the inland waterways were nationalised in 1948. The shares of the Company of Proprietors were of £50 but no one could hold more than four and it is interesting to note that the Nottingham Corporation, jealous of the town's position in relation to river trade (it had strenuously opposed the improvement at Newark) took its full quota of four. The new Company undertook to provide a channel of sufficient depth for boats carrying 30 to 40 tons. To do this required a minimum of 24 inches at the principal fords (Sawley, Wilford, Holme and Gunthorpe) and 27 inches at the shallowest places elsewhere. As a result dredging was undertaken, several weirs were built and a few cuts were made to avoid the worst shoals. The Company appears to have done its best to meet its obligations and with an ever-increasing volume of trade on the river, it prospered.

It was estimated that in 1790 total cargoes moved on the Trent above Gainsborough amounted to nearly 90,000 tons and that dues on 75,000 tons were paid to the Company at Nottingham. Reporting in 1793, William Jessop, the Company's engineer, claimed that for 63 miles out of the total stretch of nearly 70 miles the channel was three feet or more in depth; but there were several dangerous shallows and near the Soar confluence the depth was only 21 inches. Jessop urged the importance of dredging and the need for further weirs and locks, but work of this kind was accomplished only in the course of many years.

Well before the advent of the Company of Proprietors, navigation was extended along some of the tributary rivers. The Derwent was made navigable as far as Derby in 1721 and by 1767 the Soar was canalised as far as Loughborough. Even earlier, despite protestations in Nottingham, traders at Burton, situated relatively far up the river, began to send their boats down to Gainsborough and back. Thus organised river traffic began to be extended upstream from Nottingham.

At this time the use of water transport for the conveyance of coal to both local and distant markets from the Derbyshire and Nottinghamshire mining districts provided the greatest impetus to the growth of river traffic. By 1800 the majority of craft plying on the Trent were engaged in the coal trade. Boats having a capacity of 30 to 40 tons carried regular shipments to Nottingham, Newark and Gainsborough and even as far as the Humber, some being used to bring return cargoes of corn, malt, stone and timber. Besides the coal trade a notable item of traffic in the late 18th century was the transport of ale from Burton, either coastwise to London or as an export to Europe, chiefly to Baltic countries. At Burton several breweries which were to become renowned, Worthington (1744), Wilson (Allsopp) and Bass (1777) had agents in Gainsborough and Hull who shipped the ale to Danzig and St. Petersburg and arranged for return cargoes.

The canals

With the building of canals, which afforded more direct access to the Trent from the mining districts and growing industrial centres than did most of the navigable tributaries, traffic increased still further. By means of the canals, moreover, the Trent was linked with and became part of a national system of inland waterways. This was largely achieved by the completion of the Trent–Mersey or Grand Trunk Canal (1766–77) and its connection with the Severn at Stourport by means of the Stafford and Worcester canal, together with the link made *via* Leicester to the Grand Junction canal which gave access to London. The Trent–Mersey project had been urged by Liverpool merchants as early as 1755 and was in turn supported by Josiah Wedgwood in the Potteries and by Matthew Boulton in Birmingham. The canal itself, 93 miles long, left the Trent at a point between Sawley and Shardlow near the Derwent confluence and not at Burton as at first intended. Burton was given access to the canal, however, by the short Bond End Cut (1776).

Sanctioned in 1771 and completed five years later, the Chesterfield canal served to connect Chesterfield, Worksop and Retford with the tidal section of the Trent at West Stockwith. Along it, coal, as well as iron from the Chesterfield furnaces, and stone and lead from the Derbyshire hills moved to the river, while cargoes of grain, foodstuffs and timber were carried in the opposite direction. In the year 1789, out of a total traffic of 74,000 tons, 42,000 tons of coal and nearly 4,000 tons of lead were shipped to the Trent. Next came the Erewash canal (1777–79) which led northward from Trent Lock, near Sawley, along the Erewash valley to Langley Bridge, a distance of nearly 12 miles. This was built by local colliery owners to expedite the movement of their coal. Similarly a branch about four and a half miles long called the Nutbrook canal (1793) provided an outlet for coal from the Shipley district. It should also be noted that some years earlier, in 1762, the ancient Fossdyke, connecting the Trent with the Witham at Lincoln, had been improved by raising the water level to provide a deeper channel. Thus, with the construction of the Chesterfield and Erewash canals, Lincoln was able to obtain waterborne coal from Derbyshire.

Soon after 1790 the Cromford canal was opened, continuing the course of the Erewash canal beyond Langley Bridge and leading across to the Derwent valley at Ambergate, thence following the Derwent itself to Cromford. This important waterway afforded yet another route for moving coal while it also enabled lead from the Wirksworth district to be brought southwards to the Trent. For many years it was a vital factor in the growth of the famous Butterley Ironworks at Ripley and it is interesting to recall that the sections of the Vauxhall Bridge over the Thames which were cast at Butterley in 1816, were conveyed by the canal to the Trent and finally shipped from Gainsborough.

The building of the Derby canal (1795) which joined the Trent–Mersey at Swarkeston enabled navigation along the tortuous stretch of the lower Derwent to be superseded. From Derby it led eastwards to reach the Erewash canal and then afforded a direct means of bringing coal to the town. A short extension northwards from Derby served as an outlet for the stone quarries at Little Eaton.

In the same period parallel developments took place at Nottingham. Begun in 1789 and completed three years later, the Nottingham canal led westwards to the Erewash and followed the east side of the valley as far as Langley Bridge, where it joined the Cromford canal. Not only did it provide another route for conveying the riches of the Derbyshire coalfield but it served to stimulate output from the Trowell and Cossall district, only five miles from Nottingham itself. To effect its junction with the Trent, the Nottingham canal was connected to the regulated channel of the Leen, a small tributary which made its outfall immediately below Trent Bridge. A short extension to Sneinton Hermitage, of which no trace exists today, served the eastern part of the town. On the Trent itself above Nottingham navigation had always been hampered by the shoals at Wilford. To avoid these, especially at a time when canal traffic was promoting a great increase in the use of the river, the Beeston canal (1795) was cut, leading from the Nottingham canal at Lenton and rejoining the Trent at Beeston. Thus for a short distance traffic was diverted from a persistently difficult stretch of river by means of a safe channel which has continued in use to the present day. A similar diversion, though of shorter length, to avoid the shoals near the Soar confluence, was provided by the making of the Cranfleet Cut at Trent Lock.

With Nottingham maintaining its position as a focus of water transport, a scheme for linking it with the agricultural areas to the east was brought to fruition by the completion of the Grantham canal (1793–97), some 30 miles in length. Starting from the right-bank of the Trent at a point almost opposite the entrance to the Nottingham canal, this waterway followed a winding course around the margin of the Vale of Belvoir to reach the Witham valley at Grantham. Coal could now reach the farming areas far more readily than hitherto and agricultural produce could as easily find its way to the industrial centres across the Trent. Much of the traffic in each direction passed through Nottingham.

The period of canal construction and of many improvements made to the river itself was chiefly between 1775 and 1798. It was this short span of 23 years which witnessed the 'canal mania' so far as the middle Trent region is concerned. From this brief survey of the period certain general points emerge. In the first place, once the Trent and its associated waterways became linked with the main system, chiefly by means of the Grand Trunk and Grand Union connections, traffic on the Trent itself steadily declined, for the canals offered more direct access to London and to other parts of the Midlands. Coal traffic was an exception, however, for shipments down-river to Gainsborough and Hull and coastwise to the Thames and other east coast ports continued to increase without setback until the railways were firmly established. In fact an additional impetus was given to the coal trade by the advent of steam vessels in 1814 on the lower Trent. Three years later a twice-weekly steamer service between Gainsborough, Newark and Nottingham was inaugurated. In 1816 some 940,000 tons of coal from Derbyshire mines and nearly 500,000 tons from Nottinghamshire were brought to the Trent. Although a proportion of this huge quantity was absorbed either locally in Nottingham and Derby or sent on by canal to Leicester and London, most of it was conveyed by river to Gainsborough and the Humber for coastwise distribution.

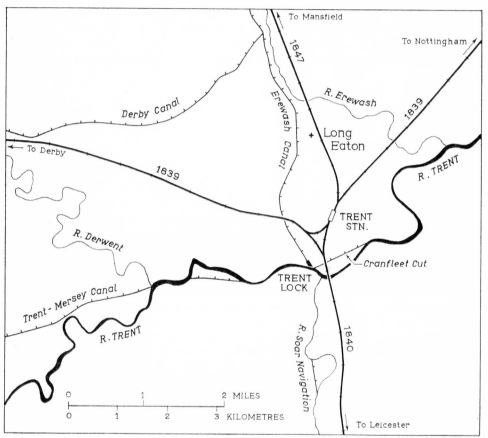

Fig. 57   Trent Lock (Waterways) and Trent Junction (Railways) as a communications focus

Another point to bear in mind is the prolonged inferiority of the navigable channel on certain sections of the Trent compared with the canals. On the latter a fixed depth was invariably maintained. The Trent–Mersey, for example, provided for craft carrying up to 25 tons, yet on portions of the river a load of only 10 to 12 tons was possible and in dry seasons even this had to be reduced. In this respect the dredging undertaken by the Company of Proprietors after 1783 was of major importance to all carriers.

Present-day Trent navigation

Present-day commercial navigation on the Trent extends from Shardlow, 13 miles upstream from Nottingham, to the Humber, a distance of almost 100 miles. From Shardlow to Gainsborough (68½ miles) the waterway falls under the jurisdiction of the British Transport Commission (Waterways) but beyond Gainsborough the controlling authority is the Humber Conservancy Board. In relation both to physical and economic conditions the stretch of river between Shardlow and Gainsborough may be divided into three sections. Upstream from Gainsborough as far as Cromwell Lock, four miles below Newark, the Trent is tidal and presents no special problems other than the maintenance of an adequate depth of channel. From Cromwell Lock to Nottingham the river in its natural condition has a comparatively sharp fall. In fact, over a 14-mile stretch between Holme Pierrepont and Fiskerton, the fall is 21 feet, giving a gradient of over 17 inches per mile. To provide for a modern waterway, with access to Nottingham at all seasons of the year, this difficulty has been overcome by the provision of a series of six locks and weirs at intervals between Nottingham and Newark. This channel, like that on the tidal reach, affords passage for standard Trent craft of 82 feet 6 inches length and 14 feet 6 inches beam. As a result of improvements consequent upon a flood prevention scheme recently undertaken by the Trent River Board just below Nottingham, boats of 140 feet length and 18 feet 6 inches beam can now reach the city terminals. A depth of six feet is maintained throughout. On the third section, that from Nottingham to Shardlow, the waterway is limited to what are termed upper Trent craft having maximum dimensions of 71 feet 6 inches by 14 feet 6 inches and 3 feet 6 inches draught. To reach Shardlow it is still necessary to use the Beeston canal and part of the Nottingham canal, both dating from the heyday of canals more than a century and a half ago, but there is now very little traffic on this section.

Profitable use of the Trent depends upon economic and technical conditions very different from those of former times. Essentially, waterborne cargoes are now moved on the river between terminal points from which road vehicles can undertake further distribution. Commercial navigation is in fact a product of the motor age. Loads are carried by diesel-powered barges and are transhipped at places organised to handle road haulage and operations are mostly independent of rail transport. At Nottingham, railway sidings, made available at one of the new river terminals in the 1930s, were abandoned in 1958. Traffic is virtually confined to the river, for most of the tributary canals are now disused and in some cases partially filled in. The Erewash canal as far as Ilkeston and the Soar navigation to Loughborough remain open but traffic on them is negligible. The Trent–Mersey canal can still be used by narrow boats. Nottingham has therefore reverted to its ancient role as head of river navigation, while Newark and Gainsborough are the only significant trading points downstream.

British Waterways own a fleet of nine diesel-powered vessels, each having a carrying capacity of about 120 tons, in addition to 20 'dumb', i.e. engineless, craft with a capacity varying from 100 to 130 tons. Normally one or two of the latter are towed by a powered vessel. All the craft are designed for the transport of general merchandise. At each of the off-loading points warehouses, together with transit sheds for short period storage, are found. These are located as follows:

Table XLIII

Off-loading point	Storage capacity (in tons)
Gainsborough	4,000
Newark	1,750
Nottingham (Wilford Street) ..	10,000
(Trent Lane) ..	10,500
(Meadow Lane) ..	4,250
Shardlow	2,250

Most of the traffic originates at Hull and the main movement is therefore upstream. At Hull, Goole and Grimsby river craft have direct access to ocean-going vessels from which bulky, non-perishable commodities such as grain, timber, pulp, strawboard, cattle-cake and tinned foodstuffs are transhipped. Other craft on the Trent are operated by independent carriers, the largest of these being the petrol tankers which carry oil in bulk from Saltend (Hull) and Killingholme (Lincolnshire) to storage tank depots owned by some of the principal oil companies at Colwick (Nottingham) and Torksey. There is also a much smaller storage depot at Newark. The movement of oil is in fact the outstanding feature of commercial traffic on the Trent and accounts for well over half the tonnage carried (other than sand and gravel). As a result Nottingham is the leading distributing centre for the East Midlands. Several companies convey general merchandise to Nottingham, as well as along the Fossdyke to Saxilby and Lincoln. Since 1963, moreover, some revival in the use of narrow boats has occurred, carrying timber from Boston to Nottingham and Leicester. Given a favourable tide the journey from Hull to Nottingham can be made in 24 hours. Oil-carrying craft, however, cannot convey a return load.

Downstream traffic is both smaller in volume and less regular in occurrence. It consists chiefly of relatively bulky manufactured goods such as hardware and machinery. Coal finds no place in the river trade, not even to supply the riverside electricity generating stations, for its shipment has long been in the hands of the railways. Coal, the source of power in the first industrial age, was once the outstanding commodity carried down the Trent but today the rival source of power, which is imported, must be conveyed up the river.

During recent years British Waterways have undertaken a considerable programme of modernization on the Trent. The locks below Nottingham have been converted to mechanised operation and equipped with sodium lighting and electric traffic signals.

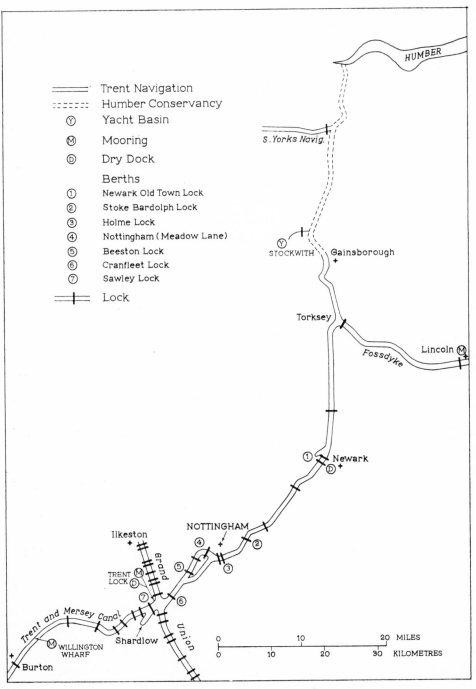

Fig. 58 The Trent Waterway today
(*By permission of British Waterways*)

Weirs have been reconstructed with steel piling and concrete infilling to give a greater depth of water in the river, enabling craft to load to full capacity at most periods of the year. Hazleford weir (300 feet long) was rebuilt in 1957; Cromwell weir in 1959, to replace the one breached by floods in 1955; Gunthorpe (375 feet) and Averham (1,000 feet) in 1960; Stoke (400 feet), Sawley (370 feet) and Beeston (520 feet) in 1962. Steel piling has also been used in places to protect the banks from erosion caused by the wash of passing craft. New workshops have been built at Newark, together with a two-berth dry dock. Constant dredging is necessary to maintain the channel and the sand and gravel removed in this way make an important contribution to the concrete-making industry. The amount dredged has increased from 184,000 tons in 1954 to 287,000 tons in 1964.

Table XLIV

The nature and quantity of commodities carried on the Trent in 1964

Commodity	*From*	*To*	*Tons*
BULK OIL	Humber	Torksey	112,000
		Colwick	170,400
		Newark	9,600
GRAIN AND FLOUR	Hull/Goole	Nottingham	15,000
		Newark	10,300
		Gainsborough	46,638
		Lincoln	11,900
FERTILISERS	Hull/Goole	Saxilby	19,700
GENERAL GOODS (chiefly paper, preserves, wire rods, timber, plywood, ale, strawboards and ferro silicon)	Hull/Goole	Nottingham	46,200
GENERAL GOODS	Nottingham	Hull/Goole	2,900
SAND AND GRAVEL	Lower Trent	Humber	491,700
	Middle Trent	Humber	45,400
STONE, SLAG AND CHALK	Various places		70,300

The future of our canals and inland waterways is a much-discussed question. It is common knowledge that most of the canals are both unsuited to modern needs and are, with some exceptions, totally uneconomic for commercial transport. As already mentioned, some canals, or sections thereof have already been closed. There remains the problem of their possible maintenance for other uses. Stretches of the Trent, like some of the canals, are used considerably by anglers, mainly for coarse-fishing. For pleasure-cruising the Trent is a popular river and even British Waterways operate one pleasure craft, the *Water Wanderer*, on the lower section and along the Fossdyke. The river supplies quantities of water for agricultural, industrial and power-station cooling purposes but for all of these uses the revenue obtained is insignificant. Along canals and rivers alike there are stretches which form attractive features in the rural scene and many would feel that they should be preserved for their amenity value alone. A recent report on the future of British Waterways (1964) suggests that portions of the old Trent–Mersey and Grand Union canals might fall into this category. Pending further consideration in official quarters the outcome is still uncertain.

AIRWAYS

Until very recently, air transport has played little part in the communication of the Nottingham region apart from a few regular services, together with charter flights, which were operated from the Derby airport at Burnaston. Yet Nottingham itself made an early start in providing for this form of transport, the municipal airport at Tollerton, opened in 1928, being the second in the country to receive a licence for this purpose. Until the outbreak of the second World War, when it was immediately requisitioned by the Air Ministry, this airport was operated by a private company organising charter services to London and other leading centres such as Birmingham, Hull and Grimsby, and, in the holiday season, to Skegness. Tollerton's use as a municipal airport, however, did not survive the war, despite its highly convenient location barely four miles from the city centre. Years later, an experimental service by helicopter between Nottingham, Leicester and Birmingham was also shortlived. Thus, apart from the limited services available at Derby, mainly to the Channel Islands, to reach London airport from Nottingham for international travel has entailed an overground journey of more than 50 miles to the Birmingham terminal at Elmdon. Nevertheless many passengers did so.

Not long ago a combined project for an East Midlands airport, sponsored by a group of local authorities comprising the Corporations of Nottingham and Derby, and the County Councils of Nottinghamshire, Derbyshire and Leicestershire, was proposed. Apart from Nottingham's interest in the scheme, strong support came from Derby, for the Burnaston airport, established in 1938, restricted to a grass landing strip, was becoming inadequate and for Derby Aviation Ltd. (now British Midland Airways), founded in 1949, improved facilities were becoming urgent. A consortium of local authorities was a novel means of promoting a regional airport. It proved equal to the task and the result must be counted as a notable achievement of local authority co-operation. The site chosen for the project was the former Royal Air Force station at Castle Donington, less than 10 miles from Derby and about the same distance from Nottingham. Loughborough is only five miles away and Leicester 15 miles. Apart from new buildings the airfield itself had to be entirely reconstructed. The main terminal building was erected under the CLASP system (see page 436). The concrete runway is 5,850 feet (1782 metres) long and can be extended to 7,400 feet and even more if required. The location of the East Midlands airport, which is at an elevation of 305 feet above sea-level and some 195 feet above the neighbouring Trent valley, is one of the most favourable in the country for road access, for it lies within a mile of the London–Yorkshire motorway (M.1), a similar distance from the London–Manchester trunk road (A.6) and the Nottingham–Birmingham road (A.453).

The airport became operational on 1st April 1965 and provides for internal and international traffic, both scheduled services and chartered flights. In the first six months 98,600 passengers were carried, compared with a predicted number of 75,000 and in terms of aircraft movement, instead of an estimated 750 per month over the same period, the actual number was well over 1,400. Regular connections throughout the winter are maintained with Belfast, Dublin, Glasgow, Leeds and Paris, with freight services only to Jersey and Guernsey. In summer the services are augmented and are extended to other continental countries. Freight traffic has developed rapidly, especially exports, which include manufactured goods from the region.

SELECTED REFERENCES

ROADS

Cossons, A. The Turnpike Roads of Nottinghamshire. *Historical Association Leaflet* No. 97 (1934).

Osborne, R. H. The London–Yorkshire Motorway: its route through the East Midlands. *East Midland Geographer* No. 13 (June 1960).

RAILWAYS

Birks, J. A. and Coxon, P. *An Account of Railway Development in the Nottinghamshire Coalfield.* Mansfield (1949) (published privately).

Edwards, K. C. The Nottingham and Derby Railway, 1839. *The Railway Gazette* (30th June 1939).

British Railways Board. *The Reshaping of British Railways.* H.M.S.O. (1963).

British Railways Board. *The Development of the Major Railway Track Routes.* London (1965).

WATERWAYS

Wood, A. C. The History of Trade and Transport on the River Trent. *Transactions of the Thoroton Society of Nottinghamshire* Vol. 54 (1950).

British Waterways Board. *The Future of British Waterways* (Interim Report). H.M.S.O. (1964).

ACKNOWLEDGMENTS

Grateful acknowledgment is due to the Divisional Manager, British Railways (London Midland Region), Nottingham, for information concerning rail traffic in the district. Similar acknowledgment is due to officers of the British Waterways Board (Northern Region) and to the Manager of the East Midlands Airport for their kind help.

Fig. 55 was compiled by G. T. Bloomfield and R. H. Osborne.

XX

POPULATION AND SETTLEMENT

AT the time of the first census in 1801 the distribution of population and settlement in Derbyshire, Nottinghamshire and the adjacent part of Lincolnshire still bore a fairly close resemblance to the pattern established by the Anglian and Danish colonization, although total numbers were, of course, much greater. Villages tended to be closer together in areas where natural conditions for cultivation and settlement had originally been most favourable, as in the Keuper Marl and Lower Lias country. Agricultural settlement was less dense on the Coal Measures, owing to their rather indifferent soils. Areas of very sparse settlement included the Bunter Sandstone country of Nottinghamshire, the gritstone moors of the Derwent basin (contrasting with the better-populated shale valleys), and those parts of the Carboniferous Limestone of Derbyshire where water-supply was scanty. In Lincolnshire the belt of limestone known as the 'Heath' was almost devoid of settlement and villages were strung out in a line at the foot of the Lincoln scarp or 'Edge'.

Enclosure of the common fields for pastoral farming had led to the reduction or disappearance of certain villages at various times prior to the 18th century. The Enclosure Movement of the 18th and early 19th centuries affected the surviving open-field villages, with the notable exception of Laxton in Nottinghamshire, but little is known about the precise demographic effects. Only a minority still remained unenclosed by 1801. Of 71 parishes enclosed in Derbyshire and Nottinghamshire between 1801 and 1821 only six declined in population in this period and of these one was a lead-mining village and one a coal-mining village. In fact, local population decreases were rather exceptional in the early decades of the 19th century. Where enclosures of large areas of 'waste' were involved, relatively high, though short-lived, rates of increase sometimes occurred.

The old-established pattern of agricultural villages had already undergone some modification as a result of the expansion of industry and mining. In parts of the Carboniferous Limestone country lead-mining had for centuries provided a means of livelihood, so that here a fairly close scatter of villages contrasted with the rather modest agricultural potential. In the Coal Measure districts of east Derbyshire and adjoining parts of west Nottinghamshire the coal and iron industries were expanding rapidly in the latter decades of the 18th century, leading to local population increases.

Water-powered cotton-spinning mills pioneered by Arkwright and Strutt were causing significant changes in the Derwent basin, where once obscure hamlets such as Belper, Cromford and Milford were now rising to prominence. Similar, but less impressive, developments were occurring on streams near Mansfield and Nottingham. Occupying a wide zone on either side of the Derbyshire–Nottinghamshire county boundary was the domestic knitwear industry, which had become important in a large number of towns and villages in the 18th century. The zone extended from beyond Matlock and Mansfield in the north to the Derby–Nottingham area in the south, covering much of the coalfield and the country on either side of it. Southwards the zone continued along the Soar valley into Leicestershire, to include Loughborough and Leicester and related villages. Many agricultural settlements had thus become miniature industrial centres.

Superimposed on this changing rural pattern were the urban centres, ranging from the county-towns of Nottingham, Derby and Lincoln, to smaller market-towns that were often little more than villages. Greater Nottingham (with a population of 45,900 in 1801), consisting of the town itself (28,800) and a number of growing industrial parishes beyond the common lands (particularly Basford, Bulwell, Lenton and Radford, all in the Leen valley), was a leading centre of knitwear production, with machine-lace also becoming important. Derby (10,850) was noted for its silk spinning, and the town and neighbouring villages also engaged in the production of silk knitwear. With their newly-created canal connections, giving access to coal and iron in the Erewash valley, and radiating road systems, both towns exercised a strong influence on the economic life of the region.

The third and fourth towns were the market-centres and river-ports of Lincoln (7,200) and Newark (6,700). Next was Mansfield (6,000), where cotton-spinning and knitwear were important. Other towns of over 2,000 inhabitants were Alfreton (2,300, including neighbouring industrial villages), Ashbourne (2,000), Chapel-en-le-Frith (2,500), Chesterfield (4,300), Grantham (c 4,000), Ilkeston (2,400), Matlock (2,400), Retford (2,300), Southwell (2,300), Wirksworth (3,000) and Worksop (3,000). All of these performed commercial functions for their surrounding areas, and some also had a considerable industrial element, such as textiles, coal or iron. More specifically industrial in character were the cotton town of Belper (4,500) and the knitwear town of Sutton-in-Ashfield (2,800). Just beyond the county boundary, Burton upon Trent (3,700) acted as a market-centre for part of south Derbyshire.

RURAL CHANGE

The census returns of 1831 and subsequent years show an increased incidence of population decline in agricultural parishes. Where growth took place it was often only very moderate in degree. Natural increase, which had apparently been rapid for some time, had obviously outstripped local employment opportunities, while in towns and coal-mining areas, on the other hand, the demand for labour was increasing. In 1834 the reform of the Poor Law removed the prop of subsidies from the able-bodied unemployed and reduced the restrictions on mobility caused by the settlement laws. Shortly afterwards the development of the railway network facilitated the physical mobility of the population. A great rural exodus continued throughout the remainder of the 19th century, both in the prosperous years of the 50s and 60s and in the period of depression beginning in the 1870s.

However, it was not only from the agricultural parishes that migration took place. Some of the lead-mining villages of Derbyshire were already beginning to lose population in the early years of the 19th century and there is evidence of movement to the coalfields when lead mines either failed or became uneconomic to work. The closure of small country cotton-mills affected other villages (e.g. Cromford, Langwith, Linby, Papplewick, Tissington, Wessington) well before the testing years of the 'cotton famine' in the 1860s, caused by the American Civil War. Certain parishes on the exposed coalfield near Nottingham, where shallow coal-pits had existed for centuries, declined in the first half of the century, when their workings were abandoned (e.g. Bilborough, Cossall, Strelley, Wollaton). Small canal ports declined when traffic was taken by the railways, notably Shardlow. Of greater importance was the chronic depression in the domestic knitwear industry, so well documented in the report of the Royal Commission in 1845. Many villages were severely affected and population declined or stagnated. When new local employment opportunities were subsequently created as a result of developments in industry or coal-mining, or when towns began to spread beyond their ancient limits, the existing trends were often dramatically reversed. Such revival was most frequent in the Nottingham–Derby area and in the coalfield to the north.

In the first decade of the 20th century the rural exodus began to diminish in volume, both regionally and nationally, and the incidence of population decline was reduced. Agriculture was, temporarily at least, more prosperous, suburbanization (aided by local train and bicycle) was gathering momentum, and the cumulative effect of the loss of so many young persons seems to have reduced rural rates of natural increase. The scale of the movement from the countryside before 1911 may be seen from Table XLV, which shows the experience of seven Registration Districts in Derbyshire and Nottinghamshire having considerable agricultural populations. In Ashbourne, Bingham and Southwell Districts not only had there occurred a 'shedding' of the equivalent of the entire natural increase over the 70 years concerned, but the population was actually lower in 1911 than it had been in 1841.

In the inter-war period the effect of the car and the motor-bus was to facilitate still further the growing divorce between place of work and place of residence and thus to enable certain villages increasingly to draw their livelihood from employment in nearby towns. Nevertheless, in 1931 many parishes in Derbyshire and Nottinghamshire still had lower populations than they had 100 years previously in 1831. According to the present writer's calculations, 112 parishes with more than 50 persons in 1931 had declined over this period in Derbyshire. Their combined population fell from 53,800 to 42,450, i.e. by 21 per cent. In Nottinghamshire 150 parishes declined, from a total of 51,000 to 39,000, i.e. by 22 per cent. In both counties the declining areas held about 23 per cent of the population in 1831, but only about six per cent in 1931. The modal year of peak population for such parishes was 1841 in Derbyshire and 1841 and 1851 equally in Nottinghamshire. The declining parishes, where often, admittedly, partial recovery had already occurred by 1931, constituted about half the respective area of each county. The Derbyshire parishes lay chiefly in the rural west; the Nottinghamshire ones in the rural east. Between these two major areas of depopulation lay the quadrilateral Worksop–Nottingham–Derby–Chesterfield, roughly bisected from north to south by the county boundary. In this area the growth of industry and mining had attracted migrants from the rural districts, and natural increase had generally tended to be high, at least until the first World War. The two counties had thus become mirror images of each other as regards population distribution and patterns of change.

Table XLV   Migration from rural areas, 1841–1911

Registration District	Population 1841	Population 1911	Net migration*
Ashbourne ..	21,357	19,516	—17,952
Bakewell ..	29,393	36,866	—15,089
Belper	46,233	72,612	—34,619
Bingham ..	16,196	14,707	—12,796
East Retford ..	21,376	27,103	—14,527
Newark ..	27,350	32,711	—19,469
Southwell ..	25,014	19,573	—20,082

*Population in 1911 minus population in 1841 and recorded natural increase 1841–1911. As the number of births is known to have been significantly under-registered until the last quarter of the 19th century the migration balances were probably rather higher than indicated here. Belper Registration District included part of the east Derbyshire coalfield.

NOTE—After 1911 Registration Districts were no longer used for the publication of population data.

During the second world war the evacuation of city children to rural areas and the setting up of military camps and other establishments concerned with the war effort often led to temporary population increases. The immediate post-war housing shortage had the effect for several years of inhibiting renewed migration from the countryside. In the period 1951–61, however, rural population decline again showed itself, although it was still much less widespread than in the 19th century, when natural increase was in any case higher. In certain villages, especially the smaller agricultural ones, it may be suspected that decline between 1951 and 1961 was due, at least partially, to an excess of deaths over births. On the other hand there were a number of villages where substantial growth had taken place, especially those where suburban development had occurred, or where local councils had deliberately concentrated both their own housing projects and private building schemes, or where 'institutions' of various kinds had taken over large country houses. Even in villages where close planning control prevents large-scale new housing development, existing property is often bought up by commuters and a slow process of sociological replacement is thus set in motion.

THE COALFIELD AREAS

The Derbyshire–Nottinghamshire coalfield has a western boundary running approximately from Chesterfield to Derby. The exposed field, where surface outcrops have been worked since medieval times, extends eastwards to the Magnesian Limestone belt. In the south the latter lies well within Nottinghamshire, but in the north it passes through the Bolsover salient of Derbyshire. The latter county thus includes part of the concealed field and the former part of the exposed. Generally speaking the progression of mining activity has been from west to east, and population has shifted in response, thus entailing some movement of Derbyshire mining families into Nottinghamshire, especially since the end of the 19th century.

In the early decades of the 19th century the chief areas of expansion in mining and iron-working in the exposed field lay in the Erewash valley or on its margins. Not until the 1840s did a comparable surge of activity begin in the Chesterfield area, further north in the Rother basin. Railways now provided the transport link to the south that was not possible from this area in the canal age. The leading districts of growth were around Chesterfield, Clay Cross, a new community on the Derwent–Rother watershed, and Staveley. The first mine in the concealed field was sunk as early as 1859 at Shireoaks (Worksop), but it was some time before the eastward shift of mining became pronounced and, indeed, it often happened that new sinkings were still being made in the rear on the exposed field while others were being made a few miles to the east on the concealed field. The middle decades of the century also witnessed increased activity in the small south Derbyshire coalfield, lying between Burton (Staffordshire) and Ashby-de-la-Zouch (Leicestershire), around Swadlincote in the 'toe' of Derbyshire. In the period between about 1870 and the first world war a great expansion of mining took place to the east of Chesterfield around the small decayed market-town of Bolsover, in the Mansfield area, and in the Leen valley near Nottingham, including Hucknall. In the period between the first world war and the 1930s there was a notable development of new mining villages in the Bunter Sandstone district east of a line running approximately through Worksop, Mansfield

Y

and Nottingham (e.g. Bilsthorpe, Blidworth, Clipstone, Edwinstowe and Ollerton). The migration of mining families to these places and, more particularly, the depressed condition of the coal industry for much of the inter-war period, led to some decline of population, or only negligible growth, in the older mining districts, especially in those where other employment opportunities were lacking. Even the new villages themselves experienced economic difficulties. Since the second world war the buoyant condition of East Midland coal-mining has led to some curtailing of population loss, although certain older mines have closed down. Such population decreases as occurred in the 1950s were often partly due to rehousing policies involving short-distance migration.

In many mining communities it is possible to discern a cycle of population change extending over several decades. First would come the manning of a new mine, sometimes located in an agricultural village or a former knitwear village, when a fairly youthful population would move in. A high rate of natural increase would then ensue, but the second generation might have difficulty in obtaining employment unless mining employment was still expanding locally, and outward migration might thus result. Then there might come a stage when mining employment contracted or ceased. Population would then stagnate or fall, unless other nearby mines or industries could absorb displaced labour and school-leavers.

The effect of the exploitation of the east Derbyshire–Nottinghamshire coalfield has thus been to stimulate an eastward-moving tide of population and settlement, extending over the last 100 years. At the same time it is clear that during the present century there has been a net outward migration movement from the coalfield as a whole. In the Erewash valley, for instance, there has been very little growth of population in Alfreton, Heanor, Ilkeston and Ripley since 1921, nor has there been suburban supplementation, except at Ilkeston to a slight extent. In the south Derbyshire field the population of Swadlincote was lower in 1961 than in 1921.

Local government boundaries have often been slow to change in conformity with new settlement patterns. In the Erewash valley the Derbyshire village of Ironville, a company town, grew up in the 1830s and 1840s in Alfreton parish. It served the adjacent Codnor Park ironworks in the parish of the same name. Also adjoining the works was the village of Jacksdale in the Nottinghamshire parish of Selston. The ironworks was eventually transferred to Alfreton in the 1930s. Elmton parish, near Bolsover, includes a tiny hamlet of this name, but most of the population lives in the modern mining village of Creswell. In Sherwood Forest a large part of the new mining settlement adjoining the old village of Ollerton stretches into Boughton parish. The Urban Districts are often composite in character as regards settlement, either because the original parish was very extensive or because amalgamation has taken place. Thus Alfreton is only one of several places within the Urban District of the same name and this feature is also true of Heanor, Ripley, Swadlincote and others.

COMPARISON OF URBAN GROWTH-RATES

Fig. 59, A to E, shows the growth of population in certain selected urban areas between 1801 and 1961, and also that of England and Wales. The use of a logarithmic vertical scale means that slope is proportionate to rate of change: comparability of towns one with another and with the nation as a whole is thereby facilitated. Comparability over time is ensured by the retrojection of present municipal boundaries to include places absorbed since 1801. Some adjoining parishes are also included. The population figures for selected years are given in Table XLVI.

Table XLVI Urban populations, 1801–1961

Area	1801	1851	1901	1921	1931	1951	1961
			(a)				
1 Greater Nottingham ..	45,900	115,500	286,000	335,600	364,300	436,800	460,500
2 Greater Derby ..	15,700	50,200	125,800	143,700	164,400	197,500	213,200
3 Lincoln	7,900	19,000	53,700	69,700	70,800	77,200	86,500
			(b)				
4 'Erewash'	18,600	41,200	111,800	138,400	141,400	151,000	153,400
5 Greater Mansfield ..	12,200	23,900	59,900	111,200	115,400	129,800	135,500
6 Chesterfield–Staveley	12,100	23,100	70,500	86,600	94,900	102,500	106,700
			(c)				
7 Newark	8,400	13,900	18,800	22,300	23,900	29,300	33,100
8 Grantham	5,100	12,700	19,500	21,200	21,700	26,800	28,300
9 Retford	4,200	7,400	12,700	13,700	14,600	16,700	18,300
			(d)				
10 Worksop	3,300	7,200	16,100	23,200	26,300	31,000	34,300
11 Long Eaton ..	1,200	1,900	14,800	23,000	23,300	28,600	30,500
12 Hucknall	1,500	3,000	15,300	17,000	17,800	23,200	23,300
			(e)				
13 Buxton	1,800	2,700	14,900	17,600	17,900	19,600	19,200
14 Matlock	6,800	9,200	14,600	15,700	16,600	17,800	18,500
15 Belper	4,500	10,100	10,900	12,300	13,000	14,500	14,700

Composition (retrospective)

1 City of Nottingham, Urban Districts of Arnold, Beeston and Stapleford, Carlton, West Bridgford

2 County Borough of Derby, Civil Parishes of Allestree, Alvaston and Boulton, Breadsall, Chaddesden, Chellaston, Darley Abbey, Littleover, Mickleover, Spondon

3 City of Lincoln, Civil Parishes of Bracebridge Heath, North Hykeham, Skellingthorpe

4   Municipal Borough of Ilkeston, Urban Districts of Alfreton, Eastwood, Heanor, Ripley (except Ambergate and Heage), Civil Parishes of Awsworth, Brinsley, Cossall, Greasley, Kimberley, Nuthall, Selston, Strelley, Trowell (Nottinghamshire) and Dale Abbey, Mapperley, Pentrich, Pinxton, Shipley, Smalley, South Normanton, Stanley, Stanton-by-Dale, West Hallam (Derbyshire)

5   Municipal Borough of Mansfield, Urban Districts of Mansfield Woodhouse, Kirkby-in-Ashfield, Sutton-in-Ashfield

6   Municipal Borough of Chesterfield, Urban District of Staveley, Civil Parishes of Brampton, Brimington, Calow, Hasland, Walton, Wingerworth

7   Municipal Borough of Newark, Civil Parishes of Balderton, Coddington, Farndon, Hawton, Kelham

8   Municipal Borough of Grantham, Civil Parishes of Belton and Manthorpe, Great Gonerby, Londonthorpe and Harrowby Without

9   Municipal Borough of East Retford, Civil Parish of Clarborough

10 Municipal Borough of Worksop

11 Urban District of Long Eaton

12 Urban District of Hucknall

13 Municipal Borough of Buxton

14 Urban District of Matlock

15 Urban District of Belper (excluding Milford)

It will be seen that Nottingham, Derby and Lincoln (Fig. 59) grew at rates at or above the national rate in nearly all the intercensal periods. Two of Nottingham's lace booms, in the 1820s and the 1870s, are clearly reflected. Derby's growth was smoother than that of Nottingham, but the overall growth rate was higher for the whole period. It must be admitted, however, that Nottingham's figures exclude physically detached suburbs, such as Radcliffe and Keyworth, that have grown rapidly in recent years. In both Nottingham and Derby continuously rapid expansion was possible not only because staple industries were prosperous for long periods, but also because eventual stagnation or contraction in them was offset by the successful growth of new kinds of manufacturing. In Nottingham the lace industry offered prosperous conditions in the 19th century, even though the domestic knitwear industry was undergoing periods of crisis, followed by extinction. By the time the lace industry was declining, in the 1920s, the bicycle, pharmaceutical, telephone and tobacco industries were all well-established, and the factory knitwear industry had been flourishing for over 60 years. Derby's railway engineering industry was already important when the textile sector was declining after the middle of the 19th century, and in the 20th century activity in other engineering trades, especially aero-engines, and in artificial fibres, more than compensated for the lack of expansion in railway engineering. In the smaller towns it was often this lack of available 'replacement industries' that brought a pause in population growth when specialized economic activities declined. Lincoln's industrial growth largely reflects the fortunes of its engineering firms and the success of their transfer of interest from agricultural machinery to other products. Its overall rate of growth matched that of Nottingham, but the pace of change varied considerably. The boom of the 1870s should be compared with the stagnation of the 1920s, when the engineering industry languished.

Fig. 59 shows the experience of three large population clusters on the coalfield. 'Erewash' consists of the coal, iron and textile settlements in the middle and upper part of the Erewash valley and its fringes, an area extending for about 12 miles from north to south and about six from west to east. For the group as a whole, decennial growth rates did not decisively overtake those for England and Wales until after 1851, while since 1921 growth has been consistently below the national average. The respective contributions made by individual places have, of course, varied considerably over the period. Greater Mansfield may usefully be compared with the Chesterfield–Staveley group. Both had approximately the same population in 1801. The latter, situated on the exposed coalfield, grew rapidly after 1841, while the former, lying further east on the concealed field, was growing only moderately in the 1840s and declining in the 1850s, owing to the depression in the domestic knitwear industry. As a result the growth curve of Chesterfield overtook and crossed that of Mansfield soon after 1851. As mining advanced eastwards and factory employment increased, so population growth in Mansfield gathered momentum, with the result that between 1881 and 1921 numbers more than tripled. The growth curve of Mansfield crossed that of Chesterfield in the early years of the present century. Mansfield's rate of growth slackened off in the 1920s, when new colliery villages were built to the south and the east, while in Chesterfield the rate of growth was maintained, largely due to the expansion of the iron and chemical complex at Staveley. Since 1931 both groups have broadly conformed to the national average.

Worksop (Fig. 59), like Chesterfield and Mansfield, is an example of a coalfield town with market functions and a considerable range of industry. Here, after steady 19th century expansion, there was a steepening of the rate of growth in the 1890s, chiefly owing to the eastward advance of mining, since when growth rates have continued to be above the national average. Hucknall and Long Eaton (Fig. 59) grew rapidly as specialized industrial satellites of Nottingham in the second half of the 19th century. Hucknall concentrated on woollen veils and coal-mining and Long Eaton on lace. The former failed to grow as rapidly between 1891 and 1931 as in the period 1861–1891, owing to the decline of the veil trade and the cessation of expansion in mining. Renewed vigour between 1931 and 1951 has been followed by a stationary condition. Long Eaton's rate of growth weakened substantially in the period 1911–31, when there was a contraction in the lace trade, but the subsequent expansion of other industries enabled an upward movement to recur.

In the Derwent basin the new industrial town of Belper (Fig. 59) grew briskly up to 1841, after which its cotton industry failed to expand and its silk glove industry declined. As a result, it was not until 1891 that the 1841 population level was surpassed. Since then growth has continued, but at only a moderate rate, based on

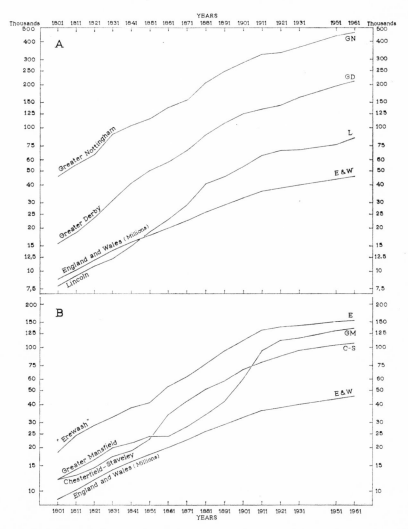

Fig. 59 Population change in selected urban areas and in England and Wales, 1801–1961

(*For composition of urban areas see Table XLVI*)

a more diversified industrial structure. Buxton and Matlock (Fig. 59) expanded as spa towns in the second half of the 19th century, after railway connections had been established, but in the inter-war period they became less popular and today their spa functions are negligible. The modern urban district of Matlock contains not only Matlock Bath to the south and Darley to the north, but also several neighbouring villages, which in the 19th century engaged in cotton spinning, domestic knitwear

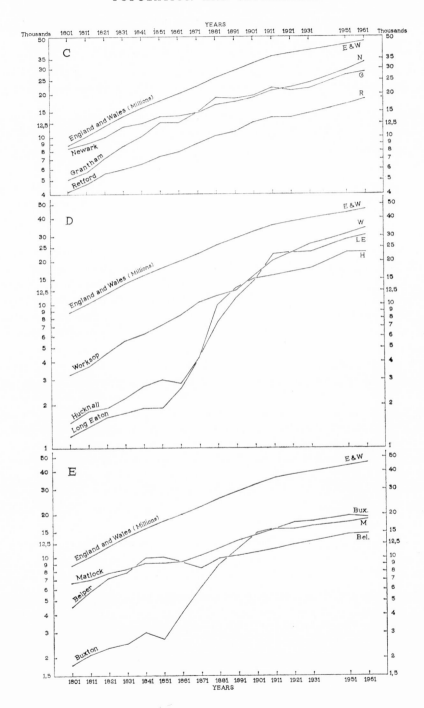

and lead-mining, all of which proved to be declining activities. Before 1841 growth rates in the urban district as a whole were very slight, while between 1841 and 1861 population was stationary. Thereafter Matlock's population grew continuously, but not dramatically, up to 1911. Since then growth has been only moderate, despite a varied economic structure and the transfer from Derby to Matlock of the County Council offices in 1958. Buxton grew rapidly between 1851 and 1901, but since 1921 growth has been only moderate, and there was a slight decline between 1951 and 1961.

The market-towns of Grantham, Newark and Retford, situated on the 'east coast' rail route to the north, also invite comparison (Fig. 59). Since 1801 Grantham has achieved an overall rate of increase similar to that of the nation as a whole, but this has been the outcome of rather striking fluctuations related to the economic health of its engineering industries, initially agricultural machinery. Growth in Newark was particularly sluggish between 1831 and 1871, when railway transport undermined its river traffic. After 1901 parity of growth with England and Wales was reached, while since 1921 growth has been progressively higher than the national average in each successive intercensal period, mainly as a reflection of the prosperity of its engineering industries. Even so, Newark's overall growth-rate failed to equal the national average for the entire period. The same is true of Retford, where, apart from stagnation between 1911 and 1921, growth was remarkably smooth, but undistinguished, despite, or perhaps because of, a balanced range of activities.

Finally mention may briefly be made of some of the smaller towns. Wirksworth had a population in 1961 (4,200) that was scarcely any higher than that in 1841 or 1831. The decline of lead-mining and of its market functions was responsible. On the other hand growth has been continuous since 1931 (3,600). Also in upland Derbyshire are the two market-towns of Ashbourne and Bakewell, which have grown steadily in recent decades, in spite of there being little population growth in their rural hinterlands. Chapel-en-le-Frith, near Buxton, owes much of its recent growth to its brake-linings industry. In Nottinghamshire Southwell's population remained stationary in the period 1841–61 (3,500) and did not surpass this figure until the 1950s.

THE PRESENT DISTRIBUTION

General aspects

Fig. 60 (facing page 360) shows the 1961 distribution of population in a territory extending for about 30 miles north of the Nottingham–Derby area and for about 20 miles to the south. The west–east span is about 60 miles. The map may also be regarded as showing a generalized version of the settlement pattern. The extreme north of Nottinghamshire and the extreme north–west of Derbyshire are both excluded, while neighbouring parts of Yorkshire, Lincolnshire, Rutland, Leicestershire and Staffordshire are included. Not all the population shown on the map is tributary to Nottingham or to its smaller neighbours of Derby and Mansfield. In particular Sheffield, to the north, and Leicester, to the south, would claim large areas if the spheres of influence of major towns were demarcated.

It will be seen that there is a broad zone of well-populated country stretching southwards from Yorkshire to the Derby–Nottingham area and largely coincident with the east Derbyshire and Nottinghamshire coalfield. Southwards this zone becomes rather wider in extent, but less concentrated in terms of population and settlement. This populous zone, which links Yorkshire to the West Midlands, may be roughly delimited by an easterly line passing through Worksop (34,311), Nottingham (311,899) and Leicester (273,470), and a westerly line passing through Chesterfield (67,858), Derby (132,408) and Burton upon Trent (50,751). A salient is formed on the west by the loose group of settlements included in the urban districts of Matlock (18,505) and Wirksworth (4,931), while to the east there is some blurring in the Bunter Sandstone area of Sherwood Forest, owing to the 20th century development here of coal-mining communities. Within these limits there remain considerable tracts of open country and even a few villages that may still be called agricultural in character, but generally speaking non-agricultural interests predominate. Despite the great changes of the last two centuries pre-industrial patterns are still discernible. Thus along the Derwent and the lower Soar lines of villages on terraces or other rising ground can still be detected, although today they are often industrial or suburban in character.

In the predominantly rural areas to the east and the west the general pattern has changed very little. Parts of the Peak District and Sherwood Forest continue to show sparse peopling, while along the Trent and at the foot of the Lincoln Edge strings of agricultural villages still persist. The rural areas continue to be served by traditional market towns, such as Bakewell (3,606), Ashbourne (5,660) and Uttoxeter (8,185), in the west, and the much larger centres of Retford (17,792), Lincoln (77,077), Newark (24,651), Grantham (25,048) and Melton Mowbray (15,914), in the east. Today these are also industrial towns in their own right, especially Lincoln.

In the north-west of the map Buxton (19,155) and Chapel-en-le-Frith (6,460) represent outposts of the Greater Manchester area. In the south a line approximately through Burton upon Trent, Loughborough and Melton Mowbray would mark the limit of the influence of either Derby or Nottingham. Burton and the adjacent Swadlincote Urban District (19,221) have associations with Derby, but further to the south-west Birmingham's influence is paramount. Ashby-de-la-Zouch (7,460), Coalville (26,156), in the Leicestershire coalfield, Loughborough (38,638) and Melton Mowbray all have bus or rail communications (or both) with Nottingham but, on balance, their closest links are with Leicester. In the north of the populous zone the Chesterfield and Worksop districts feel the influence of Sheffield, as also do Retford to the east and the Peak villages north of Bakewell to the west. In the Chesterfield district Dronfield (11,303) is increasingly becoming a residential satellite of Sheffield, while the parishes of Beighton (23,056) and Eckington (20,047) have large dormitory housing estates.

Our attention narrows, therefore, to the Nottingham, Derby and Mansfield areas, and the Erewash valley, which together may be said to constitute the greater part of a Nottingham 'city region', exhibiting a close concentration of population and settlement and also a considerable degree of functional cohesion.

The Nottingham–Derby–Mansfield area

Nottingham, eighth largest city of England, had a population of 311,899 in 1961, but within 10 miles of the Old Market Square there is a total population of about 700,000, of whom less than half, therefore, live in the city itself (Table XLVII). Immediately adjoining the city are the five Urban Districts of Arnold (26,829), Beeston and Stapleford (55,995) (which also includes Attenborough, Bramcote, Chilwell and Toton), Carlton (38,815), Hucknall (23,269), and West Bridgford (26,973), with a combined population of 172,000. Only Hucknall, up the valley of the Leen, can claim to be physically separate from the city, and even here the break in urban development is very slight. Further away, to the north-west and west, are the Urban Districts of Eastwood (10,607), Heanor (23,870) and Long Eaton (30,476) and the Municipal Borough of Ilkeston (34,672), all situated in the Erewash valley. Eastwood is in Nottinghamshire and the others in Derbyshire. Their combined population is about 94,000 (excluding part of Heanor Urban District lying beyond the 10-mile radius). The remaining population is located in 84 Civil Parishes of Rural Districts, 31 of which have over 1,000 inhabitants, with a total population of 97,000. Some are purely residential in character, while others have industrial or mining activities. The remaining 53 parishes have a total population of only 19,000 and they account for less than three per cent of the numbers within the 10-mile radius. Of these smaller parishes, 24 have less than 250 inhabitants and, perhaps rather surprisingly, five of them are only five miles or less from the city centre (Barton-in-Fabis, Gamston, Stoke Bardolph, Strelley and Clipston).

Table XLVII Estimated population within 10 miles of Nottingham, 1961

City of Nottingham	311,900
Five adjoining Urban Districts	171,900
Eastwood, Heanor (part), Ilkeston and Long Eaton ..	93,700
URBAN POPULATION	577,500
Civil parishes with over 1,000 inhabitants	96,900
Smaller parishes	19,000
'RURAL' POPULATION	115,900
TOTAL	693,400

Continuous urban or suburban development extends westwards from Nottingham into Derbyshire, through Beeston, Bramcote, and Stapleford, as far as Sandiacre (6,794) and Risley (767), and also through Beeston, Chilwell and Toton to Long Eaton, Breaston (3,626) and Draycott (1,995), the latter being situated nine miles from Nottingham. Long Eaton and Toton, at the lower end of the Erewash valley, have almost fused with Sandiacre and Stapleford, further up the valley to the north. These in turn are linked to Ilkeston, through Stanton Ironworks and the large village of Trowell (1,877) respectively. Between Nottingham and Trowell, however, there is open country for about a mile along the main Nottingham–Ilkeston road (A.609). West of Ilkeston are the straggling villages of Stanley (2,359) and West Hallam (1,925), near the south–western extremity of the coalfield.

North-westwards from Nottingham there is continuous urban landscape extending along the A.610 to Eastwood and Heanor, through the parishes of Nuthall (3,721), Greasley (5,321) and Kimberley (4,642). South of the Trent, West Bridgford is connected through Wilford with Nottingham's post-war housing estate of Clifton, forming a south-bank salient of the city's administrative area. Clifton adjoins the large village of Ruddington (5,158). In an easterly direction Carlton Urban District is succeeded by the residential village of Burton Joyce (2,447). Radiating fingers of urban development, of varying age, character and breadth, thus extend in a number of directions, often leaving between them, however, substantial rural wedges. In terms of bricks and mortar there is certainly a Nottingham conurbation, but the problem of arriving at a satisfactory delimitation cannot be dealt with here.

Even those villages not strictly forming part of the continuous built-up area are nevertheless closely associated with the city, such as the residential villages of Radcliffe-on-Trent (6,468) and Bingham (2,457), to the east, and the parishes of Keyworth, Normanton-on-the-Wolds, Plumtree and Tollerton, which form a sprawling group to the south (combined population 5,079). Planning policy has deliberately stimulated growth in these two areas and both enjoy quick road access to Nottingham. Other large villages south of the Trent are East Leake (2,856) and Gotham (1,434), with their gypsum workings and associated industries. Cotgrave (641), where a new coal-mine was opened in 1964, may be expected to grow rapidly. In the lower Soar valley are Kegworth (Leicestershire) (2,645) and Sutton Bonington (1,154), where the School of Agriculture of the University of Nottingham is located. North of the river there are a number of parishes where coal-mining is, or has been, important, including Awsworth (1,529), Brinsley (1,915), Cossall (1,149) and Selston (9,904), on the exposed field, and Bestwood Park (1,690), Calverton (5,658) and Newstead (2,569), on the concealed field.

A 20-mile radius from the centre of Nottingham takes in a further 830,000 people and comfortably embraces both Greater Derby and Greater Mansfield (Table XLVIII). The County Borough of Derby and a dozen adjoining residential suburban parishes form a compact urban concentration with a population of about 220,000. The largest are Allestree (7,298), Alvaston and Boulton (13,855), Breadsall (4,904), Chaddesden (15,622), Littleover (11,867), Mickleover (9,709), Ockbrook (including Borrowash) (5,278), and Spondon (11,541). Settlement is almost continuous between Derby and Nottingham along the road route (A.6005) passing through Long Eaton, the only break being one of half a mile between Borrowash and Draycott. It is thus possible to travel for over 25 miles from Mickleover, south-west of Derby, to Burton Joyce, north-east of Nottingham, without leaving a predominantly urbanized landscape. However, along the more direct route between Derby and Nottingham (the old A.52) there is a clear break of nearly two miles between Borrowash and Risley.

Table XLVIII

Estimated population within 20 miles of Nottingham, 1961

County	0 to 10 miles	10 to 20 miles*	Total
Nottinghamshire ..	582,300	224,100	806,400
Derbyshire ..	108,400	418,500	526,900
Leicestershire ..	2,700	180,900	183,600
Lincolnshire ..	—	5,600	5,600
TOTAL	693,400	829,100	1,522,500

*Excluding any part of the City of Leicester

Northwards from Derby there is rather more spasmodic settlement along the Derwent valley from Allestree to Belper (14,722), through Duffield (3,375) and Belper's outlying village of Milford (830). To the east of the Derwent the valley of a small tributary, the Bottle brook, runs almost parallel to the Derwent and lies just within the coalfield. Here there are several large villages situated between Derby and Ripley (12,940), at the head of the valley, including Little Eaton (1,733), Holbrook (1,386), Kilburn (2,631) and Denby (1,805). Ripley, whose Urban District (17,617) also includes Heage (2,007) and Ambergate (2,670), situated to the west, merges southwards into Codnor and Loscoe, forming part of Heanor Urban District. Northwards, Ripley is almost continuously linked to Alfreton (8,984), through the village of Swanwick (3,724), which is included in Alfreton Urban District (22,999). The latter also includes Ironville (1,739), Riddings (3,100) and Somercotes (5,452), to the south-east, which join up with Pye Bridge, Pye Hill and Jacksdale in the Nottinghamshire parish of Selston. Adjoining Alfreton on the east are the large mining villages of South Normanton (6,946) and Pinxton (4,556), the latter being located near the head of the Erewash valley.

In short, therefore, the west–east Derby–Nottingham 'axis' along the lower Derwent and the Trent has northward–branching extensions following the valleys of the middle Derwent and the Bottle brook (from Derby), the Erewash (from Long Eaton and Toton), and the Leen (from Nottingham). The longest of these, that of the Erewash valley, differs from the others in that it has no spinal road serving its settlements, and thus transverse connections to Derby and Nottingham are particularly important. While the valleys discussed above are well-populated and frequently show fusion of settlements, the interfluves often remain rural in character, such as the area around Strelley and Cossall, between Nottingham and Ilkeston, or the much larger one between the Erewash and the Bottle brook. It is this fragmentation that makes it inappropriate to speak without qualification of an entire Nottingham–Derby–Erewash conurbation.

Straddling the watershed between the upper Erewash and the Maun, a tributary of the Idle, is Greater Mansfield, consisting of the Municipal Borough of Mansfield (53,218), 13 miles north of Nottingham, and the Urban Districts of Mansfield Woodhouse (20,197), Kirkby-in-Ashfield (21,686) and Sutton-in-Ashfield (40,441). These form an amorphous built-up area, beyond the limits of which are other large communities, chiefly committed to coal-mining, including the Urban District of Warsop (11,606) and the parishes of Blidworth (7,308), Clipstone (3,947), Edwinstowe (3,666) and Ollerton (6,903, with adjoining Boughton), in Sherwood Forest, and Ault Hucknall (1,746), Blackwell (4,084), Glapwell (1,676), Pleasley (2,754), Shirebrook (11,635) and Tibshelf (3,620), in Derbyshire. Pinxton, Selston and South Normanton, already mentioned, also lie close to Greater Mansfield, which is thus connected on the south-west to the Erewash valley by a landscape of mining villages and collieries. On the other hand, in a southerly direction there are considerable tracts of well-wooded country between Mansfield and the approaches to Nottingham. North–westwards from Greater Mansfield and its satellite mining villages the Urban Districts of Bolsover (11,772) and Clay Cross (9,163), 20 and 18 miles from Nottingham respectively, tend to have closer relationships with Chesterfield than with Mansfield, especially Clay Cross. Together with Staveley (18,070) they thus form part of a north-east Derbyshire group of industrial and mining settlements that falls more logically within a Sheffield region than a Nottingham region.

Eastwards from Nottingham, a 20-mile radius also takes in Newark and its suburban villages, while in a southerly direction most of the northern half of Leicestershire is included; indeed the city boundary of Leicester itself is impinged on. If we exclude the whole of the population of northern Leicestershire, virtually all the remaining population of about 1·3 millions living within 20 miles of the Old Market Square is either tributary to Nottingham or else is associated with the two smaller neighbouring conurbations of Derby and Mansfield. Even beyond this radius, however, there are populations that generally look to Nottingham, Derby or Mansfield for certain facilities.

REGIONAL CHANGES IN THE NATIONAL SETTING

Despite much urban and industrial growth in Derbyshire and Nottinghamshire during the 19th century their share of the population of England and Wales showed remarkably little change between 1801 and 1901. Derbyshire's share rose from 18·2 per 1,000 to 19·1, but losses of territory from the ancient county to Leicestershire, Staffordshire and Yorkshire reduce this to 18·3 for the modern county. Nottinghamshire's share was the same in both years, at 15·8.

In view of the national migration loss to overseas countries which was typical of the 19th century, it is not surprising that between 1841 (the first census year after the introduction of civil registration) and 1901 the decennial balance of migration was usually outward for both Derbyshire and Nottinghamshire Registration Counties. The exceptions were 1871–81 and, in Nottinghamshire only, 1891–1901. Between 1901 and 1951 Derbyshire continued to lose population and the gain for 1951–61 (12,400) is cancelled out if short-distance 'overspill' movements from Sheffield are subtracted. Derbyshire's share of the national population was thus only slightly higher in 1961 (19·0) than in 1901. On the other hand, Nottinghamshire has been gaining population during the present century, although admittedly only to a rather small extent in 1951–61 (7,600). As a result the county's share of the national total had risen to 19·6 by 1961. In 1961 the population of Derbyshire (877,620) was 5·4 times that of 1801, compared with 6·4 times for Nottinghamshire (1961 population 902,988) and 5·2 for England and Wales.

The role of Nottinghamshire in the redistribution of the national population is particularly interesting, since in the 19th century it was losing population to the northern industrial counties, while in the first half of the 20th century it was gaining from them. In both periods it was losing to London and the south-east. These movements and others, such as the pronounced inflow from Derbyshire since about 1900, are illustrated in Fig. 61, based on the 'county of birth' data published in the 1861, 1901 and 1951 census volumes. Net movements from county of birth to county of enumeration, in respect of all English and Welsh persons alive in these three years, can be calculated for individual counties in relation to each other. Thus in 1951 there were 23,000 more persons of Derbyshire birth living in Nottinghamshire than there were Nottinghamshire-born persons living in Derbyshire.

It will be seen that in the years prior to 1861 Nottinghamshire had been gaining from Leicestershire, but losing to Lancashire and Yorkshire, the London area and the West Midlands. The county had lost nearly 14,000 persons on balance. By 1901 many of the migrants alive in 1861 had died and new movements of population had taken place. By now Lincolnshire had become the chief single source of immigrants (13,900 on balance), the loss to the West Midlands had been reversed, and the movements to the north and to the London area had increased somewhat. The outcome was a net gain from the rest of the country of 13,100.

By 1951 significant changes had taken place. Large numbers of persons had moved into the county from Derbyshire, while the Lincolnshire inflow had diminished. The gain from Staffordshire had increased, but there was now a loss to Warwickshire (including Birmingham and Coventry). More striking was the reversal of the pre-existing movement to the northern counties; these now showed substantial losses

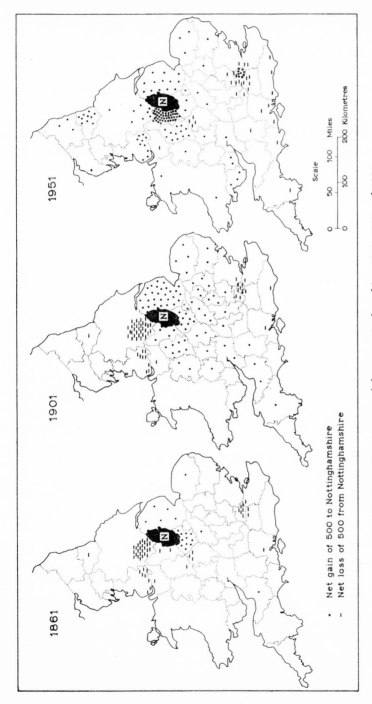

Fig. 61 Net migration to and from Nottinghamshire, 1861, 1901 and 1951

The net balances are in respect of English and Welsh persons enumerated in each of these years. Only balances of over 250 persons are shown. Movements from Nottinghamshire are assumed, for cartographical purposes, to have been directed to the nearer major urban concentrations in the counties concerned. Movements to Nottinghamshire are assumed to have originated either from such concentrations or from widespread places if the population of the county concerned was well distributed

• Net gain of 500 to Nottinghamshire

– Net loss of 500 from Nottinghamshire

Scale

1951

1901

1861

to Nottinghamshire, presumably owing to their less prosperous conditions. Welsh persons had also, no doubt, been affected in the same way. Rather surprisingly, perhaps, there had been no very great increase in the 'drift south' between 1901 and 1951; indeed the County of London had lost on balance to Nottinghamshire. The latter was not exceptional in this respect, as nearly all counties had favourable migration balances with London in 1951, owing to wartime dispersal and also to the fact that migrants to the London area tend to settle in the Home Counties rather than in London itself. Within the south of England, however, the number of counties gaining from Nottinghamshire increased. The outcome of all these movements was a net gain of 52,000, to which Derbyshire was the leading contributor.

In several ways the general experience of the region illustrates trends common to many parts of the country, although over the whole period, 1801–1961, the population of Derbyshire and Nottinghamshire has admittedly grown at a rather higher rate than that of England and Wales as a whole. Within the region population redistribution, caused by migration and differential rates of natural increase, has led to an impressive growth of towns and of industrial, mining and suburbanized villages. These have shown varying rates of change in different periods in accordance with contemporary economic conditions. Agricultural villages have usually shown little upward movement since the middle of the 19th century and some have declined, except where functional conversion has taken place. A concomitant of the growth of population has been the spread of built-up areas. These reach their greatest extent in the Nottingham and Derby districts and in the coalfield stretching away northwards. Nevertheless important elements of persistence from the pre-industrial era cannot be overlooked; thus the general distribution of the rural population still reflects early settlement patterns. Nottingham and Derby are still the largest towns in their respective counties (as also are Leicester and Northampton to the south). Lincoln, however, has been supplanted by Grimsby, and may in time be superseded by Scunthorpe. Within this general context, Nottingham itself, the largest county-town in England, has remained an important regional centre and has maintained its place among the leading provincial cities.

SELECTED REFERENCES

Couzens, F. C. Distribution of population of the mid-Derwent basin since the Industrial Revolution. *Geography* Vol. 26 (1941) pp. 31–38.

Osborne, R. H. Population concentrations and conurban tendencies in the Middle Trent counties. *East Midland Geographer* Vol. 1 No. 2 (1954) pp. 30–37.

Powell, A. G. The 1951 census: an analysis of population changes in Derbyshire. *East Midland Geographer* Vol. 1 No. 2 (1954) pp. 13–23.

Powell, A. G. The 1951 census: an analysis of population changes in Nottinghamshire. *East Midland Geographer* Vol. 1 No. 4 (1955) pp. 29–42.

Wallis, B. C. Nottinghamshire in the nineteenth century: the geographical factors in the growth of the population. *Geographical Journal* Vol. 43 (1914) pp. 34–61.

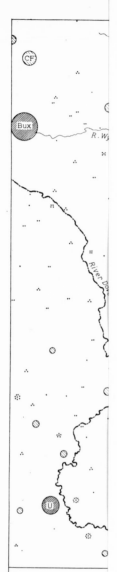

CF

Bux

R. W

River Dove

U

Places with more th
950 inhabitants
500.0

PART III

THE CITY OF NOTTINGHAM

XXI

THE GEOGRAPHICAL DEVELOPMENT
OF NOTTINGHAM

POSITION AND SITE

Position

Nottingham occupies a significant geographical position in the Midlands and in the country as a whole. Like the two larger cities of Leeds and Sheffield, as well as the neighbouring town of Derby, it stands near the east or south–east margin of the Pennines, where the hill country of northern England gives way to the lowlands of the English Plain. While Sheffield is in closer contact with the hills, Nottingham is more distinctly a lowland city, deriving its importance from the fact that, throughout its long history, it has controlled one of the principal crossing points of the Trent, a river large enough to have been a serious obstacle to movement between north and south. For centuries, moreover, Nottingham has been the effective limit of navigation on the Trent, so that from early times the value of its position was enhanced by the convergence of land and water routes. Again, Nottingham lies at the southern extremity of the largest coalfield in Britain, and is situated at the point of contact between the great industrial area which has developed along the eastern flank of the Pennines and the predominantly agricultural area lying to the east and south. Much of Nottingham's importance is due, therefore, to its position close to the junction of the highland and lowland zones of Britain, as a place of exchange between the different resources and economies which these contrasted environments have promoted.

Site

The location and early growth of Nottingham exhibit an exceptionally close relationship to the physical conditions afforded by the site. A glance at the geological map (Fig. 2) shows that several different rock formations converge upon the position occupied by the town on the north side of the Trent valley. The city now spreads over parts of all these outcrops, including the alluvial deposits of the valley itself and, with the possible exception of Bristol, embraces within its boundaries a greater diversity of surface materials than any other city in England. The central member of this group of outcrops, i.e. the Bunter Sandstone, provided the site for the original township. This formation, extending southwards through Nottinghamshire, terminates abruptly in a river-cut cliff, about two miles long, overlooking the Trent floodplain. Apart from minor occurrences like those at Rugeley, Staffordshire, and

Repton, Derbyshire, both of which lie on the south bank of the Trent, the appearance of the Bunter Sandstone at Nottingham is without parallel in the long course of the river from The Potteries to the Humber, for, with these exceptions, the Trent has carved its valley entirely in the red clays of the Keuper Marl. At Nottingham the Bunter formation is chiefly represented by the Pebble Beds, a buff-coloured sandstone containing bands of quartzite pebbles. A lower division of the Bunter, known as the Lower Mottled Sandstone, occurs only as a narrow fringe to the west of the main outcrop. The Pebble Beds sandstone is coarse-grained and highly porous, giving rise to a prevailingly dry surface and infrequent streams. Thus, in contrast to the ill-drained, often marshy, nature of the floodplain, the comparatively elevated dry ground afforded by the Pebble Beds (from which, nevertheless, supplies of pure water could readily be obtained from wells), offered favourable conditions for early settlement. The sandstone surface, however, was far from uniform and its detailed configuration greatly influenced the development of the town. Reference to Fig. 62 shows that the cliff forming the southern edge of the outcrop is in fact discontinuous, for it is broken by three small dry valleys, or depressions, grading to the floodplain. Separating the most westerly of these (Park Valley) from the next is a spur which tapers southward to form the massive crag known as the Castle Rock, while between the central depression and that to the east of it, the cliff is again high and abrupt, with the ground to the north rising still higher. On either side of the central hollow, therefore, hill sites commanded the approaches from across the Trent valley, and in each case a cliff provided security from attack on this side.

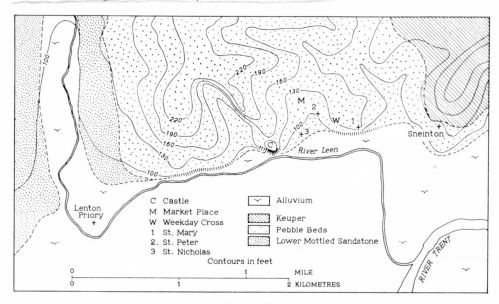

Fig. 62   The site of Nottingham

The earliest documentary reference to Nottingham is that in the *Anglo-Saxon Chronicle* which points to the existence of an Anglian settlement in A.D. 867 which soon afterwards fell to the Danes. The Anglo-Danish *burh* occupied the more easterly of the two hills, the summit of which (150 feet O.D.) is about 80 feet above the floodplain. While little is known about the Anglian settlement prior to the Danish incursions its subsequent importance is beyond doubt, since it became one of the Five Boroughs of the Danelaw and, about A.D. 920–924, during the time of the Anglo-Saxon reconquest under Edward the Elder, the route from the south was improved by the erection of a bridge over the Trent.

Following the Norman Conquest, the strategic value of Nottingham's position was further recognised by the building of a castle on the western hill (192 feet O.D.), which reached some 110 feet above the floodplain. Adjoining the castle, a second township developed which was predominantly military and Norman-French in character, contrasting with the purely civil township of the Anglo-Danish borough a few hundred yards to the east. Earthworks and eventually walls were raised eastwards of the castle to protect the lower ground between the two centres and ultimately these were extended to enclose the whole. As the two settlements developed together, at first uneasily and later more peacefully, the intervening depression became the focus of fairs and markets and developed into the Great Market Place which was one of the largest in the country. The dual nature of early Nottingham, consisting of two separate boroughs is clearly revealed in Speede's map of 1610 (Plate XV), produced long after the original elements had been combined into one.

THE GROWTH OF THE CITY

Medieval

The pre-Conquest borough was roughly rectangular in shape and occupied about 39 acres. Its perimeter was defended in part by ditch and earthwork and in part by a wall, though on the south side no evidence of either form of defence has come to light. A track leading from across the Trent and Leen entered near the south–east corner by cutting obliquely through the cliff face—it is still called Hollowstone—and then struck northwards through the settlement, dividing it into two more or less equal parts. In the western half were the church and market-place, the one on the site of the present St. Mary's, which dates mainly from the 15th century, and the other at what is still called Weekday Cross. A cross stood at this point until it was removed in 1884. The road which bisected the town is called Stoney Street and, together with Hollowstone, must be the oldest thoroughfare in the city. Its name may well refer to the banks of pebbles which occur in the sandstone and some of these are still exposed in the cutting through which Hollowstone ascends the hill. Some street names reflect the existence of ancient trades and crafts in the medieval town, though in some cases the form of the name has undoubtedly changed in the course of time: Woolpack Lane, Barker Gate, Fletcher Gate, Pilcher Gate. Others occur around the Old Market Square and relate to extensions of the original street plan: Goose Gate, Poultry, Bridlesmith Gate, Smithy Row, Lister Gate, Wheeler Gate. At a later but unspecified period another entry to the town was made at the south–west corner, leading to Bridlesmith Gate by means of the steep path known today as Drury Hill. Nottingham, as an Anglian settlement, derives its name from *Snotinga- ham* (the homestead of Snot's people). To the east of it a second settlement sited on another sandstone spur appears to have been established not long afterwards. This is now known as Sneinton (Fig. 62), derived from *Snoting-tun* (the *tun* associated with Snot). The name retains the initial 'S', whereas in the case of Nottingham it has been lost. Sneinton was long a separate settlement, with its own church, but later growth made it virtually a part of Nottingham and it was eventually absorbed into the city (see p. 392).

The Norman borough, some 80 acres in extent, included not only the castle but the churches of St. Nicholas and St. Peter, as well as the Great Market Place. A group of streets spread fanwise from the castle towards the open ground of the Market Place. These streets survive today as Mount Street, St. James's Street, Friar Lane, Hounds Gate and Castle Gate. Just as Bridlesmith Gate was aligned just outside the west side of the old *burh*, so the present-day Park Row marks the outer side of the Norman wall.

The castle, probably in rudimentary form, was founded in 1068 and given by the Conqueror to the custody of William Peveril. It was rebuilt in stone and further elaborated in the time of Henry II. The two churches appear to have been founded early in the 12th century, presumably to meet the needs of the growing community in the French borough. St. Nicholas's was situated close to the Leen and its dedication suggests a connection with medieval trade conducted in boats along the navigable Trent. The present church dates from 1678, its predecessor having been destroyed in the Civil War. In the mid-13th century a Franciscan friary (Greyfriars) came to occupy the low ground bordering the Leen marshes east of the castle, while, somewhat later, a Carmelite community (Whitefriars) settled in the area between the castle and the market place near the present Friar Lane. Another important feature of the locality, though it was established outside the town, was the great Cluniac priory of Lenton, which became the richest and most influential of all the monastic houses in Nottinghamshire. The priory was founded about 1109–12, probably by William Peveril, and was situated within the sharp bend of the Leen where the stream enters the Trent floodplain a little more than a mile from the castle (Fig. 62). In view of the recurrent flood menace this would seem to have been an unpropitious site, yet the institution prospered and some 50 years later Henry II granted the right to hold an annual fair in addition to the two already held in Nottingham. In time this became one of the great fairs of the country, achieving almost national importance and attracting leading traders from London and other towns.

Within the Norman borough, lying between the castle and the Anglian township, was the open ground, nearly six acres in extent, which became the common market-place for the two communities. When regular markets were first held is not known, nor is it clear when they effectively supplanted the daily market at Weekday Cross, for the latter continued to be held on a small scale until the year 1800. A charter of the 12th century, however, confirms the use of the Great Market Place as a Saturday market. An interesting feature of later date was the wall, breast high, which ran across the Market Place, dividing it into two sections. While it is clearly indicated on Speede's map (Plate XV) its purpose is unknown, though it may have served to divide the area occupied by livestock from that containing the stalls for the sale of corn, malt, bread, ironware and other such commodities, but even this is conjecture. The wall remained in existence until the early 18th century.

The occurrence of two adjacent boroughs is to be found elsewhere, as at Norwich and Northampton. In the former case, as in Nottingham, the two markets remained distinct for a long period, but in Nottingham the large size and central position of the Market Place in the Norman borough, besides the relatively low flat ground which it occupied conspired to make it a natural focus for the town as a whole and as such it has persisted to this day, providing the city with an impressive centre.

Throughout the Middle Ages some contrasts between the English and Norman communities lingered on long after the town became unified in the physical sense and earlier animosities forgotten. The terms 'English borough' and 'French borough' remained current until the mid-15th century. Separate juries sat at quarter sessions until the end of the 17th century and the custom of electing two sheriffs continued until as late as 1835. Even today the Sheriff of Nottingham on ceremonial occasions bears two maces as a reminder of the city's dual origin. One of the most significant differences was the matter of inheritance, for in the Norman borough descent went to the eldest heir, while in the English borough the pre-Conquest practice of descent to the youngest son was maintained. 'The latter custom', of Borough English, remarks Professor A. C. Wood, 'was not peculiar to Nottingham . . . . . but the actual name of Borough English seems to have been derived from the English borough of Nottingham'.

In economic terms medieval Nottingham played a twofold role. It developed as a general trading centre and source of supply for a large tract of country reaching from parts of Derbyshire to the Vale of Belvoir. From districts to the east, across the Trent, cattle provided meat and hides for tanning; barley was brought in for a brewing industry which later became famous. Charcoal from the timber of Sherwood, and coal, even closer at hand, provided fuel for use in the town and for sale to other parts. Secondly, Nottingham shared in the wool trade which was the basis of the national commerce during the period. The town was an important outlet for wool produced on the Derbyshire uplands and elsewhere in the Midlands, whence it was conveyed on the Trent to ports such as Hull, Lincoln and Boston. Cloth-making was also a leading pursuit in the town itself, for a gild of weavers was one of the earliest to be established and a charter of Henry II supported the dyeing of cloth by restricting the process, within a certain radius, to the borough itself.

In the 15th century, Nottingham's general importance and its position among the leading towns of the country was recognised by its advancement to the status of a county on its own by letters patent from Henry IV, usually referred to as the Great Charter of 1449.

Post-medieval

In the early 17th century, at the time of Speede's map (Plate XV), the population of Nottingham was about 4,000. The map shows the town essentially as it had been for several centuries. In fact the outstanding feature of post-medieval and early modern Nottingham was the persistence of its small size, despite a steady, and later on an accelerated, population growth. For a period embracing the latter part of the 17th century and the first half of the 18th century Nottingham was an outstandingly attractive town, almost a garden city. Around 1720, when there were about 2,000 dwellings and 10,000 inhabitants, the town was noted for its spaciousness and the great number of houses with gardens and orchards. At this time also its architectural heritage was handsomely enriched. In 1674 William Cavendish, Duke of Newcastle, began to build his mansion on the site of the castle ruins and soon many other elegant houses appeared. Among those surviving are Newdigate House (1675), Bromley House (1732), Willoughby House (*c.* 1743) and Lord Howe's house (*c.* 1790). In 1724 the Exchange Building was erected at the eastern end of the Market Place and remained until it was replaced in the 1920's by the present Council House. Among several charitable bequests were the graceful Abel Collins Alms Houses (1709), one of the most beautiful buildings in the Midlands, but these were demolished some years ago, not without a storm of public protest. This was indeed an era of urban splendour and Nottingham was acclaimed by visitors from home and abroad as the pleasantest of towns and the cleanest outside London. Prosperity was combined with urbanity and, in the words of Professor J. D. Chambers, 'Nottingham was basking in the full Augustan sun'.

Pre-Enclosure

In the latter half of the 18th century, however, an unmistakable change set in, leading to a marked deterioration of conditions in the town. As the late G. M. Trevelyan remarked, 'Golden ages are not all gold and they never last long'. The beginnings of industrialization, which might have extended the golden age, did otherwise. Framework-knitting, the town's staple industry and precursor of the modern knitwear industry, continued to grow, both as a domestic activity and in the new factories, while machine-made lace soon gave further scope for manufacturing. Labour was in constant demand, drawing unlimited numbers of men, women and children from the surrounding area. The urban population increased

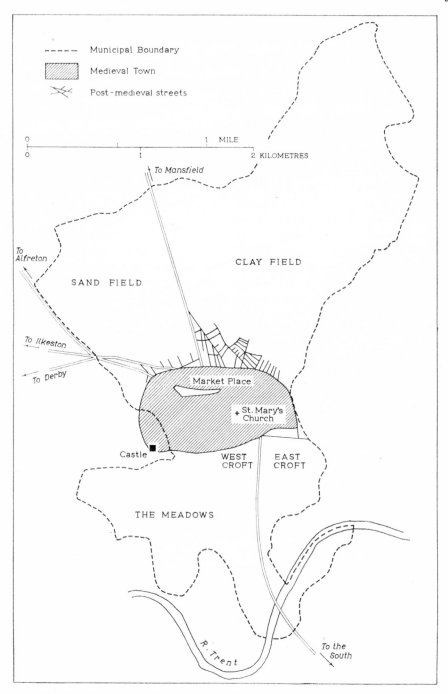

Fig. 63   The common lands of Nottingham, c1480 (based on R. M. Butler)

alarmingly yet had to be accommodated within the small compass of the medieval town which covered a bare 800 acres. In the course of time, narrow streets and alleys lined with miserable hovels were made between the existing thoroughfares and every interior space was filled with dwellings and workshops. Squalor was rampant. This phase of intensified growth within, unaccompanied by any outward expansion, exercised a profound influence upon later development, even to the present day, for, without affecting the size and shape of the town, it substantially altered the urban texture.

By 1831, with a population of well over 50,000, the town had become appallingly overcrowded. The map of the same date, by Staveley and Woods (Plate XVI) shows that the only extensions of the built-up area since medieval times were a narrow fringe on the south, between the Leen and the Nottingham canal, a ribbon-like prolongation northwards along the road to Mansfield; the beginnings of development outside the old western gate at Chapel Bar; and, on the east, a group of streets filling the gap between the old town and Sneinton. Yet industrialization itself was not the main reason for the dismal condition. The primary cause was the persistent opposition of the burgesses and freemen to the enclosure of the commonable lands which lay around the town. These lands consisted chiefly of the Sand Field and Clay Field to the north (their names reflecting the contrast between the two major geological formations, namely the Bunter and Keuper respectively), together with the East Croft, the West Croft and the Meadows which formed part of the Trent flood-plain to the south. In addition there was the Forest (124 acres) and the Duke of Newcastle's park (150 acres) most of which was still open and let out for grazing to local farmers and butchers (Fig. 63). The total extent of common land falling within the municipal boundary, but outside the built-up area, amounted to some 1,400 acres.

Apart from forfeiting the privilege of common rights, many influential citizens owning property in the town feared the loss of their rents if expansion took place. Repeated attempts at local elections to dislodge the obstructionists were made without success. Eventually, pressure of public opinion, aided by an extension of the franchise following the Reform Act of 1832, led to the passing of the Nottingham Enclosure Act in 1845. The town at last broke its bounds and entered on a new phase of growth (Fig. 66).

Enclosure and expansion

The effect of Enclosure upon urban expansion has been closely examined by Professor J. D. Chambers and it is relevant here to quote fully from his study entitled *A Century of Nottingham History, 1851–1951* (Figs. 64 and 65):

> With the Enclosure Act of 1845 began a phase in the development of Nottingham to which the key has only recently been found. It consists of the Enclosure Award, drawn up by the three commissioners appointed under the Act of 1845, and it gives the distribution of the allotments of the various owners and their names, and also the lay-out of the new streets.

The plan drawn up by the commissioners is substantially the plan of a very large part of Nottingham today, and is worthy of the closest study. It took them twenty years to complete their work, for it was not until 1865 that they laid down their office and handed over the area which they had marked out to the jurisdiction of the Corporation. In the meantime, development had taken place in many parts, although the roads were not made up, and bitter complaints were made that communications were almost impossible owing to the roads being reduced to a sea of mud in winter time. This, as we might expect, was especially serious in the case of the Meadows and above all Arkwright Street, the condition of which in times of flood can be imagined. But the commissioners were unperturbed, and continued on their leisurely way, not merely laying out new streets, but conditioning the development of Nottingham in the Meadows, the Sand Field and the Clay Field from that day to the present. Briefly, their method was to set out allotments according to the claims of the various owners, of whom there were about 400. They had to arrange the allotments according to the road plan which seems generally to have followed the pre-enclosure field paths; and these go back to the Middle Ages and beyond . . . . . Within the pattern thus laid down by history or by nature the allotments of all shapes and sizes were set out, each in the possession of a separate owner. This system was followed over the entire area of the Meadows and the Sand Field and Clay Field; and of course each one of the new owners had an un-fettered right to develop his allotment subject to the provision of the Enclosure Act. Since there were about four hundred owners there were, in effect, four hundred little town planners at work, each busily engaged in the development of his allotment according to his own ideas and without reference to what was taking place on the allotment of his neighbour . . . . . Although the streets were laid out without design or intention—except to get the maximum number of houses on the available land—each street formed a community of its own, centring on the public house or the chapel, a unit that might well be more intimately bound together than the modern housing estate or neighbourhood. The new Nottingham was drab and depressing beyond description to the modern eyes; but it was vastly more healthy and not less intimate than the old . . . . . So the Lammas Lands and Meadows were enclosed and a wilderness of Victorian bricks and mortar took their place; and since Victorian building was solid, it remains with us today ugly but habitable.

In other directions, too, the development of Nottingham proceeded rapidly in the second half of the 19th century and, on the part of the Corporation, with remarkable enlightenment. Almost the first step to be taken following the Enclosure Act was the allocation of 130 acres for public recreation which resulted in the creation of the Arboretum and the Forest as public open spaces, perhaps the earliest statutory provision of this kind in the country. Later, in 1875, lease of the Castle was acquired from the Duke of Newcastle and the building opened as a museum and art gallery and its grounds converted into another public park. In 1871 the medieval bridge over the river was replaced by the modern Trent Bridge. Between 1882 and 1884 the construction of the 60-feet wide tree-lined roads known as the Boulevards (Gregory, Radford, Lenton and Castle Boulevards) which made a rectangular circuit of the town on the north, west and south sides, was a far-sighted project, still of immense value. At the close of the century, the town having already spread southward to the Trent, plans were made to build the Victoria Embankment which resulted in the present riverside promenade, opened in 1901.

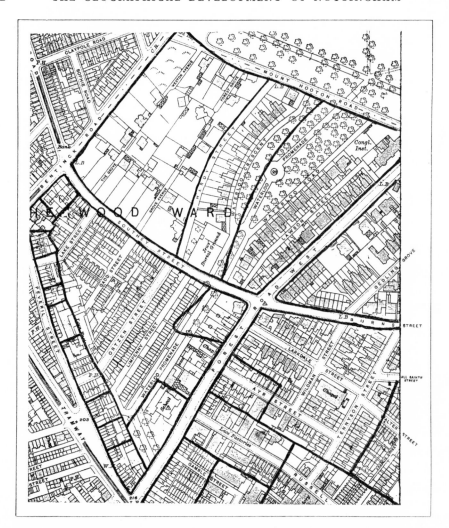

Fig. 64   Urban development on the Sand Field

In the historic core, which remained congested and blighted with slums, progress was for a time less evident, although improved access to the Market Place on the north side was made by the construction of Market Street (1865) and King Street and Queen Street (1892). These operations also removed at least a fraction of the worst slums, including the ill-famed 'Rookeries'. In 1884 improvement to Parliament Street itself, which ran east–west along the line of the north wall of the medieval town, enabled it to become one of the main shopping thoroughfares. Onwards from 1850 much of the area which contained the original Anglo-Danish borough was

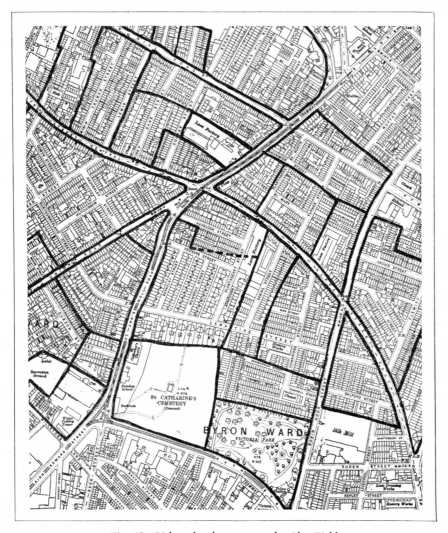

Fig. 65   Urban development on the Clay Field

transformed into the specialised quarter known as the Lace Market (see p. 386), while the privately-developed residential district called The Park, immediately to the west of the Castle (see p. 389) was begun in 1854.

These are only some of the more outstanding features of Nottingham's development following the release from its prolonged confinement within its medieval bounds. With a major boundary extension in 1877, some 20 years of growth by accretion was succeeded by growth by amalgamation. The incorporation of the outlying centres of Lenton, Radford, Basford and Bulwell along the Leen valley to the west and north–west, Carrington and Sherwood to the north and Sneinton to the east, brought a large additional population and proportionately an even larger acreage of land (Fig. 66). In 1871 the population was 86,600, but with the areas added in 1877 it was 157,000. Growth thereafter continued to be rapid and by 1891 it reached 213,800 and soon after the turn of the century it exceeded 250,000.

The second half of the 19th century was also the period of greatest industrial expansion in Nottingham. By this time the factory system was well established as the basis of manufacturing. With the piecemeal development of the town following the Enclosure Act of 1845, industry profited as much as housing from the sites made available on the former common lands. As a result the new areas of working–class dwellings were interspersed with factories mainly devoted to lace- and hosiery-making and some to light engineering. In particular, however, industrial premises, especially the large ones and those concerned with heavier forms of production, became concentrated on the flat valley floors of the Trent and Leen adjacent to the railways (Fig. 68). Eventually industrial activity came to overshadow most other forms of land use along the Trent valley north of the river, from Netherfield (Carlton Urban District) in the east to Long Eaton (Derbyshire) in the west, a distance of nearly 10 miles. Along the Leen, for a distance almost as great, a similar ribbon of industrialization emerged, though narrower and a little more intermittent.

South of the Trent, little development of any kind took place along the valley, save for the growth of West Bridgford as a residential suburb across the bridge. This expansion began shortly before 1890 and, in 1891, with a population of 2,600, of which the great majority earned their living in Nottingham, West Bridgford was granted the status of an independent Urban District. The Trent, already an administrative boundary between city and county, now became a sociological boundary separating the middle-class, non-artisan community of West Bridgford from the wholly working–class industrial area of Nottingham known as the Meadows, which lay between it and the city centre.

20th-century growth

The problems of housing which Nottingham inherited from the grim period of overcrowding before 1845 remained a pressing one in some parts of the city for many decades afterwards. As old property deteriorated further, slum conditions continued to spread or to intensify even until the first World War. Conspicuous advances in slum clearance and re-housing, however, were made by the local authority between 1920 and 1939, but the task was hampered, largely by the continued increase in population, as it has been since the last war, aggravated, too, by building shortages and other difficulties. It is not surprising, therefore, that for the past 40 years the Corporation has been pre-occupied with housing schemes. A determined policy of local-authority development has resulted in the creation of numerous housing estates

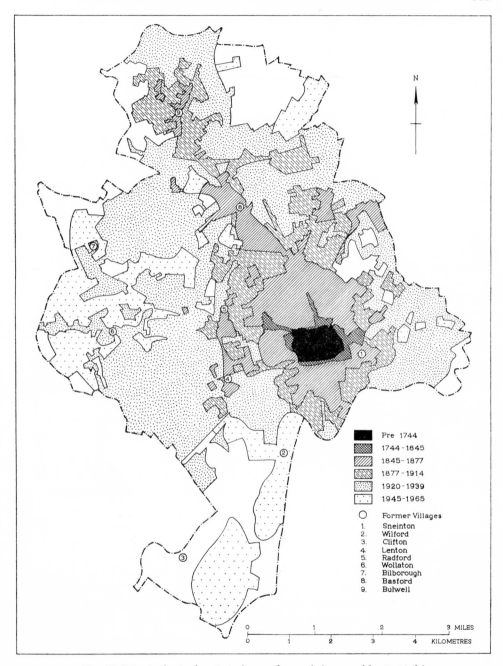

	Pre 1744
	1744-1845
	1845-1877
	1877-1914
	1920-1939
	1945-1965

○ Former Villages
1. Sneinton
2. Wilford
3. Clifton
4. Lenton
5. Radford
6. Wollaton
7. Bilborough
8. Basford
9. Bulwell

Fig. 66 Nottingham, showing phases of growth (prepared by S. Little)

of varying size, distributed especially on the western and northern fringes of the city. A boundary extension in 1935 enabled further expansion of this kind to take place in the same general directions, while a further extension across the Trent in 1951 resulted in the building at Clifton of the latest and the largest of the housing schemes, which will accommodate 30,000 people (Fig. 66). Between the wars the Corporation erected nearly 17,500 dwellings and since the second World War it has built a further 15,600. Some 124,000 people, or well over one-third of the total population, now live in council-built homes (Appendix VI).

The outward movement of population from the centre since the early part of the century is clearly shown in Fig. 67. During the inter-war period (1931) residential growth took place rather more to the east, in the Mapperley Ward, and in the Urban District of Carlton, than to the west; but more recently this trend has been reversed, largely because of the boundary extension which provided land for large-scale housing development, especially in Broxtowe. It is worth noting, however, that population in the interior wards is again increasing as in Market and St. Ann's Wards where, after clearance, re-housing in modern types of accommodation is taking place.

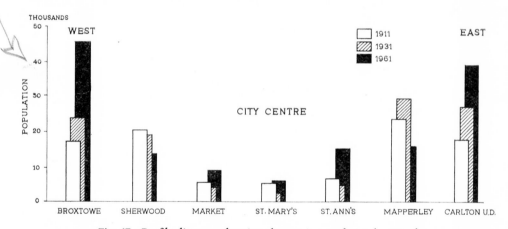

Fig. 67   Profile diagram, showing changes in population by Wards

While estates became typical of all large towns following the Housing Subsidy Act of 1919, the earliest of those in Nottingham set an example to other local authorities in lay-out and in the design and quality of dwellings. Wollaton Park (1926) may be cited as an example, although its bisection by a major highway which now forms part of the western ring road, would not be acceptable under present-day planning practice.

The extensive spread of municipal housing planned, for the most part, at comparatively low densities per acre, has consumed a huge acreage of land and, as was shown by the need for a site at Clifton, no large undeveloped areas remain within

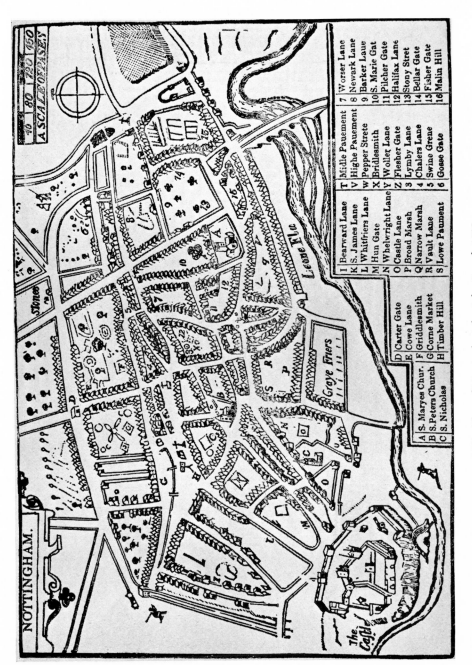

XV Plan of Nottingham by John Speed, 1610

XVI   Plan of Nottingham by E. Staveley and H. M. Woods, 1831

the city. The former policy which opposed the construction of flats has been relaxed in recent years and in districts of re-development near the centre considerable use is now being made of multi-storeyed blocks. Since 1945 there has been comparatively little building by private enterprise, although a good deal has taken place in the adjoining urban districts and in country areas beyond, attracting people in the middle and higher income groups from the city. In this respect the economic and social interdependence existing between Nottingham and the four contiguous urban areas has been further consolidated.

Industrial development, while becoming more diversified during the present century, has shown no marked change in distribution. More intensive use of the Trent and Leen valleys has been made by the expansion of existing firms and the coming of new ones. In the Trent valley the enlargement of Boots' chemical works near the Midland Station has also been accompanied by the building of additional factories at Beeston onwards from 1932, again on the floodplain. The development of the Royal Ordnance factory, now to accommodate a substantial transference of work from Woolwich Arsenal, is another example. On the Trent bank itself large extensions to the North Wilford electricity generating station (with an adjacent source of coal from Clifton colliery) have been made, and close to the new bridge at Clifton (1958) an estate for future light industry has recently been prepared. At Colwick, eastwards beyond the city boundary, the production of beet-sugar was started in 1924. In the opposite direction, the telephone and electronic equipment works of Ericssons at Beeston and the Royal Ordnance Corps mechanical transport depot at Chilwell have also expanded. Along the Leen valley, the growth of Raleigh Industries (formerly the Raleigh Cycle Company) and the development of light industry along Triumph Road to the west of the railway have resulted in the building-up of one of the few remaining sites in this portion of the industrial zone.

The largest of the new sites for industrial development is that situated on Glaisdale Drive, in the heart of the extensive housing estate area in west Nottingham, adjoining the railway which runs westward to the Erewash valley (Fig. 68). On the north side of the line, actually dependent on road and not railway access, is a group of miscellaneous factories located there for the purpose of giving employment to those living in the vicinity. To the south of the railway is Wollaton colliery, which is about to be closed.

Before concluding this section, brief mention should be made of one of Nottingham's most distinctive features as a town, the use made for many purposes of its man-made caves. Wherever the Bunter Sandstone forms the bedrock, past generations, especially in the area of the medieval town, have excavated the sandstone so extensively that a labyrinth of underground caves and passages has been produced. Most of these date from medieval times and onward and it is doubtful if any were of prehistoric origin, although there is a record of Neolithic implements being found in a cave discovered during the construction of Victoria Station in 1900.

AA

The most famous of the passages is that known as Mortimer's Hole, which afforded a secret entrance to the Castle through the Castle Rock. Among the caves shown to sightseers the most popular are those belonging to the ancient inn called 'Ye Olde Trip to Jerusalem' built into the foot of the Castle Rock. Deep cellars are a feature of many of the older inns for the exceptional dryness of the rock and the constant air temperature of about 11°C (52°F) were highly advantageous in the days of home brewing. Beneath one of the inns is a large regularly-cut cave which served as an arena for cock-fighting with a small ante-chamber for the bird-pens.

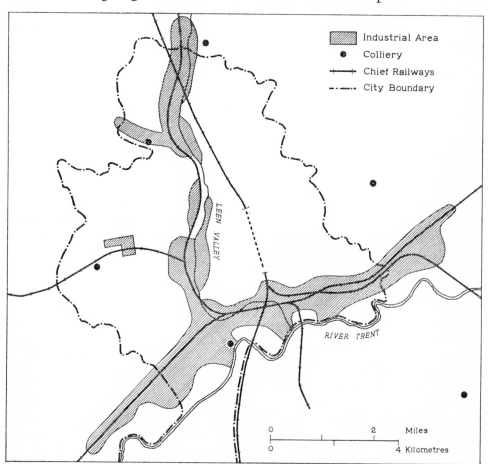

Fig. 68 Nottingham, showing the chief industrial areas

Most of the caves were situated under business premises and were used for the storage of goods, as indeed they still are. Some have at times been used for dwellings. Others at or near the surface have been used for burial, as in the Rock Cemetery

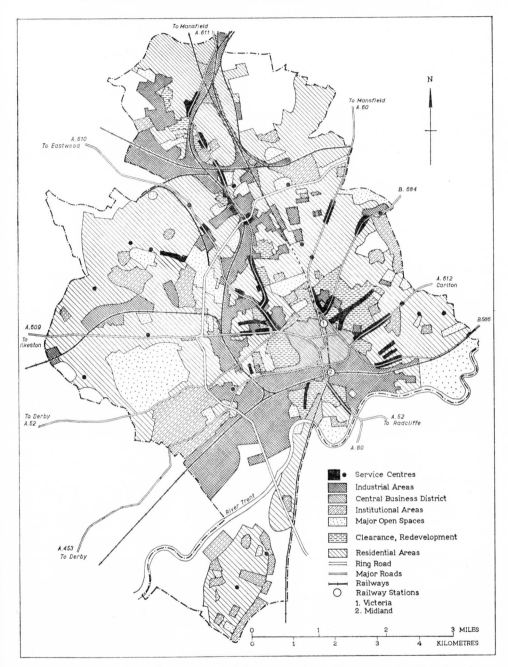

Fig. 69 Nottingham, showing principal forms of land use, 1965 (prepared by J. A. Giggs)

on Mansfield Road, and a still more recent use is for the garaging of cars. An interesting example of the use of deep cellars for commercial purposes dates from the late 17th century, when Thomas Smith, a Nottingham merchant, founded the well-known Smith's Bank (later absorbed by the National Provincial Bank). Smith utilised rock cellars under his premises on the south side of the Market Place for the safeguarding of customers' goods, deposited with him during their absence from the town, and later on, as confidence in his reliability grew, he was entrusted with money as well.

Under what circumstances so many of the cellars became interconnected by underground passages, often tortuous in plan, is not clearly understood. Such accommodation was nevertheless put to good use as public air-raid shelters during the last war, some of them being large enough to hold over 1,000 people. It is likely that a complete survey of Nottingham's underground world has never been made, nor ever could be. As a result, re-development in the central area often necessitates careful preliminary boring before large structures are erected.

THE FUNCTIONAL PATTERN

Having traced the broad stages in the growth and development of the city a brief summary of the present-day functional pattern, as shown in Fig. 69, can now be made. The central business district is focussed on the market place, now officially termed Old Market Square, and extends for a limited distance along the streets leading out from it. It also includes Parliament Street, on which is Theatre Square. Broadly speaking, the area lies between the Castle and the Lace Market in one direction, and between the two main railway stations in the other. One important extension is that leading westwards along Castle Boulevard where, on both sides of this thoroughfare, is the greatest concentration of motor-vehicle sales and service facilities to be found in the city (Fig. 70). This specialisation of function is due to a number of closely related circumstances, namely, the position of the highway as part of the main route from Trent Bridge to the north and west, avoiding the town centre, the availability of comparatively cheap land on sites previously not fully developed, together with the favourable breadth of the road and the absence of any gradient. The market place was largely transformed in the 1920's by the removal of the stalls to a covered building on Parliament Street and by the erection of the present Council House, with its formal approach. So great is the emphasis upon retailing in this area that the ground-floor arcade of the Council House was also designed for shops. North of Parliament Street, a further grouping of central functions, including municipal services, occurs as a result of late-19th century development: the Guildhall (1888) contains offices of the Corporation departments and the Courts; the Public Library (1881) and the former University College building, now incorporated in the Regional College of Technology; and the Police and Fire Service stations (rebuilt in 1940). As re-development proceeds in this quarter this assemblage will form part of a planned civic centre.

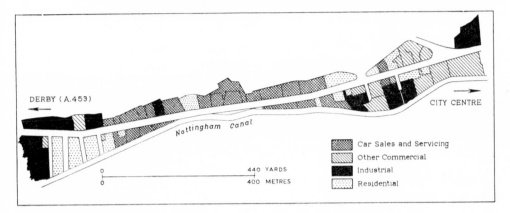

Fig. 70   Land use on Castle Boulevard, Nottingham

A more detailed analysis of functions is shown by the first three maps in Fig. 71. Since much of the central area is now undergoing re-development, the fourth map in this series shows the distribution of recently erected buildings, some of them tall office blocks, as well as older building sites in which obsolete property contains vacant floor-space either in advance of demolition or in cases where leases are running out.

Around the central business district, except immediately on the south, is a zone of poor-quality 19th-century housing, interspersed with older industrial premises. To the south this is represented by much of the Meadows district, which lies within the industrial belt. This is the typical 'zone of decay' to be found in so many cities and in Nottingham, as elsewhere, much of it is now in process of clearance and re-development. Beyond this zone stretch the major tracts in the city devoted to residential use, varying in age from late Victorian days to post-war housing estates. Of these, the areas lying outside the ring road chiefly represent the expansion of the town since 1920. Similarly, to the south of the Trent, parts of Wilford and the entire Clifton estate are of very recent date (see p. 376). Within this residential zone, as shown in Fig. 69, are numerous institutional areas. These are chiefly occupied by schools, but the two largest, lying adjacent to the ring road, are the sites of the University (south–west) and the City Hospital (north). Between the roads leading to Derby (A.52) and Ilkeston (A.609) is Wollaton Park (774 acres), by far the largest of Nottingham's public open spaces. The Park, including Wollaton Hall, the large mansion dating from 1588 (now the Natural History Museum), was purchased from the Willoughby family by the Corporation in 1925 (see p. 419) and a portion of the land used for the Wollaton Park housing estate.

The industrial areas of the city have already been referred to (p. 377 and Fig. 68), but in Fig. 69 their distribution is indicated in greater detail.

Lace Mkr.

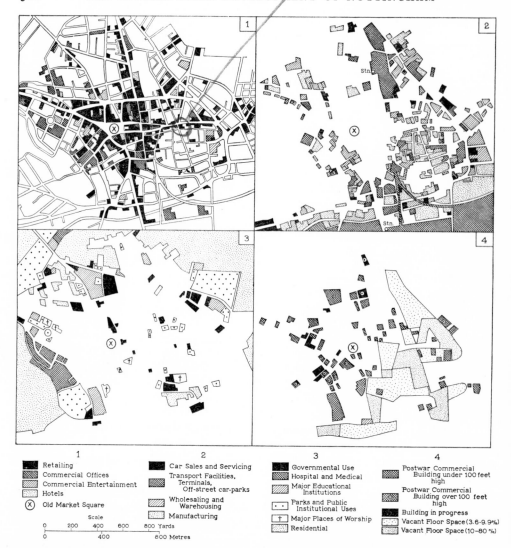

Fig. 71   Aspects of land use in the central area of Nottingham, 1965 (from J. A. Giggs)

As the regional centre for the East Midlands (or North Midlands), Nottingham is the headquarters of various Government departments and nationalised undertakings. Some of these are housed in a group of offices built for the purpose near Western Boulevard, while others have found accommodation in buildings more widely scattered, the latest being the Department of Economic Affairs.

In functional lay-out Nottingham is distinctive and perhaps unique on account of the two contrasted and highly specialized districts which lie immediately to the east and west of the centre: the Lace Market and The Park estate respectively. The former is a commercial quarter, having its own particular character, the limits of which are broadly coincident with those of the old English borough. The Park is a private residential district, planned in mid-Victorian days and redolent of the social characteristics of that age. Between the Lace Market and The Park is the historic market-place, now known as Old Market Square, which also contains some interesting features. All three areas merit somewhat fuller description.

Old Market Square

Reference has already been made to the origin and development of the market-place (see pp. 365, 367). Early descriptions repeatedly stress its size and impressive appearance. Thus, Leland, writing in the first half of the 16th century, claims that 'both for the buildings on the site of it, and for the very great wideness of the street and the clean paving of it, it is the fairest without exception of all England'. More than a century later, the historian Deering recorded a similar impression: 'The west entrance to Nottingham (i.e. at Chapel Bar) offers to the traveller's view a market-place in spaciousness superior to most, inferior to few, if any, in the kingdom, graced with many beautiful buildings'.

Although today the various markets are dispersed to other parts of the city and there are now few buildings which date back earlier than mid-19th century, Old Market Square remains *par excellence* the leading shopping centre. Nevertheless, there are many surviving details of its past form and character and many reminders of its earlier contributions to Nottingham's economic development. Firstly is the obvious fact that the extent and general plan of the 'square' has remained almost unchanged since the medieval period, the principal exception being the encroachment at the eastern end by the present Council House and its predecessors (Fig. 72). Secondly is the survival of many narrow streets and passages which lead off the Square to adjoining parts of the city. Some of these are of medieval origin, others date from a later period. Some now serve merely as pedestrian thoroughfares, others lead only to a small half-hidden court, such as that giving access to Bromley House. A few contain old-established business premises, for example tailors and milliners, dealing in specialised high-quality goods for a small but regular clientele. Others again have been widened to give easier access to the former market-place, Market Street itself being an example, although Exchange Walk, dating from 1868, was designed for pedestrians alone.

A third feature of the old market-place which persists as a present-day characteristic is the colonnade (*piazza*) which runs almost continuously along the north side (Long Row), though only intermittently on the south. This certainly existed in the early 18th century but the time of its first appearance is indefinite. Besides affording shelter, the colonnade allows the upper storeys of buildings to be extended outwards.

Yet another reminder of the past consists of the names applied to the streets which fringe the open space. Many of these denote sections of the market which were allocated to particular trades and commodities. Thus, on the south side, eastwards from Chapel Bar, are Beastmarket Hill, South Parade (formerly Timber Row) and Poultry. Opposite the last-named is Cheapside, now forming the south side of the Council House, the north side of which is Smithy Row. In the old Exchange Building (erected in 1724 and rebuilt in 1814), which preceded the Council House, was a butchers' market known as the Shambles, which was also of early origin. In comparatively recent years, however, this was moved to one of the narrow streets leading from Chapel Bar to Parliament Street and was known as the West End Meat Market. Still more recently the latter has become the West End Arcade, with only one or two butchers left. Angel Row, between Chapel Bar and Beastmarket Hill, is probably derived from a connection with one of the medieval religious institutions which stood close to the market-place.

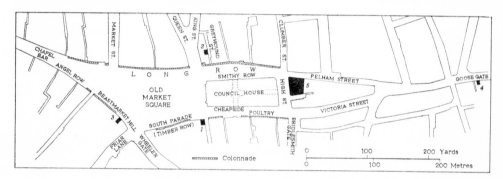

Fig. 72   Features of Old Market Square

Key

1   Thomas Smith, 1658 (Smith's Bank, 1688; National Provincial Bank, 1917)
2   J. and R. Morley, Stockingers, *c.*1785 (later I. and R. Morley Ltd.)
3   John Player, Tobacconist, 1877 (succeeded William Wright, 1828)
4   Jesse Boot, Herbalist, 1877 (Boots Pure Drug Co., 1887)
5   Boots' Chemists, head store

    Around Old Market Square are some of Nottingham's oldest inns and hotels. On Long Row West, the Talbot Inn, with its sign depicting a talbot, or hunting dog, probably dates from the 14th century, though it was rebuilt about 1600 and again last century. On Long Row East, Maypole Yard marks the site of the Maypole Inn, which, in coaching days, was the terminus of the service between Nottingham and Derby. Further on is the Black Boy Hotel, also a coaching inn, with Black Boy Yard at the rear once providing the stabling and the exit to the north. Opposite, on the south side of the Council House, is the Flying Horse, bearing the date 1483. Though restored, the present hotel is of the Elizabethan period, but it rests on the foundations of a much older building, beneath which are extensive rock cellars. The Bell, once called The Angel, on Angel Row, is an ancient inn whose origin is obscure. Well over 500 years ago it was a refectory belonging to a religious institution and it is claimed that the flagstones in the main passage-way date from that time. The cellars in the rock below are regarded as being older still.

Last among the details which recall the past are the sites on which some of Nottingham's best-known trades and industries originated. These are shown on Fig. 72 and include the premises at the corner of Exchange Walk (identified by a plaque) where Thomas Smith founded the 18th-century bank; the stockingers' workshop and first warehouse in Greyhound Street belonging to John and Richard Morley, later the hosiery firm of I. and R. Morley Ltd.; John Player's tobacconist shop on Beastmarket Hill, which he took over from William Wright, the previous owner; in Goose Gate, little more than a stone's throw from the market-place, the small herbalist store which in 1863, Jesse Boot, as a boy of 13, began to manage on behalf of his widowed mother; and in High Street the first of Boots branch shops (1883), still the leading one in Nottingham.

With the expansion of modern Nottingham and the accompanying increase in traffic, the role of the market-place changed. Stage by stage its market functions were withdrawn. As long ago as 1870 the entire livestock section was removed to another site; in 1900, largely to allow for the passage of electric tramways, the wholesale activity in fish, fruit and vegetables was transferred to Sneinton; finally, in 1928, with the erection of the Council House, the retail stalls were transferred to the new Central Market building, adjoining Parliament Street. The year 1927, moreover, was the last in which the famous Goose Fair was held in the market-place. The Fair had taken place here almost without interruption since the 13th century and possibly earlier. Beginning on the first Thursday in October, it lasted for several days and drew vast crowds. In 1704, Marshall Tallard, who was captured at Blenheim and brought to Nottingham for internment, wrote to the French king after seeing the Goose Fair, advising him to end the war, for he had seen as many men congregated in one English market-place as could conquer the whole of France! The Fair is now held on the Forest recreation ground.

Devoid of its markets and fair the great market-place remains as the natural focus for much of Nottingham's business activity and public entertainment. For diversity of shopping facilities it is unexcelled and this is particularly true of Long Row on the north side. Long Row has a tradition to maintain in retail enterprise and the supply of fashionable goods. Perhaps this reputation for enterprise reaches back to the time when, in 1615, the George and Dragon Inn, where Long Row adjoins Chapel Bar, was the first brick building to be erected in the town, or to 1838, when one of the shops was the first to use plate-glass for window display. Others might argue that Long Row, on slightly higher ground than the south side, derives advantage from its southerly aspect, which gives it a greater amount of sunshine. In terms of trade and traffic, however, these differences are of little consequence.

Besides its shops, banks, offices, inns and hotels, two of the three largest cinemas are located in Old Market Square, the third being in Theatre Square. Nottingham's three theatres, although not in the Square, are all at short distances from it. Similarly, for historical reasons already made clear, none of the older churches nor any other large place of worship stands in the Square. St. Peter's is just beyond the south side, while the Roman Catholic Cathedral (1844) and the Albert Hall Methodist Mission are a little beyond Chapel Bar. As a focus of communications Old Market Square is still the terminus for some of the municipal bus routes, but the increasing pressure of traffic in recent years has resulted in the re-routing of some services and the use of peripheral termini for others.

From the architectural standpoint, the present-day appearance of Old Market Square poses a dilemma, quite apart from the general unharmonious blend of old and new. On the one hand, the buildings around the margin present a miscellaneous assemblage of differing styles, while on the other, an entirely unrelated element is introduced by the Council House and the formal lay-out of a large portion of the open ground intended to harmonise with it.

The Lace Market

The Lace Market occupies the relatively high ground around St. Mary's church. Functionally and architecturally it forms a highly distinctive quarter, unique among English towns, consisting of a massed concentration of warehouses and offices of the leading lace merchants. The gradual change from domestic lace-making to factory production in the early 19th century not only brought about an expansion in output but it promoted the rise of many firms engaged in merchandising. In the early and mid-Victorian period the area around St. Mary's was transformed from a residential district containing large and elegant houses with spacious gardens into one of gaunt, towering, brick buildings, five or even six storeys high, for the storage of huge quantities of lace and lace fabrics. The Lace Market came to occupy the greater part of the early Anglian town site, bounded by the cliff below High Pavement and Hollowstone on the south, by Goose Gate to the north, by Bridlesmith Gate to the west, and by Carter Gate (now Lower Parliament Street) to the east. It also included part of Broad Street and Heathcoat Street which lie north of Goose Gate. These large buildings were erected almost without a break along Stoney Street, St. Mary's Gate and Fletcher Gate, and on all the narrow streets and passages connecting them. In time most features of the pre-industrial age in the old town disappeared to make way for the new development. Plumptre House, built in 1714 as a residence by John Plumptre, the descendant of one of Nottingham's most illustrious families, was demolished in 1855 to provide space for Broadway; the town theatre in St. Mary's Gate, dating from 1760, was removed, to be followed later on by the ancient Guildhall in Weekday Cross. Only St. Mary's and the Shire Hall (1770) remained, as they do to this day. Interspersed with the warehouses were a few lace and hosiery factories. Similar warehouse accommodation, less concentrated and on a smaller scale, also appeared further west towards the Castle on Hounds Gate and Castle Gate.

Not all the warehouses were gaunt and forbidding in appearance and some of the wealthiest firms, like Thomas Adams, whose offices can be seen in Stoney Street, even contrived to make them ornate. Not long before the transformation began, Nonconformist bodies had begun to establish chapels in the district, but they do not appear to have been deterred by the continuing change in its character. Hockley Methodist Chapel was built in 1782; the Baptist Chapel in Broad Street in 1815; Wesley Chapel, also in Broad Street, in 1839; the Methodist City Temple, in Halifax Place, in 1847; and the Unitarian Chapel, on High Pavement, in 1876. In George Street there was another chapel as well as a Catholic church and school (1828) and on the corner of Broad Street and Old Lenton Street a Sunday school for the religious and secular instruction of poor children, dated 1819. A People's Hall appeared in Heathcoat Street in 1854. Of all these only one survives today as a place of worship.

From the 'eighties until the first World War, the period covering the heyday of Nottingham's famous industry, the Lace Market became renowned; indeed, the small area which it encompassed represented a large proportion of the city's wealth. The importance of the export trade and its international connections and the coming of immigrant trading firms, especially from France and Germany, some of whose names survive, gave to this specialised quarter a distinctly cosmopolitan air. By 1874, 75 per cent of all those owning property on Stoney Street were connected with the lace trade; in Pilcher Gate, 74 per cent were similarly concerned, while in St. Mary's Gate the proportion was 82 per cent and on Broadway 100 per cent. The position in 1885 was even more striking. From this congested area, with its army of office workers and warehousemen, every package of lace and fabric had to be conveyed to the railway-station for despatch. Much of this movement was concentrated on the Thursday of each week, the early-closing day for shops, so as to take advantage of reduced traffic in the town. There are still elderly people in Nottingham who can recall the processions of heavily-laden horse-drawn vehicles clattering along the cobbled streets on their way to the station.

Today the Lace Market is again in the throes of change, a process which has been sharply accelerated in recent years. For a long time past the decline in business of the great export houses has resulted in a progressive sub-letting of offices and warehouse capacity to other firms. Increasingly, buildings have been converted to other uses, such as hosiery, clothing and light engineering factories. One of the commonest among the newcomers is the small printing firm, of which there are now more than half-a-dozen, although a few printers had always found it advantageous to have their works in an area so largely devoted to office activities. Moreover, as the city population spread outward into the suburbs, the chapels were found to be inconveniently situated and most of these have been put to other uses or left to decay. War damage, chiefly the result of air attacks in 1941, which left derelict sites in its wake, added further to the spectacle of change. Some of these sites, like those resulting from the current demolition of older property, have provided useful car-parking space. In Barker Gate, the East Midlands divisional headquarters of the Central Electricity Generating Board occupy one of the former lace-market buildings. On Broad Street, the Nottingham Co-operative Society's Education Centre has replaced the old Wesley Chapel, and on Stoney Street a new Post Office has been built.

Fig. 73   Land use in the Lace Market, Nottingham, 1965
(*Survey by D. Turner*)

Although the first stages of re-development are now in progress, the future role of the Lace Market is far from evident. A number of lace, hosiery and clothing factories continue to function successfully, while the lace trade itself, though operating on a smaller scale than formerly, is still in a flourishing condition, making full use of most of the remaining office and warehouse capacity. Thus, the area still serves the essential purpose for which it was created. Despite considerable diversification of interests, it is still indisputably the Lace Market. As such it continues to exhibit one very distinctive feature as a specialised quarter within the city: while by day it is busy, even bustling with activity, by night it is silent, almost without traffic and empty of people.

The Park estate

The Park is also an area of quite exceptional character. It is a private estate, planned in the mid-19th century to accommodate well-to-do citizens. Though much of its glory has faded and many of the houses converted into flats, it is still a strictly residential area, with gated entrances, closed one day in the year to preserve the right of private access. Its large red-brick dwellings, ornamental with Gothic and, to a lesser extent Tudor detail, and gardens and rockeries often stepped on sharp declivities, are tangible evidence of Victorian enterprise and ostentation. Yet, with all this, few large cities can exhibit such an elaborate example of residential planning situated so close to the centre.

The site on which The Park estate was built has an interesting history. It formed part of several hundred acres of land lying adjacent to the Castle which, by permission of the Crown, was enclosed in the 12th century for the use of the Castle commander. Part of the area was on the higher ground afforded by the sandstone and part on the Trent floodplain, later known as the Meadows. Following the Restoration in 1660, when the Castle had already fallen into disuse, Charles II granted an extensive acreage to William Cavendish, the first Duke of Newcastle, in return for services rendered to the Stuart cause. The Duke then built a mansion on the site of the Castle (completed in 1679), replanted his land with trees and stocked it with deer. Thus was developed a ducal residence and park flanking the heart of the town. In 1831, over a century and a half later, the house was pillaged and burned by a mob during the Reform Bill riots and the ruined building was not restored until 1875–78, when it was acquired by the Nottingham Corporation and opened as the first municipal art museum in England. The fifth Duke, whose father had suffered the loss of the house, eventually received £20,000 in compensation from the Government and in 1851 began to plan The Park estate on 155 acres of his land to the west of the Castle. By this time the low-lying portion of the Newcastle lands had been severed from the higher parts by the Nottingham–Derby railway line and with the further acquisition of land for railway development south of the Castle the unity of the ancient enclosure was entirely lost. It is interesting to note that before the coming of the railway the berths for river craft on the Nottingham canal (1795) at Wilford Road, beneath the Castle Rock, were called the Duke's Wharfs. One social link between the two areas did, however, survive, for as streets crowded with working-class dwellings spread over the Meadows beyond the canal and the railway, this community provided a supply of domestic servants for the large houses of The Park. Indeed, many domestics who did not 'live in' had their homes in the Meadows.

The Duke's enterprise in planning The Park was opportune. While, at one extreme, poverty persisted in Nottingham, at the other, rising incomes were increasingly common. Substantial profits were coming from local industry, especially from the lace trade; the coal trade was remunerative; investment in factories was proving successful and increasing dividends were coming from the railways. The new middle class of traders and *entrepreneurs* required better houses and they needed large houses for their large families. The site for the estate lay between Derby Road on the north and Lenton Road (opened in 1828), on the south. The surface was uneven, with a large, pronounced hollow sloping southwards. On the east side, between the Castle and Derby Road, the ground dropped abruptly. The lay-out was nevertheless geometrical and based on two circuses, Lincoln Circus, the more northerly, and Newcastle Circus, around which ran a series of 'Crescents', these in turn being flanked to the east and west by more or less parallel 'Drives'. The main axis connecting Derby Road with Lenton Road, passing the two circuses was formed by North Road and South Road. On one of the circuses a church was planned, in the hope of making the estate an independent parish, but it was never built. The scheme was designed by Thomas Hine, a local architect, who received the advice and support of W. E. Gladstone. Building proceeded onwards from 1854 and Hine himself, together with his assistant, C. I. Evans, was responsible for some of the larger houses, such as Peveril Towers, Clumber Court, Gladstone House and Haddon House. Though Clumber Court was demolished a few years ago, the others survive. In all, about 650 houses were built, the scheme being completed by 1887. On the north–west edge of the estate Barrack Lane recalls the existence of barracks built for the local militia in 1792 and demolished in 1855. Two minor features of The Park might be noted. One is the long flight of steps for pedestrians, leading up the steep slope from Park Valley to the entrance at the Hospital, providing the only public right of way through the estate. The other is a tunnel cut through the sandstone from an entrance in Derby Road, which gave residents possessing a key a direct route to the centre of the town, but in 1962 this was closed. In 1938 the Newcastle interests in The Park were acquired by the Nuffield Trust and passed thence to the University of Oxford, the present owners of the estate. It is still operated as a private estate, the owners still being responsible for the maintenance of roads and sewers, but for some years past residents have been able to convert their property from leasehold to freehold and now about three-quarters of the total are freehold. Today The Park is rapidly changing in character, though it remains strictly a residential area and under present planning policy it will continue to do so. In some respects it is in decline for, with some exceptions, the larger houses can no longer be maintained by individual families. As a result, many have been converted into flats and at present about a quarter of them are let in this way. A few houses have been demolished, a few new ones built. Some of the roads are in disrepair and many of the gardens are less well cared for than they once were. On the other hand, tennis courts, squash courts and bowling greens have been provided. It is estimated that some 3,250 people now reside in The Park.

SECONDARY SERVICE CENTRES

In Nottingham, as in all large towns, local or district service centres having retail, banking and post-office facilities, and in most cases provision for entertainment, are to be found in addition to the central business area. Despite the obvious attraction of the latter, many of the secondary service centres have continued to increase in importance, largely because of rising transport costs, traffic congestion in the heart of the city and the outward spread of residential development. Some of the older secondary centres, moreover, exhibit a strong local community tradition. A survey of the service centres in Nottingham (excluding Clifton), made some years ago by I. G. Weekley, revealed the existence of more than 40 of these, having various degrees of importance. They were grouped in accordance with simple quantitative criteria, reflecting the strength and variety of their service functions. On this basis six classes or orders of importance could be distinguished. Centres of the first order were those possessing at least three banks, a post-office, a Woolworth store, a Boots chemists and a cinema. Those of the second order possessed three banks, a post-office, a chain grocery store and a cinema, while for those of the third order the same criteria were adopted except that the number of banks was only two. All centres, whatever their order, possessed some general shopping facilities, those of the sixth or lowest order having only a small cluster of shops supplying day-to-day needs.

The survey (Fig. 74) showed that there are four centres of the first order (Sneinton, Hyson Green, Sherwood and Bulwell), four of the second order (Arkwright Street, St. Ann's Well Road, Alfreton Road and Basford) and two of the third order. Of some 30 centres belonging to the fourth, fifth and sixth orders, many are of relatively recent origin, located in municipal housing estates or in other areas of newer residential growth. In fact, the distribution of secondary service centres in general shows a close relationship with particular stages in Nottingham's growth. Some of them originated to serve outlying places long before the latter were absorbed into the city and they have persisted, not only to meet the needs of their own population but of the inhabitants of the areas which later grew around them. Sneinton, Basford and Bulwell afford good examples. Again, where residential development took place along radial roads leading out of the town, local service facilities often grew up in linear fashion on the main thoroughfares themselves. Arkwright Street, St. Ann's Well Road and Sherwood (Mansfield Road) are typical instances. Later still, on the planned housing estates, service facilities have been deliberately sited at convenient points, either centrally within the estate or marginally at the junction of a main road and a feeder road leading into the estate.

The district service centre forms a significant element in the internal structure of the large town, but there is space here only for a brief description of the first and second order centres in Nottingham, together with reference to the somewhat special case of the retail facilities to be found on Hockley and Goose Gate, a street which is immediately adjacent to the central business area of the city, yet in several respects distinct from it.

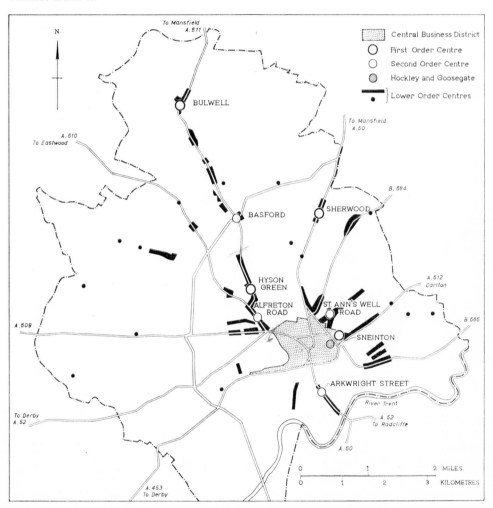

Fig. 74   Secondary service centres in Nottingham
Centres described in the text are named

First-order centres

Sneinton

Of the several outlying places which eventually became absorbed into Nottingham, Sneinton was by far the nearest, being less than half a mile to the east of the old Anglo-Saxon town (p. 366). It was the birth-place of William Booth, the founder of the Salvation Army.

XVII   View of Nottingham from the south, 1784

XVIII   View of Nottingham from the south today

During the first half of the 19th century, because of the shortage of room in Nottingham itself, factories and workers' dwellings began to spread towards Sneinton into the district to which the name New Sneinton was given. Here a small retail market appeared about 1850 which has remained active ever since. As the district grew into a densely inhabited artisan quarter this market developed in importance, while the streets adjoining it became increasingly occupied by shops and other service-providing premises. Old and New Sneinton were incorporated by the city in 1877 and control of its market passed to the municipal authority. Adjacent to the Sneinton retail market is the Nottingham wholesale market. Wholesale marketing was formerly conducted in the Old Market Place, but towards 1900, when electric tramways were introduced, it was transferred to Sneinton. In 1938, the opportunity provided by a local slum clearance scheme allowed the wholesale market to be rebuilt on a larger scale. While it was designed to give more efficient handling, the traditional three-fold division was retained; a section for fruit, vegetables and flowers; one for fish, game and poultry, and a third for country produce. The market is the main source of supply, not only to retailers throughout the city, but to the urban districts beyond. The continued expansion of this activity has reached a point when it is now felt necessary to reconstruct the market on an even larger scale.

With Nottingham's central retail market only a stone's throw away, market functions are heavily concentrated in this part of the town. The Sneinton retail market, held twice weekly, is itself distinctive on account of the wide range available, including the sale of all kinds of miscellaneous articles, both new and second-hand. As a result, it draws people from all parts of the city, leaving the shops on adjoining streets to serve the needs of the local population during the rest of the week.

Hyson Green (Radford)

Hyson Green is a shopping area of considerable importance situated to the north-west of the city centre on Radford Road above and below the intersection with Gregory Boulevard. Long before the building of St. Paul's church at Radford (1844) and the construction of Gregory Boulevard (1882), Hyson Green was the focus of activities connected with the large race-course, dating from 1690, which extended westwards from the present-day Forest Recreation Ground into the adjoining parts of Radford and Lenton. Here were concentrated the saddlers, wheelwrights and straw dealers and nearby were tea-gardens patronised by fashionable townsfolk, whether race-goers or not. With 19th-century industrial development along the Leen valley came the spread of artisan housing over much of the Radford district and with this a reduction in the size of the race-course area and the appearance of better-class houses along the western end of Gregory Boulevard. In 1895 the race-course was removed to its present site at Colwick, on the east side of Nottingham. As these changes took place Hyson Green was transformed into a shopping centre to serve a rapidly expanding residential district, though it was eventually linked with the city by a tramway route. The tradition of providing for entertainment, however, was maintained in another form by the Grand Theatre, which served successively as a music-hall, a repertory theatre (made prominent by the Compton family of actors), and a cinema, until it was demolished in 1964. Today, as a general retail centre, Hyson Green possesses a multiple store and a supermarket among its half-mile of shops, as well as a branch of the public library and a police station.

Sherwood

Sherwood is a residential district, largely of middle-class character, lying on either side of the Mansfield Road about two miles north of the city centre. The Mansfield Road is the principal outlet from Nottingham to the north, although much of the ' through traffic' is now diverted from the Sherwood section by means of the western ring road, which leaves the main road at Daybrook. Sherwood is essentially a late-19th and 20th-century extension of Carrington which originated within the angle formed by the Mansfield and Hucknall Roads about 1830. Carrington Church dates from 1842, and in the same period a few small lace and framework knitters' factories appeared. A small market-place, which can still be seen, was provided for Carrington's working-class inhabitants. Eventually, groups of suburban villas appeared at intervals along the Mansfield Road and it is to these developments that the beginnings of Sherwood can be traced. Housing extended along new streets laid out on either side of Mansfield Road, so it is not surprising that the main thoroughfare itself developed into an axis of retail activity and other service facilities. These functions extend almost continuously on both sides for a distance of over half a mile. The relatively high-grade shops, together with a suburban cinema, reflect the character of the residential neighbourhood, while the volume of trade has risen substantially since the building of the Edwards Lane housing estate (1935) and the more recent housing to the north of it. For the inhabitants of the latter, however, a small alternative shopping centre has grown up at Daybrook, also on the Mansfield Road.

Bulwell

Before its incorporation by the city in 1877, Bulwell was a small industrial township with some 4,000 inhabitants situated in the Leen valley about four miles north–north–west of Nottingham. Its separate identity was emphasized by the fact that it had its own market dating back to a much earlier period when a settlement developed at the point where the Leen passed through a stretch of the old forest waste. Bulwell Forest, now a large public recreation ground, is a remnant of the waste. Industrialisation in the mid-19th century, encouraged by direct access to two railways (Midland and Great Northern) was based on textile working, utilising old mill sites on the Leen, stone-quarrying and brick-making. Numbers of miners employed in local collieries later formed significant elements in the growing community. Though the market at Bulwell came under the control of the Nottingham Corporation, it has remained active and is held twice weekly. Around the market-place and along Main Road in the direction of Hucknall, a considerable range of shops and other service facilities are to be found, providing all the characteristic elements of a small town centre. With the extension of residential areas and further industrial development during recent decades, the Bulwell district now has a population of over 20,000. Despite good bus services to the city centre, local retail trade continues to expand and, largely as a result, a scheme for the enlargement of the market place is in preparation. It is intended to exclude vehicles from the market itself, and to provide for a new car-park and bus station. Approach roads will be widened, affording more scope for retail purposes, and a by-pass to carry 'through' traffic will be built. A project of this kind clearly reflects the importance of the local service centre as an element in the structure of a large city and the improvement it provides for must be regarded as being complementary to, and not merely competitive with, the process of renewal which is taking place in the central area of the city.

Second-order centres

Arkwright Street

Turning now to local service centres of the second order, the first to be described is Arkwright Street. This is a thoroughfare of modern origin running south-eastwards from the Midland Railway Station as a main artery leading to Trent Bridge and the south. It was built in 1848, four years after the construction of Carrington Street, of which it is a continuation. The latter was built to give access to the railway station from the old town when the first railway, the Midland Counties line from Derby, was opened in 1839. It was not until the rebuilding of the Midland Station in 1904 that the road formed by Carrington Street and Arkwright Street was carried over the railway by a bridge, thus replacing an obstructive level-crossing. Arkwright Street itself, originally named Trent Bridge Road, led across the flat, low-lying area of meadowland which, though now a densely built-up district, is still called the Meadows. Building developments on either side of Arkwright Street were at first slow but spread rapidly in the 'sixties, covering a large area with artisan housing, interspersed with lace and hosiery factories and engineering works. On the main highway itself St. Saviour's church was built in 1863, and soon afterwards the Methodist Bridgeway Hall, which has just been rebuilt on the same site. Thus, the Meadows was transformed and Nottingham was literally brought to the bank of the Trent.

A few reminders of the once rural character of this district survived after the turn of the century. Buildings belonging to a small farm near the southern end of Arkwright Street have disappeared only a few years ago. The farm contained a pool where kingfishers and waterfowl could be found and part of its six-acre field was the ground of Nottingham Forest Football Club until 1898. One of the streets leading off Arkwright Street is named Crocus Street, recalling the crocuses which bloomed in the Meadows and which continued to grace the few remaining patches of sward until almost within living memory. They are referred to in a poem of the first World War written by a soldier in Flanders, which contains the lines:

> Out here the dogs of war run loose,
> Their whipper-in is Death;
> Across the spoilt and battered fields
> We hear their sobbing breath.
> The fields where grew the waving corn
> Are heavy with our dead;
> Yet still the fields at home are green
> And I have heard it said, that
> > There are crocuses at Nottingham
> > Wild crocuses at Nottingham
> > Blue crocuses at Nottingham
> > Though here the grass is red.

Nearly 200 years previously the noted traveller Celia Fiennes had observed with delight the crocus-studded meadows as she rode into Nottingham after crossing the Trent. Along Bathley Street, which leads off Arkwright Street not far from the river, mid-Victorian working-class housing is succeeded by that which characterised the period prior to the first World War and immediately afterwards. This area, with St. Faith's church, built in 1915, represents the last phase in the development of the district of which Arkwright Street is the principal axis.

As a shopping thoroughfare, Arkwright Street has certain distinctive features. Its shops are small, mainly owner-occupied until very recently, and characteristically Victorian in appearance. The range of goods obtainable is unusually diverse, more so perhaps than in any other of the city's subsidiary retail centres. Prices tend to be slightly lower than elsewhere and result in a large patronage. This is partly due to low overhead costs and partly to a tradition of personal attention to customers. Besides regular trading by the local population, there is a considerable casual trade by shoppers from other districts, the position of the main railway station at one end of the street and Trent Bridge, which gives access to West Bridgford, at the other, being factors which help to promote it.

St. Ann's Well Road

St. Ann's Well Road, once called Wood Lane, provides another example of the linear concentration of service facilities, though in this case it is based on an ancient highway. The road follows the line of an old track used, from medieval times onwards, to reach a group of springs situated to the north–east of the town which was known as St. Ann's Well. From the mid-14th century until the period of the Civil War the mayor and town elders went in procession to the Well at Easter and the scene became one of public merry-making. Later, the springs gained a reputation for their curative properties and in the 19th century the Well became a local pleasure resort. The site of the springs was eventually buried beneath the embankment constructed to carry the suburban branch of the Great Northern Railway and the stream which issued from them was culverted underground, but its course is recalled by two local street names, Brook Street and Beck Street.

St. Ann's Well Road was developed as a main thoroughfare in the late-19th century to serve the large working-class area which grew up between the Hunger Hills gardens and Carlton Road. Retail premises and other service provision, originally focussed on the junction of Union Street with the main road, now extend for three-quarters of a mile along the latter. Small and rather old shops still predominate over the few modern stores which are now appearing.

Alfreton Road

From the centre of the city, Derby Road, mainly lined with shops except for the frontage of the Roman Catholic Cathedral, leads uphill to Canning Circus. Here, at the summit of the hill, three main roads diverge. Derby Road itself continues in a south–westerly direction and is predominantly a residential thoroughfare; the Ilkeston Road runs westward and Alfreton Road north–westward. The areas lying within the angles formed by these roads, now undergoing redevelopment, consist of numerous streets crowded with Victorian artisan housing and occasional factories. Shopping facilities have inevitably become concentrated along the Ilkeston and Alfreton Roads as axial highways long served by tram and bus routes. Those on Ilkeston Road, however, are fewer in number and less varied in range of goods than those on Alfreton Road and rank only as a fifth- or sixth-order centre. Alfreton Road, for a distance of three-quarters of a mile, provides a considerable diversity of shops as well as banks, cafes, restaurants and places of entertainment, although one cinema has recently been demolished. Though comparatively close to the main business area of the city, Alfreton Road serves a distinct and densely-populated district in which local loyalties are strong. This same social characteristic also largely accounts for the survival of a subsidiary cluster of shops on Denman Street, lying between Ilkeston Road and Alfreton Road.

Basford

Like Bulwell and Sneinton, Basford was incorporated in 1877. Prior to that date, however, like Lenton, Radford and Bulwell, the other villages in the Leen valley, Basford was an early settlement, having its own identity and local life. The church of St. Leodegarius (St. Leger) dates back to the 12th century and in later medieval times stone quarrying from the Magnesian Limestone to the west of the village, as at Bulwell, provided a useful building material throughout the Nottingham area. There is a record of Basford stone being used in 1458 for repairing the Trent Bridge. Quarrying continued intermittently until rather more than a century ago, but old stone dwellings are a feature of Basford, as they are of Bulwell. Towards the dawn of the 19th century, when corn mills on the Leen were supplemented by cotton mills and bleaching and dyeing works, industrialisation proceeded rapidly and Basford soon became a leading centre of framework knitting. By 1844 there were well over 500 stocking-frames in and around the village, while lace manufacture, too, had already made progress, following the erection of Biddle and Birkin's small factory in 1825 and Birkin's larger works 10 years later, in which steam power was applied to Leavers lace machines for the first time. Further industrial development, continuing until the present day resulted in a huge expansion, at first to the east in the district known as New Basford and later to the north and south. Even by 1877 the population of Basford had reached 15,000. Basford also has local administrative functions, for it is the headquarters of the Basford Rural District, which extends around the city both to the north and south of the Trent. The offices of the former Nottinghamshire Miners' Association were situated in a building on Nottingham Road, erected in 1900. The area of retailing and other service facilities is now in two parts, separated by the Nottingham Road and the railway running alongside it. On the one side, close to the church, are the old and rather small shops along Church Street, while on the other, at the intersection of Nottingham Road and the western ring road (Valley Road), is a modern concentration of shops, banks and a cinema.

Hockley and Goose Gate

Brief reference, as mentioned earlier, should be made to the somewhat special case of the retail functions of Hockley and Goose Gate which lie close to the main shopping centre around the Old Market Place. The name Hockley originally applied to the pastures on the north side of the hill on which the early Anglo-Danish town was built. The present street so named was once called Walkergate, after the cloth-makers who felted their material by stamping on it, and is a continuation of Goose Gate. Together they form one of the several shopping thoroughfares which radiate from the Old Market Place, at the same time preserving a separate identity. This is partly because of the constricted width of Carlton Street, which links Goose Gate with Victoria Street and the Old Market Place, which has always prevented the operation of a tram or bus route, and partly because of the distinctly lower density of retail premises on Victoria Street. On the other hand, Hockley and Goose Gate serve no large residential district in the immediate vicinity, for they are bounded on the south side by the Lace Market and on the north by an area dominated by offices and factories. Among the latter is an important cutlery and tool-sharpening works, founded in 1840, which is now largely engaged in sharpening equipment used in the hosiery industry. The firm's premises include the building in which Richard Arkwright set up his frame on coming to Nottingham from Lancashire in 1769. Street widening at the lower end of Hockley a few years ago, however, has given easier access from Sneinton and the numerous streets of artisan dwellings off Carlton Road. The shops vary greatly in appearance, some old-fashioned, dating from 1850–60, others very modern, but they provide a wide diversity of goods. They include a few chain-stores, including Woolworth's and a supermarket. It was in Goose Gate in 1877 that Jesse Boot, the founder of the great firm of chemists, began business as a herbalist. His first shop was actually next door to the present branch of Boots chemists.

MUNICIPAL TRANSPORT

Municipal transport in Nottingham began in 1878 with the introduction of horse-drawn trams on two routes leading southwards from St. Peter's Square, one to Trent Bridge *via* Carrington Street and the other *via* Station Street to London Road. Two years later a third route was opened from the Market Place to Basford along the Derby, Alfreton and Radford Roads, necessitating the use of additional horses for the steep hill on Derby Road. Soon afterwards the route from the Market Place to Carrington along the Mansfield Road was opened. The Basford and Carrington routes were then linked by another which followed the entire length of Forest Road. These services were operated by the Nottingham and District Tramways Co., which, incidentally, experimented with a steam tram on the Basford route for a short time in 1884. The undertaking was acquired by the Corporation in 1897 and in 1901 electric trams began to supersede the horse-drawn vehicles.

During the next 25 years further tram routes and extensions were added, the last being along Derby Road to Wollaton Park in 1927. Already, however, the Corporation were planning the conversion of the tramways to trolley- and motor-bus services, the process being completed by 1936. The first motor buses appeared in 1920. Although the trolley-bus possessed distinct advantages as a passenger-carrying vehicle, its limitations during the period of rapid increase in the volume of road traffic have rendered it less and less suitable and in the past few years, on one route after another, it has been superseded by the motor bus. The first trolley-bus route was opened in 1927 and the last remaining vehicles of this kind were withdrawn in 1966.

Apart from local train services, one of the earlier forms of transport carrying people between the city and the more distant outskirts was the electric tramway connecting Nottingham with Ripley, in Derbyshire, over a distance of 17 miles through the densely-populated settlements of the coalfield. This route, which had its terminus in Queen Street in the very heart of the city, was opened in 1914 and was in use until 1932. A journey in the Ripley tram is the subject of one of D. H. Lawrence's short stories (*Tickets, Please*) and the author's opening description affords a graphic yet authentic picture of the route:

> There is in the Midlands a single-line tramway system which boldly leaves the county town and plunges off into the black industrial countryside, up hill and down dale, through the long ugly villages of workmen's houses, over canals and railways, past churches perched high and nobly over the smoke and shadows, through stark, grimy, cold, little market-places, tilting away in a rush past cinemas and shops down to the hollow where the collieries are, then up again, past a little rural church under the ash trees, on in a rush to the terminus, the last little ugly place of industry.

From the beginning of the century the Urban District of West Bridgford across the Trent grew rapidly as a residential suburb, developing mainly as a dormitory for people employed in Nottingham. Public transport to and from the city, however, was long restricted to the tramway which terminated on the Nottingham side of the river. In 1908 a proposal for a railway station on the Midland line at West Bridgford was rejected through lack of local support. Three years later a privately operated horse-drawn bus service plying between West Bridgford and St. Peter's Church was started, but it was not until 1913 that an effective solution to the problem was found. In that year the Urban District Council obtained parliamentary consent to operate its own motor omnibus services as far as the city boundary at Trent Bridge. West Bridgford was the first of the small number of urban district authorities in the country ever to acquire such powers. Regular services on four routes were started in 1914. The drawback of having to change buses at Trent Bridge persisted until 1927, when agreement was reached for the West Bridgford buses to run to the city centre and for those of the Corporation to serve the Urban District. Since that date the two authorities have jointly operated the routes serving both sides of the river. In addition, by co-ordinating its fares and time-table with those of the Corporation and one of the private transport concerns, West Bridgford operates one of the routes to Clifton, the city's large new estate south of the Trent.

Reference to Fig. 75 shows that Nottingham Corporation bus routes, besides supplementing the services to West Bridgford, serve much of the area in the other adjoining urban districts of Arnold, Carlton and Beeston and Stapleford. In the case of the last-named, part of Beeston and almost all the Stapleford portion of the Urban District are served not by the Corporation but by the large private company known as Barton Transport, the headquarters of which is in Chilwell. This company operates many country services which are focussed on Nottingham. Other concerns which serve the districts beyond the city boundary and connect Nottingham with neighbouring towns are the Trent Motor Traction Company, the Midland General Omnibus Company, the East Midland Motor Services and the South Nottinghamshire Bus Company.

Within the area served by the Corporation transport system there is naturally a close correlation between the direction and destination of bus routes and the distribution and density of residential areas. The pattern of routes as shown in Fig. 75 is essentially radial in character, with an emphasis upon those leading northward and north-westward to the large housing estates and southward to the dormitory area of West Bridgford. Some of the routes indicated operate only at peak periods and at the weekend. At the city centre some routes terminate in the Old Market Place, and some pass either through it or near to it, while others terminate within a short distance of it, at Hanley Street (north) and Granby Street (south). Adjacent to the latter is the Mount Street bus station, which is shared by the independent transport concerns operating westwards, as also are the bus stations at Huntingdon Street and Broad Marsh for north- and east-, and south-bound services respectively.

Services around the periphery are not greatly developed except along the two inner roads, Castle Boulevard and Lenton Boulevard. Those along the ring road (Valley Road–Western Boulevard–Middleton Boulevard–Clifton Boulevard) vary in

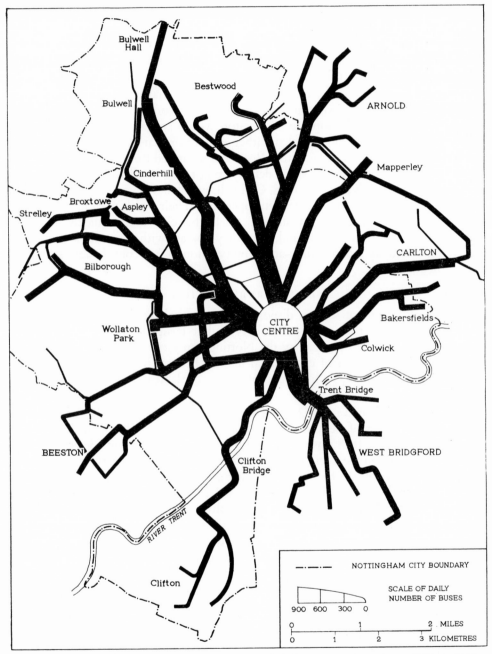

Fig. 75   The pattern of Nottingham Corporation daily bus services (Monday to Friday), 1965
(*Map by R. E. Pearson*)

Note post-war housing App VI.

frequency on different sections and there is only one continuous route which operates at peak periods. This has been extended in recent years to pass across the new Clifton Bridge and on to the Clifton housing estate. The eastern outskirts of the city are served by a circular route leading from the centre *via* Carlton and Westdale Lane to Mapperley Plains and returning *via* Mansfield Road.

In serving areas beyond the city boundary some anomalies arise as a result of the system by which municipal transport is protected from competition. Thus, for example, despite its large population, Beeston would appear to be less well served both in routes and in frequency than either Arnold or Carlton, though it must be noted that, unlike Arnold and Carlton, Beeston is separated from central Nottingham by the 'green' area of low population density comprising Wollaton Park, University Park and the Highfields Playing Fields. Chilwell, which lies beyond Beeston, is linked with Nottingham solely by independent operators. Their buses, with few permitted stopping points after leaving Chilwell, reach the city more quickly than the Corporation buses from Beeston and, since they operate with comparable frequency, Chilwell has actually a better time-accessibility, though it is considerably smaller in traffic potential.

SEWAGE PURIFICATION

An effective means of sewage disposal is an essential requirement of a civilized community and, in urban areas particularly, public health largely depends on such provision. The scheme operated by the Nottingham Corporation on behalf of the city and adjoining areas is of exceptional interest because it incorporates a modern sewage purification plant, with disposal of sludge on land in rotation for profitable agriculture.

The scheme originated in 1872 under the Leen Valley Sewerage Board, covering the suburban villages of Lenton and Radford in the Leen valley and the town of Nottingham itself. In 1878 it was absorbed by the Corporation and 638 acres of land at Stoke Bardolph, on the Trent floodplain downstream from the city, were acquired for the disposal works. In the following year areas which now comprise the urban districts of Arnold and Carlton were included in the scheme and others, such as Hucknall, West Bridgford and part of the Southwell Rural District, have since been added (Fig. 76). The total drainage area is 42,700 acres (nearly 66 square miles), with a population of nearly 450,000, of which nearly 320,000 are in the city. Two trunk sewers discharge at the works, one originating from Hucknall, at the northern extremity of the drainage area. It follows the course of the Leen as far as Bobbers Mill, passing thence through the centre of the city to Stoke Bardolph. The other leads from Roughill Wood, on the slope of Colwick Hill, and conveys sewage pumped into it principally from the low-lying southern portions of the city and the Urban District of West Bridgford. A third main sewer serving the Southwell district leads into the works from Lowdham. The average daily flow of sewage for treatment during the year 1964–65 was 28·6 million gallons.

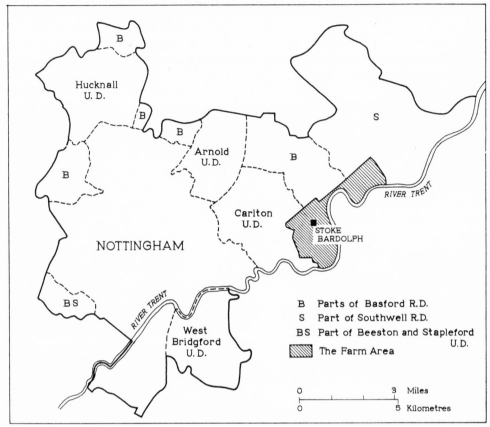

Fig. 76   The drainage area of the Nottingham sewage disposal unit and farm

The site for the works at Stoke Bardolph was chosen by the enlightened engineer, M. Ogle Tarbotton, in order to utilize the river gravels for the downward filtration of sewage material. Broadly there are two distinct aspects of sewage working; firstly, the clarification of water acceptable to the standards of the Trent River Authority, and, secondly, the disposal of accumulated sludge. In the Nottingham scheme water clarification is achieved by modern aeration methods with final discharge into the Trent, but with regard to the sludge a system has been devised by which this material is fully utilized as a fertilizer on the Corporation's own estate. For this, an initial advantage lies in the fact that use of the gravels avoids the necessity for capital expenditure on either drying beds or vacuum filters as well as for finding sites for deposition. Instead of building up a mass of dry sludge of little or no value, therefore, a process of controlled irrigation covering a large area allows the otherwise unwanted material to support the regular cultivation of crops and pasture. Wheat, oats and barley, sugar beet, potatoes and grasses are grown. The entire estate, comprising the sewage plant and the farm, now covers approximately 2,000 acres, of which nearly 1,700 acres are farmland. Each year some 200 to 250 acres are sludged and eventually each field will be treated once in seven years. Part of the crops raised is used to maintain an attested herd of Friesian dairy cattle, together with some beef cattle and and a considerable number of pigs. The farm is largely mechanized and grain drying, cleaning and storage facilities are now being developed, along with a milking parlour and improved housing for dairy cows.

On the cultivated area the soils are so rich in manurial content, chiefly in phosphate and nitrogen, that they are temporarily out of balance in relation to crop requirements and correction is made by the application of potash and other salts. Two further points of interest are, firstly, the utilization of purified effluent for spray irrigation and, secondly, conservation of methane gas produced during the process of sludge fermentation. This gas is collected and used to generate all the electricity required for the sewage purification plant, which amounts to a continuous load of some 1,200 Kw. Some partially dried sludge is sold to local farmers and market gardeners. Thus, as far as possible, everything is turned to profitable account. With income derived from farm profits and from charges made for the treatment of industrial waste, together with saving on the cost of power, the charge to the ratepayer for sewage disposal in the Nottingham area is the low figure of a little over one-third of a penny per head per day. In the year 1964–65 it was slightly less than this amount.

SELECTED REFERENCES

Brown, P. A. The Local Accessibility of Nottingham. *East Midland Geographer* No. 11 (June 1959).

Butler, R. M. The Common Lands of the Borough of Nottingham. *Transactions of the Thoroton Society* Vol. 54 (1950).

Chambers, J. D. *Modern Nottingham in the Making*. Nottingham (1945).

Chambers, J. D. *A Century of Nottingham History, 1851–1951*. University of Nottingham (1952).

Edwards, K. C. Some Location Factors in the Development of Nottingham. *East Midland Geographer* No. 5 (June 1956).

Edwards, K. C. The Nottingham Conurbation. *East Midland Geographer* No. 18 (December 1962).

Gray, D. *Nottingham: Settlement to City*. Nottingham (1953).

Large, D. C. Nottingham: its urban pattern. *East Midland Geographer* No. 6 (December 1956).

Weekley, I. G. Service Centres in Nottingham: a concept in urban analysis. *East Midland Geographer* No. 6 (December 1956).

Wood, A. C. *A History of Nottinghamshire*. Nottingham (1947).

Important historical works dealing with the growth of and early conditions in the Nottingham area are the following: R. Thoroton, *The Antiquities of Nottinghamshire* (1677); C. Deering, *Historical Account of Nottingham* (1751); J. Blackner, *History of Nottingham* (1815); Wylie, *Old and New Nottingham* (1853 and also 1865 edition). The authoritative work on early local textile manufacturing is W. Felkin, *History of Machine Wrought Hosiery and Lace* (1867).

ACKNOWLEDGMENTS

Mr. A. R. Stone, Manager of the Nottingham Corporation Sewage Purification Works, kindly provided information concerning the disposal plant at Stoke Bardolph. Details of the Nottingham Park Estate were given by the Manager, Mr. G. E. Cole.

XXII

INDUSTRIAL STRUCTURE

NOTTINGHAM is an outstanding example of a local community with a well-balanced employment structure. In the city and its neighbourhood there are light and heavy industries, capital goods and consumer goods industries, industries providing jobs for women as well as men. Although Nottingham industries contribute to the country's export trade, they are not unduly dependent on overseas markets. Some local industries are dominated by big firms, but in others small-scale enterprise is characteristic. All these features contribute to the impression of a balanced industrial community. In addition, there are, of course, the usual service trades supplying local needs and the numerous activities that make up the infrastructure of an urban area.

This fortunate constellation of industries and related activities is due partly to the facts of physical geography described elsewhere and to the influence of economic forces. But chance has played an important and beneficent part in the industrial history of Nottingham. Our oldest industry, hosiery manufacture, became established in Nottingham because the stocking frame happened to be invented at nearby Calverton in 1589. Similarly, the inventors of machine-made lace, for which Nottingham became famous in the 19th century, were men who lived in and near Nottingham, many of the pioneers being connected with the older textile industry. The three great enterprises to which modern Nottingham owes so much—Boots, Raleigh, Players— were all located here as the result of historical accident.

Before the first World War Nottingham was pre-eminently a textile centre. More than half the total employment in what may be called the characteristic industries was accounted for by lace, hosiery, clothing and textile finishing. Lace was by far the most important member of the group. It employed 22,000 in 1911, including a high proportion of skilled workers, many of them women, and in good times earnings were high. But the trade was notoriously unstable. It was particularly susceptible to fashion changes and also heavily dependent on overseas markets, where there was often strong competition from protected domestic manufacturers. Hosiery manufacture was less important than lace in Nottingham, being widely distributed in the counties of Nottingham, Derby and Leicester and having its main centre in Leicester itself. But hosiery, too, was subject to fluctuations, partly seasonal in character, but also reflecting the influence of fashion changes.

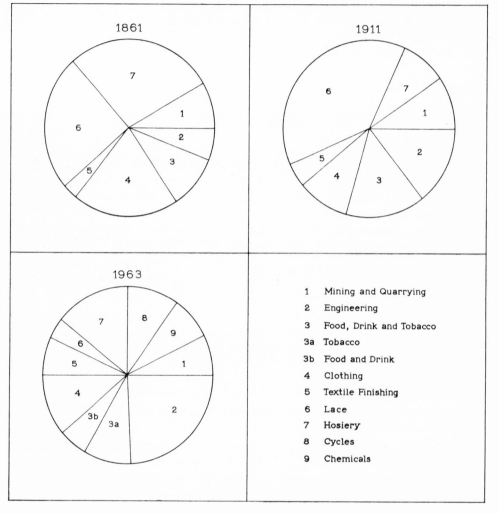

Fig. 77

Changes in the relative importance of the principal industries of Nottingham, 1861, 1911 and 1963

These diagrams exclude those industries and services which are found in all large towns. They illustrate the characteristic industries of Nottingham

    If Nottingham had continued to depend on its lace trade as it did in the 19th century, it might well have become a depressed area in the 1920s. For few trades can have suffered so sharp a decline as occurred here after the first World War. It was precipitated by fashion changes more sudden and more sweeping than anything previously experienced. Hitherto there had been changes in styles and in the purposes for which lace was used. Now there was a veritable revulsion from lace. There had been so much of it: lace curtains, lace tablecloths, nets and bedspreads, lace anti-macassars and the lace insertions, flounces and frills on feminine garments. The post-war generation admired austerity in dress and furnishings; it didn't want lace. The trade by no means disappeared. Some lines, like the new curtain nets and hairnets did quite well and in the later 1930s there were signs of revival in the demand for the more traditional products such as dress laces. But employment in the Nottingham lace trade fell to less than half its pre-war level and the decline proved to be permanent.

In contrast to the lace trade, the hosiery industry expanded rapidly between the wars. Fashion favoured hosiery. It accentuated the importance of stockings, which must be fine-gauge and therefore less durable. Knitted underwear and outerwear became popular with women. Men's demands increased too, especially for coloured socks, sports shirts and pullovers. The effects of all this were seen in the growth of employment and the building of new factories. By 1931 there were nearly twice as many hosiery workers in Nottingham as before the war.

Garment making, or 'making-up' as it is called locally, is another trade that was favoured by the changes of the inter-war years. Ready-made clothing became popular with both men and women. For the concentration of tailoring and dress-making in factories greatly reduced the cost of making and the benefit was shared by the consumer through the chain and department stores which provided the complementary large-scale retailing system. This trade had been growing in Nottingham before the war and now it rivalled hosiery in its speed of expansion. Its development owed much to the enterprise of firms in the older textile industries and to the local tradition of women's employment in factories and warehouses.

These changes within the traditional trades were only part of a process that was re-shaping the whole structure of employment in the Nottingham area and improving its balance. The process was profoundly influenced by the growth of the three enterprises already mentioned, each in a different industry and so contributing to the diversification of employment.

They had all started at about the same time, in the 1870s, each in a small way. The beginning of Boots was a little chemist's shop in Goose Gate run on the principle of low prices and quick turnover and aided by unconventional forms of advertising. A company was formed in 1883 and more shops were opened by what was now Boots Cash Chemists. Five years later Boots Pure Drug Company was established and manufacturing began. By the end of the century Boots had 60 shops in 28 towns, but it was still only in the early stages of its growth.

Players began in 1877 when a small tobacco-manufacturing business, established some 50 years earlier, passed into the hands of John Player. He was a pioneer in the production and sale of tobacco and cigarettes sold under advertised brands, a development which was to transform the trade, not only in tobacco, but in many

other lines of consumers' goods. Under the new conditions of sale tobacco manufacture was admirably suited to large-scale operations and Player saw the possibilities.
He built three factories in anticipation of a greatly expanded business, letting two
of them in the meantime to lace manufacturers.

The origin of the third great enterprise, the Raleigh Cycle Company, is particularly
interesting, for the founder of this business did not live in Nottingham, and it was
only by chance that he established himself here. Frank Bowden, the founder, after
a profitable 15 years in Hong Kong returned home in 1887 to die, or so his doctors
told him. Instead of dying he took to cycling and within six months was quite fit
again. In his enthusiasm he set out to trace the makers of the machine he had been
riding and found them in a small workshop in Raleigh Street, Nottingham, where
12 men turned out three bicycles a week. The cycle boom had not yet begun, but
Bowden saw the possibilities. He took over the business in Raleigh Street, founded
the Raleigh Cycle Company and soon afterwards built his first factory in Lenton,
not far from Players.

Later on, at the turn of the century, another new industry was brought to the
Nottingham area by a firm destined to become a major enterprise. This was Ericsson
Telephones, established at Beeston, a semi-industrialised district with a few lace
factories, some three miles to the west of Nottingham. Here land was cheap, labour
plentiful and communications good.

Fortunately for Nottingham all these enterprises prospered. They represented what
were to become the growth industries of future years. This stake in the growth
industries and the widening range of employment opportunities that opened up
imparted a notable resilience to the local economy. The foundations had been laid
of an industrial structure that proved remarkably well adapted to the economic
environment of the inter-war period, which favoured, especially, industries producing
consumers' goods for the home market.

Boots is an outstanding example of such an industry. In explaining its growth we
must not, of course, exaggerate the effects of environment. The firm is, indeed, a
remarkable instance of the influence of personality on industrial development; but
the trend of economic and social conditions between the wars was particularly
favourable. The standard of living was rising; people were better fed, better clothed,
better housed than ever before; and they were healthier, partly for these reasons, but
also because of the rapid advance of medical science, which in turn created the demand
for medicinal supplies. The demand was partly stimulated by National Health
Insurance, but there was a big increase in voluntary spending on pharmaceutical
products, and also on toilet goods and cosmetics. All these things were made and
sold by Boots.

In its method of distribution, too, Boots was in line with current tendencies; it
was among the pioneers of chain store retailing and with many products it had

become price leader. The administration of the retailing side of the business remained centred in Nottingham, where it was served by a large office staff. The printing department had become bigger than most printing firms and the company was now a large employer of labour in the engineering and woodworking trades. Boots was almost an industry in itself. By the middle of the inter-war period the firm had 8,000 employees in Nottingham. It had far outgrown the accommodation on the original site in the heart of the city and most of the manufacturing departments were now removed to fine new factories on the Nottingham side of Beeston. It was fortunate that these factories were completed before the war, especially as the older premises suffered severed damage, for the war made heavy demands on Boots's resources. An additional factory was built during the war for the manufacture of penicillin. The firm was a pioneer in this process as it had been earlier in the production of insulin.

The growth of John Player and Sons, as a branch of the Imperial Tobacco Company, was almost as impressive. Here again it was a case of responding to market demand, and also of enterprise in demand creation. The extraordinary increase in tobacco consumption which began in the first World War was reinforced by the continued growth of population and its changing age structure. The effect of increased consumption was most marked on the demand for cigarettes and Players had long been established in this branch of the trade. A big new cigarette factory was built on land which was fortunately available on the opposite side of the road to the existing factories and a great new bonded warehouse was completed in the same neighbourhood.

Except for leaf stripping, which is done by hand, the manufacture and packing of cigarettes and pipe tobacco is highly mechanised and much of the work requires little skill. It is, however, well paid, wages forming only a small proportion of the selling price of the product. The presence of this expanding industry, therefore, contributed substantially to the maintenance of employment and the level of wages in Nottingham between the wars.

The experience of the Raleigh Cycle Company in the same period is similar to that of Boots and Players. The first of the present factories, built in 1896, was designed to employ 850 people and was reputed to be the biggest cycle factory in the world. The demand for cycles continued to increase and Raleigh secured an increasing share of the growing market. The high reputation of their machines was publicised by effective advertising. They absorbed a number of smaller firms and at the same time developed an important trade as suppliers of components, particularly the Sturmey-Archer gear, to other cycle makers. With the growth of motoring in the 1920s it seemed likely that the demand for pedal-cycles would dwindle, and a Raleigh motor cycle was introduced; but, contrary to expectation, pedal cycling increased. Population was spreading out and many had to travel farther to work; cycling was cheaper and often more convenient than the bus. The roads were improved and many of the younger generation took to cycling for pleasure. Wherever the standard of

Cc

living was rising, as it was in Britain and other countries, there was an increasing demand for cycles among the millions of people who, as yet, could not hope to own a car or even a motor cycle. Eventually Raleigh decided to concentrate on this side of their trade and, in the late 1930s, they were still increasing production making pedal cycles only.

Other light engineering trades in the Nottingham area were similarly favoured by the trend of demand between the wars. Ericsson Telephones at Beeston is an outstanding example. Although Britain lagged behind other advanced countries in the use of telephones, the demand was rapidly increasing and Ericssons had a substantial share of the market. Moreover, they were well placed for expansion in Beeston, where they had acquired an extensive site in the midst of a growing residential area.

The picture of industrial Nottingham between the wars is not one of unclouded prosperity. Unemployment was severe in the two depressions of the early 1920s and the early 1930s. This reflected the deterioration of economic conditions throughout the country, indeed throughout the world. When conditions improved Nottingham's industrial expansion was resumed. Unemployment in Nottingham was mainly cyclical unemployment, as distinct from the structural unemployment that became a chronic problem in some industrial areas. The only serious case of structural unemployment was the lace industry. This brought hardship to older men with highly specialised skills. For younger workers there were opportunities in the other textile trades, including the new rayon industry, represented by British Celanese, at Spondon, 12 miles to the west of Nottingham. Women and girls had little difficulty in finding alternative employment, for there was an increasing demand for machinists in the hosiery and making-up trades and all the newer industries employed a high proportion of female workers.

In some areas the decline of coal mining was a serious cause of structural un-employment, but the East Midlands was already emerging as one of the most productive coalfields in the country. Nottingham itself had several pits and during the first World War employment reached a peak of about 9,000. The following years brought some decline but this was partly due to mechanisation. In the wider region coal was still an expanding industry and the fall of employment in Nottingham was compensated by increases in other parts of Nottinghamshire and Derbyshire. There was thus little structural unemployment attributable to coal-mining; indeed, the comparative prosperity of the East Midlands coalfield contributed to Nottingham's growth as a commercial centre.

Since the second World War Nottingham's industrial structure has undergone a further process of adaptation. The changes are partly a reflection of the tendencies already described; but there have been, in addition, some important new developments which will help to shape the future distribution of employment in the city and its immediate neighbourhood.

Of the traditional industries lace maintains the relatively minor position which it occupied in the 1930s. Its labour force in the Nottingham area is about 4,000. It is, however, represented by a number of firms in Long Eaton, over the Derbyshire border, and also in Derby. On its diminished scale the trade is flourishing. Its products range from curtain nets to dress laces, made in a variety of materials, and though there are frequent shifts in demand from one line to another employment has been on the whole well maintained since the war.

The hosiery industry, which grew so rapidly between the wars, has not added much to local employment in recent years. There are three main reasons for this. In some processes technical progress has greatly reduced the labour content per unit of output. In particular, the speed of knitting machines has increased and they have become more automatic in action; machines for making fully-fashioned hose have also grown in size, thus raising the operative's capacity. In some branches of the trade changes in the style of garments have reduced the demand for labour. For instance, the making of seamless stockings involves fewer processes than that of the fully-fashioned type; underwear, too, is simpler in style, and knitted outerwear, now an increasingly important part of the industry's output, requires little in the way of machining and handwork after the knitting is done. Apart from these general influences, the expansion of the hosiery industry's employment in Nottingham has been checked by the acute shortage of female labour. This has persisted since the early post-war years and it has further encouraged the dispersal of the manufacture in the smaller towns of the Nottinghamshire–Derbyshire coalfield, many of which are old centres of the industry. The same is true of the making-up trades. Here the processes, based on the sewing machine, are more labour-intensive than in most manufactures and the opportunities for economising labour are less evident than in the hosiery industry.

Another Nottingham industry in which expansion has been checked in recent years is tobacco manufacture. This is in marked contrast with experience between the wars. Although Players appear to have at least maintained their position in the industry, they have been affected by the generally downward trend of demand in recent years. It is, indeed, hard to see how the consumption of tobacco could have increased much more, even at pre-war prices; post-war prices, enhanced by heavy taxation, have had an adverse effect. After allowing for price changes, tobacco consumption in 1953 was no higher than in 1947 and it has since fluctuated about that level. Anti-smoking propaganda may have had some effect too, and its impact on the rising generation may depress demand still more in the future.

Employment at Players has fluctuated in accordance with these changes in demand, women being more affected than men. In 1947 there were 4,000 female workers and a slightly larger number of men; but, while the male labour force has remained at about the same level, female employment has fallen. The displacement of labour has been effected by reducing the number of part-time workers, with a corresponding improvement in the productivity of labour. Productivity has also been raised by continuing technical progress, for example, in the design of cigarette-making machines, and this has reduced the demand for labour in some processes. There are signs that this hitherto highly specialised industry may find opportunities for further growth in diversification. If these are realised, the former upward trend of employment at Players may well be resumed.

The outstanding feature of post-war industrial development in the Nottingham area is undoubtedly the growth of its engineering trades. Before the war, Nottingham was not regarded as an engineering centre, like the neighbouring town of Derby, for instance. As we have shown, however, engineering was already well represented. In 1939 nearly 15 per cent of the working population was employed in the group, as compared with nine per cent in 1929. The 1939 position was, of course, influenced by preparation for war, but in the main it indicates the expansion of normal business in the important concerns already mentioned and in many smaller firms covering a wide range of products.

This development, which is, of course, in line with post-war changes in the national pattern of industrial activity, provides a further illustration of that capacity for adaptation which has been such a marked characteristic of Nottingham's economic growth. Nottingham's prosperity between the wars derived mainly from the production of consumers' goods for the home market. Now, with increasing emphasis on the production of capital goods, not only for the home market but also for export, we see the local structure adapting itself to the changing needs of the national economy.

Post-war experience also shows the recurrence of a feature in the process of adaptation itself. Nottingham's growth between the wars owed far less to the introduction of new firms in new trades than to the expansion of firms already here, and which benefited from the market trends of that period. So again, in the last 20 years, the changing employment structure reflects, in the main, the activities of existing firms, and now, particularly, in the engineering trades.

As might be expected, the character of the local engineering trades was influenced, in the past, by Nottingham's importance as a textile centre. Nottingham became famous for the building of lace machines and it has equipped most of the countries where lace manufacture is carried on. A parallel development was hosiery machine building. Both these industries have declined. Lace machines have a very long life, and although machines and accessories are still being made the demand is now small. Some firms have expanded in other lines, however. One example is the Jardine Group. Another old-established firm, Manlove Alliott and Company, which began by supplying the lace dressing trade with machines for extracting moisture by centrifugal action now produces laundry machinery, chemical plant and sterilizers for hospitals, in which it does a considerable export trade. Hosiery machine building is now concentrated in Leicester rather than Nottingham and much knitting machinery is now imported from America, Germany and, lately, Italy. The making of machine parts and accessories occupies several firms, some of which have branched out into other products requiring similar labour and equipment, such as machine tools, refrigerator parts and gear components. Thus, the direct influence of textile manufacture on the Nottingham engineering trades, though important historically, is less marked than it used to be. Nevertheless, machine building did establish a tradition of skilled engineering work, which has assisted more recent developments in the engineering trades.

The main contribution to these developments has come from the continued growth of the two concerns whose progress between the wars has already been described. The Raleigh Cycle Company, which was turning out 400,000 cycles a year in 1938, emerged from the war with a potential output of 600,000; but, after complete re-organisation and the introduction of an improved conveyor system, the pre-war output was doubled in 1949. Then more factories were added and as Raleigh Industries Limited, the firm achieved an output of over a million cycles a year, to which was added a huge production of lighting sets and hub gears. The labour force increased by 50 per cent to about 8,000, and for an engineering firm the number of women employed, nearly 1,700, is unusually high. This is accounted for by the amount of assembly work, which can be appreciated from the statement that a bicycle contains between 1,500 and 2,000 parts.

Raleigh's expansion has been checked recently. Overseas sales, which had absorbed 80 per cent of output, have declined owing to tariff restrictions and increased competition, and the home market demand has fallen too. However, under Tube Investments, Raleigh has been merged with other cycle firms and some redistribution of production has taken place. Other lines have been introduced, including mopeds, and the firm's position has at least been stabilised at a high level of activity.

The other concern, Ericsson Telephones, is still expanding and employment now exceeds 5,000. About a quarter of the workers are women, who are engaged mainly in operating semi-automatic machines and on the less skilled forms of assembly work. The still increasing demand for telephones and the conversion to automatic exchanges provides an assured outlet, and a particularly encouraging feature of post-war trade is the big increase in exports. Both Ericsson and Raleigh give special attention to industrial training and thus make an important contribution to the future supply of skilled labour in a number of occupations.

The chief representative of heavy engineering in Nottingham is the Royal Ordnance Factory, occupying works originally owned by Cammell Laird. Employment in recent years has remained steady at about 2,500, and the decision to close Woolwich Arsenal and retain Nottingham may mean some increase in the labour force. Two other important sources of employment connected with the national defence programme are the Central Ordnance Depot at Chilwell and a research and development branch of Rolls Royce at an airfield a few miles north–west of Nottingham.

The rest of the metal and engineering firms in the Nottingham district cover such a variety of products that classification is difficult. There are four firms engaged in structural metal work. Of the two larger, one makes window panels, radiator grills and ventilators, while the other specialises in the design and erection of structural steelwork. Machine-tool making and precision work are represented by several firms, and there is the old-established firm of Smith Brothers, well-known for its production of valves and pressure gauges. Another important member of the engineering group is the Beeston Boiler Company, which has expanded considerably in recent years.

It is unnecessary to describe the many industries that are 'local' in the sense that they exist mainly to serve the area in which they are located. In all large centres of population such industries employ a big proportion of the total labour force, but they do not contribute to the distinctive character of an industrial area. There are, however, many instances of firms that began as members of a 'local' industry but which now serve a much wider market. Such a firm is Thomas Forman and Sons. This was originally the jobbing printing side of a business whose main activity was the publication of a local newspaper. In the 1920s it split off from the parent enterprise and it is now one of the best-known colour printers in the country. Other examples are to be found in furniture making and in tanning and leather work, as well as in engineering where, as mentioned earlier, many existing firms were set up originally to serve the local textile trades.

As in all large urban areas, the numerous services that support the infrastructure of the local economy account for an increasing proportion of total employment. About 41 per cent of the occupied population in the Nottingham area are engaged in transport and public utilities, the distributive trades, banking, insurance, educational and professional services and public administration. Since nearly half the workers in this field of employment are women and girls, the manufacturing industries have faced increasing competition for female labour. The traditional industries of Nottingham have always been heavily dependent on female labour and this is also characteristic of the newer trades, including light engineering. Thus, Nottingham has always had a high proportion of women and girls in its gainfully occupied population. The proportion for the country as a whole, 34·5 per cent, is, of course, higher than before the war; but for Nottingham it is 38·4 per cent, and it can hardly be expected to go much higher. The shortage of male labour is rather less acute, though there are often unfilled vacancies in skilled occupations, and Nottingham's unemployment percentage is consistently below the national figure. Thus, labour supply, and particularly the supply of female labour, is a serious limiting factor to further industrial expansion.

The position has been relieved to some extent by immigration, including a considerable influx from the West Indies and Asia, and also from central Europe. The growth of population by immigration and natural increase creates other problems: the spreading out of housing over an ever-widening area, the lengthening of the journey to work and the intensification of traffic congestion around the city centre. A solution of these problems must be sought in the further dispersal of industry on the lines described in the survey of the Nottingham region (Chapter XVII).

XXIII

CULTURAL PROVISION

City library

Nottingham is fortunate in its library provision. The city library, with the central library and 18 branch libraries, an unusual number for a city of just over 300,000 people, was founded in 1868, and moved into its present premises in 1881. Over the years both stocks of books and readers have increased greatly, with the result that today a service of great depth of resource and flexible growth is possible, and is used by 70,000 citizens who between them read 2¾ million books a year. Half a million volumes are available, the only restriction on future growth being physical limitations of space within the present building, now quite outgrown. Across the Trent at West Bridgford is the headquarters of the Nottinghamshire County library which serves a population of 360,000 in county villages and Urban Districts.

In the city library, the reference section which has 150,000 volumes, is under constant pressure from students, and is devoted chiefly to the humanities. It is responsible for the issue of regular booklists, that in greatest demand being the monthly list for architecture and town planning, which is read as far afield as Finland and Japan. The need to meet the requirements of specialist readers had led to the development of the commercial and technical library which contains the entire concentration of reference works relating to business and management, together with both pure and applied science. Approximately 700 periodicals are currently taken, and in 1963 the department became the headquarters of NANTIS (Nottingham and Nottinghamshire Technical Information Service), an organisation similar to those in other regions of the country, designed to make available to industrial firms all the technical material held by the co-operating members. One million books and periodicals are thus tapped for use by members, and a rapid system of inter-loan enables material outside the region to be readily accessible *via* telephone and telex. In addition, as agents of the National Lending Library of Science and Technology, the public library opens the way to the state's largest reservoir of scientific literature.

Other major departments of the city library are the local history library and the archives department. In the former a collection of 27,000 books and pamphlets relating to Nottingham and Nottinghamshire has been assembled over the last century. Photographs, slides, maps, special gifts of material relating to stage history, church history, the study of the flora and fauna of the region, the geology and natural history of the county, are all maintained in the library. The recently acquired Doubleday Index to articles and references to Nottinghamshire has been of immediate benefit in opening up the riches of the local collection. Of particular importance are the collections of local authors: D. H. Lawrence, strong in first editions and variants, and continually increased by the addition of critical works; the Byron collection of every edition of the poet is enhanced by the special collection of autographs and rare items of world-wide repute, housed at Newstead Abbey, and given to the city by Herbert Roe. The Robin Hood collection comprises the many ballads and legends, together with studies attempting to place the outlaw historically. Contemporary local authors' work is continually included, notably that of Alan Sillitoe and Stanley Middleton. A local history library is always a large factor in the make-up of a municipal library, and only by the patient accumulation of years can an irreplaceable collection be made of lasting interest and value to researchers, historians and laymen alike. The latest addition to this department is a tape recorder on which has been recorded examples of the Nottinghamshire dialect and interviews with representative local people in many walks of life. In the fullness of time the sound archive will have an obvious dimension of value to the future. In 1968, centenary year of the founding of the public library, it is proposed to issue a Nottinghamshire Bibliography.

The archives department is the official repository for family, personal and business MSS. They cover the entire history of the city as registered in deeds, conveyances, wills, accounts, memorial records, genealogies, letters, diaries, indentures, the records of firms, families, religious and professional bodies, to the present time. These are the original source materials to which any student has recourse, whether in writing the history of the framework knitters, or in taking a period or family history.

Other important departments are those of music and children's work. Special services include books for old people's homes, the mentally ill, and partially-sighted readers. Additionally, books are loaned to local adult classes.

Specialist libraries in the city

Nottingham has for a long time been a city of varied industries, the most celebrated being tobacco (John Player's); chemical preparations (Boots'); cycles and engineering products (Raleigh); telephones (Ericsson's), and the many lace and hosiery firms. Each of these enterprises has its own special information section, and below there follows a brief description of some of them:

Boots Pure Drug Co. Ltd. has a research library of approximately 50,000 volumes covering medicine, biology, chemistry, biochemistry, pharmacy, chemical technology, agriculture, veterinary science, etc. The two main libraries are in the medical sciences building and the chemical sciences building of the research department at Pennyfoot Street; smaller libraries are at the Agricultural Research Station, Lenton, the Veterinary Research Institute at Thurgarton, and the Beeston factory. The research library is maintained primarily for employees of the company.

Ericsson Telephones Ltd. began a research library in 1958, has a book stock of 3,600 volumes, 2,000 reports and takes 400 periodical titles. The library serves all staff in the firm, including the factory at Sunderland, the main users being the research and development departments. The principal subject field of the library is telecommunications, but it covers a wide range of fringe topics such as physics, chemistry, management, accountancy, etc.

Hosiery and Allied Trades Research Association library, founded in 1949, is concerned mainly with the periodical and patent literature of textiles. Over half the books in its small but comprehensive collection on knitting are foreign language works. Its own '*Hosiery Abstracts*' includes items on all aspects of the knitting industry and, as part of a co-operative scheme with other textile research associations and the Textile Institute, forms the hosiery section in a national abstracting service which covers the whole field of textiles. Most of the library's facilities are available only to members of the Association though, each year, loans to other libraries and individuals account for about 10 per cent of the total.

There are two other libraries of a quite different kind. One is the *Bromley House Library*, a private circulating library founded in 1816, which has occupied its present premises since 1822. It has a bookstock of approximately 40,000 with strong local history coverage. The other is the library of the *Mechanics Institute*, with its own valuable collection which has functioned since 1837. This is still a centre of vitality in Nottingham with a wide membership. It is also strong in local history.

At *Newstead Abbey*, in the salon, is housed the Roe-Byron collection of first editions, rare pieces, and autographs relating to the poet and his circle, acquired by Herbert Roe, a Nottingham businessman. The collection was presented to the city in 1937 and is available to scholars and students on application to the Curator.

MUSEUMS IN NOTTINGHAM

The Nottingham city museums consist of the Castle Museum and the Natural History Museum at Wollaton Hall, as well as Newstead Abbey, where relics of the poet Byron are preserved and exhibited.

The Castle Museum, in the centre of the city, occupies the site where the original medieval castle stood. This was dismantled during the Civil War; the present building is a house, built in 1674 on the same site by the 1st Duke of Newcastle. In 1831, Reform Bill rioters set it on fire; the walls were left standing but the interior was completely destroyed. In 1878 it was opened as the first provincial municipal art museum, the interior having been remodelled as a two-storey building instead of a three-storey building, as it had been in the 17th century. The collections now include fine arts (paintings and sculpture from medieval times to the present day), the applied arts (ceramics, glass and textiles) and historical and archaeological material. The display of English pottery is one of the most comprehensive in the country, and the textile section includes a large collection of lace, both hand-made and machine-made and, on permanent loan, the beautiful 17th-century embroideries and costume belonging to Lord Middleton. Bonington and Sandby, the most important artists which the Nottingham vicinity has so far produced, are both well represented in the fine art section.

In the same building is the museum of the Sherwood Foresters. It is fitting that Nottingham Castle, which has many associations with the regiment, should house its interesting relics, which include uniforms, documents, weapons, trophies, colours and medals.

The Sherwood Foresters museum is on a mezzanine floor which was built specifically for the purpose. Although this is a modern addition it does, to some extent, restore the 17th-century proportions to that part of the building. The floor that was inserted into the empty shell to make the museum that was opened in 1878 cut across the middle tier of windows; this was in accordance with the 19th-century museum fashion for high ceilings, but it made nonsense of the windows, and destroyed the original proportions of the rooms. The mezzanine floor, inserted just above the top of the lowest windows, gives the visitor some idea of how the 17th-century ground floor must have looked.

As well as the permanent collection the Museum also shows a number of temporary exhibitions; every year an exhibition is held of the works of local artists, and, of the other exhibitions which are shown, the most important one to be held in recent years was the comprehensive exhibition of the works of Richard Parkes Bonington, shown April–May 1965.

More temporary exhibitions are shown at the smaller gallery in Victoria Street, which, like the Castle, has the advantage of being in the middle of the city. A great variety of exhibitions is shown; there are one-man displays by contemporary artists, picture exhibitions circulated by the Arts Council and the Art Exhibitions Bureau, and exhibitions of other sorts of material from the Circulation Department of the Victoria and Albert Museum. Also there are occasional exhibitions by local societies, photographers and schools. The Victoria Street Art Gallery is administered by the Castle Museum.

The Natural History Museum is housed in Wollaton Hall. The building is the finest example of domestic architecture within the city boundary. It was built by Sir Francis Willoughby, between 1580 and 1588, the architect being John Thorpe, and the house is magnificently situated on an elevated position in its own park. The Willoughbys, who acquired the title Middleton in 1711, lived in the house until it was bought by Nottingham Corporation in 1925.

Vertebrate animals are shown in natural habitat groups on the ground floor, and one room is devoted to comparative anatomy. Invertebrate animals and geology are on the first floor. Through lack of exhibition space, much of the botanical collection has to be in store and can only be seen by special arrangement. On the lower ground floor, the former servants' hall, is the H. G. Scott collection of cycling historia, opened to the public in June 1965. Already this collection has been augmented by the loan of a number of old cycles from the Raleigh Industries Limited and additions to the series of bells, gears, hubs, cyclometers, lamps, etc., will be made as historical pieces become available. Prints and photographs dated as far back as 1817 are included in the display.

Above the first floor is the central prospect room, not open to the public. It is a single chamber, originally the ballroom, with windows on all sides, from which there are magnificent views of the city and its surroundings.

Nottingham's other interesting museum, Newstead Abbey, is not under the Art Galleries and Museums Committee but the Libraries Committee. Situated outside the city, on the north side, it consists of a house on the side of the old priory, set in beautiful grounds, and at present used to house and display the relics of Byron. The Byron family were there from the 16th century to 1817, so it is particularly fitting that the Corporation should use the house to commemorate the famous poet.

There will be in the foreseeable future another municipal museum in Nottingham, the Industrial Museum, which will preserve and display material relating to local industries. A Curator has been appointed and material is being collected, but a suitable site has yet to be found.

THE THEATRE IN NOTTINGHAM

Nottingham has a long and interesting theatrical history. There are now two theatres, the Theatre Royal and the Nottingham Playhouse, both of some importance in the national picture. Each has roots in the past, connections with earlier buildings and with a web of activities, professional and amateur. There are also two amateur theatre buildings.

A small theatre in St. Mary's Gate was built in the 18th century and housed, until the 1860s, companies playing a circuit of East Midland towns. Exactly 100 years ago it was replaced by the Theatre Royal, built by the Lamberts, a local family. This theatre still stands, Victorian and portico'ed, at the head of Market Street. It was first operated by the Robertsons, an old theatrical clan, of whom Tom Robertson, the playwright, was one, and his sister Madge (later Dame Madge Kendal) another. It was she who sang 'God Save The Queen' on that opening night, whose centenary was celebrated last year. A performance of *The School for Scandal* followed.

Soon, however, the late Victorian and Edwardian theatrical pattern had established itself in Nottingham, a pattern which soon became uniform throughout the country, touring companies sent out by London managements to visit weekly the theatres of all our cities and towns. These theatres for the most part ceased to be locally owned, and were built or acquired, Nottingham's Theatre Royal among them, by a number of national combines. It is now owned by Moss Empires. It is, in its auditorium, older and handsomer than most, with all the glitter and atmosphere of the late Victorian period. Every actor of importance in the past 100 years has played on its stage.

By the '90s Nottingham had another touring theatre, the Grand at Hyson Green, built to house second companies and melodramas. Then came two music halls, the Empire, built in 1898, which adjoins the Theatre Royal, and a second very large house, the Hippodrome (now the Gaumont cinema), built in 1908 to replace a smaller building in Market Street, which became the Scala cinema.

Each of these later theatres, providers of lighter entertainment, has succumbed, one by one, to alternative methods of provision by the mass media, cinema and radio, then 'talkies' and finally television. Now, of this older order the Theatre Royal alone survives, still housing Christmas pantomime and companies sent from London, 'try-outs' and touring seasons following a London run, with visits from the big national and subsidised companies of drama, opera and ballet, playing an important part in the picture. In this way, though unhappily in a diminishing number of towns, the stars and names of the theatre and the big musical shows can still be seen by a provincial public. Large theatres are needed for this purpose and the Theatre Royal at Nottingham is one of the 20 or so in the country which remain.

The Grand Theatre had turned over to films by 1923 but the final phase in its history was of fascinating interest in itself and for its links both with the past and the future. In 1921 it was acquired by Mrs. Edward Compton. She was the widow of a successful actor-manager whose Compton Comedy Company had for many years provided a repertoire mainly based on Sheridan, Goldsmith and Shakespeare for provincial audiences, and occasionally for London. She had herself, with her sisters, played leading lady to Irving in his first seasons at the Lyceum. She was the mother of Compton Mackenzie and Fay Compton. Now, with her daughters Viola and Ellen she wished to spend what she had inherited from her husband in establishing in a provincial city, and in a working-class area at that, a repertory theatre on the same lines as those recently created by her friends Miss Horniman in Manchester, Miss Cons and Miss Lilian Bayliss at the Old Vic, and Sir Barry Jackson in Birmingham. By the end of three years the inheritance had vanished. The strong religious principles and high social purpose of Mrs. Compton, typical of the attitude to 'repertory' at that time, and the devoted and skilled professional work of her daughters and her company, were not enough to drag Nottingham audiences in sufficient numbers to Hyson Green, to plays which, while they included Shaw (still regarded as dangerous and *avant-garde*) and threatened to include Ibsen, were nevertheless performed by a company whose style was rooted in a past tradition. There were frequent productions of Shakespeare and the classics and an occasional new play. W. G. Fay, of the Abbey Theatre, Dublin, directed a number of the productions and in many ways the venture was well ahead of its period. The failure seemed tragic at the time, but those three years had a lasting effect on quite a number of Nottingham people, gave them a feeling for the theatre and a determination to see in course of time another repertory theatre established in their city. A quarter of a century passed before this happened but the seeds had been sown.

Their first crop was a spate of amateur activity at a rather high and serious level. Outstanding among these efforts in the late 'twenties and throughout the 'thirties was the Philodramatic Society (now the Theatre Club) which from the first had its own theatre, dedicated to theatrical adventurousness and experiment of the most daring and sometimes reckless kind, ranging from Shelley's *Cenci* to the Auden-Isherwood drama of the 'thirties; from the obscurer Elizabethans to Clifford Odets, or Plautus to home-made revue. Its founders had known, and in some cases been associated with, the Compton venture. The original tiny theatre in Alfred Street was succeeded by a larger one and the Club still flourishes with vitality in a third. Another group, the Playgoers Club, had been formed as a supporting body to the Compton theatre, and remained in being to promote an interest in drama in general and the creation of a professional repertory theatre in particular, until it merged with the Philodramatic Society just after the war. These groups represented the peaks of aspiration, and sometimes of achievement, but there were on the lower slopes some 60 societies in the 'thirties, buzzing with activity in the city and its surrounding areas.

The Compton theatre had come into being three years after the first World War ended: the new professional repertory theatre came at last in the Nottingham Playhouse, three years after the ending of the second. Again the link with the spirit of the times was clear. But before this happened there was one more manifestation of that spirit, very much in its 1945 form, in the amateur field. This was the provision of a new theatre and arts centre on a quite lavish scale by the Nottingham Co-operative Society, to provide a home for the theatrical and musical activities of its members, and the facilities of a real theatre for amateur dramatic events, drama festivals, youth drama competitions and the rest. This theatre, situated in George Street, still makes a major contribution to that side of the theatrical life of the city, and particularly of its young people, in its own adventurous programmes and in the facilities it offers to others.

Nottingham is certainly active and well provided in the amateur sphere, but the strength of these activities has not, as in some other cities, drained off the effort needed to promote a professional theatre. It was mainly from people whose interest in the drama had been fostered in these activities that this effort came. Just before the war ended, a Civic Theatre Committee came together, with representatives from the amateur theatre community, from the University and from people generally interested in the arts in the city. They prepared a scheme for the inclusion of a professional theatre in Nottingham's post-war town plan, which was submitted to the City Council and rejected within a week. The next move came also from the amateur sphere. A businessman well known in the local amateur theatre world acquired a small building in Goldsmith Street, a former cinema, ran it for a short time in conjunction with commercial weekly repertory managements, and then offered the lease to a trust which was promptly set up by more or less the same people who had constituted the Civic Theatre Committee. This was in 1948. The Trust was very much on the post-war model. The local government Act of that year had just been passed. So had an Act authorizing the building of a national theatre—when time was ripe. No longer need repertory theatres be gallant causes for earnest 'do-gooders'. War-time CEMA had given the precedent for the spending of public money on the arts, including the 'entertainment' arts, drama, music and ballet. The Arts Council of Great Britain came into being and the Trust received from it a small amount of money and a great deal of help and guidance from the start. Two other links of an official kind were formed. One was with the University. Its Vice-Chancellor, Mr. B. L. Hallward, became the Chairman who guided the Trust's fortunes for 15 years, and two senior members of the University staff joined the board. The second was with the local authorities. The difficult and stormier passages in the relationship between the City Council and Theatre are not unknown but they tend to obscure the fact that there has always been a close and practical relationship, which showed itself at once in a gift of £1,000, to get the Trust on its feet, a loan at a later stage, and above all in an arrangement which has continued ever since for the provision of some 15 to 20 special matinees for school-children every year. A similar arrangement was made with the county Education Authority, with whom relations have also been most close and friendly, and they too have enjoyed a similar number of matinees and a yearly tour of the county by a specially formed company. This formed a wonderful basis for future audiences whose special quality has been their youth. Finally the Playhouse Club was formed to support the new theatre and has given useful help in many ways ever since.

The Trust raised a small fund locally to supplement the city and Arts Council gifts and acquired the lease of the Goldsmith Street building. Built in the late 1900s as one of the first permanent cinema buildings in Nottingham, it had, but only just, a stage and dressing rooms. During the last war the building was first used regularly as a theatre by Tod Slaughter and his company and several weekly repertory companies which followed. It seated 467 and in spite of its deficiencies was not without the qualities and atmosphere which make an intimate theatre.

Nottingham Theatre Trust, having acquired the building, improved it, christened it the Nottingham Playhouse and engaged André Van Gyseghem as the first Director of Productions. In three years he established this theatre as one of the outstanding ones among the already strengthening group of the country's repertory theatres. Because the artistic policy was clear—Shakespeare and the classics, modern classics like Shaw, Wilde and Maugham, and lively and interesting contemporary plays, English and foreign, actors of ability and promise were willing to work here in spite of low salary, and worse working conditions. The policy was not too rigid to allow an occasional farce, thriller or modern West End success. But their place was never a dominating one. Van Gyseghem having triumphantly set the theatre on its feet was succeeded by John Harrison who, in his five years, guided it with great flair and firmness into directions in which Nottingham audiences would not easily have followed in the earliest days: more frequent new plays, lesser-known Shakespeare and Jacobean work, Chekhov and Ibsen and work from France and even Yugoslavia. His flair for choosing actors was considerable. In 1956, Val May took over the reins and continued a programme which was in some ways even more adventurous. *Peer Gynt* and *Oedipus Rex* were only two examples of a confidence that Nottingham would respond to something big.

In fact they had responded almost from the beginning. Van Gyseghem's second season, for example, virtually paid its way irrespective of subsidy. A continuance of this situation was too much to hope for, with a building whose seating capacity was too limited to exploit success and with so little to offer the audience in the way of amenities. The fortnightly—increasingly three-weekly—runs of each play, by no means always filled the theatre. There were, in fact, startling ups and downs in the audience figures, and the finances, and Arts Council subsidies were increased to meet rising costs. Nevertheless, the Goldsmith Street theatre always paid 80 per cent of its way from box-office takings.

By the mid-1950s it became obvious that the work not only deserved, but urgently needed, a better theatre. The Trust made an application to the City Council for a site and a new theatre. The full story of the struggle that followed would be too long to give here. Perhaps the important fact is that one half of the council of an important local authority stuck through thick and thin to a decision taken on a cultural issue, which moved to the centre of local life as a topic of fierce argument and feeling. Even the Conservative opposition became in time opposition, not to any scheme for a theatre, but to *that* scheme—their opponents' scheme—in particular, though the initial approaches from the Trust had been to both party leaders and to the Council as a whole, and the scheme itself architecturally, financially and in its detailed approach to the problems of a regional theatre for the 1960s onwards had the approval of the Arts Council and of eminent and expert authorities. In the end the vital resolution passed the Council by the Lord Mayor's casting vote.

The architect was Peter Moro, who had been associate architect for the Royal Festival Hall. The site is in Wellington Circus and adjoins the Albert Hall, the city's largest concert hall. The Midland Group Gallery is opposite. The architect has made extremely good use of these surroundings and the building is increasingly recognised as quite an important example of the architecture of our day. It is certainly a major contribution to the great argument as to what theatres built for the second half of this century should be like. Whether it solves the problem of flexibility and allows proscenium arch and open stage types of production within one building—whether indeed this is possible of achievement with a building beyond a certain size—remains a matter for argument. Certainly there is a degree of flexibility, together with facilities for the presentation of plays in repertoire of differing types and periods, enjoyed by few other theatres in the country. Peter Moro worked strictly to his brief, which was to design a theatre on the new model—provided by a city, to meet the needs of its citizens of all types and classes, but particularly young people. There must, however, be no whiff of the municipal. It must give the same glitter and sense of occasion which the Theatre Royal, with its stalls and circles, boxes and pit, its stucco and gilt, had given to a more class-rigid generation. But this had to be done in the idiom of today and, above all, on a very limited budget.

The briefing came almost entirely from the professional theatre people—the city were enlightened enough to allow this—mainly from Val May and his colleagues, who were occupying the Goldsmith Street theatre during the planning period, with a great deal of consultation and advice from other theatrical sources. Val May left to run the Bristol Old Vic in 1956. It was unfortunate that the Directors who were ultimately to have charge of the new theatre were appointed too late to have any say in this planning (artists' ideas are bound to differ), or in the decision to make certain much-regretted cuts and omissions imposed by a desperate need not to exceed the figure voted by the Council. Nevertheless, the space and working facilities backstage, the equipment and machinery, the workshops, scene stores, paint rooms, laundry, dressing rooms, showers, rehearsal room, green rooms and recording room (even though some dimensions had to suffer a little) are generous and efficient. The backstage area is 95 feet wide and 50 feet deep (more than double that of the Belgrade, Coventry) and the auditorium seats 756 for a proscenium production and 723 when there is the maximum stage projection.

The final cost of the furnished and equipped building was £380,000, almost exactly the contract figure: 1s. 0d. per square foot less than the new Coventry theatre built five years earlier and less than the Guildford theatre built later. A contribution of £15,000 came from the Gulbenkian Foundation and £10,000 from the Arts Council for special equipment and furniture and a further gift from the Arts Council of a piece of sculpture. The total expense of the fully equipped theatre was, therefore, just over £380,000, of which the city paid £310,000, and the building remained theirs. The Trust, helped by these donations and a contribution from the County Council, raised the balance. The gloomy prognostications of the scheme's opponents as to this 'reckless and feckless' venture had not been justified, on this side at any rate.

Nor have they on the running side. After long and somewhat painful negotiations between city and Trust it has been agreed that the theatre shall pay to the city an annual sum of £27,000 with one hand and receive £22,000 with the other. The net result is an annual sum of £5,000 plus rates for the use of the building and site. This is not small as theatre rents go but it contains a subsidy element in terms of municipal accounting under which capital spent has to be repaid. The basic capital cost, however, was met from a special fund owned by the city, so that it did not fall on the general rate fund. The Arts Council gives a subsidy for the work itself amounting in 1965–66 to £24,000, approximately the same as for the other repertory theatres of regional importance. Financial help has also come from the County Council and the smaller authorities in the area.

With these financial arrangements the theatre has so far met its costs. In fact the audiences have far exceeded expectation. The honeymoon period has passed but the theatre still plays to an average capacity of over 85 per cent; audiences roughly treble those which came to the Goldsmith Street building and their numbers are continuously increased by visitors from all over the country and from abroad.

The Directors of the theatre and the company have risen to the opportunity given by the new building. The last Director at Goldsmith Street was Frank Dunlop, although André Van Gyseghem had returned to the theatre to direct a short distinguished closing season. Dunlop, in a difficult two years, had begun to build for the future. A Director of some standing, he was able to bring regularly into the company well-known actors, producers and designers in a lively and imaginative programme. Among them was John Neville, and it was Frank Dunlop and John Neville who, with Peter Ustinov, were appointed joint Directors of the new theatre. Mr. Ustinov was not expected to give a great deal of his time, but his help in the background in the early stages was quite appreciable, and he wrote for the theatre a play which attracted attention and interest at just the right moment. The basic strategy for the new venture and the gruelling hard work of transforming a small-scale operation into quite a large and complex one was that of Dunlop and Neville and the new young Manager, Peter Stephens. As for the programme itself, a system of true repertoire was planned and put into operation. Nottingham was thus the first major theatre outside London, apart from the Royal Shakespeare at Stratford, regularly to operate a system long advocated as a better alternative to the system of short runs after which each production is scrapped. Successful plays can be kept in the repertoire while they are continuing to draw, failures can be withdrawn quickly, and plays with minority appeal have their due place. The National Theatre, which opened two months earlier at the Old Vic, and the Royal Shakespeare at the Aldwych, work on the same system and many of the leading repertory theatres are following suit. Arts Council subsidy has in each case made this system possible for it is initially costly, but there is little doubt of the artistic result or the benefit to the public. In Nottingham's case it was also possible because the new theatre had been planned with the workshops, scene stores and back-stage space to accommodate a number of productions at the same time and the housing of a large enough staff to operate them.

Above all the success of the Nottingham Playhouse is the work of John Neville. For an actor of his achievement and reputation to come to Nottingham in the first place was in itself a gesture of belief that the theatre outside London should not be a second-best affair and of the need to bring it within the reach of all ages and classes.

His appeal has been particularly to the young; he has sponsored a wide range of extra activities, jazz and poetry recitals, lunch-time performances, a youth club on Saturday mornings, art exhibitions and visits to factories and clubs and a summer arts festival, apart from the school matinees and the annual tour of the county. The company has visited Ghana and Nigeria and the Far East. Much of this has followed Nottingham Playhouse tradition, but John Neville and his team have brilliantly and tirelessly exploited the opportunity given by the building and the greater resources at their disposal. As to the plays themselves, the assumption was made that Nottingham would come to what was good, if it had vitality and quality in its performance: Shakespeare, Shaw, Ben Johnson, Wilde, Calderon, Chekhov among the classics and modern classics; Brecht, Anouilh and a series of new plays including a highly successful version of Sillitoe's *Saturday Night and Sunday Morning*, and several successes transferred to the West End. If the programme has not yet been experimental to the extent occasionally possible in the old Goldsmith Street days the mistake has not been made of aiming low, and the box-office reaction of 4,500 paying patrons week by week is the proof that the choice has been good. *Richard II* ran through a large part of one season and, revived, continued to draw large audiences in the next.

Success has been helped by the willingness of well-known actors to work here. Sir Tyrone Guthrie directed the opening production of *Coriolanus*. Leo McKern, Angela Baddeley, Alistair Sim, Michael Craig, Joan Heal, Judi Dench and many others of standing in the theatre have been in the company for periods. London critics and managers are frequently in the audience. This is already an important theatre regionally and nationally, a far cry indeed from the old conception of 'weekly Rep' churning out ill-rehearsed versions of West End successes, and is symptomatic of the way things are going theatrically in this country.

That Nottingham has given a lead here is increasingly a matter of local pride. Its theatrical activity taken as a whole has grown from local roots, sometimes painfully, but always with vigour and strength. Without Arts Council help at the national level a theatre of the quality of the Playhouse would not have been possible. Municipal recognition and provision of a building came at the right moment. For all that, it has been the enterprise of local people and the dedicated work and skill of the theatrical profession which has created something which will enrich increasingly and for many generations the life of a city, a county and a region.

XXIV

EDUCATION

RESPONSIBILITY for the provision of primary, secondary and further education in the City of Nottingham is delegated by the City Council as Local Education Authority to its Education Committee. This Committee consists of 24 members of the City Council and four co-opted members who are 'persons of experience in education', and its work is organised under seven main sub-committees covering primary, secondary and further education, special services, sites and buildings, youth employment and finance and general purposes. There are in addition a Youth Committee and sub-committees, Joint Consultative Committees for primary, secondary, further and adult education, bodies of governors for eight groups of secondary schools, for each voluntary secondary school and for the various institutions of further education, as well as managers for voluntary primary schools. The Nottingham Regional College of Technology is controlled by a Joint Education Committee, on which the city, Nottinghamshire, Derbyshire and the University of Nottingham are represented. Nottinghamshire, as well as the city, is also represented on the Governing Body of the Nottingham College of Education, and the Nottingham College of Art and Design has representatives both of Nottinghamshire and Derbyshire on its Governing Body.

Primary Education

After a period of seven years of steady fall in the birth-rate the increase which began in 1957 is now having a significant effect on the infant schools of the city. It is also noteworthy that from an almost insignificant proportion in earlier years the number of coloured immigrant births in the city in 1964 rose to nearly 10 per cent of the total. In several primary schools serving the poorer areas near the centre of the city the proportion of West Indian, Indian and Pakistani immigrant children has already risen to 20 or 25 per cent, while in two schools it is now over 40 per cent.

If the task of striking a balance between the maintenance of educational standards for native English children and the application of successful measures for the educational and social integration of immigrant children is one of the most difficult and growing problems facing primary education in the central part of the city today, another is undoubtedly the need to replace or re-model old and unsuitable primary school buildings. Many of these date back to the turn of the century or earlier and do not lend themselves readily to adaptation to meet the requirements of current educational standards and ideals.

With the Education Committee's sustained drive to provide the widest possible range of opportunity in modern and well-equipped secondary schools coming within sight of completion, attention is now increasingly focussed on the urgent need to replace old and unsuitable primary schools and high priority is being given to the provision of an educational environment for the younger children in the central areas comparable in standard with that existing in the more recently built schools on the outskirts of the city.

There are in the city a total of 125 primary schools, including four nursery and eight special schools, employing approximately 1,000 full-time, 80 part-time and 45 temporary teachers. The number of pupils, full- and part-time, in ordinary, nursery and special schools in January 1965 was over 31,000. In the last decade the number of oversize classes in infant and junior schools has fallen dramatically and the few remaining classes of 45 pupils or over result from accommodation difficulties rather than problems of teacher supply.

In the field of nursery education, which is available in the city's four nursery schools and 22 nursery classes attached to infant schools, the Committee have adopted the policy in selected schools and classes of providing half-time as well as full-time places in order to give a larger number of children the opportunity of benefitting from this form of education.

In the primary schools of the city notable progress has been made over recent years, despite staffing and accommodation problems, in widening the curriculum and developing new methods and techniques. Many infant schools are organised on a pattern of family grouping under which each class includes a complete cross-section of the age ranges in the school. The basic skills are taught with the aid of the widest possible range of practical apparatus and emphasis is placed on the importance of social development in an informal but purposeful environment. Children are encouraged and given the opportunity to experiment and discover the interest of artistic, musical and other media, and the work is aimed to meet the requirements of each individual child rather than making all children conform to a set pattern.

In junior schools many head teachers are experimenting with an 'unstreamed' organisation of classes in all or part of the four-year junior school course and the results of this approach on the progress of both the bright and the slower children are being carefully observed.

The curriculum of city junior schools has been enriched by developments in the teaching of a broader concept of mathematics rather than arithmetic alone, by the introduction of simple experimental work designed to lay the foundation of objective scientific observation, recording and conclusion, and by the growth at a number of schools of the teaching of French by modern audio-visual methods. In this latter connection Nottingham is one of the areas selected to take part in the current experimental project of the Department of Education and Science in conjunction with the Nuffield Foundation for the teaching of French from the age of eight to children in selected groups in primary schools, with continuation of the course into the secondary school.

A further recent development has been the progressive installation of television sets in primary schools as an additional aid to the educational process.

The provision of special education for handicapped children falls within the purview of the city's Primary Education Sub-Committee. There are four special schools for educationally sub-normal children and in addition separate schools for pupils who are respectively physically handicapped and deaf. The Ewing School for the Deaf was specially built in 1960 for its purpose and is equipped with the latest aids for the teaching of deaf and partially hearing children. It is, of course, impracticable for any Authority to make provision on its own for special education to meet the needs of all forms of handicap, physical and mental, which occur in children of school age and, as is the usual practice, the Committee place some of their handicapped children in independent residential schools and special schools provided by other Authorities.

Secondary Education

In the field of secondary education the city's Education Committee have extended the range of opportunity available by developing a system of bilateral schools in association with grammar schools. The bilateral schools offer courses to G.C.E. 'O' level for children admitted to their selective streams. Pupils attaining an appropriate standard in the G.C.E. 'O' level at the end of a five-year course in the selective streams are subsequently given the opportunity to transfer for 'A' level studies to the sixth forms of associated grammar schools or may alternatively proceed to specialised courses of full-time or part-time vocational study in further education.

The establishment of the bilateral system has provided a successful answer to the problem arising from the margin of error in prognosis inherent in all systems of testing academic educational potential at 11 plus. Experience has shown that a proportion of children qualify at 11 plus for grammar school places who subsequently fail to justify their admission to an intensive academic course, while on the other hand, a proportion of those not selected at 11 plus show themselves able, given the opportunity, to achieve academic success. Recent analyses made of the performance of pupils in city secondary schools have shown that on the one hand pupils who have failed in grammar schools and on the other those who have succeeded in obtaining university entrance standard after progressing through bilateral schools to grammar school sixth forms have not largely been those who were on the borderline for grammar school admission in tests taken at 11 plus.

There is a total of 20,300 pupils in the secondary schools of the city and a teaching staff of 1,179 full- and part-time teachers.

There are six county grammar schools in the city, three mixed, one for boys only and two for girls only, and a voluntary aided Roman Catholic grammar school for girls. The Committee provides places for Roman Catholic boys at the independent Becket School, and a number of places for pupils of high academic potential are also provided at the direct grant Nottingham High School for Girls (Girls Public Day School Trust) and the independent Nottingham High School for Boys. On the Clifton Estate, a self-contained area of council housing detached from the main built-up area of the city, with a population of about 30,000, the Education Committee has established a comprehensive school for boys, with a total roll in September 1965 of 1,656 pupils. Pupils in the first completely unselected entry to this school completed a five-year 'O' level course in 1964, and in the summer of that year, of 250 boys of all ranges of ability who entered the school at 11 plus, approximately 30 per cent completed the five-year course. The proportion of pupils staying on to 16, and performances in external examinations in this school are almost exactly comparable with those for the rest of the city under the 'comprehensive' system of grammar, bilateral and modern schools.

The city has 18 bilateral schools, some mixed and some single-sex, including two voluntary aided Roman Catholic schools. There are 13 secondary modern schools, three of which will be closed on the completion of a further bilateral school for 1,200 pupils now in course of construction. A third voluntary aided Roman Catholic secondary school is to open in the academic year 1965–66.

The aim of the Education Committee is in due course to replace all remaining secondary modern schools by provision in large mixed bilateral schools and consideration has been given as a possible long-term future development to the admission of all pupils at 11 plus to bilateral schools, without selection, using the existing grammar schools as sixth form colleges.

Under the Committee's present arrangements, selection at 11 plus is on a modified quota system for each primary school and is based on the results of two National Foundation for Educational Research tests in verbal reasoning in combination with head teachers' assessments. Just over 18 per cent of the age group are offered places in grammar schools and a further 18 per cent in the selective streams of bilateral schools. Subsequent transfer is effected in appropriate cases between non-selective and G.C.E. streams of bilateral schools and between modern schools and bilateral schools. The main bulk of transfer, however, is that from bilateral G.C.E. streams to grammar school sixth forms after G.C.E. 'O' level. In September 1964 105 pupils were transferred in this way, and in the same academic year 35 former bilateral pupils obtained or surpassed in grammar schools the minimum of two 'A' levels normally required for admission to university degree or comparable courses.

Fourteen secondary schools, modern and bilateral, provide elementary commercial courses for girls and in most schools boys have the opportunity of learning technical drawing in addition to metalwork and woodwork as a foundation on which vocational courses of further education can later be based. An interesting recent development is the installation of language laboratories in two grammar schools. The secondary schools of the city are active in the fields of music and drama as well as in sport and physical education. Instrumental tuition in music continues to develop, the schools take full advantage of the facilities for seeing good drama at the Nottingham Playhouse, while in physical education continual progress is made in opening up to school children an ever-widening range of sport and recreation not confined solely to the traditional team games.

An interesting development in school building and organisation is that planned in connection with extensions to sixth form accommodation at one of the city's mixed grammar schools, where provision is being made for common rooms, individual study and a more adult approach generally towards the older pupils.

From the academic year 1964–65 onwards the new Certificate of Secondary Education examination replaced throughout the country all fifth-year secondary school examinations other than the G.C.E. The city and the county of Nottingham fall within the area in which the new examination is administered by the East Midlands Regional Examination Board. The examination, for which large numbers of city and county candidates entered in 1964–65, is teacher-controlled and many local teachers serve on the controlling committees and subject panels set up to conduct it in accordance with the requirements of the Schools Council.

Further Education

The major institutions of further education in the Nottingham area under local authority control are the Nottingham College of Education, the Nottingham Regional College of Technology and the Nottingham College of Art and Design. The College of Education draws its students from all over the country, while the College of Technology and the College of Art, though predominantly serving the East Midland region in the field of part-time education, recruits students for advanced full-time or sandwich courses on a national basis. In addition the city has two colleges of further education, People's College and Clarendon College, and the first phase of a third college to be located at Basford Hall will shortly be built. The Education Committee also maintains a Nursery Nurses' College and is responsible for the staffing, equipment and curriculum of Boots' College, which was established by Boots Pure Drug Company as part of their premises at Beeston to provide general education for their young employees.

Further education in the Nottingham area, as in the country generally, is in a state of rapid change and expansion to meet ever-increasing demands on the lines of development recommended by the Robbins Committee and other national bodies. The additional courses of vocational education which will be required by local industry when the Industrial Training Act is fully implemented are likely to place a further strain on the resources of the colleges, as also will the endeavour to fulfil the recommendations of the Henniker-Heaton Committee on Day Release, which include the doubling in the next five years of the volume of day release of employees in industry and commerce to attend courses of further education.

To keep pace with the rising demand for further education a considerable building programme is planned or in progress in the city. Major extensions are currently being added to the Regional College of Technology and additions are also being made to the People's College of Further Education. The College of Education is in the course of being considerably enlarged and the College of Art and Design is to be completely re-housed in new buildings on which a start has been authorised in the financial year 1965–66. In the same financial year the first instalment of the new third College of Further Education is scheduled to begin, and Department of Education and Science approval has been received to the commencement in the financial year 1966–67 of schemes for the extension of Clarendon College of Further Education and for the provision of communal and hostel accommodation for students.

In order to achieve a reasonable and equitable distribution of courses at colleges of further education throughout the district, while at the same time leaving the regional college free to concentrate on advanced work, a rational pattern of transfer and location of courses has been devised in agreement with the county authority.

The Nottingham College of Education at Clifton was opened in 1960 and is one of the largest and most sought-after in the country. It was planned for 480 students, 320 of whom were to be resident. Considerable expansion has already taken place to meet the need for more teachers. In 1963–64, 208 students completed their three-year course at the College, which includes periods of teaching practice for which schools in the city, Nottinghamshire and Derbyshire are used. In the academic year 1964–65, student numbers total 765 and the extensions now being built will provide accommodation by 1966 for about 1,000 students, 400 of them resident. There is continuing pressure from the Department of Education and Science for the provision of yet more student places to assist in the present 'crash programme' for increasing further the number of teachers coming into the schools. From September 1965, with the approval of the Senate of the University of Nottingham, the College now offers a four-year degree course on the lines recommended in the Robbins Report.

The Regional College of Technology has departments of Mechanical and Production Engineering, Electrical Engineering, Building and Civil Engineering, Mining, Mathematics and Physics, Chemistry and Biology, Business Administration, Liberal Studies, Textiles and Printing. It is governed by a Joint Education Committee consisting of representatives of Nottingham city, Nottinghamshire and Derbyshire. The city and county have equal representation, whilst Derbyshire takes a smaller share. The College offers a wide range of full-time degree and comparable courses, and to accommodate these a substantial and phased programme of transfer of less advanced work to other institutions is in operation. The College is authorised to offer courses leading to degrees of the recently established Council for National Academic

Awards in Mechanical Engineering, Electrical Engineering and Civil Engineering, and proposals for additional courses of the same honours degree standard are under consideration. The College enrolled a total of 7,278 students in 1964–65, of whom 719 were full-time.

The College of Art and Design has recently been recognised as a centre for Diploma in Art and Design courses in Fine Art and Fashion/Textiles and it is hoped that other courses, including a course in theatre design to be commenced in the academic year 1965–66, will eventually be granted similar recognition. A further new course which began in October 1965 is a Joint B.A. Honours Degree Course in Fine Art and the History of Art arranged in conjunction with Nottingham University. The College has departments of Fine Art, Textiles and Fashion, Graphic Design, Three-Dimensional Design and a School of Town and Country Planning. Enrolment in 1963–64 totalled 1,471, of whom 386 were full-time students.

People's College of Further Education, one of the largest of its type in the country, provides courses up to Ordinary National Certificate level in Mechanical and Electrical Engineering, Building and Science as well as technicians' and craft courses. Besides servicing courses in technical subjects the Department of General Studies offers courses to G.C.E. 'O' and 'A' level. The majority of students attend the College on part-time day release from industry, but there has been a very considerable expansion of block release in the last few years with the co-operation of local firms. The College has a total student enrolment of over 5,000.

The city's second College of Further Education, Clarendon College, has departments of Commerce, Languages and General Studies, and Catering and Women's Subjects. The College has over 450 full-time students as well as over 4,500 attending for evening and part-time day and evening courses, and in a number of branches of its work serves the needs of a very wide area of the East Midlands. Courses in the Commerce Department include the Ordinary National Diploma and Certificate in Business Studies.

Notable progress is being made in the development of courses in music, speech and drama, and intensive language tuition is facilitated by the use of language laboratories. Catering students are prepared for the examinations of the Hotel and Catering Institute and other qualifications. The College also offers full and part-time courses in hair-dressing.

The Nursery Nurses' College provides a two-year course combining practical experience in nursery schools and day nurseries and similar establishments with further general education at the College. Students are drawn from a wide area and the demand for places considerably exceeds the number of students who can be accepted.

Boots' College is attended solely by employees of Boots Pure Drug Company and provides a course of general education on a one day per week basis for all young employees of the firm under the age of 18. Courses for the Certificate in Office Studies have been introduced and some students are prepared for the City and Guilds examination in Chemical Plant Operation.

In addition to the courses of further education available in its colleges the city's Education Committee provides for elementary commercial training and non-vocational and recreational classes for adult students in a series of adult education centres in various parts of the city. In addition, a considerable range of classes is provided for community associations and women's clubs.

The work of the Committee in further education also includes the administration of a constantly growing volume of university and other awards to students following courses of higher education.

The city's youth service covers 256 affiliated groups and clubs with a total membership of 13,239 young people. New youth club premises are constantly being provided, some by voluntary bodies with financial assistance from the Department of Education and Science, others by the Local Authority. Since the acceptance by the Government of the Albemarle Report, six new youth centres have been provided by voluntary organisations and two by the Local Authority. Department of Education and Science approval has been given to the provision of two further Local Education Authority centres in the 1965–66 and 1966–67 youth service building programmes respectively.

Youth Employment

The city's Education Committee provide a youth employment service in exercise of their powers under the Employment and Training Act, 1948, and the various National Insurance Acts. The duties of the service are to see that vocational guidance and careers information is made available to all young persons under 18 years of age, and beyond that age if they are still at school, and to place, as far as possible, each youngster in suitable employment.

The general pattern of the procedure is for vocational guidance officers to deliver talks in schools to groups of potential leavers during their last year, followed up later by individual vocational guidance interviews.

Careers staff in schools are responsible for maintaining, in collaboration with the youth employment service, a school careers library. School careers staff act as a daily link between potential leavers and the vocational guidance officers and are in a position to arrange educational/vocational visits to local places of employment for senior pupils. The youth employment service has, during the last few years, organised and assisted schools in arranging various careers conventions.

An increasingly important side of the careers counselling work of the service and of careers staff in schools is the provision of detailed guidance to fifth- and sixth-formers concerning opportunities for entering full-time courses of further and higher education.

EDUCATION IN THE URBAN DISTRICTS

For those parts of the Nottingham district outside the city but contiguous to it, i.e. the Urban Districts of Arnold, Beeston and Stapleford, Carlton and West Bridgford, the responsibility for education services rests with the Education Committee of the Nottinghamshire County Council. This Authority provides places for over 14,000 pupils in the primary schools of the four Urban Districts and for well over 10,000 in the secondary schools, though in each case a number of children from adjoining rural areas are included. There are two Colleges of Further Education, one serving Arnold and Carlton, the other serving Beeston and Stapleford, having a total of about 900 full-time students and nearly 6,000 part-time and day release students. Plans have been approved for a similar college at West Bridgford and a start on the building should be made in the financial year 1966–67.

The Nottinghamshire education authority pioneered the C.L.A.S.P. (Consortium of Local Authorities' Special Programme) building system, now widely known at home and abroad. Originally designed to provide a satisfactory answer to the problems of building in areas of mining subsidence, as on the Nottinghamshire coalfield, C.L.A.S.P. has developed into a most modern and efficient method of school construction. This has enabled the county to build educational establishments ranging from small village schools to large comprehensive schools at well below national cost levels yet with excellent facilities and finish.

In the peripheral area around Nottingham, the county primary schools, large and small, serve the needs of many different communities. Secondary school provision includes grammar, technical grammar and modern schools. A flexible transfer system operates between the different types of secondary school and in some districts the development of campus sites facilitates close co-operation. The county is justly proud of its residential special schools at Sutton Fields, Hopwell Hall and Ramsdale, and above all, of the unique Thieves Wood Residential School for severely physically handicapped children. Other activities which should be mentioned include the county museum service which supplies schools with a variety of items of historical interest for examination and study; the Education Committee's collection of original works of art, numbering nearly 250 items, available on loan to schools; and the County Music School at Arnold. The Music School is the Saturday rendezvous of dozens of young instrumentalists whose activities culminate in the annual performance of the County Youth Orchestra, an ensemble comparable in size and quality with many large orchestras.

ADULT EDUCATION

The great movements in adult education in the 19th and 20th centuries almost all met with a quick and ready response in Nottingham; indeed some of them had their beginnings there. Why this should be so, what gives a town or a region such a pre-disposition, is a question which could only be answered, if it could be answered at all, by a geographer, an economic historian and a sociologist working in concert. In the present state of such inter-disciplinary studies we cannot wait for their findings.

Certainly the town exhibited, throughout the first half of the 19th century, a heartily radical temper. It formally recorded its opposition to 'the Bills against Treason and Sedition' in 1795, petitioned for the reform of Parliament in 1817, protested at the Peterloo massacre in 1819, supported the Roman Catholic Peers Bill in 1822 and the Catholic Emancipation Bill in 1825, protested at the Aliens Bill in 1824, and petitioned for the repeal of the Game Laws in 1848, for 'the establishment of reformation schools for young criminals instead of sending them to prison' in 1854, and for 'entry to the Civil Service by open competition' in 1856. Nottingham marked the end of a turbulent half-century by putting up a statue of Fergus O'Connor, the Chartist leader, in a newly opened public park, the Arboretum, where it still stands.

These attitudes bred, naturally enough, an equally lively concern for education. In the period before the School Boards the Corporation seems to have been generous in its grants of lands and its financial contributions to voluntary schools, and it showed an early interest in university education by buying, in 1829, two £100 shares in London University. But a great deal of the educational life of the town flowed in more covert streams. J. W. Hudson, who in 1851 wrote a *History of Adult Education*, in effect a history of the Mechanics Institutes, remarked on the 'active thirst for information in this town' which though it 'led to a vivid perception of political rights and wrongs, to political unions and Chartism' yet 'threw off the veil that darkened the vision of the human intellect'. And he goes on: 'The desire for intellectual amusement seems to have entered into all the ramifications of society in this town, for there are several Working Men's Libraries held in *public houses*. At two of these houses political discussions are also held under judicious regulation'. We know of seven of these 'operatives libraries' from local sources (six met in public houses and one in a temperance institute) and know that they were set up in part to provide the books of political and religious controversy which were banned from the rather grand, and officially sponsored, Artizan's Library, which had been set up in 1824. Libraries presume readers, and, by the standards of the time, Nottingham seems to have been a fairly literate community. It supported a very large circulation of unstamped newspapers and journals and one of the best known radical booksellers in the country, Sutton and Sons. In 1857 the Superintendent of Police found that, of 1,105 persons apprehended during the year, only 411 could neither read nor write. Many of the more respectable citizens would have said that their literacy contributed to their downfall, and that had they not been able to read the publications of Carlile, Wooler and Hare they might not have been where they were.

This was, then, a rich soil for adult education to grow in, richer in fact than the printed records suggest. For underneath it was an even richer subsoil of educational self-help, in Chartist groups, Owenite groups, friendly societies, mutual improvement societies, Methodist class meetings, working men's associations, trade unions, a bewildering variety of small and often ephemeral organisations of which the 'operatives libraries' are, as it were, only the visible tip of the iceberg. The rest of this section will review, very briefly, the way in which new and changing patterns of adult education in the 19th and 20th centuries established themselves, or in some cases were established, here.

Adult Schools

It had not been uncommon for adults to attend day schools and Sunday schools in the 18th century, and certainly in Wales and in Gloucester special adult classes had sometimes been attached to such schools. What appeared in Nottingham at the end of the century was a school for adults independent of other institutions, as far as we know, for the records are haphazard and confused, the first of its kind. In 1789, according to J. W. Rowntree and H. B. Binns, 'an Adult Sunday School for Bible reading and instruction in the secular arts of writing and arithmetic was opened in a room belonging to the Methodist New Connection in Nottingham by William Singleton, himself a Methodist. He had help from a Quaker tradesman, Samuel Fox, who afterwards became specially identified with the School'. This school persisted into the 20th century, but it is of interest less for itself than for the influence it had upon the great resurgence of adult schools, under Quaker auspices, in the second half of the 19th century. For Joseph Sturge, whose Severn Street Men's School in Birmingham inaugurated a period of nation-wide expansion, was inspired to its foundation by a visit he had paid to the Nottingham school in 1842. He sent some of his Birmingham teachers to visit what he obviously regarded as the parent organisation in 1846. They were impressed, but evidently felt that the inclusion of 'the secular arts of writing and arithmetic' in the Nottingham curriculum was somewhat revolutionary for, they reported, 'persons who learn arithmetic on the First-day will soon think it no harm to keep their accounts or even transact business on that day'.

Mechanics Institutes

Nottingham could not fail to be caught up in the movement which swept the whole country in so spectacular a fashion in the 30 years or so following the establishment of the London Mechanics Institution in 1823; by the middle of the century there were between six and seven hundred such institutes established. After several false starts, one as early as 1824, the Nottingham Mechanics Institute was established in 1837, grew with speed and vigour, erected its own premises in 1841 and rebuilt them, on an even larger and grander scale, after a fire in 1859. It was for half a century, until the establishment of the University College, one of the largest and most splendid public buildings in the town and was certainly the major cultural and educational centre. Thus on such civic occasions as the official opening of the Arboretum in 1852 guests were given cards of admission to the grounds of the Castle and to 'the rooms and museum of the Mechanics Institute'. The building stood until 1965, when it was replaced by another on the same site; and the institution still survives, though of course in much changed form and serving purposes different from those of 1837. Most Mechanics Institutes, if they survived at all into the last quarter of the century, did so by turning themselves either into Technical Colleges or into mainly social and recreational clubs. Nottingham, like the rest, struggled for as long as it could to maintain the educational work for which it was founded. But its contribution to adult education lies less in its own work than in the central part it played in bringing into being, first, university extension classes, and then a University College.

People's Colleges

This was the one movement in 19th century adult education which in Nottingham failed to find an effective response. The first College was opened in Sheffield in 1842 by R. S. Bayley, an Independent Minister, and set out, in conscious reaction against the narrow and utilitarian curriculum of the Mechanics Institutes, to teach the humanities to working men. It was an aim that went against the grain of the time and failed in most places to attract the money and the influential support that were given so freely to the Mechanics Institutes, so that, though in many places attempts to found such Colleges were made, hardly any of them survived for more than a few years. Two notable Colleges were sustained by genius and still exist: that in London founded by F. D. Maurice in 1854 and that in Leicester founded by D. J. Vaughan (much influenced by Maurice) in 1862. Nottingham was quick off the mark, and in 1846 set up a People's College 'for the mental and moral improvement of the labouring population' but almost from the start it was diverted to the provision of basic and technical education for children and adolescents, first in evening classes and then in a day school as well. A separate section for the education of working men, with its own meeting place, was established in 1854, perhaps influenced by the example of Maurice rather than Bayley, but seems to have disappeared in the 1860s.

University Extension

It was the Extension movement of the 1870s that really made its mark on Nottingham. James Stuart's tentative excursions from Cambridge had begun in 1867 with courses given to meetings of the North of England Council for the Higher Education of Women at Manchester, Sheffield, Leeds and Liverpool, to railwaymen at the Mechanics Institute at Crewe and to the Equitable Pioneers Co-operative Society at Rochdale. The demand for such courses was so widespread that it could not long be met by the efforts of individuals, and in 1871 Stuart made a formal appeal to Cambridge that such Extension Courses should be accepted as a proper function of a university and that machinery should be set up to provide and develop them. A syndicate was appointed to explore the matter and memorials were received from the centres in which Stuart had lectured and also from Leeds and Nottingham. The Nottingham memorial was adopted at the Annual General Meeting of the Mechanics Institute in January 1873 and was submitted as from the Institute and the Trades Council. It was drafted by two men of intellectual distinction and of great local influence, Richard Enfield, a solicitor, and J. B. Paton, Principal of the Congregational Institute, and displays a persuasive combination of academic perceptiveness and local pride. The tutors whom the University was urged to appoint for this work were thus described: 'Men who could attract and really teach working men must be thorough masters of their subject and able, not only to lecture, but to discuss and reply to the questions raised in the class, especially considering the native intelligence of the artizans of this locality, the advance in elementary education and the continual discussions of political and social questions among them'.

The syndicate reported speedily and favourably, and was, according to Stuart, much influenced by the Nottingham memorial. 'There were no people connected with the University Extension movement, outside the University itself, who seized more fully its leading ideas and entered more completely into its spirit than did Mr. Enfield and Dr. Paton. Especially did they recognise a point uppermost in my mind, namely the great advantage which might accrue to the nation through the education of all classes being carried on by the same agency.' So it was that the first University Extension classes in the country were provided on a Nottingham–Derby–Leicester circuit under the scheme suggested and organised locally by Enfield and Paton. An inaugural meeting held in the Mechanics Institute was addressed by Lord Carnarvon and Henry Sidgwick, and six courses were launched straightway, three in the Michaelmas Term of 1873 and three in the Lent Term of 1874. The subjects were chosen with an eye to three potential audiences: English Literature and Geography for young women, Force and Motion and Astronomy for young men of the middle class and Political Economy and Constitutional History for working men. We do not know how accurate these judgments of class interests proved to be, but there was an average attendance in Nottingham of well over 100 in this first series of lectures.

This first series of Extension Courses was hardly ended when Enfield conveyed to the Corporation the offer of a friend, who insisted upon remaining anonymous, to give £10,000 to endow lectureships to put such work upon a permanent footing in Nottingham provided that the Corporation would, within reasonable time, put up a building to house it. This was a bold challenge but it came at the right time. Whereas the first half of the century was a time of voluntary action by a host of independent organisations, this second half was a time of civic action, with the Corporation flexing its muscles, trying out its new responsibilities and taking over the projects that had earlier been established by voluntary effort. Thus the old Artizan's Library was taken over when the Free Library and Museums Act was adopted in 1867. Its books formed more than half the stock of the new Free Library, 6,000 out of 11,000. The collections of the Naturalists Society were absorbed at the same time. The Literary and Philosophical Society was dissolved in 1882, and similarly gave its books to the Free Library. The School of Design, opened in 1843 'to provide for manufacturers artizans better educated and better able to originate and execute their respective wares' was taken over by the Corporation in 1888. And so on; it is a familiar story.

So the response to Enfield's, and his anonymous friend's, challenge was a vigorous one. First, their bold and imaginative scheme was met by one bolder and yet more imaginative: a scheme for a building to house not only the Extension Courses but also the Free Library, the Natural History Museum and the evening classes, mainly of a technical nature, sponsored by the Department of Science and Art and housed in the Mechanics Institute. Second, their scheme was modified to ensure that the Corporation had a majority on the governing body. Agreement was reached and designs were sought straight-way; those approved were for the building in a Victorian version of French Gothic which still stands in Shakespeare Street and which, whether one has a taste for such things or not, is still so much livelier and more imaginative than its 20th-century neighbours. By 1877, when the foundation stone was laid, the building was already being referred to as 'the University College' and Gladstone so spoke of it on that occasion. The College opened in 1881 and although the Cambridge Extension Courses continued to be housed there for many years, its story henceforth belongs more to the history of the University than to that of adult education in Nottingham. But it is a notable thing that so comprehensive a project in higher education, costing about £100,000 to build and, in its first year, £6,500 to maintain, the product then of a twopence-halfpenny rate, should in the 1870s have been a municipal project, promoted by the Corporation and paid for almost wholly out of public funds. Even 20 years later, when civic enterprise was more general, this was commented on by the Treasury Inspectors who visited the College in 1897: 'That a municipal corporation should recognise the needs of higher education, and that it should have the support of the community in so doing, is a very remarkable thing. It is not to be wondered at that at one time the policy should have been severely criticised and much opposed in Nottingham, but we have good evidence that the College is now thoroughly popular . . . . . The College, being supported by the rates, may be said to be the most democratic institution of its kind which we have seen.' Nor is it to be wondered at that the College in order to grow into a true university had to break out of this municipal chrysalis and had to struggle painfully to do so. It was still an astonishing piece of Victorian enterprise, which grew out of adult education and a city's concern for it.

Tutorial Classes

In the first decade of the 20th century adult education took a decisive step in a new direction. Tutorial classes, i.e. small groups engaged in sustained discussion and study for fairly long periods, were beginning to replace the relatively short series of lectures addressed to large audiences which were characteristic of many of the Extension Courses. The new movement was closely associated with the newly formed Workers' Educational Association, which by 1911 had established branches in Nottingham, Derby, Mansfield and Sutton-in-Ashfield. These new organisations turned not to Cambridge but to their local University College for the provision of tutors, and by 1913 the College was providing five three-year tutorial classes for these branches. It found, as Cambridge had done a quarter of a century earlier, that once such demands begin to be met they increase to a point at which new machinery has to be created

EE

to deal with them. A joint committee for tutorial classes, with lay as well as College representation, was set up and all seemed set for a new phase of development in adult education.

The first World War intervened, but in the hot-house atmosphere of post-war reconstruction growth was even more rapid than it might have been in 1913. In 1919 the local branches of the Workers' Educational Association combined to form the East Midland District and this new organisation, together with the committee for tutorial classes, submitted to the College Council a scheme for the development of tutorial classes in the area and for the appointment of a full-time tutor (in Economics) to teach them. But in the same year was published the Report of the Adult Education Committee of the Ministry of Reconstruction, an unusually full, prescient, and readable, document which recommended the establishment at every university or university college of 'a department of extra-mural adult education with an academic head'. So the response of the College Council went beyond the requests of its petitioners: it created the first Department of Adult Education in the country in 1920, gave the Head of the Department professorial status and a seat on Senate, and created a Chair of Adult Education in 1923. Its incumbent for 30 years was Robert Peers, who in that time exercised a decisive influence upon the development of adult education in the whole country and became without question its most distinguished figure.

The University Department of Adult Education

The Department which Peers founded in 1920 had in its first session a programme of 43 classes. In the session 1963–64 the total was 335. This figure, together with the 238 classes provided in the same session by the East Midland District of the Workers' Educational Association, must give the East Midlands a greater saturation of classes in the liberal studies than almost any other region in the country, for the total population served is less than 2,000,000. The student body it serves is a very fair cross-section of this population, both in sex and age distribution within the range 20 to 60 years of age. The distribution by educational background is of course skewed by the inescapable fact that the more education people have had in early life the more they want, and the easier they find it to get, in later life. So only 30 per cent of the students in normal, open-entry classes left school at age 14 or 15 and 25 per cent were in full-time education up to the age of 20 and beyond. To some extent this is corrected by a special programme of classes for industrial workers, both by day-release and in factories, in which the corresponding figures are 75 per cent and 2 per cent.

Adult Education by Television

Television was once seen as a threat to adult education. More recently, there has been a somewhat uncritical acceptance of the educational value of television pro-grammes which, though excellent in themselves, fail to teach because they make no provision for regular work by students and its correction by tutors. In 1964 the

Department of Adult Education conducted the first full-scale experiment in the country in teaching by a combination of television programmes, a correspondence course and face-to-face meetings with tutors. The programmes were televised throughout the Midlands by Associated Television Ltd.; teaching costs and research costs were met by grants from the Leverhulme Trust and the Department of Education and Science. Over 1,550 students, most of them new to adult education, enrolled for, and over 1,150 completed, a quite exacting one-term course in Economics. If the Midlands can nurture this as it has the other ventures in adult education which have been described here the last 30 years of the 20th century may prove to be as vigorous a period of growth in adult education as were the last 30 years of the 19th century.

THE UNIVERSITY

The vision of Nottingham as a centre of university education has a surprisingly long history. It can be found in embryo in the minds of the founders of the Mechanics Institute as early as 1851; and it was present, though only half avowed, among the pioneers of the University Extension movement when they promoted the project which culminated in the University College in Shakespeare Street. Its official title then was the Education Buildings, but at the stone-laying ceremony in 1877, Mr. W. E. Gladstone, the chief speaker, referred to the new buildings as a University College, and even spoke of the contingency that 'at some remote date, perhaps you may be speaking not of a University College, but of a University of Nottingham. That is an arduous and a soaring ambition.'

It was not made less arduous by the unusual, perhaps unique, circumstances under which the University College came into being. Apart from an anonymous gift of £10,000 from a local lace manufacturer, the entire financial responsibility—the site, the buildings and the upkeep—was undertaken by the Corporation. It was, in fact, a civic institution, a branch of municipal administration, and this position of dependence was given legal sanction in 1903 when it received its Charter of Incorporation as a University College. The independent University status which was accorded to the University Colleges at Birmingham in 1900, Manchester and Liverpool in 1903, Leeds in 1904 and Sheffield in 1905, was not to be won by Nottingham for another 40 years.

Attempts were made in the years immediately following the first world war to further the project by means of an imaginative scheme for an East Midlands University incorporating the technical schools at Derby, Lincoln, Northampton, the technical college at Loughborough, the agricultural college at Kingston and the University College which was being planned at the time in Leicester. The scheme, which had its roots in discussions going back to pre-1914 days, broke down on the problem of local loyalties, and the University College had no choice but to proceed alone. It had the generous support of the city of Nottingham and the co-operation of all the local authorities of the East Midland area with the exception of Leicester; but the financial outlook remained bleak.

In 1920, however, an entirely unlooked-for break in the clouds appeared as a result of the intervention of a relative newcomer, Sir Jesse Boot, and the situation was transformed overnight. The rise of Boots Cash Chemists is a success story with few parallels in the history of modern British business, and a series of bold strokes by which Sir Jesse now proceeded to make good the claim of his native city to be able to support an independent university was in keeping with the dazzling speed of his business career.

He began by making a gift in 1920 of £50,000 to found a Chair of Chemistry and as a contribution to the Building Fund. He followed this a year later by the gift of the Highfields Estate which he had originally thought of as a suitable site for a model suburb upon the style of Bourneville and Port Sunlight. The suggestion that it might provide a site for the proposed new university, we are told, was made to him one morning in summer as he gazed over the Vale of Trent from the slope overlooking the present Highfields lake; and on the same afternoon he conveyed the decision to Alderman Huntsman, the Chairman of the College Council, to use the site for this purpose. With the site went the name—Highfields Park or simply Highfields. It was more than a university site; with its graciously undulating contours falling away to Beeston Lane and Derby Road, it formed, along with the ancient park of the Willoughby's and the Elizabethan mansion of Wollaton Hall, one of the most pleasing urban landscapes in industrial Britain, and represented an amenity of incalculable value to the life of the city. Its importance began to be realised in more tangible form when the site itself became the scene of building operations which, by 1928, represented an investment in building alone of £438,000. This was an earnest of the vast outlay in fixed capital and services which the munificence of Sir Jesse Boot, or Lord Trent as he became in 1929, had initiated. In the post-war years it grew until, at the present time, the University constitutes one of the major industries of the city, with an annual contribution of £3,000,000 to the total income of the region. The buildings in 1928 included the central block, the Trent Building, designed by Morley Horder, and the Florence Boot Hall for women students, named after Lady Florence Boot, the founder; but for a further 20 years development plans were hamstrung by lack of local support on a scale that would realise the 'soaring ambition' of which Mr. Gladstone had caught a glimpse in 1877.

The session of 1928 opened with the Arts and Science Departments in their new quarters at Highfields. They were followed by existing Departments of Civil and Mechanical Engineering and a new Department of Electrical Engineering. Difficult problems, especially of finance, loomed ahead, and from the death of Lord Trent in 1931, the University College stood virtually alone.

The following years were occupied with attempts to provide financial security through adequate endowment funds and to effect a revision of the constitutional basis in keeping with the dignity of an institution that aspired to university status. In 1938 the College obtained a supplemental Charter which broadened the regional basis of support and provided for somewhat wider academic representation on the College

Council. It was not, however, until 1947 that the final steps were taken to dismantle the administrative authority of the Corporation and to prepare a new constitution for presentation to the Privy Council. These preliminaries were successfully accomplished under the energetic leadership of the Acting Principal, Professor Robert Peers, in a surprisingly short time. In August 1948 the coveted Charter was received and Mr. B. L. Hallward, formerly Headmaster of Clifton College, who had been appointed Principal in July, was able to take up his duties as Vice-Chancellor in October 1948. The President of the University College, Lord Trent, son of Sir Jesse Boot, was installed as the first Chancellor.

In the meantime, important decisions had been taken under the supplemental Charter. In 1945, a Technical College which had existed side by side with the University College in Shakespeare Street, became a separate institution as the Nottingham City Technical College, but the Department of Mining and Fuels was moved to Highfields while the Department of Textiles was transferred to the Technical College. The Midland Agricultural College at Sutton Bonington was incorporated in the University in 1947 as the School of Agriculture; a one-year post-graduate training course in Education had already taken the place of the former two-year Teachers' Certificate Course and an Institute of Education to associate the several training colleges in the region with the University College came into existence at the same time. The acquisition of additional sites, often with spacious houses of old standing, went on steadily and brought the area of the University park to 234 acres; and by agreement with the Nottingham Corporation Planning Department a further area of 382 acres was scheduled for future development.

The driving force behind this burst of energy was the new situation created by the post-war demand for university education. Between 1939 and 1947, student numbers had risen from 600 to 1,700; the current grant went up from £31,900 to £159,000 and non-recurrent grants reached £204,000. To cope with this tidal wave of students, temporary buildings were rapidly erected; new buildings were begun for Botany and Zoology and for Civil and Mechanical Engineering; but rising maintenance costs for which no provision had been made by the Grants Committee, proved a lion in the path of planned advance, and a restriction on spending during the last two years of the quinquennium had to be enforced. The most serious and unfortunate consequence of this decision was to hold up plans for the Students' Union and Refectory Building, the Portland Building as it was known after its opening in 1956. The worst sufferer was the library which had to endure three further years of intolerable overcrowding until the removal of the former refectory and kitchens released invaluable space for expansion. The delay in making this space available was a factor in the decision to abandon the idea of a main central library serving the whole University, and in its place to create a separate science library to serve the needs of science and technology. A new modern building to take the place of the various *ad hoc* arrangements that had been made was planned for this purpose and opened in 1964.

The opening of the second quinquennium was a signal for a further phase of planned physical expansion and its character was greatly influenced by four splendid bene-factions: a gift of £50,000 in October 1953 from Mr. C. T. Cripps, Managing Director of Pianoforte Supplies, Roade, Northamptonshire, and his son Mr. C. H. Cripps, for a Chair of Metallurgy, and another similar gift from the same donors for a Chair of Production Engineering; and two similar sums by Boots Pure Drug Company to endow a Chair of Pharmaceutical Chemistry and a Chair of Chemical Engineering. These last two gifts were made on the occasion of the retirement of Lord Trent as Chancellor owing to ill-health. He was succeeded by the Duke of Portland, the present Chancellor. In the following years Messrs. C. T. and C. H. Cripps made a further sum available, initially of £250,000 but later raised to £375,000, for building a new Hall of Residence for men. It was opened in 1959 for 200 men and named the Cripps Hall in honour of the benefactors. There were then three men's Halls, the others being the Hugh Stewart and Wortley Halls, both established in the pre-war years. These, together with the two women's Halls, Florence Boot and Florence Nightingale, and their smaller annexes brought the total number of students in residence to 833, which represented a percentage of 41 of the total student population.

A further major project was the result of a special grant by the Grants Committee for the development of science and technology. New buildings at an estimated cost of £750,000 were projected and Mr. (now Sir) Basil Spence was invited to prepare plans. They included 142,000 square feet for laboratories that were 'among the most advanced and versatile in the country', a special first-year teaching building and a Tower Block. All these projects were duly completed and brought into use between 1960 and 1964. The social sciences, forming a new faculty, were also provided for in the Social Science and Education Building completed in 1958.

The rate of expansion was accelerated further in the early 1960s when, in addition to the buildings mentioned, four new Halls of Residence were made ready for occupation in 1962–63 and the University internal road system was enlarged to include Beeston Lane. At the same time, the absorption of the department of city College of Art and Crafts into the projected Department of Architecture and Civic Planning was decided upon and the new Department was duly installed in the Tower Block in 1964. On the heels of this came the announcement that Nottingham University was to be the centre chosen for a new medical school to be built in conjunction with a new teaching hospital; and plans are now going forward to implement this scheme, the culmination of more than 30 years of endeavour. These multifarious and massive operations were the external manifestation of an expansion in the University community itself which raised many acute problems of planning and organisation. The complexity of these problems was enhanced by two factors over which the University had no control. The first was the rise of overhead costs as a result of post-war inflation and the embarrassment that this caused in trying to operate the system of quinquennial budgeting. The second was the uncertainty as to the ultimate number of students the government had in mind for university training. The University's plans had long been designed so that its main effort would come when it was most needed, that is, to meet the rise in the post-war birth-rate which would become effective between 1964 and 1966; and the annual provision of non-recurrent grants of over £1,000,000 a year since 1959 presented not only the opportunity but the obligation to make a maximum effort. With this in mind the University planned in terms of a 50 per cent increase between 1962 and 1967, but in view of the growing sense of urgency induced by the slow gestation of the Robbins Report, the University raised its sights still further and offered to increase its overall intake from 3,068 in January 1963 to 4,820 in 1967–68 (instead of the 4,500 as planned) and to build two more Halls of Residence. However the University Grants Committee allocated grants on the assumption that the target would be 4,300 and that only one further Hall would be built.

Numerous other important projects including a concert hall and theatre had to be shelved; an imaginative scheme by the Vice-Chancellor to divert some of the student growth to Sutton Bonington through the establishment there of a Faculty of General Studies was not accepted. One important new development during the period must be recorded: as a result of the generosity of Mr. C. T. Cripps and Mr. C. H. Cripps, it was possible to establish a direct link with the University of Manchester 'Atlas' Computer and bring into operation the Cripps Computer Centre in July 1963.

Vice-Chancellor Hallward expressed his intention to resign in the summer of 1965 and his successor, Professor Dainton of Leeds, took over his duties in October 1965. An epoch in the history of the University had ended, an epoch of dynamic growth which probably has no parallel in post-war university history.

SELECTED REFERENCES

Beckett, E. M. *History of University College, Nottingham* (Nottingham, 1928).

Final Report of the Adult Education Committee. Ministry of Reconstruction, Cmd. 321 (1919).

Hudson, J. W. *History of Adult Education* (London, 1851).

Peers, R. *Adult Education* (London, 1958).

Rowntree, J. W. and Binns, H. B. *History of the Adult School Movement* (London, 1903).

Wood, A. C. *A history of the University College Nottingham 1881-1948* (Oxford, 1953).

In the preparation of the section on Adult Education reference has been made to the *Records of the Borough of Nottingham* for 1947-56.

XXV

THE NOTTINGHAM CONURBATION

NOTTINGHAM, now the eighth largest city in England and Wales, is the focus of an urbanised area which forms a true conurbation. The administrative components of this conurbation are: the county borough of Nottingham (with a population in 1961 of 311,645), the immediately adjacent urban districts of Arnold (26,809), Carlton (38,790), West Bridgford (26,957), Beeston and Stapleford (56,720) and Hucknall (23,246), together with the urban district of Long Eaton (30,464), in Derbyshire, which adjoins Beeston and Stapleford to the west. (Fig. 78). These contiguous units form a more or less continuously built-up area containing over 500,000 people. They also form a highly industrialised area in which many of the principal activities, for example lace, hosiery and clothing manufacture, and dyeing and finishing trades, are interdependent, while others, including various forms of engineering, are closely interrelated.

Greater Nottingham, despite its administrative fragmentation, is a coherent, closely-knit economic and social entity and it is for the most part clearly separated from neighbouring towns, such as the Mansfield urban complex to the north and Loughborough to the south, by tracts of agricultural land. To the west, however, there are close links with the towns of the Erewash valley, for a continuation of the built-up area, although tenuous in places, extends north–westwards to Eastwood and beyond; on the other hand, nearly a mile of open country effectively separates Nottingham from Trowell, a village adjoining Ilkeston. The southern part of the Erewash valley, at Stapleford and Long Eaton, is connected to Nottingham by almost continuous building development and these places are both included in the conurbation area as defined above.

The urban districts peripheral to Nottingham, most of which developed from large villages into major industrial and residential satellites in the late 19th century, are heavily dependent upon the city for major services and to a large extent for sources of employment. They certainly look to no other centre for the services which a large city normally provides. Moreover, only a small fraction of the total working population finds employment outside the conurbation, as a result of which the daily journey to work presents a highly complex pattern of local movement. On the other hand, considerable numbers travel to Nottingham and to other parts of the conurbation from varying distances outside.

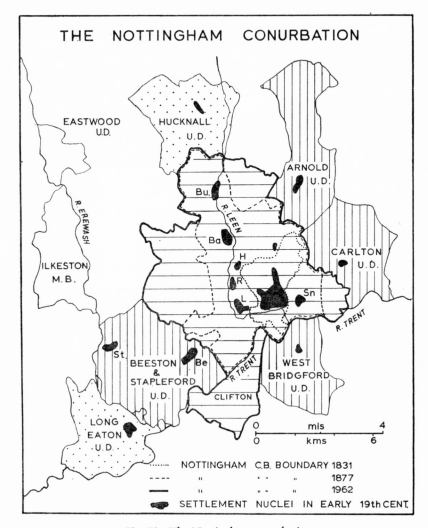

THE NOTTINGHAM CONURBATION

EASTWOOD
U.D.

HUCKNALL
U.D.

ARNOLD
U.D.

Bu.

R. LEEN

Ba

H

R

L

Sn

CARLTON
U.D.

R. EREWASH

ILKESTON
M.B.

R. TRENT

St

BEESTON
&
STAPLEFORD
U.D.

Be

R. TRENT

CLIFTON

WEST
BRIDGFORD
U.D.

LONG
EATON
U.D.

0   mls   4
0   kms   6

.... NOTTINGHAM C.B. BOUNDARY 1831
— — —   "   " "   "   1877
————   "   " "   "   1962
⬤⬤ SETTLEMENT NUCLEI IN EARLY 19th CENT.

Fig. 78   The Nottingham conurbation

Ba—Basford; Be—Beeston; Bu—Bulwell; H—Hyson Green; L—Lenton; R—Radford; Sn—Sneinton; St—Stapleford

Nottingham, as the largest city of the East Midlands, is also a regional centre serving as the focus of numerous regional organisations. The large-scale facilities for entertainment, recreation and cultural activities are nevertheless scattered in different parts of the conurbation. Thus, whilst some of these are situated in or near the heart of the city, the site on which the famous Goose Fair is held lies in a predominantly residential district well to the north of the centre. The racecourse is at Colwick

(Carlton Urban District), the Trent Bridge cricket ground and the ground of the Nottingham Forest Football Club are in West Bridgford, while the Nottinghamshire Rugby Football Club ground is at Beeston. Similarly, with regard to higher education, the University, although situated just within the Nottingham boundary, lies geographically between Nottingham and Beeston, and has outlying units in the Beeston and Stapleford Urban District. The Nottingham College of Education (like the University, recruiting its students both regionally and nationally) is located across the Trent at Clifton, which was incorporated in the city in 1952. Though there is supplementation by privately operated bus services, together with those of the West Bridgford Urban District Council, much of the conurbation is served by the Nottingham Corporation transport system.

THE URBAN DISTRICTS

The adjacent urban districts differ from one another in the degree to which they are dependent upon the city, and brief reference to each in turn may serve to indicate such differences.

West Bridgford Urban District

The highest degree of dependence upon Nottingham is shown in the case of West Bridgford which, from the beginning of its modern growth shortly before 1890, has remained almost entirely a residential area for people earning their livelihood in the city. It is a dormitory area *par excellence* and its residents fall largely within the middle-income group. Over 7,000 people daily cross the Trent to their work, whereas only 2,300 are employed within the urban district itself. Local shopping facilities and places of entertainment are inevitably limited, for frequent bus services make Nottingham easily accessible for these and many other purposes. The GEM American-type suburban shopping centre, established in 1964 on a site adjoining Loughborough Road, is located primarily to attract people from the various residential areas south of the Trent. It contains more than 50 shops and departments, occupying a single floor area of nearly 85,000 square feet and offers free parking space for 1,000 cars.

Close to West Bridgford, incidentally, is the large city housing estate at Clifton, developed since 1951, which will eventually accommodate some 30,000 people, mainly of the lower income groups. So far there is little provision for employment, although shops for daily needs, together with schools, are adequate. Thus, south of the Trent, existing development consists of two distinct units, one an urban district and the other a municipal housing estate within the County Borough of Nottingham, both overwhelmingly residential in character and heavily dependent on the city for employment and services.

Arnold Urban District

Arnold is only a little less dependent upon the city than West Bridgford, both as regards employment and social provision. The net outward daily movement, mainly to Nottingham, amounts to 65 per cent of the working population, so that Arnold, too, is largely a residential area. In fact Woodthorpe, a neighbourhood of good-quality private-enterprise housing, which adjoins the Nottingham boundary, is in effect an integral part of the city. Arnold, however, first grew as an industrialised village, but with the building of factories in the latter half of the 19th century it became an industrialised satellite of Nottingham. Hosiery, engineering and a few other light industries continue to provide local employment but the district is poorly served with shops and entertainment facilities and in these respects it is therefore heavily dependent upon the city. It is significant that, like West Bridgford, Arnold is not served by a railway and in consequence modern development has depended on motor transport, a much more effective means of integrating a city and its outlying parts.

Carlton Urban District

Carlton, likewise, developed as a late 19th-century satellite of Nottingham, being chiefly concerned with hosiery-making, which still affords a livelihood for one-third of the working population. There are, however, three other sources of employment: the railway marshalling yards at Netherfield, engineering and general manufacturing at Colwick and the large colliery at Gedling. With the exception of the colliery, these are located in the Trent valley and form part of the main industrial belt. In the older part of Carlton, hosiery-workers, miners and tradesmen form a community, pursuing local interests and activities somewhat independent of the city. On the other hand, although 7,000 people work locally, over 8,000 travel to Nottingham, so that the dormitory function is again dominant.

Much of the northern part of Carlton consists of an extension of Nottingham's eastern residential district along Mapperley Plains and has little direct contact with the older area adjoining the Trent valley.

Beeston and Stapleford Urban District

Beeston and Stapleford is the largest of the urban districts adjacent to Nottingham. It became a single administrative unit in 1935 as a result of the merging of the Urban District of Beeston and the small Rural District of Stapleford. Initially this union presented the appearance of a *mariage de convenance*, for the two areas had few common interests and the two main centres, situated three miles apart, had, and still have, no very direct means of communication connecting them. The amalgamation of Beeston and Stapleford, however, provided considerable scope for development and in this respect progress in the post-war years has been substantial, especially as regards housing. For a period immediately following the war the Urban District led the country in the erection of local authority dwellings. Such developments, together with road improvements, extension of bus services, some expansion of shopping facilities and increased educational provision (a County Council responsibility notwithstanding), have done much to integrate the two main centres and the several smaller ones.

Strong local community interests persist in Beeston and, despite close ties with the city, it might well be claimed that the urban district exhibits a greater measure of independent existence than is found in any of the other peripheral areas. Yet at the same time the Beeston and Stapleford Urban District forms an integral part of the Nottingham urban complex. The spread of residential development on the western side of the city has now reached southwards to give continuous built-up links across the Beeston boundary in the Lenton Abbey–Wollaton–Bramcote area. The only remaining 'open' land between Nottingham and Beeston is that occupied by Wollaton Park, the University estate and a large stretch of public playing fields.

In addition to lace, hosiery and clothing factories, engineering works and various forms of general manufacturing located in the older parts of both Beeston and Stapleford, there are also on the Beeston section of the Trent flood-plain the Beeston Boiler works, the large establishment of Boots (pharmaceutical products) and Ericssons (telephone and electrical equipment), the last two each employing several thousand people. Within the urban district employment provision is distinctly in excess of the resident working population and there is a net inward daily movement of 5,000 persons, including 1,300 females, chiefly from Nottingham. The integration of the whole area is shown by the fact that Nottingham and Beeston are each important dormitories for the other. On the other hand, about 40 per cent of the resident workers travel outwards, mostly to the city and in a lesser degree to Long Eaton, to the Stanton Ironworks in the Erewash valley and to the Courtauld (British Celanese) works at Spondon, near Derby.

Long Eaton Urban District

Adjoining Beeston and Stapleford, across the Derbyshire border, is the town of Long Eaton, a modern industrial centre which forms the south–western extremity of the conurbation. Long Eaton's economy closely resembles that of Nottingham and the immediate satellites and as a centre of lace and hosiery manufacturing it actually developed as an offshoot of Nottingham. In consequence, it has close ties with the latter, and a large proportion of its inhabitants depend on the city for weekly and occasional shopping, and for entertainment, while several hundreds are employed either in the city or in the Beeston and Stapleford Urban District.

Hucknall Urban District

The only other urban unit forming part of the conurbation is Hucknall, which lies to the north–north–west and which, like Long Eaton, is about seven miles from the centre of the city. It is primarily a centre of coal-mining and hosiery-making, but, apart from a tenuous ribbon extending for about a mile along the main road from Nottingham, the built-up area of Hucknall is still distinct from that of the city.

Yet, to quote from the *County of Nottingham Development Plan* (*Report of the Survey, 1952*), 'it is important to treat Hucknall as part of the Nottingham conurbation and not as an isolated town'. In support of this view the tendency for resident workers to find employment in the city should be noted and the recent move of a large clothing firm from Nottingham to Hucknall should further increase the inter-dependence of the two areas. Frequent public transport services enable the people of Hucknall to use the city for shopping and other facilities.

The effect of Nottingham's modern growth is not confined to the conurbation as defined above. As already mentioned, expansion to the north–west, through Kimberley as far as Eastwood, has all but created a continuous urban link with the mining and industrial area of the middle Erewash valley. Recent housing developments at Stapleford and Trowell bring the built-up area close to Ilkeston and the large industrial complex of Stanton Ironworks lower down the same valley. In fact, there is now comparatively little non-urban land remaining between Nottingham and the Erewash. On the other hand, for many years the rural areas to the east and south have attracted people from the city seeking to build their homes away from the industrial scene. As a result, a number of villages have been transformed into dormitory centres. The earliest to be affected in this way were Radcliffe-on-Trent, on the railway to Grantham, and Burton Joyce and Lowdham, on the Midland line to Newark. Later on the private car and local bus services favoured a similar development at Ruddington, Tollerton, Plumtree and Keyworth to the south, while other villages are now becoming involved in this trend. While, therefore, to the west of the city industrial and residential expansion is steadily creating a solidly built-up area reaching as far as the Erewash, to the east and south an increasing 'commuter' population is in process of dispersal among the larger villages.

The economy of the Nottingham conurbation continues to expand. The rate of unemployment is slight, being always well below the national average, while in some sectors there is often a shortage of labour. Under present policy the Board of Trade is unlikely to permit the introduction of further large-scale industrial enterprises, but many existing undertakings continue to grow and considerable expansion in service activities is to be expected. There is every reason to suppose, therefore, that the present rate of population growth will be maintained and that housing needs will continue to increase.

Since the population of the conurbation rose by over 24,000 between 1951 and 1961, it would seem that in a few decades the demand for housing sites may well exceed the amount of land available unless much higher densities are accepted. Even more important is the increase in the number of households, for between 1951 and 1961 the latter increased by almost 17,700. The question therefore arises as to whether, within the limits of the existing local authority areas, land suitable for residential use is really adequate, assuming planned development is to ensure satisfactory location and distribution. Apart from green belt considerations and the liability of certain areas to mining subsidence, the general distribution of future housing presents a considerable problem for, broadly speaking, land for this purpose is more likely to be obtainable across the Trent on the south and east sides of the conurbation, while expansion in employment opportunities is more likely to occur on the west. The new colliery at Cotgrave and with it the introduction of a mining community might provide a growth point for further industrial development but this has not occurred at Calverton, where the colliery has been operating since 1952, nor even at Ollerton, in mid-Nottinghamshire, which is 40 years old, despite several attempts to establish textile and light engineering.

Another factor in the situation, the effects of which cannot yet be seen, will be the completion next year of the London–Yorkshire motorway (M.1), which is to pass a little to the west of the conurbation. This may well create a change in land values and promote an interest in potential housing sites on the outskirts of the present built-up area, though not necessarily within the present local authority boundaries of the conurbation.

From what has been said concerning the different parts of the conurbation and their relationship to Nottingham, including reference to housing needs, it would appear unlikely that future development can be satisfactorily achieved under the present arrangement of local government units. The planning problem as a whole, involving not only housing but industrial sites, roads and service provision, is considerable, and the facts of the situation argue strongly for the adoption of two distinct measures. Firstly, to secure adequate land for development, some extension of the outer boundary of the conurbation is necessary. In this connection green belt provision would require reconsideration. Secondly, the task of planning and administering the area as an entity can only be satisfactorily undertaken if a single authority is created for the purpose.

PART IV

OTHER URBAN CENTRES

XIX Derby and the Derwent from the north. The river, flowing south-eastwards to the left, is crossed by the modern Exeter Bridge. The west bank shows the effect of redevelopment in the 1930s—Police Buildings, Council House, covered Morledge market, bus station and river gardens, the latter containing the outfall of the Markeaton Brook, the culverted course of which is indicated by the broken white line. In the upper left-hand corner is Traffic Street, the earliest portion of the inner ring-road, skirting an old residential area in process of redevelopment on the gentle rise of Cockpit Hill. On the right the Market Square is overlooked by the Town Hall, with the Market Hall behind. The Assembly Rooms, recently gutted by fire, are at the east end of the Square. In the upper right-hand corner is the chief street intersection, where the south-north line of St. Peter's Street—Cornmarket is crossed by the east-west line of Albert Street—Victoria Street.

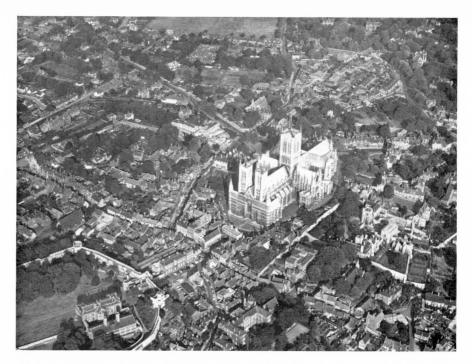

XX   Lincoln showing the Cathedral and Castle. The steep slope seen on the right
      overlooks the Witham Valley.

Photo by J. K. St Joseph

XXI   Newark upon Trent showing the Castle ruins and the bridge over the river

XXVI

OTHER URBAN CENTRES

DERBY

DERBY, with a population of 132,408 in 1961, is the second town in size and economic importance in the Nottingham region as defined in this survey. It is a near neighbour, being only 14 miles west–south–west of Nottingham, though the distance by road from centre to centre is about 16 miles. Derby is situated where the southward-flowing Derwent, having emerged from the hills fringing the Peak District, enters the Keuper Marl country of the middle Trent lowlands and turns south–eastwards in its broad flood-plain. The confluence with the Trent occurs seven and a half miles downstream, near the villages of Shardlow and Sawley.

It has always been important as a route centre. A Roman camp, later to be called Little Chester, was situated on the left (east) bank of the river half a mile upstream from the Anglo-Danish town that later developed on the opposite bank as the nucleus of Derby. At Little Chester the Roman road later to be known as Ryknild Street crossed the Derwent; this ran from *Letocetum*, on Watling Street, near Lichfield, to Templeborough, near modern Rotherham. The crossing did not, however, persist as an element in Derby's communication network. Other roads led westwards to Rocester, on the Dove, and thence into Cheshire, by way of the present 'Potteries' district; north–westwards to Buxton and Manchester; and south–eastwards to a supposed crossing of the Trent near Sawley. Certain sections of these routes are still followed by modern roads.

The subsequent Anglian settlement of *Northworthige* developed a few hundred yards up the valley of the Markeaton brook, a right-bank tributary of the Derwent, descending from the north–west. During the period of the Danelaw this settlement was enlarged and elevated in status as *Deoraby*, one of the five Danish boroughs of the occupied East Midlands. By the time of Domesday there were six churches, of which five have survived, although rebuilt or restored at various times. Until the Industrial Revolution the town's area and functions changed little; it was a county-town and market-centre, with its first charter dating from 1154, and, in addition, there were corn mills and craft trades, some of which are indicated by surviving street names, for example, Full Street, Iron Gate and Sadler Gate. Derby also handled some of the lead shipments from the Peak District, as it probably had in Roman times. There were also several religious houses until the Reformation. An early 'castle', of which no trace remains, existed for a time on what later became known as Cockpit Hill, to the south of the confluence of the Markeaton brook with the river. Close by was a market, which still survives in the 'Morledge'. Derby was never as large or important as Nottingham or Leicester, and, indeed, its standing in relation to these two neighbouring county-towns has remained remarkably constant.

The central business area of the modern town still corresponds very closely to the early nucleus and its main thoroughfares. The chief part of the town stretched northwards from the Markeaton brook on to the gently sloping interfluve between it and the river. Here the market place was located and beyond it, in close succession, the churches of All Saints' (a cathedral since 1927), St. Michael's and St. Alkmund's. From near St. Alkmund's routes led northwards into the Peak District, while Bridge Gate descended to St. Mary's Bridge over the Derwent. This bridge, located at the north end of the town and downstream from the Roman crossing, was rebuilt in 1788, but a small portion of the old bridge, with its much-restored chapel at the town end, still remains. From the east bank roads forked northwards to Chesterfield and eastwards to Nottingham. South of the brook, crossed by several bridges during its passage through the town, the land rose rather more steeply, and until modern times this part of the town was less important. Here the route to the south proceeded up St. Peter's Street, today the chief shopping street, past the church of the same name, and, reaching the top of the slope, branched out in several directions, now represented by London Road, Osmaston Road, and Babington Lane, leading on to Burton Road and Normanton Road. This southern end of Derby's main north–south axis, about half a mile long, is known as the 'Spot'. To the west of the main crossing of the brook its valley broadened out owing to the confluence of two smaller streams, and here was the church of St. Werburgh. Beyond it was Friar Gate (taking its name from the nearby Dominican Friary), which later continued westwards out of the town as the Ashbourne Road. To the south–west a route led to Uttoxeter. The Markeaton brook remained open until the middle of the 19th century, when it was culverted, thus permitting the development of the sinuous shopping streets of the Strand, Victoria Street and Albert Street. At the same time Exeter Bridge, the town's second bridge over the Derwent, was built, giving direct access to the market place from the east bank of the river (Plate IXX).

In the 18th century Derby entered upon a period of industrial growth and physical expansion, aided by improved communications, which have continued to the present day. Its population rose from about 4,000 in the 1690s to nearly 11,000 at the census of 1801. The Derwent was made navigable up to Derby in 1720; turnpike roads were established and coaching routes developed. Derby's geographical position achieved historical importance in 1745, when the Young Pretender here decided to begin a retreat rather than cross the Trent, the Rubicon to which his advance-guard had progressed. No invader has ever held an English town since. To Defoe, Derby was 'a fine, beautiful and pleasant town . . . . . a town of gentry rather than trade', the latter being 'chiefly in good malt and good ale'. But he was also impressed by Derby's great silk mill, effectively the first power-driven textile mill in England. This had been built (1718–21) by John Lombe. Sited below St. Mary's Bridge on a narrow island just off the west bank of the river it adjoined and superseded an earlier silk mill, built by Thomas Cotchett, that had proved unsuccessful. Lombe's mill used a very large water-wheel constructed by George Sorocold, an eminent local engineer, and it was concerned with the 'throwing' (spinning) of silk yarn. This was chiefly destined for the domestic framework-knitting industry, which at this time was rapidly establishing itself in the East Midlands, including Derby and surrounding villages. Later on, other silk mills were built in the town, although none seems to have attained a similar importance.

Further downstream, on a larger island (the Holmes), rolling and slitting mills for copper and iron were set up and by the end of the century there were also lead mills in the town. Other important 18th-century industries were clock-making and china manufacture. The latter industry, under the direction of John Heath and William Duesbury, also absorbed the famous Chelsea factory, the activities of which were transferred to Derby. After a lapse of some years in the 19th century the industry was revived by the setting-up of the present Crown Derby company in 1877. In the 1770s and 1780s Richard Arkwright and his erstwhile partner, Jedediah Strutt (inventor of the 'Derby rib' adaptation to the knitting frame), built a number of water-powered cotton mills at various places upstream on the Derwent, thus making supplies of cotton yarn available in Derby. Other entrepreneurs later followed suit. The Darley Abbey mill is a survivor from this period. The Strutt family also built the country's first calico-weaving mill in Derby in the 1790s, which, moreover, was the earliest example of a fire-resisting factory. This activity did not survive and the building itself has disappeared.

At the end of the 18th century further transport improvements were made with the construction in 1794 of the two arms of the Derby canal, linking the town eastwards to the Erewash canal (and thus to the Cromford and Nottingham canals) and southwards to the Trent and Mersey canal. Northwards a branch canal continued up the Derwent valley to Little Eaton, whence a tramway gave a connection to the collieries of the Bottle brook valley.

Further developments in the textile industries took place in the early decades of the 19th century, when factories for the manufacture of lace, ribbons, silk piece-goods and tapes were established. Steam-power was now becoming dominant, except in the knitwear trade, where conversion from the domestic system to steam-powered factories did not take place on a large scale until the second half of the century, by which time the industry in Derby had declined. Thus, in the late 1830s, immediately before the coming of the railways, Derby, with a population approaching 30,000, was already an industrial town, with a strong interest in textiles (involving 28 per cent of the employed population at the census of 1841), although traditional commercial functions still persisted and had been enhanced. Already, however, the growth of modern engineering trades was discernible, since steam-engines and lathes were now being produced, in addition to textile machinery, and this new interest was soon to be powerfully reinforced.

In 1839–41 three railway lines were built that terminated in Derby, running respectively from Birmingham, Leeds and Nottingham, and in 1844 the town became the headquarters of the Midland Railway Company, an amalgamation of the three companies concerned. The development of a large railway-engineering industry now created a second stage in Derby's industrial growth; it attracted a new wave of immigrants and led to important changes in the town's morphology. Hitherto the town had been expanding predominantly in a north–westerly direction in the Markeaton brook area, although there had also been some growth across the river and in the Burton Road district. The railway station and its associated workshops were built on a broad low-lying terrace between the river and the rather higher ground of the Keuper Marl, itself partly covered by old gravels, on a site beyond 'Castle Fields', about three-quarters of a mile south–east of the town-centre. Housing for the railway workers developed near the station and also spread westwards into an area lying south of the town and crossed by the London, Osmaston and Normanton Roads. A large part of this development fell within the parish of Litchurch, eventually absorbed into the borough in 1877, at which time it had a population of 18,500. Another effect was to increase the importance of St. Peter's Street through a southward pull of shopping facilities. Further growth of the town resulted in a second boundary extension in 1901, involving Normanton, Osmaston and part of Alvaston-and-Boulton. In 1875 additional rail facilities were provided through the building of the Great Northern line, from Nottingham, *via* Ilkeston, to Derby and Egginton Junction, near Burton upon Trent. After entering the town from the north–east the line passed through the western part of central Derby, with a station in Friar Gate. The effect of the introduction of this rather minor line on industry and urban development was not marked, however, and it is no longer used for passenger traffic.

While railway employment rose in the second half of the century the numbers employed in silk began to fall after 1860, when the Cobden Treaty with France exposed the industry to French competition. There was, however, some partial compensation in a limited expansion of other textile activities, especially elastic-web manufacture. Textiles, taken as a group, thus failed to maintain their dominance, so that long before the end of the century Derby had decisively become an engineering town. However, it should be noted that firms other than the Midland Railway were also partly responsible for this change of emphasis.

A number of engineering concerns established themselves in Derby during the hundred years up to the outbreak of the second World War. Most of these firms were attracted, it may be argued, by Derby's central location and good communications, its close access to coal and iron, and, not least, the strong engineering tradition amongst the labour force that the Midland Railway had obviously fostered. Derby's rail links were impressive, including direct connections to London (*via* Leicester), Birmingham (*via* Burton), Crewe (*via* the Potteries), Manchester, Sheffield (*via* Chesterfield), and Nottingham. In the 20th century the Town Council itself has pursued a deliberate policy of attracting industry. Many of the large engineering concerns selected locations in a zone curving south–westwards from the Midland station and its extensive workshops, following the railway line to Birmingham. A second, but less extensive, engineering district extends for a short distance north–wards along the line up the Derwent valley. Derby's well-marked engineering zone, within which certain other industries are also found, thus extends in almost linear fashion for over four miles. Whatever the initial advantage of location close to the railway may have been in the past, it has been shown that today road transport is used much more than rail by most of the firms concerned.

The most important of the newcomers has proved to be Rolls Royce. It has been stated that the firm, wishing to move south from Manchester, chose Derby rather than Leicester, the other location contemplated, because of a marginal advantage at the time in the price of electric power. Having opened factories in 1908 in the Osmaston Road district, it expanded greatly under the direction of Sir Henry Royce during the first World War, and again during the 1930's and the second World War, as a result of the production of aero-engines. Car production, which had now become a subsidiary activity, was suspended during the last war and later transferred to Crewe. The absorption of the Midland Railway Company into the new, large, London, Midland and Scottish Railway in the 1920's meant that, while Derby remained an important centre of railway engineering, it ceased to be a railway headquarters. Moreover, employment in the industry has ceased to grow in recent decades, although Derby has been much less affected than other railway engineering centres by the recent national contraction in this sector. 'Royce's' has thus overtaken 'the Midland' in terms of relative importance to the town's economy and the firm now has a number of establishments in Derby and district, including a research section. The research activities of British Rail are also concentrated in Derby.

The third industrial giant of modern Derby, British Celanese, now controlled by Courtaulds, developed during the first World War, when cellulose acetate was manufactured for coating aircraft fabric. The plant was later adapted for the production of artificial silk. There is thus no link with Derby's earlier participation in the natural silk industry. A large chemical, textile, clothing and plastics complex eventually developed around the original plant, located three miles south–east of the town centre in the Derwent flood-plain, on a site adjoining the village of Spondon. Here river and canal provided both a water supply and a means of effluent disposal. Steam is taken from the adjoining Spondon power-station. The activities of British

Celanese have had the interesting effect of restoring the textile sector to one of major importance in Derby.

In the inter-war period the built-up area of Greater Derby underwent very considerable growth, as a result of the proliferation of low-density residential development, in the form of both Council schemes and private speculative ventures. The scale of development reflected the relatively high degree of prosperity at this time, compared with the general national experience. Ribbon development and the suburbanization of nearby villages led to a situation by 1939 where the borough boundaries fell considerably short of the built-up area, despite extensions in 1927 and 1934. The lop-sided shape of Greater Derby was partly reduced by considerable expansion eastwards, to the north of the Nottingham Road, both in the borough and in the neighbouring villages of Chaddesden and Spondon. This was partly a response to the growth of employment at British Celanese. North–westwards, the built-up area terminated abruptly only one and a quarter miles from the centre, largely owing to the existence of the Markeaton Hall estate. However, in 1933, land here was purchased by the Council and annexed to the borough. South–eastwards, on the other hand, the built-up area extended for four miles to Shelton Lock and Chellaston (Fig. 79).

Considerable changes also took place within the town itself, anticipating the drive for 'urban renewal' that is so common a feature in all towns today. Part of the west bank of the Derwent was cleared of old premises, including the familiar landmark of the old Shot Tower, to give way to a bus-station, riverside gardens, a covered 'Morledge' market, police offices, and new Council House, while the nearby Exeter Bridge was also replaced. The eyesore of the municipal power-station, overlooking the silk-mill island, still remained, however, its chimneys contesting the skyline with the lofty tower of All Saints' cathedral. Other municipal enterprises included new schools, hospitals, technical college and public baths. An airport was opened at Burnaston, south–west of the town, in 1939. During the 1950s this became the leading airport for a large part of the East Midlands, but in 1965 it was superseded by a joint local authority airport at Castle Donington, to the south–east. Markeaton and Darley Parks were added to a list of public open spaces that had begun with Joseph Strutt's gift of the Arboretum as far back as 1840. The clearance of slums was accompanied by the construction of the first section of an inner ring-road (Traffic Street). More impressive in scale was the phased development of an outer ring-road extending for eight miles from Darley Abbey in the north to Spondon in the east. Its last stage (Raynesway), crossing a hitherto undeveloped section of the Derwent flood-plain, was completed in 1939. Here the meandering course of the river had been straightened. Another achievement was the building of a culvert to take the storm water of the Markeaton brook direct to the Derwent above Derby and thus eliminate periodic floods in the central part of the town, the last of which occurred in 1932. Flooding in Little Chester in December 1965 was caused by the Derwent itself.

Fig. 79 The growth of Derby and its suburbs

In the period since the second World War the general prosperity of Derby has probably never been greater, despite close controls by the Government on new industrial expansion. Nevertheless two new industrial estates have been sponsored by the town, at Osmaston and on Raynesway, but the former is primarily for the re-location of factories being moved from unsuitable sites elsewhere. The present (1963) structure of the employed population within the Derby Employment Exchange area is shown in Table XLIX. About 51 per cent of all employed persons are engaged in the manufacturing sector, within which the metal and metal-using industries account for nearly 70 per cent, and textiles, with clothing and footwear, for 18 per cent. The large 'Vehicles' sector includes aero-engines and the manufacture and repair of railway locomotives, carriages and wagons. Other engineering and metal trades involve the production of canning lines, chains and conveyors, coal-mining roof-supports, constructional steelwork, diesel power plant, electric cables, electric motors and instruments, grates and stoves, hydraulic and mechanical presses, lawn-mowers, pipework installations, power-station boilers, steel kitchen utensils, and sugar-mill equipment. Several firms produce iron or brass castings, some of the former being destined for the motor industry. Although the textile sector is dominated today by artificial fibres the older-established industries of knitwear, lace and especially 'narrow fabrics' (chiefly tapes and elastic web), still remain, as well as clothing. Amongst other consumer goods are beer, china, foodstuffs, medicated preparations and mineral-waters, although employment in each is relatively small. Several large building and printing firms serve national markets.

Housing development within the town since the war has been dominated by the Mackworth estate (population about 10,000), in the north-western part of the borough, which fulfils pre-war plans for expansion in this direction. Nevertheless the borough's population fell in the 1950s, as it had in the 1930s, owing to the number of persons moving to the suburbs. Between 1951 and 1961 Derby lost about 13,000 persons by net outward migration, while the suburbs gained about 20,000. In 1964 the Local Government Commission, like its abortive predecessor in 1948, proposed a large boundary extension that would affect 19 parishes and take in a population of 83,000. Such a change would raise Derby's population (1963) from 132,000 to 215,000 and its area from 8,100 acres to 19,100 acres.

As regards its wider functions Derby continues to act as a major agricultural market for mid- and south Derbyshire, particularly for cattle, while its shopping and entertainment facilities (cinemas and Playhouse) draw people from a wide area. Higher education for a large part of the county is provided at the new Colleges of Art and Technology, overlooking Markeaton Park, and replacing older premises in the centre of the town. There is also an old-established Diocesan Teachers' Training College, now partly transferred to a new site as a College of Education, and a British Railways School of Transport. The administrative seat of the County Council was removed to Matlock, which is more geographically central, in the 1950s.

Table XLIX Employment in the Derby area, 1963

	Males	Females	Total
EXTRACTIVE INDUSTRIES			
Agriculture, forestry and fishing ..	1,013	209	1,222
Mining and quarrying	377	39	416
	1,390	248	1,638
MANUFACTURING INDUSTRIES			
Metals and metal-using			
Vehicles★	24,129	2,820	26,949
Engineering, electrical, and 'other metal goods' ..	7,572	1,345	8,917
Metal manufacture†	5,726	787	6,513
	37,427	4,952	42,379
Textiles, clothing and footwear			
Textiles	5,680	3,883	9,563
Clothing and footwear	338	1,344	1,682
	6,018	5,227	11,245
Food, drink and tobacco ..	1,237	1,014	2,251
Paper, printing and publishing ..	1,256	753	2,009
Chemicals and allied industries ..	1,066	775	1,841
Other manufacturing industries ..	1,177	561	1,738
	48,181	13,282	61,463
CONSTRUCTION	7,488	384	7,872
GAS, ELECTRICITY AND WATER	3,287	426	3,713
TRANSPORT AND COMMUNICATION ..	5,900	1,918	7,818
DISTRIBUTIVE AND SERVICE TRADES, FINANCE, PROFESSIONS, PUBLIC ADMINISTRATION ..	15,273	20,727	36,000
TOTAL	81,519	36,985	118,504

Source: Ministry of Labour

★Including aero-engines, and locomotives and railway rolling-stock   †Including castings

NOTE—Self-employed persons and civil servants excluded

This was a controversial step, undertaken largely in order to obtain more spacious accommodation in a redundant hydropathic establishment, but the headquarters of the populous South–East Derbyshire Rural District remains in Derby. Derby also has the headquarters of the Derby and Burton Sub-area of the East Midlands Electricity Board, the Nottinghamshire and Derbyshire Division of the East Midlands Gas Board, and the South Derbyshire Water Board. The Trent Motor Traction Co. Ltd. operates over a large part of both Derbyshire and Nottinghamshire and its routes also penetrate into neighbouring counties. The *'Derby Evening Telegraph'* serves a population of well over half a million and the weekly *'Derbyshire Advertiser'* is also published in Derby.

The immediate sphere of influence of Derby may be said to extend as far as Matlock and Alfreton to the north, Ashbourne and Uttoxeter (Staffordshire) to the west, and Burton upon Trent (Staffordshire), Swadlincote, Melbourne and Castle Donington (Leicestershire) to the south. East-bank Burton (Stapenhill and Winshill) was part of Derbyshire until the late 19th century, and the town as a whole looks to Derby for a number of facilities, not to mention customary support for Derby County football and Derbyshire County cricket. Beyond Burton the influence of Birmingham becomes increasingly intense and beyond Melbourne and Castle Donington that of Leicester. To the east Derby's influence is quickly challenged by that of Nottingham, which extends across the county boundary of the Erewash into Heanor, Ilkeston, Sandiacre and Long Eaton. Derby people themselves travel to Nottingham to see touring West End theatrical productions and to hear leading soloists and orchestras. Adult education is organised in conjunction with the University of Nottingham. On the other hand Nottingham relies on Derby to some extent for certain specialized medical facilities and types of technical education. Such connections are reinforced by a web of cross-commuting which also involves the Erewash valley towns. The recent completion of a fast, dual carriage-way road, extending from the outskirts of Nottingham to Spondon, and due to be prolonged into the very heart of Derby, must obviously increase these inter-connections still further, and the question may therefore be posed whether the time has come for some kind of co-ordinated long-term economic and physical planning of the whole Derby–Nottingham area.

Relatively few architectural monuments of Derby's past remain today; even many of the early industrial premises have been swept away. The old silk-mill building was largely destroyed by fire in 1910. The chief surviving buildings of note include All Saints' cathedral (Perpendicular tower with rebuilt Classical church), St. Peter's medieval church, with the nearby 16th-century school-room (the forerunner of Derby School), the timber-framed 16th-century Dolphin Inn, the County Hall (Assize Court) of 1660, the 17th-century Jacobean house, St. Mary's Bridge (1788), with its restored medieval chapel, the 18th-century Assembly Rooms (façade), and Georgian houses in Friar Gate. These are all situated within, or on the margins of, the central commercial area, with its irregular pattern of busy streets. Beyond are scattered areas of industrial and residential blight, some awaiting demolition, others already cleared for redevelopment. Such areas merge into zones of regularly laid-out streets consisting of Victorian terraced housing of red brick, where monotony is relieved by the obtrusion of an occasional factory. Further out again is the residential sprawl of the 20th century, where, however, attractive elements may be found, as in Allestree and Darley Abbey to the north, and Littleover and Mickleover to the south-west.

Derby's contribution to the national heritage has, appropriately enough, been concerned less with culture than with industrial endeavour and innovation, chiefly in textiles and engineering, and with science and speculation. Moreover, Derby's leading contributor to the arts, the 18th-century painter Joseph Wright, was particularly noted for his depiction of scientific experiment, while the versatile physician, Erasmus Darwin, grandfather of the more famous Charles, is remembered for his poetry with its technological prophecies. In the field of science Derby is proud to have been responsible for the early education of John Flamsteed, the first Astronomer Royal. Nineteenth-century Derby, with its rapid economic and social change, produced two important thinkers, the eminent philosopher, Herbert Spencer, one of the founders of modern sociology, and J. A. Hobson, the economist, whose unorthodox theories were, in different contexts, to be echoed by both Lenin and Keynes, surely two of the most important influences on the economic organization of the contemporary world.

LINCOLN

Lincoln is located at the point where the north–south feature forming the Lincoln Cliff and Heath is broken by a mile-wide gap, through which now flows the river Witham before entering the fenland section of its course. Five periods are outstanding in the city's development: Roman, Danish, medieval, 19th century and post-war 20th century. The contribution of each of these periods to the present form of the city can be traced in buildings, walls and street patterns, by means of which changing site values can also be assessed.

The slope to the north of the gap is steep, in places one in four, and on the elevated site above it, at 225 feet O.D., commanding the point where the Ermine Street crossed the gap, the main garrison settlement on the east side of Britain was established in 47 A.D. This occupied 42 acres (Fig. 80). After the northward advance along Ermine Street had been resumed and the ninth legion moved on to York, in about 71 A.D., Lincoln was given the status of a *Colonia* for retired legionaries. There has been continuous occupation of this stite, forming the upper part of the present city, and parts of its walls, gateways and street plan still exist. In the third century A.D. the walls were extended southward down the slope almost to the river to enclose a further 56 acres. Beyond the walled town to the south the gap was spanned by a causeway

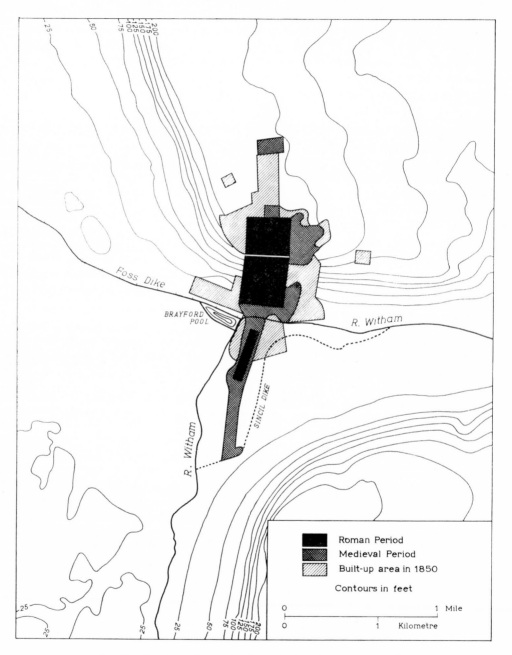

Fig. 80 The site and growth of Lincoln (based on J. F. W. Hill)

bringing Ermine Street, joined by the Fosse Way from south–west Britain, across the marshy area, with villa settlement alongside the road. Thus the north–south axis of the city was established at this early date. Sincil Dyke, a catchwater drain cut to protect the street and adjacent land from flooding, is probably of Roman origin, as is the Foss Dyke canal connecting Lincoln with the Trent. This canal, with the lower Witham, was to be Lincoln's chief commercial highway until the railway age.

Under the Danes Lincoln became one of the five boroughs of the Danelaw, along with Derby, Leicester, Nottingham and Stamford. Besides being a fortified *burh* it was an important centre for Scandinavian trade. Place-names suggest that further settlements developed outside the city walls to the south as well as on the east and west slopes.

After the Norman conquest, when the castle and cathedral were built on the high ground within the first Roman enclosure, about half the area of the upper town was cleared to make room for them. This resulted in the displacement of the Roman street pattern, with curves replacing the grid plan, an extension eastwards for the cathedral close beyond the Roman walls and the growth of a new suburb in Newport, outside the walls to the north. The whole upper town, known as the bail and close, was annexed to the castle, and was administered separately from the rest of medieval Lincoln and, in fact, remained outside its jursidiction until 1835. The second Roman enclosure on the slope leading down to the Witham was the commercial heart of the medieval city, with markets and merchants' quarters. Street names give evidence of former trade functions. Twelfth-century stone houses and 15th- and 16th-century timber-framed houses still exist here, those on the river side having ground-floor storage space. The main street is now an area of small specialised shops, mainly for antiques, and is by-passed by vehicular traffic. Old housing areas on the slopes on either side are now being re-developed. Along the High Street, south of the bridge, the line of early parish churches, as well as some other remaining medieval buildings, again emphasises the city's north–south alignment.

Lincoln's great prosperity from the 12th to the 14th centuries was based on the wool trade. The city was both port and staple town, Brayford pool was a busy inland harbour and the headquarters of the wool staple was located beside the Witham at Thornbridge. The waterway (including the Foss Dyke) was the route along which wool from the Midlands reached Lincoln for export. In 1369 the wool staple was transferred to Boston and this marked the beginning of an economic decline for Lincoln which was to last until the railway age. The population is estimated to have been about 5,000 to 6,000 at Domesday; by the early 16th century it had probably dropped to about 2,000 and by the early 18th century it was only a little over 3,000. Speede's map of 1610 shows that the settled area had not expanded since the 14th century. Plague and the Civil War, as well as economic stagnation, had all hindered progress.

Renewed vigour in the 19th century is often attributed solely to the coming of the railways, but even by 1831 the population had risen to 11,217. Enclosures and the new farming methods, including fen drainage, were undoubtedly factors in the resurgence of economic life, as were the turnpike roads in increasing traffic and bringing trade to the city. The waterway was still important for traffic.

With the advent of the railways in 1846 and 1848 new significance was given to the level land on the floor of the gap, where lines from the Midlands, Yorkshire, London and the east coast converge. Industry rapidly followed and the population, which was 13,000 in 1841, increased to 20,000 in 1861, and to 48,000 by the end of the century. The built-up area was extended on either side of the High Street, and the main economic life of the city shifted southwards. Many of the engineering enterprises originally providing agricultural machinery, steam engines and pumps for drainage, were started by men of vision and energy between 1849 and 1857, and have developed widely. During the first World War the tank was first designed and produced in Lincoln. The largest firm in the city, Ruston and Hornsby Ltd., now employs some 5,700 people in several factories. These cover over 100 acres and make diesel engines, locomotives, boilers and gas turbines, with a large export market. The allied firm of Ruston Bucyrus Ltd., making excavators and cranes, employs 3,000 in Lincoln. Others in the main industrial belt include Dawson's (belting), established 1896, with 400 employees, Robey's (1854, engines, boilers and mining equipment), Gwynne (1849, pumps), Penny & Porter (1856, grain dryers and seed drills), Clayton Dewandre (1928, road vehicle equipment).

Although engineering predominates, accounting for about 15,000 of some 20,000 industrial workers in the city, there are other forms of manufacturing located both in the main industrial area, especially along the waterside (where flour mills still use the Foss Dyke to some extent for their imported grain supplies) and on the city outskirts, on land formerly quarried for limestone or gravel, and on the line of the proposed outer ring road. The newer industries include food processing, such as Smith's potato crisps (1939), Swift's frozen chicken (1962) and others, animal feeding stuffs, plastics, joinery, electronics and paper processing.

The generalised land-use map (Fig. 81) shows, along the floor of the gap, and on the lower slopes to the north of it, a zone devoted to industrial premises, railway stations and sidings, together with areas crowded with 19th-century artisan housing. Some of this housing is now being cleared. The main commercial and administrative core today lies in the southern part of the old city and on either side of High Street, to the south of the river. Considerable traffic congestion arises in these areas through the proximity of rail and bus stations, shops and factories, though the factories now mainly use road transport. Two level-crossings in High Street, the narrow roadway over the Witham bridge and the Stonebow arch which still marks the southern extremity of the former walled city, add further to the problem. Until the opening in 1958 of Pelham Bridge, a little further east, built to span some of the railways, no alternative route through Lincoln existed without a level-crossing.

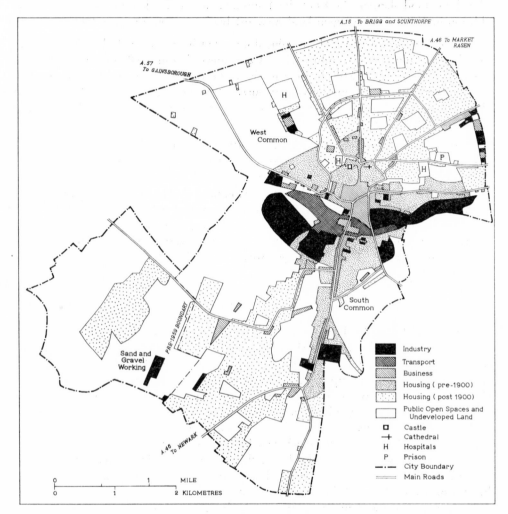

Fig. 81   Land use in Lincoln

Bailgate and Castle Square, with the Cathedral Close in the upper part of the city, form a secondary centre of different character. Shops here are small family concerns, many of them old-established. Two of Lincoln's largest hotels are located here, together with the county archives and county courts in the castle grounds. Twentieth-century housing estates with small shopping centres occur on land beyond the core, to the north on the level ground as far as the city boundary, and to the south extending beyond the boundary. The largest open spaces are the south and west commons, pre-enclosure common lands. Other open spaces near the Witham are related to flood danger. In 1959 the boundary was extended to the west by the addition of 1,390 acres of open land now gradually coming into use for housing.

The contrast between uphill Lincoln, dominated by the cathedral and castle, and downhill Lincoln, mainly industrial and commercial, can well be seen from such vantage points as the cathedral tower or the castle turret. Although industry appears to predominate, service functions (distributive, transport, building, professional and administrative) in fact account for rather more than half the total employed population (Plate XX).

There is a considerable daily movement both in and out of the city, with a balance of a net inward movement to work of some 3,000 people daily, mainly from adjacent Rural Districts. Though a number of county services are located in Lincoln (Lindsey County Offices, hospitals, etc.), the city's regional importance is limited by the fact that towns such as Market Rasen, Scunthorpe, Horncastle, Newark, Sleaford, Louth and Grantham, exerting their own urban influence, exist within a 10- to 25-mile radius. With a population of 77,000, Lincoln is nevertheless, after Nottingham, Leicester and Derby, the fourth largest town in the East Midlands.

THE MANSFIELD URBAN COMPLEX

Mansfield and its related group of urban settlements lie some 12 to 14 miles north of Nottingham. To the west of them lies the exposed coalfield of east Derbyshire, but the greater part of the urban area is located on the Permian rocks, mainly Magnesian Limestone, though to the east it extends on to the Bunter Sandstone. The Limestone and the Sandstone have both played a part in the economic life of the area, the former as an excellent building stone, still to be seen in many buildings, while the latter is actively quarried for moulding sand. It is the Coal Measures, however, which have created the urbanized area as it is today, with 12 large collieries operating in the neighbourhood, all but three of them yielding over 450,000 tons per annum each. It was the progressive advance of the collieries from west to east across the area between 1870 and the 1920s that led the separate settlements to expand and later merge to form a virtually continuous built-up area from Annesley in the south to New Clipstone in the north–east.

This urban complex, consisting of the borough of Mansfield (53,218) and the three Urban Districts of Sutton-in-Ashfield (40,441), Kirkby-in-Ashfield (21,686), and Mansfield Woodhouse (20,197), together with the parish of Clipstone (3,947), is much more than a series of large mining settlements strung across the landscape. It is true that the siting of mines has led to a sprawling pattern of housing estates, at first separated from each other and only later, in many cases since the war, joined

XXII   View of Southwell

XXIII   Southwell Minster showing the Chapter House

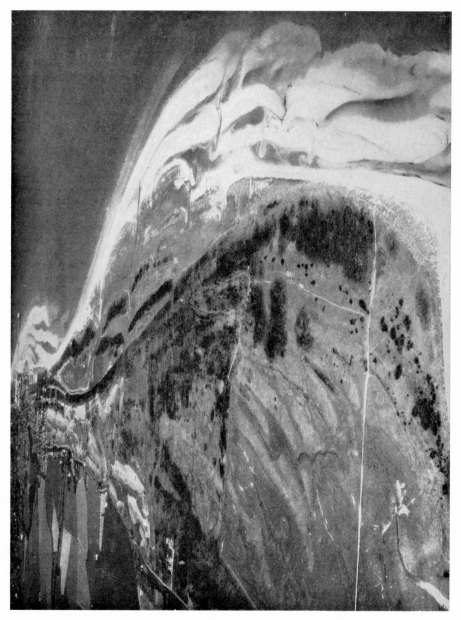

Photo by Aerofilms and Aero Pictorial Ltd.

XXIV   Gibraltar Point looking north along the main eastern dunes. In the shelter of these is the mature marsh, behind which are the western dunes. Young dunes are developing behind the present ridge and runnel beach. Part of Skegness is seen in the distance

by infilling, but both Mansfield and Sutton have urban origins and functions pre-dating the mines, whilst the others had their beginnings in rural activities and domestic industry.

Mansfield, sited in a shallow basin below the Bunter escarpment, where a small tributary joins the river Maun, has enjoyed the status and prestige of an important market centre at least since 1377, the date of its market charter. Its retail, administrative and service functions as a regional centre for west Nottinghamshire and the adjacent part of Derbyshire are reflected in its nodal position and its well-developed commercial core area with what is said to be the largest street market in England. The domestic hosiery industry, iron foundries and water-powered cotton mills along the Maun and Meden, together with agricultural processing and servicing, provided the economic base to the town for 100 years before coal-mining became important.

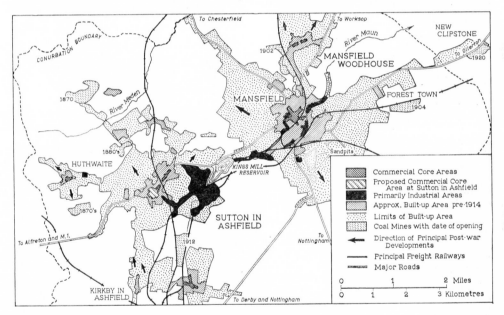

Fig. 82   The Mansfield urban complex

Although overshadowed by Mansfield, Sutton-in-Ashfield, three miles to the south–west, also had well-marked urban features, such as a market place, a complex street pattern, an industrial economy and considerable retail functions. Being less well-developed than Mansfield and being invaded by mines on all sides within a relatively short period, the old town was immersed and in the process lost its former character, as did the other smaller settlements of Kirkby-in-Ashfield and Mansfield Woodhouse. Mansfield, however, with its greater economic and social strength, coupled with the fact that no mine has ever been sunk within the 7,000 acres enclosed by the municipal boundary, survived the onslaught and retained its regional importance as well as becoming the predominant service centre for an urban area with a population now totalling some 140,000.

Mansfield and Sutton-in-Ashfield, 1866

A century ago, despite the permanent depression of the domestic hosiery industry and a decade and a half of poor trade in the cotton industry, the nine water-powered cotton mills along the rivers Meden and Maun, led by William Hollin's mills at Pleasley Vale, employed some 800 persons, while a further 4,000 were engaged in the domestic hosiery industry within the area of the Mansfield Poor Law Union. Moreover, the 'golden age' of British agriculture was accompanied in this area by the agricultural colonisation of Sherwood Forest, following enclosure, and this, too, brought prosperity to Mansfield. Some 500 men were employed in agricultural servicing and processing industries and numerous foundry workers were engaged in making agricultural machinery. Further diversity came from the predominantly domestic clothing and shoe trades, employing 1,200, of whom the majority were women. Stone and sand quarrying were active and coal-mining, although only on the extreme western fringe of the area, was beginning to expand.

This diversification of the industrial base and the well-developed commercial functions are clearly reflected in the urban morphology of Mansfield. The commercial core extended for some 200 yards along each of the five principal roads leading from the Market Place. Many of the shops were of a substantial kind and between them provided a full range of goods. There were also three banks and many large inns, including the Swan Hotel. The major industrial area was a tenuous line, some two miles in length, along the Maun valley, stretching from the large flour mill at King's Mill, downstream to the Bath cotton mill. Along this west to east axis were most of the stone quarries and 14 of the larger industrial premises, including six cotton mills, two foundries and a brewery.

The residential and social structure also reflected the truly urban form of the town. Close to the town centre and east of the Maun, in Ratcliffe Gate (A.617), were to be found numerous alleys and courtyards with poor-quality, high-density housing, the centre of much domestic industry. The commercial and professional middle classes mainly lived over or behind their shops and offices along the five principal roads, cheek by jowl with the poorer property. Two other artisan and lower middle class housing districts were to be found, one between the railway and the Nottingham road and the other along a series of streets running off Westgate, notably St. John's Street. A high-class residential area was developing in a broad arc from the Chesterfield road eastwards to the Maun valley at Car Bank (Borough Offices) and it was here that the local industrialists and gentry lived. Thus it can be seen that Mansfield enjoyed a well-balanced structure economically and socially, despite a population of only 10,225 in 1861, rising to 11,824 by 1871.

Sutton-in-Ashfield (6,483 in 1861) could boast an urban street pattern centred on a market place but the services provided did not include a bank or those of an attorney. The retail functions were essentially for the resident population and there is no evidence that Sutton possessed any recognisable urban field, unlike Mansfield, which had already a well-defined sphere of influence stretching from Alfreton to Ollerton and from Elmton to Kirkby.

Sutton also lacked the industrial diversity of its larger neighbour and in fact was heavily committed to the domestic hosiery trade, although coal-mining was by this date within a few miles of the town and some of the 900 miners recorded in the Mansfield Poor Law Union area were doubtless from Sutton.

The settlement of Kirkby-in-Ashfield (2,886) consisted of a linear village and a few scattered hamlets in the parish and, like Mansfield Woodhouse (2,263), was concerned with the domestic hosiery industry. At Kirkby, mining was close at hand in the upper Erewash valley. Neither of these settlements could be classified as more than a large village, however, and they lacked the diversity of services and functions requisite for even a small town.

The built-up areas of the four settlements were all very restricted and in no sense could they be said to form a single unit. Even between Mansfield and Mansfield Woodhouse there was almost a mile of open country.

Greater Mansfield in the 1960s

Some of the major morphological features of the conurbation today are shown in Fig. 82, which also indicates the nature and direction of its growth. As far as the extent of the built-up area is concerned, consolidation and infilling have been the dominant traits over the last 20 years. This applies particularly in Kirkby and Sutton, where earlier residential development had produced a series of fragments rather than a truly urban form. In pre-war years, apart from fragmentation, there was a high degree of ribbon development along the principal roads, especially the Chesterfield road in Mansfield and the Huthwaite–Sutton road, which, despite infilling, is still apparent. It might be argued that overall planning of the entire area could have achieved still more in terms of consolidation of the separate urban units.

Economically the conurbation is fortunate indeed, and its households have among the highest average incomes of any industrial area in the country. This can be attributed to the large coal mines, with their high productivity, over one million tons per annum has been produced by individual pits in the area and Kirkby pit is thought to be capable of raising up to two million tons per annum in the future. The long life of these pits has led to a considerable influx of Durham and Scottish miners into the area under National Coal Board schemes. Prosperity from mining is matched by prosperity in the hosiery trade, which is firmly established in mainly medium-to-small size plants, employing 60 per cent or more female labour. There are approximately 40 factories producing hosiery and allied products, the largest employing some

800 people. Although lacking a large engineering industry, the area has developed a foundry industry, which has expanded into structural steel working. The local authorities would welcome more light engineering to provide greater diversity and lighter work for men but the general prosperity and high rate of employment do not strengthen the case for the influx of new industry.

The commercial core areas within the urban complex pose some interesting questions, whose answers lie in the future. At the present time Mansfield is clearly predominant, with all the major chain department and specialist stores represented and well supported by other retail, social and professional services. The commercial core has not altered in location to any marked extent over the last century and is now in need of fairly extensive renewal if only to prevent strangulation by traffic. In contrast, the commercial centre in Sutton moved from the Market Place north-eastwards along Outram Street at about the turn of the century, but, despite the rapid growth of the town, it never rivalled Mansfield. Sutton now has plans for a central area re-development on a large scale, which will take the commercial core back to the Market Place, where it may even challenge Mansfield. The other two urban districts have smaller plans and see themselves as local service centres for their own populations. If Sutton's scheme is carried out in full it will be interesting to see whether both Mansfield and Sutton can prosper on increased trade and whether the former will keep its ascendancy. Either or both could also gain at the expense of Alfreton, in Derbyshire, only five miles away.

Communications will play a vital rôle, both in any commercial contest and in the broader economic future of the entire area. Again there are some interesting aspects. Firstly, the conurbation is now without a passenger railway service, despite the complex network of railways. The nearest places for main-line connection are Chesterfield, 12 miles distant, or Nottingham, 14 miles distant. The railways were built by competing companies for the coal traffic and it is the very heavy traffic in coal which uses them today. The severing of the rail services has been hastened, no doubt, by the fact that the only main line serving the area was the former Great Central, all the others being branch lines. More pertinent to the future of these towns, however, are the roads. Mansfield is the focus of five major roads and is easily accessible from any direction; the other towns have rather limited accessibility by main road. Sutton, however, is conscious of the likely effect of the London–Yorkshire motorway (M.1), which will pass close to the western boundary of the urban district. There will be a junction between the M.1 and A.615 and thus, of all the urban centres, Sutton will become the most accessible to the new highway.

The Mansfield urban complex, or 'Greater Mansfield' as it might be called, is really a small conurbation. In terms of population, Mansfield (53,218) is now being challenged by Sutton (40,441) and on this basis the degree of inequality between them is diminishing. The other two Urban Districts cannot hope to rival Mansfield and Sutton, if only because of their peripheral location, but Kirkby (21,686) is anxious to preserve its status and looks to its central development plan to assist in this. Mansfield Woodhouse (20,197), on the other hand, is already in two distinct sections, one lying between the Worksop road and the railway, and the other formed by Forest Town on the road (A.611) between Mansfield and Clipstone. This, coupled with proximity to Mansfield, has relegated Mansfield Woodhouse to the position of a suburb and local service centre which is unlikely to change.

SOUTHWELL

Southwell is a small town, a former market centre situated in the valley of the Greet, a tributary of the Trent, 14 miles north–east of Nottingham. Its particular importance in relation to Nottingham lies in the fact that since 1884 its large and splendid church of the Blessed Virgin Mary, has been the cathedral church of the Nottinghamshire diocese. Although Southwell is the administrative centre of a Rural District of the same name, a large agricultural area comprising 55 parishes, the town itself, with a population of only 4,300, is too small to have urban status. The history of this ancient centre is closely bound up with that of its Minster, though it is likely that a settlement existed in pre-Christian times, for a fragment of Roman tesselated pavement, said to be of the second century A.D., was uncovered beneath the south transept of the Minster and can still be seen. There was certainly a Saxon church on this site and the well referred to in the place-name, along with several others, can also be traced back to Saxon times. The evidence of Danish settlement in the vicinity, probably developing side by side with the Saxon, is seen in the names of the two hamlets Westhorpe and Easthorpe which eventually became absorbed into Southwell. Across the Greet the hamlet of Normanton falls within the parish of Southwell but as a settlement is still separate from the little town (Plate XXII).

Apart from the Minster and the buildings associated with it, including Vicars' Court and houses of the Prebends of the clergy, a number of features survive to indicate Southwell's importance as a country town in the 19th century and earlier. Along the main street, the site of the former market (Market Street) lies adjacent to the historic inn, The Saracen's Head (formerly the King's Arms) where Charles I stayed preceding his surrender to the Scots Commissioners in 1646. The town Assembly Room, built in 1806, later formed part of the inn. Nearby, the Minster Grammar School, a very ancient foundation which the cathedral choristers still attend, occupied a building erected in 1819. From about 1812 onwards Southwell also possessed a theatre. The extension of the town towards Westhorpe, along one of the two roads to Nottingham (B.6386), is reflected by Trinity Church dating from 1846, although a few years earlier the Baptist Chapel (1839) had appeared near the junction of the main Nottingham road (A.612). At the eastern end of the town on a rise of ground before descending to the Greet is the Burgage Green, a tree-lined open space, on one side of which is the Burgage Manor, a Georgian house rented by Byron's mother in the early years of the 19th century and where the poet spent his vacations when at Cambridge. On the same side of the Green is the old prison or House of Correction with its gateway dated 1809, a reminder of Southwell's past and present function as an administrative centre. When the prison became disused in 1900 it was converted and enlarged to serve as a lace-factory, by a firm from Bulwell, Nottingham, producing lace curtains. For the past eight years, however, it has been occupied by a haulage firm as a depot for general merchandise distribution.

As a market town, even in the early 19th century, Southwell was never as important as Newark, only eight miles away and Mansfield, 12 miles. Both the latter were better served by communications and eventually developed into industrial centres while retaining their market functions. Nevertheless, until its own market declined, Southwell held an annual fair, in later days a cattle fair, at Whitsuntide, and a ploughing contest is still held in September. While serving the surrounding agricultural district the town also attracted a considerable number of well-to-do people including some from Nottingham who moved there on retirement from business. John Byng, writing towards the end of the 18th century, left a curious impression of Southwell as 'a well-built clean town, such a one as a quiet distressed family ought to retire to'. The many substantial houses of Georgian and later styles certainly bear witness to the existence of a residential community living in comfortable circumstances. Yet for almost a century and a half the town's population grew extremely slowly. In 1801 it was about 2,500, by mid-century it was 3,500, and by 1901 it declined slightly to 3,200, and in 1951 was 3,300. The opening of the Mansfield-Newark line in 1871, which provided Southwell with railway communication, clearly had little effect on its growth and its expansion in recent years has been due almost entirely to increased transport by road. The station is now closed.

Today Southwell is a local service centre with a resident population which is steadily growing on account of the increasing number who commute daily to Nottingham and Newark. The replacement of older dwellings and the building of additional ones has resulted in some expansion of the town to the north along the Greet valley between the railway and the Kirklington road. Bus services link the town with Nottingham, Mansfield and Newark but the railway is now used only for goods traffic. The shopping centre, with its banks, post office, public library and Rural District offices, remains strung along the narrow thoroughfare which forms the axis of High Town. There is little industrial activity apart from the old-established flour mill which stands adjacent to the railway and to the Greet which was its original source of power. In the surrounding area several types of specialised agriculture are to be found in addition to the characteristic mixed farming. These include the production of orchard fruit and small fruit in the parishes of Halam, Edingley and Kirklington, the cultivation of nursery and horticultural products at Upton Fields, and growing of rose-trees at Southwell itself by a firm formerly noted for its apple orchards from which originated the well-known variety called Bramley Seedling.

Adding further emphasis to Southwell's close connections with the agricultural community, is the Nottinghamshire Farm Institute at Brackenhurst Hall, which is a residential school for farmers and farm workers situated about a mile to the south of the town. The racecourse on which the Southwell race meetings have been held since 1898 is on the flat ground of the Trent floodplain at Rolleston junction, where the railway from Mansfield and Southwell joins the main line from Nottingham to Newark and Lincoln. Its location reflects the days when railway access was more important than communication by road.

Southwell Diocese

The early history of the ecclesiastical jurisdiction of what was eventually to become the Diocese of Southwell is obscure. The Kingdom of Mercia did not accept conversion to Christianity till some time in the last half of the seventh century. Then this vast area became a diocese with its see at Lichfield. It was not long before this bishopric was divided into five parts, and at the time of the Danish invasions what is now Derbyshire was in Lichfield and what is now Nottinghamshire was in Stow (in Lindsey). By the middle of the 10th century it is clear that Nottinghamshire was in the Diocese of York, and that the Archbishop had much land in the county.

Thereafter Derbyshire was part of Lichfield, and Nottinghamshire remained part of York till 1837, when it was transferred to Lincoln, and so to the jurisdiction of the Archbishop of Canterbury. This transfer made new problems for Lincoln, and Lichfield also was needing relief. The outcome was the creation in 1884 of the Diocese of Southwell, including the two counties of Nottingham and Derby, with a population then of about 880,000. By 1921 this had risen to 1,355,000, and plans to make Derbyshire a separate diocese came to fruition in 1927. The two dioceses were still in the province of Canterbury, but not for long. York welcomed Southwell back in 1935, after a century's exile; and there it remains, with little likelihood of another upheaval.

Southwell Minster

On the site where the Minster now stands are Roman remains, and about 200 yards to the east more and richer work has been excavated and is now covered again. It is known that there was a Saxon church on this site, but only a few fragments remain. (Tympanum, north–west door in north transept, and capitals above the screen.) Before the new Grammar School was built on land belonging to the Church, excavations disclosed much coloured mosaic, some remarkable painted plaster, and a tiled swimming bath. The plaster is being assembled; the rest has been covered up to protect it until arrangements can be made for it to be available for inspection.

The key date for thought about the present building is 956. This is the most probable date of a charter by which King Edwy conferred on Archbishop Oskeytel lands (and therefore rights and duties) in and around Southwell. The earliest copy of this charter (in the Great White Book of York) dates from about four centuries later; and there is no certain knowledge as to why the king made this grant. It would be an impertinence to attempt to summarise in a line or two what Sir Frank Stenton spent an hour discussing in a lecture in the Minster on 22nd September 1956. Suffice it to say that the results of this grant vastly affected Southwell's future, in at least three main ways. The Archbishops of York had a house in Southwell in which they lived from time to time. There came into being a college of clergy to supervise the lands, the courts, and the other Archbishops' affairs (the 10th century use of 'Minster' means something like a semi-independent outpost of a bishop, and Southwell became one of York's Minsters); and when the time came to replace the Saxon church the new church was on a scale which matched the status of the Archbishops who ruled it.

About 1108 Thomas the Second started on the present church, and the main lines of his work can be seen today in the three towers, the nave, and the transepts. What the east end of the church was like is uncertain, for guesses based on excavations are hazardous; but it seems probable that there were apses on the east faces of the transepts.

In 1234 Walter de Grey began the building of the present choir. It is about twice as long as the earlier one. The vertical lines, the fillets on the shafts, the dogtooth decoration, and variety of bosses all compel attention. The solid yet light restfulness of the nave gives place to an almost mobile sense of stretching. The chapel at the east side of the north nave transept also belongs to this period. In it can be seen some indications of changes in its plan while it was being built.

About 1290 John Romaine ordered the chapter house to be built on the north side of the choir. Its wealth of naturalistic decoration has received minute attention by A. C. Seward (in the *Cambridge Antiquarian Society's Communications*, Vol. XXXV) and N. Pevsner (*The Leaves of Southwell*). This emphasis has tended to put into the background a wealth of other delights—dogs, pigs, lizards, a bat, a goat, a merman and so on. The absence of a central pier adds to the sense of space (Plate XXIII).

About 1330 the present screen was built. The stone came by water, from an unknown quarry, and not from the earlier source near Mansfield which is still used today. The wealth of heads, especially on the east face, are beyond description. It is interesting to compare the robust, almost licentious, work of the 14th century with the tame pious early 19th-century 'restoration'. The Sedilia on the south side of the sanctuary are about the same date as the screen.

The only other major alteration to the Minster came at the end of the 15th century, when the great west window was inserted.

The heads on the screen have already been mentioned. Other heads, inside and outside, await systematic study. In different periods of history and in widely separated parts of the world the mind of man has expressed itself in carvings of heads of striking similarity. At the top of Southwell's two western towers are 12th-century heads which are matched by recent Nigerian work, and Karnak and Cnossos are echoed in the nave. And today, as in the 14th century, the masons of Southwell are incorporating into its fabric the continuing common life, by carving and building in the heads of the head verger, the keeper of the belfry, the dog-whipper, a chorister, three of the masons themselves, and the Provost.

The property and the government of the Minster were in the hands of the Chapter until 1841. The property was then vested in the Ecclesiastical Commissioners, who were required to make 'competent provision' for fabric and services, and were empowered to seek an Order in Council to give effect to a permanent scheme. This temporary arrangement lasted for 120 years. In 1962 such a scheme was made and accepted. In the meantime various Cathedral Measures had produced new Statutes, and eventually what had been the responsibility of the Chapter was transferred to a Cathedral Council, thereby bringing into the administration of the Minster the experience and gifts of the laity.

SKEGNESS

The major natural asset which the Lincolnshire coast possesses for the attraction of holiday visitors is the continuous expanse of sand beach, narrow in the central section around Mablethorpe, but wider in the northern and southern sections of the coast. The beach is backed in many places by high sand dunes which serve as a sea defence, although these have been replaced to a large extent by artificial banks. Behind the dunes lies the coastal marshland, a low-lying farming area which suffered extensive inundation when the sea-defences broke down during the storms in 1953. Early settlement on this marshland was located on slight hummocks where the underlying boulder clay protrudes through the marsh.

Today the few towns along the coast are holiday resorts. These include Skegness (population 12,847 in 1961) and Mablethorpe and Sutton (5,388). In the 18 miles which separate them are several places which have important concentrations of holiday camp, caravan and chalet facilities, including Ingoldmells (790), Chapel St. Leonards (909) and Anderby (195).

The chief resort is Skegness, often spoken of as 'Nottingham-by-the-sea', which, in common with Mablethorpe, has depended for its growth on investment and visitors from the East Midlands, in particular from the Nottingham area. A number of streets and hotels are named after historic places and personages in Nottinghamshire and Derbyshire; branches of Nottingham shops are to be found and Nottingham newspapers are in circulation. Until the middle of the 19th century Skegness was a small fishing village of some 500 persons, but with a growing reputation as a sea-bathing place. The initial stimulus for its development into a resort was the opening, in 1873, of a branch line from the Boston to Grimsby railway. In the same year, moreover, rail excursions were first run from Nottingham direct to Skegness. Of far greater consequence, however, was the fact that most of the land in the parish of of Skegness was owned by the Lumley family, the Earls of Scarbrough. The ninth Earl initiated the design for a new town, the development of which was controlled by his estate agent, and by 1878 the first buildings were being erected on new streets forming a grid layout. Next came the construction of a sea-wall to protect the new town, which lay immediately north of the original village street, as shown on the growth map (Fig. 83). Amenities for holiday visitors were provided, including shelters, pleasure gardens and a pier, built in 1881. In the early 1900s residential development spread on the sandhills to the south of the town and this trend is continuing. In addition there has been a western extension of the urban area on to the marshlands, mainly of post-war council housing.

At first, holiday accommodation was of the traditional hotel and apartment type, but in 1937 a new concept in holiday-taking was provided by the opening of Britain's first self-contained holiday camp, the Butlin Camp at Ingoldmells, immediately north of the urban district boundary. Further developments were interrupted by the war years, but since 1945 there has been a great increase in holiday accommodation in the form of static caravans. There are now more than 12,500 caravans on several sites along the Lindsey coastline, with major concentrations in the parishes of Ingoldmells and Chapel St. Leonards.

The development of the Lincolnshire coast resorts is reflected in their population growth. Until 1871 the population of Skegness remained at about 500, but by 1881 it had risen to 1,600; during the present century it grew rapidly to over 9,000 in 1921, at which level it remained in 1931, but since the second World War it has again grown, reaching 12,847 in 1961. The population of Mablethorpe and Sutton increased steadily throughout the 19th century, from 2,000 to 4,900 between 1911 and 1921; it fell below 4,000 in 1931, but reached 5,393 in 1951, and was almost the same in 1961.

The Lincolnshire resorts are patronised mainly by family holiday parties. A survey made in Skegness in 1964 showed that 74 per cent of the visitors were in family groups; the same survey showed that the holiday catchment area of Skegness is strongly located in the East Midlands. The counties of Nottingham, Derby and Leicester provide 53 per cent of the total visitors, while the West Riding of Yorkshire supplies 25 per cent. The pattern for Mablethorpe and Sutton is similar. Sources of day-trippers to the resorts are more strongly localized in the East Midlands, for reasons of proximity and also because it is from these nearer centres that the best public travel facilities are available. Thus, in the 1964 August Bank Holiday period, the East Midlands supplied 72 per cent of all day-trippers to Skegness, the West Riding of Yorkshire contributing 15 per cent.

One of the problems facing many small coastal resorts is the possibility of the closure of their rail communications. Not long ago the whole of the east Lincolnshire railway system was threatened, including the two branch lines, to Mablethorpe and Sutton, and Skegness. Closure would inevitably mean the loss of some visitors,

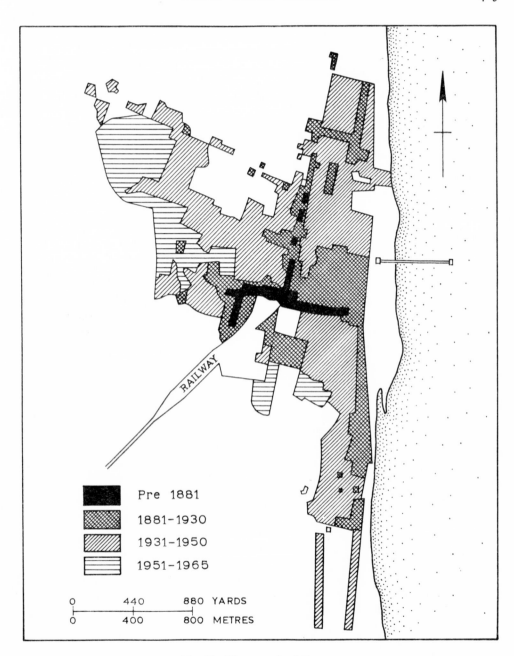

Fig. 83 The growth of Skegness

although results of the survey mentioned above suggested that the majority would adopt public or private road transport as an alternative means of travel if the necessity arose. Some 18 per cent of all visitors to Skegness used the railway in 1964, compared with the national travel figure of 20 per cent, a proportion which has declined rapidly in favour of private motoring since the war. The Minister of Transport has refused his consent to the proposed rail closures in east Lincolnshire, however, so the railway will continue to serve the resorts for at least a few more years.

Another problem facing resort towns is that of seasonal unemployment. In recent years the unemployment rate in Skegness and Mablethorpe has fluctuated from less than one per cent in the summer to eight per cent in the winter months. Between March 1960 and July 1962 the two towns were classed as a Development District and some small light engineering firms were introduced during that period, using mainly female labour but still leaving some male unemployment in the winter months. Towards the end of 1965 Government permission was obtained to expand the Skegness industrial estate.

Great pressure is exerted on coastal land for urban and other forms of development, especially caravan sites, which, with a permitted maximum of 20 caravans per acre, are extravagantly space-consuming. This results in a conflict with amenity and wild life conservation interests which are endeavouring to keep large sections of the coast free from holiday development. The first controls on coastal development were applied under the Lindsey County Council (Sandhills) Act 1932, which prohibited any further extensions of unregulated bungalows and shack development on the coastal dunes. Since the war the county planning authority has been active in establishing nature reserves south of Skegness, to the north of Mablethorpe, and in the area south of Sutton-on-Sea, where there is a conservation area with public access to the beach. Caravan camps are excluded from these areas and such development is concentrated within the scheduled holiday coast areas immediately north of Skegness and in the Mablethorpe and Sutton urban district. As part of the conservation policy much of the undesirable shanty property erected in the inter-war years has now been removed.

SELECTED REFERENCES

DERBY

Cauter, T. and Downham, J. S. *The communication of ideas: a study of contemporary influences on urban life* (A social survey of Greater Derby). London (1954).

Richardson, W. A. *Citizen's Derby* (A history of Derby compiled for its young citizens). London (1949).

Smith, D. M. The silk industry of the East Midlands. *East Midland Geographer* Vol. 3 (17) (1962) pp. 20–31.

Turton, B. J. Industry and transport in Derby. *East Midland Geographer* Vol. 2 (14) (1960) pp. 3–10.

Vollans, E. C. Derby: a railway town and regional centre. *Transactions and Papers of the Institute of British Geographers, 1949* (1951) pp. 91–112.

MANSFIELD

Groves, W. H. *The History of Mansfield*. Nottingham (1894).

Law, C. M. An outline of the industrial development of Mansfield. *East Midland Geographer* No. 20 (December 1963).

LINCOLN

Hill, J. F. W. *Medieval Lincoln*. Cambridge (1948).

Hill, J. F. W. *Tudor and Stuart Lincoln*. Cambridge (1956).

Abel, E. I. and Chambers, J. D. *The Story of Lincoln*. Lincoln (1939).

SOUTHWELL

Beaumont, R. M. *The Chapter of Southwell Minster*. Southwell (1956).

Pevsner, N. *The Leaves of Southwell*. London (1945).

ACKNOWLEDGMENT

Thanks are due to the Borough Engineer, Derby, for his advice on the compilation of Fig. 79.

PART V

NATURE CONSERVATION

XXVII

THE CONSERVATION OF NATURE
IN LINCOLNSHIRE

THE landscape of Britain has undergone many changes at the hands of man, but none as drastic or as widespread as those brought about during the last fifty years by the spread of town and industrial development as well as by the technological advances in agriculture. Inevitably the countryside has been diminished and the wild places in many lowland counties have been reduced to remnants. The 18th-century enclosure landscape with its variety of semi-natural features which supported a rich and varied flora and fauna is rapidly disappearing as intensive arable farming dispenses with features like trees, hedgerows and ponds.

Everywhere too, the by-products of these urban, industrial and agricultural developments are apparent: the lowering of water tables and the fall in the levels of ponds and lakes and in the flow of streams and rivers; pollution of the air, of watercourses and of the seas around our coasts; and in recent years the effects of chemicals used as pesticides. Whilst the value of chemicals in increasing agricultural yields is indisputable, a few of them, the persistent chlorinated hydrocarbons, have contaminated the whole environment and threaten the very existence of some of our finest birds of prey.

To all these pressures on the natural environment must be added those of a human population now highly mobile and enjoying increasing leisure, whose needs for outdoor recreation of all kinds must be met from the dwindling resources of coast and country.

LANDSCAPE CHANGES IN LINCOLNSHIRE

The impact of all these developments can be seen throughout the East Midlands. Over much of Derbyshire and Nottinghamshire it is industrial and urban growth and their by-products which have changed the environment. In Lincolnshire, the landscape has been transformed by intensive cultivation, and the coast by recreational development. Of the vast fens, which in the middle of the 18th century still covered much of the south-eastern part of the county, not a vestige remains, though fragments are left in the Isle of Axholme in the extreme north-west. The open downland of the chalk Wolds has likewise almost totally disappeared. Within the last forty years

HH

the blown-sand heaths of the north-west have been reduced to a few isolated remnants by afforestation and ploughing. Woodlands are still extensive on the boulder clays of the Middle Marsh, in the central clay vale and in the Kesteven valleys; but native deciduous woodland of the traditional standard oak with coppice type is fast becoming scarcer. So too are the oak-birch woods of the sand and gravel soils and the valley alder and willow carrs. The sand-dune coast of the county has become the playground of the East Midland holidaymaker, and few stretches of it have escaped development or remain relatively undisturbed during the summer months.

THE ORGANISATION OF NATURE CONSERVATION

These changes were, of course, inevitable and others will no doubt follow. But there is now a growing awareness of the need to conserve the interest and beauty of the environment and the natural resources of wildlife and landscape. This has resulted in the creation of the Nature Conservancy and in the expansion of the voluntary conservation movement, most notably by the establishment of County Conservation or Naturalists' Trusts which are now found in almost every county in Britain. The Lincolnshire Trust, founded in 1948, was one of the earliest. Trusts in Derbyshire and Nottinghamshire were formed in 1962 and 1963 respectively. The Trusts and the Nature Conservancy work in close association.

The first aim of the Trusts is to protect the best remaining examples of the principal natural or semi-natural habitats in each county. Some degree of protection is afforded to the most important of these by their designation as Sites of Special Scientific Interest under Section 23 of the National Parks Act, 1949. This ensures consultation between a local planning authority, the Nature Conservancy and the County Trust before any development on these sites is permitted. Unfortunately, agricultural development is not covered by these provisions and many of these sites have been destroyed or damaged as a result, including two of the most important in Lincolnshire: Manton Warren, a blown-sand heath with a dune system; and Waddingham Common, the only turf bog on limestone in the county.

THE ESTABLISHMENT AND MANAGEMENT OF NATURE RESERVES

Trusts, like the Nature Conservancy, are seeking not only to protect sites but, wherever possible, to secure their management as nature reserves. Almost all of them have been modified by man's activities, and in order to maintain or enhance their characteristic habitats and variety of flora and fauna, some form of positive management is usually necessary. This may involve the control of vegetation by traditional treatments such as mowing, grazing or coppicing, or by the eradication of scrub; or it may be desirable to maintain water levels, to excavate ponds or to plant trees. Much of this work on Trusts' reserves is carried out by conservation corps parties of volunteers, mainly young people.

Nature Reserves are being purchased or leased by Trusts with money raised by local appeal and with grants from national sources. They are established by agreement with private landowners and bodies like the Forestry Commission and the National Trust. County Councils have the same powers as the Nature Conservancy to create reserves. Few of them have so far used these powers, but with Trusts now available in almost every county to advise and assist with management, we may expect more of them to do so in the next few years. In Lincolnshire some 20 nature reserves, containing a wide variety of habitats, have been established by these various means.

NATURE RESERVES IN LINCOLNSHIRE

Heathlands

The blown-sand heaths are well represented in the Lincolnshire Trust's reserves at Scotton Common near Gainsborough, and Linwood Warren near Market Rasen. Both have a characteristic heathland flora, including species now either rare or highly localised in Lincolnshire, such as the marsh gentian, bog asphodel, butterwort and two species of sundews. Curlew and Nightjar are among the nesting birds, and Linwood is still a stronghold of Red Squirrels and has four species of reptile, including the Slow-worm. At Linwood an adequate water table has been maintained by a series of dams and sluices in the stream which runs through the reserve. There, too, a cattle grazing experiment, made possible by a Nature Conservancy grant, is being conducted to discover the optimum conditions for the varied flora of an area of wet heath.

Fens

In the Isle of Axholme, the Trust has acquired the only fen relics left in the county, the Epworth and Haxey Turbaries. Raised sphagnum bog and sedge fen with *Cladium* are both well represented in these little-known fen reserves. The bog rosemary and the Large Heath butterfly occur here at the southern edge of their range in Britain.

Chalk and Limestone grasslands

With the almost complete destruction of downland in Lincolnshire, calcicolous plants and their associated animals survive only on steep banks, road verges and in disused quarries. To these the Trust has given particular attention. At the south-eastern edge of the Wolds, chalk pits at Candlesby Hill and at Claxby-by-Alford have been acquired. On the limestone at Wilsford two more quarries have become reserves by agreement with the owner. Nearby at Ancaster, another agreement affords protection and some degree of management to The Valley, a steep-sided dry valley which may have originated as a glacial overflow channel. This is one of the most important areas of grassland on the Lincolnshire Limestone and has an excellent flora, including horseshoe vetch, clustered bellflower, dropwort, purple milk vetch, and several orchids. The principal management problems are the control of gorse scrub and the maintenance of the optimum grazing regime. In the extreme south-west, three other small but biologically rich areas of limestone grassland are protected by agreements with a private landowner and with the Forestry Commission.

Woodland

In addition to the new coniferous forests planted by the Forestry Commission in recent years on the sand and gravel soils of Lincolnshire, there still remains much woodland on the boulder clays east of the Wolds and on the Oxford and Kimmeridge clays between the chalk and the limestone. Formerly deciduous woodland, much of it managed on a coppice-with-standards system, it is increasingly being changed in character to conform with modern timber requirements. The old coppice-with-standards woods produced a great diversity of flora and fauna, and the Lincolnshire Trust has acquired Hoplands Wood at Claxby-by-Alford which will be managed in part on this traditional system. Hoplands retains many fine standard oak and ash trees, with ash and hazel coppice and a variety of other native trees and shrubs. On the edge of the East Fen at Friskney, the Trust owns a small wood, the site of a famous duck decoy. There is much birch and Scots pine, an extensive Badger colony and an interesting bird population.

Coastlands

The Gibraltar Point–Skegness Reserve

Preservation of the natural features and amenities of the Lincolnshire coast has long been the concern of the Lindsey County Council, whose unique Sandhills Act of 1932 enabled it to acquire or to control considerable stretches of shore. One of the areas thus acquired was at Gibraltar Point, south of Skegness, which in the early 1930s had been threatened by large-scale bungalow development. Since 1948 the area has been managed as a nature reserve by agreement between the County Council and the Lincolnshire Trust. The Council's original area has been greatly extended by further acquisition and by lease of the foreshore, and now covers more than 1,000 acres. A further area of about 200 acres owned by Skegness Urban District Council is similarly managed as a reserve. The County Council were the first Local Authority in England to use powers under the National Parks Act of 1949 to establish a nature reserve. The Trust is responsible for the day-to-day management and shares with the County Council the cost of employing a resident warden.

The Gibraltar Point–Skegness Reserve consists of sandy beaches, mudflats and rapidly accreting sand-dunes and salt-marshes. The development of dunes and marshes and their succession of vegetation provide great geomorphological and botanical variety and interest. Both of these are dealt with more fully later in this chapter. There are large populations of invertebrate animals in the inter-tidal zone; and the insect fauna of the dunes contains many localised species. The Reserve is now the only regular breeding place on the Lincolnshire coast of Little Terns and Ringed Plovers; it provides a high-tide roost for waders and other shore birds which feed over a wide area of The Wash; and it is a very important migratory and wintering area for many other species of birds, including a flock of up to 5,000 Pink-footed Geese.

Simple field study facilities, including a bird observatory, were provided as soon as the Reserve was established, and in 1958 the lease by the County Council to the Trust of the old Coastguard House made it possible to expand them. The value of the station was so well demonstrated that in 1964 the County Council carried out major extensions consisting of new laboratories, a class-room and domestic quarters for up to 30 students. The University of Nottingham is one of the principal users of the field station and of the Reserve. Physiographical research by Dr. C. A. M. King and Mr. F. A. Barnes and other members of staff and students of the Department of Geography has been an outstanding feature of the University's work. The Departments of Botany and Zoology have also used the Reserve extensively for research and teaching purposes, and particular mention must be made of the work of Dr. M. C. Pearson and students on Sea Buckthorn, and of Dr. M. R. Young and students on the fauna of the inter-tidal zone. In addition, the University's Department of Adult Education has provided many weekend and summer courses for amateur naturalists and teachers. Other users of the field station are the Kesteven, Nottingham-shire and Doncaster Training Colleges, and many secondary schools from Lindsey and from other parts of Lincolnshire, Nottinghamshire and Derbyshire and from even further afield. In addition to residential courses, many schools bring pupils for day visits for field work and observation. Organisations like the British Trust for Ornithology also organise training courses at the station, and many amateur naturalists stay there to carry out a variety of field studies, especially those connected with the bird observatory where migration records are kept and where migrants are trapped for examination and ringing.

The principal problem in a multi-purpose nature reserve like Gibraltar Point, which is open to the public, is to reconcile its use for education and enjoyment with the conservation of its wealth of plants and animals and natural features. It is imperative that damage and disturbance be reduced to a minimum. This requires the careful planning of educational use, the avoidance of certain areas at certain seasons, and regulations for the collecting of specimens. For the general public, access is regulated by bylaws, car parks are provided adjoining the public road, and tracks are well-made and defined. Even more important is the educational and interpretive programme designed to increase the understanding and appreciation of visitors and so enlist their interest and co-operation in conservation measures. For this purpose wardens act as guides, attractive pictorial notices are used, and in 1963 an Information Centre was opened on the main car park. It has windows on three sides in which exhibits are displayed illustrating the flora and fauna and geographical features of the

Reserve. A nature trail, explaining the features of the salt-marsh and sand-dunes, has been mounted on the main track leading to the beach.

The effects of human pressures on the flora and fauna of the Reserve and the effectiveness of the methods being used to ensure adequate conservation, are currently the subject of an investigation by the Trust, for which the Nature Conservancy has awarded a contract. This kind of research is essential for formulating policies of management which will make it possible to use reserves like Gibraltar Point without diminishing the very scientific and aesthetic interest for which they are valued.

The North Lindsey Coast Reserve

Between Skegness and Mablethorpe the Lincolnshire coastline has been subjected to severe erosion for the last seven or eight centuries and the Marshland behind has had to be protected by sea banks and, in recent years, by massive concrete walls. But north of Mablethorpe there is again accretion of sand and silt. In contrast to conditions at Gibraltar Point, there is at the present day little wind-blown sand to build new dunes, but there is a wide shore of sand and mud backed by a range of old sand-dunes which in places forms an extensive system of ridges and valleys. The mature dunes are almost certainly older than any at Gibraltar Point and have rather more floristic variety, including calcicolous species like carline thistle and pyramidal orchid and rarities like the sand-dune form of the meadow rue. The composition of the salt-marsh vegetation is also somewhat different from that at Gibraltar Point. There is more thrift and sea arrow grass, but less sea lavender.

Between the main dune ridges at Saltfleetby is a freshwater slack, a kind of maritime fen unique on the East Coast of England. Its flora is particularly rich and attractive. Over much of it the sea rush and the great water dock are abundant and, in parts, the common reed and the pond sedge are dominant. In the more open areas and along the margins there is a great variety of plants including marsh and spotted orchids, felwort, lesser water plantain, bog pimpernel and marsh arrow grass. The ponds in the slack have a variety of aquatic creatures including the Water Spider; and the Natterjack Toad occurs here in its only Lincolnshire locality.

The Trust leases 325 acres of this area from the Air Ministry and it is now designated as a National Nature Reserve for which the Nature Conservancy will become primarily responsible. A basic geographical survey of the reserve has already been made and important quantitative studies of the salt-marsh vegetation and of the ecology of sea purslane have been carried out.

The protection from development of this stretch of coastline and that of Gibraltar Point has been due to the enlightened policies of Lindsey County Council through its Sandhills Act and more recently through the exercise of its planning responsibilities by which it has secured the discontinuance of caravan sites in both areas. Elsewhere, between Mablethorpe and Skegness, much of the coast has been developed for holiday-making. In addition to the resorts more than 15,000 caravans and chalets can be accommodated on the land allocated by the Planning Authority for holiday camping.

NATURE CONSERVATION IN THE COUNTRYSIDE

Besides the reserves, County Trusts and the Nature Conservancy are seeking to promote the conservation of nature throughout the countryside. For this purpose many of the Trusts have concluded agreements with County Councils such as Lindsey and Kesteven for the protection and management of the road verges of high biological interest. Similar treatment is being sought from River Authorities for certain stretches of river and stream. Trusts are also acquiring or protecting features like old quarries of the kind already described, and ponds like the Sea Bank Clay Pits along the coast between Sutton-on-Sea and Chapel Point which have been purchased or leased by the Trust from the local River Authority and which attract a wide variety of wildfowl and other aquatic birds and animals. It is features such as these which help to maintain the variety of wild life in an intensively cultivated countryside.

In all fields of conservation there is much to be done in the East Midlands as elsewhere. Many more nature reserves are necessary to protect adequate samples of different types of habitat. In Lincolnshire, for example, an alder carr valley in the Spilsby Sandstone, a wood in the clay vale containing the localised small-leaved lime tree, as well as further calcareous and wetland sites are needed. As field studies in the life- and earth-sciences increase in importance, the demands of education for outdoor facilities must be met. Not all nature reserves are suitable for intensive use since some must be primarily for conservation or research; on the other hand special teaching areas are needed to be used and perhaps managed by schools. In view of the rapidly increasing pressures on coast and countryside, we need more interpretive services for visitors by way of field museums, nature trails and so on. Finally, we need surveys of each county's outdoor resources for conservation, education, recreation and enjoyment, to be followed perhaps by the establishment of advisory county countryside committees on which local authorities and representatives of all the principal land owners and users would be represented. These tasks require the collaboration of all organisations, official and voluntary, concerned with the countryside. They need too the support of all who care about the future of the natural environment and all it contains.

The task of conserving the Lincolnshire countryside has been outlined above. The special place which can be given to the natural features of the Lincolnshire coast are emphasised by the two accounts which follow. The first deals with the geo-morphology of the Lincolnshire coast, with particular reference to Gibraltar Point, while the second is concerned with items of botanical interest at Gibraltar Point.

THE GEOMORPHOLOGY OF THE LINCOLNSHIRE COAST

In the last interglacial period the coast of Lincolnshire consisted of high chalk cliffs. The lower part of this cliff line is now buried by till but the upper degraded part can still clearly be seen running in a north-west to south-east line through Louth. At the foot of the cliffs a marine abrasion platform slopes gently down under the till, reaching a depth of between 50 and 100 feet below sea-level along most of the present coast. The late-glacial and post-glacial development of the coast has been worked out by H. H. Swinnerton, who has shown that as sea-level rose during the Flandrian transgression the glacial deposits of the Lincolnshire marsh gradually became flooded, but not until forests had grown on the till surface and bad drainage during the Neolithic period had allowed peat to form, burying the roots and stumps of the trees. These remains can now be seen at low tide along the coast, for example at Ingoldmells Point and at Sutton-on-Sea. The continued rise of sea-level then allowed a thick layer of salt marsh clay to cover the peat. A short phase of rather lower sea-level during the Iron Age allowed an upper layer of peat to form, consisting largely of the remains of reeds (*Phragmites*). A renewed rise of sea-level then brought in more salt marsh silt, forming a thick layer of fine clay. Clearly, for this type of deposit to accumulate along what is now an exposed coast, liable to erosion, some offshore protection must have been available at the time. Swinnerton has suggested that this was provided by a morainic deposit now apparently remaining only in the Protector Outfalls, the Inner Dowsing and similar offshore shoals. These are no longer exposed because of a continued rise of sea-level. He also suggested that this offshore barrier was finally breached and destroyed during the storms of the 13th century and that some of the material from the barrier was pushed inland over the old salt marsh deposits to form a belt of dunes along the coast; thus the old clay deposits now underlie the foreshore of the modern coast. This clay is exposed on the foreshore at times of exceptional storms, such as that which occurred in 1953.

The dunes still form the best protection for this low coast, but these have had to be supplemented by man-made banks for many centuries, particularly in the area between Mablethorpe in the north and Skegness in the south (Fig. 84). Some explanation of this stretch of coast being more liable to erosion than those to the north and south has been offered by A. H. W. Robinson as a result of experiments made with sea-bed drifters which follow the tidal streams and thus indicate the movement of material. Very few of these drifters became stranded on the part of the coast most liable to erosion. This suggests that this part receives very little sediment from offshore. To the north and south, however, a considerable number of drifters became stranded on the foreshore, indicating that material can reach these parts of the coast from offshore. A. E. B. Owen has shown that the coast south of Mablethorpe has been driven back about a quarter to half a mile in the last few hundred years. The dunes have encroached over the marsh deposits, necessitating the repeated rebuilding of the sea-walls further inland.

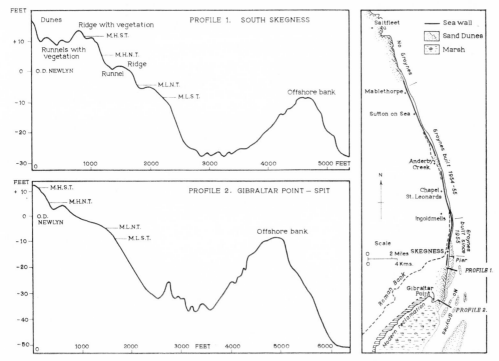

Fig. 84   The coast between Saltfleet and Gibraltar Point

On the other hand the area south of Skegness has been building out during the past two or three centuries and provides a very good example of a low coast of accretion. The processes operating in this area have also been studied in some detail during the past 15 years. The Gibraltar Point area includes a wide variety of features characteristic of a low coast of accretion and illustrates the operation of many interesting processes. Reclaimed marshland lies behind a belt of well-vegetated mature dunes that formed the coast in the 18th century. In front of these old western dunes a mature salt marsh has grown up behind a newer but already stabilised belt of eastern dunes. The latter formed the coast at the beginning of the present century, indicating that the mature marsh had been built up mainly during the previous hundred years. At its southern end the mature salt marsh ends abruptly against a feature called the 'storm-beach', which was formed as the result of a storm in 1922. This eroded the southern margin of the marsh and built up a belt of sand at its denuded end. Since this time a new salt marsh, still in the slobland state, has been developing rapidly in front of the storm-beach and is protected from the sea by a spit, prolonging the north-south line of the coast at Gibraltar Point.

The growth of this spit has been studied during the past decade and it is now being pushed west, over the new marsh. It is one of a series of spits that have developed on this coast. The western dune ridge originally ended in a spit, the remains of which now forms the ground where the Field Research Station is situated. It was then cut off from its supply of material from the north by the growth of the eastern dune ridge and, as a result, it became hooked and decayed. The present spit may well go through the same cycle, because active accretion in the form of an arcuate 'ness' is in progress to the north, where yet another environment can be seen.

In this area new arcuate dune ridges are developing, clothed only in marram and other grasses, and separated from one another by strips of salt marsh still flooded by the spring tides (Fig. 85). These young foredunes develop on a foundation of beach ridges built up on the foreshore by the action of constructive waves. The runnels between the ridges form the initial stage of marsh slack development. An earlier stage of this development can be seen at the southern end of Skegness, where since 1957 a series of high ridges have been built up on the foreshore separated from each other by muddy runnels. The ridges nearer the shore became stabilised behind newer ones growing to seaward. The beach ridges on this coast trend slightly away from the coast southwards and move steadily south along the coast, thus on any one line across the beach they appear to move gradually landwards. When the northern end has become stabilised by the growth of a ridge to seaward the southern end of the ridge continues to move shoreward, thus creating the characteristic arcuate shape. Once the beach ridge has been built up by the waves to the limit reached by spring tides, wind-blown sand can accumulate around the growing clumps of vegetation, while halophytes can grow in the muddy runnels.

The foreshore in south Lincolnshire is considerably wider than that north of Skegness, and is characterised by well-developed beach ridges down to about mean sea-level. Below this it is much flatter and near Gibraltar Point becomes muddy and soft. This type of lower foreshore can only develop where wave action is negligible at low water. This occurs south of Skegness because there are offshore banks in this area. These dry out at low water and prevent effective wave action on the foreshore when the tide is low. The offshore banks provide the final shore type found on this coast and play an important part in the development of the coastal features. Thus all the different environments in the area are acted upon and are built up by a combination of different processes.

In the offshore zone the tide is of fundamental importance in shaping the offshore banks. These elongated banks are built up in an area where the tidal streams are rectilinear, as they are off the Lincolnshire coast, flowing south with the flood tide and north with the ebb. Banks only form in an area where there is an abundance of loose sediment such as is available at the mouth of The Wash and within it. Between the banks a pattern of interdigitating tidal channels is formed by the tidal streams; the flood stream tends to continue in one channel after the ebb has set-in in an adjacent one, thus different channels become used and shaped predominantly by either the ebb or flood tide. The channel lying off the coast near Gibraltar Point is used predominantly by the flood tide which attains a speed of four knots at some states of the tide. The active flow in this channel is clearly indicated by the very coarse, poorly-sorted sediment that lies on its floor. Between the nearest bank and those further offshore is a double set of ebb channels shoaling in a northerly direction. Thus movement of sediment in the area is complex and is predominantly along the channels, to the south down the flood channels and north along the ebb channels. However, as Robinson's experiments have shown, sediment can reach the beach from offshore in the area to the south of Skegness, although by a very circuitous route, dependent almost entirely on the residual movement of the tidal currents. The banks themselves are formed of fine, firm sand and show clear evidence of tidal action in the series of ebb sand waves on their crests as they emerge at low water.

On the foreshore itself waves play the most important part in shaping the profile. The dominant waves are the long swells that come mainly from the north, and it is these constructive waves that build up the ridges on the foreshore. The slight divergence of the ridges offshore to the south is in response to the direction from which the refracted long swells approach the beach. The material that has allowed the active outbuilding in the Gibraltar Point area is probably derived mainly from the north, partly by beach drifting along the foreshore, by wave action and partly by being brought into the area by residual tidal currents along the channels. The southerly movement of material along the beach is responsible for the formation of the spit, and this is built up by the action of the constructive waves, moving the sand and shingle shoreward. Mud probably comes mainly from rivers draining into The Wash, e.g. the Steeping river which enters the sea near Gibraltar Point.

In the dunes the wind, aided by sand-loving plants, plays the essential part; in the marsh slacks, too, it is the wind carrying the sand which forms dune slacks once the tide has been excluded. These are often colonised by sea buckthorn, as are also some of the dune ridges in the stage following their colonisation by marram and other grasses. Vegetation also plays a very important part in the salt marsh, where the tide is also essential in accumulating muddy sediment. The mature marsh and the new marsh illustrate very clearly the two main stages of marsh development. The former, in the salting stage, has well-developed creeks, through which the tide gains access to the marsh, and this is only flooded at high spring tides. Salt pans are well developed and the vegetation pattern makes evident the formation of natural levées round the creeks. This marsh is only changing slowly at the present time. The new salt marsh, on the other hand, is undergoing very active accretion and is flooded by high water at all stages of the tide except extreme neaps. The rapid upgrowth of this new marsh is partly the result of the stage of development and partly due to the predominance of *Spartina townsendii* amongst its flora. This plant is an extremely effective trapper of silt and thrives in sloppy mud, such as is found in the new marsh. Thus tide, waves, wind and vegetation, together with the availability of very varied sediment, combine to create a zone of coastal accretion of great interest in the Gibraltar Point area.

THE VEGETATION OF GIBRALTAR POINT

The Lincolnshire coast shows features of the active deposition of shingle, sand and mud and of the colonisation and stabilisation of these deposits by vegetation. A site which shows these features to advantage is Gibraltar Point, an area extending southwards from Skegness to the entrance of The Wash, now managed by the Lincolnshire Naturalists' Trust as a Nature Reserve. This coastal strip consists of a series of dune ridges sub-parallel to one another and to the coast-line, the landward ridge being continuous whilst the remainder to seaward are discontinuous. The latter are separated from each other and from the continuous ridge by lagoon-like saltings which are connected with the open sea by tidal channels. Offshore are several sandbanks sub-parallel to the dunes and separated from them by a wide beach, which itself may comprise one or two low ridges of shingly-sand (see Fig. 85A). It is on such beach ridges, once they have been raised above high tide level, that sand dune formation is initiated. The supply of sand for this dune formation is brought by on-shore winds from the beach when it is exposed at low tide. The wind-blown sand may be trapped initially by tidal debris consisting largely of dead sponges lying at the various high tide mark drift lines.

The plant species form two natural groups: (i) the annual foreshore plants such as prickly saltwort (*Salsola kali*), sea rocket (*Cakile maritima*) and orach (*Atriplex hastata*); and (ii) the perennial grasses, notably sea couch grass (*Agropyron junceiforme*), marram grass (*Ammophila arenaria*) and occasionally sea lyme grass (*Elymus arenarius*), which are the major dune builders. Periodically one or more annual foreshore plants may accumulate a limited amount of sand but the development of embryo dune formation relies on the perennial grasses. The outermost of the discontinuous dune ridges (Fig. 85B) has been built up sufficiently high for a permanent plant population to be maintained, but, in addition, on its seaward side, there usually occurs a well-developed drift line whose plant population of annual foreshore species varies from year to year. (Plate XXIV.)

The vegetation above the drift zone and on the dune crest is chiefly *Agropyron junceiforme*, *Ammophila arenaria* and *Festuca rubra*. On the sheltered landward slope is a more varied collection of plants including those just mentioned, together with sea holly (*Eryngium maritimum*) and a number of plants primarily of open habitats and not specifically dune species, notably ragwort (*Senecio jacobea*). The sea buckthorn (*Hippophaē rhamnoides*) occurs as isolated bushes of three to six years old which give rise to numbers of young aerial shoots from their extensive horizontal roots. The middle dune ridges (Fig. 85C) are all rather similar, though there is a general increase in height moving landward through the series. Most tend to have an abundance of *Agropyron junceiforme*, *Festuca rubra* and *Ammophila arenaria* on their lower slopes and in open areas, and an extensive and more or less impenetrable stand of *Hippophaē rhamnoides* with dewberry (*Rubus caesius*) and cleavers (*Galium aparine*) on their broad

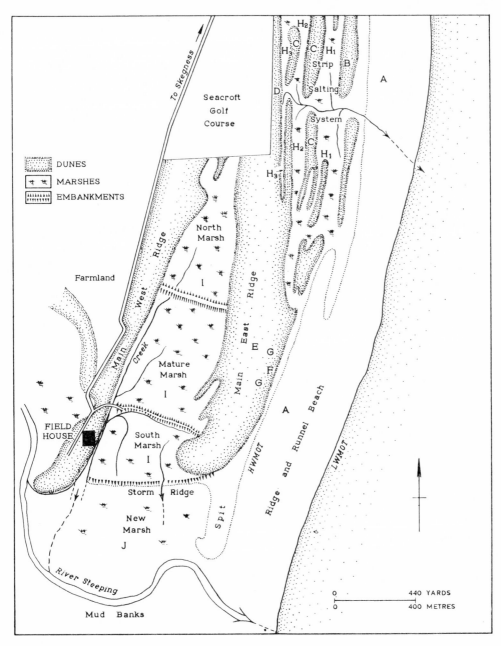

Fig. 85   Surface form and vegetation at Gibraltar Point
(*For explanation, see text*)

crests. In this central part of the coastal strip, where there are several middle dune ridges, the next landward ridge (Fig. 85D) is the highest and abuts on to the golf course, which is itself a modified complex of ridges. The seaward slope of this ridge, looking out over the others, is very steep and exposed. The *Hippophaë* bushes are smaller and the population less dense, forming an open stand with the herb associates, including *Rubus caesius, Festuca rubra, Arrhenatherum elatius, Galium aparine, Agropyron junceiforme* and *Festuca pratensis*. Further south in the Reserve the innermost of the middle dune ridges joins with the golf course boundary ridge to form another complex (Fig. 85E). This is of special interest because it supports the best dune grass-heath of the area. The principal species are *Rubus caesius* and *Festuca rubra*, while other characteristic species are *Poa compressa*, dove's foot cranesbill (*Geranium molle*), storksbill (*Erodium cicutarium*), common vetch (*Vicia sativa*), lady's bedstraw (*Galium verum*), hawksbeard (*Crepis capillaris*), ragwort (*Senecio jacobea*), germander speedwell (*Veronica chamaedrys*), *Carex arenaria* and *Anacamptis pyramidalis*. Mosses, particularly *Hypnum cupressiforme* and lichens, notably *Peltigera canina* help to makes this a very closed community. Between this ridge complex and the fore dune ridge in this locality is a hollow (Fig. 85F and 85G) with dense stands of *Hippophaë* of various ages, most of which have a fringe of young plants actively invading the surrounding dune grass-heath. The older stands, which are about 20 years of age and 10 to 12 feet high, form impenetrable thickets and consequently have few associated species, *Urtica dioica* being the most common (Pearson and Rodgers, 1962). The climax vegetation is scrub dominated by *Hippophaë* and with a small amount of elder (*Sambucus nigra*) and occasionally privet (*Ligustrum vulgare*). Elder trees both as individuals and in small groups are found infrequently throughout the fixed dune vegetation.

The saltings or salt marshes differ markedly both in their vegetation and in their substrate from those of the sand dunes. This difference is due to the direct influence of the sea which covers the habitat for varying periods of time. The substrate consists of water-borne particles, mainly fine muds and silts, and only a small amount of wind-blown sand. The plants occupying this habitat are mainly halophytes and their distribution on the floor of the salting is dependent on their ability to withstand submergence by the tide for varying periods; only marginally where the saltings abut directly on to sand dunes are exceptions found. The salt marshes at Gibraltar Point, whilst not as extensive as those bordering The Wash between Gibraltar Point and Boston, e.g. Freiston Shore, have examples of all the East Coast salt marsh communities. Often very localised changes of habitat conditions show how critically these control the distribution of the vegetation. In the lagoon-like saltings between the discontinuous dune ridges in the central part of the Gibraltar Point Reserve there is some creek and 'pan' development. Both these features may originate from the uneven nature of the surface of a marsh, brought about by the differential growth rates, growth forms and silt-trapping powers of salt marsh plants. Tidal waters meandering amongst the hummocks select the lowest pathways through the marsh and deepen and straighten them to form the main drainage channels or creeks. Those hollows, which are not drained and contain water for varying periods of time after being filled by a tide, are termed pans. This water may slowly evaporate, giving rise to high salinities and so preventing colonisation by marsh plants, or may slowly percolate away, permitting limited colonisation by plants such as *Spartina* and *Salicornia*. If the tidal scour is insufficient to keep channels open, blockages lead to the development of a series of channel pans. The floors of the creeks are the lowest parts of the saltings and have no vegetation. Where under-cutting has taken place causing parts of the banks to slump and form ledges, these support sea poa (*Puccinellia maritima*) and seablite (*Suaeda maritima*). Redeposited mud on the inside of creek meanders supports glasswort or marsh samphire (*Salicornia stricta*) and Cord-grass (*Spartina townsendii*). The name *Spartina townsendii* was given originally to a slender male sterile plant but was later applied to a more vigorous and fertile form. Whilst the latter is regarded as a different species it is still un-named and retains the name *S. townsendii*. It is this plant which is found in abundance in these Lincolnshire salt marshes. The naked creeks are often bordered by *Spartina* and where levées are present these support sea-purslane (*Halimione portulacoides*). The deeper pans have no vegetation whilst the shallow pans may have *Spartina townsendii* and sea-arrow grass (*Triglochin maritima*). The vegetation of the outermost salting (Fig. 85H₁) is typically a mixture of *Suaeda maritima*, sea aster (*Aster tripolium*), scurvy grass (*Cochlearia officinialis*), *Halimione portulacoides*, sea lavender (*Limonium* spp.), *Puccinellia maritima*, and *Spergularia marginata*. The middle saltings (Fig. 85H₂) have a turf of *Puccinellia maritima* with frequent *Suaeda maritima* and *Salicornia stricta*, and occasional *Halimione*, *Aster* and *Limonium* spp. In wetter parts is *Spartina townsendii* whilst in the sandier parts is sea milkwort (*Glaux maritima*) and sea hard-grass (*Parapholis strigosa*). The innermost salting (Fig. 85H₃) has a well-developed sward of *Puccinellia maritima* with an under-storey of *Salicornia stricta* and *Suaeda maritima*; there are a few pans with *Spartina* and abundant *Salicornia*. Collins studied the development of the salting-dune system in this central part of the Reserve, with particular reference to the influence of tides and of vegetation. In the southern part of the Reserve is an extensive mature marsh (Fig. 85I) contained behind a dune complex to the east and a storm beach to the south. Briefly this mature marsh supports three main plant communities. The first is dominated by a dense stand of *Halimione portulacoides* with *Puccinellia*, *Suaeda maritima* and *Salicornia stricta* represented by very few plants in an under-storey. The second has *Puccinellia* and *Limonium* spp. (*Limonium vulgare* and *L. humile*) co-dominant; the *Puccinellia* forming a continuous sward and the *Limonium* occurring as individuals and as clumps of varying sizes. Other species present include *Spergularia marginata*, *Aster tripolium*, *Plantago maritima* and *Cochlearia marginata*. The third community is an almost pure stand of *Agropyron pungens* and is situated on higher and better drained sites than those of the other two communities. Barnes and King, in their studies of salt marsh development at Gibraltar Point, have carried out complete surveys of the New Marsh (Fig. 85J), which lies to the south of the storm beach, on two occasions, the first in 1951 and the second in 1959. From their data and from personal records, perhaps the most striking change in the vegetation is the rapid extension of *Spartina townsendii* from a few isolated small clumps to an extensive sward and several widely scattered clumps. The original *Salicornia-Suaeda* association containing a little *Halimione*, has followed the line of normal salt marsh succession and is now becoming dominated by *Halimione* and with *Aster* and *Puccinellia* now well represented, though previously absent.

SELECTED REFERENCES

GEOMORPHOLOGY

King, C. A. M. and Barnes, F. A. Changes in the configuration of the inter-tidal beach zone of part of the Lincolnshire coast since 1951. *Zeitschrijft für Geomorphologie* Vol. 8 (1964), pp. 105–126.

King, C. A. M. The character of the offshore zone and its relationship to the foreshore near Gibraltar Point, Lincolnshire. *East Midland Geographer* Vol. 3 (1964) pp. 230–243.

Robinson, A. H. W. The inshore waters, sediment supply and coastal changes of part of Lincolnshire. *East Midland Geographer* Vol. 3 No. 22 (1964) pp. 307–321.

Swinnerton, H. H. The Post-glacial deposits of the Lincolnshire coast. *Quarterly Journal of the Geological Society* Vol. 87 (1931) pp. 360–375.

VEGETATION

Barnes, F. A. and King, C. A. M. Salt marsh development at Gibraltar Point, Lincolnshire. *East Midland Geographer* Vol. 2 (1961) pp. 20–31.

Pearson, M. C. and Rodgers, J. A. Hippophaê rhamnoides, Biological Flora of British Isles. *Journal of Ecology* Vol. 50 (1962) pp. 501–513.

PART VI

SCIENTISTS, INVENTORS AND TECHNOLOGISTS

XXVIII

SCIENTISTS, INVENTORS AND TECHNOLOGISTS

SCIENTISTS

One of the supreme figures in the culture of the western civilisation, Isaac Newton, was born on Christmas Day in the year 1642, in which Galileo, whose work he came to fulfil, died. Newton's birthplace was in the hamlet of Woolsthorpe, near Colsterworth, a few miles south of Grantham. Since the hamlet has been absorbed by the village of Colsterworth it is necessary to distinguish this Woolsthorpe from another in the same county of Lincolnshire, near Belvoir Castle.

Newton's discovery of the theory of fluxions, a pragmatic type of the differential calculus, his work on gravitation, astronomy, the binomial theorem and his *Principia Mathematica* are well-known. His unorthodox writings in religion which he regarded as important, his dabbling with alchemy and his notable services to the Mint when the currency was being changed, are sometimes forgotten. His investigations in acoustics and optics put him into the first rank as an experimenter, though even he did not see the possibility of making achromatic lens-combinations and optical diffraction phenomena which would have provided him with useful clues concerning the propagation of light.

Nevertheless, the dualism of particle and wave, which still bedevils so much physics, was inherent in his corpuscular theory. Goethe, with all his philosophy and insight into Nature, seems to be at least a century before Newton and not, in fact, a century later.

There are many associations with Newton in the Grantham district and the villages to the south of it. As a child and youth, Newton often stayed at Stoke Rochford Hall, near to his birthplace, and now the building which houses one of the Colleges of Education associated with the University of Nottingham. A large stone obelisk in the park in front of the Hall records this. In the village of Boothby Pagnall, in the year of the Plague, Newton calculated π to many places of decimals, thereby 'rectifying the ellipse', an operation closely related to 'squaring the circle'. In the market-place at Grantham there is a statue to him and near this, above the town library, a Newton museum. King's School, Grantham, where he was a pupil, still treasures the carving of his name on a window frame and he attended the parish church when he lodged nearby. On an internal wall at Colsterworth Church is a stone sun-dial which he carved as a boy. Newton died in 1727.

A mathematician whose stature has seemed to grow with the passage of years is George Boole, LL.D., D.C.L., F.R.S. (1815–1864), famous for his work on algebraical logic, sometimes called logical algebra. Boole, the son of a cobbler, whose real interests were in optics and mathematics, was born at the corner of Silver Street, Lincoln. George had lessons in Latin from a local bookseller and taught himself Greek, French and German from borrowed books. A translation, *Ode to Spring*, was his first published work, when he was 14. He became an usher in a school at Doncaster for a short time and then returned to Lincoln, where in the local village of Waddington, he continued to teach for 18 years. At the age of 20 he opened a school of his own and from 1840 his Academy was at 3 Pottergate, since then the house of the Cathedral organist.

Boole had a strong sense of the obligations of citizenship; he not only gave free lessons in classics and mathematics at the Mechanics' Institute but took an active interest in the Female Penitents' Home and the Lincoln Early Closing Association. He was a keen student of the works of Isaac Newton. His combined interest in both Latin and mathematics led him to the idea that algebraic formulae might be used to express logical relations. His contemporary C. L. Dodgson (Lewis Carroll) had similar ideas, but because he had so many other interests and perhaps smaller powers of concentration, failed to develop this work to the same degree as Boole.

Although it was suggested by his friends that he should take a Fellowship at Cambridge, he refused this in order that he could continue to support his aged parents. His mathematical papers in the Cambridge Mathematical Journal (1840) secured for him the Chair of Mathematics at Queen's College, Cork. In 1855 he married Mary Everest, niece of Sir George Everest, after whom the famous mountain is named. Of five daughters three showed exceptional ability. One became the first woman chemistry professor in England, at the Royal Free Hospital, and another, Ethel Voynich, published a number of novels and some music. Boole died on 8th December 1864 and was buried in the churchyard of St. Michael's, Blackrock, County Cork. Stained glass windows to his memory can be seen in Lincoln Cathedral and in University College, the former Queen's College, at Cork. Boole's major publications are: 'A General Method of Analysis' in *Phil. Trans.* (1844); *Mathematical Analysis of Logic* (1847); *The Laws of Thought* (1854); *Treatise on Differential Equations* (1859); *Calculus of Finite Differences* (1860). Thus was mathematical logic founded, and since then has been applied to the design of modern electronic computers. The centenary of Boole's death was celebrated in Lincoln on 7th November 1964, when his grandson, Sir Geoffrey Taylor, F.R.S., Fellow of Trinity College, Cambridge, unveiled a plaque to his memory on the house at 3 Pottergate, Lincoln.

George Green (1793–1841), one of the leading applied mathematicians of his age, might have reached even greater heights had he not been dogged by ill-health during much of his short life. He was born and died in Sneinton, an east suburb of Nottingham. His father was a man of means and a miller, and the mill was prominent in the district until it was destroyed by fire a few years ago. Green extended the work of Laplace and Gauss and was particularly interested in the problem of flow and propagation of waves in various media. His work on gravitational, electrical and magnetic attraction led him to introduce the concept of potential. Also he was an innovator of the principle of 'conservation of work'. He entered Caius College in 1833, five years after the publication of his remarkable *Essay on the application of mathematical analysis to the theories of electricity and magnetism*. Although he was placed Fourth Wrangler in 1837, as a mathematician he stood head and shoulders above all his companions in and outside of the University.

Another mathematician, Philip E. B. Jourdain (1879–1919), would have obtained greater distinction had his life not been disturbed and prematurely terminated by a rare hereditary disease of the central nervous system, Friedreich's ataxia. Jourdain was the son of a Derbyshire vicar. He was educated at Cheltenham College, at Cambridge and Heidelberg, and showed considerable creative ability as a mathematician at this time. He contributed, between 1906 and 1912, masterly papers, chiefly on the Theory of Transfinite Numbers to the *Quarterly Journal of Mathematics* and to the *Archiv der Mathematik und Physik*. He was also editor of *Isis* and *The Monist*. Jourdain was unable to walk after the age of 21 but his mind was so active that he kept two typists constantly at work. He is remembered today chiefly by his little book, *The Nature of Mathematics*, which has been reprinted lately by Professor Newman in his collection *The World of Mathematics*. Jourdain edited the mathematical works of De Morgan and Boole and wrote articles on other mathematicians such as Galois, Poincaré and Dedekind when the importance of their work was not widely appreciated in Britain. He was able to find his way in the most complex and esoteric mathematical operations and, at the same time, the clarity of his mind, his grasps of essentials and his simple, fluent style as a writer of English made him a vulgariser, in the best sense of the word.

John Flamsteed (1646–1719), the first Astronomer Royal, who established the Royal Observatory, which until recent times was at Greenwich, was born in Denby, about five miles from Derby, in August 1646. His father was a maltster. From childhood Flamsteed suffered from rheumatism and underwent operations and endured various forms of primitive treatment for it. It is surprising therefore that he lived to the age of 73. As a youth, Flamsteed spent much time at Wingfield Manor, famous for its connection with Mary, Queen of Scots, where his friend, Imanuel Halton, had a library. Flamsteed became a clerk in Holy Orders and was given a small living near Derby. His astronomical calculations and star maps were well-known in London, where he settled in 1673. Two years later he established the Royal Observatory, built by Christopher Wren in Greenwich, principally as an aid to shipping. Both as a practical observer and an astronomical calculator he achieved international fame for his accuracy and persistence. He was associated with Newton in their mutual astronomical interests, but later seems to have tried to impede Newton's work by seeking to deny him the tables necessary for his calculations. This is probably a strong reason why Flamsteed has not always been given his proper place in the history of British science. Flamsteed retired to the living of Burslow in Surrey in 1684 and died in 1719.

Henry Cavendish (1731–1810) was a descendant on both his mother's and father's sides of one of the best-known families of the region, that of the Duke of Devonshire. The Hon. Henry Cavendish was the elder of two sons of Lord Charles Cavendish, the third son of the Duke of Devonshire. He was born at Nice, went to St. Peter's College (Peterhouse), Cambridge, in 1749 but did not graduate. For 10 years there is little record of what he did. He became a Fellow of the Royal Society in 1760 and thereafter experimented with various 'airs'. He produced an eudiometer and found that hydrogen burns to water. His great metrical skill as an experimenter is seen in his researches to find, by using relatively small apparatus, the universal gravitational constant G and, therefrom, the mean density of the earth. So accurate were his measurements that there was practically no improvement in them for another century. He experimented much with the frictional and atmospheric electricity and communicated his findings to Gilbert White, the naturalist and curate of Selbourne, near Basingstoke.

Cavendish had residences at the corner of Gower Street and Montague Place, in Dean Street, Soho, and in Clapham Common, London. Cavendish was entirely ungregarious, but he had a profound respect for his fellow scientists and was free from jealousy. He would never sit for an artist and the only portrait of him was obtained surreptitiously. He was buried in All Saints' Church, now the Cathedral, in Derby in the family tomb provided by his ancestress of Queen Elizabeth's time, Bess of Hardwick. He left one and a half million pounds, a tremendous sum, which might be multiplied by a factor of 15 or 20 to give an idea of its present value. Cavendish's work was appreciated in France, even at the time of the Revolution: "le plus riche de tous les savants et probablement le plus savant des tous les riches".

Of interest in the immediate locality of the University is the Lowe family, who lived in the house which was the first existing building on the University site and is now the residence of the Vice-Chancellor. The family, one of the best-known in Nottinghamshire, traced its ancestry to George Lowe, who died in Witton, near Chester, in 1591. His descendant, Joseph Hurst Lowe, a wealthy 'landed' gentleman, was a founder of the Nottingham Mechanics' Institution and was a member of the Meteorological Society from its commencement. He built a tall, octagonal observatory, now derelict, near Beeston Station. He made daily observations of the weather and nocturnal observations of the firmament, and continued them until 31st July 1856, only 10 days before his death. Under his will, the Highfield Estate became the property of his son Edward Joseph Lowe, who was born in Highfield

House on 11th November 1825. At the age of 15 he started his daily meteorological observations and continued them until 1882 when he left the district in order to live in Shirenewton Hall in Monmouthshire.

As a young man of 21 he published an important book: *A Treatise on Atmospheric Phenomena*. Although this was written in simple language it was of considerable scientific value because for the first time a careful distinction was made between electrical phenomena in the atmosphere and meteorites (matter rendered incandescent by collision with the earth's atmosphere). The Lowes had three observatories in the district: the tall building near Beeston Station; cupolas at the top of Broadgate House, now occupied by the University Air Squadron; and instruments on the high ground near Highfield House. Simultaneous plottings of the paths of the meteorites, made from the different observatories, would enable estimates of the heights of the meteors to be obtained. In those days considerable sections of the Proceedings of the British Association were devoted to meteors and E. J. Lowe was a member of a committee which dealt with them. In association with G. Dolland, F.R.S., the founder of a firm of instrument makers which still flourishes today, he described, in the Proceedings of the year 1846, a weather station which would register its findings on paper, if not continuously, certainly at intervals. Lowe worked hard to establish an observatory in Nottingham but in spite of his efforts and financial backing the project was unsuccessful. Although Beeston, between the railway and the river, is notorious for its fogs, it used to happen that the appearance of fogs in Beeston and Greenwich was not often simultaneous. Thus, observations which were denied to the Astronomer Royal at Greenwich were made, as a result of telegraphed instructions, in Beeston. In 1867, Lowe, though a non-graduate, was elected as a Fellow of the Royal Society. He saw clearly the conditions which would be necessary for a successful system of weather-forecasting. He published in 1849 *Prognostications of the Weather*. Later he became interested in botany and geology. He published a *Conchology of Nottinghamshire* which Professor Edward Forbes incorporated in his compilation of the British Mollusca. He wrote books on British grasses and ferns. He was particularly interested in the hybridization of plants and was the first to cross successfully the British ferns *Polysticulum angulare* and *Polysticulum aculeatum*. He was one of the first to send daily weather telegrams to the Government Meteorological Office, established under Admiral Fitzroy. He was one of the last and greatest of the scientific amateurs, men of means who could devote most of their time and energies to their hobbies and the cultural subjects of which to him the most important was 'natural philosophy'. Today the weather station of the Geography Department of the University makes continuous records only a few yards from the site of Lowe's station at Highfield House.

Amongst distinguished men of science who visited and worked in the district we may mention the naturalist John Ray (1627–1705) who was a friend of the Willoughby family which owned Wollaton and Middleton Halls. Wollaton Park is separated from the University grounds by a few yards—the width of Derby Road. Wollaton Hall, an excellent specimen of domestic architecture in the Italian Renaissance style, is now a natural history museum belonging to the Nottingham City Corporation. Ray explored the Park and wrote of its flora and fauna. The French philosopher and musician Jean Jacques Rousseau (1712–1778) visited the Duke of Devonshire at Chatsworth House in Derbyshire. At that time Rousseau had interested himself in the hybridization of plants. He brought seeds from the gardens of Paris and broadcast them in Dovedale. It is probably fanciful to think that any plants which appear today in Dovedale are descended from those introduced by Rousseau.

The German chemist Robert Bunsen (1811–1899) was employed as a consultant to the Alfreton Ironworks for a short time. This Company was early in the field of utilization of furnace gases and since Bunsen had obtained European fame for his work in gas analysis, he devised the burner named after him and he visited Derbyshire to give his expert advice. It nearly proved fatal for him, because in the course of his investigations for the Company he was poisoned with carbon monoxide and was put to bed for several days until he recovered.

One of the greatest of the organic chemists of his age was Frederic Stanley Kipping (1863–1949), who occupied the Chair of Chemistry at University College, Nottingham, for 39 years. Kipping was born in Higher Broughton, Manchester, and went to Manchester Grammar School. He entered Owen's College, Manchester, in 1879 and took the London B.Sc. degree with second class honours in zoology at the age of 19. Thereafter he became a chemist in the Manchester Gas Department, and learnt the foundations of his work as an accurate and scrupulous researcher. In 1886, he went to Munich to work in Von Baeyer's laboratories where he met W. H. Perkin Junior, and thus began a long and happy association which produced, amongst other writings, two important text books. He took a Ph.D. degree in Munich and one year later, at the age of 24, the D.Sc. London. After serving as Perkin's assistant at the Heriot-Watt College in Edinburgh and H. E. Armstrong's at Imperial College, London, he was elected to the Royal Society and also to the Chair of Chemistry at Nottingham in 1897 at the age of 34.

Kipping produced a series of 'organic' derivatives of silicon, analogous to carbon compounds. This discovery came some decades too early for him to benefit from an industry worth many millions of pounds. The silicones are basic to substances which make insulators, rubber substitutes, polishes, lubricants, plastics and water-proofing and roofing media, all of which are stable under severe thermal conditions. British industry was uninterested in his discoveries and in 1932 the Dow Corning Corporation in the United States started researches into the practical applications of the silicones. The processes, like those for the production of penicillin, were patented and now our public have to pay royalties for substances discovered by their own countrymen. Kipping published his last paper at the age of 81, and died five years later.

Ambrose Fleming (1849–1935) who is remembered for his pioneer work in electrical engineering and electronics, in particular his part in the development of the thermionic valve, served the University College for a short time as its first Professor of Mathematics and Physics. Amongst other distinguished scientists and teachers who have occupied Chairs in the University College during the earlier years of the present century were H. H. Swinnerton, the geologist, whose contributions to palaeontology were of great importance, and E. H. Barton, who collaborated, as a junior, with Heinrich Hertz in his work on the properties of electromagnetic waves and was well-known as an acoustician in his later years. In recent years L. F. Bates, F.R.S., who occupied the Chair of Physics, did important work in magnetism.

The University College was a pioneer in the use of X-rays for diagnostic purposes. Mr. Simpson, a lecturer in physics, collaborated with the surgeons of the Nottingham General Hospital within a few weeks of the publication of Röntgen's paper in December 1895. *The Lancet*, 28th March 1896, printed some remarkable fracture photographs taken in Nottingham only three months after Röntgen's discovery. The original cathode-ray tubes which were used are preserved in the Electrical Engineering Department of the University.

INVENTORS AND TECHNOLOGISTS

Many of the industries of the Nottingham region have developed, directly or indirectly, from the invention of the stocking frame in the locality in the 16th century. This machine was contrived by the Reverend William Lee, a native of Woodborough (a village seven miles north of Nottingham) and subsequently curate of the adjacent parish of Calverton. The early career of this Renaissance genius is obscure. All that can be said for certain is that his invention was perfected by 1589, when he made an unsuccessful claim for a royal patent to protect his invention. Lee's frame, 'a prodigy of complicated and delicate mechanism', was not improved on for more than a century and a half, and frames built on Lee's principles continued in general use up to the end of last century. The modern power-driven machine making fully-fashioned work has the same essential features.

In the first half of the 18th century the use of the frame was extended from worsted yarn to silk and cotton and in the second half various devices were added to the frame for producing patterns in the mesh. Jedediah Strutt, a Derby hosier, patented the first of a long series of attachments to the frame in 1758. The success of his 'Derby rib' hose encouraged many other experiments to produce new meshes and garments on the frame.

William Hayne, a hosier who migrated to Nottingham from Ashbourne, Derbyshire, in 1773, perfected an open mesh known as 'point net'. The net was embroidered by women outworkers, and formed the basis of the Nottingham lace manufacture. From the time of Hayne most of the mechanical talent of the neighbourhood was employed in trying to improve the production of lace net, and after the beginning of the 19th century hosiery lost its earlier dynamism as the most talented men in the industry migrated into the infant lace industry. Framework knitting became an overcrowded occupation, and wages were so poor that the application of power to the hosiery frame was delayed until the middle of the 19th century.

The stimulus of competition from Saxony and Belgium initiated an intense period of experimenting to apply power after 1845. In the vanguard of these developments was Moses Mellor, a Nottingham framesmith who improved upon a circular frame (or *tricoteur*) invented by I. K. Brunel in 1816. The circular frame produced a tube the width of a stocking leg, which was then seamed and sewn into shape. The credit for producing the first fully fashioned hose by power must go to Mellor's workman, Luke Barton. Four shaped leg pieces, ready for seaming, were produced by an automatic device to narrow the length of hose as it was knitted. However, the greatest advances in this type of machine were made by William Cotton, a mechanic employed by Cartwright and Warner of Loughborough. Cotton's patent rights were assigned to two large Nottingham firms, Hine and Mundella (Nottingham Manufacturing Company) and I. and R. Morley. Cotton himself established a firm at Loughborough which became one of the first of a new class of hosiery machine builders. This new industry found its main centres in Leicester and Loughborough, but Moses Mellor represented the interests of the Nottingham branch of the hosiery industry in this activity. Over the last century most innovations have come from the East Midlands hosiery machine builders and their American and German competitors. During this period the Cotton patent has been developed in both size and speed. Simultaneously there has been an increase in the fineness of gauge and yarn, notably for fully fashioned nylon stockings, which are now knitted in yarn of 10 denier, i.e. 0·0014 inch diameter.

The first lace net to be produced in Nottingham, as we have already noticed, was knitted on the stocking frame. However, before the close of the 18th century experiments were being made to *twist* net, that is to simulate the motions employed in making handmade (cushion) lace. The first to achieve commercial success was John Heathcoat, a Nottingham framesmith. His genius was to incorporate a number of earlier devices with his own improvements and produce a fast and regular hexagonal net. His bobbin net machine was patented in 1809. A generation of Nottingham framesmiths and other artisans laboured to improve upon Heathcoat's success. John Leavers, after whom the modern lace machine is named, was only one of a number of mechanics who devised improvements to Heathcoat's machine.

The embroidering of the net was a handicraft occupation until the 1830s, when repeated attempts were made to incorporate simple motifs into the net. The Jacquard system was already widely used to determine patterns in powerloom weaving, and its application to the lace machine seemed feasible. Hooton Deverill, another Nottingham mechanic, building on the improvements of a host of others, successfully applied the Jacquard principle to the Leavers machine in 1841. It proved possible to apply rotary power to the Deverill machine without any adverse effects to the fancy lace it produced, so that the lace industry rapidly moved into factories in the 1840s. The Deverill machine is identical in principle with the modern lace machine, an instrument of remarkable versatility which can produce all kinds of fancy laces from narrow breadths for trimmings to wide pieces for dresses.

Another kind of lace machine, for making lace curtains, is attributed to John Livesey, a Nottingham draughtsman. In the curtain machine the jacquard principle is applied to the original bobbin-net machine to make a patterned net with a bolder design than could be produced on the Deverill machine. This machine is similar in principle to that still in use in the much-contracted lace curtain industry in Nottingham.

The hosiery and lace industries consumed increasing quantities of worsted, cotton and silk thread, and this stimulus played an important part in the technical development of silk-reeling and cotton and worsted spinning. The first silk-reeling plant to be built in Britain was opened in Derby in 1721. The capital, said to amount to £30,000, was provided by a London merchant, Sir Thomas Lombe, and the technical direction by his half-brother, John Lombe, following a successful mission to Leghorn, Italy, as an industrial spy. According to one account, John Lombe, a native of Norwich, had previously served an apprenticeship at an earlier, but unsuccessful silk-reeling factory at Derby. The engineering problems of building on the soft soil of an island in the River Derwent and providing water power for the winding engines, eight spinning and four twisting machines, were overcome by George Sorocold. This ingenious engineer erected a great undershot water-wheel, 23 feet in diameter, which powered the whole plant for more than a century. The Derby silk mill is generally recognised as the first successful power factory in England.

It appears that Richard Arkwright first became acquainted with the East Midlands as an itinerant hair dealer. It is known that he stayed in Wirksworth for a period, a visit which would lead him to recognise both the possibilities of Cromford for water-power and Nottingham, the economic centre of gravity of the region, for recruiting capital. The declining lead-mining industry in Derbyshire offered ample cheap labour to a manufacturer. Arkwright's originality as an inventor is in some doubt; the spinning of cotton by rollers was achieved by Lewis Paul nearly 20 years before Arkwright began his career in the cotton industry. Arkwright's claim to genius lies rather in his successful and striking organisation of cotton spinning in factories, which was widely imitated in Lancashire, the West Riding, Scotland and the Midlands in the last 20 years of the 18th century. He is rightly recognised as the father of the factory system. James Hargreaves followed Arkwright from Lancashire to Nottingham with his 'jenny', but was much less successful. The jenny remained a hand-operated machine, while Arkwright's roller-spinning apparatus enjoyed the superior advantages of power, at first from horse capstans, then in turn from water wheels and rotary steam engines. The jenny held its own for four or five decades in Lancashire and the West Riding because, in weaving, roller spun yarn was only suitable for the woof, but in the hosiery manufacturing districts the hand-operated machine had no comparable advantage over mechanical power. Hargreaves and his partner Thomas James became licensees of Arkwright in 1777, only eight years after the inventor had left Lancashire.

The success of the inventions of Hargreaves, Arkwright and Crompton in spinning cotton suggested applications to the spinning of woollen and worsted yarns. Worsted was the original raw material of the hosiery industry, and several of the pioneers of mechanised worsted spinning opened factories in the East Midlands in the last two decades of the 18th century. It was not difficult to adjust a roller-spinning machine to worsted yarns—the technical problem involved no more than increasing the diameter of the front rollers and adjusting the distance between the back and front rollers. The real problem for the masters of the early worsted factories was to break the bottle-neck at the previous stage of production, combing the 'slivers' of wool for the spinning machines. The hand comber was able to produce better slivers with less waste almost up to the middle of the 19th century. Worsted spinners in the East Midlands were, however, responsible for the earliest attempts to imitate this art mechanically. The Reverend Edmund Cartwright, well-known as the inventor of an early power loom, secured the first patent for a combing machine (1789). Cartwright's factory was opened at Doncaster, but he came from a landed family at Marnham, Nottinghamshire. The royalties on his combing patent were shared with John Hawksley of the firm of Davison and Hawksley of Nottingham. After Cartwright gave up his small Doncaster mill in 1793 he relied on this firm to make practical experiments with his 'Big Ben' combing machine. Other wool-combing machines were developed by Toplis and Company at Mansfield and Worksop, and Dakeyne and Company at Darley Dale, near Matlock. The initiative in this development was lost to the West Riding early in the 19th century.

We have already noticed two crucial developments in the transition to the factory system of production that were introduced in the region. Lombe's Derby silk mill had rightly been recognised as the first successful power factory in England, though for nearly half a century it had few authentic successors. Arkwright copied the Derby mill and the phenomenal success of his factories called forth a host of imitators in the textile areas of the country, thus precipitating a transition to factory production, first in cotton spinning and then in other branches of the textile industry. Until the last decade of the 18th century, the typical factory was a simple timber-framed building, most vulnerable to fire. William Strutt, F.R.S., son of Arkwright's partner Jedediah Strutt, built the first multi-storey fire-resistant buildings, the Derby calico mill and the Milford cotton warehouse, both in 1792–1793. These industrial buildings were the starting point for an entirely new form of construction, the iron-framed building, from which the modern steel-framed structures have evolved. Strutt corresponded with the engineer Charles Bage, who was shortly responsible for iron-framed mills at Shrewsbury, Salford and Leeds.

The rapid growth of the hosiery industry during the second half of the 18th century also stimulated the growth of ancillary industries: dyeing, bleaching, machine building and engineering. Until the end of the eighteenth century, hosiery, like other fabrics, was bleached by the action of sunlight, and tenter fields could be seen in all the Leen-side parishes from Lenton to Papplewick. Robert Hall, a Basford bleacher and cotton spinner, was among the first in the country to use chlorine for bleaching on a large scale. He studied the works of Black, Scheele, Lavoisier and other early chemists, and corresponded with Priestley and Henry. The manufacture of bleaching and other textile machinery was developed in Nottingham by Manlove, Alliott & Co. Edward Manlove was the son of a framesmith whose firm was for a period (c.1815) the most successful infringers of Heathcoat's bobbin net machine patent. He formed a partnership with Alexander Alliott and together they developed the standardised machinery for most of the processes of hosiery manufacture: cleaning, drying, fulling, bleaching, dyeing and dressing. The firm were among the first to make automatic circular hosiery machines. Their interest in textile machinery led them to a specialised interest in steam boilers and pressure gauges.

The rapid growth of population which accompanied industrial expansion in the second half of the 18th century and in the 19th century presented its own problems to inventors and technologists—problems of water supply, sanitation and public health. In 1845 a government commissioner recognised Nottingham as the most congested and overcrowded industrial town in the country. Thomas Hawksley, F.R.S., son of the worsted spinner John Hawksley, was appointed engineer to the Trent Water Co. in 1830 at the age of 23. He designed and supervised the construction of a constant high pressure water supply to some 8,000 working-class houses in Nottingham. Hawksley's system demonstrated both the efficiency and economy of this method of water supply over older methods of accumulated supply. In 1844 Edwin Chadwick, in his famous Health of Towns Commission Report, gave national publicity to Hawksley's success, showing that piped water supply prevented the stagnation and contamination of drinking water and that cheap water was necessary for effective sanitation and cleansing. Hawksley subsequently became engineer or consulting engineer for schemes to provide water to Liverpool, Sheffield, Leicester and other large towns.

After the middle of the 19th century the lace and cotton spinning industries reached a plateau so far as innovations were concerned; there were no further major technical developments in either industry until after the second World War. The hosiery industry saw continued technical development through the remainder of the century, but the important innovations originated in Leicester, or in Germany or America. Hosiery and lace had become the great staples of the economy of the Nottingham region. It is equally true that this was a period in which new industries were introduced into the region, among others the manufacture of motor vehicles, bicycles, telephones, pharmaceutical products and artificial fibres. However, in these new industries the region did not provide the innovators so much as the engineering skill and capital necessary to develop and create a market for new manufactures. The most striking illustration of this point is provided by the firm of Rolls-Royce Ltd., whose first works were opened at Derby. The original partners were not local men, but chose Derby because it could provide the craftsmen necessary to produce the quality of work that they aspired to. The Raleigh Cycle Company did not invent the chain-driven bicycle, nor even the famous Sturmey-Archer three-speed hub on which the firm built its reputation after 1902. The Company was formed when Frank Bowden, a cycling enthusiast with capital, recognised the skill of a group of former hosiery mechanics who had begun to build a few bicycles in Nottingham. The British Celanese Company at Spondon (Derby) were not the pioneers of the artificial silk industry in Britain; the innovating entrepreneurs were Courtaulds of Coventry. The traditional interest of Derby in the silk industry provided the trading connections to encourage the foundation of the company. The histories of many smaller firms illustrate the same theme. It was not until such firms as those mentioned, and others like Boots the chemists, Ericssons Telephones, Stanton Ironworks and the Butterley Company were able to establish their own research divisions that technical progress was resumed in the region.

SELECTED REFERENCES

Chaloner, W. H. *People and Industries* (1963) Chapters 1 and 5.

Chapman, S. D. The Pioneers of Worsted Spinning by Power. *Business History* Vol. VII (1964).

Johnson, H. R. and Skempton, A. W. William Strutt's Fire Proof and Iron-Framed Buildings, 1792–1812. *Transactions of the Newcomen Society* Vol. XXX (1955–1956).

Varley, D. E. *The Midland Counties Lace Manufacturers' Association* (1959) Chapter 2.

Wells, F. A. Hosiery and Lace. *A History of Technology* (ed. Charles Singer) Vol. IV pp. 594–604.

APPENDICES

Appendix I

HISTORICAL NOTE CONCERNING CLIMATIC OBSERVATIONS

When the British Association met at Nottingham 100 years ago the Stevenson screen was about to be introduced (1866). Rainfall measurement was not yet standardised, and 15 years were to pass before a satisfactory sunshine recorder appeared. Therefore much care is needed in relating earlier observations to modern series.

A summary list of known observers and their records in the district before 1850 is given in Table L. Excluding Thomas Barker's remarkable rainfall series at Lyndon, Rutland (1736–98) the earliest known set of reasonably consistent weather observations is that compiled at Mansfield Woodhouse, Nottinghamshire, from 1785 to 1805 by Hayman Rooke whose daily observations of wind direction, temperature readings (taken at fixed hours), averages of rain days, snow days, days of frost and thunder, and monthly rainfall figures (1800–05 afford interesting comparisons with later records of Mansfield's climate. J. Swanwick's observations of temperature and rainfall in Derby from about 1794 also form an important series. Unfortunately records for Nottingham itself in the early 19th century are fragmentary, but taken together are sufficient to give a broad view of climatic conditions, while temperature readings for the period 1819–24 from several stations in and near the town illustrate local site variations and the effect of the urban environment on temperature. The full record of Matthew Needham at Lenton House (1809–40) has not been located, but A. S. H. and E. J. Lowe (1853) used it to derive ten-year temperature means for 1810–40 which, taking account of a north-wall exposure are remarkably consistent with modern averages. E. J. Lowe regarded this series as virtually homogeneous with his own extensive record at Beeston Observatory, and Highfield House, now the University Vice-Chancellor's residence, where readings span the period 1840–81. Of special note also are the observations of rainfall and wind at East Retford by J. S. Piercy from 1822 to 1865. From 1860 rainfall records became numerous enough for Henry Mellish to construct a mean rainfall map of Nottinghamshire for 1861–90 which differs little in essentials from the modern map. Colonel Henry Mellish, of Hodsock Priory, Worksop, was a president of the Royal Meteorological Society, and his very full meteorological record, beginning in 1876, was continued by his sister after his death in 1927 to give a run of about 60 years. Major T. L. K. Edge, at Strelley (1881–1931, with a break of four years), kept a rainfall record which was continued until recently by his daughter. The late Arnold B. Tinn, first at Burford Road and later at Woodthorpe, kept records for many years.

Interest in Nottingham's own climatic record was stimulated by the British Association meeting of 100 years ago, and the Corporation began its records in 1867. Unfortunately, homogeneity has been prejudiced by site changes, but the Nottingham Castle site has been unchanged since 1887. Trent Lane (later Sneinton Pumping Station) measured rainfall from 1903, and its other instruments were transferred to the Castle in 1924. Since it is located in the Trent Vale at 76 feet, and has distinctly more extreme climatic site characteristics than Nottingham Castle, care is needed in interpreting Nottingham records. Long homogeneous rainfall records exist (periods to 1960) near Nottingham at Stoke Bardolph (1879–1960), Strelley (1880–1958), Basford Waterworks (1891–1960), Papplewick Waterworks (1891–1960), Mapperley Hill (1882–1949), Burton Joyce Waterworks (1900–60), Ramsdale Hill Reservoir (1906–60) and Wilford Hill Reservoir (1907–60). Unfortunately climatic observations on the University campus have been fragmentary, for Needham's observations at Lenton House (1809–40) and Lowe's at Highfield House and 'Beeston Observatory', now the University Air Squadron Headquarters (1840–81), were not succeeded until rainfall was measured at Lenton Hall (now Hugh Stewart Hall) from 1912 to 1915. Lenton Fields operated a full station from 1920 to 1927, and observations were taken east of the central University buildings from 1936 to 1944, north of them from 1951 to 1957 and on another site from 1962, and at Lenton Experimental Station (Lenton House), 100 yards away, from 1952 onwards.

Table L Some early climatic records

Observer	Place	Period	Phenomena
H. Rooke	Mansfield Woodhouse	1785–1805	Wind direction; temperature (fixed hours); frost; snow; thunder
		1800–05	Rain
J. Swanwick	Derby Commercial Academy	1794–?	Temperature
		1809–35	Rain
		1816–32★	Wind direction
—	Chatsworth	1777–1807★	Rain
W. Thompson	West Bridgford	1794–98 (–1809?)	Rain
—	Langar	1794–96	Rain
Rev. Blanchard?	Nottingham	1800–07	Rain
Dr. Clarke	Nottingham (near St. Peter's)	1807–11	Rain; temperature (three fixed hours); (minimum temperature from 1808); wind direction
— — —	Nottingham town Standard Hill Fox Hill	1819–24	Temperature
M. Needham	Lenton	1809–40	Temperature (11 p.m., 8 a.m. and minimum; maximum from 1820)
—	Oxton	1819–20	Temperature
—	Leicester	1821–23★	Rain
Ab. Booth	Mansfield	1821–23★	Rain
J. S. Piercy	East Retford	1822–65	Rain, wind direction
—	Horncastle	1808–10★	

Table L (continued) Some early climatic records

Observer	Place	Period	Phenomena
Gen. Johnson	Wytham-on-the-Hill Bourne	1820–62	Rain (early exposure dubious)
Rev. H. S. Neucatre	Sleaford and South Kyme	1826–39 and 1840–64	Rain
Veall and Williams	Boston	1826–	Rain
—	Pode Hole	1829–	Rain
—	Boston	1816–54	Maximum and minimum temperature
R. S. Stone	Derby	1837–38	Various
J. Davis	Derby	1843–74	Rain
R. N. Harris	Nottingham, Bromley House	1836–41*	Rainfall; temperature; weather
—	Park Hill, Nottingham	1836	Temperature
—	General Hospital	1836	Rainfall; pressure
E. J. Lowe	Highfields House	1840–81	A range including rainfall and temperature
W. Tillery	Welbeck	1840–76	Rain
W. W. P. Clay	Southwell	1844–81	Rain

*Full extent of record not known.

There are references to temperature measured at Nottingham in 1768 and in Nottingham Meadows in 1798; at Tollerton (1823), Oxton (1819–20), Langwith, Derbyshire (1823), Basford (1808); and rainfall was measured at Hathersage (Bamford) and Hayfield (Kinderscout) in 1839–41. Minimum temperature was certainly measured at Welbeck through 1804. Misterton Soss Pumping Station in the lower Trent area was measuring rainfall in 1838.

Table LI Recorded late frosts

Year	Day of April	Day of May	Day of June	Nottingham—Trent Lane	Strelley Hall	Hodsock Priory	Southwell	Buxton	Nottingham Castle	Nottingham—Burford Road	Woodthorpe	Attenborough	
1868	13	—	—	25·8	—	—	—	—	—	—	—	—	Hodsock 24·5 on 16th April with snow
1876	—	3	—	—	—	25·2	—	19·0	—	—	—	—	
1877	1	—	—	28·0	—	23·0	—	—	—	—	—	—	
	—	6	—	23·8	—	24·0	—	—	—	—	—	—	
1878	—	3	—	25·0	—	23·8	—	—	—	—	—	—	Destroyed wall fruit
1879	4	—	—	28·0	24·8	21·9	—	—	—	—	—	—	Beacon Scoop 21·0
1881	—	11	—	27·1	29·3	27·1	—	27·7	—	—	—	—	Mansfield 27·7, Oakamoor 26·6. Damage to many crops
1883	1	—	—	24·8	26·0	23·3	—	—	—	—	—	—	
1884	23	—	—	25·1	26·7	23·6	—	22·0	—	—	—	—	
1885	4	—	—	26·1	27·0	20·7	—	20·8	—	—	—	—	Belper 24·4
1887	18	—	—	28·9	—	24·6	24·2	24·5	—	—	—	—	
	—	1	—	30·8	—	26·2	24·4	22·1	—	—	—	—	
1888	6	—	—	22·8	—	23·2	22·2	23·8	—	—	—	—	Burton 25·0
1890	2	—	—	23·2	—	24·8	21·6	—	—	—	—	—	Loughborough 23
1891	1	—	—	25·2	—	23·4	22·3	—	—	—	—	—	Belper 23·1, Burton 20·6, Lincoln 25·0, Hesley Hall 20
1892	19	—	—	23·5	—	20·7	22·2	17·1	—	—	—	—	Belper 28·7, Burton 25·9
1893	—	1	—	28·9	—	29·2	23·8	27·6	—	—	—	—	Burton 24·7
1894	—	—	—	27·4	—	24·2	21·7	24·5	—	—	—	—	Belper 30·5, Burton 28·8. Great crop damage because April was warm
	—	22	—	31·0	—	26·4	30·6	—	—	—	—	—	
1895	—	—	15	32·3	—	—	—	30·0	—	—	—	—	
1898	2	—	—	23·0	26·9	25·5	—	22·5	—	—	—	—	
1900	2	—	—	26·0	25·9	24·8	—	26·9	—	—	—	—	Loughborough 23
1903	21	—	—	26·0	25·8	22·7	—	—	—	—	—	—	Belper 26·4, Lincoln 28·1. Mild March—trees damaged
1905	—	6	21	—	26·7	27·6	—	29·6	—	—	—	—	Much damage in north Nottinghamshire
1906	7	23	—	26·3	27·2	23·5	—	26·8	—	—	—	—	Belper 27·9, Lincoln 29·6
	—	18	—	28·0	—	—	—	—	—	—	—	—	Rauceby 28·0. Tree damage

Figures in italics denote potentially damaging frosts ——— indicates change of site or break in recordings

Table LI (continued) Recorded late frosts

Year	Day of April	Day of May	Day of June	Nottingham—Trent Lane	Strelley Hall	Hodsock Priory	Southwell	Buxton	Nottingham Castle	Nottingham—Burford Road	Woodthorpe	Attenborough	
1908	24	—	—	26·2	25·8	24·2	—	19·7	—	—	—	—	Matlock 21·9. Snow cover
1910	6	11	—	26·0	26·9	23·8	—	25	—	—	—	—	Matlock 24·9, Belvoir 26, Lincoln 27
1912	—	1	—	28·0	32·8	28·4	—	—	—	—	—	—	Blossom damaged
1914	—	2	—	28·0	—	28·5	—	—	—	—	—	—	Crops, fruit damaged. Trees blackened on
						23·9							low ground
1917	2	—	—	17·6	—	7·2	—	—	—	—	—	—	Welbeck 8·0. Snow. Lowest in 100 years.
													With 1879 and 1941 lowest in 100 years at
													Nottingham
1922	—	7	—	25·0	—	26·3	—	—	—	—	—	—	Mayfield 22, Fulbeck 26
1924	1	—	—	27·0	—	23·9	—	—	—	27·2	—	—	Belper 29, Lenton Fields 27, Mansfield 31,
													Mayfield 26
1926	10	9	—	23·0	—	24·2	—	30	30	28·8	—	—	
										31·8			
1927	30	—	—	—	28	24	—	26	29	—	—	—	Belper 26, Lenton Fields 23, Mayfield 22,
													Sutton Bonington 27
1928	18	—	—	—	28	—	—	25	29	27·8	25	—	Mansfield 28, Sutton Bonington 26,
													Mayfield 24, Belper 27
1929	6	—	—	—	—	—	—	—	27	27·6	—	—	Mansfield 27, Mayfield 22, Belper 24
	21				26				27	29·2	20		Sutton Bonington 23, Mayfield 22
	22							25	27	28·2			Cranwell 24, Sutton Bonington 23,
													Mayfield 22
1931	—	21	—	—	—	—	—	—	34	33·6	—	28	Mayfield 28
1932	—	7	—	—	—	—	—	—	33	33·0	—	28	Mayfield 25
1933	21	—	—	—	—	—	—	—	—	31·4	—	25	Crop damage
1934	8	—	—	—	—	—	—	—	30	31·0	—	25	
1935	—	—	1	—	—	—	—	—	31	*30·2*	—	27	Cranwell 35
1936	—	—	—	—	—	—	—	—	—	30·7	—	31	Cranwell 29
1938	11	8	—	—	—	—	—	—	29·2	24·6	—	21	Cranwell 31
									32·7	25·8			
1939	28	—	—	—	—	—	—	—	34·0	26·6	—	24	Watnall 25
1940	11	—	—	—	—	—	—	—	29·0	25·6	—	26	

Figures in italics denote potentially damaging frosts   —— indicates change of site or break in recordings

Table LI (continued)   Recorded late frosts

	1940	1941		1942	1944	1946	1949	1950	1957		1958		1961	1962
	11th April	4th May	8th May	4th May	7th May	15th May	10th May	26th April	7th May	8th May	2nd April	13th April	27th May	30th May
Nottingham Castle	29·0	30·9	—	33	33·5	32·8	33	29	—	—	29·6	31·4	34	33·0
Nottingham Woodthorpe	25·6	24·9	28	28·1	27·6	27·2	28	25·7	—	34	25·3	26·1	—	—
Lenton Experimental Station	—	—	—	—	—	—	—	—	—	—	23·9	25·4	31	—
Chandos School	—	25·0	—	34	—	—	33	—	—	—	26·0	28·0	32·5	33·0
Watnall	—	—	—	—	—	—	—	—	—	—	—	24	28	28
Sutton Bonington	—	—	—	—	—	—	—	—	—	—	—	22	29·7	—
Langar	—	—	—	—	—	—	—	—	—	31	21	—	35·1	—
Mansfield	—	—	—	—	—	—	—	—	—	28	21	—	28·9	33
Warsop (Gleadthorpe)	—	—	—	—	—	—	—	—	—	31	28	—	—	—
Cranwell	—	—	—	—	—	—	—	—	23	—	21	—	26·1	33·4
Lincoln	—	—	—	—	—	—	—	—	31	—	27	—	—	24·0
Waddington	—	—	—	—	—	—	—	—	30	—	—	—	—	—
Buxton	—	—	—	—	—	—	—	—	—	27	24	—	28·9	—
Chesterfield	—	—	—	—	—	—	—	—	—	31	—	—	30·0	—
Belper School	—	—	—	—	—	—	—	—	—	31	—	—	30·0	—
Mackworth	—	—	—	—	—	—	—	—	—	31	—	—	30·0	31·0
Morley	—	—	—	—	—	—	—	—	—	28	27	27	28·9	31·0
Derby	—	—	—	—	—	—	—	—	—	32	27	27	31·1	31·0
Shardlow	—	—	—	—	—	—	—	—	—	28	24	24	—	—
Wirksworth	—	—	—	—	—	—	—	—	32	—	29	29	—	—

Figures in italics denote potentially damaging frosts

Notes

The earlier part of the record shows that Hodsock, on low-level ground, was more susceptible to late frosts of damaging severity than Trent Lane, Nottingham; but Southwell, in a smaller valley, was sometimes even more subject to low temperature. The year of the greatest severity of late frost since 1867 was 1917, when the lowest April screen minima in a century were recorded. At Nottingham, 1917 shared the lowest May value of the record with 1879 and 1941. There was little damage in 1917 because vegetative growth was much delayed. By contrast, the much less severe frosts of 22nd May 1894 and 21st April 1903 were destructive because of earlier mildness and advanced growth.

Later figures indicate Mayfield, Attenborough, Lenton Fields, Sutton Bonington, the newer Lincoln station, Woodthorpe, Shardlow and Warsop, all in valley situations, as susceptible to late frosts.

The higher sites are much less susceptible and Nottingham Castle has not recorded a damaging screen minimum at least since 1924.

Notable late frosts in the early 19th century include those of:

1805	May and June	
1810	4th May	Nottingham
1819	May	
1820	28th April	Vegetation damage. Minima: Nottingham 28, Lenton *25*, Standard Hill *26*, Fox Hill 28, Derby *26*
	5th May	Nottingham 31, Lenton *28*, Fox Hill 30
1821	9th and 10th June	Ice of half-crown thickness in Derbyshire
1826	27th April	

Appendix II

Table LII A comparison between rainfall and equivalent run-off

Year	Month	Rainfall (inches)	Rainfall	Mean (cusec)	Mean/ square mile (cusec)	Inch rainfall equivalent	Accumulative run-off (inches)
1958	October ..	1·87	1·87	4,675	1·6175	1·8650	1·8650
	November	1·68	3·55	2,727	0·9435	1·0529	2·9179
	December	3·74	7·29	4,692	1·6233	1·8717	4·7896
1959	January ..	2·61	9·90	7,343	2·5405	2·9292	7·7188
	February ..	0·26	10·16	2,359	0·8162	0·8497	8·5685
	March ..	1·61	11·77	2,134	0·7383	0·8513	9·4198
	April ..	3·00	14·77	2,817	0·9746	1·0877	10·5075
	May ..	0·71	15·48	1,358	0·4698	0·5417	11·0492
	June ..	1·08	16·56	977·3	0·3381	0·3773	11·4265
	July ..	1·67	18·23	860·1	0·2976	0·3431	11·7696
	August ..	1·25	19·48	832·7	0·2881	0·3322	12·1018
	September	0·13	19·61	715·6	0·2476	0·2763	12·3781
	October ..	2·43	22·04	787·0	0·2723	0·3140	12·6921
	November	3·45	25·49	1,340	0·4636	0·5174	13·2095
	December	4·38	29·87	3,365	1·1642	1·3423	14·5518
1960	January ..	5·28	35·15	6,619	2·2900	2·6404	17·1922
	February ..	2·26	37·41	6,766	2·3409	2·5258	19·7180
	March ..	1·64	39·05	2,955	1·0224	1·1788	20·8968
	April ..	1·29	40·34	2,046	0·7079	0·7900	21·6868
	May ..	1·47	41·81	1,282	0·4435	0·5114	22·1982
	June ..	2·66	44·47	1,110	0·3840	0·4285	22·6267
	July ..	3·63	48·10	1,183	0·4093	0·4719	23·0986
	August ..	3·99	52·09	1,339	0·4633	0·5342	23·6328
	September	4·65	56·74	3,861	1·3358	1·4908	25·1236
	October ..	5·36	62·10	6,267	2·1684	2·5002	27·6238
	November	3·85	65·95	8,021	2·7751	3·0970	30·7208
	December	3·50	69·45	7,634	2·6410	3·0450	33·7658
1961	January ..	3·24	72·69	5,455	1·8873	2·1761	35·9419
	February ..	2·22	74·91	5,239	1·8126	1·8869	37·8288
	March ..	0·57	75·48	2,121	0·7338	0·8461	38·6749
	April ..	3·71	79·19	3,390	1·1729	1·3090	39·9839
	May ..	1·10	80·29	2,239	0·7746	0·8931	40·8770
	June ..	1·10	81·39	1,103	0·3816	0·4259	41·3029
	July ..	2·62	84·01	1,160	0·4013	0·4627	41·7656
	August ..	2·81	86·82	1,138	0·3937	0·4539	42·2195
	September	2·00	88·82	1,084	0·3750	0·4185	42·6380
	October ..	3·06	91·88	1,540	0·5328	0·6143	43·2523
	November	2·05	93·93	1,414	0·4892	0·5459	43·7982
	December	3·01	96·94	3,110	1·0760	1·2406	45·0388

Table LII (continued)   A comparison between rainfall and equivalent run-off

Year	Month	Rainfall		Run-off (equivalent rainfall)			
		Rainfall (inches)	Rainfall	Mean (cusec)	Mean/ square mile (cusec)	Inch rainfall equivalent	Accumulative run-off (inches)
1962	January ..	2·90	99·84	4,915	1·7005	1·9607	46·9995
	February ..	1·44	101·28	3,303	1·1428	1·1897	48·1892
	March ..	1·18	102·46	1,674	0·5792	0·6678	48·8570
	April ..	2·58	105·04	2,861	0·9898	1·1046	49·9616
	May ..	2·29	107·33	1,674	0·5792	0·6678	50·6294
	June ..	0·59	107·92	1,026	0·3550	0·3962	51·0256
	July ..	1·88	109·80	1,159	0·4010	0·4624	51·4880
	August ..	4·46	114·26	1,860	0·6435	0·7420	52·2300
	September	3·58	117·84	1,951	0·6750	0·7533	52·9833
	October ..	0·99	118·83	1,708	0·5909	0·6813	53·6646
	November	1·71	120·54	2,171	0·7511	0·8382	54·5028
	December	2·36	122·90	3,029	1·0480	1·2083	55·7111
1963	January ..	0·95	123·85	1,623	0·5615	0·6474	56·3585
	February ..	0·67	124·52	1,756	0·6075	0·6324	56·9909
	March ..	2·82	127·34	4,484	1·5514	1·7888	58·7797
	April ..	2·37	129·71	3,583	1·2396	1·3834	60·1631
	May ..	1·69	131·40	2,135	0·7387	0·8517	61·0148
	June ..	3·21	134·61	1,878	0·6497	0·7251	61·7399
	July ..	1·69	136·30	2,026	0·7010	0·8083	62·5482
	August ..	3·09	139·39	1,789	0·6190	0·7137	63·2619
	September	2·65	142·04	2,055	0·7110	0·7935	64·0554
	October ..	1·94	143·98	1,676	0·5799	0·6686	64·7240
	November	4·46	148·44	5,026	1·7389	1·9406	66·6646
	December	0·55	148·99	2,167	0·7151	0·8245	67·4891
1964	January ..	0·90	149·89	1,689	0·5844	0·6738	68·1629
	February ..	0·92	150·81	1,817	0·6286	0·6783	68·8412
	March ..	3·57	154·38	4,978	1·7223	1·9858	70·8270
	April ..	2·26	156·64	2,498	0·8643	0·9646	71·7916
	May ..	1·89	158·53	1,736	0·6006	0·6925	72·4841
	June ..	2·92	161·45	2,045	0·7075	0·7896	73·2737
	July ..	2·37	163·82	1,487	0·5145	0·5932	73·8669
	August ..	2·12	165·94	1,438	0·4975	0·5736	74·4405
	September	0·71	166·65	1,026	0·3550	0·3962	74·8367
	October ..	1·73	168·38	1,047	0·3622	0·4176	75·2543
	November	1·45	169·83	1,163	0·4024	0·4491	75·7034
	December	3·01	172·84	2,561	0·8861	1·0217	76·7251

AGRICULTURAL TABLES

Table LIII Acreage under crops and grass and numbers of livestock in 1914 and 1962 and in intermediate decades

	Derbyshire						Nottinghamshire					
	1914	1924	1934	1944	1954	1962	1914	1924	1934	1944	1954	1962
'000 ACRES												
Wheat	16·1	15·1	19·6	37·7	29·6	22·7	38·0	36·9	49·0	69·1	69·0	52·0
Barley	4·6	4·4	1·2	3·5	4·7	21·3	30·1	24·1	9·0	21·7	34·6	84·6
Oats and other grains	18·9	23·7	16·2	49·4	38·7	19·4	37·3	41·4	31·3	40·1	38·2	18·7
Potatoes and sugar beet	2·5†	2·8	3·9	13·3	7·0	5·0	6·3†	9·0	19·3	35·6	32·2	26·9
Other crops and bare fallow	18·7	21·8	17·7	28·1	21·7	15·4	61·3	58·1	45·8	46·5	34·0	20·6
Temporary grass	18·5	22·8	13·9	41·0	50·3	68·4	44·0	48·2	32·9	40·6	62·5	71·8
Permanent grass	405·1	373·3	372·0	246·8	264·3	255·7	222·3	212·8	225·8	146·5	131·0	120·0
TOTAL CROPS AND GRASS	484·6	463·9	444·6	419·9	416·6	408·0	439·6	430·4	412·9	400·0	401·6	394·7
'000 HEAD												
Cows and heifers	80·5	83·7	90·7	106·8	103·2	103·0	31·6	24·9	37·3	43·3	40·0	42·1
Other cattle	65·5	62·2	75·9	72·8	87·6	99·0	53·0	64·2	63·2	62·2	71·0	77·9
Sheep	133·6	100·9	123·9	110·2	123·1	204·8	163·0	128·8	127·9	66·6	72·3	130·6
Pigs	31·1	31·0	33·7	19·1	65·7	49·3	29·1	44·9	46·3	23·4	81·2	77·4
Poultry	526·0*	641·3	1164·6	506·7	1083·7	1335·1	393·5*	497·5	1023·6	444·8	1058·6	2696·3

*1921   †Potatoes only

Table LIV Percentage of holdings and acreage by size of farm groups in 1914 and 1962

Size groups Acres of crops and grass	Derbyshire				Nottinghamshire			
	Holdings		Acreage		Holdings		Acreage	
	1914	1962	1914	1962	1914	1962	1914	1962
1¼ to 19¾ ..	52·5	40·9	9·7	5·1	49·2	46·1	5·9	3·2
20 to 99¾ ..	34·7	41·4	39·1	38·5	28·8	25·8	22·1	16·9
100 to 149¾ ..	6·4	8·8	18·2	19·0	8·1	8·9	15·6	12·9
150 to 299¾ ..	5·7	7·8	26·2	27·4	10·4	13·1	32·7	32·2
300 and over ..	0·7	1·1	6·8	10·0	3·5	6·1	23·7	34·8
	100·0	100·0	100·0	100·0	100·0	100·0	100·0	100·0
TOTAL HOLDINGS AND ACREAGE ..	11,160	7,310	484,550	407,968	6,742	4,653	439,537	394,675

Table LV Percentage distribution of population, holdings, crops and stock, between the sub-areas of Derbyshire and Nottinghamshire

	Derbyshire				Nottinghamshire					Both counties	
	North-west	Central and South	East	County total	West	Central	East	South	County total	Per cent	Thousand acres, or Numbers
Total population, 1961	6·6	4·6	38·1	49·3	40·7	4·0	4·0	2·0	50·7	100·0	1743·9
Estimated agricultural population	18·3	20·9	15·1	54·3	9·4	15·1	11·8	9·4	45·7	100·0	47·5
Regular whole-time workers in agriculture	12·0	19·4	14·9	46·3	11·7	18·9	12·6	10·5	53·6	100·0	10·3
Estimated labour requirements—											
Standard man days	17·2	21·1	13·2	51·5	9·5	17·4	12·4	9·2	48·5	100·0	4651·0
TOTAL HOLDINGS	21·8	20·7	18·6	61·1	9·4	11·4	10·6	7·5	38·9	100·0	12·0
TOTAL AREA	23·1	16·3	15·0	54·4	10·6	14·6	12·5	8·3	45·6	100·0	1183·6
Cereals	1·9	13·8	13·3	29·0	12·7	24·7	19·8	13·8	71·0	100·0	218·6
Potatoes	2·0	10·4	17·1	29·6	16·9	25·1	16·1	12·4	70·4	100·0	14·5
Sugar Beet	—	2·9	1·5	4·4	14·5	32·3	29·0	19·8	95·6	100·0	17·5
Fodder crops	13·6	21·5	16·4	51·6	11·7	17·4	11·4	8·0	48·4	100·0	20·2
Horticultural crops	1·6	15·6	11·2	28·4	17·0	36·8	13·9	3·9	71·6	100·0	10·0
Bare fallow	4·2	13·1	13·3	30·6	11·0	28·6	17·7	12·1	69·4	100·0	5·2
Temporary grass and lucerne	11·0	20·6	15·6	47·2	10·3	18·7	13·2	10·6	52·8	100·0	134·5
Permanent grass	32·4	24·0	11·6	68·1	5·1	8·5	9·6	8·8	31·9	100·0	375·7
TOTAL CROPS AND GRASS	18·1	19·7	12·8	50·5	8·8	16·2	13·7	10·7	49·5	100·0	396·2
Rough grazing	83·1	10·9	2·4	96·4	1·4	1·1	0·6	0·5	3·6	100·0	85·6
Dairy cows and heifers	27·2	32·3	14·1	73·6	4·7	8·0	6·7	7·0	26·4	100·0	129·1
Beef cows and heifers	24·4	15·7	9·6	49·7	7·2	14·8	16·5	11·8	50·3	100·0	15·9
Other cattle (male)	15·3	15·8	12·7	43·8	8·4	16·0	18·9	12·9	56·2	100·0	73·8
Other cattle (female)	26·7	25·2	12·9	64·8	5·7	9·8	10·3	9·4	35·2	100·0	100·7
Sows	8·5	13·9	17·8	40·3	13·8	23·2	12·1	10·7	59·7	100·0	17·0
Other pigs	7·0	13·5	18·2	38·7	14·3	19·8	14·5	12·7	61·3	100·0	108·7
Total sheep	39·7	15·9	5·5	61·0	4·4	11·8	9·9	12·8	39·0	100·0	335·4
Total poultry	6·7	12·6	13·8	33·1	18·6	32·4	10·4	5·5	66·9	100·0	4031·4
TOTAL NET OUTPUT £	14·2	19·3	13·5	47·0	10·4	19·0	13·8	9·8	53·0	100·0	31·6

Table LVI Distribution of crops, stock and net output within each sub-area of Derbyshire and Nottinghamshire

		Derbyshire				Nottinghamshire					Both counties
		North-west	Central and South	East	Whole county	West	Central	East	South	Whole county	
PER 100 ACRES OF CROPS AND GRASS											
Cereals	acres	2·9	19·2	28·7	15·8	39·5	41·9	39·7	35·2	39·4	27·5
Potatoes and sugar beet	acres	0·2	1·3	2·7	1·3	7·1	7·2	6·7	6·2	6·8	4·0
Other crops	acres	2·2	4·2	5·1	3·7	6·6	6·7	4·3	3·1	5·2	4·4
Grass	acres	94·7	75·3	63·5	79·6	46·8	44·2	49·3	55·5	48·6	64·1
Dairy cows and heifers	No.	24·3	26·6	17·9	23·6	8·6	8·1	7·9	10·5	8·7	16·2
Beef cows and heifers	No.	2·7	1·6	1·5	2·0	1·6	1·8	2·4	2·2	2·0	2·0
Other cattle	No.	26·4	23·6	22·1	24·2	17·0	16·8	22·3	22·3	19·5	21·9
Pigs	No.	6·3	10·8	22·5	12·2	25·5	19·8	16·4	18·2	19·5	15·7
Sheep	No.	92·3	33·9	18·1	50·9	20·9	30·8	30·4	50·4	33·2	42·1
Poultry	No.	186·7	324·4	549·6	331·8	1,069·2	1,012·7	328·5	259·6	684·7	506·4
NET OUTPUT PER ACRE OF CROPS AND GRASS											
Dairying	£	18·3	19·1	15·1	17·8	8·9	8·0	7·4	9·4	8·3	13·1
Beef	£	4·8	3·8	3·4	4·0	2·7	2·8	4·1	3·3	3·2	3·7
Sheep	£	3·4	1·2	0·7	1·9	0·9	1·3	1·2	1·9	1·4	1·6
Pigs and poultry	£	3·1	4·8	8·5	5·2	9·3	6·6	6·0	4·6	6·8	6·0
Cereals	£	0·9	5·8	8·6	4·8	11·9	12·6	11·9	10·6	11·9	8·2
Cash roots	£	0·2	1·2	2·6	1·2	6·2	6·1	5·7	5·2	5·8	3·5
Horticultural crops	£	0·3	2·9	3·2	2·0	7·0	8·1	3·6	1·3	5·2	3·6
Total	£	31·0	38·8	42·1	36·9	46·9	46·5	39·9	36·3	42·6	39·7
NET OUTPUT PER HOLDING	£	1,719	2,455	1,919	2,029	2,937	4,392	3,437	3,458	3,601	2,641
NET OUTPUT PER STANDARD MAN DAY	£	5·6	6·2	7·0	6·2	7·5	7·4	7·6	7·2	7·4	6·8
NET OUTPUT OF PIGS AND POULTRY	%	10·1	12·5	20·2	14·0	19·9	16·3	14·9	12·7	16·0	15·1
Estimated agricultural population as percentage of total population		7·5	12·4	1·1	3·0	0·6	10·3	8·1	12·5	2·5	2·7
Estimated labour requirement (standard man days per 100 acres of crops and grass)		555	627	604	595	628	628	527	502	573	584
Size of holding— acres of crops and grass		55	63	45	55	63	94	86	95	85	67

Appendix IV

THE AGRICULTURAL POPULATION

Estimates of the population directly dependent on agriculture have been prepared for groups of parishes within the seven sub-areas (see Figure 43). These estimates are a summation of the following items:

A   Number of holdings of 15 acres and over (= 'farmers') × 3   }   =   farmers and their dependent families

B   Number of regular full-time male workers aged 20 years and over × 3   }   =   adult farm workers, including farmers' sons, and their dependent families

C   Number of regular full-time male workers aged under 20   }   =   youths employed in agriculture, including farmers' sons

D   Number of regular full-time women and girls   }   =   females employed in agriculture, excluding farmers' wives

NOTES

1   Source: *Agricultural Statistics*, June 1962, parish summaries.

2   Holdings under 15 acres have been assumed to be part-time or hobby farms. To the extent that this is untrue the number of farmers has been under-estimated. However, every holding of 15 acres and over is not necessarily occupied solely by a farmer; a small proportion of holdings are occupied as multiple farm units. This tends to over-estimate the number of farmers.

3   Each farmer and adult male farm worker has been assumed to be married with one dependent child (at school or under school age). This is the approximate average family composition in Derbyshire and Nottinghamshire.

4   Women and girls enumerated as agricultural workers may include farm workers' wives. This may slightly over-estimate the total.

The *total* population for the groups of parishes has been extracted from the 1961 Population Census. These have been used to assess the proportion of the total population directly dependent on agriculture.

Estimation of labour requirements (standard man days)★ and of net output

The estimated annual labour requirements, in standard man days, of the crops and stock within the area have been calculated on the following scale.

★One adult for eight hours

Table LVII

	Per acre		Per head
Cereals	2·0	Dairy cows and heifers	12
Potatoes	16·0	Beef cows and heifers	3
Fodder roots, kale, etc.	8·0	Bulls	7
Sugar beet	12·5	Other cattle ..	2·5
Horticulture ..	50·0	Sows and boars ..	4
Bare fallow ..	0·5	Other pigs	0·5
Hay	1·0	Sheep	0·75
Grazing	0·25	Poultry	0·15
Rough grazing ..	0·1	Broilers	0·01

This has been adapted from scales currently used by the National Agricultural Advisory Service and the Provincial Agricultural Economics Service in collaboration with the Ministry of Agriculture.

Net output has been estimated by using a scale of net output per standard man day for various enterprises. This scale has been adopted from one originally devised by the Ministry of Agriculture in 1960 for a preliminary classification of farms by economic type. Output has been defined for livestock as gross output less purchased and home-grown concentrates, and for fodder crops and sale crops as gross output net of seeds. It has been assumed that the net output of fodder crops has been consumed by dairy beef cattle, beef cattle and sheep and the net output of fodder crops (including grass) has therefore been redistributed to these three enterprises in proportion to the net output of each.

Table LVIII

	Net output per standard man day
	£
Dairying ..	4·6
Beef ..	6·9
Sheep ..	3·9
Pigs ..	7·3
Poultry ..	9·4
Cash roots ..	6·1
Fodder crops ..	8·2
Cereals ..	15·0
Horticulture ..	5·7

It should be noted that this is a scale of net output per standard man day 'required'. It cannot be regarded as a measure of the relative profitability of these enterprises, nor of farming in the various sub-areas for which figures are given, since it takes no account of the labour actually used and of the land and capital associated with it.

Appendix V

OIL PRODUCTION

Table LIX Production of oil in Great Britain—tons

Field	1938–54	1955	1956	1957	1958	1959	1960	1961	1962	1963	1964	Total
Eakring and Duke's Wood	624,018	32,286	36,873	35,402	28,080	23,049	19,915	18,566	17,684	16,650	13,369	865,892
Kelham Hills and Caunton	224,794	17,622	15,063	16,135	11,034	9,097	8,517	7,157	5,842	5,126	3,924	324,311
Egmanton	—	896	9,049	26,988	36,125	33,783	26,571	24,931	22,980	33,233	27,087	241,643
Bothamsall	—	—	—	—	627	7,439	18,651	16,789	14,744	14,207	14,116	86,573
Plungar	1,054	2,517	4,891	3,269	3,394	3,525	3,424	2,824	2,238	2,133	1,978	31,247
South Leverton	—	—	—	—	—	—	549	7,411	7,324	4,829	4,198	24,311
Torksey	—	—	—	—	—	—	—	—	—	1,156	940	2,096
Corringham	—	—	—	—	376	2,109	3,496	7,006	7,161	6,089	5,006	31,243
Gainsborough	—	—	—	—	—	1,211	3,958	10,160	19,162	26,432	40,434	101,357
Beckingham	—	—	—	—	—	—	—	—	—	—	1,353	1,353
Glentworth	—	—	—	—	—	—	—	2,139	3,557	1,904	1,774	9,374
REGIONAL TOTAL	849,866	53,321	65,876	81,794	79,636	80,213	85,081	96,983	100,692	111,759	114,179	1,719,400
Kimmeridge	—	—	—	—	—	2,336	44	8,738	10,180	10,977	13,142	45,417
Wareham	—	—	—	—	—	—	—	—	—	—	16	16
Formby	9,062	161	120	131	113	81	72	19	—	—	154	9,913
Other areas	2,271	—	—	1	70	13	85	31	—	28	—	2,499
EXTRA-REGIONAL TOTAL	11,333	161	120	132	183	2,430	201	8,788	10,180	11,005	13,312	57,845
GRAND TOTAL	861,199	53,482	65,996	81,926	79,819	82,643	85,282	105,771	110,872	122,764	127,491	1,777,245

Appendix VI

NOTTINGHAM'S HOUSING RECORD

The following list gives the sites, and numbers of dwellings on each, erected by the Nottingham Corporation since 1920.

Abbey Bridge	142		Hucknall Lane		32
Aspley	2,838		Ilkeston Road		18
Barnaston Road	26		King's Meadow Road		5
Bells Lane	922		Lancaster Road		14
Berridge Road	52		Lenton Abbey		880
Bestwood	1,137		Liddington Street		14
Bobbers Mill	46		Morley Avenue		42
Bilborough	686		Mundella Road		62
Brook Street	56		Northampton Street		40
Broxtowe Hall and Lane	1,558		Park Lane		56
Broxtowe Lane	308		Pym Street		12
Bulwell Hall	808		Ravensworth Road and		
Bunting Street	16		Squires Avenue		65
Canterbury Road	150		Rolleston Drive		18
Cardale Road	291		Rossington Road		2
Cliff Road	106		Sherwood		1,085
Colwick Hill	329		Sneinton Boulevard		57
Colwick Road	146		Sneinton Dale		489
Coppice Road	56		Southwold		311
Cranbrook Street	12		Springfield Street		14
Dornoch Avenue	14		St. Peter's Street		8
Edwards Lane	650		Stockhill		224
Fairfax Street	14		Sunrise Avenue		14
Fraser Road	25		Tissington Road		40
Gladstone Street	6		Waterford Street		12
Gordon Road	220		Wells Road		80
Greenwood Road	63		Wells Road		114
Hawthorne Street	16		Whitemoor		584
Heathfield	564		Windmill Lane		273
Hempshill Lane	30		Woolmer Road		44
Highbury	625		Wollaton Park		422
Highbury	50		Zulu Road		2

TOTAL PRE-WAR   16,595

POST-WAR

1946 Act—pre-war types			Greenwood Road	..	68
Aspley Lane	.. ..	222	Hyson Green (Pleasant		
Bestwood	.. ..	214	Court)	.. ..	45
Broxtowe	.. ..	338	Lime Street	.. ..	4
			Moorbridge	.. ..	16
			Quorn	.. ..	66
			Ransom Road ..	..	30
Post-war types			Rock Street	.. ..	64
Ainsley	.. ..	228	Sandhurst Road	..	210
Beechdale	.. ..	18	Sherwood Station site	..	180
Bells Lane	.. ..	22	Sneinton site	.. ..	274
Bestwood	.. ..	168	Squires Avenue	..	38
Bestwood Park	..	2,871	Strelley	.. ..	652
Bilborough	.. ..	2,676	Trowell Avenue	..	70
Blue Bell Hill	..	8	Wells Road	..	10
Broxtowe	.. ..	68	Wendover Drive	..	40
Chedworth	.. ..	53	Woodthorpe Gardens	..	18
Clifton and Glapton	..	6,828	Robin Hood Chase	..	12
Denman Street site	..	336			
Fernwood	.. ..	384	*Temporary bungalows*	..	1,000
Firbeck	.. ..	184			
Glamis Road	.. ..	36	*Small builders' schemes*	..	330

TOTAL POST-WAR	17,799
TOTAL PRE-WAR	16,595
GRAND TOTAL	34,394

(The above figures are reproduced by courtesy of the
City Estates Surveyor)

During the 20-year period 1945–65, the number of privately-built houses erected in the city was 5,954.   In the four adjoining Urban Districts of Arnold, Beeston and Stapleford, Carlton and West Bridgford, a total of 10,998 houses were privately built, compared with a total of 7,565 local-authority houses. In addition another 532 were erected in Arnold and Carlton by housing associations. It should be noted that the majority of private dwellings have been built since 1954, for prior to that year government policy demanded a ratio of 4 : 1 in favour of local-authority housing. This was modified in 1952 to a ratio of 1 : 1 and in 1954 restrictions on private building were removed.